VANITY FAIR

VANITY FAIR

SELECTIONS FROM AMERICA'S MOST MEMORABLE MAGAZINE

A CAVALCADE

of the

*1920*s AND *1930*s

Edited by

CLEVELAND AMORY

and

FREDERIC BRADLEE

Picture Editor: KATHARINE TWEED

THE VIKING PRESS · PUBLISHERS · NEW YORK

Published in 1960 by The Viking Press, Inc., 625 Madison Avenue, New York 22, N.Y.

Published simultaneously in Canada by The Macmillan Company of Canada Limited

EDITORIAL ACKNOWLEDGMENTS

Such a book as this does not reach completion without more than the ordinary amount of help and cooperation from people whose names never appear in it. The editors wish to express their profound and heartfelt gratitude to the staff of the New York Society Library; to Evelyn Raphael and Carole Kageyama, and especially to Paul Bonner and Jeanne Ballot, of The Condé Nast Publications Inc.; to Monica McCall; to Martha Hodge Amory; to our picture editor, Katharine Tweed; to the staff of The Viking Press; and above all to Bryan Holme, not only for his skill and taste in designing the book, but also for his tireless energy, his Olympian calm in moments of crisis, and his unwavering devotion to the project as a whole.

An earlier version of the Introduction by Cleveland Amory appeared in *Esquire*.

"Frank Crowninshield, Editor, Man, and Uncle" by Frederic Bradlee appeared in *Vogue*.

Library of Congress catalog card number: 60–13340

Printed in the U.S.A. by the Murray Printing Company

Contents

(Illustrations are indexed on pages 325–327)

Introduction—A Fair Kept

CLEVELAND AMORY

And the name of that town is Vanity; and at the town there is a fair kept called Vanity Fair.
—John Bunyan, *The Pilgrim's Progress*

THE story of *Vanity Fair* itself is as good a story as any the magazine ever published. There never was, nor in all probability ever will be again, a magazine like her. She was born in 1914, and she died in 1936, and, unlike the legendary gentleman of the old school who was very good at wars but not very good between wars, the lady who was *Vanity Fair* was not very good at wars and depressions, but between them, in the golden days of the twenties, she was very good indeed. And today, as we look back at her from out of the shadowy sixties, she seems, all in all and all at once, behind her time, ahead of her time, and yet, unmistakably, *of* her time.

She was behind her time, first of all, in the sense that she carried forward, into a faster and crasser age, the stately white-tie-and-tailed elegance of a fast by-going Edwardian era. And she maintained this link with the past not alone through her pages but also, in true Edwardian style, through the personality of her best beau—the man who was to her, all in all and again all at once, beau ideal and beau in person, *paterfamilias* and editor *elegantiarum*. His name was, of course, Frank Crowninshield, and he was not only a nineteenth-century man by birth and at heart, he was also no man to do violence to the past as he pioneered a future. In fact, he innately preferred, when it came to standards and values, almost any century previous to his own. It is hardly a wonder that his Fair reflected not alone the clamor and glamour of the new café society and the Great White Way; she also symbolized nostalgically to a whole generation of not-so-grown-up small-town Americans the *jeunesse dorée* of the old Gay Nineties and the Naughty Oughties. For *Vanity Fair* was America in transition—America in mid-passage, as it were, between the old Four Hundred and the new Smart Set.

If *Vanity Fair* was behind its time, it was most assuredly ahead of its time. For the magazine was pleased to take for granted the fact that its readers were cultured people, or at least people susceptible to so being—and, to prove the point, published modern art as if people were already initiated to it, which most of them were not, and was also not averse, on occasion, to publishing a piece entirely in French. If a few readers did not understand French, it was the editor's opinion that they should—and, more important, would—ask somebody who did. All the departments, not just the humorous ones, were edited on the principle that nothing in the magazine, least of all the magazine itself, should ever take itself too seriously. Famous too was the occasional "We Nominate for Oblivion" feature. Bored with years of the "Hall of Fame," the editors nominated contrasting candidates who ran the gamut from King Carol and Queen Marie (not to mention Belle Livingston, Raymond Duncan, and Cornelius Vanderbilt, Jr.) to the statue of "Civic Virtue" (which they felt was being overlooked) and the "Forgotten Man" (which they felt was being overdone). Once, indeed, one of the nominees for oblivion, the late Floyd Gibbons, complained that his treatment was manifestly unfair—only a few issues before, he pointed out, he had been enshrined in the magazine's Hall of Fame. "Then," replied Mr. Crowninshield, protecting managing editor Clare Boothe Brokaw, who thought up the idea, "what are you grumbling about? You're all even."

Above all, *Vanity Fair* was ahead of its time in the search for new talent. The list of American and foreign discoveries is unmatched by any other magazine in a similar period and reads in retrospect like a roll call of future recognition: Thomas Wolfe, Gertrude Stein, e. e. cummings, Edmund Wilson, Robert Sherwood, Paul Gallico, Corey Ford (John Riddell), Margaret Case Harriman, Clare Boothe Brokaw, and Gilbert Seldes, Allan Seager, Carl Carmer, P. G. Wodehouse, Aldous Huxley, Colette, Ferenc Molnar, and many others. Then, too, comes the roster of painters, sculptors, and graphic artists who had their coming-out parties in print form, often through the superlative color plates for which *Vanity Fair* was noted: Picasso, Matisse, Gauguin, Rouault, Epstein, Segonzac, as well as Covarrubias, Rockwell Kent, Tony Sarg, and Gluyas Williams. And finally, last but not least, there were the photographers: Steichen, Bruehl, Horst, and Beaton.

And, of course, *Vanity Fair* was of its time; indeed, it was as accurate a social barometer of its time as exists. At first the late Condé Nast, the publisher of *Vogue,* who had bought the old title *Vanity Fair*—one which had flourished briefly in (when else?) the Gay Nineties—tried his own magazine. It was called *Dress & Vanity Fair,* and its first issue was for September 1913. Nast was, however, dissatisfied with it and took it over to show to his friend Mr. Crowninshield, at that time art editor of the *Century.* (Before that he had served as publisher of *The Bookman,* 1895–1900, and as editor of *Metropolitan,* 1900–1902, and *Munsey's,* 1903–1907.) Mr. Crowninshield looked over the magazine for some time, then put it down. "There is no magazine," he said, "which covers the things people talk about at parties—the arts, sports, humor, and so forth." At once Nast asked Crowninshield if he would undertake to make his *Dress & Vanity Fair* into such a magazine. Mr. Crowninshield agreed, and America's most memorable magazine was born—one which is still, in a sense, so triumphantly alive in the minds and hearts of its readers that the stark fact that it has been dead, as of 1960, a quarter of a century, seems at once a base and a baseless canard.

Once Mr. Nast had asked Mr. Crowninshield to edit his magazine, he left him virtually alone. Even though a man of far more conservative taste himself, Mr. Nast was liberal in the extreme in the freedom he gave his editor. And Mr. Crowninshield operated equally independently—even in later days when it became apparent his severe policy of the separation of editorial and advertising departments was, in depression days, to mean his magazine's final failure. Once when *Vogue* editor Edna Woolman Chase turned over to him the idea of doing the "Well-Dressed Man" department, formerly a feature of *Vogue,* Mr. Crowninshield refused point blank—at first. "Darling," he told Mrs. Chase, "a gentleman *knows* how to dress."

Mr. Crowninshield was, of course, a gentleman by the simplest and best of all definitions—he was a gentle man. He had, however, his own definition of the term. "A man," he said earnestly, "who tries to be some help to his fellows; who is considerate of women, of the sick, the weak, and the unfortunate." Iva Patcévitch, present publisher of *Vogue,* said he always thought of him as the Last of the Mohicans. "He had all the old-world courtesies—his manners were so perfect that he seemed insincere."

Background he had, and plenty of it—but he not only kept it, in the great gentlemanly tradition, *in* the background; he dearly loved, in his waggish way, to make fun of it. In *Vanity Fair,* for example, he delighted to publish—in fact he gave Edmund Pearson the idea of writing—"The Murder of Captain White," the story of a murder committed by an ancestor of his by the name of Richard Crowninshield. "One of my collateral ancestors married his cook," Mr. Crowninshield once explained to Geoffrey Hellman, "a union resulting in Richard, a criminal of a quite colorful order."

Even in his heyday as an acknowledged *arbiter elegantiarum*— and here he not only really was the last of them but was also the only one who never became a biter—he was equally at home at the Dutch Treat Club, or, for that matter, at Schrafft's, as he was at Mrs. Vanderbilt's or in his black leather chair at the Knickerbocker Club. To Schrafft's, indeed, after he had received his pay of three hundred dollars a week—which he always received in cash— he would often repair with all the office girls. In his latter years a company lawyer took him to task, trying to prevail upon him to take out a charge account, for income-tax purposes. "At *Schrafft's?*" he asked. "The government *can't* be serious." His own favorite club was the famous Coffee House, which he founded, together with Robert Benchley, and for which he wrote the rule book. "The first rule," he wrote firmly, "is that there are no rules."

There were no rules, either, in the office of *Vanity Fair.* Here the playful spirit of "Crownie" reigned supreme, and whether the entire staff was engaged in watching him trying to match Houdini at magic tricks or whether they were all playing, the boys against the girls, the Rape of the Sabine Women, there has never been an office like it before or since.

And what a staff *Vanity Fair* boasted! Here came Robert Benchley to write his first piece, "No Matter from What Angle You Looked at It, Alice Brookhansen Was a Girl Whom You Would Hesitate to Invite into Your Own Home." Here came Dorothy Parker as a young girl; she wore a large turned-up hat and large horn-rimmed glasses which she removed quickly if anyone spoke to her suddenly. Her first job—for which she was paid ten dollars a week—was to write captions, and her first caption, designed to explain six photographs showing miscellaneous underwear, read, "Brevity is the soul of lingerie, as the Petticoat said to the Chemise." Swift on the heels of this masterpiece she sold her first poem, for which *Vanity Fair* paid the noble sum of five dollars. Here also, fresh from heroic service with the Canadian Black Watch—he had left Harvard as a Junior in 1917—came a tremendous, stoop-shouldered six-foot-seven giant of a man named Robert Sherwood —a young man so shy that in dictating a letter or a caption he was able to do so only by sitting on the floor with his back to the stenographer. And these were by no means all. There were also Edna St. Vincent Millay ("Nancy Boyd"), Elinor Wylie, P. G. Wodehouse, and a host of others—all regular contributors. It was truly a fair which kept fair company.

Looking back at the issues of any magazine published a quarter of a century or more ago, one expects to find much that is dated and little that is still refreshingly alive. But the batting average of *Vanity Fair* is superlatively high. Furthermore, so much of the other material that might be termed "dated" is so pleasantly and mistily nostalgic that it cries out to be seen again.

In retrospect most people remember *Vanity Fair* as the most sophisticated and witty magazine of our era. What they may not recall is the high quality of its stories and articles, for only later did the reputations of many of the then avant-garde writers become firmly established in this country. In a single year—1928— *Vanity Fair* published pieces by Max Beerbohm, Compton Mackenzie, André Gide, and D. H. Lawrence, all of which make just as good reading now.

The literary content of the magazine remained consistently catholic in scope and elegant in quality, a startling accomplishment for a magazine of its circulation. "White Poppies Die" by Nancy Hale appeared in 1933, and "Little Caruso" by Saroyan in 1934; the broadly comic G. B. Stern piece called "Compensation Instinct" the following year, and also, by way of contrast, the serious and moving story "The Bums at Sunset" by Thomas Wolfe. These too were ahead of their time.

Some of the features in the original *Vanity Fair* may be even more interesting to us today than they were to readers when first published—particularly so the profile of Somerset Maugham (1920), which Hugh Walpole wrote ten years before Mr. Maugham's novel *Cakes and Ale,* in which the acidly sketched portrait of Alroy Kear was reportedly none other than Mr. Walpole!

The difficulty of making selections from so much material and keeping it within practical limits for a book was considerable— only one piece, or at the most two pieces, by the same author; only one or very few of the many pictures of the same celebrity in the span of years.

Variety was, of course, one of the criteria of our choice. "The Importance of the Comic Genius," by Aldous Huxley—renowned chiefly as a mordant satirist—rather than any other of Huxley's *Vanity Fair* pieces was chosen because in this essay he makes a strong point of the fact that in great comedy, satire is not enough; comedy must have great heart as well! And "The Birth of a Great Artist" by André Maurois is reprinted not only because it is funny but because it is so unexpectedly funny coming from an author associated today with staid and distinguished biography. We were also delighted to run across a frolicking bit of nonsense called "The Mystery of Stroppingwallingshire Downs," signed by a P. G. Wylie, who turned out to be none other than the Philip Wylie who wrote *Generation of Vipers.*

In choosing one rather than another equally good article by the same author, wherever possible we took into consideration which article best suggested the year in which it appeared. This, we feel, has added nostalgic appeal to *Vanity Fair* the book. The Stark Young feature on David Garrick and John Barrymore appeared in 1923, the year Barrymore was playing Hamlet in New York, and the John Gunther article on King Carol and Madame Lupescu appeared in 1934, when their romance was still headline news.

Vanity Fair was a pioneer in so many areas that it can be said to be a significant yardstick of American culture. Not only did it publish many pieces by first-rate writers and artists before—and after—they became known, but it set a new standard for photography and picture journalism. Another thing it did "first" was to give due recognition to Negro personalities and artists. The book includes a 1925 photograph of Florence Mills, the girl who immortalized the still popular "Bye-Bye Blackbird"; a Steichen photograph of the all-Negro play *Green Pastures,* which won the 1930 Pulitzer Prize; and pictures of Paul Robeson as "Emperor Jones," of Ethel Waters in *As Thousands Cheer* (1934), and of Joe Louis, Louis Armstrong, and Jesse Owens as they appeared in 1935.

For the most part the photographs selected are of people much seen or talked about today—leaders in the world of literature, theater, art, music, sport, politics, and society. We also chose pictures of celebrities almost forgotten now but very much of that era—not purposely to provide readers with a "guess who" game, though this may be a likely outcome when families and friends pore through the book together.

You will find the name of Frank Crowninshield in few books of quotation. This is a pity, for there were few wittier men in all our literary history. "Married men," he once said, "make very poor husbands." Mr. Crowninshield himself never married. "The reason," says one of his friends, "is simply that he couldn't. He felt he had to make every girl in the world feel as if she was the only girl in the world—and he almost did, too."

One thing we did not include—and it should be here—is a *Vanity Fair* rejection. "Mr. Crowninshield's letters of rejection," says Dickson Hartwell, "were so complimentary that they usually had to be read twice to discover whether he was making a nomination for the Pulitzer Prize or expressing regret." Once he had to send back a manuscript to Paul Gallico. "My dear boy," he wrote, "this is superb! A little masterpiece! What color! What life! How beautifully you have phrased it all! A veritable gem!—Why don't you take it around to *Harper's Bazaar?*"

Mr. Gallico never did so, but he always cherished his rejection slip. For even a rejection from Mr. Crowninshield was something to prize; it was the next best to being a member of the family—one of whom, Frederic Bradlee, his nephew and my collaborating editor, we offer you next on the bill of *Fair*.

FRANK CROWNINSHIELD

1872–1947

Frank Crowninshield—Editor, Man, and Uncle

FREDERIC BRADLEE

"*VANITY FAIR was* Mr. Crowninshield," said Jeanne Ballot, his devoted secretary and associate. And indeed there may never have been a magazine more personal, more reflective of its editor's own character. Frank Crowninshield's most remarkable gift was his Geiger-counter ability to find hitherto unrecognized talent. When he published Gertrude Stein's "Have They Attacked Mary. He Giggled" in 1917, the readers of *Vanity Fair* may have been understandably startled, since this was one of the first "cubist" poems to appear in America. That same year he suavely lured away from *Vogue* a shy young copywriter named Dorothy Rothschild by publishing in *Vanity Fair* her sprightly lyric "Men: A Hate Song." Could even Frank Crowninshield have foretold that young Miss Rothschild would emerge years later as the incomparable Dorothy Parker? Could he have predicted that "The Social Life of the Newt," which he elicited in 1919 from a modest Harvard graduate signing himself Robert C. Benchley, would in due course evolve into the short film classic *The Sex Life of the Polyp*? He could surely never have envisioned what a Roman candle he was helping to set off in 1921 when he published a satirical piece written by a totally unknown English boy named Noel Coward. (When he and Gertrude Lawrence were playing Boston in *Tonight at 8:30* I met Noel Coward in his dressing-room—accompanied, as it happens, by the picture editor of this anthology. To Katharine and myself, both then in our teens, this somehow illicit backstage visit seemed a memorable oasis in the bleak desert of New England adolescence. I remember Coward's affixing me with a penetrating glance, as the famed staccato accents rapped out, "Your Uncle Frank paid me the first dollar I ever earned in America. As I was almost starving at the time, I was positively enchanted to get it.")

In the realm of painting, too, we can today more readily appreciate the pioneering aspect of Frank Crowninshield's editorship. In 1913, he was one of the organizers of the New York Armory show—that milestone in American aesthetic education in which the post-impressionist pictures created such a furor. And in 1929 he helped found New York's Museum of Modern Art. But even as late as 1930, he had to struggle to reproduce in *Vanity Fair* the now almost too familiar Picassos, Van Goghs, Gauguins and Rouaults—not to mention the sculpture of Despiau and the paintings of Braque, Modigliani, Pascin, and Segonzac, which he especially cherished and which formed the nucleus of his own collection. Many of the magazine's advertisers, in fact, threatened to withdraw their pages because of what they termed these "decadent and distorted" reproductions. We can in retrospect assess the extent of Frank Crowninshield's vindication and even triumph in this area. We need only ask ourselves whether these artists would be so familiar now—let alone so fashionable—had he not had the courage and sureness of instinct to champion them then. Would some of their "decadent and distorted" paintings fetch as much as a quarter of a million dollars at auction today, had he not first sponsored them at the Armory show and then reproduced them in the pages of *Vanity Fair*?

Significant of Frank Crowninshield the editor was his relish for the off-beat, the unexpected, the non-"square," which flavored

Vanity Fair throughout its twenty-two years. It would indeed be fanciful to suggest that this courtly gentleman was the forerunner of the "hip" movement in American culture. And yet, what other editor of his age would have invited Joseph H. Choate to write an article *not* about law or diplomacy, but about De Wolf Hopper? Or happily published a piece by Walter Lippmann not about the League of Nations, but about such colorful citizens of the time as "Peaches" and "Daddy" Browning, Ruth Snyder and Judd Gray? Or, for that matter, persuaded Arnold Bennett to forget his Five Towns long enough to devote a feature to the career woman of the 1920s? Frank Crowninshield had inherent gaiety, a zest for the absurd and the outrageous, which was reflected in *Vanity Fair* by such features as the William Cotton caricatures and the Covarrubias–"John Riddell" "Impossible Interviews." That his sense of fun was tinged with the sardonic is evidenced in the magazine by the quantity of murder articles by Edmund Pearson and Janet Flanner and the somewhat ghoulish stories by such writers as Lord Dunsany and Allan Seager.

The Crowninshield response to beauty was unorthodox and had several lacunae (he was, for instance, bored to death by music in any form). But to most sophisticated expressions of the aesthetic ethos he was highly attuned. His mind was cultivated rather than profound. He had a deep-bedded instinct, an uncanny sense of what was and would continue to be fresh, bright, fun, and appealing.

Like most of us, Frank Crowninshield was a man of many contradictions, some of which might entertain the readers of this book and perhaps shed a little new light on its progenitor.

When I first read his essay, "Ten Thousand Nights in a Dinner Coat," I remember savoring especially this description of a prisoner serving time at Sing-Sing: "The Warden, who was acting as our cicerone, drew my attention to an unhappy-looking man of approximately my own age who was completing in solitary confinement a visit of thirty years to that famous Hudson River resort. The reason for his protracted stay was that he had once dismembered the body of a lady for whom he had formerly entertained the liveliest feelings of affection." That pungent whiff of Crowninshieldiana somehow typifies all that was stately and ornate in his prose style. (It is even possible to imagine those lines flowing from the pen of that earlier *Vanity Fair* creator, Mr. William Makepeace Thackeray.) A short time after this, when I was about seventeen, I showed him a story which had been published in my prep-school magazine. Somewhere in the story, no doubt in unconscious imitation of Uncle Frank, I had written the word "verisimilitude." His eye spotted this at once and he asked me what I meant by "verisimilitude." "Truth," I told him, after a beat. "Then why," he demanded with devastating simplicity, "didn't you say 'truth'?"

Both generous and gentle with his family and his myriad friends, Uncle Frank seldom revealed the stringy thread of puritanism in his makeup. And it was a slight shock, in consequence, whenever he did. He said to me once, à propos of nothing whatever, "Say, Freddy, you've never repaid me the ten dollars I lent you during your Christmas holiday back in 1937." I must have looked a bit startled, since I probably assumed that—like most of his avuncular *pourboires*—the ten dollars had been a gift. "You might bear in mind," he continued with austere kindness, "that no matter how small the amount, people always remember *not* being paid back. I just thought I'd mention it, dear boy." Never had I seen him so forthright, so stripped of ceremony.

A further Crowninshield ambivalence was his air of belonging to an earlier era and at the same time very much to his own. One evening we were discussing a young lady to whom I had introduced him and who later became a close friend of his. "You know, it's so sad," he remarked quite seriously and in tones of wonder, "she has a quick mind and a lovely nature, but she's awfully mixed up and unhappy, and she apparently loathes her mother. Now that's the sort of thing I can't understand. I simply adored my own mother from the day I was born until the day she died." There was something beguiling in his entire innocence of the Freudian implication in what he had revealed. Later that same evening, however, he insisted I repeat to him a meaty epigram which a lady of his acquaintance had uttered at a party to describe her bridegroom's amatory prowess and versatility. With some diffidence (he was, after all, my grand-uncle and thus two generations removed from me), I told him the *bon mot*—in its unexpurgated version—which, freely translated for these refined pages, went: "This is my new husband, everybody: he makes love to me like Casanova and he titillates me like the Marquis de Sade." Uncle Frank replied instantly and without batting an eye, "Oh dear, poor darling—I'm afraid that means he does neither." And the gleam in his eye of up-to-date insight into those who are overly vocal about their sex lives need not have shamed Dr. Menninger himself.

Still another of Frank Crowninshield's dichotomies was in the realm of tact. Though renowned for his urbanity and vivid awareness of the social niceties, he could at odd but memorable moments be almost militantly tactless. Some years ago, when my brother was a fledgling reporter on a small country newspaper, Uncle Frank took my then sister-in-law and myself to lunch at the Colony restaurant. At a nearby table he spied his old friend Mrs. William Randolph Hearst. "Millicent, my dear," he intoned vibrantly across the room, "how lovely you're looking. Oh, say, Millicent, I'd like you to meet my little grandniece-in-law. You have a bond in common, you and she. You see, she also is a long-suffering, dedicated newspaperman's bride. And I thought possibly you might give her a few pointers." The subsequent hush in the restaurant was a little gray eternity that still now and then haunts my slumbers.

More often, however, the Crowninshield tact could be subtle and delicate. To any species of affliction, courage, or dilemma he responded warmly and with instinctive grace. Betsey Barton, daughter of his old friend Bruce, was one of his many protégées—not merely because of her youthful vitality and charm, but because he sensed in her from the moment they met a gift for writing. When Betsey had the tragic automobile accident that broke her back at the age of sixteen, he bombarded her with presents and jokes and tender little notes. One of the notes went as follows: "Dearest of all created beings: here is a pillow for your back and a book for your brain. I also send you love and admiration and remembrance. Your old beau, Crown." There must have been almost half a century between their ages.

This particular quality in Frank Crowninshield's character was perceptively brought home to me in a letter I received after his death from Tallulah Bankhead. (She adored him and was also one of his favorites.) She ended her letter: ". . . and he knew that despite his age and your youth, there were no years between you." It was quite true. He was precisely the same toward anyone who aroused his curiosity or interest—whether the person was twelve or eighty, simple or complicated, famous or obscure. This gave one the feeling that he himself was strangely ageless.

The much heralded Crowninshield manner was studied and its style was rococo, but he had true quality of spirit. His personal refinement and lightness of heart were constant and swift-flowing. The last time I saw him was Christmas Day, 1947, in Roosevelt Hospital, three days before he died. He was still sufficiently conscious to ask me why I was not yet rehearsing in a play for which he knew I had been engaged. I assured him that rehearsals had merely been postponed a few weeks because our star,. Jane Cowl, had broken a leg. With but seventy-two hours left in his own life, he became full of affectionate concern for Miss Cowl, his close friend for many years. When I told him that a truck had presumed to bump into that majestic lady on 44th Street, he dictated the following telegram: THIS FATAL FASCINATION YOU HAVE FOR MEN DEAR JANE EXTENDS NOT ONLY TO TRUCK DRIVERS BUT ALSO TO YOUR OLDEST SURVIVING ADMIRER DEVOTEDLY CROWNIE. It was the last wire he sent.

My favorite of all the Frank Crowninshield stories concerns the speech with which he introduced the spectacular aviatrix Amelia Earhart to the members of the Dutch Treat Club. I have saved it for the last partly because I think it is less well known than most, but chiefly because it captures so much of the kaleidoscopic Crowninshield spirit. It has his gift for rising to an occasion, his elegance, his *panache,* his mischief, his gentle yet satanic charm: "Gentlemen. Once upon a time there was a little colored girl named Eliza who died and went to heaven. She was met at the pearly gates by Saint Peter, who said to her: 'You're in heaven now, Eliza, and you're an angel in good standing. Go and pick yourself out a nice pair of wings.' So Eliza did, and in no time at all she was flashing about doing arabesques and entrechats and I don't know what all. She became, in fact, so confident that presently she thought she'd show off a bit before God. Now God and His Son were seated on Their golden thrones enjoying an afternoon nap—when Eliza came zooming into view. God awakened and watched her in mounting astonishment. At last He shook His sleeping Son and exclaimed softly and reverently: 'Jesus Christ, can that girl *fly.*' Gentlemen—Amelia Earhart."

We give you now *Vanity Fair.* We hope it is a book of which Frank Crowninshield might have been proud. We hope, too, that it will evoke joyous memories in the generation that knew its world and remembers the man who gave this world a little of its delectation. We hope finally that those born into the harsher world of today will enjoy and welcome some of the lighthearted flavor of an age gone by.

In Vanity Fair

(From the first editorial by Frank Crowninshield as it appeared in the issue of March 1914)

*V*ANITY FAIR has but two major articles in its editorial creed: first, to believe in the progress and promise of American life, and, second, to chronicle that progress cheerfully, truthfully, and entertainingly.

This is certainly a pleasant task, and not, we think, an impossible one. On every side there is helpful material at our hand; on every side there is encouragement. At no time in our history has the wonder and variety of American life been more inspiring, and, probably as a result of this, young men and young women, full of courage, originality, and genius are everywhere to be met with. This is particularly true in the arts. In our painting and sculpture a highly fertile and stimulating period is at hand. In the world of letters there are evidences of a profound activity, of originality of angle, of an inventive, forward, and reactionary spirit. New orders and readjustments confront us in the drama and in all the arts.

LET US instance one respect in which American life has recently undergone a great change. We allude to its increased devotion to pleasure, to happiness, to dancing, to sport, to the delights of the country, to laughter, and to all forms of cheerfulness. This tendency among us has been of late the subject of many parental warnings, admonitory sermons, and somewhat lugubrious editorials. For our part, it seems a bright sign in the heavens, for it argues, we believe, that we, as a nation, have come to realize the need for more cheerfulness, for hiding a solemn face, for a fair measure of pluck, and for great good humor.

NOW *Vanity Fair* means to be as cheerful as anybody. It will print humor, it will look at the stage, at the arts, at the world of letters, at sport, and at the highly vitalized, electric, and diversified life of our day from the frankly cheerful angle of the optimist, or, which is much the same thing, from the mock-cheerful angle of the satirist.

Thackeray said, in Vanity Fair

"I HAVE no other moral than this to tag to the present story of Vanity Fair. Some people consider Fairs immoral altogether, and eschew such, with their servants and families: perhaps they are right. But persons who think otherwise may perhaps like to step in for half an hour and look at the performances. There are scenes of all sorts; some dreadful combats, some grand and lofty horse-riding, some scenes of high life, and some of very middling indeed; some lovemaking for the sentimental, and some light comic business: the whole accompanied by appropriate scenery."

THIS latter angle is sometimes a little foreign to our American artists and authors, and it will be one of *Vanity Fair's* most pleasant duties to wean them from their stiff, unyielding ways and make them, as the French periodicals have succeeded in making theirs, a little more free in their technique—a shade less academic and "tight"—a trifle more fluent, fantastic, or even absurd.

FOR women we intend to do something in a noble and missionary spirit, something which, so far as we can observe, has never before been done for them by an American magazine. We mean to make frequent appeals to their intellects. We dare to believe that they are, in their best moments, creatures of some cerebral activity; we even make bold to believe that it is they who are contributing what is most original, stimulating, and highly magnetized to the literature of our day, and we hereby announce ourselves as determined and bigoted feminists.

VANITY FAIR will strive always to tell the truth about life, and to tell it tolerantly and entertainingly. With such a mission in mind we feel that we are fortunate in our title. Under no other titular banner could we battle so cheerfully. Bunyan, who first discovered the title, had, in *The Pilgrim's Progress,* an admirable and major purpose in mind—the determination to tell the truth about life, and to tell it entertainingly. Thackeray pinned the title to a novel in which he also succeeded in picturing the truth about life and in picturing it most entertainingly.

A PERIODICAL is bound to be, in a way, a family affair, and only when its family are really united does it become at all useful or successful. We hope to be useful to our family; to be permitted to aid them in many humble and practical ways, and to present to them cheerfully, month by month, a record of current achievements in all the arts and a mirror of the progress and promise of American life.

White Studio
De Wolf Hopper in The Mikado

De Wolf and Hedda Hopper with their infant son

Kazanjia
Mr. Hopper in Iolanthe

Early Memories of De Wolf Hopper

A Great Gilbert and Sullivan Comedian

JOSEPH H. CHOATE

DE WOLF HOPPER comes naturally by his remarkable powers as a comedian. It is a case of heredity, pure and simple. His father, John Hopper, was, in his way, a perfect comedian, off the stage. In my earliest years in New York he was one of my nearest and most devoted friends.

Many years before, he had married—in a runaway match—the beautiful Rosalie De Wolf, a member of a distinguished Rhode Island family. The runaway couple had lived together for twelve years, without sign of any child, when suddenly De Wolf appeared. He came upon the stage—the year was 1858—as a great surprise—just as he has done a thousand times since.

His father, as may be supposed, was wild with excitement and carried on frantically. The day before the child was born, he greeted the old apple woman at the corner and said: "You come to my house to-morrow, and, if it's a boy, I'll give you the largest plate of buckwheat cakes you ever had."

I must have seen the child the next day, but he made a public appearance—his first public appearance—on the third day of his life. His nurse had given him his bath and laid him for a moment on the bed, when John seized him by the leg and held him out of the open window over the street, naked, for all the world to see that he had a son.

John was a great walker, and one day he made his appearance in Madison Square with De Wolf in his arms. "Who has lost a baby?" he cried out to the nurses assembled there. "Has anybody lost a baby? See what a splendid baby I have found!" Strangely enough, a poor woman, who had recently lost a baby, and was quite crazed by the fact, sprang forward, exclaiming, "It is mine! It is mine!" John had to appeal to the police!

John himself had a perfect passion for the stage. As a boy he used to save up his quarters and buy a ticket to the shilling gallery. When Fanny Kemble was here

he used to see her every night. The theatre was, of course, the perfect horror of his father, that grand old Quaker, Isaac T. Hopper. One night his father caught John stealing upstairs at midnight, with his shoes in his hands. "John," said he, "where has thee been?" "To the theatre," was the reply. "Whom did thee go to see?" "Fanny Kemble." "But, John," his father asked, "I hope this is the first time thee has ever done such a thing?" But John replied, "No, father, this is the sixty-third time."

I do not see how De Wolf Hopper, being his father's son, could ever have been anything else than the comedian he is. I was on very intimate terms with the boy in his infancy, so much so that on his third birthday—his father and mother were giving him a party—he was asked, by one of the early guests, "Are you three years old yet, Willy?" (He was always called Willy in those days.) "No," he answered. "I shan't be three until Choate comes."

14

JOSEPH H. CHOATE

From a sketch by John Singer Sargent

The Force of Heredity, and Nella

A Modern Fable with a Telling Moral for Eugenists

ANITA LOOS

TWELVE years had elapsed since Nella had hung on the old gate—the old gate of the old farm not far from the old well where they kept the old oaken bucket—and had promised her old mother that, come what might, she would always be eugenic.

Twelve years had now gone by since that day, and on the last—or nearly the last —day of the twelfth year, Nella lay back among the silken cushions of her gilded *chaise longue* and wept—wept over the rash promise of her youth, and wept at the thought of all it had brought her.

Listen: When Nella had first come to New York she had secured a position as a manicure in a fine big hotel. She was quite frank with the fine big proprietor: she told him straight out that she did not know how to cure manis. He took one look at her fine big eyes and engaged her on the spot. Proprietors of such hotels are only too apt to engage manicures in that fine, impulsive way.

For many weeks Nella lived her simple, girlish life, prodding her customers with that pointed stick which manicures always wield so earnestly. And the thing that ever held the finest, biggest place in her mind was the promise she had made to her old mother on the old gate at the old farm: the promise to be eugenic.

At last He appeared—the Perfect Prince —of whom she had so honorably dreamed. And he was miraculously vouchsafed to her at dinner in an Italian *table d' hôte*. He was as handsome as handsome is, and as muscular as the *poulet du jour*. She knew that he was a poet from the way he ate his spaghetti. He had a fine, sensitive mouth.

Evidently he was poor. But he was *healthy*. They would have to begin housekeeping in a shack somewhere up among the snow-bound wastes of the Bronx, but it would be home, HOME. As for Gus, he

Foley

ANITA LOOS

was heartily in favor of it. "Lead me there unto," was the poetic way he put it. Life seemed just to have begun for him.

IT WAS within a week of the day set for the wedding of Nella and Gus when, one morning, Sigsbee van Cortland, the Copper King, hobbled into the manicure parlor where Nella sat waiting to manicure. He gave her one glance, and hobbled toward her, his hands extended. He hobbled because he had a wooden leg. Why had he a wooden leg? He never made any mystery about it: if you asked him how he had happened to lose his real leg, he would answer, quite simply and frankly, that it had been bitten off by a shark, and then change the subject.

He loved Nella from the first moment he saw her and asked her to be his wife.

Nella hesitated. Apart from the fact that she was so soon to be married to Gus and that Gus had already bought a wedding ring with the word "Mizpah" engraved on it, how could she wed a man with a wooden leg? After all the teachings of her good old mother, how *could* she? But a Copper King is not easily balked. Coming down to hard reality he can produce the tinkle: and that meant a whole lot to the sweet young girl from the fine old farm.

SO Nella made her excuses to Gus, and married the wooden-legged millionaire.

* * *

AND NOW, twelve years afterward, she lay on her silken covered *chaise longue* and wept. That morning, weary of it all and filled with a vague remorse, she had been sitting at the front window when a familiar figure passing in the street awakened a strange, sad note in her memory.

It was Gus.

In her anguish she could not stifle the little cry that escaped her lips. Gus looked up. He hesitated but a moment, then dashed up the steps and was soon at her feet. Nella looked at his fine, broad shoulders and burst into a flood of tears.

"Nella, dear," he cried, "are you happy?"

Nella staggered to her feet. Together they wavered on through one exquisitely furnished room after another and finally stopped before a door on which was a sign reading: NURSERY.

"Open it," she said. "I haven't the courage."

Gus opened the door. Inside, hobbling pitifully around the room, were eleven children. Gus looked once again and recoiled. They had all been born with a wooden leg!

NIJINSKY

A new portrait by Baron de Meyer of the celebrated Russian ballet dancer

Sarah Bernhardt Here Again

The Most Famous of Living Actresses on an American Tour

ARTHUR JOHNSON

SARAH BERNHARDT, the greatest of living actresses, is here to fill what she describes as her "last American engagement." Opening in Montreal she will reach New York at the beginning of November, and appear at the Knickerbocker Theater there for a month's engagement. She will celebrate her seventy-second birthday at Ottawa on October twenty-third. It is a pity that the American metropolis will not have the opportunity of presenting its homage to her on that memorable occasion.

REGISTERING a failure on the occasion of her début at the Comédie Française in 1862, Bernhardt left the "House of Molière" for the Porte Saint-Martin, and for the Gymnase soon after that. But she was not at all successful in burlesque. In 1867 she went to the Odéon and made a great success as Cordelia in a French version of *King Lear,* and as the Queen in Victor Hugo's *Ruy Blas.* Returning to the Comédie Française in 1872, she made one brilliant success there after another. As "sociétaire" she excited the jealousy of her colleagues to such an extent that she broke her contract with the Théâtre Français in 1879.

The French courts condemned her to pay a fine of 100,000 francs, but the Republic decorated her with the Legion of Honor, technically as a tribute to her skill as a painter and sculptor.

ARTHUR SYMONS, in speaking recently of Sarah Bernhardt and of her advanced age, remarked that the very best moment to study an artist was at the moment of his or her "decadence," when the first energy of inspiration is gone and when the method and technique alone are left.

It is easy to understand the excitement with which people went to the theater to see the slim and tigerish Sarah in her prime as Phèdre, Marguérite Gautier, Adrienne Lecouvreur, Fédora and La Tosca. Her voice, especially when employed on the noble lines of Racine, seems to be not a single musical instrument but an entire orchestra. Prose she uses as if she were playing on a rare old violin.

MADAME BERNHARDT first appeared in this country in November, 1880. Her fame had preceded her, and her early audiences were made up largely of those who were attracted there by a morbid desire to see the best advertised woman in the world, rather than through interest in her art: —but not so the playgoers of this later generation.

SINCE she first appeared here innumerable players speaking an alien tongue have come and gone without achieving enduring success. How does Bernhardt contrive to remain in full possession of this field? What are the qualities that have enabled her to succeed and how is it that, even in her old age, she can attract such enormous audiences? Perhaps these questions may be worth the consideration of the few persons now living who take the stage seriously.

DURING her first season in New York, Madame Bernhardt gave a professional matinee here. As the great audience was dispersing, a wise actor exclaimed, in the presence of the writer, "Heavens, what a wonderful *feeder!*" The actor, in that single remark, had touched the mainspring of this great artist's enduring fame. "Feeding," as it is technically called, is really only another name for the difficult art of *listening,* or paying the closest sort of attention to the actors with whom the scene is played, an art which has grown into sad decay the past few years in America.

Bernhardt is always the central figure of any play in which she appears, but, unlike many of our native actresses, she is never above listening—with rapt attention—to whatever is said to her by the actors on the stage. And it is this quality, more than anything else, that has made her a permanent favorite with American audiences.

Duse, who conquered New York in a single night, once said something so wise that very few members of the profession paid any attention to it: "An actress's greatest moments are not those in which she speaks, but those in which she listens." It was for other reasons that this incomparable artist failed on her second and last visit to this country. Another star who was highly successful here was Salvini, whose feats of listening will never be forgotten by anyone who witnessed them. Many German players have visited this country—Barnay, Agnes, Sorma, Geistinger Schratt, Josie Gallmeyer—but not one of them has ever appealed to American audiences.

SARAH BERNHARDT

From a photograph taken in August 1916 at her villa near Nice

A Memory of Eleonora Duse

And of Her Acting in La Città Morta

ARTHUR SYMONS

I LOOK back, several years, to a week I once spent in Zurich. Duse was there, playing in d'Annunzio's dramas. I had never seen *La Città Morta* on the stage, and, having translated it into English, I was particularly curious to see what impression it would make upon me as an acting play. I have changed none of my opinions about it, but some of my opinions have been a little more defined.

Everything that has to be said or done by Duse becomes much more beautiful, gains nobility and a kind of intellectual quality.

I see now all the points at which *La Città Morta,* that remarkable study in morbid and criminal nerves, becomes a representation of mere brutal madness. The whole of the second act, and particularly the confession of Leonardo to Alessandro, becomes even more unsatisfactory than it is in the play as one reads it; partly, no doubt, because the actor, whose business it was to listen in a quivering and agonized silence, listened with perfect composure, looking down calmly at his new brown leggings; but partly, also, because a confession so harrowing could not have been listened to in silence by any human being, and the play itself is at fault.

HERE, if anywhere there should have been some vivid action, some significant incident which, almost without words, should have set the truth naked between man and man; and there is little action, only words.

In *La Città Morta* d'Annunzio has neither accepted the conventional form of the drama, nor has he, like Maeterlinck, created a wholly new and satisfying form. He has transplanted the novel to the stage, and by sheer force of emotion he has made these conversations absorbingly interesting, even when they are not, properly speaking, dramatic.

La Città Morta is almost more a poem than a play, and there is in it a beauty which is to be found in the work of no contemporary writers for the stage except Maurice Maeterlinck and W. B. Yeats. And this beauty is of an entirely individual kind, a poetry of sensation, or of an emotion which is made up of a spiritual apprehension of the things of the senses.

D'Annunzio dedicated *La Gioconda* to *Eleonora Duse delle belle mani,* and, in *La Città Morta* he has made her blind, in

ELEONORA DUSE

The great Italian tragedienne

order that she may see, as the blind do, with all her senses, and most with her hands. In *La Gioconda,* the symbolism is cruder, the poetry less delicate; the hands have to be crushed, that the absence of their beauty may be realized.

But here how much of the poetry comes from that sense of touch, as the blind woman moves, with exquisite hesitations, about the room! The sense of hearing, too, the physical sense of the sun, of light and dark, not seen with the eyes, but felt through all the blood, comes into the very substance of the play, in which, for once, Duse can be herself the character which she represents.

In all the plays into which this woman comes, you watch her exist on the stage, a beautiful human thing; and she moves, is silent, thinks or speaks or listens, and it is enough. When she is silent, her face has a mystery which is more significant than anything she can say; when she speaks, her voice is like a smile, like a caress, like a person: her voice is itself a woman. It has its physiognomy, with mortal pallors, dim anxieties, strange tendernesses. And how much, how often, is this great artist, this great woman, lost under the false and confusing lights of the stage, under the burden of indifferent words, under the

mask of faces which try vainly to be the face of Marguérite Gautier, a *cocotte,* or of Magda. In *La Città Morta* she plays a part which is itself poetry, and she becomes suddenly at once herself and the part.

WHAT is acting? Is it to be oneself with the utmost intensity, and to put that self into every character, or is it to have no self and to be a speaking mirror? In seeing Duse in *La Città Morta,* one says, perhaps for the first time wholly: "This is not Duse, this is Anna;" and yet, after all Anna is Duse. For once there is nothing between herself and the character she has assumed, or only a veil which softens the outlines a little. It is Duse seen through a temperament, and the temperament is her own.

This it is, for good and evil, to be greater than one's art. Here is a woman who, in her own nature, is a great personal force, a force of beauty, subtlety, intellect, intensity, and, being more than an actress, is perhaps also less than an actress. She creates out of her own nature, her own flesh and blood and soul; and loses something of what is finest in herself as she descends to the imitation of outward realities and in her emotions, which is the business of the actress.

Have They Attacked Mary. He Giggled

GERTRUDE STEIN

Somehow, it seems as if the surest test for the detection of a modern philistine is the poetic work of Gertrude Stein. The reader who takes a delirious joy in the poem which we publish here, who constantly stops his reading to say "Isn't it great—" "Isn't it wonderful?," etc., is not a philistine. On the contrary, the individual, male or female, who begins foaming at the mouth at Miss Stein's second "page," who shrieks "This is insanity" at the third or fourth, and ends by writing a letter of protest to the Editor of Vanity Fair, IS one. Decidedly this second individual is one. Is one decidedly.

Page I

Can you be more confusing by laughing. Do say yes.

We are extra. We have the reasonableness of a woman and we say we do not like a room.

We wish we were married.

Why do you believe in me.

Including all that is sold, you mean three pictures, including all that is sold why cannot you give me that.

I do give it to you.

Thank you I was only joking.

But I do mean it.

Thank you very much.

Page II

Can you swim in a lake.

We can.

Then do so.

Page III

Have you an automobile.

Page IV

The queen has.

We asked for one.

They cannot send it now.

Cannot they.

We will see.

Page V

In memory of the Englishwoman

We will buy it together.

Not that Englishwoman.

No not that time or that one.

Page VI

We wish to go there.

Can they accept us.

We marry.

They ask.

Page VII

In the midst of the exercise.

We exercise.

We are successful.

Page VIII

Lighting.

We can see to the lighting.

Page IX

Can a jew be wild.

Page X

A great many settlers have mercy. Of course they do to me.

You are proud. I am proud of my courage.

Page XI

Can you find me in a home.

We can all find you in a hole. I hope not.

Then keep warm. I cannot have that announcement. Very well then elect him. We can be *so* suggestive.

Page XII

In the midst of refusing I have been asked to go on.

Page XIII

In the next name you mean the wife in the next name there is a mention of a ring. In the next name they have means.

What can you do to relate it.

Many ready papers many papers are taken there.

Page XIV

In the midst of the fortnight what was the wish.

We did not say others. Nor did he.

Indeed he was not observed. You mean in the time.

In the day time and at night.

And in the evening.

Page XV

Believe me in everything.

Page XVI

It is wonderful the way I am not interested.

Page XVII

What can you do.

I can answer any question.

Very well answer this.

Who is Mr. McBride.

Page XVIII

It is found out.

Not by me.

Page XIX

I told you that you were told.

Page XX

It is outrageous to mention a hotel.

Page XXI

Can you please me with kisses.

Page XXII

I cannot destroy blandishments.

That is not the word you meant to use. I meant to say that being indeed convinced of the necessity of seeing them swim I believe in their following. Do you believe in their following.

Page XXIII

Can you think in meaning to sell well. We can all think separately. Can you think in meaning to be chequered. I can answer for the news. Of course you can answer for the news.

Page XXIV

In the midst of that rain.

In the midst of that rain there was a wing. And he was not sorry. Who can be sorry there. We are.

Yes lamb.

Roger.

Page XXV

In leaning grass, in leaning grass.
Yes, in leaning grass.
Can you widen rivers there.

Page XXVI

Why am I so sleepy.

Page XXVII

Fifty boxes of matches wax matches which burn very well and strike very well and have no smell. Do you mean less smell than others.

Page XXVIII

You say he is that sort of a person. He has been here again and asked about pitchers.

Page XXIX

Can he ask about pitchers.

Page XXX

Officers do not kiss soldiers.
What do officers kiss.
Officers kiss the cross. Indeed they do.
So do soldiers, in passing.

Page XXXI

Can you see him.

Page XXXII

Particularly today.
Feel me.
A sentimental face.

Page XXXIII

Can they say no excuse. Can they say selfish brothers. Do they say we are pleased to have been taught. No they do not do so they have that very negligible quality, the station of Lyons. We were there. And books. Yes books. You did not understand a laundry-woman. Yes woman porters. Of course women porters. Why should we be proud. Because it is foolish. It is very foolish to be wrong. In that case may I beg to refer to it. You may.

The French are polite.

—◦✦◦—

Genthe

MAXINE ELLIOTT

Famed actress and international beauty

Born Jessie Dermot in Rockland, Maine, she came to New York in 1895 and joined Augustin Daly's Shakespeare repertory company as Maxine Elliott. From 1898 to 1903 she co-starred in a series of plays in New York and on tour with her second husband, the noted actor Nat Goodwin. In 1908 she became the first American actress to have a theatre built for her and named after her, and has owned and operated the Maxine Elliott Theatre with great aplomb ever since.

Men: A Hate Song

DOROTHY ROTHSCHILD (PARKER)

I hate men.
They irritate me.

I

There are the Serious Thinkers—
There ought to be a law against them.
They see life, as through shell-rimmed
glasses, darkly.
They are always drawing their weary hands
Across their wan brows.
They talk about Humanity
As if they had just invented it;
They have to keep helping it along.
They revel in strikes
And they are eternally getting up petitions.
They are doing a wonderful thing for the
Great Unwashed,—
They are living right down among them.
They can hardly wait
For *The Masses* to appear on the news-
stands,
And they read all those Russian novels—
The sex best sellers.

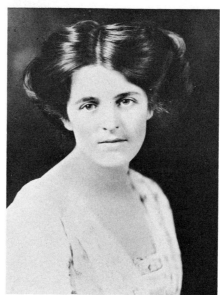

United Press

DOROTHY PARKER

III

And then there are the Sensitive Souls
Who do interior decorating, for Art's sake.
They always smell faintly of vanilla
And put drops of sandalwood on their
cigarettes.
They are continually getting up costume
balls
So that they can go
As something out of the "Arabian Nights."
They give studio teas
Where people sit around on cushions
And wish they hadn't come.
They look at a woman languorously,
through half-closed eyes,
And tell her, in low, passionate tones,
What she ought to wear.
Color is everything to them—everything;
The wrong shade of purple
Gives them a nervous breakdown.

II

There are the Cave Men—
The Specimens of Red-Blooded Manhood.
They eat everything very rare,
They are scarcely ever out of their cold
baths,
And they want everybody to feel their
muscles.
They talk in loud voices,
Using short Anglo-Saxon words.
They go around raising windows,
And they slap people on the back,
And tell them what they need is exercise.
They are always just on the point of walk-
ing to San Francisco,
Or crossing the ocean in a sailboat,
Or going through Russia on a sled—
I wish to God they would!

"They talk about humanity"

IV

Then there are the ones
Who are Simply Steeped in Crime.
They tell you how they haven't been to bed
For four nights.
They frequent those dramas
Where the only good lines
Are those of the chorus.
They stagger from one cabaret to another,
And they give you the exact figures of their
gambling debts.
They hint darkly at the terrible part
That alcohol plays in their lives.
And then they shake their heads
And say Heaven must decide what is go-
ing to become of them—
I wish I were Heaven!

"They frequent the theatre"

I hate men.
They irritate me.

Two Heavy-Weights

on a Fairbanks Scale

Here is the great screen triumvirate: the three Busy-Bertha guns on America's movie battle-front. Their combined salaries would take up the next Liberty loan —and leave something over for taxes and taxis. This three-in-one photograph recently came to us, with the following

note, from Hollywood, California: Dear *Vanity Fair*: Isn't it wonderful how strong we all are? Here is a well-balanced picture for your photograph album. Please excuse Charlie for shaving off his mustache, and Mary for wearing her Lucile rompers at half mast. Your loving son,
Douglas Fairbanks

Modern Love—by a Modern French Poet

A Few Novel Forms in Which to Address the Lady of Your Heart's Desire

PAUL GÉRALDY

Vanity Fair *rarely prints contributions in foreign languages, but it cannot, in this instance, resist the temptation of publishing a group of these verses in their original form.*

Dualisme

Chérie, explique-moi pourquoi
tu dis: "*mon* piano, *mes* roses,"
et: "*tes* livres, *ton* chien" . . . pourquoi
je t'entends déclarer parfois:
"c'est avec *mon* argent à *moi*
que je veux acheter ces choses."
Ce qui m'appartient t'appartient!
Pourquoi ces mots qui nous opposent,
le tien, le mien, le mien, le tien?
Si tu m'aimais tout à fait bien,
tu dirais: "*les* livres, *le* chien"
et: "*nos* roses."

Méditation

On aime d'abord par hasard,
par jeu, par curiosité,
pour avoir, dans un regard,
lu des possibilités.
Et puis comme au fond soi-même
on s'aime beaucoup,
si quelqu'un vous aime, on l'aime
par conformité de goût.
Pour l'amour d'aimer on s'invite
à partager ses moindres maux.
On prend l'habitude, très vite,
d'échanger de petits mots.
Quand on a longtemps dit les mêmes,
on les redit sans y penser . . .
Et alors, mon Dieu, l'on aime
parce qu'on a commencé.

Doute

Tu m'as dit: "Je pense à toi
tout le jour."
Mais tu penses moins à moi
qu'à l'amour.

Tu m'as dit: "Mes yeux mouillés
qui ne peuvent t'oublier
restent longtemps éveillés
lorsque je me couche."
Mais ton cœur est moins grisé
qu'amusé.
Tu penses plus au baiser
qu'à la bouche.

Tu ne te tourmentes point.
Tu sais sans chercher plus loin,

que nos joies sont bien les nôtres. . . .
Mais l'amour est un besoin.
M'aimerais-tu beaucoup moins
si j'étais un autre?

Abat-Jour

Tu demandes pourquoi je reste sans rien
    dire . . .
C'est que voici le grand moment,
l'heure des yeux et du sourire,
le soir . . . et que ce soir je t'aime . . . in-
    finiment!
Serre-moi contre toi. J'ai besoin de caresses.
Si tu savais tout ce qui monte en moi, ce
    soir,
d'ambition, d'orgueil, de désir, de tendresse,
et de bonté! . . . Mais non, tu ne peux pas
    savoir! . . .

Baisse un peu l'abat-jour, veux-tu? Nous
    serons mieux.
C'est dans l'ombre que les cœurs causent,
et l'on voit beaucoup mieux les yeux
quand on voit un peu moins les
    choses. . . .
Ce soir je t'aime trop pour te parler
    d'amour.
Serre-moi contre ta poitrine!
Je voudrais que ce soit mon tour
d'être celui que l'on câline. . . .
Baisse encore un peu l'abat-jour.
Là. Ne parlons plus. Soyons sages.
Et ne bougeons pas: c'est si bon
tes mains tièdes sur mon visage! . . .

Mais qu'est-ce encore? Que nous veut-on?
Ah! c'est le café qu'on apporte. . . .
Eh! bien, posez ça là, voyons!
Faites vite! . . . Et fermez la porte! . . .

Qu'est-ce que je te disais donc?
Nous prenons ce café . . . maintenant? Tu
    préfères?
C'est vrai: toi, tu l'aimes très chaud.
Veux-tu que je te serve? Attends, laisse-moi
    faire.
Il est fort, aujourd'hui! . . . Du sucre? Un
    seul morceau?
C'est assez? . . . Veux-tu que je goûte?
Là! Voici votre tasse, amour. . . .
Mais qu'il fait sombre! On n'y voit
    goutte. . . .
Lève donc un peu l'abat-jour.

Tendresse

Tu m'aimes? . . . Qu'est-ce que tu fais?
Tu ne dis rien. . . . Mets-toi plus près.
Laisse ces choses qui t'occupent,
et viens t'étendre ici, voyons!
Je ferai bien attention.
Je ne friperai pas ta jupe. . . .
Otons les coussins s'ils te gênent.
Tâchons de nous installer bien,
et donnez-moi vos mains, vilaine,
et mettez vos yeux dans les miens. . . .
Si vous saviez comme on vous aime!
Regardez-moi mieux. . . . Encore
    mieux! . . .
Ça doit bien se voir dans mes yeux
que je t'ai donné tout moi-même! . . .
Tu le vois, dis? . . . Tu le com-
    prends? . . .
Mon amour, ce soir, est si grand,
si grave, si profond, si tendre! . . .
Mais non, tu ne peux pas comprendre. . . .
Tu dis que si? . . . Tu es gentil.
Je te dis tout ça, mon petit,
c'est pour que tu te rendes compte,
que tu saches. . . . Enfin, voilà. . . .
Regarde: les larmes me montent.
Et rien n'existe, et rien ne compte
que ces yeux-là, que ce front-là. . . .
Penche ta tête un peu du côté de la lampe,
et laisse-moi, comme un bandeau,
mettre les paumes de mes mains contre tes
    tempes. . . .
Ainsi, c'est bien vrai, mon petit oiseau:
ils résument pour moi les tendresses
    suprêmes,
ces doux yeux attentifs, ce joli front égal?
C'est vrai, dis? C'est vrai? . . . Je t'aime,
    ah, je t'aime! . . .
Je voudrais te faire du mal.

Finale

Alors, adieu. Tu n'oublies rien? . . . C'est
    bien. Va-t'en.
Nous n'avons plus rien à nous dire. Je te
    laisse.
Tu peux partir . . . Pourtant, attends en-
    core, attends . . .
Il pleut. . . . Attends que cela cesse.

Couvre-toi bien surtout! Tu sais qu'il fait
    très froid
dehors. C'est un manteau d'hiver qu'il fallait
    mettre . . .
Je t'ai bien tout rendu? Je n'ai plus rien à toi?
Tu as pris ton portrait? tes lettres? . . .

Allons, regarde-moi puisqu'on va se quitter, . . .
Mais prends garde: ne pleurons pas! . . . Ce serait bête.
Quel effort il faut faire, hein? dans nos pauvres têtes,
pour revoir les amants que nous avons été!

Nos deux vies s'étaient l'une à l'autre données toutes,
pour toujours. . . . Et voici que nous les reprenons!
Et nous allons partir, chacun avec son nom,
recommencer, errer, vivre ailleurs. . . . Oh! sans doute,

nous souffrirons . . . pendant quelque temps. Et puis, quoi!
l'oubli viendra, la seule chose qui pardonne.
Et il y aura toi, et il y aura moi,
et nous serons parmi les autres deux personnes.

Ainsi, déjà! tu vas entrer dans mon passé!
Nous nous rencontrerons, par hasard dans les rues . . .
Je te regarderai de loin, sans traverser . . .
Tu passeras avec des robes inconnues . . .

Et puis nous resterons sans nous voir de longs mois . . .
Et mes amis te donneront de mes nouvelles . . .
Et je dirai de toi qui fus ma vie, de toi
qui fus ma force et ma douceur: "Comment va-t-elle?"

Notre grand cœur, c'était cette petite chose! . . .
Etions-nous assez fous, pourtant, les premiers jours!
Tu te souviens, l'enchantement, l'apothéose? . . .
S'aimait-on! . . . Et voilà: c'était ça, notre amour!

Ainsi nous, même nous, quand nous disons "je t'aime,"
voilà donc la valeur qu'a ce mot-là! Mon Dieu! . . .
Vrai, c'est humiliant. . . . On est donc tous les mêmes?
Nous sommes donc pareils aux autres? . . . Comme il pleut!

Tu ne peux pas partir par ce temps. . . . Allons, reste!
Oui, reste, va! On tâchera de s'arranger. . . .
On ne sait pas. . . . Nos cœurs, quoiqu'ils aient bien changé,
se reprendront peut-être au charme des vieux gestes. . . .

On fera son possible. On sera bon. Et puis,
on a beau dire, au fond, on a des habitudes. . . .
Assieds-toi, va! Reprends près de moi ton ennui.
Moi près de toi je reprendrai ma solitude.

CARUSO

And a new marvel in moving pictures

The Italian scientist, Lieutenant B. Bettini, has perfected an invention in motion pictures which was tried out by Enrico Caruso —a young man who has lately been attracting a good deal of attention as a singer in opera. M. Caruso sat down, posed befor the movie machine, came back in an hour, paid Bettini two dollars and received a five-by-eight-inch negative on which he saw seven hundred views of himself in action. He was handed an eight-by-ten enlargement of one of the microscopic pictures, sat down again and this time saw the pictures of himself, which had only an hour ago been posed, flash by him on the screen. The enlargement in center is of the little image indicated with a white band.

Nominated for the Hall of Fame: 1914–1918

Hoppé

HENRY JAMES

Because though, through his devotion to the cause of the Allies, he has become a British subject, we shall always insist on calling him "our Henry James." Because he has done more to reveal us to ourselves than any other American novelist. Because he has never sought for popularity; and finally because the British have welcomed him with open arms and we lose him with regret.

© *Pirie Mac Donald*

HENRY CABOT LODGE

Because he is one of our best equipped and most readable historical writers; because at the age of twenty-three, he edited the *North American Review;* because he is a wit and English scholar of high attainments; because he is one of the best living embodiments of the culture of Harvard College and of Massachusetts.

de Strelecki

MARCONI

Because he is the most conspicuous Italian man of science of our time. Because, by improving wireless telegraphy, he robbed the sea of half its terrors, in peace time. Because he is working hard for the success of his country in the war, and finally because he was the youngest man to reach the rank of Senator in the Parliament of United Italy.

IGNACE PADEREWSKI

Because he was for a great many years the most conspicuous pianist in the world; and because since the war started, he has dedicated his means, talent and energies to the welfare of the destitute people in his native Poland.

Thompson

CHARLES DANA GIBSON

Because he is the most popular figure in American illustration, but chiefly because he has mobilized the artists who are directing the pictorial propaganda of America.

VERNON CASTLE

Because he gave up an income of over fifty thousand dollars a year to go to the front and fight for his country; because he has done more for modern ballroom dancing than any living man; because two excellent musical comedies were built around his popularity as a citizen of New York; because he had the extreme good fortune to marry Mrs. Vernon Castle; because he carries modesty to the point of self-abasement; and finally because—as a daring and resourceful aviator—he has brought down his share of flying Teutons from the sky.

ARTURO TOSCANINI

Because he is one of the greatest conductors the world has known; because he introduced Wagner into Germany; because he has done more than any man to raise the level of opera in this country; because he conducts without a score.

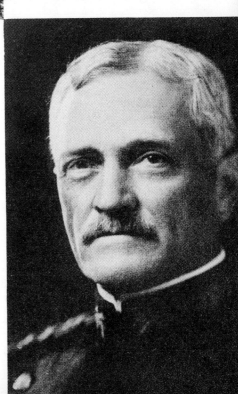

BRIGADIER GENERAL JOHN J. PERSHING

Because he is even a greater administrator than warrior; because he created the Bureau of Insular Affairs; because, by his patient forcefulness he tamed the Moro tribes and was elected to their innermost councils; because he is looking for a Villa in Mexico; and finally, because he shuns politics and does not talk for publication.

Poems

MICHAEL STRANGE

Fairchild

MICHAEL STRANGE

Fate

I am Fate,
The thrown back noose;
The lapse into unconsciousness;
The revitalized echo.
I peer from the faces of pools, at dusk,
From the up-flung eyes of praying women,
From the roar and flux of the eternal tides.
My direction speaks
In the curiosities of children,
Among the impulses of manhood,
And in the sympathies of age.
I drive all caravans
To their next resting;
I tune each instrument
For its latest song;
Since I comprise the gait
Of every purpose;
I, who am Fate,
The reins upon Time,
The inevitable way,
The brow of Destiny.

Why!

Why some down-flying bird
Shakes a slumbering rose;
Why a poet's muse—leads on—or goes,
God knows!
Why Love, juggling with gleams,
Should alight on your sill,
Singing to you—Fulfill, Fulfill,
'Til you rise, cry out—and find the air still.
Why Birth is launched amid shrieks and
  cries,
Why Life is spun from a thread of sighs,
Until Death sweeps up, on his flight of
  crows—
God knows!

Autumnal

To-night the inland sea hurls through the
  air
Her foam. The trees twist, silver-limbed
  and bare!
A new strength mutters in the wind, while
  I—
I feel the nails of Time among my hair!

Solitude

I am Solitude,
The master of thought,
The mood of sorrow,
The whistler for dreams.
I dwell in the fixed look
Of sad eyes,
And in the questioning smile
The soul gives strangers.
I live in the phrase
That is never answered;
In the ultimate Why
Of the cloistered heart.
I call my élèves
At the Autumn's moonrise;
And, during the Winter's
Snow-mad nights,
I sing to them
Of the loves of angels,
And the dying words
Of the passing Gods.

For I am Solitude,
The master of thought,
The mood of sorrow,
The whistler for dreams.

Sunset—An Impression

Columns of golden smoke,
Floating against aquamarine;
Ribbed mantles of purple rose,
Stretching across sapphire-musk;
Fissures—slate colored—
Expanding into white, and widening
Among greens. Reds!
Then wind-pulled, dust grey snow-fields,
Hardening to black.

No summary of Michael Strange's work can be counted complete without a reference to its most salient virtues and chief defects. By defects is meant, first, the occasional lack of form in her poems—perhaps the result of a contempt for technical metric formulae—and, second, a somewhat too insistent introspection. To the latter defect we attribute a feeling, as we read her outpourings, of witnessing the tortures of an intellect whose subtleties have turned back upon itself. Her introspection is at times so complete that she seems as one employing a delphic alphabet, with the meaning of which she is, alone among mortals, familiar. In this she a little resembles the futurist painters, who express themselves in symbols which convey emotions that are poignant to them, but without definite meaning to others.

The virtues of Michael Strange's work lie in the highly emotional qualities discernible in it: in the daring of her metaphors and similes, and in her power of evoking the true atmosphere of drama. She has, too, a decided gift for satire; a wit and cleverness of phrase which challenge our interest; an occasional, and charming, whimsicality; and always something of golden Youth, something intangible but none the less appealing. So that, notwithstanding the lack of clarity in their outline and the morbid introspection often so evident in them, her poems are calculated to arrest the attention of a public long swamped by the ordinary "magazine" verse of our day, verse which, though irreproachable in form, is nevertheless wholly undistinguished in thought, in drama, or in emotion.—F.C.

All About the Income-Tax

A New Parlor Game for the Family Circle

P. G. WODEHOUSE

AS I sit in my poverty-stricken home, looking at the place where the piano used to be before I had to sell it to pay my income-tax, I find myself in thoughtful mood. The first agony of the separation from my hard-earned, so to speak income, is over, and I can see that I was unjust in my original opinion of the United States Government. At first, I felt toward the U. S. G. as I would feel toward any perfect stranger who insinuated himself into my home and stood me on my head and went through my pockets. The only difference I could see between the U. S. G. and the ordinary practitioner in a black mask was that the latter occasionally left his victim carfare.

Gosh! I was bitter.

NOW, however, after the lapse of weeks, I begin to see the other side. What the Government is going to do with it, I do not know—I can only hope that they will not spend it on foolishness and nut sundaes and the movies—but, apparently, they needed a few billion dollars, and you and I had to pay it. That part remains as unpleasant as ever. But what I, like so many others, have overlooked is the thoughtfulness of the authorities in having chosen March for the final filling-up of their printed forms.

The New Indoor Sport

YOU know how it is in the long Winter evenings, if you have nothing to occupy you. You either play auction bridge, or you go in for one of those games played with colored counters and a painted board (than which nothing is more sapping to the soul), or else you sit and scowl at each other and send the children early to bed. But, last March, with the arrival of Form 10536 X-G, dullness in the home became impossible. Our paternal government, always on the lookout for some way of brightening the lives of the Common People, had invented the greatest round-game in the world. Tiddleywinks has been completely superseded.

In every home, during this past Winter, it was possible to see the delightful spectacle of a united family concentrated on the new game. There was Father with his spectacles on, with Mother leaning over his shoulder and pointing out that, by taking Sec. 6428

H and shoving it on top of Sub-Sec. 9730, he could claim immunity from the tax mentioned in Sec. 4587 M. Clustered around the table were the children, sucking pencils and working out ways of beating the surtax.

"See, papa," cries little Cyril, "what I have found! You are exempt from paying tax on income derived from any public utility or the exercise of any essential governmental function accruing to any state or territory or any political subdivision thereof or to the District of Columbia, or income accruing to the government of any possession of the United States or any political subdivision thereof. That means you can knock off the price of the canary's bird-seed!"

"And, papa," chimes in little Wilbur, "I note that Gifts (not made as a consideration for service rendered) and money and property acquired under a will or by inheritance (but the income derived from money or property received by gift, will, or inheritance) are taxable and must be reported. Therefore, by referring to Sub-Sec. 2864905, we find that you can skin the blighters for the price of the openwork socks you gave the janitor at Christmas."

And so the game went on, each helping the other, all working together in that perfect harmony which one so seldom sees in families nowadays.

NOR is this all. Think how differently the head of the family regards his nearest and dearest in these days of income-tax. Many a man who has spent years wondering why on earth he was such a chump as to link his lot with a woman he has disliked from the moment they stepped out of the Niagara Falls Hotel, and a gang of children whose existence has always seemed superfluous, gratefully revises his views as he starts to fill up the printed form.

His wife may be a nuisance about the home, but she comes out strong when it is a question of married man's exemption. And the children! As the father looks at their grubby faces, and reflects that he is entitled to knock off two hundred bones per child, the austerity of his demeanor softens, and he pats them on the head and talks vaguely about jam for tea at some future and unspecified date.

There is no doubt that the income-tax, whatever else it has done, has taught the family to value one another. It is the first

practical step that has been taken against the evil of race-suicide.

One beauty of this income-tax game is that it is educational. It enlarges the vocabulary and teaches one to think. Take, for instance, the clause on Amortization.

In pre-income-tax days, if anyone had talked to me of amortization, I should, no doubt, have kept up my end of the conversation adroitly and given a reasonable display of intelligence, but all the while I should have been wondering whether amortization was a new religion or a form of disease which attacks parrots.

Now, however, I know all about it. You should have seen me gaily knocking off whatever I thought wouldn't be missed for amortization of the kitchen sink.

You would hardly believe—though I trust the income-tax authorities will—what a frightful lot of amortization there was at my little place last year. The cat got amortized four times, once by a spark from the fire, the other three times by stray dogs: and it got so bad with the goldfish that they became practically permanent amorters.

Heaven Help the Corporations!

AS REGARDS income-tax, I am, thank goodness, an individual. I pray that I may never become a corporation. It seems to me that some society for the prevention of cruelty to things ought to step in between the authorities and the corporations. I have never gone deeply into the matter, having enough troubles of my own, but a casual survey of the laws relating to the taxing of corporations convinces me that any corporation that gets away with its trousers and one collar-stud should offer up Hosannahs.

The general feeling about the income-tax appears to have been that it is all right this time, but it mustn't happen again. I was looking through a volume of *Punch,* for the year 1882, the other day, and I came across a picture of a gloomy-looking individual paying his tax.

"I can just do it this time," he is saying, "but I wish you would tell Her Majesty that she mustn't look on me as a source of income in the future."

No indoor game ever achieves popularity for two successive years, and the Government must think up something new for next Winter.

Confessions of a Jail-Breaker

And a Few Asides on Handcuffs and Strait-jackets

HARRY HOUDINI

WITHOUT having recourse to any of these new-fashioned lessons, I am able to tell (while balancing an oil-lamp in one hand and a bank-account in the other) the exact date of the birth of Caracalla, the Roman Emperor, as well as the day of the month, in 1593, when the dissenting clergymen were hanged in Scotland. It was on the 6th of April in both cases.

"Marvelous!" you would exclaim. "Is there no limit to what this man can do?"

But I will disclose the secret of this trick (a thing I very rarely do). The 6th of April happens also to be my own birthday. It is therefore no effort to fix this date in my mind, and to tie up Caracalla and the dissenting Scotch clergymen with this chief event in my life (which occurred, by the way, in 1874). The United States Government recognized the significance of this date, in 1917, by waiting until it had arrived before declaring war on Germany.

Although I have had regular and established domiciles in Sydney and Melbourne, London, Berlin, Paris, Copenhagen, and Dublin, with front door keys and servant problems in each city, I was born in Appleton, Wisconsin. It was from Appleton that I made my first escape.

It was in Appleton, also, that I made my first public appearance. With the unassuming title of Eric, Prince of the Air, I made my début as a contortionist and trapeze performer in Jack Hoefler's Five Cent Circus—next to the railroad-tracks. My contract called for thirty-five cents a week spending money, in addition to bed and board. That thirty-five cents was practically velvet.

My training as a contortionist was, of course, the first step toward my present occupation of escaping from strait-jackets and chains, for it is chiefly through my ability to twist my body and dislocate my joints, together with abnormal expansion and contraction powers, which renders me independent of the tightest bonds. Thus, to any young man who has in mind a career similar to mine, I would say: "First try bending over backward and picking up a pin with your teeth from the floor, and work up from that into the more difficult exercises."

That was *my* first stunt.

I LEFT Appleton to go on tour through the country, arriving in New York in 1887. There was no Mayor's Committee of Wel-

United Press

HARRY HOUDINI

come to meet me, but I managed to pull through, and, in 1895, I joined the Welsh Brothers' Circus. Here my salary, over my bed and board, was $200 a year, but I would like to make note of the fact that the meals which were furnished to us by this circus were the best I have ever eaten on either of my favorite continents.

I could easily draw an incredulous crowd on a street corner today by recounting the various items in our circus menus, and draw tears to the eyes of the present generation of restaurant habitués by describing the quality of the food and cooking. It all seems like a dream to me now.

Then came Martin Beck, who introduced me to the Orpheum Circuit, booking me later with Mr. E. F. Albee, which was the beginning of the Big Push. Under this management Mrs. Houdini and I opened at Keith's in New York on December 31, 1900. Since then I have always managed to scrape a living together in one way or another. In doing so, I have escaped from drowning on over 2,000 occasions. I have extricated myself from approximately 12,-500 strait-jackets, and picked, roughly, 8,300 locks.

I would not be giving Nature her due if I did not acknowledge right here that, in addition to my natural malleability of framework, I am a born lock-picker. This is a gift. It usually lands its beneficiary in jail, but I have domesticated and refined it until it has landed me before applauding mon-

archs and paying audiences. It all depends on whose lock you pick.

IT WAS on my first European tour, in 1901, that I became an advocate of war with at least a part of Germany. I believe that I therefore can claim precedence over Mr. James M. Beck in this respect. This is the way I was made to see the light:

I was performing in Hanover, and gave a private performance before Count von Schwerin. He was determined to prevent my escaping from the strait-jacket which he and his court had selected, and commanded his henchmen to adjust it in such a manner that it was a constant source of physical torture to me every minute that I was in it. So great was the pain that I was unable to work with any degree of speed and it was 90 minutes before I finally freed myself.

I then took occasion to tell the Count that I would never forget his little joke. I am not an advocate of Bolshevism, but I would be in favor of giving the Hanover soviet *carte blanche* on the estate of the Count von Schwerin.

A much more pleasant performance was one which I had the honor of giving before Colonel Roosevelt. On this occasion I was able to mystify him with what, on the face of it, was a most uncanny trick, but which was really nothing more or less than a case of practical forehandedness on my part.

I was about to sail from London for America, and learned at the ticket office that Colonel Roosevelt was to be a fellow-passenger, although no public announcement had been made of the fact. Figuring things out in advance, I foresaw the customary request from an entertainment committee of passengers for a performance from me on board ship, and I also realized that Colonel Roosevelt would be the dominating presence in the audience. I therefore resolved to work up something which would involve some recent activity of his.

It so happened that he was returning at that time from his trip of exploration in South America with the announcement of the discovery of the River of Doubt. He had given—privately—a map of his explorations to a famous London newspaper and it was to be published three days after the steamer had sailed. No one, with the exception of Colonel Roosevelt and one or two others, knew the details of the map. I, therefore, determined to get a copy.

I will not tell you how I managed to

secure this copy, but I can say that it is always easy to get people to assist one in a trick. They feel that they are being let in "on the ground floor," and will practice all kinds of deceits to which they are unaccustomed by nature, simply for the sake of being one of the few in a large crowd who are "in" on the thing. It is a human failing which I have seldom been unable to make use of. If I were to give a list of my accomplices and their part in some of my tricks, some of my glory would be transferred to many worthy citizens in all walks of life whose only connection with magic has been when they were connected, *sub rosa,* with some nefarious little scheme of mine. So it was that I got a copy of Colonel Roosevelt's map.

On the second day after leaving Liverpool I was asked to give a séance and to answer questions. My expectations in this matter were fulfilled to the letter when the Colonel himself asked me if I would make my "spirit medium" trace, on a sheet of paper, the path of his recent explorations. I took the name of William Stead, who had shortly before been lost on the Titanic, as my supposed "control" from the spirit world, and, on a slate, reproduced the exact map of Mr. Roosevelt's travels. He was astounded and rushed up to me afterward, saying that it was the most amazing thing he had ever seen.

THE ART of making people look somewhere else when they think they are watching *you,* is one of the chief requirements for a successful magician. In this, the trained usher or attendant is invaluable. By a clumsy action on the part of an usher at the left, the attention of the audience can be distracted from the performer at the right for a second or two, or sufficient time to give the latter an opportunity to perform the necessary sly work to make the trick successful. Even without an accomplice, the magician himself can make the audience look away from him by simply shouting, "Look at this globe! You will see that it is empty." And everyone looks at the globe and not at the magician's left hand, which is probably concealing a rabbit or a bowl of goldfish in his hip-pocket.

Percy Haughton, the football coach, who has, in his way, done considerable magic with Harvard teams, once said that he took his cue from the magician, and tried to teach his charges to play football so that the opposing team would be forced to watch one end of the line while the man with the ball was going around the other.

But, of course, my particular field is much broader than rabbit concealing, and I have to go into training for such exigencies as submersion in frozen rivers, while chained and handcuffed, and stepping from the tops of buildings into vacant space.

I have, for many years, bathed in ice-water to make myself immune from the effects of my professional submarine activities. I once had an entire meal served to me while seated in a tub full of floating cakes of ice.

My average sojourn under water, while escaping from boxes and trunks and things like that, is about three minutes, although, in 1896, I made an under-water record of four minutes and six seconds. In order to keep in first-class physical condition, I neither drink nor smoke. With the advent of prohibition, and the consequent improvement in the physical condition of American men, I look for a horde of competitors in my line. I am safe, however, so long as abstinence does not carry with it the ability to dislocate the joints at will.

And just to get the jump on them, I have just gone into the movies. Edgar Allan Poe will furnish the first scenarios, as his tales contain the desired amount of mysticism, danger and opportunity for physical exertion. The combination is one that I shall not try to break. I am told out here in California, where I am working away at my scenarios and productions, that my act is bound to go well in the movies; so, if you hear that the Famous Players have made a small fortune during the year 1919, you will know at whose door to lay credit for it.

The Weather-Vane Points South

AMY LOWELL

I put your leaves aside,
One by one:
The stiff, broad outer leaves;
The smaller ones,
Pleasant to touch, veined with purple;
The glazed inner leaves.
One by one
I parted you from your leaves,
Until you stood up like a white flower
Swaying slightly in the evening wind.

White flower,
Flower of wax, of jade, of unstreaked agate;
Flower with surfaces of ice,
With shadows faintly crimson.
Where in all the garden is there such a
    flower?
The stars crowd through the lilac leaves
To look at you.
The low moon brightens you with silver.

The bud is more than the calyx.
There is nothing to equal a white bud,
Of no color, and of all;
Burnished by moonlight,
Thrust upon by a softly swinging wind.

de Meyer

IRENE CASTLE

Soon to appear in a film version of The Firing Line, *the novel by Robert W. Chambers*

MARILYN MILLER

After playing in Fancy Free, *she is now shining in the* Follies

Johnston

32

LILLIAN GISH

Has reached the height of her career in the notable production of Broken Blossoms.

The First Hundred Plays Are the Hardest

A Strenuous Effort to Keep Up with the Oncoming Dramas

DOROTHY PARKER

MUCH as the water comes down from Lodore have the new plays come upon us. New plays crashed down upon a helpless populace on all sides, not by twos and threes, but by dozens and scores. True, the late coolness between actors and managers badly stalled the season, and it is but human of the managers to wish to get their new productions under way; but if they don't have a heart, they will have a strike of dramatic critics to face. When our reviewers are mumbling, white-bearded grandsires they will hold their clustering descendants in breathless horror with grisly tales of those wild times back in '19, when if there were only four openings scheduled for a night, the critic felt that his evening was practically free.

But, outside of nervous exhaustion, the first-nighters have little to complain of. From the way it starts, the present one bids fair to be the best season in many. Even the most pretentious of last year's displays are already hopelessly outdistanced; a month that brings *Déclassée, Clarence,* and *Too Many Husbands* to the theatre is worth a lifetime of *Crowded Hours, Dark Rosaleen's,* and *Daddies.*

Unfortunately, optimism is not its own penalty. Mere worming his way through the world, tenaciously making the best of things is not in itself a bitter enough fate for the amateur Frank Crane. The one who goes doggedly about insisting that everything he sees is the best of all things in the best of all possible worlds is going to be pitiably out of luck when he encounters something really good. The cheervender whose throat is tired from shouting the praises of the commonplace has no voice left when something unusual comes along. And the reviewer who waxes lyrical over *A Voice in the Dark* and *Up in Mabel's Room,* is left dumb and adjectiveless before *Déclassée.*

Déclassée

ZOE AKINS, author of *The Magical City* and of *Papa*—which many people had the pleasure of reading, and an unfortunate few the pain of seeing last season—has made our Great American Dramatists cling desperately to their somewhat shopworn laurels by virtue of this, her first long play. In fact, it looks as if they would have to think about making over the dramatic map and putting her name on it, well up with the spaces colored to represent Pinero, Jones, and Sutro. Those who have been just on the point of putting on crepe for the American drama can take heart once more; Miss Akins has pulled it through.

Of Ethel Barrymore's performance in *Déclassée* it is difficult to write—hosannahs are heavy going, for even the doggedest reader. If, during my theatre-going lifetime, there has been any other performance so perfect as the one she gives in the role of Lady Helen Haden, poor, brave, reckless Lady Helen who gave up everything for an unreturned love—if there has been any other bit of acting like that, I can only say that I had the hideous ill luck to miss it. It takes a seasoned writer to attempt eulogy; humbler pens splutter and blot in the effort. Perhaps the safest way is to say that Miss Barrymore is at her best in *Déclassée,* and leave it at that.

It may seem over-captious, but one can't help feeling that there are discordant elements in the persons of three unlisted actors, who, in their fortunately brief roles of acrobats whom the capricious Lady Helen befriends, bring things perilously near to burlesque; and in the person of Vernon Steele, who, being the only conspicuously British person in the company, is cast by an all-wise management in the role of an American youth. However, the management gets in some really high art in the first act, when barley-water is served after dinner in Lord Haden's drawing-room. No one drinks it, but there it is, and a special line is brought in to call attention to it, in case it might have gone over your head.

Such touches of realism as this must make Mr. Belasco clutch feverishly at his clerical collar.

But all this last is merely said in a spirit of roguery. The producer who has had the foresight and the judgment to give us *Déclassée* deserves the heartfelt gratitude of the entire community.

Clarence

IT IS a long way from the somewhat somber *Déclassée* to the amazing lightness of *Clarence,* but it is a way well worth traveling. Booth Tarkington has put behind the curtain of the Hudson Theatre what he so admirably succeeded in placing between the red covers of *Seventeen.* I know that there is no better basis for a free-for-all than to ask "Who is the greatest living American author?" but we all have a perfect right to our own ideas, and, according to my rating, Mr. Tarkington is well up toward the front in the first two. And *Clarence,* in its faithful portrayal of all the absurdities and exaggerations of adolescence, is Mr. Tarkington on his own home grounds. It is a great boon to find him writing directly for the stage—for—or so it seemed to me—practically all of the charm of *Seventeen* was spilled on its way from the printed page to the footlights.

There are those who say that there is no plot to speak of in *Clarence*—that its story of a discharged soldier who takes a position in a typical Englewood family, clears up the domestic messes, turns out to be a distinguished scientist, and finally marries the governess, is far too slender. But if they are going to be that way about it, it seems only fair to call to their attention that on even more delicate supports have the most scintillant comedies been built. And after all, the gluttons for plots can always go and have an evening for themselves at *At 9:45* or *The Luck of the Navy.* They also say with an erudite curling of lips, that *Clarence* is structurally deficient; I can only answer them that, if it comes to that, so is *Misalliance,* and a very neat answer it is, too, when you stop to think of it.

Mr. Tarkington has been fortunate in finding two such skilled interpreters of male and female flapper roles as Helen Hayes and Glenn Hunter. Alfred Lunt, one of our most adroit comedians, does wonders with the title part—by the way, in *Clarence* he has the distinction of playing the first soldier hero who not only never got across, but who isn't even a non-commissioned officer.

The Girl in the Limousine

THE most densely populated bed in town is that in *The Girl in the Limousine,* at the Eltinge. Someone is either in or under it, or both, during the entire evening. The farce is the work of Wilson Collison, the erstwhile Kansas City druggist, helped out by Avery Hopwood. It was Mr. Collison, you remember, who conceived the idea of *Up in Mabel's Room.* One wonders where he gets his fancies—what do you suppose is above that drug-store?

The Girl in the Limousine is undeniably very funny, owing to the infallible John Cumberland. I should think Mr. Cumberland would loathe the very sight of a bed, out of office hours. I don't doubt that he sleeps in the park, in his leisure hours, to get away from a bed for just a little while. Zelda Sears and Charles Ruggles lend their experienced aid, and Barnett Parker starts out by being most amusing and then, unfortunately, is carried away by his prowess and over-acts vehemently. Doris Kenyon, late of the movies, looks charmingly pretty, and acts just as if she were doing it all for the camera.

Smilin' Through

SURELY the glad cohorts can gather at the Broadhurst Theatre, and give three rousing cheers for *Smilin' Through,* the play by Allan Langdon Martin, in which Jane Cowl is starring. The work treats of what a perfectly corking institution death is, anyway; according to the author, there is practically nothing to it—the idea is that we'd all go smilin' through the years, if we only knew what was coming to us in the end. In fact, so glowingly does the play speak of the Great Adventure that it might almost have been written by Dr. Berthold Baer.

The great feature of the play is, of course, Jane Cowl. It is indeed a busy evening for Miss Cowl; she appears first as a modern Irish girl, and then, rushing around behind the scenes, doubles as the ghost of her own grandmother—and if all ghosts could only look like Miss Cowl, not a woman in the audience but would gladly pass on immediately.

The Famous Mrs. Fair

AND surely not even the most hard-boiled optimist could have greeted a production with more ecstatic "Oh's" and "Ah's" than those with which the reviewers greeted James Forbes' play, *The Famous Mrs. Fair,* on its initial revealment at Henry Miller's Theatre. It was hailed on all sides as practically the ultimate achievement in American comedy. To the amateur, no matter how doggedly he polishes his rose-colored glasses, it is almost impossible to discern just what all the raving is about. However, if he will just think of what a wholesome, clean play it is, and reason out all the good it will do, and consider that not even Dr. John Roach Stratton could see any harm in it, he can soon get into his stride and brighten up about it.

The story concerns a woman who achieves fame and decorations through her war work. She embarks on a lecture tour, to find, on her return, that her husband is in the toils of a siren, her son has married a stenographer, and her daughter has fallen into the clutches of an unscrupulous fortune-hunter; whereupon, with Maeterlinckian impulsiveness, she gives up the lecture tour, returns to domesticity, and they all live happily ever after. The moral is, of course, that woman's place is in the home; would it had been taken to heart by the woman sitting in front of me, who was seized with a severe cough just as the curtain rose and who paused for neither rest nor refreshment all through the play.

Henry Miller plays the neglected husband, a part which demands but little of him, while Blanche Bates—the famous Mrs. Creel–has the title rôle. To her emotional scenes, there is no more spontaneous tribute than that which welled from the heart of some mysterious person behind me.

"Look at that," said an awe-stricken voice, as Miss Bates smote her forehead a resounding whack. "That's some acting, that is!"

It requires no self-made optimist to see good in Margalo Gillmore's performance of the daughter; even the bitterest of first-nighters had to hand it to her freely and humbly. Certainly, youth is being served in the theatre this season. Miss Gillmore has made a success to equal those of her contemporaries, Helen Hayes and Genevieve Tobin.

The Son-Daughter

WE NOW take a little jaunt to China by dropping into the Belasco Theatre, where Lenore Ulric is starring in *The Son-Daughter,* a Chinese drama by George Scarborough and David Belasco. The huge success of *East Is West* has naturally led the playwrights to suspect that there must be something in this Chinese thing; and indeed, there is a great deal in it—mandarin coats and black wigs and red screens and pidgin English do much to divert attention from the play itself. Mr. Belasco and Mr. Scarborough have played safe and followed *East Is West* almost exactly, save for the introduction of a revolution into the plot. The play is most effectively produced, with unlimited golden idols, dim red lights, and burning of joss sticks. Miss Ulric plays with commendable restraint in her sweeter moments, and commendable ferocity in her emotional scenes, and Harry Mestayer, Albert Bruning, and Thomas Finlay give clever characterizations. The long cast is supplemented by a horde of supernumeraries whose strictly correct Chinese costumes and wigs render the more piquant their strikingly Hibernian features.

If Mr. Samuel Shipman is in the house, I should be glad to have him observe me get down and crawl abjectly along the ground for anything I may have said about his brain-child, *East Is West.* Last season, in the exuberance of youth, I used to think that no play along the same lines could possibly be worse; that was before the dying year brought *The Son-Daughter.*

Caesar's Wife

STILL in the East, though fortunately safely out of China, is the setting of W. Somerset Maugham's play *Caesar's Wife,* in which Billie Burke is starred. There are but few flashes of Mr. Maugham's brilliance in the dialogue, and the evening seems a long and uneventful one. Miss Burke, in her rôle of the young wife, looks charmingly youthful. She is at her best in her more serious moments; in her desire to convey the girlishness of the character, she plays her lighter scenes rather as if she were giving an impersonation of Eva Tanguay.

The Little Blue Devil

The Little Blue Devil, at the Central, can be traced back through a maze of vulgarity (adv.) to an indistinct beginning in Clyde Fitch's *The Blue Mouse.* Harold Atteridge has badly mangled the book and lyrics and Harry Carroll has slightly rewritten most of the musical successes of the last few seasons. The resulting entertainment features both Bernard Granville and Lillian Lorraine. During one of her emotional moments in the comedy, the latter fervently declares that "she is a good woman, even though she is a bad actress." Miss Lorraine has said something. The football coaches could select an invincible All-American eleven from the line-up of show girls.

SOMETIMES, while pondering over the earnings of Dr. Frank Crane or musing on the royalties accumulated by Mrs. Eleanor H. Porter, one wonders whether this glad outlook is not the right ideal, after all. A backward glance through the pages of history reveals the fact that none of the World's Greatest Crabs ever amassed anything really noteworthy in the way of a bank account. Nietzsche's stuff was never syndicated in the evening papers throughout the country; Hauptmann never could say that seventeen road companies had been sent out in *The Weavers.* It is the really sagacious writers who lavish their ink upon exhortations to be glad, glad, glad; for that is the way to bring in something to be glad about. Gloom may be all very well for a lot of unshaven Russians, but for a good hustling American, there's nothing like chasing sunbeams. Say what you will, the pen with the smile wins.

de Meyer

HELEN HAYES

Who has scored a triumph as Margaret in Dear Brutus

LIONEL BARRYMORE

As he appears in The Jest. *Mr. Barry-more and his brother have made Sem Benelli's drama the success of the season*

Johnston

The Social Life of the Newt

What Maeterlinck Did for the Bee and Fabre for the Wasp Is Here
Done for Our Popular Amphibians

ROBERT C. BENCHLEY

IT IS not generally known that the newt, although one of the smallest of our North American animals, has an extremely happy home-life. It is just one of those facts which never get bruited about.

I first became interested in the social phenomena of newt life early in the spring of 1913, shortly after I had finished my researches in sexual differentiation among amoeba. Since that time I have practically lived among newts, jotting down observations, making lantern-slides, watching them in their work and in their play (and you may rest assured that the little rogues have their play—as who does not?) until, from much lying in a research posture on my stomach, over the enclosure in which they were confined, I found myself developing what I feared might be rudimentary creepers. And so, late this autumn, I stood erect and walked into my house, where I immediately set about the compilation of the notes I had made.

So much for the non-technical introduction. The remainder of this article bids fair to be fairly scientific.

Sexual Manifestations

IN STUDYING the more intimate phases of newt life, one is chiefly impressed with the methods by means of which the males force their attentions upon the females, with matrimony as an object. For the newt is, after all, only a newt, and has his weaknesses just as any of the rest of us. And I, for one, would not have it different. There is little enough fun in the world as it is.

The peculiar thing about a newt's courtship is its restraint. It is carried on, at all times, with a minimum distance of fifty paces (newt measure) between the male and the female. Some of the bolder males may now and then attempt to overstep the bounds of good sportsmanship and crowd in to forty-five paces, but such tactics are frowned upon by the Rules Committee. To the eye of an uninitiated observer, the pair might be dancing a few of the more open figures of the minuet.

The means employed by the males to draw the attention and win the affection of those of the opposite sex (females) are varied and extremely strategic. Until the valuable researches by Strudlehoff in 1887 (in his *"Entwickelungsmechanik"*) no one

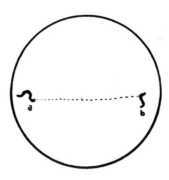

A romance among the newts, considerably magnified. The hero (a) is here seen forcing his attentions on the "best little girl in the world" (b).

The eternal triangle. Returning home unexpectedly, Newt Germ Plasm C discovers that his old college friend B has taken advantage of his hospitality.

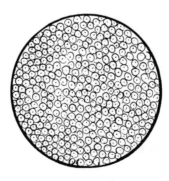

A gathering of newt germ cells in the Newtonville Town Hall to inaugurate community singing as a civic feature.

had been able to ascertain just what it was that the male newt did to make the female see anything in him worth throwing herself away on. It had been observed that the most personally unattractive newt could advance to within fifty paces of a female of his acquaintance and, by some *coup d'oeil*, bring her to a point where she would, in no uncertain terms, indicate her willingness to go through with the marriage ceremony at an early date.

It was Strudlehoff who discovered, after watching several thousand courting newts under a magnifying lens (questionable taste on his part, without doubt, but all is fair in pathological love) that the male, during the courting season (the season opens on the tenth of March and extends through the following February, leaving about ten days for general overhauling and redecorating) gives forth a strange, phosphorescent glow from the center of his highly colored dorsal crest, somewhat similar in effect to the flash of a diamond scarf-pin in a red necktie. This glow, according to Strudlehoff, so fascinates the female with its air of elegance and indication of wealth, that she immediately falls a victim to its lure.

The Courtship

BUT the little creature, true to her sex-instinct, does not at once give evidence that her morale has been shattered. She affects a coyness and lack of interest, by hitching herself sideways along the bottom of the aquarium, with her head turned over her right shoulder away from the swain. A trained ear might even detect her whistling in an indifferent manner.

The male, in the meantime, is flashing his gleamer frantically two blocks away and is performing all sorts of attractive feats, calculated to bring the lady newt to terms. I have seen a male, in the stress of his handicap courtship, stand on his fore-feet, gesticulating in amorous fashion with his hind feet in the air. Franz Ingehalt, in his *"Uber Weltschmerz des Newt,"* recounts having observed a distinct and deliberate undulation of the body, beginning with the shoulders and ending at the filament of the tail, which might well have been the origin of what is known today in scientific circles as "the shimmy." The object seems to be the same, except that in the case of the newt, it is the male who is the active agent.

In order to test the power of observation in the male during these maneuvers, I carefully removed the female, for whose benefit he was undulating, and put in her place, in slow succession, another (but less charming) female, a paper-weight of bronze shaped like a newt, and, finally, a common rubber eraser. From the distance at which the courtship was being carried on, the male (who was, it must be admitted, a bit near-sighted congenitally) was unable to detect the change in personnel, and continued, even in the presence of the rubber eraser, to gyrate and undulate in a most conscientious manner, still under the impression that he was making a conquest.

At last, worn out by his exertions, and disgusted at the meagerness of the reaction on the eraser, he gave a low cry of rage and despair and staggered to a nearby pan containing barley-water, from which he proceeded to drink himself into a gross stupor.

Thus, little creature, did your romance end, and who shall say that its ending was one whit less tragic than that of Camille? Not I, for one. . . . In fact, the two cases are not at all analogous.

The Community Life of the Newt

AND now that we have seen how wonderfully Nature works in the fulfillment of her laws, even among her tiniest creatures, let us study for a minute a cross-section of the community life of the newt. It is a life full of all kinds of exciting adventure, from weaving nests to crawling about in the sun and catching insect larvae and crustaceans. The newt's day is practically never done, largely because the insect larvae multiply three million times as fast as the newt can possibly catch and eat them. And it takes the closest kind of community team-work in the newt colony to get things anywhere near cleaned up by night-fall.

It is early morning, and the workers are just appearing, hurrying to the old log which is to be the scene of their labors. What a scampering! What a bustle! Ah, little scamperers! Ah, little bustlers! How lucky you are, and how wise! You work long hours, without pay, for the sheer love of working. An ideal existence, I'll tell the scientific world.

How They Work

OVER here on the right of the log are the Master Draggers. Of all the newt workers, they are the most futile, which is high praise indeed. Come, let us look closer and see what it is that they are doing.

The one in the lead is dragging a bit of gurry out from the water and up over the edge into the sunlight. Following him, in single file, come the rest of the Master Draggers. They are not dragging anything, but are sort of helping the leader by crowding against him and eating little pieces out of the filament of his tail.

And now they have reached the top. The leader, by dint of much leg-work, has succeeded in dragging his prize to the ridge of the log.

The little workers, reaching the goal with their precious freight, are now giving it over to the Master Pushers, who have been waiting for them in the sun all this while. The Master Pushers' work is soon accomplished, for it consists simply in pushing the piece of gurry over the other side of the log until it falls with a splash into the water, where it is lost.

This part of their day's task finished, the tiny toilers rest, clustered together in a group, waving their heads about from side to side, as who should say: "There— that's done!" And so it *is* done, my little Master Draggers and my little Master Pushers, and *well* done, too. Would that my own work were as clean-cut and satisfying.

Philosophical Conclusion

AND so it goes. Day in and day out, the busy army of newts go on making the world a better place in which to live. They have their little trials and tragedies, it is true, but they also have their fun, as anyone can tell by looking at a log full of sleeping newts on a hot summer day.

And, after all, what more has life to offer?

GEORGES CLEMENCEAU

The Premier of France in a portrait etching by Albert Besnard, head of the Académie de France in Rome.

Nominated for the Hall of Fame: 1919

THOMAS G. MASARYK *(right)*

Because it was through his skill as a diplomat that the United States and the Allies recognized the Czecho-Slovaks as a nation; because he is a scholar as well as a statesman; because this portrait of him is by Jo Davidson; but chiefly because he has just left New York to enter upon his duties as first President of Czechoslovakia.

Underwood

BOOTH TARKINGTON *(left)*

Because as a playwright he is almost as successful as in novel writing; because he understands boys better than any living writer; and finally because in *The Magnificent Ambersons* he has written one of the most notable novels of the time.

Hoppe

ANATOLE FRANCE

Because he is one of the few French writers whose reputation is world-wide; because he is a stylist of the first water, and a satirist directly descended from Voltaire; and finally because he has just celebrated his seventy-fifth birthday at his country place in Touraine where, all through the war, he acted as host to many American soldiers.

TYRUS R. COBB

Because he is the foremost figure in American baseball and therefore one of the foremost figures in America; because he was a professional athlete who joined the army during the war; and because he has just finished his eleventh season at the head of American batsmen.

GEORGE M. COHAN

Because, though only forty years of age, he is today one of the supermen of our stage; because he wrote the best of all the American war songs, "Over There"; because he is a distinguished actor, manager, composer and playwright; but chiefly because he does not produce, or act in, anything but clean, wholesome plays.

White

39

William Somerset Maugham

A Pen Portrait by a Friendly Hand

HUGH WALPOLE

WHEN I first saw William Somerset Maugham (it is a considerable number of years ago now) I was most acutely conscious of his grey top hat.

It must have been that same grey hat which figured so prominently in Gerald Festus Kelly's portrait—a grey hat set audaciously, cynically, with humor and with a quite definite pose of a dandyism in which the wearer obviously did not believe. That hat belonged to Maugham's earlier, more cynical days, the days of *Mrs. Dot* and *Smith,* the days when he was out quite determinately to make money and had put behind him for the moment the unproductive austerities of *A Man of Honour* and *Liza of Lambeth.*

I had the merest glimpse of him at that time wandering, under the grey hat, through the gardens of a Campden Hill retreat, where Violet Hunt was giving a literary garden party. How desperately those garden parties seem now to be things of the past! It was at the time when May Sinclair was showing her reverence for Henry James in her novel, *The Creators*; when untidy young men and women discussed, with bated breath, the audacities of the Vedrenne Barker management at the Cort Theatre. The days when Conrad was still despised and rejected, and Frank Harris was writing about Shakespeare, and Bernard Shaw was a freakish young thing who would write better one day.

Lord! What a long while ago and how scornfully Somerset Maugham moved amongst those shadows under the high trees and how he despised them for their highbrow sentiments and baggy-looking clothes! That garden party at which I saw him must have been I think the very last of its series. I never went to one again. I never heard of one again. The London world moved on to a new phase.

Maugham's House

THE next time that I saw Maugham was in that gay discreet bandbox of a house in Mayfair that became, for many of us, one of the happiest, most hospitable, most amusing houses in London. I was, I remember, from the very first struck by the strange contrast of the lower social part of the house and the room on the top floor where he did his work. That top floor remains, after all

these years, as the most ideal spot for a writing man that I have ever seen.

All rooms are, I suppose, symbolic of their owners. Maugham's had just that mingling of harsh reality with barbaric and preferably Eastern splendor that represents him. He

Elliott & Fry

W. SOMERSET MAUGHAM

had worn his grey top hat as the King of China might have worn it, and here was the King of China again among the squatting Eastern gods and the marvellous lacquer boxes and the heavy gold chests mysteriously engraven. And against this there was, in the very center of the wide bare room, a large rough deal table with good plain English legs and no nonsense about it. Here Maugham sat and cultivated his genius.

He was supposed, at the time of which I am speaking, to be giving himself up to the production of those merry superficial comedies that delighted the London world for so long. It was the characteristic thing to say at that time that Maugham had sold his soul for a "mess of pottage." He let the world say what it liked; admitted, if any-

one asked him, that certainly Mrs. Dot was a more profitable lady than Liza and that one could live only once. Meanwhile, how characteristically he was producing through all those years what will remain, I am convinced, not only his masterpiece, but one of the great English novels of the period— *Of Human Bondage.*

Only one or two of his friends knew of that book. He had for it that love which is beyond question the happiest thing in a writer's life, that love which is not pride nor conceit, but simply so deep an immersion in the thing that you are creating that you positively cannot pull yourself out of it. He lingered on and on over this "Pattern in the Carpet," as he called it, rewriting, adding, subtracting, knowing full well what every writer knows, that no book belongs to an author after its publication, that that intimacy of creation will never return once the world shares it with you.

He never tried during that time to persuade people of his other artistic self. That third book of his—*Mrs. Craddock*—still remains as one of the ablest, most poignant studies of woman in our generation. How many people here have read it?

Maugham never forced anyone to think about him at all, but the obtuseness of the world in general is one of his pleasantest private jokes. He prefers them obtuse.

The life of a popular and successful dramatist must be a very exciting and happy one. I should like immensely to be Mr. Hopwood, or Miss Zoë Akins or Mr. Knoblock. It has all the elements of horse-racing, Chemin-de-Fer, public oratory, the Episcopal Bench and proposals of marriage; it must make one simply conceited to death.

Maugham has never had that kind of conceit. He has, as have all artists who are any good at all, a justified sense of his own powers. He knows that he can write books that are worth the attention of serious people and plays that anyone, serious or not, is justified in going to see. He knows that he is better than Mr. Tom Noddy, who doesn't realize the first thing about stage technique, and Mr. Emery Paper, whose novel about Mormonism is being much read just now. But he also knows that Aristophanes and Aeschylus lived before him and understood quite a lot about the theatre and that Dostoevsky and Flaubert wrote pretty good novels.

Maugham in the War

INTO this happy and exciting existence then broke the war. Maugham was luckier in the war than many of us in that he found work that was exactly suited to him. The secret service job that fell to him was made for him, made for his knowledge of languages, his knowledge of human nature, his knowledge of when to speak and when to keep silent. I saw a little phase of his work in Russia. We were in Petrograd together during those months after the Revolution of March 1917. Very depressing those months were, when the idealism of some of us got some hard knocks, and when all our preconceived notions of Rus-sia and the Russian spirit fell to the ground one after another. I don't think that Maugham knew very much about Russia, but his refusal to be hurried into sentimental assumptions, his cynical pretence that "all was anyway for the worst" (he did not himself believe that for a single moment) gave him a poise and calm that some others of us badly needed. He watched Russia as we would watch a play, finding the theme, and then intent on observing how the master artist would develop it. He did not see the end of that play—the end indeed is not yet —but he sent home some pretty wise notions as to its probable last act.

It was in the last summer of the war that I caught quite a different glimpse of him. I stayed with him for a day or two in one of the loveliest houses in the whole of England, and it was at that time that he was writing *The Moon and Sixpence*. I think that he had the idea of the book in his head long before he wrote it. He had always been passionately interested in modern painting, and I remember his saying to me a long while ago what a novel Gauguin's life would make. I don't think, however, that that artist gave him more than the starting-point for his story. Maugham's Strickland is his own creation; the technique of that fine book is his own technique, above all, the poetry of it is his own poetry. It seems to me to rank among the finest novels in English of the last twenty years.

DORIS KEANE

America's prodigal daughter has returned to her native land to play Romance *on the screen after that play's five years of success in London*

Arbuthnot

The Soul of Skylarking

Thoughts on the New Renascence and the Structure of the Future

G. K. CHESTERTON

SOMETHING is necessary before we can really learn to enjoy games, or to enjoy theatres, or to enjoy things of art or invention. And that is that we should learn to enjoy enjoyment. It is this faculty that is always slipping away from men; and it slips away faster and faster in the modern mood of always looking for the latest thing. It matters nothing whether this takes a reactionary or a revolutionary form. It matters nothing whether it is a snobbish pursuit of the latest fashions and is called Capitalism, or a priggish pursuit of the latest fads and is called Socialism. It is equally true that the hurry after happiness is itself unhappy; and that a man is learning how to find enjoyments and not how to enjoy. But commonly the two things are combined; for the rich, especially the wicked rich, are very progressive; progress is another name for going the pace. It is among the wicked rich that you will find the advanced art; the portraits without faces, the statues without figures and the poems without poetry.

Now any real renewal must be based more broadly on much more simple and popular things. When I say simple things, I do not mean things like the simple life. Vegetarianism or teetotalism are obviously the very reverse of simple. I should not call a man simple if he could only eat pink things or pale yellow things; nor do I call him simple if he can only eat green things. I call him fastidious, and even luxurious. I should not consider a child beautifully child-like who, when offered a glass of milk, asked whether it contained any allotropic forms of alkaloid, or what not. Nor do I consider a man child-like who, when offered a glass of beer, asks whether it contains any alcohol; another arbitrary abstraction conjectured by a few chemists.

I mean by a simple man or child a good and sensible man or child; and I mean that a sensible child takes what he can get. And a simple man is one who can enjoy the normal and national food and drink. I do not say he should always enjoy them; or that he should not enjoy other things; I say he should be *able* to enjoy the normal things; and not be reduced, by successive and rapid reforms, into a condition in which he cannot enjoy anything whatever.

Bad Books and Bad Beer

THUS it is said, for instance, that the public likes bad books. But in England, at any rate, if it likes bad books it is very much as it drinks bad beer. It does so because it cannot get any good beer; and has to choose between bad beer and something that is not beer at all. So the ordinary reader often has to choose between bad books and things like those which Charles Lamb called books that are not books. He has to choose between a bald and badly written story, about love and murder, and a story that is not a story at all, but a medical diary describing the more minute sen-

Speaight

G. K. CHESTERTON

sations of an incipient lunatic, or the pros and cons of erecting a tin chapel for some new religion. The more refined artists have been driven to this, not so much because they are so lucky as to find nerves and new religion interesting, as because they are so lamentably unlucky as to find love and murder uninteresting. They have lost their normal power of enjoying enjoyable things, such as murder and love making. The very novelty of their art is the fatigue of their minds. The artists are trying to enjoy fresh things with a stale mind, while the public is still enjoying stale things with a fresh mind. That fresh mind is the first need of a fresh society.

It is more convenient to take a concrete case; and I will take the case of poetry, especially the poetry of nature. It is an old joke that papers and the public are tormented by a swarm of Spring poets, who come out like the birds in Spring. It is an old joke that the editor receives a million original Odes to the Skylark, and generally prints the worst of them. But even if the Spring poetry is worthless, the Spring is not worthless. Like death and first love, and the other materials of the detective story and the novelette, it is a marvel none the less real for being recurrent. In short, the little poet, like the large public, may not be occupied with great works; but he is occupied with great things. It may be tiresome to listen to the poet on the skylark, but it is not tiresome to listen to the skylark. At least, it ought not to be; but it is the whole problem of the new and fastidious artist that it is.

The Skylark and the Flamingo

HE IS tired, not of the small achievements, but of the great subjects of poetry. Probably he has heard too many odes to the skylark, and too few skylarks. Anyhow, he is in a mood to kill the skylark, as the sailor did the albatross, and to run after some more rare bird, let us say, the flamingo. The vivid colour and fantastic form of that wild fowl would have fitted it well for the decorative poems of the decadents, where "down the purple corridors the screaming scarlet ibis flew." I do not object to such screaming, even to such screaming colours. There is a poetry in the ibis and the flamingo, as well as in the skylark. The only creature without any poetry is the poet who is tired of the skylark.

What is the matter with him is that he has sought out a new screaming scarlet sort of skylark, not because his senses are keen, but because they are jaded. The bird has to be screaming because he is nearly deaf, and scarlet because he is nearly blind. Moreover, the necessity of substituting the flamingo for the skylark involves the advanced and fastidious bird-fancier in other difficulties. Perhaps the poet finds that there are not many rhymes to flamingo, and that "Jingo" and "lingo" are alien to the mood and atmosphere. Therefore he decides that rhyme is a jingling fetter unworthy of free modern verse. Or he finds the metre is disturbed by the insinuation of a flamingo instead of a lark; as it would be if we had to scan the line:

"Hark, hark, the flamingo at heaven's gate sings";

or as who should say:

"Like to the flamingo at break of day arising
From sullen earth sings hymns at heaven's gate."

And finding this to run a little awkwardly, he naturally decides that metre as well as rhyme is a meaningless convention, and that the modern spirit can only express itself in *vers libre*.

Only the poet happens to be wrong, according to the whole history of poetry. The editor may receive a million poems by minor poets about the skylark; but anywhere among them there may be one signed William Shakespeare, and another signed William Wordsworth, and another signed Percy Bysshe Shelley. Whereas it might be difficult to compile a Golden Treasury entirely about the flamingo.

It is the common subjects, not the uncommon subjects, on which the rare masterpieces of poetry have been written. It was because the major poets shared the enthusiasm of the minor poets. It was because they dealt with terms and things in the very texture of popular thought and speech. For instance, the same images are to be found not only in song, but even in slang. The very case of the skylark has a prose parallel in the expression "skylarking," pre-

supposing a verb "to skylark." It would be interesting if there were a verb "to flamingo," presumably conjugated like the verb "to go." It would be almost alarming if we said not only "I flamingo," but "thou hast flamingone," not to mention so extreme a case as "he flaminwent." This may seem to the fastidious almost to verge on the fanciful. But this is a fair parallel to the verb "skylarking," which is a perfect fragment of popular poetry to express a wild and hilarious holiday.

But a man cannot have a popular holiday all by himself; and a man cannot create a new language all by himself. He cannot even paint the town red without the consent of the townsfolk, even if he can disregard the town council. And that very metaphor brings us to the practical outcome of this primary truth. Given due and proper occasion, I have no particular objection to his painting the town as red as the flamingo. But even if he does so with the applause of all his neighbors, he will probably find that pleasing the town council is very different from pleasing the town. In short, he will come face to face with the falsity of modern politics which has next to be considered.

Poets and Politicians

I SAID that our basis must be simple and popular; and that I did not mean by simple and popular the puritanical pose of the simple life. I may add that I do not mean by popular the plutocratic corruption of the representative system. The machinery labelled "democracy" is not a popular thing; indeed, the very word "democracy" is not a popular word. How many times a day does a shoe-black or a scavenger use the word "democracy"? Yet it is on words he does use, and ideas he does understand, that we must found a really popular commonwealth.

Such a society must do what poets do for the people, and what politicians never by any chance do for the people. It must give them what they themselves desire, but cannot always devise. One poet writes love songs for a hundred lovers. One romancer writes adventure stories for a hundred boys who would like to have adventures. The new statesman must do the right thing, which we desire to have done but cannot do. The modern politician does the wrong thing, and then adds insult to injury and falsehood to folly, by telling us we have done it ourselves.

Poems by Edna St. Vincent Millay

Wild Swans

I looked in my heart while the wild swans
    went over;—
    And what did I see I had not seen before?
Only a question less or a question more;
Nothing to match the flight of wild birds
    flying.
Tiresome heart, forever living and dying!
    House without air! I leave you and lock
        your door!
Wild swans, come over the town, come over
The town again, trailing your legs and
    crying!

The Singin' Woman from the Wood's Edge

What should I be but a prophet and a liar
Whose mother was a leprechaun, whose
    father was a friar?
Teethed on a crucifix and cradled under
    water,
What should I be but the fiend's god
    daughter?

And who should be my playmates but the
    adder and the frog,
That was got beneath a furze-brush and
    born in a bog?
And what should be my singin', that was
    christened at an altar,
But *Aves* and *Credos* and psalms out of
    the psalter?

You will see such webs on the wet grass,
    maybe,
As a pixie-mother weaves for her baby;
You will find such flames at the wave's
    weedy ebb
As flashes in the meshes of a mermother's
    web.

But there comes to birth no common spawn
From the love of a priest for a leprechaun,
And you never have seen and you never
    will see
Such things as the things that swaddled me!

After all's said and after all's done,
What should I be but a harlot and a nun?

In through the bushes on any foggy day
My da would come a-swishin' of the drops
    away,

E D N A   S T.   V I N C E N T   M I L L A Y

With a prayer for my death and a groan for
    my birth,
A-mumblin' of his beads for all he was
    worth;

And there'd sit my ma with her knees
    beneath her chin,
A-lookin' in his face and a-drinkin' of it in,
And a-markin' in the moss some funny little
    sayin'
That would mean just the opposite of all
    that he was prayin'.

Oh, the things I haven't seen and the things
    I haven't known,
What with hedges and ditches till after I
    was grown,
And yanked both ways by my mother and
    my father,
With a *Which-would-you-better?* and a
    Which-would-you-rather?

He taught me the holy talk of vesper and
    of matin,
He heard me my Greek and he heard me
    my Latin;

He blessed me and crossed me to keep my
    soul from evil,
And we watched him out of sight and we
    conjured up the devil!

With him for a sire and her for a dam,
What should I be but just what I am?

Spring

To what purpose, April, do you return
    again?
Beauty is not enough.
You can no longer quiet me with the red-
    ness
Of little leaves opening stickily.
I know what I know.
The sun is hot on my neck as I observe
The spikes of the crocus.
The smell of the earth is good.
It is apparent that there is no death.
But what does that signify?
Not only under ground are the brains of
    men
Eaten by maggots.
Life in itself
Is nothing,—
An empty cup, a flight of uncarpeted stairs.
It is not enough that yearly down this hill
April
Comes like an idiot, babbling and strewing
    flowers!

Weeds

White with daisies and red with sorrel
    And empty, empty under the sky!
Life is a quest and love a quarrel;
    Here is a place for me to lie.

Daisies spring from damnéd seeds,
    And this red fire that here I see
Is a worthless crop of crimson weeds,
    Cursed by farmers thriftily.

But here, unhated for an hour,
    The sorrel runs in ragged flame;
The daisy stands, a bastard flower,
    Like flowers that bear an honest name.

And here awhile, where no wind brings
    The baying of a pack athirst,
May sleep the sleep of blessed things
    The blood too bright, the brow accurst.

Arbuthnot

BERNARD SHAW

A new portrait of the great satirist

The Golden Age of the Dandy

With a Short Note on His Unfortunate, but Inevitable Decline during the Age of Steel

JOHN PEALE BISHOP

THE first dandy was, I suppose, the son of a Macaroni and, suffering from that Œdipus complex which afflicts all artists, he promptly proceeded to kill his father. At all events, the Macaroni, or Buck as he was commonly called in England, with his monstrously broad cocked hat, his oiled and stringy hair falling over his cheeks like a spaniel's ears, his ineffable waistcoat and impossibly tight breeches, disappeared, no one knew quite where, shortly after the dandy stepped forth in polished boots and full trousers with a beaver over his ringleted hair.

If there were no further distinction between the buck and the dandy, they might safely be left to the limbo of forgotten fashion prints. But the difference between them is more than a mere matter of get-up, more than the oiling or curling of the hair. There is between them the difference of their respective ages: one "the great morning of the rights of man," the other, the weary and cynical decade that followed the Congress of Vienna. The buck represented an exuberant, even eccentric, play of the individual at a time when the world seemed about to begin anew; the dandy an elegant and inessential gesture in a world where ennui had followed disillusion, where the last hope of human liberty had disappeared into the realm of lyrical drama, presided over by Percy Bysshe Shelley—where Childe Harold had become Don Juan. Dandyism was a meaningless protest against a life without meaning, a life ordered by a Hanoverian king with a fairly correct English accent and a German queen who played her tragic rôle with the finesse of a befurbelowed hausfrau. Therein lies all the difference between a dandy and the "smart" frippery of a Ward McAllister in an age of brownstone-front aristocrats.

Dandyism was not the invention of a single man, however much it has come to be associated with the name of George Brummell, King of the Dandies, *"Roi par la grâce de la Grâce."* Its origin is not, properly speaking, English at all, for native English manners have always had something too much of the rigidity of the Puritan conscience and the heaviness of well-brewed stout. Its origin is to be found in the French influences which arrived in England with the Restoration of Charles II and continued until the Regency of George IV. The famous beaux of the eighteenth century—

Sir Robert Fielding, Chesterfield, Bolingbroke, and Nash—all affected a piquant sumptuousness in attire, a preoccupation with effect, an elegant admission of vanity, distinctly reminiscent of the French court. French, too, was that feeling for the romance of civilization, that formal crystallization of elaborate manners which characterized these men and their age. Somewhat

BEAU BRUMMELL

later came the Macaronis, likewise touched with French ideas, expressing in extravagant and fantastic costume an individual revolt against established custom; but they were too essentially imitative of the effeminate fops of the Directoire to make a serious stir in British society. They but prepared the way for the dandy by adding a touch of color to that period which seems to belong neither to the eighteenth nor the nineteenth century, when the English sat in fear from the time when the Corsican first appeared in the uniform of a general of the Convention until finally their breath came more easily at the thought of Louis XVIII driving through a quieted Paris with a blue ribbon across the puffy expanse of his Bourbon bosom.

The Vanity of the Dandy

A HERESY has long existed that the dandy was possessed of a consuming vanity, giving a meticulous attention to dress chiefly to win the notice and favors of women. As a matter of fact, the typical dandy cared far more for the gaming table than for such games of skill and chance as are played in the boudoir. Brummell himself allowed neither his heart nor his senses to interfere with his pose. In the latter days of his triumph he was accustomed to remain at a ball only long enough to make his effect and then disappear. The royal dandy, afterward George IV, spent his wedding night dining with his friends, leaving the disconsolate Caroline of Brunswick to a lonely meditation in German on her future career as queen of England.

As for the vanity of the dandy—it was vanity with a difference. He was concerned with the effect of his superior elegance upon others, because it was, after all, the only test of his success, but his vanity was satisfied in his being himself. Dandyism, as Barbey d'Aurevilly says, is something more than "the art of costume, a happy and audacious dictatorship in the matter of toilette and exterior elegance. Dandyism is a manner of being, entirely composed of nuances, which always appears in very old and very civilized societies, where comedy becomes rare and the proprieties scarcely triumph over boredom." It was indeed a sumptuous attire masking the futility of life, a graceful and tragic gesture signifying disillusion. It is Brummell who remains the perfect type of dandy, because, apart from the perfection of his manner, his consummate taste in dress and the insolence of his wit, he cannot be said to exist. And yet it was no other than Byron who said he would rather be Brummell than Napoleon.

It was only with such a man as Brummell, the grandson of a confectioner, who had successfully insulted the Prince Regent before he was thirty, that dandyism could reach its final perfection of form. But there were others who, beginning life as dandies, are now remembered for other reasons than the successful tying of a neck cloth. Byron made his first appearance in London as a dandy rather than as a poet. Thomas Moore, the Irish poet, was a member of Watier's, the club most frequented of the dandies, while Sheridan of *The Rivals* was not unknown there. George IV himself aspired to be a dandy and at the corpulent end of his reign used to have the suits of his more slender days brought out for him to touch, recalling with anecdote and queasy sentiment the affairs at which they had first been seen. There were others, too, who gave their more serious moments to politics or the army—Alvanley, Worcester, Erskine, Craven, Yarmouth—but they survive only in Burke's Peerage and a few unread memoirs.

Finally, the pleasant interlude came to an end. George IV became fat—a sort of gastronomic suicide for a dandy—and Brummell's insolence went to the point of referring to him as Big Ben, the familiar name of the prodigious footman at Carlton House.

So Brummell shortly betook himself to Calais, never again to set foot on English soil. George, on the other hand, became still fatter and shut Leigh Hunt in prison for referring to him as a "fat Adonis of fifty." Finally, he refused to be seen and drove abroad only in a closed carriage, through whose curtained windows passers-by occasionally glimpsed the scarlet-faced obesity that had once been crowned king of England.

The Golden Age of the Dandies was over.

The Silver Age

THERE was a sort of brief Silver Age under William IV. Count Alfred d'Orsay, a son of one of Napoleon's marshals, attempted to rule in Brummell's stead. A brief arbiter of fashion he might have been, but this *"Cupidon dé chaîné,"* as Byron called him, was no fit successor to the cold and superbly insolent Brummell. He was too French, too humane, too amiable. At best he was a lion, at his worst a fop. Disraeli described him in the Count Alcibiades de Mirabel of his *Henrietta Temple*—a novel which appeared about the same time that the future Prime Minister of England burst upon an astonished Regent Street in a black velvet surtout, trousers of purple with broad gold stripes at their seams and a scarlet waistcoat. He himself describes his progress between two lines of gaping spectators as like that of the Israelites passing between the walls of the Red Sea. Which shows that the dandies no longer enjoyed their former popular approval. Yet even so serious-minded a young man as Robert Browning was still able to present himself in ringlets and yellow gloves.

But the reign of the dandies was over. The young queen was about to ascend the throne and bring in a long regime of domestic virtue. Side whiskers, black broad-cloth and checked trousers laid a sober and genteel siege to languishing young ladies on haircloth sofas. Life, which had been so coolly ironic, so exquisitely vain, became a matter of high-minded seriousness and satisfied contemplation of the new mechanical industrialism, the British aristocracy and a beneficent evolution, moving, none knew how, but quietly and to the measures of a Tennysonian recital toward "one far off, divine event."

So the nineteenth century moved to its close, pervaded by only one characteristic of dandyism—extreme self-satisfaction in its own perfections. Its garments, which had begun with a sort of democratic concealment alike of well-turned leg and shriveled shank, ended by making both cylindrical and ugly. King Edward VII, as Prince of Wales, was a limited arbiter of fashion, who occasionally caught something of the true manner of the dandy. But time and circumstance were against him. His only success in relieving the general ill-grace of the period was his revival of small clothes for formal court dress.

Toward the end of the century came the Aesthetes, with Oscar Wilde at their head. Lily in hand, one eye cast wistfully toward the faded beauty of the Pre-Raphaelites, the other craftily set on publicity, he made a brief march down Pall Mall. But Wilde not only lacked the necessary taste, he violated the first principles of dandyism, which is to move with superior grace in a circle limited by convention. The successor of Brummell, when he comes, will accomplish his purpose, not through violent changes, but through a series of minute modifications of the prevailing habits.

Almost the only man living who successfully recalls the grand manner of the Regency is not an Englishman at all, but a Spaniard, in fact the King of the Spaniards. His success as a dandy is probably due not so much to an infallible taste as to his lonely position in a society very old and very complicated with aristocratic traditions.

To speak now of a Beau or a Blood, an Incroyable or a Dandy, is to evoke a smile. The man who first used starch for a neckcloth is dismissed with a sneer, while the man who invented the patent machine for taking out potato eyes is hailed as a benefactor of his country. Let who will erect statues to the useful citizens who create a demand for useless appliances, who discover a later and dryer form of breakfast food, who add fifty-seven new varieties of pickles to the already superfluous fifty-seven. I shall not subscribe. I shall save my pennies to buy a hand-carved snuff-box and, having bought it, remember between sneezes the men who regarded living as an art; possibly, since life seemed to them useless, as a fine art.

Adam and Eve

CHARLES BRACKETT

On fire, in Eden, they forgot the tree,
God's anger, and the vacancy
That had so fretted them, and she
Knew she must make him touch her:
  knew
The wisest way . . . ran. He crashed
  through
Thickets she threaded; caught her, drew
Her arms about him, and her face
Close against his, till the cool place
Sang like a burning bough. Thus-wise
Tedium ceased—and Paradise.

Moffett

GERALDINE FARRAR

The new Louise. Charpentier's opera will be added to the Metropolitan's repertory this season for the first time

MARY GARDEN

Who will revive Aphrodite *and* Salome *for the Chicago Opera company this season in New York*

Hoppe

A Handy Guide for Music Lovers

An Invaluable Aid to Those Who Would Be Critics of Music

CHARLES N. DRAKE

MUSICAL people generally, and music critics in particular, will hail with relief the appearance of this complete and compact questionnaire—the last word in musical criticism. The overworked newspaper critics, who have for years looked forward with dread to each approaching concert season, will hail with joy the publication of this condensed key to concert reviewing.

Our little guide is absolutely fool-proof. If followed carefully, the technical phraseology will stamp any amateur as an expert musical authority, and, what is still more charming, any critical article written according to the rules in this catechism is certain to meet with the rapturous approval of the musical artist under consideration, be he (or she) a singer, pianist, or violinist. With a set of our rules in his pocket and a program of the concert, the much reviled amateur may feel quite secure. If he happens to *like* music, he may attend the concert; if not, there is no need to do so.

The Song Recital

SONG recitals should be our first consideration, as they form the bulk of what is popularly referred to as "musical entertainment."

Here, then, is the raw material from which the music critic can create a column of keen and illuminating criticism—of any song recital:

Q. What filled every available inch of the hall?

A. One of the largest audiences of the season.

Q. What swept through the vast assemblage?

A. A tremor of expectation.

Q. What disclosed the diva's fine command of sustained phrase?

A. The lovely old aria by . . .

Q. What has seldom been given with deeper sympathy?

A. This beautiful early masterpiece.

Q. What did it prove her to be?

A. A true mistress of the classic style.

Q. Where was the charming artiste particularly happy?

A. In her choice of French songs.

Q. In which did she catch the real Gallic flavor?

A. (Mention any of the songs.)

Q. What was especially gratifying?

A. Her clear and polished diction.

Q. What was probably the most captivating part of the program?

A. The group of characteristic and fascinating folk-songs.

Q. In each of these what did the singer display?

A. A simple and artless charm that was wholly irresistible.

Q. Her singing of them might have done credit to whom?

A. Marcella Sembrich.

Q. What was clear, limpid and flute-like?

A. Her gorgeous voice.

Q. What has it done since last we heard it?

A. Taken on added richness and flexibility.

Q. What has also developed riper powers and finer perceptions?

A. Her great art.

Q. After innumerable recalls, what did the prima donna do?

A. Seated herself at the piano and sang "Annie Laurie."

Q. How many concerts have given a greater measure of delight?

A. Not one, it is safe to say.

The Violin Recital

THE following points will be found to cover any violin recital:

Q. With what was the opening sonata played?

A. Sustained, reposeful manner and lofty sentiment.

Q. What did the virtuoso draw from his instrument?

A. A tone of vibrant and luscious beauty.

Q. What flashed over the fingerboard with unerring skill?

A. His miraculous fingers.

Q. What did his intonation do to criticism?

A. Disarmed it.

Q. How was the . . . concerto played?

A. With brilliant effect and command of style.

Q. What characterized the slow movement?

A. Warmth of expression and elegance of phrasing.

Q. What was marked by dazzling abandon and consummate artistry?

A. The final allegro movement.

Q. What did technical difficulties do throughout the program?

A. Ceased to exist.

Q. What did the smaller numbers exhibit?

A. The master's deftness and exquisite polish.

Q. Where were all the amazing resources of the instrument set forth?

A. In the closing number by . . .

Q. What did the accompanist furnish?

A. A sympathetic and unobtrusive tonal background.

Q. How often has such a performance been heard in our city?

A. Rarely, indeed.

Q. After continuous applause what did this superb artist do?

A. Returned to play one of Kreisler's charming numbers.

The Piano Recital

IN REVIEWING any piano recital, the reporter has only to enumerate, and, if space permits, enlarge a trifle upon the following points:

Q. What did the first few chords confirm?

A. All that has been said of this great master.

Q. What swept the keyboard with marvelous dexterity?

A. His miraculous hands.

Q. How many pianists possess the secret of such a singing tone?

A. Only too few.

Q. What bespoke his superb musicianship?

A. His performance of . . . (Name any number on the program.)

Q. In what did he display rare poetry and beauty of tone?

A. In the group of Chopin pieces.

Q. What seemed to drip from his fingers in the soft runs?

A. Cascades of pearls.

Q. Who excels him in clear rhythm and richness of tonal color?

A. Probably no other pianist.

Q. What are combined in admirable proportions in his playing?

A. Strength, delicacy, and interpretative genius.

Q. What did he never attempt to do?

A. Exceed the legitimate limits of the instrument.

Q. In summing up the recital, one does not hesitate to do what?

A. Acclaim this remarkable artist a veritable pianistic giant.

The Man Who Lost Himself

Showing the Dangers of Sinking One's Identity at a Fancy-Dress Ball

GIOVANNI PAPINI

I HAVE never been fond of dancing and I frankly and cordially despise masquerade balls. I accepted the Seccos' invitation simply because the guests were asked to wear white dominoes, black masks and black shoes. A simple enough costume! And the affair promised to be more than usually amusing because the dancers were requested not to speak during the evening. I was curious and went. . . .

The Seccos lived in a large house on the skirts of the city. Lights blazed in every window. A procession of carriages drew up at the door. But, within, there was a deathly quiet—not a ripple of laughter, not a whisper—only the shuffle of feet on the polished floors and the faint rustle of many white dominoes. Every guest wore the prescribed costume. Every face was masked. Men sometimes danced with men and women with women, for it was often impossible to tell the difference between the sexes. Strange! Mysterious! A dance of pale ghosts!

I wandered about alone, uncertain and depressed. It was hot. My head ached. The glittering lights dazzled and bewildered me. I was caught in the crowd, shouldered and buffeted and stepped upon. I longed to escape and, feeling faint, pushed my way toward what I thought was a door.

Imagine my surprise when I found myself face to face with an enormous mirror. In it, I saw reflected the dizzy whirling of the white phantoms. And, wondering how I must look in the absurd costume, I glanced more closely into the mirror. . . .

Glanced . . . stared . . . searched for the reflection of myself. . . . In vain! Where was I? Who was I? Which was my body among all those identical bodies? I could not find myself. Could not! And the horrible thought occurred to me: "Suppose I were lost forever?"

I knew that I was standing directly in front of the mirror, facing it. But dozens of other white dominoes were doing the same thing. I was tall and thin. And with a terrible contraction of my heart, I realized that all the others were tall and thin, too—tall and thin and motionless. I moved, and a dozen like me moved at the same instant.

Which, then, was I? Where was I, myself, among that silent throng? All in white with black masks and black shoes. I, too. But I wanted *myself!* I wanted to hear my own voice, to look again into my own eyes, to know that I was different from the others. But I was lost. I had lost *myself.*

I felt dizzy, sick with apprehension, and staggering forward toward that terrible mirror, I fell headlong.

GIOVANNI PAPINI

II

WHEN I recovered consciousness it was the third day of Lent. I was in a black iron bed—and I saw, glancing about me, that I occupied one of many beds, all made of black iron. And each bed contained a being like myself tall and thin with a pallid face and staring eyes. . . . A doctor came running and regarded me with curiosity and asked me how I felt.

I told him I had no idea. I explained that I had lost myself at a masquerade ball, and wanted to find myself as quickly as possible. The doctor advised me to be calm. Excitement was dangerous for people in my condition. I saw at once that he did not believe a word I had said, and, closing my eyes, I vowed to make my escape.

The next day, several doctors examined me and agreed that I had lost my reason. But I knew that I had lost, not my reason, but my very self. My reason had been mislaid, perhaps—but I was not mad so long as it was somewhere in the world. I had only one desire—to escape. And this I accomplished by taking advantage of the visitors' hour to slip unseen into the corridor and thence to the street.

I went at once to the Seccos' house, hoping to find myself in the ball-room. Mr. Secco was at home and, when I had explained my predicament, very graciously offered to search the house for me.

"My dear fellow," he said sympathetically, "I know how it is. These doctors—they have so little imagination. By all means, let us leave no stone unturned."

But I was nowhere to be found. We went from garret to cellar and there was no trace, no shadow of me.

III

I WANDERED all day about the city, staring at every passer-by to assure myself that he was not I. I called on every one of Mr. Secco's guests—but the first would not admit me; the second was out; the third insulted me; the fourth tried to summon an ambulance; the fifth gave me the address of a famous alienist; the sixth advised cold water and plenty of sleep; the seventh was polite but refused to hear my story; the eighth denied having been at the ball; the ninth swore that he could remember nothing about it; the tenth was sick in bed and discussed his symptoms; the eleventh recalled having seen one of the masks swoon before a mirror; the twelfth grew pale when I mentioned the ball and offered me money; the thirteenth. . . .

But what's the use? No one knew what had become of *me!* At nightfall I turned toward home, crying piteously: "Where am I?"

The pathetic search continued, day after day. I haunted the streets, the shops, the churches. I looked into a million faces; I questioned thousands of strangers—always hoping to discover myself, always in terror for fear I should not recognize myself! And yet I thought I should be able to know myself again by the furtive and guilty look in my eye.

I cannot explain how acute, how atrocious my suffering was! I was so thin and pale that children laughed at me on the street. My friends avoided me. And yet I wanted nothing but myself! What had I done to merit such a fate? I put an advertisement in the "Lost and Found" column of a daily paper, reasoning that it was no more absurd to hope for the return of a soul than for the return of a dog or a pocketbook. I went to the police. I consulted the Street Cleaning Department. I interviewed the Mayor. He listened to me patiently, looked wise, and, after much consultation, gave me—my own address! "You will find yourself there," he assured me.

AND then, one day, a ray of hope penetrated the darkness of my life. Scanning the "Lost and Found" column for an answer to my advertisement, I happened to see the following notice:

"*Found. A white domino and a black mask. Owner can obtain same by applying at number 127 —— Street, today.*"

I flew to this rendezvous with Destiny. It was indeed my own domino—the very one I had worn on that fatal night! It had been found, the morning after the ball, in a street near the Seccos' house. . . . I paid the reward and, with the precious garment beneath my arm, jumped into a taxi and hurried home, with a frantically beating heart.

There, breathless with excitement, I put it on, and adjusting the black mask over my face, stared at myself in a long, old-fashioned mirror that hung in the drawing-room.

As soon as I looked into the glass, behold, I was I! I! Myself! I had found me again. My body was within that white garment, my face behind that sable mask. I recognized myself.

There could be no doubt about it, for there was no one else in the room. I wept. I laughed aloud. I kissed my own familiar hands. And I danced. . . .

But, from that day to this, I have never dared to remove the domino and the mask. I never go out. I stay indoors, alone, forgotten, fearful of losing myself again. . . . And, in all the mirrors in my rooms I see, confronting me, a white figure with a black face and staring, terrified eyes. . . .

JANE COWL

The happy heroine of her own new play, Smilin' Through

Steichen

BILLIE BURKE

Who is soon to appear in The Frisky Mrs. Johnson, *a motion picture based on Clyde Fitch's comedy*

Johnston

Van-Riel

PAVLOVA

Currently appearing in Paris and Monaco in a new series of dances

Nominated for the Hall of Fame: 1920

SERGEI RACHMANINOFF

Because he not only writes his music, but also plays and conducts it; because he is at present giving a series of piano recitals in America; because he is the author of the very famous and popular C-sharp-minor Prelude; but chiefly because though strangely unaffected by modern tendencies, he is the greatest living exponent in music of Russian Romanticism.

LADY ASTOR

Because she was one of the famous Langhorne sisters of Virginia; because she is a wit of the first magnitude; because she relinquished Cliveden, for war purposes, during the war; because this portrait of her is by John Sargent; but chiefly because she has contributed to the British Parliament its first feminine member and note of light-hearted gaiety.

FRANZ LEHAR *(below)*

Because he began his brilliant musical career as a military bandmaster; because his failure as a composer of serious operas drove him into the field of light opera; because he is the composer of *The Merry Widow,* which created a furore all over the civilized world; and because he is soon to pay America a welcome and long-deferred visit.

Melinda

W. B. YEATS *(left)*

Because he has been a force in the Irish renaissance; because, unlike many poets, he has kept on experimenting and has achieved in his latest book, *The Wild Swans at Coole,* a Dantesque beauty quite different from his early iridescence; because he is the greatest poet writing English today.

Jones

JOHN MASEFIELD

Because he has done more than any other living English poet to restore the narrative poem to its native importance; because he has made a brave and lonely attempt to reinstate heroic tragedy on the modern stage; but chiefly because in his latest book, *Enslaved,* he reaffirms his right to be considered a noble inheritor of the great tradition in English poetry.

Hoppe

Rhyme and Relativity

Parodies Showing the Possible Influence of the Einstein Theory on Our Contemporary Poets

LOUIS UNTERMEYER

The following verses are examples of what, after a course of Easy Lessons in Einstein, one might expect from a few of our most representative poets.

The Dance of Dust

By Conrad Aiken

So to begin with, ghosts of rain arise
And blow their muffled horns along the
    street . . .
Who is it wavers through this nebulous
    curtain,
Floating on watery feet?

Wind melts the walls. A heavy ray of
    starlight,
Weighed down with languor, falls. Black
    trumpets cry.
The dancers watch a murder. Cool stars
    twinkle.
In a broken glass, three faded violets die.

And so, says Steinlin, the dust dissolves,
Plots a new curve, strikes out tangentially,
Builds its discordant music in faint rhythms
Under a softly crashing sea.

"I am the one" he cries, "Who stumbles in
    twilight,
I am the one who tracks the anfractuous
    gleam . . ."
The feeble lamps go out. The night is a
    storm of silence . . .
What do we wait for? Is it all a dream?

Einstein among the Coffee-Cups

By T. S. Eliot

Deflective rhythm under seas
Where Sappho tuned the snarling air;
A shifting of the spectral lines
Grown red with gravity and wear.

New systems of coördinates
Disturb the Sunday table-cloth.
Celestine yawns. Sir Oliver
Hints of the jaguar and sloth.

A chord of the eleventh shrieks
And slips beyond the portico.
The night contracts. A warp in space
Has rumors of Correggio.

Lights. Mrs. Blumenthal expands;
Diaphragm and diastole.
The rector brightens. Tea is served;
Euclid supplanted by the sole.

The New Atom

By Louis Untermeyer

And suddenly analysis
Grows futile; thought and language rasp.
And all dimensions are contained in this
One restless body that I clasp.

Atoms disintegrate while drums
Beat their red lightnings through each vein,
And every crowded molecule becomes
A world, a bleeding battle-plain.

A thousand orbits twist and glow,
The flesh reveals its secret den . . .
And so (in rhyme) I leave the earth,
    and so
I come to your white breast again.

Guessers

By Carl Sandburg

Old man Euclid had 'em guessing.
He let the wise guys laugh and went his
    way.
Planes, solids, rhomboids, polygons—
Signs and cosines—
He had their number,
Even the division of a circle's circumference
    by its diameter never fazed him—
It was Pi to him.
Galileo told 'em something.
"You're nuts," they said, "you for the
    padded cell,
    you for the booby hatch
    and the squirrel cage."
"Have your laugh," he answered.
"Have your laugh and let it ride.
    Let it ride . . . for a thousand years
    or so."
Newton let 'em grin and giggle.
He smiled when they chuckled, "Nobody
    home."
He looked 'em over
    and went on listening to damsons, lis-
    tening to autumn apples falling with
    their "now you see it, now you don't."
"Maybe," is all he told 'em, "perhaps is
    all the answer . . . perhaps and . . .
    who knows . . . in a thousand years."
And now, bo, here's this Einstein;
Good for a laugh in all the funny sections,
Sure-fire stuff in the movies, comic-operas,
    burlesque, jazz parlors, honky tonks,
    two-a-day.
Somebody asks him "How about Eu-
    clid? . . . Was he all twisted? . . .

And is it true your kink in space will
    put the kibosh on Copernicus?"
Einstein looks 'em over and tells 'em
    "Maybe . . . and then again . . . per-
    haps."
He says "The truth is all—supposing . . .
    the truth is all . . . come back and
    ask me . . . in a thousand years."

From The Ohm's Day-Book

By Edgar Lee Masters (later style)

Take any spark you see and study it:
It brightens, trembles, spurts and then goes
    out.
The light departs and leaves, we say, be-
    hind—
Who knows?
    Succinctly, then, great men and little
    sparks
Are all the same in some vast dynamo
Of humming ether, ringed with unseen
    coils.
Now here am I, the smallest unit of
Electrical resistance. What to me,
You'd say, are systems of coördinates,
Or spectral lines, or *vibgyor* or all
The Morley-Michelson experiments?
Just this, the tiniest flash of energy,
Started beyond the furthest reach of space,
Makes ripples that will spread until the
    rings
Circling in that black pool of time, will
    touch
All other forms of energy and light.
Everything is related, all must share
Uncommon destinies.
    The problem is
To find the hidden soul, it's with our-
    selves—
Within ourselves, if we know where to
    look,
A fourth dimension of reality.
But let us take an instance: Some one's shot.
Where? At Broadway and Forty-second
    Street.
The place is fixed by two coördinates,
Crossing at sharp right angles in a plane.
But was it on the ground or in the air,
Below the surface or the thirtieth floor
Of that gray office-building? Knowing this,
Fixes the third dimension. But we must
Still find a fourth to make it definite;
Concretely, time. If then we trace the
    source
And, having clearly mapped the physical,
The soul . . . America . . . (*and so on*)

Memoirs of Court Favourites

Brief Biographies of Some Famous Beauties of the Past, Written in the Inevitable Manner

NOEL COWARD

Madcap Moll

(THE ENGLISH SCHOOL OF BIOGRAPHY)

NOBODY who knew George I could help loving him—he possessed that peculiar charm of manner which had the effect of subjugating all who came near him into immediate slavery. Madcap Moll, his true love, his one love, adored him with such devotion as falls to the lot of few men, be they kings or beggars.

They met first in the New Forest, where Moll spent her wild, unfettered childhood. She was ever an undisciplined creature, snapping her shapely fingers at bad weather, and riding for preference without a saddle—as hoydenish a girl as one could encounter on a day's march. Her auburn ringlets, ablow in the autumn wind, her cheeks whipped to a flush by the breeze's caress, and her eyes sparkling and brimful of mischief and roguery! This, then, was the picture that must have met the King's gaze as he rode with a few trusty friends through the forest for his annual week of otter shooting. Upon seeing him, Moll gave a merry laugh and crying, "Chase me, Laddie," in provocative tones, she rode swiftly away on her pony. Many of the courtiers trembled at such a daring exhibition of *lèse majesté*, but the King, provoked only by her winning smile, set off in hot pursuit. Eventually he caught his roguish quarry seated by the banks of a sunlit pool. The King cast an appraising glance at her shapely figure and tethered his horse.

"Are you a creature of the woods?" he said.

Madcap Moll tossed her curls. "Ask me!" she cried derisively.

"I *am* asking you," replied the King.

"'Odd's fudge—you have spindle-shanks!" cried Madcap Moll irrelevantly. The King was charmed. He leaned toward her.

"One kiss, mistress!" he implored. At that she slapped his cheek good-naturedly. He was captivated.

"I, faith, my daring girl!" he cried delightedly. "Knowst that I am George the First?" said the King, rising.

Madcap Moll blanched.

"Sire," she murmured, "I did not know—a poor unwitting country lass—have mercy!"

The King touched her lightly on the nape.

"Arise," he said gently, "you are as loyal and spirited a girl as one could meet. Hast a liking for Court?"

"Oh, sire!" answered the girl.

Thus did the King meet her who was soon to mean everything in his life—and more.

Muray

NOEL COWARD

Maggie McWhistle

(THE SCOTCH SCHOOL OF BIOGRAPHY)

BORN in an obscure Scotch manse of Jacobite parents, Maggie McWhistle will go down to immortality as perhaps the greatest heroine of Scottish history.

And perhaps not.

What did Maggie know of the part she was to play in the history of her country? Nothing. She lived through her girlhood, unheeding; she helped her mother with the baps and her father with the haggis; and occasionally she would be given a new plaidie.

A word must be said of her parents. Her father was known all along Deeside as Handsome Jaimie—and oh, how the light-hearted village girls mourned when he turned minister; he was high, high above them. Of his meeting with Janey McToddle, the Pride of Bonny Deeside, and the mother of Maggie, very little is written. Some say that they met in a snowstorm on Ben Lomond, where she was tending her kine; others say that they met on the high road to Aberdeen, and that his collie Jeannie bit her collie Jock—thus cementing a friendship that was later on to ripen into more and more.

History tells us that Maggie's griddle cakes were famous adown the length and breadth of Aberdeen, and that gradually a little path came to be worn between the manse and the kirk, seven miles away, where Maggie's feet so often trod on their way to their devotions. She was an intensely religious child.

One dark night, so the story runs, there came a hammering on her door. Maggie leapt out of her truckle, and, wrapping her plaidie round her—for she was a modest girl—she ran to the window.

"Wha is there?" she cried in Scotch.

The answer came back through the darkness, thrilling her to the marrow.

"Bonnie Prince Charlie!"

Maggie gave a cry and, running downstairs, opened the door and let him in. She looked at him by the light of her homely candle. His brow was amuck with sweat; he was trembling in every limb.

"I am pursued," he said, hoarse with exertion and weariness. "Hide me, bonnie lassie, hide me."

Quick as thought, Maggie hid him behind a pile of cold griddle cakes, and not a moment too soon, for there came a fresh hammering at the door. Maggie opened it defiantly and never flinched at the sight of so many men.

"We want Bonnie Prince Charlie," said the leader of the crew in Scotch.

Then came Maggie's well-known answer, also in Scotch.

"Know you not that this is a manse?"

History has it that the men fell back as though struck dumb, and one by one, awed by the still purity of the white-faced girl, the legions departed into the night. Thus Maggie McWhistle proved herself the saviour of Bonnie Prince Charlie for the first time.

There were many occasions after that in

which she was able to save and hide him. She would conceal him up a tree or in an oven at the slightest provocation. Soon there were no trees for miles around in which she had not hidden him at some period or other.

Poor Maggie—perchance she is finding in Heaven the peaceful rest which was so lacking in her life on earth. For legend hath it that she never had two consecutive nights' sleep for fifteen years, so busy was she in saving and hiding her Bonnie Prince Charlie.

La Bibi

(THE FRENCH SCHOOL OF BIOGRAPHY)

HORTENSE POISSONS—"La Bibi" the dancer. What memories that name conjures up! The incomparable—the lightsome —the effervescent! Her life, a rose-coloured smear across the history of France; her smile—tier upon tier of sparkling teeth; her heart, that delicate organ for which kings fought in the streets—but enough. Let us trace her to her obscure parentage. You all know the Place de la Concorde— she was not born there. You have all visited the Champs Elysées—she was not born there. And there's probably no one who doesn't know of the Faubourg St. Honoré —but she was not born there. Sufficient to say that she was born. Her mother, poor, honest, *gauche,* was an unpretentious seamstress; she seamed and seamed until her death in 1682 or 1683. Bibi at the age of ten, flung upon the world homeless, motherless, with nothing but her amazing beauty to save her from starvation—or worse. Who can blame her for what she did—who can question or condemn her motives? She was alone. Then Armand Brochet (who shall be nameless) came into her life. What should she do? Refuse the roof he offered her? This waif (later on to be the glory of France) was a leaf blown hither and thither by the winds of Destiny. What was she to do?

Enough that she did it.

Paris, a city of seething vice and corruption—her home, the place wherein she danced her first catoucha, that catoucha which was so soon to be followed by her famous Peruvian minuet. Voltaire wrote many books, but he didn't mention her; Jean Jacques Rousseau never so much as referred to her; even Molière was so reticent about her charms that no single word about her can be found in any of his works.

Her life with Armand Brochet—three years before she stepped on the boards—how well we all know it. Her first appearance on the stage was in Paris, 1690, at the Opera when this airy, fairy thing danced her way into the hearts of the multitudes. Oh, Bibi—"Bibi, Coeur d'Or," as she was called so frequently by her adorers—would

that in these mundane days you could revisit us with your girlish laugh and supple dancing form! Look at the portrait of her, painted by Coddlé, at the height of her amazing beauty; note the sensitive nostrils, the delicate little mouth, the graceful neck and shoulders, and those eyes—the gayest, merriest eyes that ever charmed a king's heart.

In November, 1701, she introduced her world-famed Bavarian fandango, which literally took Paris by storm—it was in her dressing room afterward that she made her celebrated *bon mot* to Maria Pipello, her only rival. Maria came ostensibly to congratulate her on her success but really to insult her. *"Ma petite,"* she said, *"l'hibou est-il sur le haie?"* Quick as thought Bibi turned round and replied with a gay toss of her curls, *"Non, mais j'ai la plume de ma tante."*

Oh, witty, sharp-tongued Bibi!

A word must be said of the glorious ballets she originated which charmed France for nearly thirty years. They were, "The Life of a Raindrop" and "Angels Visiting a Ruined Monastery at Night." People flocked to the Opera again and again in order to see them and applaud their ravishing originator. Then came her meeting with the King in his private box. We are told she curtsied low and glancing up at him coyly from between her bent knees, gave forth her world-renowned epigram, *"Comment ça va, papa?"* Louis was

charmed by this exquisite exhibition of drollery, and three weeks later she was brought to Versailles.

La Belle Bibi was certainly not one to miss opportunities, and only one month later she found herself installed at Court —the King's right hand. Then began that amazing reign of hers—short lived, but ho, how triumphant. Dukes, duchesses, countesses, even princes paying homage at the feet of La Bibi, the dancer, now Hortense, Duchess de Mal-Moulle. Did she abuse her power? Some say she did, some say she didn't. Every afternoon, Louis was wont to visit her apartments; together they would pore over the plans and campaigns of war drawn up and submitted by his generals. Then, when Louis was weary, Bibi would put the maps in the drawer, draw his head on to her breast and sing to him songs of her youth. Meanwhile, intrigue was placing its evil fingers upon the strings of her fate. Lampoons were launched against her, pasquinades were written of her. When she went driving, fruits and vegetables were hurled at her.

Absinthe was her one consolation. Her gay humour remained with her to the end. As she lay on her death-bed she uttered the supreme *bon mot* of her brilliant life. Stretching out her wasted arm to the nearly empty absinthe bottle by her bed, she made a slightly resentful mouth at the physician and murmured, "Encore!"

Oh brave, witty Bibi!

Love Song

ELINOR WYLIE

Lovers eminent in love
Ever diversities combine;
The vocal cords of the cushet-dove,
The snake's articulated spine.

Such elective elements
Educate the eye and lip
With one's refreshing innocence,
The other's claim to scholarship.

The serpent's knowledge of the world
Learn, and the dove's more naïve charm;
Whether your ringlets should be curled,
And why he likes his claret warm.

American Novelists Who Have Set Art above Popularity

A group of authors who have consistently stood out against Philistia

THEODORE DREISER

Whose crudely written but relentlessly truthful records of life are among the most extraordinary phenomena of American letters.

Hoppe

WILLA CATHER

Who has brought a careful and sure technique to her novels of the Middle-Western countryside and her short stories of the musical world. H. L. Mencken calls her *My Antonia* the best novel ever written by an American woman.

JAMES BRANCH CABELL

The champion of romance against realism. Mr. Cabell has turned from his study of the American South in its decay to a strange medieval dream-world of his own, quite unlike anything else in American fiction. The irony, beauty and urbanity of his style achieved their greatest success in *Jurgen*, idiotically suppressed by the Anti-Vice Society.

EDITH WHARTON

The greatest living American novelist, who has brought to her pictures of New York and New England life the mastery of form and the intensity of feeling of the French novelists.

SHERWOOD ANDERSON *(left)*

Foremost among those who are using the novel as a means of criticizing American civilization. His new novel, *Poor White*, presents with an uncompromising fidelity the life of the industrial towns of the Middle West.

Hutchinson

Foster

The Ballad of Yukon Jake

Begging Robert W. Service's Pardon

EDWARD E. PARAMORE, JR.

Oh, the North Countree is a hard countree
That mothers a bloody brood;
And its icy arms hold hidden charms
For the greedy, the sinful and lewd.
And strong men rust, from the gold and
the lust
That sears the Northland soul,
But the wickedest born, from the Pole to
the Horn,
Is the Hermit of Shark Tooth Shoal.

Now Jacob Kaime was the Hermit's name,
In the days of his pious youth,
Ere he cast a smirch on the Baptist Church
By betraying a girl named Ruth.
But now men quake at "Yukon Jake,"
The Hermit of Shark Tooth Shoal,
For that is the name that Jacob Kaime
Is known by from Nome to the Pole.
He was just a boy and the parson's joy.
(Ere he fell for the gold and the muck),
And had learned to pray, with the hogs and
the hay
On a farm near Keokuk.
But a Service tale of illicit kale—
And whiskey and women wild—
Drained the morals clean as a soup-tureen
From this poor but honest child.
He longed for the bite of a Yukon night
And the Northern Light's weird flicker,
Or a game of stud in the frozen mud,
And the taste of raw red licker.
He wanted to mush along in the slush,
With a team of huskie hounds,
And to fire his gat at a beaver hat
And knock it out of bounds.

So he left his home for the hell-town Nome,
On Alaska's ice-ribbed shores,
And he learned to curse and to drink, and
worse—
Till the rum dripped from his pores,
When the boys on a spree were drinking it
free
In a Malamute saloon
And Dan Megrew and his dangerous crew
Shot craps with the piebald coon;
When the Kid on his stool banged away
like a fool
At a jag-time melody,
And the barkeep vowed, to the hardboiled
crowd,
That he'd cree-mate Sam McGee—

Then Jacob Kaime, who had taken the
name

Of Yukon Jake, the Killer,
Would rake the dive with his forty-five
Till the atmosphere grew chiller.
With a sharp command he'd make 'em
stand
And deliver their hard-earned dust,
Then drink the bar dry, of rum and rye,
As a Klondike bully must.
Without coming to blows he would tweak
the nose
Of Dangerous Dan Megrew,
And becoming bolder, throw over his
shoulder
The lady that's known as Lou.

Oh, tough as a steak was Yukon Jake—
Hardboiled as a picnic egg.
He washed his shirt in the Klondike
dirt,
And drank his rum by the keg.
In fear of their lives (or because of their
wives)
He was shunned by the best of his
pals.
An outcast he, from the comraderie
Of all but wild animals.
So he bought him the whole of Shark Tooth
Shoal,
A reef in the Bering Sea,
And he lived by himself on a sea lion's
shelf
In lonely iniquity.

But, miles away, in Keokuk, Ia.,
Did a ruined maiden fight
To remove the smirch from the Baptist
Church
By bringing the heathen Light.
And the Elders declared that all would be
squared
If she carried the holy words
From her Keokuk home to the hell-town
Nome
To save those sinful birds.
So, two weeks later, she took a freighter,
For the gold-cursed land near the Pole,
But Heaven ain't made for a lass that's
betrayed—
She was wrecked on Shark Tooth Shoal!

All hands were tossed in the Sea, and
lost—
All but the maiden Ruth,
Who swam to the edge of the sea lion's
ledge
Where abode the love of her youth.

He was hunting a seal for his evening
meal
(He handled a mean harpoon)
When he saw at his feet, not something to
eat,
But a girl in a frozen swoon,
Whom he dragged to his lair by her drip-
ping hair,
And he rubbed her knees with gin.
To his great surprise, she opened her eyes
And revealed—his Original Sin!

His eight-months beard grew stiff and
weird
And it felt like a chestnut burr,
And he swore by his gizzard—and the
Arctic blizzard,
That he'd do right by her.
But the cold sweat froze on the end of her
nose
Till it gleamed like a Tecla pearl,
While her bright hair fell, like a flame from
hell,
Down the back of the grateful girl.
But a hopeless rake was Yukon Jake
The Hermit of Shark Tooth Shoal!
And the dizzy maid he rebetrayed
And wrecked her immortal soul! . . .

Then he rowed her ashore, with a broken
oar,
And he sold her to Dan Megrew
For a huskie dog and some hot egg-nog—
As rascals are wont to do.
Now ruthless Ruth is a maid uncouth
With scarlet cheeks and lips,
And she sings rough songs to the drunken
throngs
That come from the sealing ships.
For a rouge-stained kiss from this infamous
miss
They will give a seal's sleek fur,
Or perhaps a sable, if they are able;
It's much the same to her.

Oh, the North Countree is a rough coun-
tree,
That mothers a bloody brood;
And its icy arms hold hidden charms
For the greedy, the sinful and lewd.
And strong men rust, from the gold and
the lust
That sears the Northland soul,
But the wickedest born from the Pole to
the Horn
Was the Hermit of Shark Tooth Shoal!

GEORGE ARLISS

Goldberg

As the ruthless Rajah of Rukh in the now famous play The Green
Goddess, *Mr. Arliss has found his best and most sardonic role to date*

Lenglen the Magnificent

The French Woman Tennis Player Is One of the Marvelous Products of Sport

GRANTLAND RICE

AN AMAZINGLY symmetrical figure replete with grace and litheness, arrayed in a white silk dress that barely flutters below the knees. White silk stockings with white shoes. Above this background of white, hair as black as a raven's wing bound with a brilliant orange band. Perfectly molded arms, bare and brown from many suns—the entire effect being one of extreme vividness—an effect immediately to catch and hold the eye.

Herein you have the briefest sort of pen-sketch of Mademoiselle Suzanne Lenglen, the marvelous girl tennis player of France, who has a record unsurpassed in sport.

This picture is quite incomplete until Mademoiselle Lenglen begins to move about the court, when the court seems entirely too small for her. She is all over it in a brace of agile leaps, which proclaim her a combination sprinter, hurdler and high jumper any time she cares to abandon her chosen sport and seek another field for conquest. Her agility is amazing. As we sat by the low railing at St. Cloud, just outside of Paris, and watched her astounding mid-air flutterings, as of some brilliantly colored bird, with the orange band flashing like a flame of yellow fire, we could only think that Solomon, meeting the late Queen of Sheba, beat us to it with the proper phrase—"The better half has never been told."

THE mere fact that Mademoiselle Lenglen is a great tennis player is one thing. Great tennis players have been around before. It was her impressive vividness that held most of our attention.

When play began we found our attention divided between Lenglen the picture and Lenglen the tennis star. We had always thought of her as a brilliant, slashing type whirling about the court and winning by the sheer dash of her game, despite many errors. The dash and speed were there. But it was the uncanny accuracy and control of her game that featured her play. She was fast, flashy and spectacular. But she was true.

Her bare, brown arms as they glistened in the sun worked with perfect rhythm. The first effort of service, played with a hard smash, was almost invariably in. She rarely served a fault, despite the amount of speed she put upon the ball.

SUZANNE LENGLEN

The same was true of her cross court strokes and of every other stroke she played. Whether upon ground strokes or when taking the ball high in the air, the same accuracy prevailed. This versatility of stroke was one of the leading features of her play. We began to sum up the returns—speed, dash, accuracy and versatility. We wondered how she could ever be beaten and then we glanced through the program, where her record in the French championship up to the final match was printed. It ran 6–0, 6–0, 6–0, 6–0, 6–0, 6–0, 6–0, 6–1. Out of the forty-three games played to that point she had won 42 and lost 1. The wonder was not over the 42 won, but of the single game lost.

WELL, we thought, this is against women. Wait until she appears in the mixed doubles with a man to meet. On her second appearance the orange band around her black hair had given way to one of flaming crimson. This is her custom. Orange for the first appearance—crimson for the second, each striking in its effect.

The first service that came to her from the male server happened to be in. It came over like a shot. A sure ace, we thought. But, without any attempt to hurry her stroke, she not only returned the service but put something on the ball.

Mademoiselle Lenglen, paired with Decugis, one of the male stars of France, looked to be fully as effective as her masculine partner. At first she was selected as the weak spot in the combination. But this selection did not appear to be aptly made. She was not only extremely fast

on her feet but the quickness of her hand was abnormal. No matter where the ball came nor at what speed, she always had her racket in front of it. Her quick smashes down the lines, in only by inches, but seemingly always in, began to roll up points until she was no longer the target of any concentrated attack. Her knack of leaping off the ground from two to three feet was taken by many to be more for spectacular effect than for effective play. But it was both spectacular and effective. Just how she could leap to such heights, even when a leap of such proportions was not precisely required, and still retain all her accuracy was an astonishing thing. After one of these mid-air hurdles you were confident that she would hammer the ball far out of line, but her perfect control was maintained as well in mid air as upon the ground.

If France had been turning out women tennis stars for several generations it would be a simple matter to recognize Mademoiselle Lenglen as the rare product of a big school, such as we recognize the Californians. But France among her women has had no such tennis development. When Mademoiselle Lenglen was in her early 'teens she gave promise of future greatness, although no one at the time seems to have prophesied that a world beater was on the way. She was coming swiftly into her own as a youthful premier when war broke out and her tennis days were supplanted by her service as an army nurse. When peace came again to France and she resumed play, only a few weeks seemed to be needed to bring her back to top form, further proof of an inborn knack that is often more important than long training and instruction. And for the three years that have intervened since the armistice Lenglen has been not only unbeatable, but so far superior to all rivals that no one could be listed in her class. She has dwelt in another world of tennis, and when big crowds in America watch her speed, control and all-around versatility they will understand why the best of women players are helpless before the power and accuracy of her play.

They will understand why she is called Lenglen the Magnificent and why France, working hard to develop and extend its sporting glory, looks upon her as one of its greatest inspirations.

Nominated for the Hall of Fame: 1921

Janvier

H. L. MENCKEN

Because he wrote one of the first and best books on Nietzsche in English; because he has for years been almost our only bold assailant of the national Puritanism; and finally, because he has taken his place as one of our most important living critics.

Kabel & Herbert

GERTRUDE VANDERBILT WHITNEY

Because her sculptures have recently been seen on three continents; because she has been a good friend to all the arts; and because she has now sent a fine group of American paintings to London and Paris.

MARIE SKLODOWSKA CURIE

Because the Nobel Prize for physics was awarded, in 1903, jointly to Madame Curie and her husband for their discovery of radium; because alone she carried out the tedious experiments to determine the atomic weight of the newly discovered element; and finally because she has come to America to receive the public gift of one gram of radium to continue her experiments.

Manuel

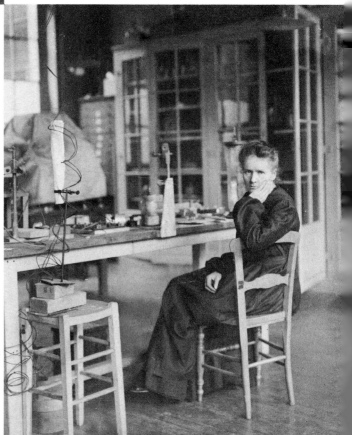

Vandamm

MAUDE ADAMS

Because, beginning as a child actress, she has long been a well-loved ornament to the American stage; because she has been the chief instrument in making Barrie the most popular of English playwrights; because, as a woman, she is unbelievably sensitive and retiring; because her reading and erudition are prodigious; and finally because she is soon to introduce us to a wholly new development in motion pictures.

Floyd

WALTER HAMPDEN

Because he has believed, firmly and always, in the importance of the classical drama; because he is a theatrical producer and manager of high distinction; but chiefly because he has been, for the past few years, one of the foremost of Shakespearean actors, and quite the most inspiring Hamlet.

Thompson

J. PIERPONT MORGAN

Because, like his father, he is the banker of the widest vision and soundest ability in America; because he is a lover, collector and connoisseur of art; because he is a sportsman of the best type, and has kept the *America*'s Cup in America; but chiefly because he is ever ready to help a friend, a worthy civic movement, or a deserving work of charity.

GEORGE JEAN NATHAN

Because the *Mercure de France* has said that he is the greatest dramatic critic America has produced since Poe; because, with H. L. Mencken, he is one of the editors of the *Smart Set;* because he is the most inaccessible literary figure in New York; because he is an adept in igniting dinners and evening parties; but chiefly because, in his new book, *The Critic and the Drama,* he dispenses with his wit and satirical gifts in order to explain the seriousness of his critical position.

Hoppe

The Incredible Jeritza

The Viennese Soprano Who Has Fallen Heir to Caruso's Popularity at the Metropolitan

DEEMS TAYLOR

MARIA JERITZA

Setzer

THE opera season in New York opened on November 15th under the shadow of Caruso's death. Everybody was wondering who would replace the great tenor and predicting that his loss spelled the doom of grand opera as a paying undertaking in New York.

For the afternoon of Saturday, November 19th, Director Gatti-Casazza had announced the first American performance of a new opera, *Die Tote Stadt,* by the youthful Austrian composer, Erich Korngold. It had been written for a Viennese soprano, Maria Jeritza, who had, it was announced, been engaged by the Metropolitan to sing the principal rôle here. Nobody knew much about her, except that she was a popular prima donna of the *Hof Opera* in Vienna, and that a few traveled opera-goers who had seen her there had brought back wondrous tales of her voice and beauty.

THERE was no applause when the audience first saw that tall, graceful, radiant figure flash upon the dim stage. Instead, one heard the strange, long sigh that a crowd gives when its eyes are startled by some sudden, breath-taking wonder. Later there was applause, and cheering, too. For

that afternoon Maria Jeritza achieved a triumph that has not been equaled since Olive Fremstad first took the Metropolitan by storm. New York had found the thing dearest to its heart—a new personality: an opera singer who combined statuesque height and beauty with a voice of glorious quality and power, and was, in the bargain, an actress of extraordinary grace, emotional fire, and variety of mood. Her stage personality was one of such vitality that it was an exciting and exhilarating adventure simply to watch her. The miracle had happened. Caruso's successor had been found.

Not that the chorus of praise after her first appearance was unanimous. It was all very well, some said, to pronounce her great after a single performance in one new opera. Wait until she sang some rôle whose traditions had been established by a long line of famous singers. Then we should see of what stuff she was made.

Her answer to that was a performance of *Tosca* that swept her hearers off their feet. She first sang the rôle on Thursday night, December first. Her very entrance established a new tradition. The time-honored Toscas have always appeared in the church

scene gorgeously attired in dark velvet and wearing a broad plumed hat. This Tosca wore the palest and most innocent of blue gowns, and her head was covered only by a light scarf. Her complete triumph came in the second act. The aria, *Vissi d'arte,* has always been rather a nuisance. It comes just after Scarpia has named his terms for releasing Cavaradossi, and Tosca, shamed and beaten, has accepted them. Whereupon librettist and composer make the heroine step forward and sing, "I have lived for art, I have lived for love, heaven help me"—or words to that effect, while suspense withered and died.

Jeritza made it one of the high points of the drama. She shrank back on the sofa, from which Scarpia roughly pushed her, so that she slipped off and lay prone on the floor. It was from this position that she began the aria, lying crushed and limp, face downward. She finished it kneeling by the sofa, with her face buried in her arms—a figure of pitiful helplessness and despair. The last few notes were sobbed, rather than sung. Half her audience were in tears. Scotti played Scarpia that night as he had never played it in his life before. He was in the presence of a great artist, and he knew it.

Jeritza in Wagner

AFTER that *Tosca* performance there was little talk of her limitations. We merely waited to see what she would do next. On December 16th she sang Sieglinde in *Die Walküre*. There is nothing spectacular in this part. It is, in fact, rather an ungrateful one. Sieglinde is technically the heroine, simply because without her there would be no Siegfried, but it is Brünnhilde who has all the great scenes. A woman who was less of an artist than Jeritza might easily have ruined everything by overacting. Not she. She sang and acted the rôle with a restraint and simplicity as perfect as it was effective. Her first-act Sieglinde was a heroic figure of tireless repose and sculpturesque beauty. When she walked, it was as one of the Elgin marbles might have walked.

On the night of January 6th Jeritza sang Elsa in *Lohengrin*. Her singing in the second act was a marvel of limpid beauty, and the scene with Lohengrin in the bridal chamber was a moment of passionate and wistful tenderness. They stayed to cheer her that night, after the last curtain, until the other singers conspired courteously and charmingly to abandon her before the great drop curtain, leaving her to take three calls alone.

She is a great artist. It is not altogether easy to describe the secret of her greatness. She is tall, graceful, and beautiful. She has a lovely, warm soprano voice, which she handles well—barring a few slight technical imperfections—and colors with marvelous skill: she sings a rôle as an actress would read her lines. She is an actress of tremendous intelligence and subtlety. But the thing that makes her great is something beyond all these attributes. Chaliapin is the only other opera singer I know of who has it. It is a power of conveying a sense of reality in everything she does. When she comes upon the stage as Tosca, or Elsa, you see Tosca or Elsa. For the moment there is no Jeritza, only the character she has become. She says, in effect, "I am Elsa," and you believe it. Instantly and unquestioningly you believe it. This is the mysterious power, that genius of personality which enables a few men and women in a generation to sway the imaginations and emotions of countless others. Eleonora Duse has it. Theodore Roosevelt had it. Napoleon must have had it.

Like all great people, she is simple. Off the stage she is a charming, rather shy young woman, utterly unaffected, and much more concerned with her work than with her press notices.

Jeritza knows fifty-nine operatic rôles, and can sing any of them on twenty-four hours' notice. American singing voices, she thinks, are remarkable. "Never have I heard such voices, especially the women's voices. You have the most wonderful operatic material in the world here; if only there were someone here to tell your young singers what to do."

What she did with one young singer is worth retelling. When she appeared in *Die Walküre* the part of Hunding was sung by William Gustafson, a young American basso of the Metropolitan, who has a fine voice but lacks Wagnerian experience. "In his scene with Siegmund in the first act," she said, "he kept moving up too close. I told him 'No, you must stand still,' and showed him how. But I was dreadfully afraid that he would move, after he started singing, and spoil his scene. And so," she explained gleefully, "when the night of the performance came, as soon as he began to sing, I stood on his foot!"

New Hampshire Again
CARL SANDBURG

I remember black waters.
I remember thin white birches.
I remember sleepy white hills.
I remember riding along New Hampshire
  lengthways.
I remember a station named Halcyon, the
  brakeman calling on passengers "Hal-
  cy-on! ! Hal-cy-on! !"
I remember having heard the gold diggers
  dig out only enough for wedding rings.
I remember a stately child telling me her
  father gets letters addressed, "Robert
  Frost, New Hampshire."
I remember an old Irish saying, "His face
  is like a fiddle and every one who sees
  him loves him."
I have one remember, two remembers;
  I have a little handkerchief bundle of
  remembers.

One early evening star just over a cradle
  moon.
One dark river with a spatter of later stars
  caught;
One funnel of a motor car headlight up
  a hill;
One team of horses hauling a load of wood,
  and a boy (and a red yarn stocking
  cap) whistling, going skating.
One boy on skis picking himself up after
  a tumble—
I remember one and a-one and a-one riding
  along New Hampshire lengthways; I
  have a little handkerchief bundle of
  remembers.

CARL SANDBURG

The Public and the Artist

Reflections on Music, Painting and the Creative Arts in General

JEAN COCTEAU

I AM working at my wooden table, seated on my wooden chair with my wooden penholder in my hand, but this does not prevent me from being, in some degree, responsible for the course of the stars.

A dreamer is always a bad poet.

Nietzsche was afraid of certain "ands"; Goethe *and* Schiller, for example, or, worse still, Schiller *and* Goethe. What would he say at seeing the spread of the cult of Nietzsche and Wagner or, rather, Wagner *and* Nietzsche!

The opposition of the masses to the elite has always stimulated individual genius. This is the case in France. Modern Germany is dying of approbation, carefulness, faithful application and a scholastic vulgarization of aristocratic culture.

Let us keep clear of the theatre. I regret to have felt its temptation and to have introduced to it two great artists. "Well, then, why do you write for the theatre?" That is precisely the weak point about the theatre; it is forced to depend, for its very existence, upon *immediate* successes.

When I say that I prefer certain circus or music-hall turns to anything given in the theatre, I do not mean that I prefer them to anything that *might* be given in the theatre.

One day I was looking at a children's puppet show in the Champs Elysées when a dog came on the stage, or rather a dog's head, as big in itself as the two other actors put together. "Look at that monster," said a mother to her child. "That is not a monster, it is a dog," said her little boy. Men, as they grow older, lose—when in a theatre —the clairvoyance they had as children.

Tradition appears at every epoch under a different disguise, but the public does not recognize it under its masks.

That which makes the public laugh is not inevitably beautiful or new, but that which is beautiful and new inevitably makes the public laugh.

"Cultivate those qualities in thee for which the public blames thee: they are Thyself." Get this idea well into your head. This advice ought to be written up everywhere like an advertisement of "Pear's Soap." As a matter of fact, the public likes to "recognize" what is familiar. It hates to be disturbed. It is shocked by surprises. The worst that can happen to a work of art is to have no fault found with it, so

Isabey

JEAN COCTEAU

that its author is not obliged to take up an attitude of opposition.

The public only takes up yesterday as a weapon with which to castigate today.

There are people who are considered quite intelligent, but who do nothing but *lean* toward good things in art. Their heads get near them, but the rest of their bodies remain rooted.

A favorite phrase of the public is: "I don't see what that's meant to be." The public wants to understand first and to feel afterwards.

A fall makes people laugh. The mechanism of falling plays an important part in causing the laughter which greets a new work. The public, not having followed the curve which leads up to this work, stumbles suddenly from where it was standing, down on to the work which it is now seeing or hearing. Consequently a fall takes place— and laughter.

A short phrase quickly spoken and full of meaning traverses the brain like a surgeon's lancet. Ten minutes later it is no longer there.

We have in our keeping an angel whom we are continually shocking. We must be that angel's guardian.

One does not blame an epoch; one congratulates oneself on not having belonged to it.

Instinct and the Artist

ART is science—in the flesh.

Genius, in art, consists in knowing how far we may go too far.

There is a house, a lamp, a plate of soup, a fire, wine and pipes at the back of every important work of art.

Instinct, in art, needs to be trained by method; but instinct alone helps us to discover a method which will suit us, and thanks to which our instinct may be trained.

In feeling his way, an artist may open a secret door and never discover that, behind that door, a whole world lies concealed.

When a work of art appears to be in advance of its period, it is really the period that has lagged behind the work of art.

There is a moment when every work, in the process of being created, benefits from the glamour attaching to uncompleted work. "Don't touch it any more!" cries the amateur. It is then that the true artist takes his chance.

Sculpture, so neglected on account of the current contempt for form and mass, is one of the noblest arts. To begin with, it is the only one which obliges us to move round it.

"Look," said a lady to her husband in front of one of Claude Monet's paintings of a cathedral. "It looks like melting ice-cream." In this particular case the lady spoke the truth, but she had not acquired the *right* to do so.

The artist must always be partly man and partly woman. Unfortunately the woman part is almost always unbearable.

Every masterpiece having once been in the fashion goes out of fashion, and, long afterwards, finds an everlasting equilibrium. Generally it is when it is out of fashion that a masterpiece appeals to the public.

Music—Good and Bad

THE musician opens the cage-door to arithmetic; the draughtsman gives geometry its freedom.

Beethoven is irksome in his developments, but not Bach, because Beethoven develops the *form* and Bach the *idea*.

The bad music, which superior folk despise, is agreeable enough. What is really intolerable is what they think *good* music.

Wagner's works are long works which are not only long, but *long-drawn-out,* because this old sorcerer looked upon boredom as a useful drug for the stupefaction of the faithful. It is the same with mesmerists who hypnotize in public. The genuine "pass" which puts the subject to sleep is usually very short and simple, but they accompany it with a score of sham passes which impress the crowd. The crowd is won by lies; it is deceived by the truth, which is too simple, and not sufficiently shocking.

The public is shocked at the charming absurdity of Erik Satie's titles and system of notation, but respects the ponderous absurdity of the libretto of *Parsifal.*

Satie does not pay much attention to painters, and does not read the poets, but he likes to live where life ferments; he has a flair for good inns. Debussy established, once for all, the Debussy atmosphere. Satie evolves. Each of his works, intimately connected with its predecessor, is, nevertheless, distinct and lives a life of its own. They are like a new kind of pudding, a surprise and a deception for those who expect one always to keep on treading the same piece of ground. Satie teaches what, in our age, is the greatest audacity— simplicity.

Nothing is so enervating as to lie and soak for a long time in a warm bath. Enough of music in which one lies and soaks. Enough of clouds, waves, aquariums, water-sprites, and nocturnal scents; what we need is a music of the earth, every-day music. Enough of hammocks, garlands, and gondolas; I want some one to build me music I can live in, like a house. Music is not all the time a gondola, or a race-horse, or a tight-rope. It is sometimes a chair as well.

We may soon hope for an orchestra where there will be no caressing strings. Only a rich choir of wood, brass and percussion.

All good music *resembles* something. Good music arouses emotion owing to its mysterious resemblance to the objects and feelings which have motivated it.

Pelléas is an example of music to be listened to with one's face in one's hands. All music which has to be listened to through the hands is suspect. Wagner is typically music which is listened to through the hands.

Too many miracles are expected of us; I consider myself very fortunate if I have been able to make a blind man hear.

Muray

EUGENE O'NEILL

The American dramatist whose Anna Christie *has been awarded the Pulitzer Prize as the best play of the year*

Custer's Last Stand

An Exciting Event in American History as Viewed by Edith Wharton from the Continent

DONALD OGDEN STEWART

IT WAS late afternoon and the gas street lamps of the Boulevard St. Michel were being lighted by a, for Paris, or at least for Paris in summer, somewhat frigid looking allumeur, when Philip Custer came to the end of his letter. He hesitated for an instant, wrote "Your——," then crossed that out and substituted "Sincerely." No, decidedly the first ending, with its, as is, or, rather, as ordinarily is, the case in hymeneal epistles, somewhat possessive sense, would no longer suffice. "Yours truly"—perhaps; "sincerely"—better; but certainly not "Your husband." He was done, thank God, with pretenses.

Philip sipped his absinthe and gazed for an instant through the café window; a solitary fiacre rattled by; he picked up the result of his afternoon's labor, wearily.

"Dear Mary," he read. "When I told you that my employers were sending me to Paris, I lied to you. It was, perhaps, the first direct lie that I ever told you; it was, I know now, the last. But a falsehood by word of mouth mattered really very little in comparison with the enormous lie that my life with you had become."

Philip paused and smiled, somewhat bitterly, at that point in the letter. Mary, with her American woman's intuition, would undoubtedly surmise that he had run off with Mrs. Everett; there was a certain ironical humor in the fact that Mary's mistaken guess would be sadly indicative of her whole failure to understand what her husband was, to use a slang expression, "driving at."

"I hope that you will believe me when I say that I came to Paris to paint. In the past four years the desire to do that has grown steadily until it has mastered me. You do not understand. I found no one in America who did. I think my mother might have, had she lived; certainly it is utterly incomprehensible to father."

Philip stopped. Ay, there was the rub— General Custer, and all that he stood for. Philip glimpsed momentarily those early boyhood days with his father, spent mainly in army posts; the boy's cavalry uniform, in which he had ridden old Bess about the camp, waving his miniature sabre; the day he had been thrown to the ground by a strange horse which he had disobediently mounted, just as his father arrived on the scene. Philip had never forgotten his father's words that day. "Don't crawl, son–don't

whine. It was your fault this time and you deserved what you got. Lots of times it won't be your fault, but you'll have to take your licking anyway. But—take your medicine like a man—always."

Philip groaned; he knew what the general would say when the news of his son's desertion of his wife and four-year-old boy reached him. He knew that he never could explain to his father the absolute torture of the last four years of enervating domesticity and business mediocrity—the torture of the Beauty within him crying for expression, half satisfied by the stolen evenings at the art school but constantly growing stronger in its all-consuming appeal. No, life to his father was a simple problem in army ethics—a problem in which duty was *a,* one of the known factors; *x,* the unknown, was either "bravery" or "cowardice" when brought in contact with *a.* Having solved this problem, his father had closed the book; of the higher mathematics, and especially of those complex problems to which no living man knew the final answer, he had no conception. And yet——

PHILIP resumed his reading to avoid the old endless maze of subtleties.

"It is not that I did not—or do not—love you. It is, rather, that something within me is crying out—something which is stronger than I, and which I cannot resist. I have waited two years to be sure. Yesterday, as soon as I reached here, I took my work to the man who is considered the finest art critic in Paris. He told me that there was a quality to my painting which he had seen in that of no living artist; he told me that in five years of hard work I should be able to produce work which Botticelli would be proud to have done. Do you understand that, Mary—Botticelli!

"But no, forgive me. My pæan of joy comes strangely in a letter which should be of abject humility for what must seem to you, to father, and to all, a cowardly, selfish act of desertion—a whining failure to face life. Oh dear, dear Mary if you could but understand what a hell I have been through—"

Philip took his pen and crossed out the last line so that no one could read what had been there.

"You should have no difficulty about a divorce.

"You can dispose of my things as you see

fit; there is nothing I care about keeping which I did not bring.

"Again, Mary, I cannot ask you to forgive, or even to understand, but I do hope that you will believe me when I say that this act of mine is the most honest thing I have ever done, and that to have acted out the tragi-comedy in the part of a happy contented husband would have made of both of our lives a bitter useless farce.

"Sincerely,
Philip."

He folded the pages and addressed the envelope.

"Pardon, Monsieur"—a whiff of sulphur came to his nose as the waiter bent over the table to light the gas above him. "Would Monsieur like to see the *journal?* There is a most amusing story about——The bill, Monsieur? Yes—in a moment."

Philip glanced nervously through the pages of the *Temps.* He was anxious to get the letter to the post—to have done with indecision and worry. It would be a blessed relief when the thing was finally done beyond chance of recall; why couldn't that stupid waiter hurry?

On the last page of the newspaper was an item headlined NEWS FROM AMERICA. Below was a sub-heading: HORRIBLE MASSACRE OF SOLDIERS BY INDIANS—BRAVE STAND OF AMERICAN TROOPERS. He caught the name "Custer" and read:

"And by his brave death at the hands of the Indians, this gallant American general has made the name of Custer one which will forever be associated with courage of the highest type."

He read it all through again and sat quietly as the hand of Polyphemus closed over him. He even smiled a little—a weary, ironic smile.

"Monsieur desires something more, perhaps"—the waiter held out the bill.

Philip smiled. "No—Monsieur has finished—there is nothing more."

He repeated slowly, "There is nothing more."

PHILIP watched his son George blow out the twelve candles on his birthday cake.

"Mother," said George, "when I get to be eighteen, can I be a soldier just like grandfather up there?" He pointed to the portrait of Philip's father in uniform which hung in the beautiful dining room.

"Of course you can, dear," said his mother. "But you must be a brave boy."

"Grandfather was awful brave, wasn't he, father?" This from little Mary between mouthfuls of cake.

"Yes, Mary," Philip answered. "He was very, very brave."

"Of course he was," said George. "He was an American."

"Yes," answered Philip. "That explains it—he was an American."

Mrs. Custer looked up at the portrait of her distinguished father-in-law.

"You know, Philip, I think it must be quite nice to be able to paint a picture like that. I've often wondered why you never kept up your art."

ISADORA DUNCAN

The famous dancer—apostle of beauty—shown appropriately enough on the steps of the Parthenon

Steichen

69

Leavetaking

A One-Act Play

FERENC MOLNAR

On a remote path far out in the park a man and a woman are strolling.

SHE: So now it's over. The moment has come to part. There is nothing else to do. So kiss my hand, and let us part friends.

HE: As you wish.

SHE: And we need have none but the most pleasant and kindly memories of each other. We met—and loved—and kissed a while—and then we grew tired of each other. Basta!

HE: You are right.

(*He kisses her hand.*)

SHE: Now I shall take the path to the right. You wait a moment and then take the one to the left. It would be quite too awful for my husband to find us out now, just as we are parting forever.

HE: Good-bye.

(*Neither of them moves.*)

SHE: Why don't you go?

HE: There is something I'd like to ask.

SHE: What is it?

HE: I first met you at a winter resort. Do you remember? You were with some women friends, wintering there without your husband. And so I didn't meet him.

SHE: I remember.

HE: We were interested in each other immediately, as you will recall, and later, in the city, our intimacy continued. Still I never met your husband.

SHE: No.

HE: Then one day you brought me a photograph of a very handsome man. You said, "I brought you a portrait of my husband. I thought you might want to know what he looks like." I studied the photograph carefully. The man was as handsome as Dorian Gray, as elegant as Edward VII. I didn't tell you, but that evening I could scarcely eat a mouthful.

SHE: I thought as much.

HE: And I couldn't sleep either. I was so madly in love with you at the time that I couldn't help making comparisons humiliating to myself. I would scan my face anxiously in the mirror. I know that I am neither good looking nor bad looking—just a commonplace face, the sort you see on any lieutenant. This realization troubled me and angered me. I was determined that somehow I must make myself handsome.

SHE: I noticed that.

HE: During all those sleepless nights I used to ask myself what you, who had a husband like that, could possibly see in me.

"Perhaps her husband is a blockhead," I told myself. That comforted me until, on further analysis, I had to admit that my own intelligence was nothing uncommon and, moreover, the face in the picture had every sign of wit and intellect. Less and less was I able to understand how you could possibly love me. I was jealous of the man in the picture; and gradually I began to enter into feverish competition.

SHE: I knew it.

HE: I had my clothes made by the best tailor. I had my hair waved. Wildly jealous of you every minute, I gave scrupulous care to every detail of my personal appearance, until, really, I began to pass for handsome. Sometimes you would say you were going to a ball with your husband. That always made me savage, thinking how imposing he must look in evening clothes.

SHE: I knew it.

HE: Every free moment of your time I demanded for my own. Do you remember? I begged you to let me meet your husband. I asked only for the opportunity of seeing him. You refused. Then it happened.

SHE: What?

HE: I can confess it now. One afternoon at my apartment you dropped a note. After you had gone I picked it up and read it. It was a note to your mother saying that your husband and you had a box for the opera the following evening and that you would stop for her and take her. You had intended to send this note to your mother, but it must have dropped out of your purse.

SHE: Really? Did I lose it in your apartment?

HE: Yes. And the next evening, of course, I went to the opera too. And I saw you all there in your box—you, your mother—— and your husband.

SHE: Did you?

HE: Is that all you have to say about it?

SHE: What do you expect me to say?

HE: Come now, don't pretend. In the opera house that night I found out—I won't say you lied to me—but that there had been a mistake. Your husband is between fifty and fifty-five years old, incredibly ugly, crooked, hairy—pardon me—but he *is* incredibly ugly.

SHE: Now—now——

HE: You can't deny he was your husband. I made sure by hunting up someone who knew who he was.

SHE: It was my husband.

HE: Well then, why did you play this comedy with me? Who was the handsome young man whose portrait you showed me?

SHE: I don't know. I bought the photograph in London. For a few shillings. Some English aristocrat or other I imagine.

HE (*puzzled*): But why?

SHE: You've answered that question yourself. It was a little deception of mine that succeeded brilliantly. Once you started to compete with the portrait you rose fifty per cent in worth. You improved incredibly. That picture actually made you handsome, elegant and witty. I was very much in love with you then. Hence it was a joy to me to improve your good qualities.

HE: Clever! I admit it. Yet it was typically feminine cleverness. So short-sighted.

SHE: How do you mean?

HE: Because, as you see, a mere accident, a note inadvertently dropped out of a purse, destroyed the entire fabric of lies. The day I saw your husband—your real husband—and knew you had lied to me, I lost all impulse to make myself attractive to you. Gradually I began to neglect my appearance. My jealousy abated. Love itself began to cool, and finally it died. Yet, if you had not dropped that note I would still be madly in love with you.

SHE (*softly*): And do you think a woman like me could drop a note in your apartment unless she really wanted to drop it?

HE: What do you mean?

SHE: A woman who deceives her husband is not likely to be careless about notes. Why, he would have found me out long ago.

HE: You mean you dropped it intentionally?

SHE: Of course.

HE (*angrily*): Why?

SHE: You've answered that question, too. I wanted you to see my husband and gradually cool off—until you were quite cold—because—because I hate scenes. When I grew tired of you—I dropped the note. Thereupon you lost interest in me. And so our intimacy came to a friendly end.

HE: You wanted to end it because——

SHE: Because I had already made up my mind to give the photograph of the handsome Englishman to someone else. Good-bye, dear. Don't be angry, but any man's heart can be managed like that—with a photograph and a note—notre cœur, as Maupassant said. Good-bye.

(*Reflectively he watches her as she takes the path to the right and disappears.*)

Nominated for the Hall of Fame: 1922

Hoppe

VAN WYCK BROOKS

Because he is Literary Editor of *The Freeman;* because the liberating influence of his early critical writings has already made itself felt in American letters, notably in the work of Sherwood Anderson; and finally because his *Ordeal of Mark Twain* is not only the most competent study of the great American humorist, but likewise provides a devastating criticism of a whole period in American life.

HENRY FORD *(below)*

Because he has changed the whole rural life of America by lowering the price of motor cars; because he has made some of the most ludicrous statements ever conceived by a public man; and finally because the benevolent paternalism prevailing in his factories is enormously applauded and admired by everyone except his employees.

CHALIAPIN

Because he has, for the last four years, remained aloof from political factions and continued to sing at the Marinsky in Petrograd and the Great State Theatre in Moscow; because he has been director of the former; because without his unrivaled voice he would still be the greatest actor since Salvini; and finally, because his recent performances at the Metropolitan Opera House created so unprecedented a sensation.

DOUGLAS FAIRBANKS

Because before he became a movie actor he had already become famous as an excellent light comedian on the stage; because he was the first to develop a new, acrobatic movie which made him one of the favorites of the world; because he married Mary Pickford; and finally because, under his own direction, he has produced this film, *Robin Hood.*

HAVELOCK ELLIS *(right)*

Because he was the Editor of the Mermaid Series of Old Dramatists; because in *Affirmations* he presented the first adequate study of Nietzsche in English; because in his *Studies in the Psychology of Sex* he wisely avoids proposing solutions for insoluble problems; and finally, because he combines scientific precision and patience with the pity and understanding of a humanist, in a way not incomparable to the great French savants.

Bain

71

David Garrick to John Barrymore

An Imaginary Letter from One Celebrated Hamlet to Another

STARK YOUNG

SIR: Great applause has come to your Hamlet, as it did once to mine. But, as I saw you, from the start to the finish of your beautiful performance, I understood more and more that you and I set out for this creation from opposite poles. So that what you have to do to perfect your creation is precisely the reverse of what I did.

At the beginning, my playing of Hamlet was irregular and vehement and pettish. But my performance improved almost nightly. At first I made Hamlet struggle violently with his friends when the ghost beckoned him. Later I made him remain awe-struck and motionless before the be-

loved spirit. At first I left out the advice to the players; I restored it later, though I always spoke it too pedantically. With Ophelia I was at first too rough and violent, with Polonius too rude. But these and other defects I softened and corrected, and at length perfected my conception of the part. Certain passages in my reading stood out always as affecting and sublime. When I taunted myself with a cowardly and pusillanimous heart, I swept the whole theatre along with me. When, by a sudden transition, I began to unfold my plan to catch the King's conscience, the house listened breathlessly. The horror and the terror of the ghostly visitation I expressed incomparably;

I acted for the ghost. At the line

*But break my heart, for I must
hold my tongue*

I paused before the last word and dropped my arm to my side; then, with the force of that gesture, I spoke the word as if I could scarcely give it utterance. These and many other effects were universally admired. But to the last I kept some odd pieces of business, as when, for example, where Hamlet has to say that some must watch while some must sleep, I walked backwards and forwards twirling a white handkerchief in my hand. My performance was superb; but it continued always to be very vivid, very much underscored.

DAVID GARRICK

The greatest English actor of the eighteenth century (1717–1779), who toned down Shakespeare, in deference to the non-romantic taste of his time.

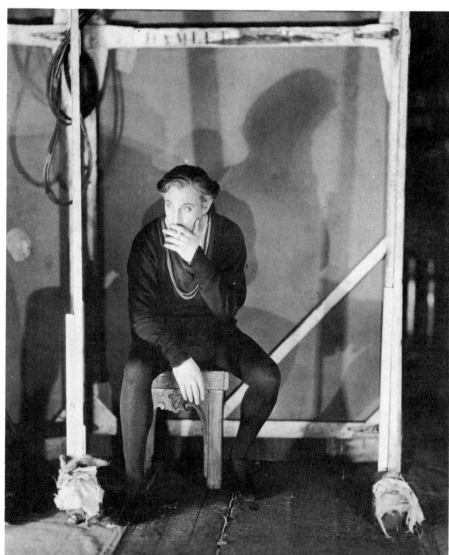

JOHN BARRYMORE

The celebrated American actor who has brought to the role of Hamlet an almost naturalistic method, which makes a break with Shakespearian traditions of the past.

Abbé

Barrymore's Continuity

SIR, you began, not with heavily marked passages; you began with no disproportionate accentuation, but with an outline already finished, distributed, even. From the moment the curtain rose on you sitting there, the picture of pale thought and brooding dear loss, to the end, when you were carried by death and the strong arms of action up that flight of stairs and out beyond that high arch, you made of your idea one perfect and complete line.

One thinks not so much of any particular business of yours or any one scene, as of a distinguished continuity and taste. What you will have to do, then, Sir, reverses my necessity. You will have to fill in your design. Put more pressure against your outline. Keep this final outline that you have discovered, but force against it a hidden violence of detail. Gradually make the part rich with meaning, with inexhaustible life.

Sir, I erred—as I see now—and you err, in making this character and life of Hamlet too simple. Neither of us would admit it whole. My age, which was the age of Dr. Johnson and Sir Joshua Reynolds, followed close on the heels of an age of reason, of Mr. Pope and Mr. Addison and the social philosophy of the French. To us Shakespeare's creation seemed a little barbaric, confused. And the graveyard scene was a vulgar muddle; I used to refer, indeed, to the rubbish of the fifth act. I cut that scene, left out the grave-diggers entirely. I altered the scenes with Ophelia and wrote in lines to make them more intelligible. I made the aspect of the character elegantly familiar, dressing Hamlet in the French fashion of the time, the black coat, knee breeches, the waistcoat with flaps; I wore my own hair. In sum, I reduced Shakespeare's play to the thought of my century. You, Sir, simplify the play overmuch by making Hamlet too easy to understand; by putting him in terms too satisfactory to your public. A part of your success is due to your presence and magnetism and to your many capital achievements in playing.

An Inexplicable Hamlet

BUT a part of it also is due to your making Hamlet so easy to digest. Your audience feel that, for the first time, they understand what it all means. But, Sir, Hamlet is the dreamer, the human soul beating itself out against limitations, the scholar, prince, lover, wit, poet, clown, the mystery. And so he remains not real but, as it were, super-real. The very essence of Hamlet is that we could never understand him. You must put into the part more zest, more of an infinite and happy nurture of the mind, more of intellect driving outward, of lyrical cry, of

bitter darkness. With your fine, clear outline, give Hamlet the nuance of more shadow, more of a fitful magnificence, more confusion, more inexplicability.

Sir, the whole theory of an art of acting that the Europe of my day held, was not that which obtains in your generation. Under that theory acting was fundamentally a separable thing from the actor's state of feeling. Technique in itself was highly considered; sheer mentality played a conspicuous part in an actor's effects and the audience' pleasure. The test of a great actor lay in his possession of a general talent, the ability to do all rôles with an equal truth.

A Strange Story

ELINOR WYLIE

When I died in Berners Street
I remember well
That I had lights at head and feet
And a passing bell.

But when I died in Hounsditch
They would not lay me out
Because they said I was a witch;
The rats ran about.

When I died in Holborn
In an old house and tall
I know the tapestry was torn
And hanging from the wall.

When I died in Marylebone
I was saying my prayers;
There I died all alone
Up four flights of stairs.

But when I died near Lincoln's Inn
The small gold I had
Surrounded me with kith and kin;
I died stark mad.

When I died in Bloomsbury
In the bend of your arm
At the end I died merry
And comforted and warm.

Toward this versatility, the equipment of an actor consisted, first of all, of mimetic powers and of a face and figure that are capable of every variety of expression. And finally he must have an intelligence that can build up out of reality an idea to be created. For such an art I had every gift. In my first season I astounded London by acting with the same success Richard III, a rascally valet, a uxorious Puritan, a fop, a conceited author, and finally in one evening Lear and Master Johnny, a country lout. My mimetic gifts, my eyes, nose, mouth and voice, were such that I could pass through many characters and emotions in a few minutes, completely different in each.

In the salons of Paris, where I was adored, I acted the dagger scene from Macbeth with overwhelming and tragic beauty, and passed from that into a cook's boy letting fall a tray of pies into the gutter. My body was in perfect proportion; and I seemed to be present in every muscle. My very presence on the stage had an air of life. I was, of all things, first an actor.

Technique and Genius

TO YOUR ears and your public such details of technique and physique may sound merely external. But, Sir, never believe that I went no further. I knew the uses of these resources. And I knew that the actor must have his idea and his effects prepared and ready. But I knew also that great acting could never stop there. I knew that from genius there must be the life blood that bursts forth and, like a flame, shoots through the spectators' veins. I knew that in the greatest moments in acting, the actor has the feeling of the instant come upon him unexpectedly. I testified that the greatest strokes of genius have been unknown to the actor himself till circumstances and the warmth of the scene have sprung the mine as it were, as much to his surprise as to that of the audience. This I made the difference between great genius and good playing: good players give pleasure by their strong power and good sense; the great genius will always realize the feelings of the character and be transported beyond himself.

Sir, your art, and the theory of art that your age maintains, are more private than mine, less social and general and separable from the actor. You have not so many of these external acting gifts as I had. You have an admirable presence, but you are not mimetic; your pantomine could mean little in itself. Your body and your face are not eminently flexible and expressive. Your features are incisive, delicate, significant, rather than mobile. Your voice is admirable but not yet a great instrument. You of all things are first, not the actor, but the artist. And yet you attain to beautiful acting. But the fundamental principles of your art and mine remain the same. Your business, as mine was, is to labor toward finding in your art a language suited to the finest reaches of your time.

And, Sir, you have already things impossible to my century or to me that I envy in you. I envy you your even continuity, and what a painter might call the fine drawing of your scenes. I envy you that kind of high tact with which your art approaches the secret nature and spirit of the man you must reveal. I envy you most the outward simplicity of your method, and your power to create on the stage not so much the action as the air of a compelling mood.

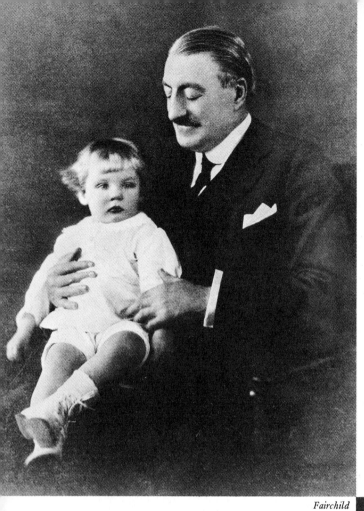

JOHN DREW

*And, seated on his lap, his grandson
and namesake, John Drew Devereux,
a white hope of the drama*

Fairchild

J. HARTLEY MANNERS

and

LAURETTE TAYLOR

*Mr. and Mrs. Manners — author and
star of the apparently immortal play
Peg o' My Heart*

Steichen

Clarke

ETHEL BARRYMORE

*John Drew's gifted niece and one of the brightest stars
of the English-speaking theatre*

The Ten Dullest Authors: A Symposium

A Group of Eminent Literary Specialists
Vote on the Most Unreadable of the World's Great Writers

We have had so many symposiums on the Ten Greatest Books in the Last Fifty Years, on the Ten Books One Has Most Enjoyed Reading, etc., etc., that Vanity Fair *has thought it might be interesting to reverse the investigation and to ask a number of prominent literary experts to name the ten great writers whom they find most thoroughly boring—whom they find that, in spite of all moral and intellectual temptations to plow through or pretend to admire, they absolutely cannot read. We have all heard the people who "don't know much about art, but know what they like." Here we present you with a number of people who know a great deal about art, and who know what they* don't *like.*

H. L. Mencken

IT IS hard for me to make up a list of books or authors that bore me insufferably, for the simple truth is that I can read almost anything. My trade requires me to read annually all the worst garbage that is issued in *belles lettres;* for recreation and instruction I read such things as the *Congressional Record,* religious tracts, Mr. Walter Lippmann's endless discussions of the Simon-Binet tests, works on molecular physics and military strategy, and the monthly circulars of the great bond houses. It seems to me that nothing that gets into print can be wholly uninteresting; whatever its difficulties to the reader, it at least represents some earnest man's efforts to express himself. But there are some authors, of course, who try me more than most, and if I must name ten of them then I name:

1. Dostoevski
2. George Eliot
3. D. H. Lawrence
4. James Fenimore Cooper
5. Eden Phillpotts
6. Robert Browning
7. Selma Lagerlöf
8. Gertrude Stein
9. Björnstjerne Björnson
10. Goethe

As a good German, I should, I suppose, wallow happily in *Faust;* I can only report that, when I read it, it is patriotically, not voluptuously. Dostoevski, for some reason that I don't know, simply stumps me; I have never been able to get through any of his novels. George Eliot I started to read too young, and got thereby a distaste for her that is unsound but incurable. Against Cooper and Browning I was prejudiced by school-masters who admired them. Phillpotts seems to me to be the worst novelist now in practice in England. As for Lawrence and Miss Stein, what makes them hard reading for me is simply the ineradicable conviction that beneath all their pompous manner there is nothing but tosh. The two Scandinavians I need not explain.

George Jean Nathan

1. Dostoevski
2. Paul Claudel
3. Paul Bourget
4. Paul Heyse
5. Charles Dickens
6. Sir Walter Scott
7. Nathaniel Hawthorne
8. Knut Hamsun
9. Charles Rann Kennedy
10. Woodrow Wilson

Elinor Wylie

WITH my hand upon the famous Vanity Fair Chain Bible, I hereby swear that the following statement is the truth and nothing but the truth; though space does not permit it to be the whole truth.

1. William Shakespeare as a Comic Writer. Because I am sadly deficient in humor.
2. Dante Alighieri. Because I can't read Italian.
3. Walt Whitman. Because I can't read Whitman.
4. George Eliot. Because her dark brown binding got into her style.
5. Robert Louis Stevenson. Because his admirers call him R. L. S.
6. Walter Pater. Because of his infinite capacity for taking pains.
7. Selma Lagerlöf. Because an English lady read her aloud to me.
8. Henry James. Because of Mrs. Wharton and Mrs. Gerould.
9. Paul Claudel. Because he has a beautiful mind.
10. Gertrude Stein. Because . . .

James Branch Cabell

ABOUT every author in my list I am, in all likelihood, entirely wrong. For I find that, somehow, I have listed only such writers as have their recognized "cults" of perfervid admirers, and such writers as a respectable lapse of time has attested—perhaps—really to make some sort of mysterious appeal to a largish number of persons. One may, of course, in private, assume that aesthetically these persons bemuse themselves with notions of their own superiority and refinement. Such anaesthetic notions still enable self-complacency to pull through many pages that are perused with rather less admiration of the author than of the reader. But, for that matter, the majority of generally acknowledged and most permanent literary reputations would seem to be based upon some similar innocuous self-deceit.

Anyhow, here are the ten "established" authors endowed with "cults" who just now appear to me the most violently uninteresting:

1. Jane Austen
2. George Borrow
3. Miguel de Cervantes
4. Henry James
5. Herman Melville
6. George Meredith
7. Friedrich Nietzsche
8. Thomas Love Peacock
9. François Rabelais
10. Walt Whitman

I submit this list without any comment save that I have made all suitable endeavors toward Melville since 1907; the antipathy is not newborn. And upon consideration, Peacock has not, really, ever annoyed me with the relentless and deep tediousness of the others. I for the moment incline to strike out his name in disfavor of that of Marcel Proust or of James G. Huneker or of W. H. Hudson; but refrain because the moment's pother about any of these three may, after all, very well and speedily prove transient.

Christopher Morley

IT IS quite obvious that the editor of *Vanity Fair,* in asking this appalling question hopes to be answered, not by a list of such classic bores as Carlyle or John Stuart Mill or Dryden or Dr. Frank Crane, but by the names of contemporaries. This, obviously, will lead to a rousing hullabaloo and healthy irritation.

As a matter of fact, I don't let anyone bore me, dead or living. If he bores me, I don't read him, though very likely I continue to love him. Many of the writers who cause me the most painful ennui in print are people for whom I have warm personal regard or affection. I don't know, of course, if they are great-minded enough to hear the truth without being angry. This is a chance to find out.

The chaps I should like to vote for are the really first-class Sedatives who can fatigue you in a paragraph. You don't have to plow through pages and pages to know whether they weary you or not. No: these fellows are considerate, they ring the gong instantly. Some fine preservative instinct tells you at once that though this may be great art, it is Not For You. For instance, W. L. George on Women, or Hal Stearns on Why Young Intellectuals Leave Home, or waggishnesses by Donald Ogden Stewart, or Community Masques by Percy Mackaye, or biographies by Edward Bok, or novels by Rupert Hughes, Bernard Shaw or Theodore Dreiser. But these fellows are Olympians; they are out of bounds.

Confining myself to the more temperate zones of achievement, I compose my list as follows:

1. Arthurian poems by Edwin Arlington Robinson
2. Books about Eugene Field
3. Plays by William Vaughn Moody
4. Poems by Cale Young Rice
5. Ectoplasm stuff by Conan Doyle
6. The second half of *Zuleika Dobson*
7. Posthumous collections of O. Henry's odds and ends
8. Domestic verse by Eddie Guest
9. *Fantazius Mallare* by Ben Hecht

That, as you observe, is only nine items. I thought it best to leave one place open in case Burton Rascoe should publish a book.

Burton Rascoe

1. John Milton
2. D. H. Lawrence
3. P. Virgilius Maro
4. W. D. Howells
5. Marcel Proust
6. Sir Francis Bacon
7. H. G. Wells
8. William Wordsworth
9. Henry James
10. Marcus Aurelius Antoninus

If I am to be frank, these are the authors who have bored me beyond all others. And in making out such a list I must explain it a little. A great many writers among the classics and among my contemporaries might have bored me to a greater extent had I not made short shrift of their endeavors to entertain and instruct me. But since I came of age, I have not permitted many writers to bore me. Ordinarily I give them a fair trial and if I find them dull I am rude enough to turn my attention elsewhere. When I was very young that was not the case. My eagerness for knowledge made all books, good or bad, dull or lively, seem wonderful in my eyes. For a long time I did not know what it was to be bored. At the age of sixteen I read that intolerable compendium of tediousness, Kant's *Critique of Pure Reason,* from beginning to end, understanding scarcely a word of it, and yet I was enchanted.

Nowadays I am occasionally bored out of a profound loyalty to a writer, or from a vague sense of duty. Milton, who bored me at college (except in his shorter poems and in his prose), bores me now on an average of once every six months.

My loyalty to writers whose works I have admired and loved grants these writers full liberty to bore me. I do not admit the right of others to presume so much. Henry James is so favored, and George Moore, and D. H. Lawrence, and Joseph Conrad. Few writers charm me as much as Moore, no one I think has a more seductive prose style, and yet I could not read *In Single Strictness* and foundered on *A Story-Teller's Holiday.* I could feign attention to D. H. Lawrence during the interminable spinning of *Women in Love* and *Aaron's Rod* because I consider *Sons and Lovers* among the great novels of our time. I keep on reading Wells with great weariness and exasperation because of *Tono-Bungay* and *The Island of Dr. Moreau.* I have taken stimulants to listen out Henry James because with him a seeming quality of boresomeness is only the legitimate demand he makes upon the reader's undivided and intelligent attention.

Ernest Boyd

ONE is tempted to begin at the beginning and list all the five-foot bookshelf geniuses, Homer, Vergil, Victor Hugo, Alexandre Dumas, and so forth, but here is an opportunity to be indiscreet. So, instead of taking refuge amongst the defenseless dead, I will mention my imperfect sympathies amongst the moderns:

1. Robert Louis Stevenson, the father of all contemporary bores, the archetype of the literary gent with illusions about the life of adventure.
2. Thomas Hardy's *The Dynasts,* an unpoetic poem and an undramatic drama, a lapse on the part of a great novelist.
3. Rudyard Kipling, as intolerable to a civilized mind as the professional Tommies of the British army whose mentality he so perfectly reflects.
4. Gilbert K. Chesterton, the cheap punster in excelsis, strenuously engaged in persuading clean-limbed Englishmen that there was ever such a place as "Merrie England," full of beer and Catholicism.
5. J. M. Barrie, the sentimental Scot raised to the *n*th degree, Harry Lauder without kilts.
6. Joseph Conrad, the perfect example of the "romance" of the sea, born in Poland and the greatest maritime glory in modern English literature.
7. D. H. Lawrence—the average Briton in the toils of sex, a sad spectacle.
8. George Santayana, platitudes across the sea.
9. Paul Claudel, pseudo-simple religiosity in the worst French style for two hundred years.
10. Giovanni Papini's *Story of Christ,* the collapse of a remarkable mind into intellectual Fascismo, an attempt to rebuild the Church of God with the bricks previously hurled by anticlericalism.

Carl Van Vechten

1. Dr. Sigmund Freud
2. Gabriele d'Annunzio
3. Edith Wharton
4. Walter Pater
5. Gerhart Hauptmann
6. James Joyce
7. Pierre Loti
8. D. H. Lawrence
9. Amy Lowell
10. J. M. Barrie

Edna Ferber

NARROWING such a list down to ten is a thing that requires gifts of selection and elimination, neither of which I possess. Still, here are some books that nothing could make me read again:

1. *Plane Geometry*
2. *Eat and Grow Thin*
3. *The Book of Job*
4. *Elsie Dinsmore*
5. *Jurgen*
6. *The Genius*
7. *Pollyanna*
8. Anything of F. Scott Fitzgerald's written since his first novel and first book of short stories
9. *The Congressional Record*
10. *Bleak House*

Poems by T. S. Eliot

Burbank with a Baedeker: Bleistein with a Cigar

Tra-la-la-la-la-la-laire—nil nisi divinum stabile est; caetera fumus—the gondola stopped, the old palace was there, how charming its grey and pink—goats and monkeys, with such hair too!—so the countess passed on until she came through the little park, where Niobe presented her with a cabinet, and so departed.

Burbank crossed a little bridge
Descending at a small hotel;
Princess Volupine arrived,
They were together, and he fell.

Defunctive music under sea
Passed seaward with the passing bell
Slowly: the God Hercules
Had left him, that had loved him well.

The horses, under the axletree
Beat up the dawn from Istria
With even feet. Her shuttered barge
Burned on the water all the day.

But this or such was Bleistein's way:
A saggy bending of the knees
And elbows, with the palms turned out,
Chicago Semite Viennese.

A lustreless protrusive eye
Stares from the protozoic slime
At a perspective of Canaletto.
The smoky candle end of time

Declines. On the Rialto once.
The rats are underneath the piles.
The jew is underneath the lot.
Money in furs. The boatman smiles,

Princess Volupine extends
A meagre, blue-nailed, phthisic hand
To climb the waterstair. Lights, lights,
She entertains Sir Ferdinand

Klein. Who clipped the lion's wings
And flea'd his rump and pared his claws?
Thought Burbank, meditating on
Time's ruins, and the seven laws.

The Boston Evening Transcript

The readers of the *Boston Evening Transcript*
Sway in the wind like a field of ripe corn.

When evening quickens faintly in the street,
Wakening the appetites of life in some
And to others bringing the *Boston Evening Transcript*,

T. S. ELIOT

I mount the steps and ring the bell, turning
Wearily, as one would turn to nod good-
    bye to Rochefoucauld,
If the street were time and he at the end
    of the street,
And I say, "Cousin Harriet, here is the
    Boston Evening Transcript."

La Figlia Che Piange

O quam te memorem virgo . . .

Stand on the highest pavement of the stair—
Lean on a garden urn—
Weave, weave the sunlight in your hair—
Clasp your flowers to you with a pained
    surprise—
Fling them to the ground and turn
With a fugitive resentment in your eyes:
But weave, weave the sunlight in your hair.

So I would have had him leave,
So I would have had her stand and grieve,
So he would have left
As the soul leaves the body torn and bruised,
As the mind deserts the body it has used.
I should find
Some way incomparably light and deft,
Some way we both should understand,
Simple and faithless as a smile and shake
    of the hand.

She turned away, but with the autumn
    weather

Compelled my imagination many days,
Many days and many hours:
Her hair over her arms and her arms full
    of flowers.
And I wonder how they should have been
    together!
I should have lost a gesture and a pose.
Sometimes these cogitations still amaze
The troubled midnight and the noon's
    repose.

A Cooking Egg

*En l'an trentiesme de mon aage
Que toutes mes hontes j'ay beues . . .*

Pipit sate upright in her chair
    Some distance from where I was sitting;
Views of the Oxford Colleges
    Lay on the table, with the knitting.

Daguerreotypes and silhouettes,
    Her grandfather and great great aunts,
Supported on the mantelpiece
    An Invitation to the Dance.

*   *   *

I shall not want Honour in Heaven
    For I shall meet Sir Philip Sidney
And have talk with Coriolanus
    And other heroes of that kidney.

I shall not want Capital in Heaven
    For I shall meet Sir Alfred Mond:
We two shall lie together, lapt
    In a five per cent Exchequer Bond.

I shall not want Society in Heaven,
    Lucretia Borgia shall be my Bride;
Her anecdotes will be more amusing
    Than Pipit's experience could provide.

I shall not want Pipit in Heaven:
    Madame Blavatsky will instruct me
In the Seven Sacred Trances;
    Piccarda de Donati will conduct me . . .

*   *   *

But where is the penny world I bought
    To eat with Pipit behind the screen?
The red-eyed scavengers are creeping
    From Kentish Town and Golder's Green;

Where are the eagles and the trumpets?

Buried beneath some snow-deep Alps.
Over buttered scones and crumpets
    Weeping, weeping multitudes
Droop in a hundred A. B. C.'s *

* An endemic teashop, found in all parts of London. The initials signify: Aerated Bread Company.

On the Approach of Middle Age

W. SOMERSET MAUGHAM

IT IS like any other of the necessary trials of life, such as marriage or death; you think of it vaguely as something that must be endured, but you seldom give it serious consideration till you are face to face with it. A man will hardly wait to learn swimming till he is thrown into the sea, but he will take no thought for his conduct in a crisis which is as dangerous and, unlike the other, by no prudence to be avoided.

Before he knows where he is, he finds himself floundering in the perilous forties. He is now that baldish, stout person whom twenty years before he jeered at when he saw him dancing, a little out of breath, with girls who might be his daughters. He is now the gentleman in the Rolls-Royce, smoking a long cigar, whom he used to outdrive at golf by thirty yards and who wilted not a little towards the end of the second round. Yesterday, he was a young man, and today he drinks lithia water.

Because, as a lad, I had seen much of the world and traveled a good deal, because I was somewhat widely read and my mind was occupied with matters beyond my age, I seemed always older than my contemporaries; but it was not until the outbreak of the Great War that I had an inkling of the horrid truth. I learned then, to my consternation, that I was a middle-aged man. I consoled myself by reflecting that I could be thus described only militarily, so to speak; but not so very long after, I had an experience which put the matter beyond doubt. I had been lunching at a restaurant with a woman whom I had known a long time, and her niece. This was a girl of seventeen, pretty, with blue eyes and very pleasing dimples. I found it vastly agreeable to look at her, and I did my best to amuse her. She rewarded my sallies with rippling laughter. Well, after luncheon we took a taxi to go to a matinee. My old friend got in, and then her niece. But the girl sat down on the tip-up seat, leaving the empty place at the back beside her aunt for me.

Painful Discriminations

FOR a moment I stood rooted to the pavement. Amid the clatter of street cars and the screams of klaxons I heard the ominous tolling of a bell. It was the knell of my dead youth. In the gesture of this maiden, I discerned the civility of youth (as opposed to the rights of sex) to a gentleman no longer young. I realized that she looked upon me with the respect due to age. Re-

spect: it is a chilling thing for a girl to give to a man. The boat had given a sudden lurch, and there was I, all unprepared, struggling for my life in an unknown sea.

It is not a very pleasant thing to recognize that for the young you are no longer an equal. You belong to a different generation. For them your race is run. They can look up to you; they can admire you; but you are apart from them: for boys you are no longer a competitor, for girls you are no longer marriageable. It is only the widow of a certain age who still casts an inquisitive eye on you. You may just as well marry and have done with it.

I think I have always been more conscious of my age than most men. It is generally supposed that the young live in the present, but I know that I lived only in the future. I was ever looking forward, generally to something I proposed to do in some place other than that in which I found myself; and no sooner was I there, doing what I had so much wanted, than it became of small account, for my fancy raced forward and I busied myself with what next year would bring. I never enjoyed the daffodils of today, because I was always thinking of the roses of tomorrow. Sometimes I think that it is the unimaginative who get the most out of life, for to them alone the fleeting moment is all in all.

My youth passed me unnoticed, and I was always burdened with the sense that I was growing old. To me, nothing is more wonderful than the consciousness of youth which in these days the young have. They are deeply aware that it is lovely and fugitive. They know, as we of a past day did not, that it is precious, and that they must make the most of it. I was young in an elderly world. Then people shrugged their shoulders at youth; it was an indisposition which time would cure, and the young were impatient to grow older.

The Compensation of Age

BUT middle age has its compensations. One is that, on the whole, you feel no need to do what you do not like. You are no longer ashamed of yourself. You are reconciled to being what you are, and you do not much mind what people think of you. They can take you or leave you. You do not want to impose upon them with false pretenses. Youth is bound hand and foot with the shackles of public opinion.

I was never of great physical strength,

and even as a lad long walks tired me; but I went on them because I would not confess my weakness. I do not mind now, and so I save myself much weariness. I hated cold water, but for many years I took cold baths and bathed in cold seas because I wanted to be like everybody else. I used to dive from heights that made me nervous, because I was afraid of seeming afraid. I was mortified because I played games less well than my companions. When I did not know a thing, I was ashamed to confess my ignorance; and it was not until quite late in life that I discovered how easy it is to say: I don't know. I am prepared now to admit cheerfully that I never can tell where I and J come in the alphabet. I find that my neighbors do not expect me to walk five and twenty miles, or to play a scratch game of golf, or to dive from a hateful board thirty feet from the water. That is all to the good, and makes life much less unpleasant; but I should no longer care if they did. It is discreet even in middle age to treat the opinion of your fellows with a show of politeness, but in your heart you can cock a snook at them.

When I left school (gathering my passion for freedom into a compact symbol), I said to myself: henceforward, I can get up when I like and go to bed when I like. That, of course, was an illusion; and I soon found that the trammelled life of civilized man only permits a modified independence. When you have an aim, you must sacrifice something of freedom to achieve it. But by the time you have reached middle age, you have discovered just how much freedom it is worth while to sacrifice in order to achieve the aim you have in view.

Though I find the young in the mass charming, I do not find them good company. For they take themselves with a seriousness which is only unintentionally diverting. Humor is rooted in disillusion, and golden illusions press them around about. It is middle age that laughs, since it is difficult to laugh at the world until you have first learned to laugh at yourself.

So here are at least two good things that middle age gives you: the inestimable boon of freedom, and the precious gift of laughter. What makes youth unhappy is its desire to be like everybody else: what makes middle age tolerable is its reconciliation with oneself.

But frankness well becomes the man who is no longer young: I would sooner be a fool of twenty-five than a philosopher of fifty.

Nominated for the Hall of Fame: 1923

THE COMTESSE DE NOAILLES

Because she is probably the most distinguished living woman writer in France; because her first volume of poems, published in 1901, immediately established her as a poet of distinguished merits; because she has written novels of extraordinary excellence, as well as short stories and sketches; because she is a Chevalier of the Legion of Honor; and finally because she has been mentioned as possible candidate for the French Academy.

RING LARDNER

Because he is quite unaware of the approval he is receiving in erudite circles; because he is covered with bruises from representing the Yale football team against his Harvard-bound boys; and finally because with a rare true ear he has set down for posterity the accents of the American language.

MARCEL PROUST

Because as a profound parodist he achieved in France a distinction comparable to that of Beerbohm in England; because he introduced Paul Morand to the public; but chiefly because of his enormous novel *A la Recherche du Temps Perdu*, dealing with the mysteries of consciousness.

PAUL WHITEMAN *(left)*

Because he began his musical career, at the age of nineteen, as a violin player in the Denver Symphony Orchestra; because, when thirty, he created the first dance orchestra with symphonic effects; because he first used the saxophone and banjo to maintain tempo and rhythm; and because he makes the most infectious phonograph records.

ELEANOR ROBSON BELMONT

Because she was for many years one of the most distinguished actresses on our stage; because even before we entered the war, she greatly helped the American cause abroad; because she is an adroit and finished speaker; because she is the wife of one of the best of American sportsmen; and finally because she is the author of a play which will appear in New York in the fall.

Fred Stone and W. C. Fields

A Comparison of the Comic Art of These Two Popular Exponents of the Old School

GILBERT SELDES

THERE has never been a fragment of mystery about Fred Stone. To ask why he is popular is like asking why black is black. Certain things arrive naturally and easily in the course of events, leading us to a refreshing belief in the ways of Providence; and the legend of Fred Stone is one of them. It simply isn't in his nature to be other than popular, and the degree of his popularity, the tightness of his hold, is all the more striking as he becomes the last of his type. Every two years he arrives in New York with a show—sometimes good, never bad; and every other year he goes out on the road with it—events as regular, and as little calling for surprise, as the precession of the Equinoxes.

Mr. Gilbert Chesterton has probably indicated already that the precession of the Equinoxes is the only thing in the world worth being surprised at; he has probably said that the man who would not be surprised at the regularity of this cosmic phenomenon is a fool, if he is not a knave. But to most of us, the arrival of summer when spring is done is pleasant, but not noteworthy. And the arrival of Fred Stone when summer is over is an equally agreeable, but not surprising phenomenon.

In his present curtain speech, Stone gives himself away—and gives his audience away. It isn't much of a secret, but it is entertaining to watch. He speaks with apparent feeling of the nature of his vehicle—*The Stepping Stones*—and says that it proves that the public wants nice, clean plays; at which point the audience bursts into applause (at the spectacle of its own morality, presumably), and Stone's little joke—"the kind of show a girl could take her mother to see"—is lost. Quite properly, for even that feeble touch of cynicism is out of character. Stone lives and breathes—and sings, and dances, and does stunts—in the air of the Brothers Grimm and Hans Christian Andersen. Indeed, there are pages of Andersen a little too bitter for him. He creates a modern fairy tale with mechanical hobgoblins, and radiolite spirits, and good fairies blazing with electricity. It is the world in which miracles happen, and he himself is the half-conscious worker of the miracle.

It is easy to underestimate what he does, because so much of it is in the exploitation of his agile body. There seems to be no position he cannot assume, no leap or tumble

or step he cannot take; and he has peculiarities of gait and gesture which make all his tricks particularly agreeable. He is a humanized Jack-in-the-Box; you feel his astonishing virtuosity in being so mechanically perfect and so humanly attractive at the same time.

This is a quality not always appreciated in America, where acrobats are dismissed with a sniff and where, as a result, most acrobats spend their golden hours, not in trying to do difficult things beautifully, but in trying to do still more difficult things, whether they are beautiful or not. It will not be news to Fred Stone, but to many of his admirers it may be news, that work on the trapeze can be enchanting to see.

Stone is a mixture of acrobat, eccentric dancer, and clownish entertainer; and in the first two of these activities, he always managed to add something to the mere difficulty of the stunt he was doing. Sometimes he added humor, sometimes grace; but he has never called on an audience to admire a difficult stunt merely because it was difficult. He is naturally less of an acrobat now, but everything he does has the skill of the acrobat, the exact amount of exertion that always produces the exact result.

FRED STONE

W. C. FIELDS

It is very hard to judge the quality of humor in a man who is compelled nightly to say that he can't be shot at dawn because he doesn't get up that early. The fact that Stone goes by the book indicates that he hasn't a creative mind for verbal humor, his real fun is in the odd and inappropriate things he does—in his old-time parody of Paderewski; in his "Very Good, Eddie" as a ventriloquist; in his present division of himself into two characters, one stealing and eating tarts, the other watching and preventing him. It is beautifully timed, the slide across the stage to assume the guardian character just as the last crumb is swallowed, and back again. Everything he does goes back to his physical agility; he has a disarming simplicity.

W. C. Fields – a Rare Comedian

AND these qualities in the highest degree keep him where he is, although the qualities themselves no longer have intense appeal. Quite at the other extreme from Stone is W. C. Fields, who was so long known as a comic juggler that one would fancy him, also, dependent upon physical means for his efforts. It is astonishing to discover that they hardly matter at all.

Fields has a great many of the necessary physical qualifications of a comedian—his bulk, his expressive face, his delicate control of hands and features. In his famous scenes —pool, or golf, or even in the Ford—his gravity of demeanor held out against the most perverse accidents. He was silent, but you felt his spirit cry out.

In *Poppy*, he found voice; it had piped up once or twice before. The voice issues from him, and he seems as much surprised as any one to realize that he has one: that it is really out of his own mouth that the sounds are coming, and that they are a useful addition to hands and feet and eyebrows and elbows as means of self-expression. Fields is playing the part of a sharper, a follower of circuses, skilled in the shell-and-pea trick, "the old army game," the various devices used for separating the boobery (Mr. Mencken's nice name for us) from their money. An ideal part, it gives him scope for all his old devices; and, surprisingly, it allows him to create a rather romantic character. He does it in the Dickensonian vein, by a gesture broad in sweep, but delicate in execution. The great fawn-colored coat with huge buttons is exaggerated as the moustache is inversely exaggerated; the gentleness of his sentiment is out of all proportion to the unscrupulous mountebankery of his schemes. When he is accused of forgery, abduction, and attempting to secure an inheritance by false pretences, his reply is the preposterous statement that "this is no time for idle twitting."

What proves him genuinely an artist in his vein is that his physical humor is as exquisite as his characterization. A fight with sheets of fly paper is, contrary to general opinion, not easy to make supremely funny. It can't help being somewhat funny; Fields intensifies the fun ten times over by creating a sort of character sketch out of it—the nightmare of a man attacked by fly paper; the cosmic tragedy of a man against whom all inanimate nature is in league. His beautiful scene with a yokel assistant is as good. Here he lets you feel, by the slightest variation in a droop of the eye, all the arrogance of an expert juggler and all his fatuous pride. It is all perfectly finished, proportioned, balanced creation.

The same words might be used of Stone, but the connotations would be different. Because everything in Stone gives the impression of a pure, native gift—a talent which is graceful and right in execution, because that is its natural and easy way to be; and everything in Fields speaks, indeed, of a gift and a talent—but speaks also of material worked over and rendered effective by arduous calculation of means and ends. The two are at the extreme of their profession—and the younger men are following the more sophisticated of the masters. Possibly they haven't the gifts of Fred Stone; but the likelihood is that, following the tendency of the comic stage, they would take even the richest endowment to school with the harder teacher.

"CHARLOT'S REVUE"

In which this young lady, Gertrude Lawrence, will soon appear in New York, singing "Parisian Pierrot," for which she is costumed here, and "Limehouse Blues"

The Importance of the Comic Genius

Showing That True Comedy, like Genuine Tragedy, Is an Invention in the Grand Manner

ALDOUS HUXLEY

THE history of literature and art provides us with more examples of fine serious than fine comic achievements. A list of the world's great creators of comedy turns out, when one takes the trouble to compile it, to be surprisingly small. Aristophanes, Chaucer, Rabelais, the Shakespeare of Falstaff, the Balzac of the *Contes Drolatiques,* Dickens; and among the pictorial artists, Daumier, Rowlandson, Doré, when he was not wasting his talents on horrible and unsuccessful religious compositions, and Goya, in certain moods. These are the names that first occur to one; and though it would, of course, be possible to lengthen the list, there would not be so very many more to add.

True, we might compile a very long list of the writers and draughtsmen who make us laugh, but few of them would be what may be styled makers of pure comedy. The number of our physiological reactions to emotion is strictly limited, and we go through the same bodily convulsions in response to very different stimuli. Laughter, for example, is provoked in us by a number of quite distinct emotions. There is the laughter of mockery—the laughter that is a social punishment, applied by the sane majority to those whose crime it is to be unlike their fellow-beings. Go out in an exceptionally large hat or an exceptionally bright tie, and you will hear plenty of that kind of laughter. Satire, whether in art or literature, provokes this cruel laughter. The fact that it is generally written by the exceptional man against the only too sane majority does not prevent it from having fundamentally the same source as the mockery of the majority against the exception. And then, there is the laughter that is our response to the smoking-room story—the laughter that is a safety-valve for letting off innocuously a part of our somewhat excessive interest in the blushful mysteries. There is, also, the laughter released in us by sudden surprise—the loud and rather nervous laughter of children when they hide and pounce out on one another from dark recesses; the hysterical, involuntary laughter that seizes one when stout old Uncle Ebenezer slips on a banana skin and comes thudding to the pavement. Its surprising, startling quality is, perhaps, the principal reason why verbal wit makes us laugh.

Satire, sex, wit—all these things make

ALDOUS HUXLEY

us laugh, and they may all be present in a work of pure comedy. But they are not, themselves, pure comedy. It is not right to include in one's list of pure comic geniuses the savage satirist, such as Swift; or the mild satirist, like Sheridan, who writes the comedy of manners; nor have the masters of verbal ingenuity, like Congreve; the hardy pornographers of Wycherley's stamp; or the subtler, sniggering suggesters, like Sterne. Your great comic genius is much more copious, much larger, and more inclusive than a mere satirist, or writer of comedy of manners, or a creator of wit. And he is, accordingly, much rarer than the satirist or the wit. He is as rare as the great tragic genius—and, perhaps, even rarer than he.

THE pure comic genius must be a great inventor. That is why he is so rare; the gift of invention is not a common one. You can be an admirable satirist or a fine serious writer, and not be an inventor—only an interpreter of actual life. Tolstoy is the supreme example of the latter class. But to create a coherent, satisfying, comic universe, you must be an inventor. You cannot stick very close to reality—particularly, the inward, spiritual reality—and make pure comedy. And the same applies to pure tragedy—though with this difference, that pure tragedy moves in the internal world, and largely ignores the externals from which pure comedy starts its flight. The characteristic creations of pure comedy, as well as of pure tragedy, are really not human

beings at all. They are inventions of the poet's mind, living not in our world, but in a parallel world; similar, but not the same. The Wife of Bath, Panurge, Falstaff, Mr. Pecksniff; Medea, Macbeth, Ivan Karamazov—these are all creatures of fable, larger than life, as befits mythological beings; and living, not with the everyday life of men, but more intensely—with the prodigious and god-like life infused into them by their creators. Serious realistic art is not creative, like pure tragedy. It depends on actual life, of which it is a picture and practical interpretation. Similarly, satire, the comedy of manners, and wit are not creative, like pure comedy. Satire and the comedy of manners depend on the actual life they portray and mock at, with greater or less ferocity; while wit is an affair of verbal ingenuity. The difference is important.

All these varieties of what we may call contingent art are less eternally interesting than the two great creative and absolute types of art. For though, to contemporary readers, a book which deals directly, and so to speak scientifically, with the life they know may be immensely valuable, it will lose much of its interest and value when the conditions of life on which it is based have changed. Only the ideal, perfected world, that is parallel to the real world, remains forever comprehensible and fresh. It is difficult not to believe, for example, that Dickens will outlast Tolstoy; though Tolstoy, in certain respects, is much more interesting and valuable to us at the present time.

It would be absurd, of course, to pretend that great comic creations are as profoundly significant as the great creations of tragedy. Comedy necessarily leaves out of account some of the most important elements of man's spiritual life. It is of the earth, earthy—its strength, its size, its colossal energy—and these are the essential characteristics of all great comic creations, from Gargantua to Micawber, from Falstaff to the fabulous Burgesses of Daumier's impassioned invention. There are the strength, size, and energy of earth-born things; there is something superbly animal, something sappy, full-blooded, and earthily un-self-conscious in pure comedy. We seem to be looking on at the gamboling of mastodons, the playing of young whales, the tumbling of a litter of dinosaur puppies. The mind, the troubled spirit of man, have but little place in comedy, the stage is occupied by his healthy body and its natural instincts. But this does not prevent a comic creation from being, in its own sphere, a delightful, and even a grand, magnificent, and beautiful, thing. Comedy deserves to be taken seriously.

THIS is a fact too frequently forgotten; a fact that is not even understood by the second-rate practitioners of comedy. These lesser exponents of comedy humiliate their art to an association with triviality, ugliness, and vulgarity. The great mass of what passes nowadays (or that has passed, for that matter, at any other period) for comic literature or art is stamped with this pettiness and vulgar hideousness. The average comic drawings, comic novels, comic plays, comic films—how small and grubby they all are! One has only to compare these little horrors with the creations of the genuine comic geniuses to see how miserably debased, how unworthy of the name of comedy, they are. A great comic work can be as large, as magnificent, and, in its own way, as beautiful, as a work of serious art.

The fact is that the *beau idéal* and the grand style are not exclusive possessions of serious art. There is also a comic *beau idéal* and a comic grand style. Comic poetry can be genuine poetry; that is to say, beautiful poetry. Comic art can be grand. A huge scale, a colossal, earthy energy, are, as we have seen, the characteristics of comedy. The comic grand style is, accordingly, a rich, emphatic style, that chiefly differs from the grand style of serious art by being too rich and too emphatic.

The step is short from the sublime to the ridiculous—and in much art that is intended to be serious, that short step has been taken. The baroque style in the plastic arts, for example, is essentially a comic grand style; its extravagance is unfitted for use in serious, tragic art. The rich, turgid prose of the seventeenth century is essentially a prose for the expression of comedy. The best passages in Milton's prose works are those in which he is making some enormous joke (the portentous phenomenon occurs more than once in the *Areopagitica,* and produces overwhelming effects). This clotted, extravagant style of prose, which the critics have agreed to call "poetic," is seen in Urquhart and Motteaux's translation of Rabelais to be the most perfect medium for comic expression. And the gorgeous rhetoric of the Elizabethans, which, when employed in serious passages, trembles perilously all the time on the verge of the ludicrous, is seen, when used for comic purposes, to be perfectly suitable.

RETURNING to pictorial arts, we find that practically the only good artist produced by the romantic movement is Gustave Doré; and he is good, not when he is being romantically serious, but in his masterly comic works (the illustrations to Balzac's *Contes Drolatiques* are a typical and noble example). The romantic style, with its extravagance, its picturesqueness, its violent contrasts, is, like baroque, an essentially comic grand style. Briefly to sum up, we may say that the principal difference between the comic grand style and the tragic is that the comic grand style is the grander. It is ludicrous in its exaggerated vehemence, but beautiful.

The great comedians have all combined comedy with beauty and magnificence. Aristophanes was one of the finest of Greek poets. In the *Canterbury Tales,* you will find the richest comedy, expressed in terms of a limpid beauty hardly rivaled in all literature. Ben Jonson's *Volpone* and *The Alchemist* are positively heroic in scale; in them, the sublime is fused indissolubly with the ridiculous.

We see the same beauty, the same grand style, in the works of the great comic artists. All Goya's sense of beauty appears in his comic work. He was, in his comedy, an intensely *serious* artist: witness his admirable series of "Caprices." Daumier, in the world of comic art, is what Michelangelo is in the world of tragic art. His comic conceptions are on the same grand scale, and exhibit the same prodigious energy, as the frescoes on the roof of the Sistine Chapel. Doré, as we have seen, makes the grotesque romantic. And the best of Rowlandson's drawings and engravings—for example, the marvelous *Soirée at Burlington House*—are marked by a force and grandeur of scale that would do credit to a great tragic creation.

It is unnecessary to speak here of our contemporaries. A few men of real comic talent are producing books and pictures at the present time. Not many, however. Most of our comic literature is mere satire, mere comedy of manners, mere wit. Most of our comic art is either not intrinsically comic at all—it is a mere accurate illustration of a funny scene, corresponding to the comedy of manners in literature—or else, when it tries, by distortion and an energetic exaggeration, to become intrinsically comic, it achieves only a petty ugliness and a mean and irritating vulgarity.

JOSEPH CONRAD

A posthumous bust by Jacob Epstein

Steichen

AMELITA GALLI-CURCI

The celebrated coloratura soprano; now touring the western coast in concert recitals, she will soon go to London to sing there for the first time

JUDITH ANDERSON

She is the cobra in the play of that name—and so fine an actress that she will star for Mr. Belasco during the coming season

Goldberg

JOHN WEISMULLER

GERTRUDE EDERLE

DEVEREUX MILBURN

Great Modern Athletes

CHARLES PADDOCK

The choice of these heroes and heroines of the sport world has been made, not by this magazine, but by the greatest sport writers and sport authorities in America—such eminent authorities as Hugh Fullerton, Ring Lardner, Grantland Rice, Christy Mathewson, Walter Trumbull, Patterson McNutt, Fred Hawthorne, W. O. McGeehan, Bozeman Bulger, Hype Igoe, O. B. Keeler, and others of equal note and fame.

Gertrude Ederle (*top left*) is the world's champion swimmer for distances up to 880 yards and rated the best woman swimmer of all time. John Weismuller (*top center*) is the world's fastest male swimmer. Devereux Milburn (*top right*) is the most commanding figure in American polo. Charles Paddock (*left*) is America's sprint champion. He holds half a dozen world's records. Bobby Jones (*below, extreme left*) is the U.S. male golf champion, and Glenna Collett (*below, left*), aged only twenty-one, is the most outstanding feminine golf champion America has produced. William Tilden (*below*) is the world's most outstanding male tennis player, and Suzanne Lenglen (*below, right*), from France, the ranking woman tennis player.

Photographs by Levick

BOBBY JONES

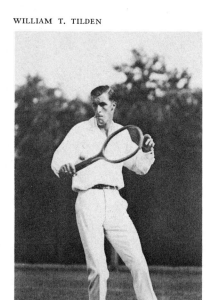

GLENNA COLLETT

WILLIAM T. TILDEN

SUZANNE LENGLEN

Mrs. Fiske: An Artist and a Personality

MARY CASS CANFIELD

MRS. FISKE, like every fine artist, has a secret and one which, as always, is directly dependent on personality. Duse had a secret and so had Réjane. Duse's secret was, finally, her religious influence, the blessing cast upon us by her crystal clear divination, her exquisite sympathy and the austere integrity of her spirit. Réjane's magic, as Yvette Guilbert's, lay in a tragi-comic, realistic facing of life.

Mrs. Fiske, compared to Réjane and Guilbert, seems more exclusively a comedian. In this, she is very American. Perhaps she is *the* American attitude intellectualized; the resolute American habit of humor has, in her, been transmuted into an unflagging wit. She never stops her play, as would Réjane or Guilbert, to hint, almost moralistically, at darker elements, to show the hideous painted face of vice, the wan masks of deprivation and despair; she is too American for that, too Yankee—yes, too Puritan. The New England propensity for suppression of all emotion survives today in our deliberate cheerfulness, our insistence on the trivial and external and commonsensible, our terror of any dangerous plunges below the surface of things.

MRS. FISKE, then, is not cruel, probing, poignant like the French comic artists; she is simply amazingly funny. She is funny almost every second, there is no let up in her action; when she has no line to speak she will make a gesture or stand in a certain way or twist her face. Her principle is continuity of effect. Her art is an escape from life as determined and sustained as jazz or Charlie Chaplin's work. Her evasion is brilliant and complete and unshakable.

What intrigues us, in Mrs. Fiske, is, perhaps, this conviction of hers—certainly racial, but in her so precisely expressed—that fireworks are better than fire.

On whatever play, whether a production with lamentable holes in it, or such a compact and trim piece of foolery as St. John Ervine's *Mary, Mary,* Mrs. Fiske manages to impress the stamp of distinction. And this is because wit, although infinitely sociable, is intrinsically aristocratic. The rapier has ever been its symbol and its action is delicate fencing, the opposite of buffoonery's heavy bludgeoning. Wit is reflective, discreet, remote; it smiles where others laugh; it walks with delicate discrimination and wears red heels and a curled white wig. Mrs. Fiske belongs spiritually in Sheri-

Steichen

MINNIE MADDERN FISKE

dan's comedies and would have waved a wicked fan at the Hôtel de Rambouillet. She has the brittle grace and exactitude of Mozart's melodies. One thinks her capable of Madame de Pompadour's dying speech to the priest leaving the bedside: "One moment, Monsieur le Curé, and we can take our departure together." She has the indifference, the elegance and the intrepid frivolity of the eighteenth century.

And she wields the rare rapier to tilt at its eternal antagonist—sentimentality. Indeed she is always curiously "on guard" in this respect. She will give us no commonplace exhibition of emotions, hardly any emotion except gaiety. She will not bathe us in any comfortable glow of sentiment. She will not relax from her light walking of a tight rope perilously distant from the earth as we know it. Her art—inasmuch as it is fireworks and not fire—is concerned with the artificial and is, in this sense, art for art's sake. She will not give us life; but she will give us, presented with beautiful self-exacting technique, a good time.

A good time we had when she strode upon the scene in *Mary, Mary,* clad in rubber boots, sou'wester and disheveled evening dress and produced her account of a night out in an open row-boat with a disgruntled elderly beau. A good time was again had by all during the moment she pretended to become much intoxicated, for her son's benefit and to his horror, in *Helena's Boys.* Mrs. Fiske, unlike most women and like every real histrionic humorist, is willing to make a caricature of herself; Beatrice Lillie, that subtle artist, shares this glory with her.

One would trade all the broad humors of the typical American farce, or the comedy of manners which is, interestingly enough, growing up among us, to hear Mrs. Fiske rap out, with classic incisiveness, such a line as:

"Well—why do you—all—stand there—like stalactites?"

THAT is because Mrs. Fiske has a precious thing—style. Style, we are told, is the man. Mrs. Fiske's style grows out of herself. Its clear outline is the result of her sharp intelligence, its economy springs from her concentration on essentials. She plays with lines as a juggler with knives and has his trick of gradually accelerated motion, so that her comic climaxes are whirlwinds worked up with almost incredible pace.

But when we have admired her technique, we have not really got to the root of the matter. Granted that Mrs. Fiske is a clown, that she is an eccentric, that she is a finished actress; beyond that she is a person. She ranks first in the American theatre not because she is clever, or educated, or experienced, or charged with vitality, although all these elements must have contributed to her success; she emerges because, like Duse, Réjane and Guilbert, she is a personality in the sense of being a point of view.

She baffles and leads us on. We cannot play on her nor learn her every stop. But she can play on us. She is, as I have said, because of her wit, mentally an aristocrat; she is also, thanks to her wit, sociable. She is never, if an architecturally faulty metaphor may be allowed, above the gallery. Humor is a common element; the gallery plunges in after her.

And yet, she is odd and alone, which endears her to the crowd. She moves in her own orbit and compels others to revolve around her. We conclude that if we feel a tonic glow on rising from one of her performances, this is to be laid to the fact that we have received the electric shock of a definite philosophy. No significant artist is without one. Mrs. Fiske makes her own world. And that is a universe founded on a peculiar refusal. "We must laugh about it," she seems to say, "in order not to cry." She laughs at others with kindly aloofness; she laughs at herself systematically and without giving quarter. But her creed's conscience is, fatally, that she excludes more than she admits.

Nominated for the Hall of Fame: 1924

Muray

EDNA FERBER

Because her first novel, *Dawn O'Hara,* written when she was twenty-one, is still selling; because after creating Mrs. Mac-Chesney and winning easy recognition as one of the first short-story writers in the language, a divine discontent turned her to the writing of so magnificent a novel as *The Girls;* because her play *Minick* (which she wrote with George Kaufman) is a success on Broadway and her novel *So Big* is the most popular one of the year.

REBECCA WEST

Because she is politically one of the most active women in Europe, not hesitating to take the stump in behalf of a cause she believes to be right; because she has contributed support at once wise and intrepid to the cause of female suffrage in England; because, having gained an admirable reputation as a critic, she turned to fiction and in *The Judge* achieved a unique distinction; because she is now on a lecture tour of the United States; but chiefly because, for all the richness of her gifts, she remains young, beautiful, brilliant, genuine and feminine.

Vandamm

GRANTLAND RICE

Because he is a writer of verse of imagination and sympathy; because we have no better sports writer in America; because he is a golfer of the first magnitude; because he is the editor of a successful golfing periodical; but chiefly because his personal following is so extensive that we wonder at the failure of the Republican party to nominate him for President.

SERGE KOUSSEVITZKY *Vandamm*

Because he is the foremost orchestral conductor in Russia, and it is largely due to his efforts that symphonic music has become popular in his native land; because he is himself a celebrated virtuoso on the bass viol, and because he will direct the Boston Symphony Orchestra next season.

Muray

ROBERT BENCHLEY

Because he is one of the most adroit and original of American humorists; because his gift for after-dinner speaking has saved many a soul-blighting banquet; because he is a discerning dramatic critic; because he is now a diverting feature in the *Music Box Revue;* but chiefly because he has mercifully injected into our national humor the quality of sophisticated and cultivated good taste.

Vandamm

FRANKLIN P. ADAMS

Because his initials (F.P.A.) are familiar to all American readers; because he is a wit and has done more than anyone else to create the profession of column-conducting; but chiefly because, in any field of poetry whatever, he may always be counted on to write a happy and distinguished thing.

Keystone

WILLIAM ALLEN WHITE

Because, as editor of the *Emporia Gazette,* he has become nationally known as a leader of the Fourth Estate; because he is an author of distinction; but chiefly because he is a daring champion of human rights as opposed to mass prejudice, witness his recent conflict with Governor Allen on the issue of free speech, and his candidacy for Governor in this election, based on opposition to the Ku Klux Klan.

WILL ROGERS

Because in all his comedy he breathes the essential spirit of America; because he has brought the lariat and the lasso into the highest society in America; because he is a well-loved figure in movies; because the Ziegfeld *Follies* have long successfully revolved around him; but chiefly because as an author and political observer he is as shrewd, satirical and clever as they make them.

Steichen

Muray

JASCHA HEIFETZ

Once a child prodigy with the fiddle, Mr. Heifetz, now twenty-three, is one of the most prodigious of living concert artists

THOMAS HARDY

The last of the great writers of the nineteenth century, now in his eighty-fifth year, has lived to become one of the greatest of the twentieth

Ediss

One Evening

A Story, Typically French, by One of the Most Subtle French Writers

COLETTE

AS SOON as the gate had closed behind us and we saw the lantern bobbing along in front, in the gardener's hand, under a covering of clipped yews so thick that only an occasional spatter of rain could penetrate it, we began to feel that a hospitable refuge must be at hand, and that the accident to our motor which had left us stranded out in the open country must be classed as a blessing in disguise.

And, indeed, it actually came to pass that Mr. B., the master of the house, who received the two dripping and unexpected female tourists on the steps, was a lawyer who knew my husband slightly, and that I had met his wife, formerly a pupil at the Schola Cantorum, at the Dominican concerts.

When we were finally seated at the hearth, in front of the first wood fire of the year, a spontaneous babble of gaiety broke forth. Nothing would do but that Valentine and I should eat a pick-up of cold meat and champagne—our hosts, it seemed, had just finished their dinner. An ancient vintage of plum brandy and steaming hot coffee put us immediately on intimate terms. They had electric lights, which were very unusual in that region, and I savoured the familiar fragrances of yellow tobacco, ripe fruit, and the resinous wood they were burning, as if they had been wafted from some newly discovered, enchanted isle.

MR. B., robust, stocky, scarcely tinged with grey, and blessed with a flashing smile as radiant as the noonday sun, immediately engaged Valentine in conversation; and I— well, I talked rather less with Madame B. than I stared at her. She was small and blond, dressed as one might be for a banquet instead of to receive stray motorists; but it was her eyes that so astounded me. They were so clear and limpid that their natural pale blue varied with every breath of thought or feeling. One moment they would become violet, like her dress; the next green, like the silk material of her chair; and when, for an instant, they looked troubled, they turned, in the reflection of the lamplight, almost red, as the blue irises of angora cats are seen to do when they are angry. I asked myself if these almost too translucent eyes did not give to the whole face its air of absent-mindedness, of empty amiability, its smile at times almost that of a somnambulist. A somnambulist, at all

Manuel

COLETTE

events, singularly attentive to our pleasure, and careful to make the two or three hours pass quickly in which our chauffeur and Mr. B.'s mechanic would be occupied in repairing the car.

"We have a room at your disposal," said Madame B., "why not spend the night here?" And her eyes expressed only an utter loneliness, a loneliness devoid even of a thought.

"You're not so badly off here," she resumed. "Just see how well my husband is getting on with your friend."

She laughed, but her eyes, wide and empty, seemed scarcely cognizant of her words. For the second time she made me repeat some slight phrase, trembling a little as she did so. What was it, morphine, opium? An inebriate would never have had those rosy lips, that smooth forehead, that soft, cool hand, or that flesh so young and tender, swelling up from beneath the low-necked gown.

Was I dealing with a mute victim of marital unhappiness? It could not be. The most Machiavellian tyrant could not have uttered the name "Simone" so tenderly, or rested upon his slave a glance of such affectionate admiration.

"Yes, Madame, they really do exist," Mr. B. was saying at that very moment to my friend, Valentine. "There really are families that live in the country eight months of the year, never are separated for so much as a week, and yet do not find anything to complain of in their lot. Isn't that so, Simone?"

"Yes, thank heavens, there are," said Simone, and her pale blue eyes held nothing but a tiny yellow flame, very far away, caught from the reflection of the lamplight on the bulging side of the samovar. Then she rose and poured us some hot tea, dashed with rum, for a nightcap.

A young man came in, bare-headed, and, without being introduced, gave some opened letters to Mr. B., who excused himself to Valentine and ran rapidly through his mail.

"It's my husband's secretary," said Simone, who was cutting a lemon into thin slices.

I spoke my thought:
"He's a nice young fellow."
"You think so?"

SHE raised her eyebrows in the surprised manner of one who should say, "Really, I never thought of that before." But this slim young man, not in the least embarrassed, struck one with his air of willfulness, with his trick of lowering his eyelids, which, when he suddenly raised them, made his abrupt, keen glance—quickly veiled, and more disdainful than shy—extremely compelling. He took a cup of tea and sat down before the fire beside Madame B. in one of those atrocities of the eighties, consisting of two attached seats in the shape of an S, which they used to call tête-à-têtes.

There was a moment's silence, when I feared that we might have exhausted the hospitality of our kind hosts. I murmured, to break the pause, "What solid comfort! I shall remember this charming house in which I have passed an evening without even knowing what it looks like from the outside. This fire will warm us again, will it not, Valentine, when, in a few minutes, we shut our eyes against the wind and . . ."

"If you go, it will be your own fault," cried Madame B. "But if I were in your place I shouldn't complain. I love the open road, the night, the rain that streaks the air in front of the headlights, the drops on one's cheeks like tears, oh I love all that!"

I looked at her in amazement. She was aglow with a delicious human flame that shyness had, perhaps, smothered during the early hours of the evening. She did not withdraw again into herself, and the most appealing candour showed her to us as gay, witty, conversant with the politics of the locality and with the ambitions of her husband, whom she pretended to tease by mimicking him in the manner of little girls who are playing at make-believe. There was no lamp on the mantel-piece; and only the wavering glow from the hearth, at some distance from the central illumination, touched or left in shadow this young woman, whose sudden animation made me think of the liveliness of canaries wakened in their cages when the lights are turned on at nightfall. The black back of the secretary leaned against his half of the S-shaped chair in which he sat with Madame B.

WHILE she was talking to her husband and my friend, turning towards them, I rose to set my empty cup down, and I saw one hand of the young man, which was concealed from their view, pressing her bare arm in a grip steady and motionless, just above the elbow. Neither of them moved. In his unoccupied hand, the young man held a cigarette, and in hers Madame B. toyed with a fan. She chatted gaily, attentive to everyone, her eyes clear, and in a voice in which her rapid breathing sometimes made a little catch, such as one experiences when one wants to laugh. And I saw the veins of her hand swell under the firm, passionate pressure.

As if he realized that he was being observed, the secretary suddenly rose, bade us goodnight and withdrew.

"Isn't that our motor I hear outside?" I asked a moment later.

Madame B. did not answer. She was looking at the fire, with her head bent a little to one side, seeming to listen to an all but inaudible sound, and looking, in the drooping of her whole body, like a woman who had been stunned. I repeated my question. She trembled.

"Yes, yes, I think so," she answered quickly. She raised her eyelids and smiled a mechanical smile—her eyes again cold and wide and empty—"It's too bad!"

We left, carrying late roses and dahlias from their garden. Mr. B. walked beside the automobile, which rolled along gently, as far as the first turn in the lane. Madame B. stood on the lighted steps, smiling at us with a face from which the desire to live seemed to have passed—one hand, beneath a transparent scarf, was pressed upon her bare arm just a little above the elbow.

Three Poems

WALTER DE LA MARE

Life

Hearken, O dear, now strikes the hour we
    die;
We, who in one strange kiss
Have proved a dream the world's realities,
Turned each from other's darkness with
    a sigh,
Need heed no more of life, waste no more
    breath
On any other journey, but of death.

And yet: Oh, know we well
How each of us must prove Love's infidel;
Still out of ecstasy turn trembling back
To earth's same empty track
Of leaden day by day, and hour by hour,
    and be
Of all things lovely the cold mortuary.

The Old House

A very, very old house I know—
And ever so many people go,
Past the small lodge, forlorn and still,
Under the heavy branches, till
Comes the blank wall, and there's the
    door.
Go in they do; come out no more.
No voice says aught: no spark of light
Across that threshold cheers the sight;
Only the evening star on high
Less lonely makes a lonely sky,
As, one by one, the people go
Into that very old house I know.

Silver

Slowly, silently, now the moon
Walks the night in her silver shoon;
This way, and that, she peers, and sees
Silver fruit upon silver trees;
One by one the casements catch
Her beams beneath the silvery thatch;
Couched in his kennel, like a log,
With paws of silver sleeps the dog:
From their shadowy cote the white breasts
    peep
Of doves in a silver-feathered sleep;
A harvest mouse goes scampering by,
With silver claws, and silver eye;
And moveless fish in the water gleam,
By silver reeds in a silver stream.

Song

HELEN CHOATE

Shall I love you a little forever?
Or love you superbly a day?

There are hearts that can bear up an in-
    finite love,
But ours were not ever as they.

Those hearts that are shiningly girded
Can withstand such a pressure and stay;
But the heart that is weak under infinite
    love,
Must break if it turn not away.

We are young—we are flippantly hearted—
Answer, beloved, and say,
Shall I love you a little forever?
Or love you superbly, a day?

Memorabilia

E. E. CUMMINGS

stop look &

listen Venezia: incline thine
ear you glassworks
of Murano;
pause
elevator nel
mezzo del cammin' that means half-
way up the Campanile, believe

thou me cocodrillo—

mine eyes have seen
the glory of

the coming of
the Americans particularly the
brand of marriageable nymph which is
armed with large legs rancid
voices Baedekers Mothers and kodaks
—by night upon the Riva Schiavoni or in
the felicitous vicinity of the de l'Europe

Grand and Royal
Danielli their numbers

are like unto the stars of Heaven. . . .

i do signore
affirm that all gondola signore
day below me gondola signore gondola
and above me pass loudly and gondola
rapidly denizens of Omaha Altoona or what
not enthusiastic cohorts from Duluth God
    only,
gondola knows Cincingondolanati i gon-
    dola don't

—the substantial dollarbringing virgins

"from the Loggia where
are we angels by O yes
beautiful we now pass through the look
girls in the style of that's the
foliage what is it didn't Ruskin
says about you got the haven't Marjorie
isn't this wellcurb simply darling"
          —O Education: O
thos cook & son

(O to be a metope
now that triglyph's here)

The Dempsey-Firpo Fight

George Bellows' most ambitious canvas of the ring, painted shortly before his death

The death of George Bellows, on January 8, 1925, was a blow from which American art will find it hard to recover. He had been ranked as the most vigorous of living American painters. Some of this feeling of strength in his work, this radiation of vitality and power, may have been due to the fact that Bellows was himself a first-rate athlete, and a great lover of sport. His enthusiasm for the prize ring amounted to a passion. Shortly after the Dempsey-Firpo fight, Bellows made a lithograph which portrayed the bout, and which was one of his finest prints. Last summer, in Woodstock, the idea came to him of attacking the same subject in oil. The result was the picture shown on this page. The painter half-humorously included himself in this vigorous canvas and may be recognized as the bald gentleman at the extreme left of the composition.

FLORENCE MILLS

She leads a Harlemquinade. The exotic rhythm and accelerated pace of the Negro Revue have reached a climax in Dixie to Broadway

JACKIE COOGAN

Young Mr. Coogan has been one of the idols of our country ever since he appeared with (and opposite) Charlie Chaplin in the immortal film The Kid

The Black Blues

Negro Songs of Disappointment in Love—Their Pathos Hardened with Laughter

CARL VAN VECHTEN

THE Negro, always prone to express his deepest feeling in song, naturally experiences other more secular emotions than those sensations of religion published in the Spirituals. Perhaps the most poignant of all his feelings are those related to his disappointments in love, out of which have sprung the songs known as the Blues. These mournful plaints occasioned by the premature departure of "papa," these nostalgic longings to join the loved one in a climate of sunlight and color—although in at least one instance the singer indicates a desire to go back to Michigan—are more tragic to me than the Spirituals, for the Spirituals are often informed with resignation, or even a joyous evangelism, while the Blues are consistently imbued with a passionate despair.

Like the Spirituals, the Blues are folksongs and are conceived in the same pentatonic scale, omitting the fourth and seventh tones—although those that have achieved publication or performance under sophisticated auspices have generally passed through a process of transmutation—and at present they are looked down upon, as the Spirituals once were, especially by the Negroes themselves. The humbleness of their origin and occasionally the frank obscenity of their sentiment are probably responsible for this condition. In this connection it may be recalled that it has taken over fifty years for the Negroes to recover from their repugnance to the Spirituals, because of the fact that they were born during slave days. Now, however, the Negroes are proud of the Spirituals, regarding them as one of the race's greatest gifts to the musical pleasure of mankind. I predict that it will not be long before the Blues will enjoy a similar resurrection which will make them as respectable, at least in the artistic sense, as the religious songs.

THE music of the Blues has a peculiar language of its own, wreathed in melancholy ornament. It wails, this music, and limps languidly; the rhythm is angular, like the sporadic skidding of an automobile on a wet asphalt pavement. The conclusion is abrupt, as if the singer suddenly had become too choked for further utterance. Part of this effect is indubitably achieved through the fact that the typical Blues is created in three-line stanzas. As W. C. Handy, the artistic father of the Blues, has pointed out to me, the melodic strain can thereby be set down in twelve bars instead of the regulation sixteen. Not only are the breaks between verses and stanzas frequent, but also there are tantalizing and fascinatingly unaccountable—to any one familiar with other types of music—gaps between words, even between syllables. These effects are more or less characteristic of other Negro music, but in the case of the Blues they are carried several degrees further. When these songs are performed with accompaniment, the players fill in these waits by improvising the weirdest and most heart-rending groans and sobs, whimpers and sighs, emphasizing, at the same time, the stumbling rhythm. Extraordinary combinations of instruments serve to provide these accompaniments: organ and cornet, mouth organ and guitar, saxophone and piano; sometimes a typical Negro jazz-band—and by this I do not mean the Negro jazz-band of the white cabaret—is utilized by a phonograph company to make a record. Many of these men do not read music at all. Many of these songs have never been written down.

Notwithstanding the fact that the musical interest, the melodic content, of these songs is often of an extremely high quality, I would say that in this respect the Blues seldom quite equal the Spirituals. The words, however, in beauty and imaginative significance, far transcend in their crude poetic importance the words of the religious songs. They are eloquent with rich idioms, metaphoric phrases, and striking word combinations. The Blues, for the most part, are the disconsolate wails of deceived lovers and cast-off mistresses, whose desertion arouses the desolate one to tell his sad story in flowery language. Another cause has contributed to the inspiration of symbolic poetry in these numbers. Negroes, especially in the South, indulge in a great deal of what they themselves call "window-dressing," in order to mislead their white employers. This is the reason for the prevalent belief in the South that Negroes are always happy, for they usually make it a point to meet a white man with a smile and often with a joke. It is through this habit of window-dressing that the Negroes have grown accustomed to expressing their most commonplace thoughts in a special tongue of their own. For example, a Negro boy who intends to quit his job surreptitiously sings to his colored companions: "If you don't believe I'm leavin', count the days I'm gone."

A favorite phrase to express complete freedom has it: "I've got the world in a jug, the stopper's in my hand."

THE Blues bulge with such happy phrases: "The blacker the berry, the sweeter the juice," referring to the preference yellow girls frequently bestow on extremely black men, or the contrasting refrain, which recurs in a score of these songs, "I don't want no high yella." Other picturesque locutions are: "I've put ashes in my papa's bed so that he can't slip out." "Hurry sundown, let tomorrow come," "Blacker than midnight, teeth like flags o' truce."

Certain refrains, for a perfectly logical reason, recur again and again in these songs. For instance, "I went down to the river":

> I went down to the river, underneath the willow tree.
> A dew dropped from the willow leaf, and rolled right down on me.
> An' that's the reason I got those weepin' willow blues.

or Goin' to the river, take my rockin' chair.
> Goin' to the river, take my rockin' chair.
> If the blues overcome me, I'll rock on away from here.

or Goin' to the river, I mean to sit down.
> Goin' to the river, I mean to sit down.
> If the blue-blues push me, I'll jump over and drown.

So many of the papas and mamas depart on trains that the railroad figures frequently in the Blues:

> Got the railroad blues; ain't got no railroad fare.
> Got the railroad blues; ain't got no railroad fare.
> I'm gonna pack mah grip an' beat mah way away from here.

or Goin' to the railroad, put mah head on the track.
> Goin' to the railroad, put mah head on the track.
> If I see the train a-comin', I'll jerk it back.

or I went up on the mountain, high as a gal can stan',

An' looked down on the engine that took away mah lovin' man.

An' that's the reason I got those weepin' willow blues.

THERE are many Blues which are interesting throughout as specimens of naïve poetry, related in a way it would be difficult to define, but which it is not hard to sense, with oriental imagery of the type of The Song of Songs. Such a one is that which begins:

A brown-skinned woman an' she's chocolate to the bone.

A brown-skinned woman an' she smells like toilet soap, etc.

A typical example of this class of song is "The Gulf Coast Blues," which also possesses a high degree of musical interest which, unfortunately, I cannot reproduce here.

I been blue all day.
My man's gone away.
He went an' left his mama cold
For another girl, I'm told.
I tried to treat him fine,
I thought he would be mine,
That man I hate to lose,
That's why mama's got the blues.

The man I love he has done lef' this town.
The man I love he has done lef' this town.
An' if he keeps on goin', I will be Gulf Coast boun'.
The mailman passed but he didn't leave no news.
The mailman passed but he didn't leave no news.
I'll tell the world he lef' me with those Gulf Coast Blues.
Some o' yo' men sure do make me tired.
Some o' yo' men sure do make me tired.
You got a handful o' gimme an' a mouthful o' much oblige.

In connection with this depressing lament, Langston Hughes, the young Negro poet, has written me:

"The Blues always impressed me as being very sad, sadder even than the Spirituals, because their sadness is not softened with tears, but hardened with laughter, the absurd, incongruous laughter of a sadness without even a god to appeal to. In 'The Gulf Coast Blues' one can feel the cold northern snows, the memory of the melancholy mists of the Louisiana lowlands, the shack that is home, the worthless lovers with hands full o' gimme, mouths full o' much oblige, the eternal unsatisfied longings.

"There seems to be a monotonous melancholy, an animal sadness, running through all Negro jazz that is almost terrible at times. I remember hearing a native jazz-band playing in the Kameroon in Africa while two black youths stamped and circled about a dance hall floor, their feet doing exactly the same figures over and over to the monotonous rhythm, their bodies turning and swaying like puppets on strings. While two black boys, half-grinning mouths never closed, went round the room, the horns cried and moaned in monotonous weariness —like the weariness of the world—moving always in the same circle, while the drums kept up a deep-voiced laughter for the dancing feet. The performance put a damper on the evening's fun. It just wasn't enjoyable. The sailors left. . . .

"Did you ever hear this verse of the Blues?

I went to the gipsy's to get mah fortune tol'.
I went to the gipsy's to get mah fortune tol'.
Gipsy done tol' me Goddam yore unhardlucky soul.

"I first heard it from George, a Kentucky colored boy who shipped out to Africa with me—a real vagabond if there ever was one. He came on board five minutes before sailing with no clothes—nothing except the shirt and pants he had on and a pair of silk socks carefully wrapped up in his shirt pocket. He didn't even know where the ship was going. He used to make up his own Blues—verses as absurd as Krazy Kat and as funny. But sometimes when he had to do more work than he thought necessary for a happy living, or, when broke, he couldn't make the damsels of the West Coast believe love worth more than money, he used to sing about the gipsy who couldn't find words strong enough to tell about the troubles in his hard-luck soul."

The first Blues to achieve wide popularity was "The Memphis Blues," by W. C. Handy, who lived at that time in Memphis, and was well acquainted with life on the celebrated Beale Street. For this song— published in 1912, a year after "Alexander's Ragtime Band"—Mr. Handy received a total of one hundred dollars. Since then he has issued so many of these songs, "The St. Louis Blues," "Hesitation Blues," "John Henry Blues," "Basement Blues," "Harlem Blues," "Sundown Blues," "Atlanta Blues," "Beale Street Blues," "Yellow Dog Blues," etc., that, taking also into account that he was the first to publish a song of this character, he is generally known as the father of the Blues. Nevertheless, Mr. Handy himself has informed me categorically that the Blues are folksongs, a statement I have more than fully proved through personal experience. To a greater degree than other folksongs, however, they have gone through several stages of development. Originally, many of these songs are made up by Negroes in the country to suitably commemorate some catastrophe. As one of these improvised songs drifts from cabin to cabin, verses are added, so that not infrequently as many as a hundred different stanzas exist of one song alone. Presently, these ditties are carried into the Negro dives and cabarets of the Southern cities, where they are served up with improvised accompaniments and where a certain obscene piquancy is added to the words. Many of the Blues, as a matter of fact, are casual inventions, never committed to paper, of pianist and singer in some house of pleasure. This does not mean that composers and lyric writers have not occasionally created Blues of their own. For the most part, however, the Blues that are sung by Negro artists in cabarets and for the phonograph are transcribed versions of folksongs. Even with such Blues as are definitely composed by recognized writers, their success depends upon a careful following of the folk formula both for words and music.

So far as Mr. Handy's own Blues are concerned, he admits frankly that they are based almost without exception on folksongs which he has picked up in the South. Occasionally he has followed the idea of an old Blues, more frequently he has retained a title or a melody and altered the words to suit Broadway or Harlem's Lenox Avenue. For example, the tune of "Aunt Hagar's Blues"—Aunt Hagar's Children is the name the Negroes gave themselves during slave days—is founded on a melody he once heard a Negro woman sing in the South to the words, "I wonder whar's mah good ol' used to be." The "Joe Turner Blues" is based on the melody of an old Memphis song, "Joe Turner come an' got mah man an' gone." Peter Turney at the time was Governor of Tennessee. His brother, Joe, was delegated to take prisoners from Memphis to the penitentiary at Nashville, and the Negroes pronounced his name Turner. Mr. Handy has utilized the old melody and the title, but he has invented the harmonies and substituted words which would have more meaning to casual hearers.

So far as I know there has been as yet no effort made—such as has been made with the Spirituals—to set down these songs, verses and music, as they are sung under primitive conditions. To me this is a source of the greatest amazement. Any Negro recently from the South knows at least half a dozen of them. I myself have heard as many as fifty in Lenox Avenue dives and elsewhere that have never been put down in any form. They are not only an essential part of Negro folklore, but also they contain a wealth of eerie melody, borne along by a savage, recalcitrant rhythm. They deserve, therefore, from every point of view, the same serious attention that has tardily been awarded to the Spirituals.

Big Casino Is Little Casino

A Three-Act Play

GEORGE S. KAUFMAN

THIS play is designed to contain a little bit of each of the many things that have been keeping people away from the theatre in recent years. Although its title might indicate that it is aimed at a particular playwright addicted to paradoxical titling, the play as a whole is intended to cover a much wider ground. The idea has been to get square with everybody in three two-minute acts.

The only performance took place in New York with the following cast, during a professional show called *No-Siree*.

HENRY C. ARCHIBALD, a Multi-Millionaire
John Peter Toohey
DREGS, a Philosophical Butler
Alexander Woollcott
GEORGE W. HARPER, a Broker
J. M. Kerrigan
JOHN FINDLAY, a Rising Young District Attorney.............*George S. Kaufman*
O'BRIEN, of the Central Office
Franklin P. Adams
MARGARET, Archibald's Daughter
Mary Kennedy
A COMMON FELON........*Marc Connelly*
BROKER'S BOY.........*David H. Wallace*
THE GOVERNOR OF NEW YORK
Robert E. Sherwood
FIRST RICH GUEST........*Neysa McMein*
SECOND RICH GUEST.....*Alice Duer Miller*

ACT I

The scene is the library in the home of Henry C. Archibald, a multi-millionaire. It is a beautiful room, with books in it. As the curtain rises the door-bell is ringing. Dregs, the butler, enters and opens the doors for the guests, all of whom are rich, and some very rich. Among them is George W. Harper, a broker. As the guests arrive, Mr. Archibald enters from an adjoining room.

DREGS: Mr. Archibald, here are some of the 214 fashionable guests for your exclusive party.

ARCHIBALD: Thank you, Dregs. You are a very good man, indeed.

DREGS: I'm glad you think so, sir. There are two kinds of married women—those who get up in the morning and those who don't.

ARCHIBALD: Good evening, everybody!

ALL: Good evening!

HARPER: We have come to the party you are giving—one of a series of lavish affairs for which you are famous.

ARCHIBALD: Indeed, I thank you.

FIRST RICH GUEST: Is this not a magnificent room, with red plush hangings?

SECOND RICH GUEST: Yes, I once read about a room like this in a volume.

HARPER: I understand that you are a very rich man and that you have some novel theories about crime.

ARCHIBALD: Yes. I believe that crime is the fault of the criminal. If you will follow my man, Dregs, who has served me for fifteen years, you may put your things in the rococo room. Dregs, tell the ten-piece orchestra from Delmonico's to begin.

DREGS: Yes, sir. Life is a puzzle and very few are able to unravel it. (*Exit Dregs and all except Archibald and Harper*)

HARPER: Have you heard anything about that ardent young reformer, John Findlay?

ARCHIBALD: Yes, I have invited him here tonight.

HARPER: He is not in sympathy with your views of the criminal. (*Enter John Findlay, a Rising Young District Attorney*)

FINDLAY: No, I am not. I believe that crime is responsible for the criminal, not the criminal for crime. Remove crime and there will be no criminals.

ARCHIBALD: Ah, Mr. Findlay! And how are you?

FINDLAY: I am well. But have you stopped to think that while you give this elaborate party here tonight, which is but one of a series for which you are celebrated, that your own daughter Margaret, whom you cast out years ago, is perhaps starving?

ARCHIBALD: I have no daughter. She ceased to be my daughter when she opposed my views of the criminal.

FINDLAY: But have you no interest in what she is doing since you cast her out?

ARCHIBALD: No, I am a hard man. She does not believe in riches, so let her work out her life herself among the poor.

FINDLAY: She is, indeed, among the poor.

ARCHIBALD: I know that you are in love with her and have kept track of her, although you are a rising young district attorney with peculiar views about crime. (*Music is heard in the rococo room*) There is the music. Suppose, while my 214 guests are dancing, that we three play a little game of casino? Or are you afraid to gamble with me?

FINDLAY: I am not afraid. But the thought of your daughter, working among the poor—

DREGS (*Enters*): You were about to ring, sir?

ARCHIBALD: Yes. Cards. (*Dregs produces a deck of cards, which he has brought with him. The three men sit at the table*) See that my 214 guests have everything they want. This is to be a night of gaiety, for that is all that there is in the world.

DREGS: Yes, sir. He who interferes in the quarrel of a neighbor is doubly foolish, for he shall have no neighbors. (*He goes*)

FINDLAY: You are a heartless man, to be gay when there is so much misery in the world.

ARCHIBALD: It cannot touch me.

FINDLAY: Who knows? Perhaps disaster is stalking into your house at this very minute. I seem to have a premonition.

ARCHIBALD (*Who has been dealing*): Nonsense! Take up your cards! There! The deal is completed. (*He turns white*) Good God! (*They all spring to their feet*)

FINDLAY: Aha! Even as you spoke!

ARCHIBALD: What fiend's work is this? Give me his name and I shall—(*Dregs rushes on*)

DREGS: Is there anything the matter, sir?

ARCHIBALD: Yes! There are only fifty-one cards in this deck! (*There are general exclamations. Dregs is about to summon help*) No! Wait! (*He turns to Findlay*) You think I cannot meet trouble face to face? Then I will show you! Dregs!

DREGS: Yes, sir! A man is as old—

ARCHIBALD: I've heard that one! No one is to know that anything has happened! My 214 guests must go ahead and enjoy themselves! The music must play on!

HARPER: God! What a man!

ARCHIBALD: I've got to think—to think! (*A pause*) Dregs, close every door! No one must leave this house until the police arrive!

DREGS: Yes, sir.

FINDLAY: Good God, you're not—

ARCHIBALD: I am going to see this thing to the bottom! Dregs, you have the slip that came with this deck of cards, marked with the number of the person who packed it!

FINDLAY: For God's sake, Archibald—

ARCHIBALD: Give it to me! (*Dregs does so, momentously*) And now bring me paper, pen and ink! (*He pauses*) And a blotter!

FINDLAY: I tell you you mustn't do this thing! I can't tell you why, but you mustn't.

HARPER: Good God, what are you going to do?

ARCHIBALD (*His face set*): Write to the American Playing Card Company.

FINDLAY: My God!

(*The curtain falls*)

ACT II

The scene is the same, three days later. Archibald is seated, deep in thought. Dregs enters.

DREGS: It is a bright day, sir.

ARCHIBALD: Yes.

DREGS: That is the reason I never married.

(*There is a ring. Dregs admits O'Brien, a detective*)

O'BRIEN: Mr. Archibald?

ARCHIBALD: Yes. You are a detective. Have a cigar!

O'BRIEN: Thanks! I'm O'Brien, Central Office! Who's this?

ARCHIBALD: Dregs, my man. He has been with me fifteen years—I would trust him implicitly.

DREGS: Thank you, sir.

O'BRIEN: I'll come to that in a minute. First, I want you to show me just where you were sitting the other night when you discovered that this card was missing.

ARCHIBALD: Right here. I began to deal, little thinking that anything was going to happen, when suddenly—

O'BRIEN: Well, Mr. Archibald, the Central Office has not been idle. We've been all through the deck and discovered what the missing card is!

ARCHIBALD: Yes?

O'BRIEN: It's the ten of diamonds! Does that mean anything to you?

ARCHIBALD (*Awestruck*): Big Casino!

DREGS: Big Casino!

O'BRIEN: Big Casino is right! And we've done more than that. Your letter to the company resulted in the arrest of the girl who packed the deck!

ARCHIBALD: Ah!

O'BRIEN: She is outside now with her lawyer, waiting to see you. We got special permission to stop here on the way to the penitentiary. Do you want to see her?

ARCHIBALD (*Pauses*): Yes! Bring her in. (*O'Brien goes*)

DREGS: After all, sir, the higher one climbs for a bird's nest, the nearer one is to God.

(*O'Brien re-enters with Margaret, handcuffed to a man in stripes. Findlay comes along*)

ARCHIBALD: Good God! Margaret!

MARGARET: Yes, Margaret!

FINDLAY: Your own daughter! So now you see your work!

ARCHIBALD: Margaret, my little Margaret, whom I used to dandle on my knee! In company with a common felon!

DREGS (*Looking closely at the felon*): Good God, sir, it's my brother! (*They embrace*)

ARCHIBALD: But how was I to know? How was I to know when this terrible thing happened, that it was you—you!

MARGARET: You should have known! You knew it would be *some* one, and that you would drag her down, down!

ARCHIBALD: Margaret!

MARGARET: Oh, it's too late now! I am on my way to the penitentiary, sentenced for five years. But before I go I am going to tell you something! This is the result of your system, your society that you think so much of! You think that riches are everything, that it is the criminals who are responsible for crime! Well, let me tell you something! *You* make money out of it! You are one of the biggest stockholders of the American Playing Card Company! Now their stock will go up and up, and you will make money—out of me! Out of my body! And all because Big Casino was missing from the deck! Well, my soul is clear, but yours isn't! You have always been Big Casino and I have always been Little Casino, but from now on our positions are reversed! It is you who will suffer! For, thank God, Big Casino is Little Casino at last!

(*The situation is tense; the curtain falls*)

ACT III

The scene is a broker's office, two days later. Harper is seated at a desk. Archibald is bowed down in a chair. At the rear a boy is calling quotations.

BOY: H. J. Heinz, 57! Compressed Air, 26! Playing Card, 52!

ARCHIBALD: What was it before?

BOY: 51.

ARCHIBALD: Good God, going up!

BOY: American Playing Card, 53.

HARPER: They put in the joker!

ARCHIBALD: We must drive it down, down! Sell another million shares!

HARPER: But good God, Mr. Archibald, you are going to bankrupt yourself!

ARCHIBALD: Do as I tell you—drive it down! Sell another million shares—sell two million!

(*A little old man enters. He wears a long coat and a slouch hat, and has whiskers*)

LITTLE OLD MAN: Buy two million American Playing Card!

HARPER: Yes, sir. (*The old man goes*)

ARCHIBALD: Who is that man?

HARPER: I don't know, sir—he's very mysterious. He gives his orders and disappears.

BOY: Playing Card—40!

ARCHIBALD: Ah!

BOY: 35—30—25—20!

ARCHIBALD: Sell another million!

HARPER: Yes, sir.

LITTLE OLD MAN (*Popping in and out*): Buy one million Playing Card!

HARPER: Yes, sir.

BOY: 15—10—5—nothing!

ARCHIBALD: Sell three million at nothing!

HARPER: Yes, sir.

LITTLE OLD MAN (*In and out*): Buy three million at nothing!

HARPER: Yes, sir. Mr. Archibald, you are ruined. You have not a dollar left in the world! (*Dregs enters*)

DREGS: Mr. Archibald, I am only a servant, but I have a little money saved. Will you not take it?

ARCHIBALD: No, I cannot take your money.

DREGS: Thank you, sir. (*He leaves*)

ARCHIBALD: I have no money, but I am rich. I have kept faith with my daughter. I am Big Casino again.

HARPER: That's all right, but you must get out of here. We can't have any beggars around. Go on—get out!

(*The little old man enters*)

LITTLE OLD MAN: Wait! He is not a beggar! He has millions!

HARPER: What!

ARCHIBALD: Who are you?

LITTLE OLD MAN (*Stripping off the disguise*): I am Margaret! As fast as you sold American Playing Card I bought it! Everything that you have lost I have made! And now I give it back to you, for you have proved yourself Big Casino!

ARCHIBALD: Margaret! But I thought you were in the penitentiary. How did you get out? (*The Governor of New York enters, accompanied by Findlay*)

GOVERNOR: I let her out!

ARCHIBALD: And who are you?

GOVERNOR (*Majestically*): I am the Governor of the State of New York.

FINDLAY: And a boyhood friend of my father's.

MARGARET: John!

FINDLAY: Margaret!

(*Dregs rushes on*)

DREGS: Mr. Archibald!

ARCHIBALD: Well, Dregs?

DREGS: My brother! He was not a convict after all, but a novelist seeking local color. (*O'Brien enters*)

O'BRIEN: What is going on here? (*Grabs Margaret*) You are under arrest!

HARPER: Oh, no! *You* are under arrest! (*Grabs O'Brien*)

ARCHIBALD: What does this mean?

HARPER: It means that he is not a detective after all, but the real thief!

FINDLAY: And who are you?

HARPER: I am the detective!

ARCHIBALD: Margaret, you have taught me a great lesson. Big Casino is Little Casino, after all!!!

(*The curtain falls*)

Beck and MacGregor

GLADYS COOPER

The beautiful and gifted English actress is successfully reviving Pinero in London

RAMON NOVARRO

In Ben Hur

The mammoth movie has been two years in the making in Rome, longer than any other film in our memory. In the film with Mr. Novarro, Francis X. Bushman will be Messala, May MacAvoy Esther, and Carmel Meyers Iris.

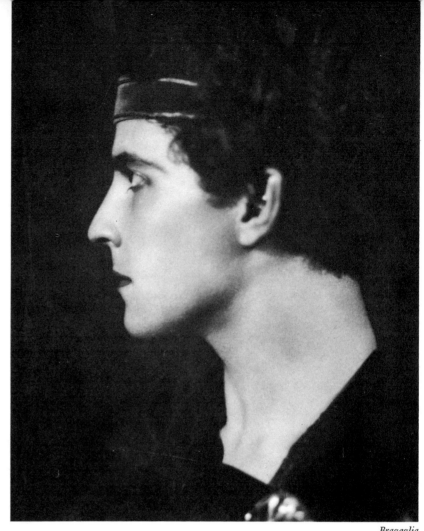

Bragaglia

MARY ASTOR
and
JOHN BARRYMORE

They are planning soon to appear in a film version of *Paolo and Francesca*. Mary Astor appeared with Mr. Barrymore in *Beau Brummell* (and more recently with Douglas Fairbanks in *Don Q, Son of Zorro*). This photograph shows two "million-dollar profiles" of filmdom in an idyllic moment before the studio camera.

Albin

JOHN BARRYMORE

"There she blows!"

Following his successive stage triumphs in *Peter Ibbetson, The Jest, Richard III* and *Hamlet,* the first actor of our theatre has recently completed a season in London, where *Hamlet* duplicated its brilliant New York success. Mr. Barrymore, now acting in films, appears here in the role of Captain Ahab in *The Sea Beast,* a screen version of Herman Melville's classic, *Moby Dick.*

A Group of Artists Write Their Own Epitaphs

Some Well-Known People Seize the Coveted Opportunity of Saying the Last Word

---

HERE LIES
Michael Arlen
AS USUAL

HIC JACET
Elsie Janis
"AND HER MOTHER CAME, TOO."

Emily Stevens, NERVOUS, "BRITTLE",
IS STILL AT LAST, BUT SHE CARES LITTLE.
THE CURTAIN'S DOWN, THE SHOW IS OVER.
REST, POOR EMILY! YOU'RE IN CLOVER!

HERE LIES
Rex Beach
TEED UP, 1877   BUNKERED, 1967
HE WORKED A LITTLE, AND PLAYED ENOUGH
ARRIVED AT THE FAIRWAY, BUT FETCHED
THE ROUGH.

HERE LIES THE BODY OF
Harry Hirschfield
IF NOT, NOTIFY GINSBERG & CO.,
UNDERTAKERS, AT ONCE!

Zoë Akins

SHE LOVED
   SHAKESPERE'S SONNETS,
   PARIS BONNETS,
   COUNTRY WALKS,
   ALL-NIGHT TALKS,
   OLD TREES AND PLACES,
   CHILDREN'S FACES,
   SHAW AND KEATS,
   OPERA SEATS,
   LONELY PRAIRIES,
   TEA AT SHERRY'S,
   SUNLIGHT AND AIR,
   VANITY FAIR

HERE LIES
Zona Gale
I'M IN THE SUN, THE MOON, THE SKY
I'M NIMBLY PERCHING ON THE BOUGH,
I'M EVERYWHERE AT ONCE, BUT I
AM MUCH TOO MODEST TO TELL HOW.

LET **Frank O'Malley's** TOMBSTONE
MOTTO
SAY SIMPLY THAT HIS RACE, HALF RUN,
WAS ENDED, AND HIS WORLD WENT BLOTTO
WHEN MUNSEY BOUGHT THE SUN.

HERE LIES
George S. Kaufman
"OVER MY DEAD BODY!"

Sherwood Anderson

GOOD NIGHT,
'TWAS FUN ENOUGH, AND LIFE WAS DEAR
I TRIED TO GET MY WISH.
I DID NOT WANT TO DIE—
BEFORE THEY PUT ME HERE.

Maxfield Parish

READ, DEAR, KIND FRIEND, THIS TOMMY-ROT,
TO M. P. IN MEMORIAM:
OH, VERY SURE IT MATTERS NOT;
THE LONGER DEAD THE MORE I AM.

George Arliss

ALL MY OLD JUNK GONE TO THE
STOREHOUSE,
HERE I AM, GOD, STARTING FOR
YOUR HOUSE.
IN ORDER TO PREVENT POSSIBIL-
ITY OF RUCTION
AM BRINGING YOU BACK YOUR
ORIGINAL PRODUCTION.

HERE LIES **Wallace Irwin** OF GENIUS
SO BRIGHT
HE FLASHED LIKE A SUN WHERE THERE
MIGHT HAVE BEEN NIGHT;
POET, PHILOSOPHER, NOVELIST, SAGE,
O! WHAT ADORNMENTS HE LENT TO HIS AGE!
GIFTS SUCH AS HIS CANNOT WITHER AND DIE,
THOUGH HE HAS JOINED THE IMMORTALS
ON HIGH
FOR HIS WORKS GLOW LIKE PEARLS ON A
SEVEN FOOT SHELF.*

*(NOTE, BY THE SEXTON: "HE WROTE THIS
HIMSELF.")

HERE LIE THE
Four Marx Brothers

THE FIRST TIME THEY EVER
WENT OUT TOGETHER.

HERE LIES
Clare Briggs

AT REST.
THAT GUILTIEST FEELING

Avery Hopwood

LIVING AND DYING I LOVED THE
TRUTH
AND I'LL SPEAK IT NOW, THOUGH
IT SEEM UNCOUTH:
I WROTE THIRTY PLAYS, AND
PRODUCED THEM AS WELL,
SO I DON'T CARE MUCH IF IT'S
HEAVEN OR HELL.

Roland Young

RESTING

Kathleen Norris

THIS MODEL MOTHER, SISTER, WIFE,
BELIEVED, THROUGH ALL HER JOYS AND
WOES,
THAT LIFE IS DEATH, AND DEATH IS LIFE—
AND NOW SHE KNOWS.

HERE LIES THE CLAY OF
Fanny Hurst

BORN—YES.   DIED—YES.

HERE LIES
W. C. Fields

I WOULD RATHER BE LIVING IN
PHILADELPHIA

HERE LIE
THE EARTHLY REMAINS OF
George Shepard Chappell
"HE HAS JOINED THE SPIRITS,
OF WHICH HE WAS ALWAYS SO
FOND."

HERE **Percy Hammond** LIES
AT LEAST HE HAD A PRETTY
NAME

Don Marquis

I AM NOT HERE! NOR LIFE NOR
DEATH MIGHT BIND
THE SCORNFUL PINIONS OF MY
LAUGHING MIND!

HERE LIES THE BODY OF
George Gershwin
AMERICAN COMPOSER.
* * * *
COMPOSER?
AMERICAN?

HERE LIES
Hendrik Willem Van Loon
"OH, WANDERER, IF MY WISH
COULD COME TRUE
THEN YOU WOULD BE I, AND I
WOULD BE YOU."

CI-GIT
Dorothy Parker
"EXCUSE MY DUST!"

HERE LIES THE BODY OF
May Wilson Preston
SHE MOVED FROM NEW YORK
TO RELIEVE THE CONGESTION

Drawings by
BENITO

Charlie Chaplin and His Film "The Gold Rush"

R. E. SHERWOOD

WHENEVER anyone starts to pan the movies (and if you can name me one who doesn't I shall be pleased to send you an autographed copy of the photograph which appears on this page, done in handsome tinto-gravure and wholly suitable for framing)—whenever, as I observed at the start, a man starts to pan the movies, he qualifies his bitter condemnation with the patronizing concession, "Of course I always go to see the Chaplin, Lloyd or Keaton comedies." As much as to say, "The middle-class suburbs bore me to tears, but I never miss a chance to visit the slums."

His meaning is obvious: the movies, as such, are less than an art, but in their crudest and vulgarest forms they do provide entertainment *of a sort*.

THAT is nonsense. No one is qualified to judge the moving picture by the so-called "photoplays"—"heart dramas," "society dramas," "epic dramas" and other trash—for these are not truly moving pictures. You have seen Miss Corinne Griffith defending her honor against Dr. Lew Cody in his rooms at the Albany, or Mr. Rudolph Valentino leading the Arab horsemen across the burning sands, or little Miss Baby Peggy bringing Daddy and Mumsie together in tearful reconciliation, or Mr. Conway Tearle, as Sergeant O'Malley of the Mounted, getting his man—but in these instances you have not seen real moving pictures. You have seen a cheap, celluloid imitation of some scene or situation that originated on the stage or on the printed page.

When the movies declare themselves independent of all other forms of expression, they approximate an art; this has been done most notably by the comedians, who express their own ideas, in their own manner and in the medium that they know best. They don't take their material second-hand from Broadway or from Grub Street.

I am not announcing that I have discovered Charlie Chaplin; that important feat has already been accomplished by almost every literary Columbus—from Gilbert Seldes to Minnie Maddern Fiske (and, incidentally, by the general public, some twelve years before). But I do believe that the movie producers themselves have yet to discover the secret of Chaplin's art; they have yet to realize that he, and the other comedians, have given the moving picture an identity of its own. They have used the camera as an artist would use his pen or a

Vandamm

ROBERT E. SHERWOOD

painter his brush; they have made it an instrument of creation.

There are, of course, exceptions. In Germany they have caught the idea, and have made such pictures as *The Cabinet of Dr. Caligari* and *The Last Laugh*. Douglas Fairbanks has done much the same thing in *The Thief of Bagdad* and *Don Q*. James Cruze did it once in a picture called *One Glorious Day*. But the great majority of the movie moguls have been content to go on, dealing in damaged goods because that, at the moment, seems the most profitable thing to do.

Mention art to a film magnate, and he will laugh in your face. "Listen, brother," he will say, after the guffaws have subsided, "the motion pictures are made for the square-heads out in Kalamazoo, not for the highbrows in Greenwich Village—and the square-heads want entertainment, not art."

It is useless to argue that art may conceivably be entertainment; art, in Hollywood, is regarded as a dull, dry, esoteric and highly unprofitable property which is to be shunned religiously by all those who have the best interests of the exhibitor's box-office at heart.

Charlie Chaplin is, and always has been, the living refutation of this absurd doctrine. For Chaplin is an artist, who expresses himself as he damned well pleases, regardless of the bankers, the distributors and the sales executives; and Chaplin's pictures are incredibly profitable. You can take any ten screen heart-dramas—all of them "box-of-

fice knockouts" in the most offensive sense of the word—and you will find that they did not, collectively, measure up to *Shoulder Arms* in earning capacity.

An examination of Chaplin's methods will prove that he is absolutely independent, that he is as free and untrammeled as the most violent *vers librist* who ever defied tradition in poetry.

Instead of buying stories that have been successful as novels and plays, and therefore possess proved circulation value, he creates his own ideas from his own mind. Instead of producing a definite number of pictures on schedule each year (so that they may be sold to exhibitors in bunches, like so many Lily Cups), he works when he feels like it and doesn't bother to release a picture until he believes that it is complete.

In the last three years, Chaplin has produced only three pictures—*A Woman of Paris, The Pilgrim* and *The Gold Rush*. The last of these was started in January 1924, and finished in May 1925.

It is the proud boast of a famous director that he recently completed a six-reel feature picture in a total of eighteen days. Chaplin frequently takes that much time for the photography of one scene, doing the thing over and over again until he is certain that it is as nearly right as he can make it.

IN PHOTOGRAPHING his new film, *The Gold Rush*, Chaplin used up nearly half a million feet of film, which subsequently had to be cut down to approximately ninety-five hundred feet. That represents a frightful waste, but it may have something to do with the fact that *The Gold Rush* is Chaplin's greatest picture.

Charlie Chaplin has produced *The Gold Rush* as a sort of symbolical autobiography. He has dramatized himself—just as he has dramatized himself in every picture he has ever made. It is the story of a stampede in the Klondike, with an enormous mob of eager prospectors storming the heights of Chilnook Pass in a wild scramble for gold. With the procession, and yet utterly detached from it, is a lonely figure in a derby hat and a burlap Inverness cape, who carries a bamboo cane to aid him in his perilous climb up the icy slopes.

He would like to mix with the others, but they will have none of him; they are too busy, too anxious to get down to business, to bother with him. So he must go his way alone. He finds the gold, but the dance-hall girl of his heart jilts him—and he is compelled to return home with nothing but vast wealth to show for his efforts.

THUS does Charlie Chaplin take his sardonic fling at the world which has been generous to him, but never sympathetic; and the world, as usual, will roar with laughter at his antics and will pay several million dollars into the theaters where *The Gold Rush* is shown.

Chaplin says that his next picture will be called *Pierrot;* this, too, will presumably be a symbolical autobiography. For the great Charlot is introspective to a painful degree, and whenever he starts a new comedy he does so with the promise, "This is to be my great work. In this I shall bare the soul of Charlie Chaplin." He does so, invariably, and because the soul of Chaplin is the soul of genius, his comedies are notable and distinguished. For with all his instinct for Russian grimness, his nebulous whimsicality, his blind groping for an elusive ideal, with all this goes the basic

knowledge that a policeman's posterior is the funniest property known to man—and that, when a well-directed toe or a lighted candle is applied to this nether locality, people will laugh.

CHAPLIN'S influence has been exerted, in an emphatically apparent manner, on the other comedians—Buster Keaton and Harold Lloyd in particular. Both of these gifted young men follow religiously in Chaplin's footsteps; they have both declared themselves independent of the moneyed aristocracy of the movies, and have made this declaration valid. They both approach each picture as an individual creation; they never promise that it will be done on schedule time, or in any particular length or according to any preconceived form. It seems to me that both Lloyd and Keaton are artists; and they are so not merely because they are clever, but because they are sincere and, above all, because they are free.

It has come about, then, that the movies have touched the highest art through the lowest forms. Where they have failed miserably (except in a few isolated instances) to achieve any genuine tragedy or sentiment or fantasy or even melodrama, they have lifted crude, slap-stick humor to heights that it has never known before. The eminence of Aeschylus, Sophocles, Shakespeare, Molière and Ibsen has not been seriously shaken by anyone in Hollywood as yet, but there is no humorist, from Aristophanes down, who must not bow to Charlie Chaplin. And the strangest part of it all—to those who cannot associate art with prosperity—is that out of some hundreds of pictures, Chaplin has met financial failure but once.

That was in *A Woman of Paris,* a film which he directed but in which he did not appear. This, above all others, demonstrated Chaplin's superb indifference to the commercial considerations which so completely dominate the movie business.

CHARLIE CHAPLIN
In a scene from his forthcoming film The Gold Rush

Nominated for the Hall of Fame: 1925

Vandamm

MINNIE MARX (below)

Because, as the daughter of a German magician, she felt inner promptings which bade her snatch her five sons from their boyhood occupations (bellhops and the like) and drive them onto the stage. She was not content until the Marx Brothers shone in electric lights on Broadway. Then, feeling suddenly idle, she went into the ginger-ale business.

Goldberg

AL JOLSON (left)

Because, without aspiring to art, he is one of the great artists of the American theatre; because he is the biggest attraction on the American stage; because he encourages the best of his blackface imitators; and finally because he is an important factor in the gaiety of nations.

Steichen

SIDNEY HOWARD

Because he is a writer of eminence and charm; because his investigation of the opium traffic in America was perhaps the ablest ever undertaken; because he wrote *Swords;* but chiefly because, in *They Knew What They Wanted,* he has written one of the most engrossing plays by an American playwright.

Steichen

FANNY BRICE

Because, from the humblest beginnings on the East Side of New York, she came to be acclaimed as the best comedian on the musical-comedy stage; because she made the trial of Nicky Arnstein, her husband, one of the most diverting on record; because she is a financial genius of high rank; and finally because her mastery of pathos, mingled with her extraordinary sense of the comic, has brought her to stardom for Belasco.

CHRISTOPHER MATHEWSON

Because for seventeen years of service in the National League he has a winning average of .665, winning 372 games and losing 187; and because, throughout his connection with baseball, he has been a conspicuous standard-bearer of honesty and the best sportsmanship.

The Murder of Captain White

The Notorious Case in Salem—Daniel Webster Appearing for the Prosecution

EDMUND PEARSON

TODAY, if a man commits a murder, and if he takes care to do it in an atrocious and notorious manner, and if, moreover, he is a person of wealth and prominence, there is a great rush of learned lawyers and scientists to explain things. He is a helpless victim of heredity, it seems, and should not be held responsible for anything; or he is at the mercy of his glands or his neuroses. He is far too interesting for us to lose by way of the gallows or the electric chair: he should be preserved alive so that the alienists may have a good time with his phantasies.

Our great-grandfathers were crude. The murderer was explained by them in simple terms: "not having the fear of God before his eyes but being moved and seduced by the instigation of the Devil," he proceeded to the commission of his crime. This Devil used to seem to me rather an undignified creature. As he presented himself to the witches of Scotland, and of Salem, there was in him more fun than harm—a low-comedy character impossible to take seriously. He became fixed in my mind as a personage in red tights, like the one on the tins of potted ham.

Reading, however, the speeches of some great criminal lawyers of today, and the testimony of the alienists, I get a new respect for the Devil of our fore-fathers. I doubt if he can be any funnier than the modern explanations of evil will seem to the world in one hundred and fifty years. At least, he offers a convenient and fairly plausible formula in the discussion of the mystery of crime.

As a stage-manager, he showed varying degrees of care in his productions. He was responsible for brutal slaughters, and for refined poisonings, for stupid assassinations, and for puzzles involving subtle problems of psychology. Ninety-five years ago he chose to set a perfect melodrama; to resurrect, in the year 1830, the apparatus of the older romance; to show that he could beat the old writers of the tale of terror, and at the same time anticipate a favorite device of the modern detective story: the murdered millionaire alone in his house.

THERE was hardly one omission of scene, of cast, or of stage property. There was the highly respectable and extremely horrified community of Salem; there was a dark conspiracy, involving hired desperadoes and the black sheep of two good families; there was a white-haired and blameless old gentleman—a man of wealth—asleep in the moonlight in his bed-chamber; there were dirks and doubloons; and there were lurking figures of men in "camblet" cloaks.

There was even talk of a cave in the woods, where a gang of "harlots, gamblers and sharpers" used to gather. (What a romantic place was my native county of Essex fifty years before I was born!) One excitement followed another in that spring and summer of 1830. Convicts were brought "in chains," to testify; there was a suicide and four capital trials. Three juries sat in awe while the deep voice of America's greatest orator resounded through the court-room; one of those groups of twelve honest countrymen listened to the most celebrated speech ever delivered during a murder trial in this country. And at the end, there were two dismal processions to the gallows; two executions of the sentence of death, and in public, before thousands of spectators. The feeling of shame which settled upon the town has not altogether lifted today: the murder of Captain White is still discussed in Salem and as a scandalous horror which is not dead, but very much alive.

CAPTAIN Joseph White was a man over eighty, and accustomed to go to bed early. In his house—still standing on Essex Street—there lived only himself (he was unmarried), his niece, Mrs. Beckford, who was also his housekeeper, and two servants, a man and a woman. On the night of April 6, 1830, Mrs. Beckford was visiting her daughter in Wenham. Early the next morning the man-servant found a parlor window open, and a plank resting on the sill so as to allow entrance and exit to the back-yard. He searched the house for traces of burglary, but discovered nothing amiss until he entered his master's bedroom. Captain White was lying in a bed drenched with blood; he had been dead for hours. His death was caused by a heavy blow on the temple, but he had also been stabbed thirteen times, and there was more than one knife wound which would have been enough, in itself, to cause death. There had been no robbery; plate in various rooms was untouched, and a "*rouleau* of doubloons" in an iron chest in the bed-chamber, were left undisturbed.

The seemingly causeless and brutal murder of an inoffensive old man, in a fine house in the center of the town, made a tremendous and painful impression upon the folk of Salem. The usual idea got about: that nobody's life was safe. Business became brisk in sword-canes, dirks, cutlasses, and fire-arms; dealers in watch-dogs could not supply the demand; and the continuous sound of hammering indicated that householders were having extra bars and bolts put on their doors and windows. Captain White's funeral was celebrated with impressive ceremony, because of the deep damnation of his taking off. Among the afflicted relatives was his nephew, the Hon. Stephen White, one of the principal heirs. Others present included some connections by marriage, one of whom was a young ship-master named Joseph J. Knapp, Jr., whose wife was the grand-niece of the late Captain White. It was the young Mrs. Knapp whom Mrs. Beckford had been visiting in Wenham, the night of the murder. Mr. Knapp, a well-dressed gentleman of respectable and sorrowing demeanor, had watched for one night beside the dead body of his wife's great-uncle; he now followed the hearse as one of the chief mourners. He had been on familiar terms with the old man, and was frequently at the house on Essex Street.

To discover the wicked man who could have committed this unexplained murder, a public meeting was called, and twenty-seven citizens were chosen to form a Committee of Vigilance. These met every night, and doubtless found much to talk about. For nearly three weeks, however, their talk led nowhere at all. Then something happened which suggested that the world was being made unsafe for the family and connections of Captain White. Joseph J. Knapp, Jr., and his younger brother, John Francis Knapp, appeared before the Committee, and told a stirring tale of an attack made upon them by night, near Wenham Pond (then a famous source of ice). Three ruffians had held them up, as they drove home in a chaise, and Salem nearly had another tragedy. One of the rascals wore a sailor's jacket, he had two black smudges on his face resembling whiskers, and he carried an ivory-handled dirk; another was very "tall and square," he had "stout whiskers," apparently false. These and other corroborative details gave much artistic verisimilitude to the narrative. Except still further to alarm the Committee—and possibly to give a fresh spurt to the sale of cutlasses and watch-dogs—the nocturnal adventure of the brothers Knapp did nothing to clear the original mystery.

After another delay of some weeks, light began to dawn from an unexpected quarter: a jail in New Bedford. A shoplifter, there in confinement, expressed a desire to talk about the Salem crime; he was brought "in chains" and gave testimony before the Grand Jury. It resulted in the arrest of some former associates of his: a Richard Crowninshield, Jr., of Danvers, together with his brother, George. The shop-lifter averred that he had often heard Richard say that he intended to kill Captain White. Crowninshield, so writes a Salem author, had never been convicted of any offense, but was suspected of several "heinous robberies." He was "of dark and reserved deportment, temperate and wicked, daring and wary, subtle and obdurate, of great adroitness, boldness, and self-command. He had for several years frequented the haunts of vice in Salem; and though he was often spoken of as a dangerous man, his person was known to few, for he never walked the streets by daylight. Among his few associates he was a leader and a despot." So says the Salem writer, the Hon. Benjamin Merrill, from whom I learn, for the first time, that there were ever haunts of vice in that city. I have recently read a contemporary biographical sketch of Crowninshield; it paints him in many colors—all somber—and endows him with the characteristics of Peck's Bad Boy, and of Milton's Satan, of Wild Bill Hickok and of Don Juan. His was, indeed, a reprehensible character, but that his versatility in wickedness was so wide, there must be doubts. The pamphleteers of 1830 were the ancestors of the yellow journalists of today. Crowninshield is represented, in a picture reproduced with this article, at his moment of greatest infamy. So far as I know, he has one remarkable distinction; he is the only man who ever committed murder in a frock coat and high hat: a peculiarity of costume which makes it clear that if the White case were put into motion pictures, the rôle of Crowninshield should be enacted by Mr. Raymond Griffith.

When clues began to develop, they fell like snow-flakes. Captain Joseph J. Knapp, Sr., father of the young men who had so fortunately escaped the bandits of Wenham Pond, now received a peculiar, blackmailing letter from one "Charles Grant" of Belfast, Maine. The writer hinted that Captain Knapp had been in some discreditable enterprise, and made threats of disclosures if a thousand dollars were not paid over. The Captain, to whom the letter was meaningless, showed it to his son, Nathaniel Phippen Knapp, who found it equally obscure. The two then rode over to Wenham, and handed it to Captain Knapp's other sons—Joseph J., Jr., and John Francis. The son who was his father's namesake—and for whom the letter from Belfast was really intended—wove another strand in the noose which was awaiting him, by advising his father to give the letter to the Vigilance Committee! This suggestion the elder Knapp promptly and innocently obeyed. Meanwhile the younger Joseph Knapp, with extraordinary fatuity, mailed two letters—one of them to the Committee. It purported to come from "Grant," and it confessed to having done the murder at the instigation of Stephen White.

"Grant" of Belfast proved to be an ex-convict named Palmer. He was arrested in Maine, whereupon he disclosed his knowledge of a conspiracy on the part of Joseph Knapp, Jr., and Francis Knapp, to hire Crowninshield for $1000 to kill Captain White. These two Knapps—others of the family were innocent of all knowledge of the plot—were promptly arrested, and three days later Joseph made a full confession to a clergyman. His interest in the death of Captain White lay in his hope that his mother-in-law, if the Captain died intestate, would inherit nearly $200,000. He had stolen a will of the Captain's—a will by which Mrs. Beckford received only a small legacy—and burned it after the murder. He had arranged for Mrs. Beckford's absence, and had unlocked the window through which the assassin entered. His brother Francis was present in Brown Street, at the rear of the Captain's house, on the night of the murder, and was recognized by one or two people, as he hovered in the vicinity, in his "camblet" cloak. Crowninshield had never received the money promised him by the Knapps, but only one hundred five-franc pieces. Joseph made numerous blunders: he was mistaken in thinking that his mother-in-law would receive half her uncle's property if he died without a will; he was mistaken in the will which he stole, as it was not the last and true testament; and he blundered unbelievably in advising his father to give the Grant letter to the Salem Vigilance Committee.

WHEN the Knapps were arrested, and when Palmer was brought to the Salem jail, Richard Crowninshield saw that the game was played out. He wrote contrite letters to his father and brother, and hanged himself in his cell, by means of two handkerchiefs. The State was now in a quandary. According to the Massachusetts law at that time, an accessory in a murder could not be tried until the principal was convicted. And the actual murderer, Crowninshield, was dead. Francis Knapp was therefore put on trial as the principal, in the second degree—that is, as an aider and abettor to the murderer; while Joseph Knapp and George Crowninshield awaited trial as accessories. Anticipating difficulty, the State called in, to assist in the prosecution, the greatest lawyer of the day, Daniel Webster. It was his task to prove that Francis Knapp was not only present at the murder, in a legal sense, but that he was there to aid and abet in the deed. Joseph Knapp had been promised immunity if he would appear as State's Evidence, and repeat in Court the confession which he had made to the clergyman in jail. He now made his final blunder, and refused to testify, but stood mute in Court, thereby placing the noose irrevocably around his own neck and his brother's. He may have acted from a noble motive that would not allow him to swear his brother's life away; but he was mistaken, for if he had testified neither could have been convicted. He had the protection of the State's promise; while his testimony (which the State would have to accept) would have shown that Francis was in Brown Street that night merely as a spectator, not as a helper. Crowninshield had told him to go home; he had done so, but had returned to the scene. And as an accessory, not as a principal, he could not even be tried.

Despite all Webster's ability in argument and in examination of witnesses, the jury disagreed. Francis Knapp was promptly put upon trial again, and at the close Webster delivered the speech in which occurs the famous description of the murder:

"Deep sleep had fallen on the destined victim, and on all beneath his roof. A healthful old man, to whom sleep was sweet, the first sound slumbers of the night held him in their soft but strong embrace. The assassin enters, through the window already prepared, into an unoccupied apartment. With noiseless foot he paces the lonely hall, half lighted by the moon; he winds up the ascent of the stairs, and reaches the door of the chamber. Of this, he moves the lock, by soft and continued pressure, till it turns on its hinges without noise; and he enters, and beholds his victim before him. The room is uncommonly open to the admission of light. The face of the innocent sleeper is turned from the

JEANNE EAGELS

After four years of Rain *she will soon appear in a new play,* The Garden of Eden

Steichen

murderer, and the beams of the moon, resting on the gray locks of his aged temple, show him where to strike. The fatal blow is given! and the victim passes, without a struggle or a motion, from the repose of sleep to the repose of death!"

Webster closed this part of his speech with the remark that when the murderer's conscience begins to torture him, the crime "must be confessed, it will be confessed; there is no refuge from confession but suicide, and suicide is confession."

THE great advocate's mastery of the twelve men in the jury box won the verdict and the prisoner was found guilty. From the point of view of technical procedure, the conviction was perhaps a judicial blunder, but of its justice, and of the verdict in the trial which followed, there is no doubt. The Knapps were guilty, and their escape would have been a scandal. Francis, who was barely twenty, was hanged on September 28, in the presence of three or four thousand spectators. The *Salem*

Register recorded its satisfaction that "a very small proportion of these were inhabitants of the town."

Joseph Knapp, Jr., was tried five weeks later. His confessions in jail, excluded at the trial of his brother, were essential. Webster again appeared, and the defense fought an impossible battle. At the other trial the State had to convince the jury that Francis Knapp was present in Brown Street not merely as a curious spectator, but as one actually giving assistance. At the trial of Joseph, the task of the prosecutor was to convince the Court of the admissibility of the prisoner's confessions. This was done, and the case was over. Joseph was found guilty and hanged on the last day of the year.

George Crowninshield, the murderer's brother, though accused, in Joseph Knapp's confession, of a guilty knowledge of the plot, proved an alibi on the night of the murder, and was acquitted on his trial. Mr. Webster, by the way, did not appear.

On the other hand, some ten or twenty

years after the murder, a wandering exhibitor of a group of wax figures did a lively business on Boston Common. He showed in a tent, for the fee of ten cents, the ghastly form of Captain White, lying in bed, and weltering in his gore. Over him, with knife raised, and with menacing face held close to the dead man, leaned the sinister figure of "Crowninshield, the hired assassin." A gentleman who had paid his admission fell into conversation with the showman. The latter admitted that business was good.

"You see," said he, "lots of folks want to see the figgers, and some of them pays again and goes in twice."

"You have to find board and lodging, of course," suggested the visitor.

"Victuals, yes," said the proprietor. "But lodging—well, the nights are warm and pleasant now here on the Common, and I don't have to go nowheres. I lets Crowninshield stay where he stands, you see, and I just takes the Captain out of bed, and gets in, in his place!"

A Western Disunion

A Tragedy Occurring among the Smarter Weekend Set of Long Island

GEOFFREY KERR

Port Washington Long Island
John Rushing
   III East Eightieth Street New York
CAN YOU COME DOWN ON THE FOURTH AND
SPEND THE WEEKEND
              CLARA BAURE

Port Washington Long Island
Miss Mildred Loveleigh
   Mt Kisco New York
CAN YOU COME DOWN ON THE FOURTH AND
SPEND THE WEEKEND JACK RUSHING IS COMING
              CLARA BAURE

Mt Kisco N Y
Mrs Edmund Baure
   Port Washington Long Island
EVER SO MANY THANKS YES WOULD LOVE TO
      MILDRED LOVELEIGH

New York N Y
Mrs Edmund Baure
   Port Washington Long Island
VERY SORRY IMPOSSIBLE WOULD HAVE ADORED
IT BUT AM SPENDING THAT WEEKEND WITH THE
GAYS AT WESTBURY MANY THANKS FOR ASKING
ME
         JACK RUSHING

New York N Y
Sydney Gay
   Westbury Long Island
HAVE JUST REFUSED PERFECTLY TERRIBLE INVI-
TATION FOR WEEKEND AFTER NEXT SAYING I
AM SPENDING IT WITH YOU MAY I DO SO
           JACK

Westbury Long Island
John Rushing
   III East Eightieth Street New York
YES OF COURSE
         SYDNEY

Port Washington Long Island
Bertram Gest-Atwill
   New York Club New York
CAN YOU COME DOWN ON THE FOURTH AND
SPEND THE WEEKEND
            CLARA BAURE

New York N Y
Mrs Edmund Baure
   Port Washington Long Island
YES DELIGHTED
       BERTRAM GEST-ATWILL

Mt Kisco N Y
John Rushing
   III East Eightieth Street New York
SO GLAD YOU ARE GOING TO THE BAURES TOO
NEXT WEEKEND WE OUGHT TO HAVE SOME FUN
LOVE
         MILDRED

New York N Y
Miss Mildred Loveleigh
   Mt Kisco New York
WHY DIDNT THOSE BLITHERING IDIOTS TELL ME
YOU WERE GOING TO BE THERE I REFUSED THEIR
INVITATION AND AM GOING TO THE GAYS AINT
LIFE TRAGIC LOVE
         JACK

Mt Kisco N Y
John Rushing
   III East Eightieth Street New York
THINGS HAVE GOT TO BE FIXED LOVE
         MILDRED

New York N Y
Mrs Edmund Baure
   Port Washington Long Island
MY DATE WITH THE GAYS HAS FALLEN THROUGH
COULD I POSSIBLY RECONSIDER MY REFUSAL OF
YOUR INVITATION
         JACK RUSHING

Port Washington Long Island
John Rushing
   III East Eightieth Street New York
BERTRAM GEST-ATWILL IS COMING DOWN SO I
AM AFRAID WE HAVE NO ROOM
         CLARA BAURE

New York N Y
Bertram Gest-Atwill
   New York Club New York
DO YOU HAVE TO GO TO THE BAURES THIS
WEEKEND
         JACK RUSHING

New York N Y
John Rushing
   III East Eightieth Street New York
ALAS YES THEY ARE THE ONLY PEOPLE WHO
HAVE ASKED ME
       BERTRAM GEST-ATWILL

New York N Y
Bertram Gest-Atwill
   New York Club New York
IF YOU GET A BETTER INVITE WILL YOU ACCEPT
IT AND NOT GO TO THE BAURES
         JACK RUSHING

New York N Y
John Rushing
   III East Eightieth Street New York
NATURALLY
       BERTRAM GEST-ATWILL

New York N Y
Sydney Gay
   Westbury Long Island
FIND I CANNOT MAKE NEXT WEEKEND AFTER
ALL SO SORRY BUT BERTRAM GEST-ATWILL IS FREE
SO HOW ABOUT HAVING HIM INSTEAD
         JACK

Westbury Long Island
John Rushing
   III East Eightieth Street New York
I DONT LIKE HIM
        SYDNEY

New York N Y
Sydney Gay
   Westbury Long Island
NOR DO I BUT COULDNT YOU PUT UP WITH HIM
THIS ONCE
         JACK

Westbury Long Island
John Rushing
   III East Eightieth Street New York
WHY SHOULD I MARGARET DOESNT LIKE HIM
EITHER
        SYDNEY

New York N Y
Sydney Gay
   Westbury Long Island
NOBODY LIKES HIM BUT PLEASE AS SPECIAL
FAVOR ASK HIM DOWN THIS WEEKEND
         JACK

Westbury Long Island
John Rushing
   III East Eightieth Street New York
DONT BE A FOOL HE MIGHT COME
        SYDNEY

New York N Y
Sydney Gay
   Westbury Long Island
IT MAY CHANGE WHOLE COURSE OF MY LIFE
TOO COMPLICATED TO EXPLAIN BY WIRE BUT
REMEMBER YOUR OWN YOUTH AND OUR AN-
CIENT FRIENDSHIP
         JACK

Westbury Long Island

John Rushing
   III East Eightieth Street New York
THE SACRIFICE SHALL BE MADE WE ARE WIRING
LITTLE BERTIE
                    SYDNEY

New York N Y

Sydney Gay
   Westbury Long Island
THANKS OLD PAL
              JACK

Westbury Long Island

Bertram Gest-Atwill
   New York Club New York
WONT YOU COME DOWN AND SPEND THIS NEXT
WEEKEND WITH US SYDNEY AND I BOTH HOPE
YOU CAN
            MARGARET GAY

New York N Y

Mrs Sydney Gay
   Westbury Long Island
THANKS YES DELIGHTED
        BERTRAM GEST-ATWILL

New York N Y

Mrs Edmund Baure
   Port Washington Long Island
REGRET EXCEEDINGLY THAT I WILL BE UNABLE
TO COME DOWN THIS WEEKEND AFTER ALL I
HAVE TO ATTEND A FUNERAL IN CHICAGO HOPE
YOU WILL UNDERSTAND
        BERTRAM GEST-ATWILL

Port Washington Long Island

John Rushing
   III East Eightieth Street New York
BERTRAM GEST-ATWILL CANT COME AFTER ALL
ARE YOU STILL FREE
           CLARA BAURE

New York N Y

Mrs Edmund Baure
   Port Washington Long Island
NEVER FREER MANY THANKS WILL DRIVE DOWN
FRIDAY AFTERNOON
        JACK RUSHING

Mt Kisco N Y

Mrs Sydney Gay
   Westbury Long Island
COULD I POSSIBLY COME TO YOU FOR THIS
WEEKEND
          MILDRED

Westbury Long Island

Miss Mildred Loveleigh
   Mt Kisco New York
YES DEAR OF COURSE COME ANY TIME
        MARGARET GAY

Mt Kisco N Y

Mrs Edmund Baure
   Port Washington Long Island
DEAR CLARA AN UNCLE AND AUNT ARE
SUDDENLY ARRIVING FROM CALIFORNIA
SATURDAY AND I HAVE TO BE WITH THEM SO
I CANNOT COME DOWN PLEASE FORGIVE ME
BITTERLY DISAPPOINTED
        MILDRED LOVELEIGH

Mt Kisco N Y

John Rushing
   III East Eightieth Street New York
HAVE GOT OUT OF MY WEEKEND WITH THE
BAURES AND AM COMING TO THE GAYS ISNT
THAT SPLENDID LOVE
          MILDRED

New York N Y

Miss Mildred Loveleigh
   Mt Kisco New York
HAVE GOT OUT OF MY WEEKEND WITH THE
GAYS AND AM COMING TO THE BAURES ISNT
THAT SPLENDID LOVE
          JACK

Mt Kisco N Y

John Rushing
   III East Eightieth Street New York
THIS IS TERRIBLE WHAT ARE WE TO DO
          MILDRED

New York N Y

Miss Mildred Loveleigh
   Mt Kisco New York
DONT WORRY LET YOUR DATE WITH THE GAYS
STAND I WILL CHANGE MINE
          JACK

New York N Y

Mrs Edmund Baure
   Port Washington Long Island
TERRIBLY SORRY BUT SUDDEN EMERGENCY HAS
ARISEN MAKING IT IMPOSSIBLE FOR ME TO
COME DOWN FOR THIS WEEKEND TERRIBLY
SORRY TO GIVE YOU SUCH SHORT NOTICE AND
TERRIBLY SORRY NOT TO SEE YOU PLEASE
FORGIVE ME TERRIBLY SORRY
        JACK RUSHING

New York N Y

Sydney Gay
   Westbury Long Island
MAY I COME TO YOU THIS WEEKEND AFTER ALL
          JACK

Westbury Long Island

John Rushing
   III East Eightieth Street New York
HAIR TURNING GRAY COME OR NOT AS YOU
LIKE BUT FOR LOVE OF PETE DECIDE
          SYDNEY

New York N Y

Miss Mildred Loveleigh
   Mt Kisco New York
WILL PICK YOU UP IN THE CAR FRIDAY
AFTERNOON AND WE CAN DRIVE DOWN TO
WESTBURY TOGETHER LOVE
          JACK

Mt Kisco N Y

John Rushing
   III East Eightieth Street New York
SPLENDID LOVE
          MILDRED

New York N Y

Sydney Gay
   Westbury Long Island
MILDRED AND I WILL DRIVE DOWN TOGETHER
FRIDAY AFTERNOON
          JACK

New York N Y

Sydney Gay
   Westbury Long Island
ARRIVING IN TIME FOR LUNCH SATURDAY
        BERTRAM GEST-ATWILL

Port Washington Long Island

Mrs Sydney Gay
   Westbury Long Island
CAN YOU AND SYDNEY COME OVER TO LUNCH
SUNDAY
          CLARA BAURE

Westbury Long Island

Mrs Edmund Baure
   Port Washington Long Island
MILDRED LOVELEIGH JACK RUSHING AND
BERTRAM GEST-ATWILL WILL BE STOPPING HERE
SO WHY DONT YOU COME OVER TO US
          MARGARET GAY

Port Washington Long Island

Mrs Sydney Gay
   Westbury Long Island
THANK YOU WE WILL IT OUGHT TO BE A
WONDERFUL PARTY
          CLARA BAURE

EDITORIAL NOTE: It was!

Rudolph Valentino

The Career of the Dead Actor Which Ended Dramatically at Thirty-One

JIM TULLY

VALENTINO, the Italian screen lover, was a graduate of the Royal Academy of Agriculture. His full name was Rudolpho Raffaele Pierre Filibert Guglielmi di Valinetina d'Antonguolla. His mother was the daughter of a Parisian doctor. His father was sometime captain of cavalry in the Italian army. He was later a veterinary surgeon.

The young film player was that rare thing in Hollywood—an actor with emotional force and brains. Success in his profession gave him the poise of the cultivated continental. He was well grounded in the arts and literatures of his native Europe.

Innately honest, he would, I think, if left to himself, have been above the cheap pretenses of his accidental calling. Valentino, like most foreign screen personalities of the first class, was superior to his American contemporaries. The American director or player does not survive the chromo art stage of his childhood. Griffith is an example. De Mille is a twig from another branch,

Victor Seastrom, the great Swedish director, von Stroheim, Emil Jannings, Pola Negri, Nazimova, George Fitzmaurice and Matt Moore are examples of people in the

film business born on foreign soil who can talk of something besides gas-lit opera houses on narrow-gauge railroads.

Valentino was married twice. Both sacraments were failures. The first girl was the mistake of a youth who danced for a living. She was one of the many zeros in the arithmetic of life. Valentino had a great deal of trouble in erasing her.

HIS second wife, Winifred Hudnut, was the daughter of the well-advertised perfumer. A member of a Russian ballet, she danced under the name of Natacha Rambova.

While living with her husband in Hollywood Miss Hudnut became so dictatorial that men associated with Valentino in the making of films did not wish to have her about. It was said that a clause in one of the Italian's contracts forbade her on the set.

Miss Hudnut had that superficial culture which led her to talk of a "career" as though it were something not of this earth. A career is generally ephemeral to those who talk too much about it. Valentino wanted a home. They agreed to disagree.

It would seem that nearly all screen people spring from the Salvation Army

bread line. Valentino was no exception. He arrived penniless in America during the year 1913. Being an agriculturist, he dreamed at the time of a great farm in the West. He secured a position doing landscape work on the estate of Cornelius Bliss, Jr. He was discharged before any of the women saw him. He then worked a month for the New York Park Department. Discharged again.

With no money, and a slight knowledge of English, he was forced out of one lodging house after another. During that winter he touched all the shores of destitution with hunger for a comrade.

To keep alive, he cleaned the brass railings in front of the ugly box-like homes of the *nouveaux riches*. He had learned how to dance in Italy, but it had not occurred to him that he might make a living with his feet in cultured New York.

Valentino was an intense individual. And one suffers little on the ragged edges of life without possessing intensity. A Bernhardt who was not intense would be just an ordinary woman.

For a year in New York Valentino was a menial of sorts. It is hard to imagine it now. A fellow in the cellar of fortune is not the same person who views the

Valentino in The Sheik, *his most famous role*

scenery from the heights. But this is certain—Valentino was not cast in an ordinary mold. A fire burned in him. That it would have blazed him to even greater success at a later period of his life there is no doubt. He was really an actor. He had character.

Many life-hungry women have literally been turned out of theatres in which Valentino appeared on the screen. Half the answer of this phenomenon may be seen in their own warped lives. Many of them were possibly club-women. That they saw in Valentino that which their tired hearts craved is not, to me, an evidence of bad taste. They might have traveled a longer road and loved the shadow of a lesser man.

It had been said in Hollywood that, once a waiter's helper, he was ashamed of it. One day, feeling he was impulsively off his guard, I asked him . . .

"Is it true that you were a bus-boy in New York?"

His heavy hand hit the table.

"No, by God, it's not true—but if I had been I'd be damn proud of it."

At this point, Fitzmaurice, the French director who receives seventy-five thousand dollars for each film directed, said, "That's right, Rudy—it's nothing to be ashamed of. I drove a truck in New York."

I ONCE asked Valentino which character he would like best to play on the screen.

"Cesare Borgia," he answered.

Surprised, I watched him closely as he continued.

"It would not be popular, but I want to play it for my very own. Borgia was not the man they say he was. His story was written by his enemies."

Forgetful of an interviewer who might deal with him unkindly, he quoted Machiavelli, Villari, Gregorovius and Sabatini to prove his points.

Thinking of American women I ventured, "But Cesare had a mustache."

"I'd play him with one."

After that first terrible winter in New York when he was unable to find work of any kind, Valentino went in a mood of desperation to the headwaiter of a famous restaurant. He was given a position as a dancer.

Within a year he was Joan Sawyer's dancing partner.

But still—such are the whims of humans —Valentino wanted to become a farmer on a large scale. He felt that he might find his opportunity in the West. With this idea in mind he joined a musical comedy company headed for California. The troupe stranded in San Francisco and the agriculturist-dancer tried to sell bonds for a living.

He failed.

Steichen

This last photograph of Valentino was taken August 6, 1926, shortly before his untimely death in New York

Despondent, a chance meeting with an actor decided his career. The actor suggested that the young dancer try motion pictures. The trouper, with the generosity of his craft, also loaned him money upon which to live a few weeks in Hollywood.

In three months, Valentino was unable to get even the lowest form of screen work —that of an extra player. Emmett Flynn, an ex-bell boy, then, as now, one of the most successful film directors, gave him his first work—at five dollars a day.

It was a start. Flynn later gave him a better part, but the picture was in litigation for some years, and Valentino gained nothing but experience. But that, of course, was important.

Followed in time two leading parts with Mae Murray. Miss Murray's leading men are not supposed to act. They are merely good-looking automatons around which the butterfly woman flies . . . and dances.

Wearily the Italian made the rounds of the studios. He could obtain nothing but mediocre parts until chance threw him across the path of one of the brainiest and most artistic men who ever directed a picture—I refer to Rex Ingram.

He was selected by Ingram to play the part of *Julio* in Ibañez's *Four Horsemen*

of the Apocalypse. The picture finished, the ex-dancer was famous. He had, to speak in the colorful parlance of the film industry, "stolen the picture."

Following this picture he played in *The Conquering Power* and in Nazimova's screen version of *Camille*.

He was next engaged by Famous Players-Lasky, for which firm he appeared in the most popular film he ever made, *The Sheik*. Followed other sex-ridden and ordinary pictures until he was given an opportunity to do real acting in *Blood and Sand*.

A dispute over salary arose with Famous Players-Lasky and he remained off the screen for nearly two years. Students of the industry felt that the long "lay-off" would ruin his career. Being one of the most popular entertainers in the world, he retained his reputation. His return to the screen was a national event in the hearts of many women. His death was to them a poignant tragedy.

The madness to cast Valentino in romantic pictures persisted.

But through all this maze of bad taste Valentino groped. None of it helped him as he wished to be helped.

The last picture of the man who wanted to play Cesare Borgia was *The Son of the Sheik*.

The Ideal Woman

Yessir, That's My Baby! Wherein Several Experts Define the Perfect Female

Vanity Fair, *with other optimists, has always felt that somewhere behind the sad, kaleidoscopic décor of our disillusions, there exists THE PERFECT WOMAN. The notion is a pleasant one; for, though disenchantment may ensue, it frequently wears an aspect of comfortable melancholy; and tragic lovers are notoriously the most engaging. Yet it is a difficult notion, too, for what two men will agree upon the Perfect Woman? In literature, for instance, and in the theatre, heroines range from grave to gay and from pole to pole, so that it is absurd to say of any woman, "Here, and here only, is perfection." So, in their perplexity, the editors of* Vanity Fair *have asked a group of men prominent in literature, art, and the drama to define, each one, his own ideal of the Perfect Woman. We are, therefore, happy to present, dispiriting though it may be to our feminine readers, the results of this symposium of opinions by connoisseurs.*

Charles Chaplin

MR. CHAPLIN'S contribution to the symposium strikes a rather acid note at times, for one so versed in the poignancy of simple sorrow. He writes:

1. When in my company, she never admires other men.
2. If I am obliged to leave her in order to keep another engagement, her disappointment is always keen enough to be flattering to me, but never quite keen enough to keep me from going where I am going.
3. Her diamond bracelets never need cleaning.
4. Her shoulders are never shiny.
5. She never takes advantage of a voluptuous situation to narrow her eyes.
6. She always reads all of the Sunday papers (the funny sheet first) but, having read them, she refolds them neatly and leaves them as they were.
7. She knows the words of no popular dance music, or, if she does, never sings them in my ear when dancing.
8. She uses only a faint *eau de toilette* during the day, but sprays herself plentifully with *L'Heure Bleue* upon retiring.
9. I am not exactly in love with her, but
10. She is entirely in love with me.

THE IDEAL WOMAN—400 B.C.

Ring Lardner

CAN it be that Mr. Lardner, the famous humorist, is not taking this symposium seriously? *Vanity Fair*'s eyebrows rise well into its hair at this suspicion; but our contributor's fourth requirement may possibly mitigate that failing on our part.

1. Lockjaw.
2. Hereditary obesity.
3. Shortness of breath.
4. Falling arches.
5. Mechanical Engineering.
6. Draftsmanship.
7. Absolutely Fireproof.
8. Day and Night elevator service.
9. Laundry sent out before 8:30 A.M. will be returned the same day.
10. Please report to the management any incivility on the part of employees.

George Jean Nathan

AND HERE is a bachelor, and a critic, who also prefers, with a languid wave of the hand, to sit, neatly tailored and fairly lush with tolerance, upon a not too rustic fence. An engaging picture! Herr Nathan, then, having left everything abundantly to his *confrères,* is wandering down dim vistas on the wings of ennui, in search of an idyll which may wholeheartedly occupy his attention. He goes on to say:

"The Perfect Woman? I leave the description of her beauty to Cabell, of her charm to Hergesheimer, of her humor to Huxley, of her manner to Anatole France, of her

heart to Willa Cather, of her voice to Synge, of her age to Max Beerbohm, of her philosophy to Hermann Bahr, of her sensitiveness to Chesterton, and of her innocence to Sacha Guitry. Then, *Vanity Fair,* you will have the Ideal Woman you are seeking."

Rudolph Valentino

TO THOSE of us who have watched the cinema screens grow mellow with Mr. Valentino's peculiar charm, it seems that he has depicted a rather grave creature for his ideal woman. Here is his list of the ten attributes necessary for the Perfect Woman:

1. Fidelity.
2. The recognition of the supreme importance of love.
3. Intelligence.
4. Beauty.
5. A sense of humor.
6. Sincerity.
7. An appreciation of good food.
8. A serious interest in some art, trade, or hobby.
9. An old-fashioned and whole-hearted acceptance of monogamy.
10. Courage.

Florenz Ziegfeld

IT IS estimated—with this magazine's customary conservatism—that the publication of the following requirements will produce 54,000 yards of tape-measure in American homes and 9,000 girls, all of whom will be found palpitating upon the doorstep of Mr. Ziegfeld's New Amsterdam Theatre before November first. Mr. Ziegfeld says that the ideal woman should average:

Height—5 ft., 5½ inches
Weight—117 lbs.
Foot size—5
Height—7½ times length of the head
Head—4 times length of the nose
Arms—hanging straight, ¾ length of body

He goes on: "Of course there are still men who favor girls four feet two inches high; a few who prefer the Amazon. They are decreasing. Most of the girls in the *Follies* range in weight from ninety-five to one hundred and ten pounds, a few up to one hundred and thirty-five, and occasionally one hundred and forty. A girl weighing 100 to 105 pounds has ten more chances of marriage than the 135-pounder, and twenty-five more chances than the 150. The Dresden-china girl, petite, piquant, light on her feet, has a thousand chances against the 160-pound weight.

"She must have:

1. Native refinement. Where this exists, education is not necessary.
2. Poise—an ability to walk, stand and manage herself with easy dignity. To modulate her voice, moods and movement with that sustained restraint which is characteristic of breeding and distinction.
3. She must have health, be wholesome and *look* so.
4. She must have strength, be vigorous, not flabby, and she must have reserve force.
5. She must have symmetry. Proportion is inseparable from beauty.
6. She must have spirit; that is, a definite animation indicative of personal power, resources and adaptability. Above all other women in the world, the American girl is spirited.
7. She must have style, know how to wear clothes—not so much expensive clothes, but any garments that fit her resources and are appropriate to her type.
8. She must appeal to both sexes—for complete beauty and personal magnetism—a great stage requirement—charm and compel both men and women.
9. She must have femininity, an overworked term, but indicative of loveliness, grace and imagination.
10. She must have the quality of glory —that elusive something as definite yet intangible as the perfume of flowers."

Arnold Genthe

"MERE facial beauty—no matter how perfect the symmetry of features—is of only minor importance if it is not illumined by a mobile, radiant spirit, without which surface-beauty remains dull. Her strong and slender hands will be as expressive as her face. She will not be a slave to fads and fashions, but wear whatever suits her individual taste; a becoming hat or dress may last longer with her than one season. If she bobs her hair, it will not be for fashion's sake, but because it is less of a burden for the charming contour of her head. A fine sense of humor, based on a just perception of values, will help her avoid the usual emotional difficulties; she will never indulge in any form of jealousy, nor in violent outbursts of temper. She will prefer an animated talk with intelligent people to the gossip of a woman's luncheon. Finally, an eager desire to understand, without preju-

dice and prudery, what is going on in the world will make her a sympathetic judge in every phase of life."

Al Jolson

HERE is an essay vibrant with all the pathos of Mr. Jolson's celebrated cantatas. One feels, quivering through its delicate web of words, the yearning, the accurate nostalgia which has made Al Jolson probably the most melancholy and yet exciting singer upon the American stage:

"The physical attributes of my ideal woman don't interest me. For instance, she may weigh four hundred pounds, if her heart is of gold. She may have a mouth like a torn pocket, if from it come kind words. What good is the softest hand if it clasps a rolling-pin? Where, when you are hungry, is the lure of a shapely leg—unless it be that of a turkey?

"Therefore speaking as a husband, my ideal woman must have:

1. The gift of stretching a can of sardines into a banquet.
2. A thorough dislike of all actors— save one.
3. An appreciation of the fact that, in all the important affairs of life, and in the trivial ones as well, I am, for some curious reason, invariably *RIGHT*.
4. A disinclination to be taken out— unless she had bid 'one club.'
5. A hearty laugh for all my jokes, including the very old ones.
6. A loathing for cross-word puzzles.
7. An inability to block a straight left.
8. Complete ignorance of the existence of the Lucy Stone League.
9. A million dollars.
10. A cough."

THE IDEAL WOMAN—1926 A.D.

Franklin P. Adams

She must be fond, she must be fair;
She must have eyes and lips and hair;
She must be firm as any stone,
And softer than a flower full-blown.
She must be weak, she must be brave,
And varying as the ocean's wave.
She must be witty and alive;
She must have finer traits than I've.
And—not without enthusiasm—
All these here qualities—she has 'em.

Lee Shubert

NUMBER fourteen on the following list of qualifications for the ideal woman will explain to the inquiring playgoer the presence of all those intellectual, old-fashioned girls in *The Great Temptations* at the Winter Garden. Listen to Mr. Shubert:

"In a career of theatrical production that has extended over many years it has been my good fortune to have known and admired thousands of beautiful women, many of whom approached, if they did not attain, perfection. With this knowledge and experience as a background it is impossible—for me at least—to limit the perfect woman to ten points. No less than fourteen points are necessary if one is to do justice to so great an ideal. It is not an easy task.

1. She must be tall but—I hasten to add—not too tall.
2. She must be brunette—the dark, splendid beauty of, let us say, Maxine Elliott.
3. She must have an interesting face— a face of mobility and expression.
4. She must be agreeable.
5. She must have a beautiful figure.
6. She must be intelligent.
7. She must be intellectual, but not a *poseuse* or a *précieuse*.
8. She must be witty but not sarcastic; able to see a joke but, more important, take one.
9. She must be calm, but not phlegmatic.
10. She must be tolerant, but never indifferent.
11. She must be charming, and by that I mean she must possess graciousness of manner as well as that overworked symbol of the theatre—personality.
12. She must be able to adapt herself to her environment and to her associates.
13. She must possess good taste in her clothes, in the cultivation of her mind, in her conformity to the material aspects of civilization.
14. She must reverence the best traditions: that is, she must not be afraid of being *thought* old-fashioned.

Poems of Youth and Age

THEODORE DREISER

The Far Country

Lo,
I will go me aside
Into the Land of Youth,
The Land of Promise,
By the shores of the Sea of Wonder,
At the feet of the Mountains of Ambition,
And there will I dream
That I have youth,
And all the whips of want
And necessity—
Hunger,
And that food would make me whole;
Loneliness of heart,
And that love would heal it;
Poverty,
And that riches
Would supply my direst needs;
Inconsequence,
And that fame would repair
The indifference
Of men.

*   *   *

Yet never, never, never,
Would I part from them more.
Oh, never!
Neither from hunger,
Nor poverty,
Nor inconsequence,
Nor loneliness of heart.
Oh, never.

*   *   *

Lest satiety come
And the fullness of the years
That is the end of youth
And dreams,
And that
Never, never, never,
Should I again know youth
Or hunger,
Or hope,
Or the wonder,
And the fulfillment
Of dreams.

Youth

Proud of my warm flesh
That is firm
And perfectly molded,
Proud of the make and fashion of my being
That I did not make
And cannot retain.
Proud of my lightness,
My little feet—
The light, sure feet of the young
That touch the grass so sportively.
Proud to show the coy spirits of my youth
And beauty,
That can
At any moment
Make a gay sun to shine
In the dim hearts of those,
Who find my beauty
A need.

Little Moonlight Things

Little moonlight things of song—
Little pools of dream and beauty in youth
    and maidenhood.
Sweet, sweet minor ballads and arias.

*   *   *

A realm between a mansion and river—
An ever-blue sky and a rare garden—
Great, cool patches of wooded beauty—
A fountain and a statue—
Moss roses and stone benches—
Magnolia trees, crepe myrtle and fronds of
    palms—
The flash of a scarlet wing in a thicket of
    jasmine.
And then—
    Men and women, perfect, perfect.
    And love that never, never dies.

*   *   *

Little pools of dream in youth and maiden-
    hood.
Little moonlight things of song.
Sweet, sweet minor ballads and arias.

Where?

Whither the old passions?
The fire? The zest?
I had them in my youth,
After the shadowland of childhood
Through which I darkly stumbled,
Feeling an uncertain way,
And adolescence,

With its passions
And its dreams—
(I had them);
Life reared itself aloft
To craggy, glistening eminences,
Veritable peaks of thought,
Himalayas of character,
Splendid mounting roads
Of dream
That seemed to lead to a solution.
My tongue was wet with hunger,
My eyes agleam.
But now, in age,
As in that early shadowland of youth
By which I came,
I seem to sink—and sink—
Back into the shadows now
(And as in childhood, blunder),
From which but yesterday I came.
Into that shadowland of fancy
My soul, as then,
Applies itself to phantasy.
It dreams of blending things,
As in the old, beginning way.
The thick, warm ways of shadow—
It sleeps long sleeps,
Oh, long, long sleeps,
And dreams sweet dreams
That are half sleeps.

*   *   *

Whither the brief passions?
The fire? The zest?
The knowledge?
Whither have sunk
The Himalayas of character,
The peaks of thought?

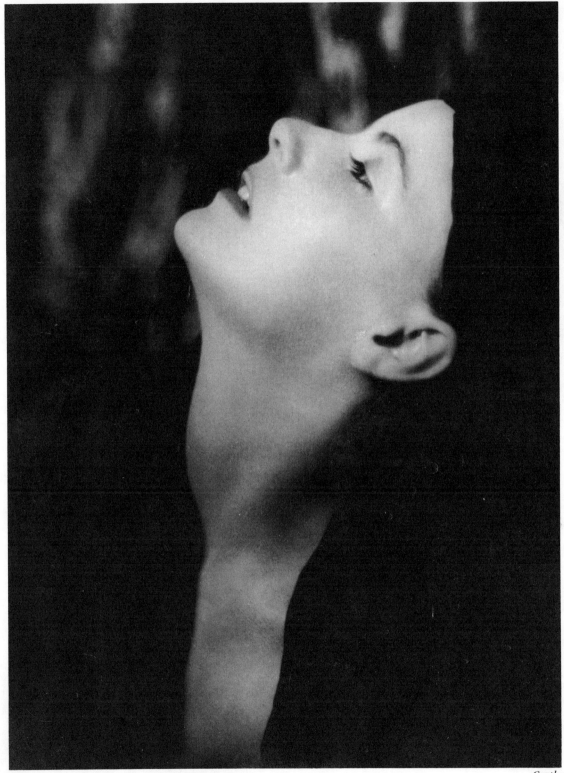

Genthe

GRETA GARBO

Visiting screen star. A study of the young Swedish actress who has recently completed Ibañez's The Torrent

Steichen

JACK DEMPSEY

For seven years the world's heavyweight champion

Born at Manassa, Colorado, in 1895, the incomparable William Harrison ("Jack") Dempsey was, at various times, a brakeman, a miner, and a hobo. And he learned in his youth to fight with surpassing speed and power. He has fought seventy-seven professional battles, no less than forty-seven of which he won by knock-outs. He wins his fights by means of furious and tigerish attacks, onslaughts that brook no sparring for openings. It was his unrelenting and killing attack which, in 1919 at Toledo, overwhelmed Jess Willard, then champion. And it was this same fury which enabled him to knock out Georges Carpentier at Jersey City in 1921, and Luis Angel Firpo at the Polo Grounds in 1923.

GENE TUNNEY

Champion boxer of the A.E.F.

James Joseph ("Gene") Tunney was born in New York, on May 25, 1898. Beginning life as a truck-driver he may have found that there was need in that occupation for good fighting qualities, but it was not until he entered the Marines, in '17, that he discovered his amazing prowess as a fighter. He soon became the undisputed champion of the American Military Forces in Europe. At the close of the war he became a professional pugilist and in 1922 won the American Light-Heavyweight Championship from Battling Levinsky. He has fought sixty ring battles—half of them knock-outs. In recent years he has put on twenty pounds, and is now a full-fledged heavyweight.

Steichen

Sheeler

HELEN WILLS

A girl of the Golden West

The pretty California tennis star has come out of retirement to win for America, for the first time in twenty years, the British Amateur Championship at Wimbledon.

Nominated for the Hall of Fame: 1926

Pach

Wide World

GEORGE F. BAKER *(left)*

Because he is, at eighty-six, the acknowledged dean of American financiers; because he is a most discerning and generous patron of the fine arts; and finally because he is celebrating his seventeenth year as Chairman of the First National Bank of New York.

VINCENT YOUMANS

Because, with *Two Little Girls in Blue* and *Wildflower,* on which he was a collaborator, to begin with, he has in the short space of three years, and at the age of twenty-six, become one of our most popular musical-comedy composers; and because he wrote *No, No, Nanette.*

IVAN MEŠTROVIĆ *(left)*

Because he is generally estimated the most notable of Central European sculptors; because, having begun life as a shepherd boy in Serbia, he finds himself, in middle age, a famous figure in all the capitals of the world; because three imposing exhibits of his work have been seen in New York; but chiefly because there is in his sculpture no suspicion of derivation.

GEORGE KELLY *(left)*

Because he is a brother of Walter C. Kelly, known in vaudeville as "The Virginia Judge," and "Jack" Kelly, the single-scull rower; because he wrote *The Show-Off;* and finally because his play *Craig's Wife* won the Pulitzer Prize for the season of 1925–26.

RUTH DRAPER

Because she is an expert monologist and impersonator; because audiences in London, Paris and Madrid, as well as New York, hail her as a whole Art Theatre in her own person; and finally because she is the only woman to whom Hamilton College ever gave a degree.

Muray

H. R. H. GUSTAVUS ADOLPHUS

Because, Prince Royal of Sweden and heir apparent to the throne, he is rivaled in popularity in younger court circles only by the Prince of Wales; because he is a Doctor of Philosophy; because he is an erudite archaeologist; because, like his father, he has gained a formidable reputation as a tennis player; because he is the husband of Lady Louise Mountbatten; and finally because he is the first scion of the Swedish royal house to come to these shores.

Hara

RUDYARD KIPLING

Because he is undoubtedly the most widely read of living writers in English; because, in *Kim,* he has produced one of the most picturesque of all studies of native India; because his gift for story-telling has seldom been excelled; and because his *Barrack-Room Ballads* have given to the world a colorful picture of the British army private.

Elliott and Fry

120

Blazing Publicity

Why We Know So Much about
"Peaches" Browning, Valentino, Lindbergh and Queen Marie

WALTER LIPPMANN

THE publicity machine will have become mechanically perfect when anyone anywhere can see and hear anything that is going on anywhere else in the world.

We are still a good long way from that goal, and the time has not yet come when the man in quest of privacy will have to wear insulated rubber clothing to protect himself against perfect visibility. That is something for posterity to worry about. It may even be that when men have lived for a few more generations in the modern apartment house they will have become so habituated to sharing their neighbors' joys, their neighbors' sorrows, their neighbors' jazz and the odors of their neighbors' cooking, that the race will no longer have any prejudices in favor of privacy. They may enjoy living in glass houses.

We can see this promised land, but we shall not enter it. Yet we have made great progress in a somewhat different direction. We can transmit sound over great distances. We can transmit photographs. We can make moving pictures. We can make moving pictures that talk. Tomorrow we shall have television. The day after tomorrow we shall have a combination of the radio-telephone and television. These inventions combined with the facilities of the great news-gathering organizations have created an engine of publicity such as the world has never known before. But this engine has an important peculiarity. It does not flood the world with light. On the contrary it is like the beam of a powerful lantern which plays somewhat capriciously upon the course of events, throwing now this and now that into brilliant relief, leaving the rest in comparative darkness. The really important experiments with the modern publicity machine have been made since the war. During the war itself the machinery was not yet sufficiently developed, and the censorship was too active, to allow more than a few trials of its possibilities. The war, therefore, was never reported to the people at home as we now understand reporting. The non-combatants never knew the war as they have since had an opportunity to know the precise behavior of Judd Gray, when he testified in the Snyder case. The epoch-making events in the experimental stage of our modern publicity machine have been, if I remember correctly, the visit of the Prince of Wales, the death of Rudolph Val-

entino, the channel swimming of Gertrude Ederle *et al.,* the amours of "Peaches" Browning, the Hall-Mills case, the Dempsey-Tunney fight, the Snyder case and the reception to Lindbergh. These events have really been *reported,* in the modern sense of the word.

No one can say we have not been neutral in our choice of the subjects on which we have cast the full brightness of the publicity machine. It is after all a mechanical device. It does not have and could not have an automatic governor to regulate its use according to accepted standards, or any standards, of good taste and good policy. The machine can no more be made so as to regulate itself in a civilized fashion than an automobile can be made which will refuse to run if there is a drunken driver at the wheel. Our publicity machine will illuminate whatever we point it at. If we point it at the "Peaches" Browning affair, it will ruthlessly and efficiently flood the consciousness of men with swinishness. Point it at Lindbergh and it will transfigure the mundane world with young beauty and unsullied faith.

THE machine itself is without morals or taste of any kind, without prejudice or purpose, without conviction or ulterior motive. It is guided by men. More specifically it is guided by newspaper men. They are the watchers who scan the horizon constantly looking for the event which may become the next nine days' wonder. They set the special writers and the batteries of photographers hurrying to the scene of action. If their judgment has been good, that is to say if they have picked a sensation which the public finds fascinating, the lead is taken up by the auxiliary services, the moving-picture people, the managers of the chains of broadcasting stations, and the Mayor's committee on the reception of distinguished visitors. In the providing of these sensations many are offered and few are chosen. The public interest works somewhat mysteriously, and those of us who serve it as scouts or otherwise have no very clear conception as to just what will go down and what won't. We know that the best sensations involve some mystery, as well as love and death, but in fact we work on intuitions and by trial and error. We know that sensations have to be timed properly

for the public cannot concentrate on two sensations at the same time. It is no use trying to tell the public about the Mississippi flood when Ruth Snyder is on the witness stand. These excitements have to be taken in series with a certain interval of quiet during which public attention can relax and refresh itself for the next exertion. The opening of the Hall-Mills prosecution had to be delayed two weeks, I believe, until the front pages could be cleared of the clutter of news about a subway strike. Chamberlain and Levine, for example, flew too soon after Lindbergh, even if they had been as charming and had had fewer relatives, to arouse the interest which their exploit would otherwise have justified.

THE search for subjects on which to employ the new publicity machine is conducted under highly competitive conditions. This is a matter of business. As a result of this competition we have seen the development of some weird devices for stimulating the interest of readers whose imaginations do not soar unaided. For the literate who cannot quite translate words into visual images there is now the synthetic photograph made by scissors, paste, and hired models. It tells a story, if not *the* story, almost without words. But above all there is the personal narrative which gives the illusion of intimacy and inwardness. This personal narrative is, of course, rarely written by the person involved: by the ladies who are still dripping wet from their channel swim, by the ladies waiting for the electric chair, by the flyers caught in a jam of kings and prime ministers. Even journalism is not produced under such conditions. And as for the recently published memoirs of Rudolph Valentino from the spirit world, even the most trusting smile as they read eagerly about his love-life there. The competition is fierce, and the rules are few. The go-getters of the publishing world set the pace.

But in those enterprises where they run foul of such critical public opinion as still exists they are usually aided and abetted by the law and its officers. The worst cases, the ones which have really aroused protest, are almost invariably based on court proceedings. It is here that we have all gone mad. On the theory that any act involving a public official may legitimately be published in a free country by a free press we have made the divorce courts and murder trials a privileged source of material for these sensations. The ordinary rules of libel and laws about decency do not prevail apparently where the pretense can be employed that only matters of record are being published. It is here, if anywhere, that some attempt is likely to be made to control the whole business.

THE suit against Charlie Chaplin furnished a striking example of how abominable the thing can become. The unproved allegations of his wife's lawyers, having become a matter of record, could be published to the world without fear of punishment for the outrage, and without the possibility of adequate remedy to Mr. Chaplin himself. Fortunately in this instance friends of Mr. Chaplin in the responsible press rose in their wrath and mitigated the outrage. But that is exceptional. The whole proceedings in divorce cases are essentially private matters, certainly as to details, and if it is not possible to adopt some sort of self-denying ordinance against the exploitation of divorce cases, we may be driven to experiment with some law like the recent English law which forbids the publication of all the juicy scandal, and confines the report of a divorce case to the barest legally relevant facts.

In murder trials the thing has also gotten altogether out of hand. The Snyder trial was conducted by Mr. Justice Scudder with extraordinary dignity inside the court room. Yet the trial was a scandal by every established standard of justice. No doubt the pair were as guilty as Satan. It was nevertheless a scandal to have the trial conducted to an accompaniment of comments by celebrities seated in the bleachers who took the case out of the hands of the judge and the jury, and rendered a daily verdict at so much per column on the precise guilt of the two defendants. Justice cannot be done if this is to be the normal atmosphere of great trials, and some day I believe a courageous judge will have us up before

him for that contempt of court of which we are unquestionably guilty. Some judge will have to do this, I am afraid and hope, before the bench can restore that atmosphere of deliberation to which the most contemptible criminal is entitled.

The modern publicity machine will not be destroyed by such regulation as this. It will still have a world of excitements on which to work. There is no way of imagining where it will take us. We do not, for example, know how to imagine what the consequences will be of attempting to conduct popular government with an electorate which is subjected to a series of disconnected, but all in their moments absolutely absorbing, hullabaloos. There is no apparent logic in the series; once it is like a peep show with vast multitudes looking through the keyhole of the bedroom door; and then again it is like a religious festival with the multitude worshiping sublime youth. We observe that through it all the important and prosaic affairs of mankind, government and diplomacy and education, are rather completely ignored by the participating crowd. It would be idiotic to pass judgment on something about which we know so little. And yet one wonders, I at least with some anxiety, what would happen if some day the lights of this engine were suddenly set blazing upon our sectional and our sectarian irritations, or upon some great and delicate controversy with a foreign power. For once the machine is running in high, it evokes a kind of circular intoxication in which the excitement about the object of it all is made more furious by fresh excitement about the excitement itself.

THE old adage of our salad days about the curative effects of publicity under popular government seems rather naive in this age of publicity. The light we now throw on events can burn as well as heal, and somehow we shall have to learn to apply it gingerly. The question is whether we can. The perfecting of the machinery will not wait upon our acquiring the wisdom to use it. In all probability we shall only

very slowly acquire the wisdom we need by trial and error in the use of the machine itself. The human mind is not prophetic enough to pursue the problem and solve it theoretically in advance. There is no use grumbling then about the character of some of our hullabaloos. They should be regarded frankly as experiments.

The philosophy which inspires the whole process is based on the theory, which is no doubt correct, that a great population under modern conditions is not held by sustained convictions and traditions, but that it wants and must have one thrill after another. Perhaps the appetite was always there. But the new publicity engine is peculiarly adapted to feeding it. We have yet to find out what will be the effect on morals and religion and popular government when the generation is in control, which has had its main public experiences in the intermittent blare of these sensations. There is something new in the world of which we can but dimly apprehend the meaning.

THAT it means the turning away of popular interest from a continuing interest in public affairs seems fairly clear. Whether one is to regard this as a good thing or a bad depends, I suppose, at least upon one's feeling about how desirable it is to have the people take a direct part in public affairs. I am inclined to ask myself whether in view of the technical complexity of almost all great public questions, it is really possible any longer for the mass of voters to form significant public opinions. The issues are not understandable to anyone who will not give extraordinary effort to studying them. The usual rhetoric of politics has in the meantime gone stale, and it cannot begin to compete in vividness and human interest with the big spectacles of murder, love, death, and triumphant adventure which the new publicity is organized to supply. The management of affairs tends, therefore, once again to rest in a governing class, a class which is not hereditary, which is without titles, but is none the less obeyed and followed.

YVONNE PRINTEMPS

A favorite of the Boulevards and the captivating wife of Sacha Guitry. It was for her that he wrote the dainty play Mozart, selected for the Guitry debut in New York

Abbé

THE ZIEGFELDS

A portrait of Billie Burke with her husband, Florenz Ziegfeld, the genius of the Follies, the annual revue which in mere looks has led the way for twenty years on the New York stage

Steichen

Neighbors at Antibes

Some visitors to a Riviera town that has become Broadway's most popular outpost

THE LAST OF MRS. CHEYNEY

After two long seasons of Lonsdale humor, the dazzling Ina Claire fled to the Azure Coast and leaped wildly into turquoise pajamas.

REFUGEES FROM "SUNNY"

Marilyn Miller and Clifton Webb could have been seen any day this summer baking in the unwinking sun that beats on the Cap d'Antibes.

THE WARBLER

Throughout two summers Grace Moore has annoyed the local Antibes nightingales by practicing the scales all morning in her blue and pink villa.

For years the herd of Americans in France followed the sanctified custom of going to Deauville or some Channel port for the summer and to the Riviera for the winter, without stopping to think that even in the summer Deauville is bleak and uninviting while the Riviera is never more bland. As recently as 1925, a July visitor to the Cap d'Antibes, which juts out into the Mediterranean a short distance from Cannes on the road to Nice, would have found its paths deserted, its villas shuttered, its hotels almost empty. Such a visitor might have seen Roland Young asleep, like some local lizard, on one of the opalescent rocks or have descried in a translucent pool the two small amphibious sons of Robert Benchley. Then suddenly the next year it seemed as if everyone must needs go to Antibes and the surprised hotels prospered. By this past summer, the migration had become such a mass movement that old Antibes devotees knew they themselves would have to pack up and move on. The crowd had discovered their retreat and they must find another or be trampled to death.

LADY MENDL

Finally infected with the Antibes fever to the point of deserting Versailles and Sutton Place, the erstwhile Elsie DeWolfe invested in a villa and a sunshade.

A Sort of Defense of Mothers

A Brief for the Old-Fashioned People Who Still Respect the Best Traditions of the Home

HEYWOOD BROUN

WHAT are you going to do if you love your mother? For that matter what are you going to do if you hate her? The boys with the new psychology will get you if you don't watch out. They will get you in any case.

Of course, at this late date I do not need to point out what happens to men who love their mothers—spots before the eyes, sudden giddiness, and even discomfort after meals. And the hair falls out.

Not even a painter of the acid courage of Whistler would dare today to paint a portrait of his mother or if he did so his obligation would be to blacken at least one eye and make the nose a flaming scarlet. So boldly I declare that the young gentlemen in the schools of advanced writing, versifying and painting have gone too far. No man need accept this modern rule and hate his mother. To me there is nothing necessarily neurotic in the statement, "I think my *mater,* when in good health and sober, has her moments."

To write, as some have done, in novel and in play, as if maternal affection were only slightly less painful and fatal than a hanging, is to betray suspicious emotion. The Freudians will get you on the rebound. No man is free from a fixation when he has a tendency to tantrums. And when anyone tells you, "Frankly I dislike my mother" put him down as one not yet free from the rope marks of the silver cord.

I AM all for much more calmness concerning mothers. The day set aside by the florists and confectioners as a holiday of adulation does not appeal to me but even if one neglects to proffer candy he need not send bombs. I would not deny that I have known men who suffered in body and in soul from a surplus of maternal affection and interference, but I think that modern thought is not quite fair to the extreme difficulties of the situation. Being a mother is just about the last job in the world I would choose to take. Shower attention on the infant and he becomes dependent and grows up with an inferiority complex. Neglect him and he loses ego satisfaction, becomes dependent and grows up with an inferiority complex. It's all very complicated.

Moreover a parent can't forever go around saying to himself, "Just what effect will my present phrase have upon this young one twenty years from now?" There

Vandamm

HEYWOOD BROUN

are a few standard devices for curbing the exuberance of infants and some of them are probably harmful. "If you're not a good little boy I'll take you out and give you to the great big policeman." Doubtless this has been said in millions of homes and the scar of the scare is with us yet.

The curious thing is that people threatened by the policeman bogey do not all behave similarly in later life. Some grow up with a terrific respect and fear of authority. It is possible to find poor psychic cripples who go about the world saying, "Yes, sir" to assistant managing editors and the vice-presidents of small banks. But it isn't always that way. In the spring of the year there will be somewhere along the Atlantic seaboard a collegiate riot in which certain students will steal the clubs and helmets, too, of the officers sent against them. Analyze the wild fury in the most savage student and without much doubt you will find a young man whose nurse or old black mammy threatened to ship him to a policeman when he whimpered. But this particular individual did not grow up with any marked respect for authority. Instead of being afraid that cops would get him he made it his business to get the cops. This process is known as over-compensation and is on the whole delightful.

ONCE, when I was small and finicky in feeding, they took the lunch with which I coyly toyed and gave it to a black spaniel. Rover was his name. The whole thing comes back to me as if it were yesterday.

Unfortunately the incident has marred my later life to a considerable degree. Now when I dine at any house where dogs beg about the table there is always danger of a situation. If my host or hostess happens to hand down so much as a partridge wing to the poor pets a sudden and uncontrollable wave of anger surges over me. It is the memory of that ancient incident. My unconscious mind whispers to me, "They are going to take your dinner and give it to the dog." It was actually lunch that Rover got but things do become a little twisted in the unconscious. And in a fit of buried rage and fear I lash out with both feet. With my right foot I kick the host and with my left the hostess. At times this is resented and there are houses to which I never have been asked more than once. However, they occasionally take the gesture to mean, "Why not a highball?" and so my complex has its compensations.

BUT to get more close to the subject I want to contend that the present-day realists have put too much emphasis on the tribulations of children who are coddled, frustrated, stifled and misunderstood by their parents. Is nobody ever any more going to pay tribute to the amount of stifling a woman must endure in raising a child? Any mother who takes care of an infant for fifteen or twenty years without throwing him into the pond deserves a medal. What if she has marred his psychic life? If that is all that happens to him I think the young person has an exceedingly lucky break.

Now I have known grown persons, some of them parental, who said that they loved children. The statement is silly. Anybody who loves children in the large lacks discrimination. Some of the most unpleasant bores, cads and bounders I have ever met were little fellows less than five years old. It is reasonable and possible to be fond of a few carefully selected children. But even in this instance there must be some limit as to the amount of time you wish to spend with them. No grown person can spend twenty-four hours a day with a child and have any honest emotion toward him except great repugnance. Indeed I doubt if a sensitive adult can spend more than five.

There is no use denying the self-evident fact that the habits of children are horrid. Much has been written of fundamental sex-antagonism. I suppose it does exist but it is no more deeply rooted than the inevitable opposition of infant and adult. Although an adult myself, I don't want to appear prejudiced in the matter. There is much to be said against adults. The issue between child and grown person has nothing of morality in it. The gulf fixed between them is one of taste. A child of six months shares no interests in common with me. He likes food and drink for which I have no fondness. There is no intellectual bond. His idea of a good time is to seize upon my nose and twist. There are a hundred things which I like better.

THE pity of it all lies in the fact that the community refuses to recognize the fact that these infants in our land are aliens. Never is the cry raised, "If they don't like it here why don't they go back where they came from?" And it is obvious that the infants do not like the civilization which we have prepared for them. There's no grumbler like a young one. It has been said of me that under proper stimulus I grow grouchy. A legend is abroad that as soon as I get $100 behind I go in for moaning and for groaning. This may be true and yet I remain a saint compared to a child into whom a pin is sticking. I'm a saint even compared to a child into whom no pin is sticking. The only remedy for the whole sad mess is segregation. Let us have separate Pullmans and smokers on all the trains. No child should be allowed into an adult waiting room and the better hotels and restaurants ought to bar them. Nor does one have to be all child to fall into the proscribed classification. One drop of infantile blood and you have a kiddie even though he may wear a thirty-four-year-old size.

Accordingly I call upon all men, including the modernists, to take off their hats to the American mother. If there were no children the world would not go on. There could be a debate as to whether or not it should but after very careful deliberation I should be inclined to say "Yes." Rearing children is not a pleasant job. Maybe it isn't a woman's work but fortunately that tradition has been set up. Mother love can be at times a destructive thing but I don't know that children, the little nuisances, deserve anything better.

BERTRAND RUSSELL

Grandson of Lord John Russell, the great Victorian champion of parliamentary reform

Mr. Russell is one of the most brilliant of living mathematicians and philosophers. One of the few men alive who really understands Einstein, he served a term of imprisonment for his pacifist political opinions and—as a result of his recent visit to the Orient—he has just published a characteristically lucid and illuminating book: *The Problem of China.*

Vandamm

Cecil

H.R.H., EDWARD ALBERT, PRINCE OF WALES

Presenting the apparently fragile but really indestructible heir to the British throne

How truly speaks the ancient proverb: "All things are not what they seem!" Or, in other words: who would suppose —on encountering this delicate physiognomy—that its owner was possessed of a fortitude and endurance unexampled in human history? Probably no one. Yet statistics prove that His Royal Highness has survived 2,754,911 snapshots and 15,450,217 feet of newsreel pictures; that he has officially laid 7003 cornerstones and fallen off his horse no less than 2431 times; that he has been proposed to by 4187 young ladies and has kissed, at various moments, 1791 babies and 2329 blondes; that he has quaffed, in toasts, precisely 19,218 quarts of champagne, and—finally —that he has traveled eleven times around the world in 1819 uniforms and 3601 assorted hats. Beside such heroic twentieth-century accomplishments, do not the mythological exploits of Hercules pale into utter insignificance? Then let us line up all the cameramen and cry: Long Live Edward Albert! Hats off to the indestructible Dancing Drinking Tumbling Kissing Walking Talking and Sleeping—but not Marrying—idol of the British Empire!

Irving Thalberg

The Astounding Career of the Youngest of the Film Magnates

JIM TULLY

IN AN industry so chaotic as the motion picture, a "boy wonder" was sure to emerge. His name is Irving Thalberg. He is considered a genius by many of the leading citizens of Hollywood.

In the cinema world the word genius is more common than a threadbare plot.

Thalberg entered pictures obsequiously enough as an employee of Carl Laemmle, an ex-clothing dealer in a little Wisconsin town, and now an aging potentate in the jungles of moronia.

There is a latent spiritual quality in Thalberg. It even survived a business course in Brooklyn.

Not strong physically, he gives one the impression of the poet. There is about his eyes a twinkle blended of mirth and sadness. His fingers are long, sensitive, and delicate—the fingers of a Richelieu—or a Machiavelli.

After graduation from the Boys' High School in Brooklyn, he became ill and was confined to his bed for six months. Upon recovery, he attended New York University for one year. Followed a position in a Brooklyn store. During spare hours he taught himself the rudiments of typewriting. He also attended a business school to learn shorthand and Spanish. In six months he was considered an expert stenographer and had a fair knowledge of Spanish. Thus equipped, he entered upon his career. He placed an advertisement in the *New York Journal of Commerce,* which read:

SITUATION WANTED: Secretary, stenographer, Spanish and English. High School education, inexperienced. $15.00.

In twelve months he was assistant manager of the organization which was fortunate enough to engage him. Aware of the sad fact that further advancement would be slow, he sought a new outlet.

While visiting his grandmother at Edgemere, L. I., he was introduced to Carl Laemmle, President of the Universal Pictures Company. They do say that Laemmle saw genius in the boy at once. A harder historian of shadows would be more apt to say that Laemmle, a genial, kindly old man, was captivated by the boy's personality. The clothing dealer from Oshkosh offered the young stenographer from Brooklyn a position. Thalberg refused.

But the story goes on . . . I quote from a Metro-Goldwyn-Mayer publicity sheet . . .

"A week later he was walking past the Mecca building in New York, which at that time housed the Universal executive offices. He happened to glance up and see the sign and decided to go in and try for a job. He was successful and obtained employment at thirty-five dollars a week. He did not mention that he had ever met Laemmle.

"After he had been with Universal for several weeks Laemmle returned from a trip to California and while walking around the office saw Thalberg seated at a typewriter.

"'Well,' exclaimed the President of the company, 'How did you get here?' After a short talk he asked Thalberg to come into his office that afternoon.

"As the youthful stenographer did not report he was sent for the following day. This time he went into the executive office and he remained there as Laemmle's private secretary.

"He worked about the industry with which he was associated—and also because he liked Carl Laemmle and wanted to prove to the great executive that he had made no mistake in selecting him for the position. After two years in the New York office Thalberg accompanied Laemmle to Universal City and was left there to look after his boss's interests while the latter made a trip to Europe. He studied production and the people who were connected with it and before long he was made general manager of the huge plant. . . ."

We will now leave the publicity writer.

Within six months Thalberg was called "a boy wonder" and a "genius." A series of ordinary pictures were made—among them *Conflict, Outside the Law, Human Hearts,* and *The Hunchback of Notre Dame.*

There was one man above the ordinary on the Universal lot at this time . . . Eric von Stroheim. He was directing *The Merry Go Round.* Irving Thalberg won a complete victory over him, and Rupert Julian finished directing the picture.

Somewhere in bygone reading I remember a great man once said that the hands on the clock of the world were turned back a hundred years when Napoleon lost Waterloo. The same can be said when the bullet-headed monster of intensity lost to the young man from Brooklyn.

I AM one who is fond of Thalberg personally—and I write with no rancor. I would have considered him a real boy wonder had he curbed with understanding the torrent that was Stroheim. For, in that far day, when those who follow us will be able to get a perspective on film history, Stroheim is likely to be considered the first man of genuine and original talent to break his heart against the stone wall of cinema imbecility.

Thalberg is boyish, kindly, and intuitive. He has a quick mentality that runs in narrow grooves. If it were deeper and vaster and more profound, he would be a financial failure in the business of films. To Thalberg all life is a soda fountain. He knows how to mix ingredients that will please the herd on a picnic. It is doubtful if such an attribute can be listed among the great talents. It was possessed by Barnum and Bailey. Morris Gest, David Belasco, Aimee Semple McPherson, Billy Sunday and Wayne B. Wheeler also have the same quality.

Thalberg has piled one piece of clay upon another until he has succeeded in building a hill for the commonalty. Upon this hill his co-workers, being lesser people than himself, and more near-sighted, see a mirage which they call genius. It often takes the form of a young man with a sad expression, leading sheep to a withered pasture.

Thalberg is the epic of the common man.

He has inspired and sponsored such productions as *The Big Parade, The Merry Widow, Tell It to the Marines; The Scarlet Letter,* and *Flesh and the Devil.* He has been a firm rung in the ladder that led to the success of such stars as Lon Chaney, John Gilbert, Greta Garbo, William Haines and many others.

His eighteen-hour day involves editing, cutting, titling, casting, advising millionaire stars, giving fatherly advice to directors, script writers and authors; passing on problems of real estate, exhibitor control, and promotional values in his productions. He is the big "idea" man of his shadow world, the seer of syndicated screen stories, self-made, self-taught—pig-headed at times but never big-headed.

But of course there are other sides of Irving Thalberg. No person could dominate a world of cheap intrigue and fierce economics with a set of emasculated virtues. He can be relentless and suave. He can strike back from any angle. In a world where friendship is as shadowy as figures on a screen, Thalberg relies on no man.

He has retained a level head and a clear course through the helter skelter of the cheapest form of intrigue known to mankind—studio politics.

The astounding thing about him is his gentle, dreamy air; his almost placid personality—except in the midst of an argument. A frail boy, he has terrifying energy—enormous vitality.

In conversation he is often an iconoclast. But he makes films which please the millions. With a colossal income—nearly a million dollars a year—he lives the simple home life of the Jewish middle class. He has that strange admixture of weaknesses which are to be found in most extraordinary people.

Modest, almost to the verge of bashfulness, there is no pretense in him . . . and no vulgarity. An aesthete in everything.

He is as fond of candy as a child. His health is bad, so he often dines on the simplest meal . . . a sandwich and a glass of milk, and then hurries to some conference in his car—alone.

His chest, unusually large, is the store house of his energy.

He is so wan, so tired looking and so appealing, that women, ever on the alert to evade logic, often become sentimental about him. The feeling is wasted. Caesar Borgia was no better able to take care of himself.

THALBERG, charming, naïve, lovable and sincere, is the biggest little man in pictures. He may even outgrow Hollywood. But his mind is not greatly creative. It reflexes, by a highly developed intuition, that which pleases the people. Jacob Wasserman visits his studio and remains but a few hours. John Colton comes, and, with a Shanghai gesture, adjusts his spectacles, and remains many months. Thalberg knows which one to retain.

He appraises human nature shrewdly. When I asked him why it was possible for a young woman in his employ who is ten years old mentally to receive forty thousand dollars a year as a "writer" he replied, instantly and decisively, "Because she reflects what the people want."

When the Mayer-Thalberg army first camped on the Metro-Goldwyn lot it found a few men of some literary talent. They soon left. Thalberg knew, in the words of the blessed Irish, that such men were neither "fish nor fowl."

He is credited with discovering many film players. Perhaps his greatest discovery is John Gilbert, a good-looking young man, literally born on the stage.

IN 1925 and 1926 Thalberg was responsible for *The Big Parade, The Scarlet Letter,* and *He Who Gets Slapped.* When I asked him for a success slogan he said, "I just guess."

When he saw the first shots of *The Big Parade* in the projection room he decided to enlarge it into a patriotic spectacle. The stolid director, King Vidor, then imbued it with Laurence Stallings' gusto and personality. When I asked Vidor where he learned about the war he said, "I read it in a book."

It is said that when Thalberg saw *He Who Gets Slapped* in the projection room he walked out in despair. The picture was directed by Victor Seastrom, who knows what compassion is, even if he sometimes allows it to wander into meadows of sentimentality. It was, contrary to expert studio opinion, a great financial success. Thalberg had apparently guessed wrong—but is now credited with guessing right. The process becomes simple. Seastrom was given *The Scarlet Letter* to direct. Save for some splendid acting by Lillian Gish in a part for which she was well fitted, the picture was not as successful as *He Who Gets Slapped.* But Thalberg's guessing average was still very high.

The young supervisor's outstanding achievement for 1927 is *Flesh and the Devil.* The director, Clarence Brown, must be given full credit for this excellent film. He was ably assisted by the fine work of Greta Garbo. If Mr. Thalberg guessed these two people into their respective roles, which is quite likely, he should be given full credit.

Irving Thalberg is too modest. There are many who claim that he does not guess. He possibly has more flashes of good guessing than any man in pictures.

HE FOLLOWS a film through all its various stages of production, from the time the idea is conceived or the story purchased. He works with cutter and director while it is being titled and edited. He sees it previewed, at a theatre adjacent to Los Angeles. He watches the reactions of the audiences. He follows the box office returns after the film is released. All this is in no way remarkable. Every other producer does the same. But Thalberg every now and then does make a film which is worth pre-viewing.

In one respect Thalberg is superior to most producers. He reads books.

"Dreiser is a greater writer than Wasserman—not so superficial," he comments.

Further, "I can't see the young highbrows—what have they got that other people haven't—except a feeling of superiority?"

I agreed with him and he went on talking, swiftly. "A young woman came to me from one of the fan magazines and said, 'Mr. Thalberg—I realize that you are of the new order in films—a young man with ideals.'

"I interrupted her. 'If you mean that I think I'm superior to the so-called cloak and shoe and glove manufacturers who have really given their lives and their pocket-books to this business in order to allow us something to build on—why then—you are wrong. I respect them very much—they had ideals also.'"

The interview was a failure.

Thalberg has essentially the beginnings of the artist in his make-up. But as a corporation official, he must give to money the first and last consideration.

Sheeler

GLENN HUNTER

After two seasons on the road, the noted actor who scored in Merton of the Movies *and* Young Woodley *is returning to New York in* Behold This Dreamer

JOHN GILBERT

The popular screen actor has recently completed a celluloid version of Anna Karenina *in which he appears opposite Greta Garbo*

Steichen

The Last Day

Wherein a Brave Little Woman Makes the Worst Worse by Gaily Inviting the Deluge

MICHEL CORDAY

HUDDLED in the back of her coupé, Mme. Corvette was thinking over events. This very morning she had seen her husband re-enter the room with a bundle of mail in his hand. The paper shook. "Marthe, we are ruined, utterly. We have just enough left to get away on. Will you go with me?"

Of course, she would go with him. She felt that twenty years of feminine luxury had made her an accomplice in this ruin. . . . But how had Corvette ever been brought to the point of flight? Not once since taking her from the family warehouse (*objets d'art* and old tapestries) had he refused her whatever sum she had asked of him. And heaven knows . . . Nor had she ever bothered herself as to the source or the state of their income. "My husband makes what he wants on the Exchange," she modestly confided to her friends.

Ruined. . . . She accepted the adventure with a sigh and a smile. Bah! A man like Corvette could make another fortune in some new country. Finally they would return to Paris, and would buy a new home. It would be quite amusing to begin all over again furnishing a place.

ALAS! How many years would she have to wait for this joyous round of shopping which would mark their return? It was all so delightful: the pleasant excitement of buying recklessly, the eagerness of the clerks, the lengthy deliberations before the counters, those brief delicious pangs of remorse when yielding to some mad caprice. . . .

And of a sudden an ingenious and treacherous idea popped into this little head. Why not spend her last day before their flight in doing the shops once more and piling up orders without limit, without restraint? . . . This would give her a double satisfaction: for besides experiencing this precious indulgence for one more time, she would be making fools of all those grasping salespeople, who would find the door closed when they came to-morrow with their goods and their bills. She would dupe them to a standstill, for the sheer pleasure of buying things.

"Jean, to Gramadoc's." And the supple carriage took her to the Corvettes' upholsterer and furniture dealer. Gramadoc came rushing up servilely to his rich client. He

had an enormous forehead, bilobate and fleshy. It overwhelmed his dry features, which were also encroached upon by his steel-grey beard.

For once Mme. Corvette was enough at ease to be amused at this botch of a face. As a rule she was nervous and felt a kind of religious awe on entering this temple of tapestries and knickknacks.

She sat down, and began to invite temptation. Gramadoc leaned his insinuating forehead towards her. Beneath his soiled thumb, the materials came to life, rustling, gaining relief, and acquiring a richer play of colour. "Madame Corvette should get new hangings for the sitting-room. This is a rare opportunity." And rare opportunities multiplied beneath Gramadoc's grey fingers—a tankard *sans pareille,* a cabinet which had turned up by the greatest good fortune (there being a god for furniture dealers), and a delightful little table with three twisted legs, just made as a pedestal for this little silver statuette.

Mme. Corvette listened, gently nodding her head. She took the tapestry, the tankard, the cabinet, and the statuette. Her delight grew keener with each new object that Gramadoc foisted upon her. Indeed, it was the upholsterer who was the first to weary.

IN HER carriage, Mme. Corvette maliciously pictured how Gramadoc's forehead would look tomorrow when all these objects which he had disposed of with such dexterity were brought back to him.

"Jean, to Archimbault's."

And she passed hours as breathless and intense as hours of forbidden love, at the hands of the celebrated tailor. When she left, with her cheeks on fire, her skin moist, and her voice tremulous, she had ordered gowns for a whole year, including voyages. Archimbault thought that he had hit upon one of those blessed days when the customer is without resistance to temptation, when her entire life is centered about the thrill of buying.

And Mme. Corvette, descending the stairs, thought of all those lovely robes which she had caressed with eyes and hands but which she would never have a chance to wear.

"Jean, to Madame Tallier's."

Oh! the joy of picking the little hat-flowers from the tops of their high stems, adjusting them just so, admiring one's self

gravely and steadily—in profile, three-quarter and full face—with mirrors set at varying angles.

Mme. Corvette ordered a hat for each gown. And again she sighed to think that she would never wear them, though it made her smile to imagine the expression on Madame Tallier's elephantine face when these hats came back to her unsold.

"Jean, to Beauvais'."

WITH the powerful jeweler, while she is caressing the precious stones laid out before her on the felt-covered counter, Mme. Corvette's enjoyment becomes sharper, verging on ecstasy. She decides on a "dog collar" with five rows of pearls, a dazzling string of diamonds, some small rings and brooches. She gives her name. The clerk bows. Everything will be delivered tomorrow.

She pauses on the sidewalk. Her head is swimming. She well knows that she will never wear these things: but no matter, it has been a pleasure to buy them.

There are still a few hours left before her return. She abandons herself to her whims. She inspects a large house on the *Rue de l'Elysée,* her dream, and leases it. She orders two new cabs. She mingles with the crowds in the big department stores, purely for the joy of passing into the hands of a hundred successive clerks and buying everything that she lays her eyes upon. After Archimbault, Gramadoc, and Beauvais, this gives one a little savour of "the people," which enchants Mme. Corvette.

And everywhere they bow, and everywhere they promise that her purchases will be sent to her tomorrow.

In her carriage on the way home, Mme. Corvette yields to a delicious fatigue. She stretches herself out like a cat. Ah! what a splendid day, despite the prospect of the train they are to take at midnight. In the space of these last few hours she has spent more than during a whole year of prosperity. And now it was these villainous shopkeepers' turn to be cheated a bit. . . .

She enters. And of a sudden Corvette rushes in and enfolds her in his arms:

"*Chérie, chérie,* we are no longer leaving. I have scraped together . . . not a great deal, but at least enough to meet the amounts due, and to give us another chance. We will remain, my brave little Marthe . . . we will remain."

The Birth of a Great Artist

A Story Dedicated to Painters Who Desire to Rise to the Top of Their Profession

ANDRÉ MAUROIS

PIERRE DOUCE, the painter, was just finishing a still life—flowers in a chemist's jar, egg-plant on a plate—when Paul-Emile Glaise, the novelist, entered the studio. For some minutes Glaise contemplated his friend at work, then he said emphatically:

"No."

The painter interrupted the polishing of an egg-plant and looked up in surprise.

"No," Glaise repeated with rising emphasis. "No, you will never get there. You have skill, you have talent, and you are in earnest. But your painting is flat, old man. It has no flash, it does not cry out. In a salon of five thousand canvases, what is there to halt the sleepy procession in front of your work? . . . No, Douce, you will never get there, I am sorry to say."

"Why?" sighed honest Douce. "I paint what I see; I have never hoped for more than that."

"That is just the point. You have a wife, old man, a wife and three children. Milk costs eighteen sous a litre and eggs are one franc each. There are more pictures than there are buyers, and the blockheads outnumber the connoisseurs. How under the circumstances is it possible, Douce, to emerge from this vast horde of the unknown?"

"Work?"

"Be serious. The only way, Douce, of arousing the imbeciles is to do something outlandish. Announce that you are going to paint a picture at the North Pole. Go about dressed like an Egyptian king. Found a new school. Mix up some learned words like exteriorization and dynamism in a hat and compose manifestoes. Deny movement, or repose; white or black; the circle or the square. Invent Neo-Homeric painting which recognizes nothing but red and yellow, or cylindrical painting, or octohedral painting, or fourth-dimensional painting."

AT THIS point a waft of strange sweet perfume announced the entrance of Madame Kosnevska. She was a Polish beauty whom Pierre Douce admired for her great charm. A subscriber to expensive reviews which reproduced at considerable cost the masterpieces of three-year-olds, she never noted the name of our honest Douce in them and she disapproved of his painting accordingly. Stretching herself out on a divan, she inspected the canvas on which he was working, shook her blond hair, and smiled not without malice.

"Yesterday," she said, with her suave and purring accent, "I went to see an exhibit of Negro art. Ah! the sensibility, the plasticity, and the power there!"

Turned to the wall was a portrait which the painter had liked. He showed her this.

"Very nice," she said dutifully; and suave, purring, and perfumed, she disappeared.

Pierre Douce tossed his palette into a corner and dropped on the divan. "I am going to get a job," he said, "as an insurance inspector, or a bank clerk, or a policeman. Painting is the lowest of trades. To be successful you have to appeal to a lot of idlers, and resort to all kinds of antics. Instead of respecting the masters, the critics encourage the barbarians. I have had enough of it, and I'm through."

Paul-Emile listened to him, then lit a cigarette and for some time pondered in silence.

FINALLY he spoke. "Would you like to give the snobs and the pseudo-artists the rough treatment they deserve? Do you feel as though you could, with an air of mystery and high seriousness, announce to Kosnevska and a few other aesthetes that for the last ten years you have been preparing to carry your manner of painting another step forward?"

"I?" said honest Douce in astonishment.

"Listen. . . . I am going to tell the world, in two articles judiciously placed, that you are founding the ideo-analytic school. Previous to you, all portraitists have in their ignorance emphasized the importance of the human physiognomy. Nonsense! For on the contrary, what really makes a man is the ideas which he evokes in us. Thus the portrait of a colonel would be five enormous stripes against a background of blue and gold, with a horse in one corner and crosses in another. The portrait of a manufacturer would be a factory chimney and a clenched fist on a table. Do you understand, Douce, what you are bringing into the world, and can you paint me in one month twenty ideo-analytic portraits?"

"In one hour," he said, "and the sad part of it is, Glaise, that it might succeed."

"Let's try it."

"I couldn't put up the front."

"Then, old man, when any one asks you for an explanation, simply take your time, launch a whiff of your pipe-smoke in the face of your interlocutor, and say these simple words: 'Have you ever studied a river?'"

"And what does that mean?"

"Nothing," said Glaise, "and as a consequence they will consider it wonderful."

TWO months later, the private showing that precedes the public opening (the *vernissage* of the Exhibit Douce), was closing in triumph. Suave, purring, and perfumed, the beautiful Madame Kosnevska was inseparable from her latest great man.

"Ah!" she repeated, "the sensibility, the plasticity, and the power there! What intelligence! What revelation! And just how, dear, did you arrive at these astounding syntheses?"

The painter paused for some time, then exhaled a cloud of smoke from his pipe and said, "Have you ever, dear Madame, studied a river?"

In a rabbit-fur overcoat the young and brilliant Lévy-Coeur was haranguing a group. "Very strong!" he was saying. "Very strong! As for me, I have been repeating for a long time that it is the height of absurdity to paint from a model. But tell me, Douce: the revelation. Where did you get the idea? From my articles?"

Pierre Douce took his time, blew a triumphant cloud of smoke in his face and said, "Have you, Monsieur, ever studied a river?"

"Admirable!" the other man exclaimed approvingly. "Admirable!"

At that moment, a celebrated art dealer who had just finished the rounds of the pictures plucked the painter by the sleeve and dragged him into a corner.

"Douce, my friend," he said, "you are a clever fellow. We could make this the beginning of a career. Give me exclusive rights to your whole output. Don't change your manner until I tell you, and I will take fifty pictures a year. Agreed?"

Enigmatically, Douce smoked and said nothing.

Gradually, the studio was emptied. Paul-Emile Glaise went and closed the door behind the last visitor. From the stairs came a retreating murmur of admiration. Left alone now with the painter, the novelist gaily thrust his hands in his pockets and broke into formidable laughter.

The painter frowned, and as the other

kept laughing, he said brusquely, "Imbecile!"

"Imbecile?" the novelist exclaimed angrily. "When I have just succeeded in the greatest hoax since the one perpetrated by the notorious Monsieur Bixiou."

The painter cast a proud glance at the twenty analytic portraits and said, "Yes, Glaise, you are an imbecile. There is something in these paintings."

The novelist contemplated his friend with extreme astonishment.

"That is too much!" he shouted. "Douce, remember. Who suggested this new style of painting to you?"

Then Pierre Douce took his time and exhaled an enormous cloud of smoke.

"Have you ever," he said, "studied a river?"

"MOTHER AND CHILD"
BY PICASSO

This modern Madonna, painted on a tinted gray background and very lightly colored, was signed by Picasso in 1922. It belongs in Picasso's period of great simplicity and classical feeling. It is an eloquent sample of his authority as a draftsman and one of the most tender of his monumental figure pieces.

"WHITE PLUMES" BY MATISSE

Henri Matisse, born in 1869, began "White Plumes" in Paris in 1919. The painting, completed when he was fifty and was in full command of his original style, is considered one of his most notable more formal and decorative portraits.

The Theory and Lizzie Borden

O. Henry Sends a Sheriff to Snoop Around an Old Murder Mystery

ALEXANDER WOOLLCOTT

WHEN the incomparable Lizzie Borden, America's most interesting woman, passed to her reward a few weeks ago, we all read with something of a pang the final chapter in the most absorbing murder case in the annals of America. And when, a few days later, her last will and testament was published in the newspapers, a good many of us recalled with a start a certain short story tucked away somewhere along the murmurous shelf left behind by O. Henry.

That story was the one he called "The Theory and the Hound" and you will find it in the posthumous collection entitled (for reasons which escape me) *Whirligigs*. It tells how, once upon a time, a Blue Ridge sheriff landed on a lazy, forgotten morsel of an island off the coast of South America. In his pocket were the warrant and extradition papers for one Wade Williams, wanted back in Kentucky for the murder of his frail, pretty wife two years before. From an intercepted letter, the sheriff knew his man was living on that island, even knew the fugitive was growing cocoanuts to ship by the occasional fruit-steamers putting in at that tiny harbor. And though he had no photograph to clinch his identification, he carried in the back of his head a rough description of the murderer, a word-sketch as to age, height, habits of drink and speech, coloring and the like. There were, he learned from the consul, but two Americans on the polyglot island and this made his search seem easy. But each of the two exiles dealt in cocoanuts and the rough description fitted one just as neatly as the other.

SHERIFF PLUNKETT must depart next morning with the fruit-steamer and he meant to take Wade Williams with him. He merely had to find out somehow within the next few hours which of the two was Williams, for it would be a sorry day for justice (and, incidentally, for the sheriff's bondsman) if he were to take the wrong man by the scruff of the neck and drag him halfway across the world to answer a charge of murder. Mild-eyed but wary, he sat with the two men, broke bread with them, drank with them, O. Henry, as he spun the tale, being careful that you should know no more than the sheriff himself which of the two—Morgan or Reeves—was, in truth, the

LIZZIE BORDEN

fugitive Wade Williams. Then the tale takes this swift turn:

A dog walked into the room where they sat—a black-and-tan hound, long-eared, lazy, confident of welcome.

Plunkett turned his head and looked at the animal, which halted, confidently, within a few feet of his chair.

Suddenly the sheriff, with a deep-mouthed oath, left his seat and bestowed upon the dog a vicious and heavy kick, with his ponderous shoe.

The hound, heart-broken, astonished, with flapping ears and incurved tail, uttered a piercing yelp of pain and surprise.

Reeves and the consul remained in their chairs, saying nothing, but astonished at the unexpected show of intolerance from the easy-going man from Chatham county.

But Morgan, with a suddenly purpling face, leaped to his feet and raised a threatening arm above the guest.

"You—brute!" he shouted, passionately; "why did you do that?"

Quickly the amenities returned, Plunkett muttered some indistinct apology and regained his seat. Morgan with a decided effort controlled his indignation and also returned to his chair.

And then Plunkett with the spring of a tiger, leaped around the corner of the table and snapped handcuffs on the paralyzed Morgan's wrists.

"Hound-lover and woman-killer!" he cried; "get ready to meet your God."

It was the next morning, when the sheriff was pushing the captive Williams into the dory, that he enlightened the still puzzled consul.

"I'm a Kentuckian," he said as the boat put out to sea, "and I've seen a great deal of both men and animals. And I never yet saw a man that was overfond of horses and dogs but what was cruel to women."

This sharp, characteristic tweak at the end of "The Theory and the Hound" spread many an amused or perhaps malicious smile in its day, but more than one eminent neurologist nodded grave assent. For it is, I am told, a pet theory among many latter-day psychiatrists that a peculiarly ardent concern in behalf of our feathered or four-footed friends is a tell-tale token of some old brutality undergoing compensation and atonement or at least is an outward scar of some ancient impulse of cruelty towards human beings, never satisfied, perhaps, and long since suppressed.

These modern psychologists are pretty trying that way. If they catch you so far obeying a scriptural injunction as to honor your father and your mother, it is a signal for them to get together and give the cheer of their school of thought—"*Oedipus Rex, Co-ex-Co-ex*"—or if you are so transparent as to rebuke a hulking driver for beating his poor nag, they pounce on you and try to wring from you a confession that, back in your foul and brackish childhood, you had slain a little baby for the coral on its neck. Any one at all familiar with their tricks and their manners knows that they chuckled when Lizzie Borden's will was offered for probate the other day.

IT WAS on a sweltering August morning five and thirty years ago that old Andrew Borden came moseying up Second Street in Fall River and, for the last time, walked acrossed the threshold of his house at No. 92. He was a lean, lanky miser, his fringe of whiskers already whitened by his seventieth New England Winter. He had just been a-prowl downtown on business, happily foreclosing mortgages, maybe. Now he was homing for his noon siesta and it was not quite eleven when the hired girl unlocked the front door to let him in. His wife, the second Mrs. Borden, had gone out, he was to be told later, on a sick call. His elder daughter, Emma, was visiting friends over Fairhaven way. But Lizzie was on the premises. Indeed as Bridget came through the hall to unlock the door for him, she had heard Miss Lizzie laughing all by herself upstairs. To some who turn from time to time the yellowing pages of this fathomless New England tragedy, that solitary and enigmatic cackle floating down the darkened stairway lifts the Borden legend to the plane of Shakespeare and Sophocles.

The morning's work about the house was done. The beds were made, the windows washed. The kitchen was to rights. The breakfast (it had consisted of bread, mutton, mutton broth, johnny-cake, sugar-cookies, bananas and coffee) was long since cleared away. After letting the master in, Bridget (they called her Maggie only because the hired girl at Borden's was always called Maggie) toiled up the back-stairs and flopped down for a rest on her bed under the hot roof. A few minutes later—ten minutes, perhaps, less than fifteen, certainly—she was summoned below by the panicky voice of Miss Lizzie spreading the alarm. On the sofa in the sitting-room, killed while he was taking his snooze, lay old man Borden. His blood was smeared all over the room and his head had been hacked with such deep, prolonged and insatiate ferocity that his oldest friend would not have known it was his. Upstairs, beside the precise, starchy, spare-room bed she had been making, the hurriedly gathering neighbors found the body of Mrs. Borden, struck down, they assumed, by the same fierce hand and probably by the same weapon, but already so clotted and cold in death that, after killing her, the slayer must have lain in wait for full ninety dreadful minutes to make the job complete by killing her husband.

The preposterous trial that followed the slaughter in the Borden house focused and held the eyes of this country as no other trial ever did before or since. The fact that no weapon was ever produced by the police and no testimony ever admitted pointing to any splotch of blood on Lizzie Borden sent her out into the world on the arm of her minister, a free woman, an innocent heiress.

So, since the state has no second chance against the incompetence of a prosecution, the bias of a judge nor the folly of a jury, the Borden case passed into history, leaving the households of this country hopelessly divided as to the guilt of the inscrutable daughter whom the police had accused. There were those who felt it was not hu-

manly possible for this young woman, with all the bad will in the world, to have accomplished the murder and effaced every evidence of her guilt (who would have thought the old man had had so much blood in him?) in the few fleeting moments when no eye was on her. There were as many others who found it even harder to imagine how some motiveless stranger could have entered, struck, and gone his way without Lizzie seeing or hearing him, even though, as she calmly swore at the inquest, she had elected to spend that critical quarter of an hour in a solitary and prolonged visit to the sweltering loft out in the barn.

This cleavage of opinion has persisted to this day and it is that which has kept the Borden case alive long after those who attended the trial had themselves followed old man Borden to the churchyard. The Elwell case, for instance, and the gaudy yellow-back killings out in De Russey's Lane fade from memory dull as a fox chase when the scent has been lost.

Within the past few years, I have heard a great and profoundly wise man argue earnestly that Lizzie Borden was innocent but it is impossible to read Edmund Pearson's analysis of the case without seeing that he at least had no reasonable doubt of her guilt. His fascinating chronicle of the Borden murders—the finest thing of its kind I ever read—is the first chapter in *Studies in Murder* and it is so inexorable an indictment of the late Miss Lizzie Borden that at least one Fall River bookseller refused to allow the horrid tome to be sold from his shelves, thus in one gesture expressing loyalty towards a fellow townswoman and tactful consideration of a customer who ordered liberally from him every year.

So it was to one of the great mystery stories in the American legend that the wills of the Borden sisters were lately added as an appendix. They had lived estranged for more than a quarter of a century, Lizzie standing her ground in a large, ugly, shuttered house in her own Fall River, Emma moving over to Newmarket, N. H., whence she made two trips a year up to Boston, once in the Spring to put her fur coat in storage and once in the Fall to take it out again. Emma's death followed nine days after the death of her more distinguished sister. They each left a considerable fortune, for the Borden girls came into some hun-

dreds of thousands by the sudden and (to him, at least) unexpected death of their acquisitive father.

What will interest the psychologists most is the evidence in Lizzie Borden's will that she had spent much of her recluse life in animal rescue work. Half her residuary estate seals a friendship formed in that work. Then she made two bequests to charity, but neither beneficiary was an organization touched by merely human woe. The sum of $2,000 went to the Animal Rescue League of Washington, D. C., and the sum of $30,000 went to the Animal Rescue League of Fall River. I think O. Henry would have smiled a knowing smile.

THIS statement of the theory and Lizzie Borden is set down here as a forecast of what the psychologists would say. Personally I have no patience with such codified interpretation of human vagaries, certainly not with this particular crotchet. These pundits would have thrown St. Francis into the Assisi lock-up and have given Androcles a mighty bad name. I most earnestly disown them. For my own part, I can think right off of a dozen people (names furnished on request) whom I would rather kick than any dog that ever bayed the moon. And was it not in a benefit in behalf of sundry animal protective societies that I once donned the costume of Henry VIII and endured the pangs of being hissed for four minutes? It was.

No, I am merely outlining a standard theory and so enamored are theorists of their notions that the single line in Emma Borden's will also leaving a few paltry thousands to still another animal rescue league would probably have led the aforesaid Sheriff Plunkett into promptly charging the older sister as an accessory before the fact. One can almost sketch the scenario of the indictment. Emma, of course, stood to profit as much as Lizzie by the murders, and the Sheriff, I am sure, would have us believe that her absence from Fall River when the slaughter was accomplished was no accident at all but that she had been packed off by the sterner sister. "Infirm of purpose, give me the kitchen-poker. Go you to Fairhaven."

Lizzie Borden was buried beside her father. In her will she set aside $500 for the care of his grave forever.

Abbé

FRED and ADELE ASTAIRE

Returning from London to appear in the latest Gershwin musical comedy, Funny Face

Nominated for the Hall of Fame: 1927

Durand

MAURICE RAVEL

Because he is one of the foremost of contemporary composers; because, although he is a Frenchman, much of his music has been Spanish; because one of his operas has a libretto by Colette; and finally because next season he is to appear in America for the first time.

COLONEL THOMAS E. LAWRENCE

Because he is, perhaps, the truest adventurer of our day; because, while still an undergraduate, he lived as a native in the desert for two years; because he not only inspired, but unofficially directed, the stirring revolt in Arabia; because his desire for anonymity has made him re-enlist in the British Army, where he is serving as a private; and finally because his vivid account of his almost legendary activities, *Revolt in the Desert,* has been one of the most talked-of books of the year.

Muray

WALTER GIESEKING

Because he is one of the finest of living pianists; because his interpretations of Debussy and Mozart have won superlatives from all critics; and finally because he is the first new pianistic star to appear on our musical horizon since the end of the Great War.

ELLEN TERRY

Because she is the most famous member of a distinguished acting family; because she has played more rôles than any other living actress; because she is a Dame Grand Cross of the British Empire; because her son, Gordon Craig, is an artist of distinction; and because it is now seventy years since she made her debut on the stage.

Muray

CARL VAN VECHTEN *(left)*

Because he was for four years music critic on the *New York Times;* because he revived American taste for the Negro Spiritual; because his latest novel, *Nigger Heaven,* paints a masterful picture of Negro life; and finally because, as an authority on music, cats, and Harlem, he tranquilly refutes the acid theories about dilettantes.

MARIE LAURENCIN

Because she is probably the most sophisticated (and naïve) of living women painters; because she has founded a new school of French art; and because her work has influenced the world of fashion as well as that of the galleries.

JOHN HELD, JR. *(left)*

Because, as a caricaturist, he invented the modern flapper; because last year he was almost elected a Member of Congress from Connecticut; because he is a syndicate artist who has not lost his flair for drawing and satire; and because he is a born comedian.

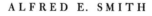

Muray

GRACE COOLIDGE *(below)*

Because she is the first lady of the land and the wife of the President of the United States; because she is one of the best-liked and the most charming hostesses in Washington; because she was an expert in the education of the blind, the deaf and the dumb; and finally because she has just completed her fourth season at the White House, each year having strengthened her popularity.

Vandamm

WINTHROP AMES

Because he was a successful editor and publisher before he became a theatrical producer; because he was director of the New Theatre; because he produces plays for the discriminating; because he has established a Gilbert and Sullivan repertoire; and finally because his next production will be Galsworthy's last play, *Escape*.

HAROLD ROSS

Because he spent his youth leaving the staff of practically every newspaper in the country; because after the mutiny on *The Stars and Stripes,* during the war, he was the private elected by the other mutineers to edit that rebellious A.E.F. weekly; and finally because he is now editor-in-chief of *The New Yorker*.

Muray

ALFRED E. SMITH

Because his long career in New York politics has been a succession of personal triumphs; because he is probably the worst golfer in the Democratic party; and finally because his election last November to a fourth term as Governor of New York suggests the possibility that he may have to forsake Manhattan and take up residence in Washington.

Wide World

Three Americans

Exceedingly Personal Glimpses of Sinclair Lewis, Texas Guinan and Clarence Darrow

CHARLES G. SHAW

Charles G. Shaw, the composer of these sketches, is the author of a recently issued satirical novel, Heart in a Hurricane. *In the trio of microscopic portraits following he has adopted a form originally invented by the late Owen Hatteras, the biographer. By this formula Mr. Shaw has endeavored to depict the characters of the Americans under analysis, through the means of idiosyncrasy, triviality and minutest detail.*

Sinclair Lewis

HE POSSESSES enormous nervous energy which carries him—at lightning speed—to a certain point. At that point he sometimes wilts, suddenly and without a struggle.

He does not like Japanese head-waiters. His favorite American resort is Bill Brown's health farm at Garrison, N. Y. His favorite foreign resort is München.

When wishing to be really swank he affects wing collars, bow ties, and doe-skin spats. Otherwise he dresses like a gentleman.

He stands over six feet in his stockings and has the complexion of a New Bedford skipper.

He is an excellent mimic and is constantly giving imitations.

He likes applause.

SINCLAIR LEWIS

It has long been a matter of debate whether *Main Street* or *Babbitt* could be classed as the earnestly sought great American novel. Certainly throughout America "Main Street" has passed into the vernacular as a term symbolizing and satirizing smug complacency, and "Babbitt" has come to represent the too-familiar type of average man, reaching greedily after success. Despite the discussion occasioned by these mordant satires, *Main Street* has sold over 800,000 copies and *Babbitt*—published two years later—already more than 500,000. Then in *Arrowsmith* Mr. Lewis found a hero to admire as well as satirize. His latest novel, *Elmer Gantry,* has also achieved international success.

Walking is his favorite exercise and, every so often, he will tramp the countryside for miles around! He is apt at impromptu lyrics and enjoys motoring.

The degree of Doctor has always fascinated him greatly.

His pet cigarettes are Lucky Strikes, though he is able to smoke almost anything.

When last in England, Philip Guedalla declared that unless he were immediately recalled to the United States there would be war between the two countries.

He is extremely fond of milk.

He will not tolerate rudeness on the part of inferiors.

His memory is an astonishing one; indeed, he is able to recall, at an instant's notice, the most trifling details of incidents long past. He takes notes, as a rule, on the backs of envelopes.

At 11:45 P.M. he is invariably drowsy; though, soon after that, he often attains the height of his eloquence and powers.

He can make excellent caricatures of himself.

From a rich Minnesota argot he is able to switch into a Whitechapel Cockney without a second's hesitation—much to the annoyance of all present. He also knows German and French.

He is highly pleased by anyone who favors his clothes and he looks best in evening raiment.

He is keenly interested in the art of boxing and will, now and then, place a wager on the outcome of a fistic encounter. He usually loses.

Possessed of great vivacity, he will, not infrequently, discourse for hours. On the lecture platform he is arresting and very effective.

He is not a good judge of character.

He admires anything well done, and is particularly keen about the mode of living of the English gentry.

His favorite piece of music is Brahms' waltz in A Major.

He is considerably impressed by titles and likes British clothes. He is proud of being a son of Old Eli, although a firm believer in the European system of education. Of his birthplace, Sauk Center, Minnesota, he has comparatively little to say.

To work for an ideal is perhaps his chiefest aim. He will sometimes work for ten hours without stopping.

He adores parties and likes people to make a great fuss over him. Strangers to whom he takes a shine he will address by their Christian names a minute after making their acquaintance.

He is a complete agnostic.

Gladly would he delve into the field of business—as he might plan a book—purely as an experience.

He is full of plots. The themes for most of his stories he first tries out upon his friends.

He is quite unable to write a play, knowing little of the technique of the theatre, though a past-master in the art of dialogue.

To Germany he is most devoted and is proud of his knowledge of German. England and Italy charm him also. He admires those who are proficient in languages.

He is highly conscious of his worth and is exceedingly irritated by those who are unable to appreciate his abilities.

He is constantly making plans that never materialize.

He claims to be heartily in favor of the Double Standard—under the present state of affairs.

Strangers interest him enormously—which has led, now and again, to certain altercations. He always wants to know the nationality of a waiter.

He prefers Europe to America, though he will defend the land of his nativity with vigor and vehemence, as soon as a foreigner attacks it.

He is a remarkably early riser.

He is the son of a physician and, at one time, acted as editor for a publishing house.

He almost never writes long-hand, doing practically all of his work upon the typewriter.

He is a great admirer of Thomas Hardy. He carries a monocle though he rarely wears it.

He firmly believes that anyone who passionately wants to write will do so, despite every obstacle.

In general, he is against reform. Except when at work or asleep, he detests being alone.

He is particularly fond of old wines, but is not much on Holland gin.

He rarely attends the moving-pictures.

He has been married only once.

He cannot abide formal functions of any sort but is especially partial to little-neck clams on the half shell.

He has been writing since he was eight years old.

He favors suspenders rather than a belt and is often to be seen carrying a walking stick.

He is a gracious host and loves introducing people to one another.

He plays no games.

He is a fellow of tremendous independence.

Some day he hopes to settle down, though just when and where he hasn't the vaguest notion.

He is extremely agile and of erect carriage.

He is a mass of contradictions.

Texas Guinan

MARY LOUISE CECILIA GUINAN was born in Waco, Texas, thirty-nine years ago (according to the date on the Thirty-seventh Street Police Station blotter), and was the first to glorify the American "sucker."

She lives with her mother, her father, and her brother (Tommy), and worships them all. Her mother's name is Bessie and her father's Michael. Her six uncles are Catholic priests.

She adores horses and will often, immediately after the closing of her "club," ride a horse for an hour in Central Park.

She has been married twice, her first husband having been Julian Johnson, a scenario editor, whom she met in Hollywood while making Wild West pictures; her second—David Townsend, a business man.

Every Sunday, she goes to early mass.

Her house, located on the northern edge of Greenwich Village (where she has lived for the last fifteen years), contains thirty-two rooms in all, and is furnished with knick-knacks, bric-a-brac, and *bibelots* gleaned from all over the world. Each of these possesses an extremely colorful history of its own.

Her household also contains a varied assortment of parrots, dogs and cats.

She has a distinct *béguin* for things Chinese.

She is on the go every minute and once lost forty pounds in a single month!

Four of her "clubs" have already been padlocked. The fifth, however, is going strong.

It was she who first laid claim to coining the phrase: "Butter and egg man."

She has no personal vanity and is not in the least afraid to show her face while swathed in cold cream.

Her repartée is instantaneous.

Among her cherished possessions is a neat bronze medal, presented to her by Field Marshal Joffre, in tribute to her services while under fire at Verdun, in November, 1916.

Hectic love affairs, she believes, are almost always fatal in the end. She also believes that people should not marry unless they are willing to sacrifice everything for their partner in wedlock.

The concert of human voices surrounding her is, she thinks, the greatest symphony in the world.

She adores crowds.

"Stool-pigeons" and "double crossers" are her pet dislikes.

Her favorite piece of music is *"Träumerei."*

She seldom gets enough sleep.

Her only game is poker, which she loves, and at which she is usually successful.

She considers Mary Pickford the greatest

living American and Jim Tully a "cruel, fierce kiss."

Her mail, which arrives by the carload, is answered by her father and her brother Tommy, who likewise manage her finances as well. She is firmly convinced that a money-making woman should never marry a successful business man.

All her dressing gowns are of gay-colored *crêpe-de-Chine,* and her living room suggests a cross between a Hong Kong hop-joint and a pawn shop in Deauville.

In her time she has done a little of nearly everything, including the show business, moving pictures, circus work and the selling of cattle. She has also ridden in Western rodeos and won a singing scholarship.

She has been the subject of many sermons throughout the country.

By her family she is called Texas. She was once known as the "Female Bill Hart."

She delights in ermine, dim lights, and oriental perfumes.

Every year she gives away a large sum of money.

Her father and mother are both Irish.

She declares that, after the first $100,000, money doesn't mean a thing. However, she adds, were she to lose every cent and be offered a million to retire and become a "nice old lady," she would refuse and start all over again on a borrowed four dollars.

Not until she reaches ninety, she avers, has she the slightest intention of "settling down."

She hopes her funeral will be the speediest ever held in New York, and she wants a cop, on a motor cycle, to lead it.

Clarence Darrow

CLARENCE DARROW was born on the eighteenth of April, 1857, in the town of Kinsman, Ohio. His father was a miller and a great reader.

As a small boy he yearned to be an orator. He also took a keen interest in fishing. He always loathed the study of Latin.

He believes that the chief virtues are pity, charity, and love; just as he believes that the greatest sins are hardness, cruelty, and selfishness.

In 1902 he was elected to the Illinois Legislature.

As a child, two things irritated him exceedingly: (1) having to go to bed so early, and (2) having to get up so early.

He considers baseball one of the few

Beaton

TEXAS GUINAN

Out of a perambulating night-club, an Irish wit, a knack for always landing on her feet and a genius for finding words to throw into any void, Texas Guinan of New York has emerged as a nationally known trade-mark for indoor fun after midnight. Her battle-word is "Curfew shall not ring tonight" and her current night-club draws to its Musical Mornings those who know they're wise and those who are willing to get wise; the very young and the very middle-aged. With the technique of a circus "spieler," Miss Guinan makes her revival meetings a melting pot for Broadway and the Farm Belt. She sits atop the piano in a kind of savage Parcae glory, maintaining an unceasing and genuinely funny running comment, keeping everything going at one and the same time—and somehow actually rejuvenating the weary formula that all the world loves a butter-and-egg man. This Circe remains the eternal, hopping, screaming, tireless Life of the Party, *every night from eleven to seven.*

CLARENCE DARROW

The marks of battle are all over his face. He has been through more wars than a whole regiment of Pershings. And most of them have been struggles to the death. Has he always won? Superficially, yes; actually, no. Did Darrow beat Bryan at Dayton? There, I think, he came closest to a genuine victory. The thing was inconceivably dramatic: two ancient warlocks brought jaw to jaw at last. It was superb to see Darrow throw out his webs and prepare his baits. His virtuosity never failed. In the end Bryan staggered to the block and took that last appalling clout. It was delivered calmly, deliberately, beautifully. Bryan was killed as plainly as if he had been felled with an ax. Imbecilities, you say, live on? They do. But they are not as safe as they used to be. Some day, let us hope, they will be put down. Whoever at last puts them down will owe half his bays to Clarence Darrow.—*H. L. Mencken*

Muray

things in life that ever came up to his hopes and expectations.

He believes, in his innermost heart, that no one really enjoys work.

He is unable to use a typewriter, though his long-hand is so illegible that he himself is at times unable to read it.

He possesses a winning smile and a charming manner.

Ordinarily, he wears a black fedora, a low, turned-down collar, and a loosely tied cravat.

He considers lecturing enormous fun, and his debates are usually held to capacity audiences.

He nearly always needs a haircut.

As a relaxation he occasionally busies himself with cross-word puzzles.

He is an inveterate reader of all varieties of literature, especially biology.

He is heart and soul opposed to capital punishment. He always *defends;* he has never prosecuted since he has been practicing law. What's more, none of his clients has ever been hanged.

He uses the simplest phraseology.

His dream in life is twofold: (1) to impress upon the world the fact that the criminal himself is never wholly responsible, and (2) to abolish capital punishment. He believes that all jails should be transformed into hospitals.

He is strongly against the Negro prejudice and has, on numerous occasions, spoken before large colored assemblies with great success.

He is tremendously popular and is regarded everywhere as a "good sport." When he dies he hopes that "all his friends will be in both places."

The Belmont is his favorite New York hotel.

He is devoted to his friends and loves discussions with them. Now and then he likes to sit in a poker game.

He has always been an ardent admirer of George Bernard Shaw. He is also attracted to the Russian novelists.

He considers marriage purely an individual contract and that one of the great evils of our present civilization is that it is taken too seriously. He also thinks many marry too young and that divorce should be made easier.

He is extremely impatient of details and is not in the least orderly or methodical.

For the last forty-one years he has been living in Chicago.

He rarely eats any luncheon.

He normally needs eight hours' sleep a night but under stress is able to get along with very much less.

He is the author of *Farmington; Crime, Its Cause and Treatment; Persian Pearl and Other Essays; Resist Not Evil;* and *An Eye for an Eye.*

He thinks it no nobler to die fighting on the battlefield than to die in any other fashion.

He weighs one hundred and eighty-five pounds and has weighed it for years.

In all his life he has never worn a pair of gloves or mittens. Neither does he affect tan shoes. His only jewelry consists of a simple gold watch and chain.

He detests receiving long letters—the very sight of which causes him to groan—and he frequently postpones reading them for months, sometimes forever.

Though he preaches agnosticism, he practices Christianity.

Genthe

RUTH ST. DENIS

The famous American ballerina makes her California garden a mise-en-scène for classical dances

LEOPOLD STOKOWSKI

The iconoclastic conductor returns after a year abroad to lead the Philadelphia orchestra

Steichen

A Very Critical Gentleman

Reporting the Impressions of an Afternoon and an Evening with the Great Andrew Lang

MAX BEERBOHM

THE first of my two glimpses of Andrew Lang was in the summer of 1896, at an afternoon party given by Mr. and Mrs. Edmund Gosse at their house in Delamere Terrace. I think this was also the first time I was at that delightful house. My *Works* had just been published; and to Gosse, whom I had already met often enough, I had sent a copy. He was not quick to patronize young men who had done nothing, nor those who had done nothing good. Sidney Colvin would sit demurely benign, exquisitely trustful of the outcome, on any egg—on any number of eggs. Gosse cared but for the fledged and able-bodied chick. I remember that when I received my summons to Delamere Terrace I felt that my little book really had not fallen at all flat.

The drawing-room was very full when, carefully dressed for the part of brilliant young dandy, and very calm, and very shy, I made my entry. Mrs. Gosse had been reading the *Works* and introduced me, as author of them, to some lady at hand. I stood talking to this lady about the weather, inwardly hoping that she was thinking how kind it was of me to talk down to her level, and that she was not guessing that I would have liked very much to dazzle her if I had known how. But, while I talked, I thought less of the impression made by me on this lady than of the deep impression made on me by Mr. Andrew Lang.

I HAD instantly recognized him from the photographs. He was leaning against an angle of the wall. One might almost have supposed he had been placed there as an ornament. From the buzzing human throng he seemed to be quite as detached as any palm in any pot. Slender and supereminent, he curved, he drooped, he was a very beautiful thing in the room. And it was even more in colour than in form that he was so admirable. To think that Nature, and not some cunning handicraft of staining and bleaching, had produced these harmonious contrasts! The long nut-brown neck was not more sharply relieved by the white of the turned-down collar than was the nut-brown forehead by the silvery hair that wavily caressed it, than were the nut-brown cheeks by the silvery vapour they had of whisker. And the moustache was jet-black, and jet-black were the eyebrows and the eye-lashes. In such surroundings the whiteness of the eye-balls and the darkness of the brown eyes "told" tremendously, of course. But in a spiritual sense the eyes told nothing at all. They shone, they flashed, but with no animation to belie the general look of inanimateness. Their lustre was as lovely and as meaningless as that of jewels. Nature had in some corner of the earth produced two large brown diamonds, of which she was very proud; and it had seemed to her that Andrew Lang's face would be the best of all possible settings for them. So there they were. I wondered whether, with things of such fabulous value exposed on his person, he went about armed, or unarmed but very heavily insured.

Now and again, as he stood propped against the angle of the wall, he inserted with long brown fingers a monocle through which the rays of the eye were refracted with surpassing brilliance. And his manner of doing this seemed to indicate, not that there was any one whom he particularly cared to inspect, but that he took a languid pleasure in the gesture. If to superficial observers the fixing of that monocle might have convicted him of curiosity, the marked way he had of letting it drop promptly down again to his waistcoat must have acquitted him of having found the slightest profit in the investigation. With his white waistcoat he wore a pale blue tie. That was the note he had added to Nature's colour-scheme; and it was well chosen. It was good, too, as a symbol. It suggested just that detachment from Oxford which (since your thorough Oxford man is superior to everything, not excepting Oxford) stamped Andrew Lang as one of the most inalienably Oxfordish persons of his time.

NOW that I saw him in person, I was loath to lose sight of him, but I did with a good grace escort my lady down to the dining-room, where were refreshments. When we came up again, Lang was no longer visible: the palm had been transplanted—whither?—and the corner where it had stood looked very bare. Presently my host came up to me and said, "Come out on the balcony. I want you to know Andrew Lang."

There he was, gazing across the balustrade to the canal whose nymphless waters flow very near to Delamere Terrace.

"The angler aroused!" murmured Gosse. And "Yes," he said to Lang, in that tone of mock-lyric ecstasy which his friends know so well, "that is where I always go a-fishing, the first thing in the morning. Oh, you should breakfast with us! Trout, salmon, dace—I know not what! . . . But now I want you to know Mr. Max Beerbohm, whose *Collected Works* have recently been issued."

"Yes, I've just been hw-eading them," Lang drawled in a tenor voice to Gosse. (To me he tendered a graceful hand, and his gaze wandered.) "Ve-wy amusing," he faintly added.

"Why, Sir, I have read them and found neither amusement in their folly nor in their precocity the symptoms of salubrious growth" is what Dr. Johnson would have said, and is what Lang conveyed. But those words might have been for me the beginning of a life-long friendship with Dr. Johnson, whereas Lang's "ve-wy amusing" was clearly a *cul-de-sac.*

And yet I daresay he meant to be kind. I have heard from people who knew him intimately that he was a really kind man. He may even have had the wish to please. But it is certain that one had to know him intimately before his wish could, in regard to oneself, be gratified. No man can easily be popular who has the Oxford manner in even a rudimentary degree: the perfection of that manner is a sovereign charm against popularity. I have praised it in one of my books; but the eulogy was a trifle insincere —was a throw-back to the time when I had not yet outgrown my undergraduate self. Oxford I have never ceased to love; but its manner—as exemplified not in writing, but in social intercourse—I began to abhor very soon after I went down. It is no wonder that Lang was not beloved by people at large.

Especially was he not beloved by the eminent creative writers of his time. Indeed, very few critics get on well with creators. There is, no doubt, a point at which criticism does merge into creation, and it is always hard to say just where this point is —to determine whether this or that piece of fine criticism may or may not truly be called creative. But to this point, assuredly, Lang was never near. With all his gifts, he had of imagination not one spark. Fancy and wit he had in his earlier work; and grace he never lost; but for the rest he had only an immense quantity of that "cleverness" which to the creative artist is of all qualities the most repellent. And this cleverness, which was always at the disposal of the classics, was never used in service of any great contemporary writer.

He helped Stevenson, because Stevenson was a Scotsman imitating Scott (instead of following the true bent of his own fantastic genius, alas). For Browning and Meredith and Swinburne, for Henry James, for Bernard Shaw, for any spirit that was new or vital in current work, he had at best a chilly tolerance. Himself remote by nature, he could enjoy masterpieces only at a distance: their proximity jarred him. He loved "Mr. Thackeray," but he loved Jane Austen more: she was further off. And Homer he loved most of all, because Homer was further off than anyone. I think there was moreover in him (with his Gypsy blood) a strain of pure mischievousness that impelled him to poke fun at any great man who was alive to be annoyed. And this I take to be the reason why he would write now and again a sudden rhapsody about some obviously third-rate new talent.

I REMEMBER old Theodore Watts-Dunton thumping the table in his back-dining-room and saying in his most sonorous accents, "I never yet knew a genius who didn't loathe Lang." He himself was the perfect type of the critic whom men of genius love. I am not a man of genius; but this did not prevent me from loving old Theodore. It did, however, prevent me from loathing Lang. I merely shared the common lot of men who met him for the first time: I did not like him very much.

Some years elapsed before I saw him for the second time. This was on a summer evening and in the court-yard of the Hotel Cecil. I had been invited to the annual dinner in aid of the Printers' Pension Fund. As I drove up, Lang was standing bare-headed on the steps, gazing brilliantly and blankly across the court-yard. He had not changed in the interval of years; the harmony of his silver and black and brown was all unimpaired. I don't suppose I had changed much either, but it never struck me that he would remember me. I was surprised when he held out that languid hand, with no sign that we had not parted from each other only a few hours before. I think I should have felt a little flattered, had not his manner seemed rather to imply that he had not taken the trouble to forget me. He said "These dinners are hw-ather a bore, aren't they?" "Well, they're not compulsory," I might have answered; but I never wanted to put an elder man—or, for that matter, a coeval or junior—at a disadvantage. Or again, I might have said truly that I myself always rather enjoyed any sort of public dinner, provided I was to be seen at the high table. But of course I did not make this confession of innocent vanity. I merely

echoed Lang's opinion that these dinners were rather a bore.

At the meal I found myself next to Sidney Lee. It appeared that Lang and he and I (a strange triad) had been invited as representatives of Literature. Lang had been placed on the right-hand side of the Chairman—Mr. Somebody M.P., an eminent Nonconformist (I was told) and, with his full black whiskers and prolonged shorn upper lip and stout short body, a perfect type of British bourgeoisie, a marvellous foil to Lang. Lee and I were further along the table, and I had an uncomfortable feeling that Lee felt he ought at least to have been placed on the Chairman's left. This was not the first occasion on which I had sat next to him. I had been his guest at a dining-club—the Tatlers. I think that he rather liked me, and that this sentiment was on the whole sufficient consolation for his being, as it were, bracketed with me, as a representative of Literature. Certainly I liked him. He had for me the same sort of charm as had poor Churton Collins. One expected him to be dry and overbearing, as in his books he pre-eminently was, and to appall one with his erudition. One found a cheery, cosy, ruddy fellow, with a great zest for food and wine, a great capacity for receiving trivial gossip, and a great love of good cigars. My own appetite for food was always, to my regret, small. I loved the idea of a lot of it. The prospect of a very long dinner always kindled me. But in the actuality I was a weakling, unless, by good fortune, my neighbour were a tower of strength —in which case, by sheer force of example and of my own quick sympathies, I too could eat a great deal with much enjoyment and with no evil result. Even if on this particular evening I had been going to make a speech, I think my nervousness would not have prevented me from eating heartily.

AFTER dinner, in one of the intervals between the toasts, Lang came and talked to us. He was presently to respond for Literature—a duty which he described as rather a bore. Lee, whose mind was more remarkable for massive grasp and sincerity than for quickness, agreed, through a puff of cigar-smoke, that it must be rather a bore. "For *you*," I said to Lang, implying that Lee and I and the other three or four hundred diners were looking forward to a great treat. Lang smiled wearily, and said; "The Chairman's a te-wible fellow. It seems he's a Member of Parliament or something of the sort," and wandered back to his place. To me the Chairman did not seem "a te-wible fellow" at all. In the two speeches already made by him he had quite won my heart. He seemed so simple and good and solid; and, sentiment aside, I judged him, despite

his mutton-chop whiskers and his dropped h's, so very much more necessary to the national welfare than Lang or myself or—no, not than Sidney Lee. And Lang's gibe at the House of Commons seemed to me a silly relic of those 'seventies and 'eighties during which the younger literary gentlemen really thought that not to be a literary gentleman was to be something rather lamentable and absurd. Lang's gibe at poor Mr. Somebody was not jarring only because it was pathetic. I wondered whether his speech would exasperate the audience or provoke their pity. I foresaw no other alternative.

Meanwhile, our Chairman was on his legs, dealing inimitably with "Litrachur." He called it all sorts of names, the lodestar of youth, the solace of the busy man, the hand-maiden of religion—I know not what. "And though," he wound up, "we cannot all 'ope to climb those dizzy 'eights which 'ave been scaled by Mr. Randrew Lang, by (glance at notes) Mr. Sidney Lee, and (glance at notes) by Mr. Max Beerbohm (I drooped my head and faintly snorted, in deference to Lee), yet in our 'umble way every one of us may" etc.

Lang, received with cheers, made merciless fun of the Chairman, but the fun was so light and good that the cruelty really did not matter. His public manner was very much better than his private one. The necessity for talking out and up into the air, so as to be heard in a large dining-hall, greatly improved him—gave him somewhat that air of vitality and geniality of which his lack was so chastening elsewhere. He left the Chairman for dead, but the death, one felt, had been painless; and he proceeded to deplore the invention of printing. Printing had been the bane of letters. All the magic of Homer, of Chaucer, of the Hebrew Prophets, was directly traceable to this immunity from the fear of being printed. . . . The idea was worked out very wittily. Public speaking seemed to galvanize not merely Lang's manner, but also his mind: his speech was as delightful as one of those *causeries* or those leading-articles with which, many years before, he had made his name in journalism, and by virtue of which he had so long thriven, in journalism, on his name.

The audience—composed entirely of men who had to do with printing—did not laugh nor cheer, and evidently took Lang's speech as a wholly serious rebuke of their calling. But, not less evidently, there was no resentment—merely an awed hearing for the views of a personage. Lang went on to regret that such a trifler as himself had been deputed to respond instead of Mr. Sidney Lee or Mr. Max Beerbohm. He pronounced a great eulogy on Lee (to Lee's intense discomfort) and, if I remember rightly, spoke of the immense debt owed him by Shakespeare. The audience cheered respectfully. Then came a yet warmer panegyric of myself, with an elaborate parallel between me and Leonardo da Vinci—our passionate detachment from the follies and strifes of the outer world, our passionate devotion to the subtle labours we had set ourselves. Again the audience cheered, still quite respectfully. But the odd thing, as it seemed to me, was that I was inwardly pleased—almost as pleased as I should have been if Lang had paid me some tiny true compliment. To the really vain person (especially if he be also really modest) ironic praise is better than no praise at all. I remember my brother Herbert once said, "I can stand any amount of flattery—if it's only fulsome enough." And I replied "Oh, I make no conditions of any sort."

Ever after that speech at the Hotel Cecil I felt more cordial towards Lang. Had I met him again in person, perhaps I should have been chilled.

But I met him only in print. The place where I most frequently thus met him was *The Illustrated London News.* There he appeared, week by week, in circumstances that touched sharply one's sense of pathos. Week by week, there was Chesterton rolling and rollicking up and down the columns of the front page, reeling off ideas good, bad, and indifferent—but always ideas, and plenty of 'em, and plenty more where they came from. And there on one of the back pages was Andrew Lang also, his words interspersed by the Editor with numerous little photographs of things in general—circular photographs, ovals, quadrangles, around which his words had to trickle as best they might. And the sad truth was that these words deserved no better treatment than they got—such tired words as they were about such trivial points in such tedious subjects of research: Did Angus MacNob wait for Prince Charlie at the back door of the inn, as Professor Chittabob declares, and not at the side door, as tradition has it? I wondered whether Lang

himself cared about such things any more than the public which skipped what he had to say about them.

Would Chesterton some day fall back on such things? Once upon a time Lang had been as alive and alert as Chesterton. A terrible thing, Time. I wondered what Lang felt about Chesterton. What, in the fourth row of the ballet, while the vigorous prima ballerina pirouettes along the footlights, is felt by the faded and emaciated woman who in her day was prima ballerina? Perhaps she is merely glad she is still able to earn *something* . . . I thought it likely that Lang, for his name's sake, was paid quite as much as Chesterton. Still, that he had to go drearily on, pointing in that public obscurity his superannuated toes, was an odious matter for reflection. When I learned, after his death, that he had left twelve thousand pounds, I was glad his need had not been so pressing as I had supposed—glad it was rather the force of habit that had kept him so constantly "at it."

A terrible thing, Time, nevertheless.

HERBERT HOOVER

and

MRS. HOOVER

Presenting one of the foremost American presidential possibilities—and his wife

Muray

The Outlived Thing

An Inquiry into Fashions and Immortalities in Clothes, Books and Popular Taste

COMPTON MACKENZIE

THERE can be few men who have avoided the discouraging experience of trying on an old suit only to find that the world is too much with them now, that the buttons have turned into battens and what was once a garment has become a camphorated prison. Women are spared these humiliations which the conservative male inflicts upon himself and which, one cannot help believing, the cynical female delights to provide for by laying away in lavender for him these pledges of a youthful prime. I never heard of any woman keeping her old frocks; her charity begins abroad at jumble sales and in the wardrobes of poor relations. She wants no testimony to the circumference of her waist twenty years ago. She sheds her plumage as the wise birds moult while it is still summer. I understand that wedding-dresses are often kept; but no woman commits the solecism of putting on her wedding-dress again. She knows that her waist line has gone the way of her virginity, and probably the only reason she had for keeping her wedding-dress was that there was never anything else to be done with it. However, if women can escape this discouraging experience that men bring upon themselves in the matter of outlived clothes, they are not less vulnerable to other reproachful conundrums of the past. "Can I really once upon a time have imagined myself in love with that man or that woman?" But this is hardly a fair example, because after all the object of our early affection will almost certainly not have retained its shape like the clothes; on the contrary the object will quite conceivably have expanded unduly while our own capacity for emotion is more than likely to have shrunk.

WHAT about our old intellectual loves? What makes us at thirty turn over the pages of a novel we remember as having thought so marvellous at eighteen, only to find our former state of mind incredible? The obvious answer is that our taste has developed meanwhile. Experience has taught us that what the innocence of youth accepted as life was in fact completely unreal. A wide reading has spoiled our zest for that sickly style we once fancied so luscious. Yes, but when we go a little further into the question we encounter a paradox. How are we to explain the effect of the outlived author? In my own case I have reached a point of not being able to read any book by Dickens, Balzac, or Scott—to mention three

giants—which I have not previously read in youth. Yet whatever novels of these writers I have originally read I can read again and again. Put *Pickwick* or *Eugénie Grandet* or *Ivanhoe* beside my bed tonight and I will read any of them with excitement. Give me *Little Dorrit* or *La Peau de Chagrin* or *Kenilworth* (you see how fairly I am choosing from what are considered among the best of their authors' works) and I shall be asleep in five minutes.

The only explanation seems to be that one re-reads the outlived author with the remembered emotions of youth. But in that case why cannot I read again a novel like *The Gadfly* by E. L. Voynich which once upon a time thrilled me as an alchemist would have been thrilled by discovering the stone that transmuted base metals to gold, but which I opened the other day to find as absurd a farrago of melodramatic nonsense as ever was concocted. I suppose that the Behaviourists who can tell us all about God and man and the endocrine glands in small octavo volumes could solve this as slickly as they solve the major problems of life and death and human destiny. Meanwhile I remain puzzled, as in parentheses I may as well admit that I remain puzzled about some of the major problems of life and death and human destiny after reading the chief works of the Behaviourist apostles. We are all ready to accept re-reading, as the test of a book's vitality; but before relying upon this for our final judgment we ought to be sure that our own development meanwhile has not proceeded too far in the opposite direction.

For instance I believe I would suffer most things sooner than to read through the *Brothers Karamazov* again, and that is the book that twenty years ago I would without hesitation have named as the greatest novel in the world. Yet, I should never dream of denying its greatness because for me it has turned into a vast foggy boredom. The fact that a man like Arnold Bennett, who is so far from the cant of enjoying what he thinks he ought to enjoy, still writes with obvious enthusiasm of the *Brothers Karamazov* shows that it is not one of those works of art which perpetually appeal to youth but lose their power in middle-age. It may be that I shall reach again a period when I can enjoy the *Brothers Karamazov*. But I do not think so. I find myself with the years turning more and more to Greece for my literary pleasure, and is it possible for anybody to

enjoy Sophocles and Dostoevsky equally at the same time?

THE progress of taste is easier to register in music than in literature. So many accidental associations interfere with our literary progress, and the finest critic is not secure against the effect of matter when he should be considering only that of form. The regularity with which pilgrims along the high road of music enter by the gates of Schubert's *Unfinished Symphony* and Chopin's *Nocturnes* and proceed through Beethoven's *Fifth Symphony* is remarkable. You cannot find any such recognized route in literature. And equally remarkable is the regularity with which these pilgrims disown those old-fashioned ivy-covered gateways when they have the key to the convulsive wrought-iron portals of Stravinsky or Schönberg. Warned by my experience in poetry I resolved never to forsake old favourites in music, because I do find these ghosts of youthful loves haunt age with increasing reproachfulness. I can never again declaim Longfellow's "Psalm of Life" with the passionate abandon of boyhood. Indeed I can never again declaim it at all. And I do not intend to let myself be fossilized out of Chopin or Schubert. Of course, it will mean being careful not to hear them too often. Music is more exposed to the effects of surfeit than literature. If you could count the number of times you listen to a famous composition and measure them against the times you read a famous poem, you will realize this. In the problem of why we outgrow certain works of art the solution will often be the contempt of familiarity—a mere question of getting tired of a good thing by having too much of it. That presumably is the cause of a popular song's mortality, not any development in ourselves. What is strange, however, about popular songs is that they should never be revived. There may be instances of some revivals, but if there be I do not know them. They die when their season is over with the completeness of flowers. But why should the surfeit of one generation extend its effect to succeeding generations? Even if the words are dated why may not once popular tunes be given new words and with them a new lease of life? But no, it seems forbidden to a real best seller like *If Winter Comes* or *The Green Hat* to survive or revive. *The Green Hat* was obviously doomed to a brief life. Every line in it was as much dated as the cut of a skirt or the shape of the heroine's own green hat. But why can we feel safe in prophesying that a new generation will ignore *If Winter Comes?* It was a book so completely old-fashioned when it first appeared that it might seem to be safe against time's revenges. There will be as many unsophisticated readers fifty years hence as there are now. Why should it not live? All one can say is that some law of nature is against its survival.

BUT after all can any work of art really survive on its own power of eternal appeal? I used to think that what we called a "classic" was a work of art whose reputation with a minority was endorsed by the appreciation of the majority. But I am coming to think that a "classic" is a work of art whose reputation with a minority is accepted in text books by the majority. Occasionally some *enfant terrible* of criticism calls out like the child in Hans Andersen that the Emperor has no clothes, and then a frantic effort is made to give him a genuine suit of new clothes. We have just been dressing *Macbeth* in khaki in response to such a clamour. But the fact is, and we may as well face it, unpleasant though it be to conservatives like myself, that the break with the past during this century is already more definite than anything since the Renaissance, and all the signs are that it will become far more complete than that before it is finished. Every age is an age of transition, said Goethe. That may be true, but he was thinking of transit in terms of contemporary locomotion. Transition is hardly the word for the rate at which we are now moving. The circumstances of the present are all in favour of outgrowing and outliving everything more rapidly than ever before in the history of humanity. In a world which is fast preparing to outgrow God one may be allowed to feel skeptical about the chance of Shakespeare's up-to-date appeal, even if you sent the actors onto the stage wearing nothing at all. And the disconcerting part about this outgrowing and outliving is that there is no perceptible development of the inward man that is pretending to keep pace with the development of the outward man. We are like children who have too many toys, and we outgrow our old toys not because our imagination has exhausted itself in playing with them, but because we are continually being presented with new toys. I write pessimistically, because I do feel pessimistic about the future of art. I cannot believe that children so well supplied with new toys are going to need grown-up people or even other children to amuse them much longer. We have yet to see the effects of radio on a generation brought up from birth to be aware of its eternal intrusion. We are faced with the certainty of television and the effect of that on another generation. The artist is made in childhood, and if children are left with no desire to dream a world of their own, I cannot believe they will ever be able to dream a world for others. Besides, dream worlds will not be wanted. There was never a moment when it was so necessary for the artist to gather that fleeting moment and never has that fleeting moment been so rich.

Perhaps with our increasing bewilderment before the future and despair after the past we shall achieve again that exquisite sense of the present which was the real secret of the greatness of Greek art. The architecture of modern America is the nearest thing that humanity has achieved to the sculpture of Hellas.

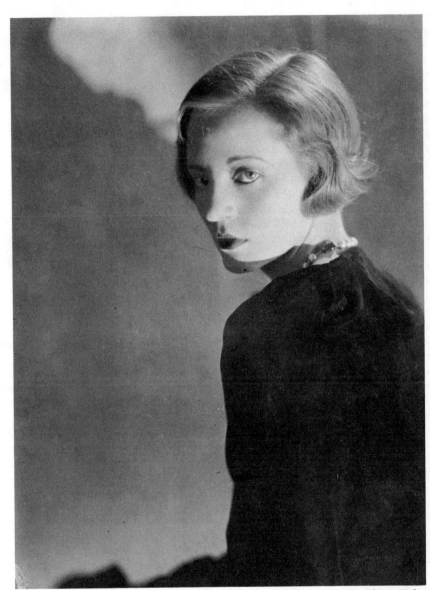

Hoyningen-Huhne

TALLULAH BANKHEAD

An American actress who has become one of the foremost stars of the English stage

Miss Bankhead has startled London with her spectacular triumphs in *The Dancers, Fallen Angels, The Green Hat, They Knew What They Wanted* and *The Gold Diggers.* She is the daughter of one U.S. Senator, the niece of another, and she is the only actress on either side of the Atlantic who is immediately identified by her first name.

Deserted Battlefields

A Polemic Against Mass Thinking and Men's Modern Indifference to the Ancient Rewards

D. H. LAWRENCE

WE STILL are ruled too much by ready-made phrases. Take for example: A man must be master in his own house. There's a good old maxim, we all believe it in theory. Every little boy sees himself a future master in his own house. He grows up with the idea well fixed. So naturally, when his time comes and he finds, as he does pretty often, that he's *not* master in his own house, his nose is conventionally out of joint. He says: These overbearing modern women, they insist on bossing the show, and they're absolutely in the wrong.

What we have to beware of is mass thinking. The idea that a man must be master in his own house is just a mass idea. No man really thinks it for himself. He accepts it *en bloc,* as a member of the mass. He is born, so to speak, tightly swaddled up in it, like a lamb in its wool.

In fact, we are born so woolly and so swaddled up in mass ideas, that we hardly get a chance to move, to make a real move of our own. We just bleat foolishly out of a mass of woolly cloud, our mass ideas, and we get no further. A man must be master in his own house. Feed the brute. An Englishman's home is his castle. Two servants are better than one. Happy is the bride who has her own little car in her own little garage. It is the duty of the husband to give his wife what she wants. It is the duty of a wife to say "Yes, darling!" to her husband:—all these are mass ideas, often contradicting one another, but always effective. If you want to silence a man, or a woman, effectively, trot out a mass idea. The poor sheep is at once mum.

NOW the thing to do with a mass idea is to individualize it. Instead of massively asserting: A man must be master in his own house, the gentleman in question should particularize and say: I, Jim, must be master in my own house, *The Rosebud* or *The Doves' Nest,* over my wife, Julia. And as soon as you make it personal and drag it to earth, you will feel a qualm about it.

You can storm over the breakfast coffee: A man must be master in his own house! But it takes much more courage to say: My name's Jim, and I must be master in this house, *The Rosebud,* over you, Julia, my spouse! This is bringing things to an issue. And things are rarely so brought. The lord and master fumes with a mass idea, and the spouse and helpmeet fumes with a mass resentment, and their mingled fumings end by making a nice mess of *The Rosebud.*

Muray

D. H. LAWRENCE

As a matter of fact, when Jim begins to look into his own heart, and also to look *The Rosebud,* which is his own house, firmly in the eye, he finds—O shattering discovery!—that he has very little desire to be master in *The Rosebud.* On the contrary, the idea rather nauseates him. And when he looks at Julia calmly pouring the coffee, he finds, if he's the usual Jim, that his desire to be master over that young dame is curiously non-existent.

And there's the difference between a mass idea and real individual thinking. Jim finds the idea of being master in *The Rosebud* rather feeble, and the idea of being master over the cool Julia somehow doesn't inspire him. He doesn't really care whether *The Rosebud* has pink bows on the curtains or not. And he doesn't care really what Julia does with her day, while he's away at his job. He wants her to amuse herself and not bother him. That is, if he's the ordinary and representative Jim.

So that man being master in his own house falls flat when the man is indifferent to his mastery. And that's the worst of mass ideas: they remain, like fossils, when the life that animated them is dead. The problem of mastery in a house is today no problem, really, because the man is hopelessly indifferent about it. He feels mere indifference; only now and then he may spout up the mass idea, and make an unreal fume which does a lot of harm.

We may take it for granted that wherever woman bosses the show, it is because man doesn't want to. It is not rapacity and pushing on the woman's part. It is indifference on the man's. Men don't really care. Whenever they *do* care, there is no question of the intrusion of women.

Men really care still about engineering and mechanical pursuits, so there is very little intrusion of women there. But men are sadly indifferent to clerking pursuits, and journalistic pursuits, and even to parliamentary pursuits. So women flood in to fill the vacuums. If we get a House of Commons or a Congress filled with women members, it will be purely and simply for the reason that men, energetic men, are indifferent; they don't care any more about being Congressmen or Members of Parliament and making laws.

Indifference is a strange thing. It lies there under all the mass thinking and the mass activity, like a gap in the foundations. We still make a great fuss about government—and, underneath, most men are indifferent to it. All the fuss about a home of your own and a wife of your own: and underneath, the men are only too often indifferent to the house and the wife both. They are only too willing for the wife to do the bossing and the caring, so that they need neither care nor boss.

Indifference is not the same as insouciance. Insouciance means not caring about things that don't concern you; it also means not being pinched by anxiety. But indifference is inability to care; it is the result of a certain deadness or numbness. And it is nearly always accompanied by the pinch of anxiety. Men who can't care any more feel anxious about it. They have no insouciance. They are thankful if the woman will care. And at the same time, by a kind of infantile perversity, they resent the woman's caring and running the show.

THE trouble is not in the women's bossiness, but in the men's indifference. This indifference is the real malady of the day. It is a deadness, an inability to care about anything. And it is of its nature that it be always pinched by anxiety.

And whence does the indifference arise? It arises from having cared too much, from having cared about the wrong thing, in the immediate past. If there is a growing indifference to politics on the part of men, it is because men have cared far too much about politics.

If Jim is really indifferent to his little home, *The Rosebud,* if he leaves it all to Julia, that is because his father and grandfather cared far too much about their little homes; made them a bit nauseating. If men don't care very vitally about their jobs, nowadays, and leave them to women, it is because our fathers and grandfathers considered the job sacrosanct—which it isn't—and so wore out the natural feeling for it, till it became repulsive.

Men leave the field to women, when men become inwardly indifferent to the field. What the women take over is really an abandoned battle. They don't pick up the tools and weapons of men until men have let them drop.

And then men, gnawed by the anxiety of their own very indifference, blame women and start reiterating like parrots such ideas as: "Man must be master in his house."

GLORIA
SWANSON

The star has made a film version of "Miss Thompson," the Maugham story which is better known as Rain

Steichen

Barakovitch

ROSAMOND PINCHOT

The leading lady of The Miracle *turns from pantomime to acting in Shakespeare à la Reinhardt*

"THE FRONT PAGE"

The latest play of newspaperdom (by Ben Hecht and Charles MacArthur) stars Osgood Perkins and Lee Tracy as its super-journalists

Steichen

CLARA BOW

En plein air

Ladies and gentlemen (not to mention children): regard, observe and otherwise behold—in an informal pose—the vivacious, the audacious, the orchidaceous Clara Bow! Feast your weary optics upon this super-flapper of them all—the hyper-reality and extra-ideality of a million or more film-goers. Thus in one person, in one pose, we have the *genus* American girl, refined, washed, manicured, pedicured, permanent-waved and exalted herewith. We have all watched the little lady prancing and dancing in her own entrancing way upon the silver screen. Do you wonder that for the nonce she is almost the most popular of the movie stars? And a writer, too, if you please! Yes, indeed; for dainty Clara has recently completed the only authentic story of her life, beginning with a statement whose veracity will surprise her most ardent admirers—"My father is the only person I care for, really" (sic). What can one add—except that she has red hair?

Dyar

The Too General Public

Showing the Degeneration of Art from an Ancient Social Necessity to an "Art for Art's Sake"

ANDRÉ GIDE

IT WAS a dangerous thing for art to withdraw from life—a dangerous thing for both art and life. The day on which the artist no longer felt the nearness of a public, the day on which art no longer found its justification, its meaning, and its use in society and morals, art was not destroyed, as one might have expected. It did not die, because the laurel of Apollo is hardy, and will not perish until the very race in which it has found sustenance for its deep roots has perished. No, art did not die of this: it fell a-doting. The history of modern art is inexplicable otherwise: the artist who is out of touch with his public is prompted, not to cease producing, but to produce works devoid of destination. The painter paints without knowing on what walls his paintings are to hang; a sculptor cannot tell how the light will fall upon his statues; the poet, singing, hears his own voice.

I do not claim that the great artists of the Renaissance or of Antiquity would have censured the doctrines which are known as "art for art's sake." I claim that they would not even have understood them. For obviously these doctrines are born of an era in which art, no longer having a place, being now unable to participate actively or find its stimulus in life, isolates itself with hauteur, becomes infatuate, and despises all who cannot value it sufficiently. And while the artist is deprived of all external tests for the excellence of his work, being forced to look solely within himself for approbation, we see the birth and development of a new form of criticism (it has been called "subjective criticism") which finds no grounding in a society without taste, but judges works (since the need to judge persists) in terms of its own personal taste and of the greater or lesser amount of pleasure which it derives from them.

IT IS remarkable how strong our hatred is for all dogmatic criticism (or criticism which seems dogmatic to an age no longer unified by dogma). A very significant thing. All the great periods of lofty artistic production are based wholly upon a kind of criticism which is dogmatic to the utmost, and which in turn derives its strength from the assurance of a cultivated society behind it. Criticism once spoke in the name of such a society, furnishing it with reasons for applause or hisses, though the choice had already been made spontaneously in accordance with good taste.

Abbott

ANDRÉ GIDE

Its function was to create, with as little artificiality as possible, a certain idea of the beautiful (we might say: a certain ideal), fixing certain rules and formulating certain attitudes within or beyond which art would seem to perish or lose caste.

The manifestations of art are endless. Its schools are legion, but I doubt whether a civilization is capable of producing and nurturing more than one of them at a given moment in its history. When Louis XIV, who was shown some pictures by Téniers, exclaimed, "Away with such ugly things," this was a case wherein narrowness was intelligence. Were Téniers four times as great, this dictum would still be justified—or even if it concerned Rubens or Velasquez. It was not at all necessary for Louis XIV to have an accurate knowledge of painting. A society derives an art not from a greater or lesser comprehension, but from its need of art. In refusing to understand Téniers, French society was able to produce Poussin; and conversely, a society capable of producing Téniers, or Rubens, would necessarily fail to recognize Poussin.

OUR age lays claim to more intelligence, especially to more eclecticism. In the rooms of our museums, these great burial grounds of art, we of today know how to bring Poussin, Velasquez, and Rubens together.

We enjoy Kranach and Dürer; but we also enjoy Delacroix and Goya; and that is taken for granted; and we are right to enjoy them; and it would be stupid not to enjoy them in our times; one does not re-learn ignorance. And similarly we are right when, at a concert, we can applaud a "Ride of the Valkyries" after a Mozart quartet. . . . But it must be admitted that this intelligent eclecticism, on which we congratulate ourselves, is proof—alas!—that art has ceased to be a natural product, that it no longer answers a definite need of the public, and that our disintegrated society, lacking a distinct ideal for formulation in some particular style, can accept imprudently and by chance encounter all the ideals of the past and any new ones which contemporary artists bring forward. And artistic tradition, which so many successive generations had carried so far, seems like a tree whose powerful main trunk is finally dying because society is no longer in a position to trim it, to clear away the mass of suckers springing up from the roots, which live forever. Often these shoots, each taken by itself, are admirable; but finally they divert all the sap, yet come to nothing beyond themselves.

An artist can do but little by himself. Who will say how much persistent and continuous effort was required of an attentive and industrious society through its successive generations to shape Hellenic beauty, for instance, in both art and life? The expression of its ideal (that is to say, the tracing of its portrait) remained like a moral and civic obligation for this admirable little people in whom morals, civilization, and art all came together.

We are astonished today at the polychrome architecture of the Greeks, and our "good taste" is offended. Our temples and public monuments are white because they no longer respond to anything but abstract needs. We no longer realize that the Greek temple, born of the soil, should not be distant from the earth, and that the gods who inhabit it should assume the colours of life.

Art, despite the modicum of heaven that it reflects, is something wholly human. As it remains in close contact with man's beliefs, nothing will affect it more injuriously than a rationalized religion. A people without art is a people whose gods are far removed from man and rule him without love. Similarly, when the abstract reason of man dares to brand as false the numberless mantles of form, this divine hypocrisy, religion, reascends into the retreating sky. Earth is abandoned by divinity; the colour of the temple pales.

Art can only flourish at those points where heaven and earth touch—at those times, I mean, when gods become men and men become gods. Neither Jewish nor Arabian monotheism could engender art; and in order that Christianity might be empowered to give the earth a new imagery, the formless God of the prophets had to descend in human incarnation. Even that was not enough. Instead of subjecting itself to Christianity, art made Christianity serve the purposes of art, by seizing upon everything that was amenable to human form. Apostles, prophets, male and female saints, a whole people of demi-gods. Could the Holy Ghost or the theological virtues be painted? Christian art, as such, scarcely exists; possibly it is a contradiction in terms. But society (to which we must revert) demanded that art be Christian. Art promptly made a pretence of being so, and the artist performed the services that were expected of him.

THROUGH a singular misunderstanding, the merit of sincerity in the work of art is extolled nowadays above all else. The artist is asked to be sincere, though no one feels quite competent to say what he means by the term. The artists of the Renaissance never bothered much about it. Do you think that society's insistence upon outward conformity to a common religion could injure their personalities? On the contrary, the cloak of Catholic hypocrisy under which they were compelled to hide their naturally pagan sensuality served the purposes of art; and we have seen the greatest of them resorting to the most hypocrisy. Art has been most brilliant in the most hypocritical eras. Hypocrisy is one of the conditions of art. It is the public's duty to force hypocrisy upon the artist.

The important thing was that a society should exist and should make demands. It demanded glorification, exaltation, intoxication. And it had the good taste to demand that the result be artistic, because it was a cultivated society. The artist served as cup-bearer. Before this thirst for art could arise, it was first necessary that society should no longer be hungry. Its material hunger was sufficiently appeased; and as for the hungers of mind and soul, the Church took care of

them. For none but well-fed societies, where the mind is at rest in the calm acceptance of some dogma or religion, have arts. Scepticism may be the beginning of wisdom; but where wisdom begins, art leaves off.

Panem et circenses, cried the Latin populace: first bread, then the games. The free play of art is not enjoyed when the stomach is empty. It is after the repast that the artist is called upon the scene. His function is not to feed, but to inebriate.

I love to recall that Plato, whose love of truth leads him in his Gorgias to make Socrates rail against flattery—that is, against intoxication—is the same man who would banish poets from his Republic and who, in speaking of Orpheus, calls him mean, "like the musician that he was."

The work of art is a flattery. And the mistake of the artist is not flattery, but flattery in the wrong place. Flattery is no better than the value which the person for whom it is intended puts upon himself. Thus the public must demand flattery that is exquisite, refusing to accept any but the best. The public does not make the artist, but at least it can make demands of him, and can make its demands exacting. Finally, it can withhold encouragement from the mediocre, exalting none but the superior; its culture will entitle it to be strict.

This public, I say, must not be hungry; it must be cultivated; I will add that it must be few in number. The Greeks of the Periclean age were few—and the *honnêtes gens* of Louis XIV, the Italian nobles of the Renaissance, the notables of the court of Weimar. So few in number that the individual could feel himself directly flattered by the work of art.

The danger of the mob, of this "totally unpolished" public which Goethe spoke of, does not derive solely from the fact that its uncultured condition makes flattery too easy, but also from the fact that it is too numerous. How flatter a heterogeneous, hodge-podge public which has no culture or traditions in common, neither tastes, ideal, nor duties? One cannot flatter it as a whole except in places most common to all men—yes, in places most common. That is observable especially in the theatre. Praised be the society of Weimar, which could find its flattery in *Iphigenia* and *Torquato Tasso!* It is good for the artist to know whom he is addressing. In our days, when he can no longer tell, he either breaks

with his age and retires within himself, as we have seen the best men do, relying on the future to recompense him for the present, and ideally flattering an unknown public which is vaguely scattered over the future; or indeed (but does he then deserve the name of artist?) he flatters the mob at random—and I shall not name the results, but you know them.

Another danger of the mob, alas! is the fact that it is hungry. It asks to be fed. The old dogmas no longer suffice. The contemporary mind rejects them like foods without savour. The oldest questions, on which the *élite* public of the past was quite tacitly and unostentatiously in agreement, have been raised again and call for new answers. Moral questions, social questions in particular. (May Weimar be spared them!) Henceforth, there is nothing disinterested in the work. The thesis play is invented. It is unsubstantial food. But what is the difference!—so long as the mob is satisfied.

And these adulterators, who are incapable of a pure work of art, despise it; and accordingly the mob despises, in the name of utilitarian art, the work of art which is unutilized.

WHEN Joseph was in prison, two prisoners like himself, two officers of Pharaoh, spoke to him—the Bible tells us. They had dreamed a dream both of them, each man his dream . . . and behold, they were sad. Now Joseph interpreted their dreams. When the first man had spoken, "This is the interpretation," Joseph explained. "Within yet three days shall Pharaoh lift up thine head, and restore thee unto thine office: and thou shalt give Pharaoh's cup into his hand, after the former manner when thou wast his butler."

And when the second man had spoken, "Within yet three days," said Joseph, "shall Pharaoh lift up thy head from off thee, and shall hang thee on a tree."

The first was the butler, the cup-bearer, the man who pours that other men may drink. Pharaoh, remembering him, recalled him to his court. Such was Ganymede, who bore intoxicants for the banquets of the gods.

The second, the chief baker, who provided food, was hanged. Such was Prometheus, who was enchained upon the Caucasus.

Nominated for the Hall of Fame: 1928

PABLO PICASSO

Because, although a Spaniard, he is one of the leading French artists; because he achieved world-wide fame and misunderstanding as the creator of Cubism; and finally because although a few years ago he was an artistic anarchist, he is now named with Matisse as a dean of modernism.

Muray

LOUIS BROMFIELD

Because he is one of the most prominent of our younger novelists; because his first novel, *The Green Bay Tree,* which he recently dramatized, gained him immediate recognition; and finally because his *Early Autumn* won the Pulitzer Prize last year.

Geiringer

THOMAS MANN

Because he is an eminent German novelist who has recently become popular in America; because he was editor of *Simplicissimus*; and finally because his next book is being eagerly awaited in America.

Bengsch

JED HARRIS

Because he is probably the youngest and most successful of theatrical producers; because in a year he produced *Broadway, Coquette,* and *The Royal Family,* which brought him a fortune and also a reputation as one of the most discriminating theatre people; and finally because he proposes to found a repertory theatre, in the European manner.

MAX REINHARDT

Because he is the world's best-known stage director; because he has made the Salzburg Festivals a mecca for tourists; because his productions in the last twenty-five years have had a profound influence on stage technique; and finally because he has recently staged *A Midsummer Night's Dream* in New York.

Moholy-Dessan

WALTER GROPIUS *(left)*

Because he is one of the leading German architects and the founder of the Bauhaus in Weimar; because his work has effected untold improvements in living conditions in Germany; and finally because his recent visit to the United States made even stronger his belief in the modernism of future architecture.

Barré

SERGE DIAGHILEFF

Because he is the director of the Russian Ballet which is now in its twenty-first season; because this portrait of him was painted by Léon Bakst; and finally because he plans to bring the Ballet to America for the first time in ten years.

S. M. EISENSTEIN *(above)*

Because, although a young man, he is the pioneer motion-picture director of new Russia, having made three internationally acclaimed films, *The Strike, Potemkin* and *Ten Days That Shook the World;* because he started his career as a professor of mathematics; and finally because he has introduced in his films a new and dynamic idea.

ERNEST HEMINGWAY

Because in two years he has become one of the leading American novelists; because identifying his characters has become a national pastime; because he followed *The Sun Also Rises* with the equally successful *Men Without Women;* and because although he lives in France he writes about Americans.

Breaker

COUNTESS DE CHAMBRUN

Because she is a noted Shakespeare scholar; because she is a sister of Nicholas Longworth and the wife of General de Chambrun (shown with her here); because her book *Shakespeare—Actor, Poet* was awarded the Prix Bordin by the French Academy; because she is prominent in diplomatic and literary circles in France and America.

157

The Captain's Memoirs

For Which an Artichoke, Some Indian Pudding and a Little Coffee Are Offered as Appetizers

ALEXANDER WOOLLCOTT

IT IS related of DeWolf Hopper that that incorrigible bridegroom likes few things in this unsatisfactory world so much as a dish of Indian pudding. For years it has been the custom, when engagements (to act, that is) or rehearsals have brought him to New York, to hurry to the Hotel Algonquin, escorting each new wife in turn and introducing her to the sacred mysteries of his favorite dish. On the subject of this homely confection Hopper would always grow lyrical. George, the head waiter, became so familiar with this not particularly secret passion that he could read the look of inquiry on the famous Hopper face the moment the gigantic comedian appeared between the curtains of the dining-room. The rising eyebrows meant "Is there Indian pudding or is there not?" If George nodded affirmatively, Hopper would make the rounds of the tables in his neighborly fashion, singing the song of his beloved pudding, urging one and all to forego mere lemon pie or floating island and join him in the dish of dishes. On one occasion, only Raymond Hitchcock rebelled, protesting moodily that he preferred rice pudding. Hopper stood aghast. He poured forth his aesthetic contempt for one who would eat an uneventful dish that could be had any day of the year when there was such an alternative as Indian pudding.

"All right, have it your own way," said Hitchcock weakly, "I'll take Indian pudding."

WITH a glow of the successful missionary warming his heart, Hopper then sat him down and whetted his appetite with soup and meat, saw the table cleared for the great event, and then announced in a voice that boomed across the hotel, "Now George, bring me the Indian pudding."

It was after an interval that George came back, pale with fear.

"I'm sorry, Mr. Hopper," he said, "but we just served the last dish to Mr. Hitchcock."

Which parable is one of a thousand traditions of this hotel on a New York side street which has become legendary in its time as the gastric gathering place of writers and players; the inn which, by the working of those forces that give any tavern its character, has long stood at the windy corner where New Grubb Street crosses the Rialto. So many are the kindred traditions that one is tempted to suggest (and

in fact this one hereby does suggest) that some midwife of beautiful letters might do worse than look around the Algonquin for a book of memoirs.

Frank Case, the proprietor for this past quarter of a century, might write such a book. Or Sarah, the coal-black mammy who, in snowy cap and apron, deals out the pies and pastries she has concocted in the invisible kitchens below. But the occasional glimpse of her extending a dark and affable hand to some such passing old-timer as Lew Fields or David Warfield is eloquent rather of the more eventful days when, for twenty years, Sarah was the maid in the dressing room of that most ample of American comediennes, May Irwin.

Or one might get a book of memoirs out of Victor, the Castilian coatroom boy, who will be leaving this Spring to study painting in Paris. It was not Victor but his immediate predecessor who entranced the Algonquin clientele by studying with disfavor the "No Hat Tip, Please" legend painted on the lintel over his domain. After some days, however, he felt that he had hit upon the aspect of that legend which displeased him, and, getting a brush and paint pot, he mounted a ladder and edited it slightly by painting out the first word.

All these observers of the scene might have their tales to tell, but I would be inclined to favor the memoirs of George Jacques, captain for many years past of the dining-room recently caricatured by the frivolous weekly *Judge*. In that weekly a page was given over to a cartoon by Ellison Hoover, an ironical fellow who has a good deal of quiet fun making sketches of places like Hollywood, Moscow and Paris as they must be visualized by one who has never been there. This latest flight of his fancy was a hotel dining-room, with a little group of serious eaters—Henry Ford, for instance, and Barbara Frietchie and Hannibal—all lunching at one Round Table. Nearby, the Smith Brothers were gravely sharing an omelette and anecdotes about cough-drops with Mary, Queen of Scots. At the next table, Jack Dempsey, Abd-el-Krim and Joan of Arc made an interesting, though faintly implausible, group of battling types. And, in a far corner of the lobby, Von Hindenburg was morosely waiting to go in to lunch with Lady Godiva who, providentially, was sitting in the shadow of a pillar. The picture was entitled, "The Algonquin,

by One Who Has Heard All About It."

Though marked by a faint exaggeration, this picture of George's realm has enough truth in it to suggest that his autobiography might be entertaining. If ever he returns to his native Aegean isle to sit in the sun and remember, I trust he will tell us whether, if he were ever to become captain of a dining-room again, he would not rather serve, let us say, in the Bankers' Club, where, it may be guessed, the captain profits by an occasional suggestion about Radio or General Electric. For his years of service, George's old age must be chiefly comforted, I fear, by an unrivaled set of contemporary first editions, autographed to him by such oddly assorted clients as Gertrude Atherton, Carl Van Vechten, Ernest Boyd, Heywood Broun, John V. A. Weaver, Rex Beach, Joseph Hergesheimer, Rabindranath Tagore, Robert Benchley and Dorothy Parker, to say nothing (unless you insist) of Jim Tully and Konrad Bercovici.

HIS memoirs might also advise us whether, in case he were ever to open an inn of his own, he might not prefer a less leisurely clientele. It is the other dining-room, where there is sometimes a chance of a second sitting, that makes the Algonquin's profits, if any. Most of George's clients can spend so much time over a few stalks of endive that, by comparison, the members of Christopher Morley's Three-Hours-for-Lunch Club seem to be bolting their food.

When *My Life in Art* by George Jacques eventually appears upon the book stalls, I hope to find in it not only the parable of the Indian pudding but the story of Jack Barrymore and the cup of coffee, and also the story of the artichoke which, for a brief period, made a reluctant impresario out of a hotel proprietor. The episode of the disastrous artichoke goes back to the days when Mr. Case's tavern was more conspicuously a haven for those writers and actors whose ships, perhaps already visible on the horizon, had not yet come in to port. As he himself had no money at the time and the hotel was not yet out of debt, I suppose he had a fellow-feeling for young hopefuls. Of course the really daring poker player is the one who has nothing to lose. And somewhat on that principle, the Algonquin, in its youth, used to allow certain fledgling writers and artists to run up the most staggering bills.

One young dramatist—he has since become celebrated both here and in London, but he must be nameless in this chronicle—stayed on for weeks and weeks, the bill being allowed to mount past the two thousand mark just because there was an air about him of one who could write a brilliant play if ever he put his mind to it. There were times when the worried proprietor was moved to drop gentle hints that the needy genius might better surrender his room in favor of someone who, although only the author of a vaudeville sketch, was living in the enjoyment of royalties actually coming in.

But he was never goaded to drastic action until one night when, feeling especially low-spirited and hard up, he glanced into his dining-room and saw his self-appointed protégé at supper. It was what the protégé was eating that brought on the storm. With the air of one who knows no worry, he had ordered the most costly luxury on the menu. He was eating an artichoke. Case fled from the scene and, while the unconscious guest was still dipping the tender and expensive leaves into a pool of *sauce Hollandaise,* the outraged boniface was upstairs, ordering the fellow's bed dismantled, taken apart and hidden away in the storeroom. After all the gentle hints, this final gesture had the effect of informing the young man that he was no longer wanted, and off he went, protesting his undying affection for his host and pressing into his hands at parting the only valuable thing he could leave as hostage for his bill. It was the manuscript of an unproduced play. Trunks have been seized since the first trunks were made, but this is probably the first case of a bill being settled with a rejected play.

The surprised recipient mulled over it for a time, then took it down the hall to Eugene Walter, induced him to re-write it for a mere 75 per cent of the possible royal-ties, and finally got his own share of the proceeds only by a suit at law, during which he heard himself denounced in court as a mere crass dealer in lodgings and nourishment who would fall like a vulture upon the dream children of artists. The play in its final form was called *Fine Feathers.*

THE story of the aforesaid cup of coffee tells not of that Jack Barrymore who became, and for a brief time remained, the foremost actor of the English-speaking stage, nor even of that lesser person who is part of the circus in the town called Hollywood. It is rather the Jack Barrymore who, after tentative and unsatisfactory experiments in drawing cartoons for the *Evening Journal,* and also in doing nothing at all, came wandering into the theatre as a lackadaisical wastrel who, everybody felt safe in predicting, would certainly come to no good end. George need feel no delicacy about thus reverting to the days of the great Barrymore's vagabondage, because they are the very part of his life which the great Barrymore himself most likes to dwell upon whenever he puts pen to paper or puts his lips close to the Boswellian ear of Karl Schmidt. In those days Barrymore used to stop at the Algonquin because his famous uncle was always lodged there during the Drew season at the Empire, and because of the proprietor's seemingly endless patience in the matter of bills. The management did try (unsuccessfully) to shake this touching confidence. On one occasion the cheerful Barrymore's trunk was being held by the less pally Bellevue-Stratford in Philadelphia for a little matter of $35.00. It came on to the Algonquin only when Mr. Case promised over the telephone to send his own check for that embarrassing amount. Case did feel, however, that for the good of his own soul the young sinner should at least make this amount good. So when, forgetting all about it, Barrymore left blandly for a song-and-dance engagement in Chicago that evening, the hotel was moved to experiment in administering the salutary shock of a suit at law. The process server was guided to the very door of Barrymore's hotel room in Chicago, and was left there to apply the aforesaid shock. As nothing seemed to come of it, however, the discouraged Mr. Case investigated and found that Barrymore (through the keyhole of his bathroom) had welcomed the surprise party with the affable offer of a drink, that this unstable minion of the law had thereafter sat him down to wait for the morning bath to be over, and when last seen the process server and the defendant were weaving through Chicago, arm in arm.

Amused but exasperated, the baffled plaintiff tried again, somewhat in the spirit of a man who keeps plugging away at Canfield until at last he runs it out. When next the elusive young player put foot in New York another and more abstemious process server was set on his track. That night, while hurrying to the theatre, Barrymore dashed up to Case, feeling distractedly in his pocket as he approached him, retrieving at last a crumpled piece of paper, and thrust it into Case's hands.

"Won't you look after this for me?" he asked with the successfully appealing reliance a child can show. "It's a legal something or other. You know all about such truck." And off he went, with a that's-that expression on his face and, as like as not, a comfortable sense of having been extremely competent and business-like for once in a way.

When Case got a spare moment an hour later he took out and examined the document thus confided to him. It was a summons. In fact it was *his* summons. He gave up.

CHARLES MacARTHUR and HELEN HAYES

Another wedding in the wings

Mr. MacArthur is the erstwhile Chicago reporter who wrote *Lulu Belle* with Edward Sheldon, *Salvation* with Sidney Howard and most recently that roaring and mischievous comedy *The Front Page,* wherein he and Ben Hecht, in skylarking mood, set forth their gigantesque memories of the Chicago newspaper business. *The Front Page* was in the first week of its engagement in New York when MacArthur and Helen Hayes hunted up a magistrate in his office and there were quietly married. Miss Hayes will continue her triumphant tour in *Coquette* until Spring, and will then take the play to London for her first appearance on the English stage.

Steichen

LYNN FONTANNE and ALFRED LUNT

The couple are currently appearing in Caprice

The Lunts, who triumphed together in *The Guardsman* by Molnar, *The Second Man* by S. N. Behrman and *The Doctor's Dilemma* by Bernard Shaw, are devoting their combined talents to the new Viennese comedy by Sil-Vara.

ARTURO TOSCANINI

The Italian conductor comes to America once more this season to lead the Philharmonic

Vaghi-Parma

Steichen

GERTRUDE LAWRENCE

*The English actress who is deserting the musical
stage to play in P. G. Wodehouse's By Candlelight*

Mental Hazards of Golf

Stray Thoughts on Worry, Nerves, Temperament and Lack of Concentration in the Game

ROBERT T. JONES, JR.

GOLF is assuredly a mystifying game. Even the very best players cannot step onto the first tee with any assurance as to what they are going to do. Even Walter Hagen may have a putting slump from which he cannot recover in an entire round. It would seem that if a person has hit a golf ball correctly a thousand times he should be able to duplicate the performance almost at will. But such is certainly not the case.

The golf swing is a most complicated combination of muscular actions, too complex to be controlled by objective, conscious mental effort. Consequently we must rely a good deal upon the instinctive reactions acquired by long practice. It has been my experience that the more completely we can depend upon this instinct—the more thoroughly we can divest the subjective mind of conscious control—the more perfectly can we execute our shots. I have even had the experience that when I played some of my best shots in trying situations I had not the slightest recollection of hitting the ball. That intense concentration upon results (to the absolute exclusion of all thoughts as to method) is the secret of a good shot. Few great shots are played when the mind is fixed on the position of the feet, the behavior of the left arm, etc.

Since I began playing golf, I have played three iron shots that I shall always remember. Each of them won an open championship for me—at Inwood, at St. Andrew's and at Columbus. Of the shot at Inwood I have no recollection whatever other than that of seeing the ball in the air against a black cloud on the horizon. But I remember distinctly that on the two other occasions my knees were actually knocking together as I addressed the ball. I think it may have been pure nervousness and unadulterated fright that made me hit those shots correctly.

The great match-players among the amateurs are of the nervous type. Von Elm and Sweetser are as high-strung as thoroughbred race horses. It is that quality which makes it certain that they will never descend to plodding mediocrity.

Almost every contestant leaves the first tee with a certain amount of apprehension in his soul. But a lot of them make the mistake of trying to assume an indifferent attitude. In trying to quiet a pounding heart or still a trembling hand, it is quite possible to fall into a lazy slackness which can-

not be shaken. The competitor who can keep himself concentrated and "on edge" is the hard man to beat.

In playing any golf shot it always helps if the player can shut out from his mind all worry over the result of the effort, at least while he is in the act of playing the shot. It is well to be apprised of all dangers, and the chances of failure (and the penalty likely to be incurred in the event of such a failure) ought to be weighed carefully before deciding upon the shot. But, after taking the stance, it is too late to worry. The only thing to do then is to hit the ball.

I DO not believe it is possible to stress this point unduly. It is not easy, even with the assistance of a first-class teacher, for a man to develop a sound golfing style. But it is possible and practicable for a person to cultivate a mental attitude toward the game which will enable him to get everything possible out of his own capabilities.

Medal competition is the most diabolical sort of golf because it puts so many worries into the player's head. Unseen rivals are pictured as never missing a shot. When we ourselves make a slip, we feel that every man in the field is going to take advantage of it. We cannot conceive that the others are also having their difficulties. Strangely, too, every report borne about among the gallery which reaches the player's ears has to do with some other man's marvelous start, or his "three birdies in a row." If a man listens to all these reports he can hardly be blamed for stumbling a bit.

Suppose your opponent, in match play, plays a fine shot dead on the flag and, from the place where you stand, his ball appears to be within a few inches of the hole. What will you do? Very likely you will strain every muscle and nerve to lay your ball inside of his. You will try so hard to do this that you will probably hook or slice into a bunker and permit your opponent to win the hole without the necessity of holing his putt.

What you should do is to tell yourself that your opponent's ball is not likely to be as close to the hole as it appears to be. Probably he is short, and at least he may have left himself a very missable putt. Tell yourself also that you are going to try to hit your shot well in order to get close to the hole, but that you will make sure that you get on the green somewhere within reasonable holing distance so that your op-

ponent will at least have to hole out his putt in order to win the hole.

An approach may stop only six or eight feet away from the hole, yet there still remains the putt to be holed, which is not always a simple procedure. The man who, in playing his approach, keeps one eye on the ball of his opponent which is already on the green is simply looking for trouble.

On the putting green, too, it is often hard to keep from thinking about the importance of the putt rather than about hitting the ball properly. The thought that a miss may mean defeat or at least an almost hopeless position is often an absolute bar to concentration. The observer can usually tell what is in the player's mind by the way the player strokes the ball, even when the putt, by good fortune, tumbles in. A quick, nervous jab betrays the player's anxiety.

I am sure it has been a source of wonder to many how even a first-class golfer can go out in an exhibition match on a course he has never before seen, and equal or beat the par for the course the first time around. I remember watching Leo Diegel shoot a sixty-five over the Louisville Country Club course the day after the National Open at Detroit. He had never played the course before, yet his score was two or three strokes better than the existing course record.

In playing various charity matches I myself have gained a little experience along that line. I have found that if the putting greens are good and the distances not too hard to judge, I usually play better on the first round than I do on the next four or five.

The ability to hit the shot for the flag and to let trouble take care of itself is a rare attribute among golfers. I think it is one of the chief *fortes* of Walter Hagen and Harry Cooper. Neither appears to give a thought to what may happen to the shot. I am sure that they see only the green as the inevitable destination of the ball.

On the seventeenth hole at Brae Burn, in the first qualifying round, I hit one of the worst shots I can ever remember hitting. The seventeenth hole is 255 yards and requires a very accurate brassie shot. The more serious difficulty there lies to the right, and this was the side I determined to avoid. But, as I addressed the ball, I was thinking more about keeping away from the danger on the right than about driving to the green, and, as I hit the ball, I did something—Heaven knows what—that sent

Sanders

"BOBBY" JONES

the ball an inconceivable distance into the very woods I was trying to avoid. I was very lucky to get out of that scrape with a four. This desire to *guide* the shot is the most difficult fault in golf to overcome.

To think too much of the swing while playing a golf shot is usually disastrous. It is a difficult matter to be conscious of every detail of the stroke and still retain a modicum of concentration upon driving the ball to a desired spot. It is this difficulty which leads the average golfer to believe that the expert player must have nothing to worry about except hitting the ball.

The expert has to make use of his golfing intelligence and experience every time he strikes a ball, and it is his ability quickly to discover, and remedy, the defects in his swing which enables him to widen the space that separates him from the ordinary player.

"God Rest You Merry, Gentlemen . . ."

A Few Lingering Praises of Journey's End

GILBERT W. GABRIEL

THE theatrical season in New York was barometrically ripe for the burst of *Journey's End*. Something sultry and angrily vacuous could be scented in the air above Broadway. An extraordinary play of any sort would whirl in surrounded by electrical salutes. An extraordinary war play would start a cyclone. A *Journey's End* would cause such storm as only a *Journey's End* could cause, this time of year, this season, any season, any place on earth where men have once gone forth to war and cannot yet forget their going.

This *Journey's End* is by all odds (and every artistic right, too) the most assertive success of the year in drama. It had been no sooner seen and cheered and enormously loved in London than a second company was on its way to a similar Spring festival in New York. Soon France and Germany, Italy, the Scandinavian countries, will all be in its path. Its fire has the velocity of gunpowder's. Its tragedy has the lilt in it of such ballad loveliness as all the present-day world must immediately memorize and sing in husky chorus.

I FEAR I may be making *Journey's End*, a fine little play about the Great War, out to be a great play against war. On the contrary, it is a play as emotional about that war as Shakespeare could be about Agincourt . . . emotional, comic, heroic, commiserative, terrific. Young Mr. Sherriff, I'm sure, wanted neither to praise nor to bury war. He had no intention to push us one sob nearer to pacificism, or to start any such wrangle as honored another such war piece, *What Price Glory?*, a few years back. This had once been his life. It was now his play. He had, it seems, to write it.

The smallest occasion brought *Journey's End* forth. By now the incident is public property of how this R. C. Sherriff, an unmarked English insurance clerk scarce thirty-one years old, first composed it as a drama to save his local cricket and rowing club from having to pay royalties on their annual show. Before that he had tried it as a novel. The thought of eighty thousand words had bullied him down, he says. Wherefore, a play instead.

All this makes handsome press material —and Mr. Sherriff says it's true enough. He seldom adds that he was sixteen years old when he went to war and when all these things burned their way into his brain . . . these things which he retells so quietly, with such a rebellious simplicity, such grim delight and hard-lipped rue, in *Journey's End*. Sixteen is an open sesame to all one life's thereafter. Had these things happened to Mr. Sherriff at thirty-nine, would he—indeed, must he—have written them into such a play?

Every incident that is retold in this "dugout in the British trenches before St. Quentin" truly happened. Mr. Sherriff need not have assured me of that, but he did. His thin, rather tight and anxious face lost its good looks for the moment. Youth and success and all laughter went out of his eyes. The pain of remembering penciled his mouth suddenly with twenty black creases. Actually he was only telling how he had found his play's name, *Journey's End,* daubed on a door-plank over a German dug-out. Inevitably he was explaining how he had had to weed this play out of a dead, corrupting past—this play, and none other, and in no other or less self-raking style.

HE HAD not wanted to write a war play first and foremost, he said. He had hoped that the war would be taken only as its backdrop, as its flourish, whilst a trimmer and more saving conflict of man against man wrestled down-front in a manner that all great plays have learned from the Greeks. He had hoped we'd all see it as a clash of human personalities, war-time, peace-time, any time at all.

That may have been his hope. If so, the author must have felt his play a failure. The author alone is entitled to do so. The rest of us, even if to his chagrin, must go on seeing it primarily as the finest stage picture yet painted of the late war: of the mud and seeping glooms, bad food, bad nerves, the clumsy fellowship, the wry, barb-wired humor and whiskey-breathed heroism, that made this war of shop-clerks, farmers and minor poets the war of abysmal holiday it was for us all.

There have been war plays aplenty. There will be good ones to come, no doubt. *The Case of Sergeant Grischa* was a play before Zweig rewrote it into novel form—and before I see that play of Grischa translated and done for us over here I would reserve at least one or two trenchfuls of superlatives. But, to date, *Journey's End* tops them all, smothers them lifeless, leaves them revealed as mere circuses and synthetic claptrap.

Mr. Sherriff knows how little plot he needs. That is wonder number one about *Journey's End*. To this dark, scabrous dugout, home of a British infantry company's officers and many bewildered cockroaches, comes a brand new subaltern, a babe out of home, formerly schoolfellow of the captain. The captain is almost as young, a juvenile hero breaking under the strain, already a ruined souser. Their meeting is cruel. It has all the jaggedness of war-worn pride, the terror of just such terrible things as turned these golden lads into creatures of verdigris. The new boy is sent out almost at once on a raid. He is brought back shell-pierced, broken, for his hasty death. That, plot for plot, is about all.

But upon this bare, ironic truss of a tale the little group of characters—all men, of course, and almost all officers—are hung up in such full view, they cannot help taking on the looks of the last of the demi-gods. This wretched hole which has been scratched beneath the heaving ground is like a buried Ararat, ultimate refuge of a few living remainders from the hell that is fuming and flaring overhead. They, too, will finally all go out into it . . . up and out, to be shriveled and torn in the same impromptu, almost jovial way of this man-made cataclysm. And the very dug-out itself, where even the young dead cannot be allowed to lie in peace—but here are Mr. Sherriff's own last stage directions:

" . . . The whine of a shell rises to a shriek and bursts on the dug-out's roof. The shock stabs the candle-frame; the timber props of the door cave in slowly, sandbags fall and block the passage to the open air. There is darkness in the dug-out. Here and there the red dawn glows through the jagged holes of the broken doorway. Very faintly there comes the dull rattle of machine-guns and the fevered spatter of rifle fire."

THE characters—there are but ten of them in all, eight in addition to the captain and the young lieutenant; and only a half-dozen with much to say. Minor officers and noncoms, mostly; men plucked out of London and vicinity and put down here in charge of the foolish fate of a company of other, unseen, unreckonable men. There is one among them who is, I do believe, the most exquisitely drawn of all men I've seen in the modern theatre. This is the gentle, oldish, gray-haired Osborne, second-in-command, commonly and affectionately known to the whole mess as "Uncle."

These "Uncles" were not peculiar to the English army. Our own was filled with them. They were salt of the earth, helpmeets and guardians, comforters, mainstays, men of Indian summer chivalry and infinite understanding. In most cases—like this Osborne's—the very business of their joining up had had a touch of quixotism and automatic sacrifice about it. They were past the brass-band period of life. They weren't pounding out after glory. But, without them and the ballast of their natures, it would have been an even sorrier war for all.

This Osborne is the one who must accompany the new lieutenant on the first raid. It means death for Osborne; he knows it; he sits reading. There's a touch for you. He holds up the book—a little apologetically—for one of the inquisitive others to see. It is *Alice's Adventures in Wonderland*. If there is a peep-hole Earthward from the Heaven to which Lewis Carroll's soul has gone, I'm sure its edges must be wetted nightly with the old Reverend's tears at that small episode.

But such episodes abound, and all as stabbing and bravely springy and poignant as that, and as finely sure of their effects. Listen to Trotter, a fat, red-faced Cockney lieutenant reminiscing into his coffee-mug and porridge:

" . . . I remember one morning last spring—we were coming out of the salient. Just when it was getting light in the morning—it was at the time when the Boche was sending over a lot of that gas that smells like pear-drops, you know? . . . We were scared to hell of it. All of a sudden we smelt that funny sweet smell, and a fellow shouted 'Gas'—and we put on our masks; and then I spotted what it was . . . Why, a blinkin' may-tree! All out in bloom, growing beside the path! We did feel a lot of silly poops—putting on gas masks because of a damn may-tree!"

So the talk goes. It has, quite all of it, that same restless, careless air, that same protesting ache of the tongues of normal humans who can only chatter tensely, abashedly, in the face of an olive-drab death. These are all Britons, all supposedly unsentimental, inarticulate. They drag out their farewells as laconically as clumsy children. Self-consciousness dampens their every handclasp. Their hearts shriek within them of homes they'll never see again, and they can only go on matter-of-factly about their old back-gardens, where they'd formerly sat in carpet-slippers over their pipes and watched the 'olly-'ocks grow.

THIS, then, is what is to be seen and heard through Mr. Gilbert Miller's enterprise at his theatre in New York. It is superbly acted. Its performance is as precise, as natural, more fundamentally stirring than any I can recall in my several drama-going days. The last quarter-hour of it, roaring with doom and imminent destruction for them all, mounted for me into a frenzy which was almost a release from grief.

Only a little while ago one of them had been telling the rest of having heard "a bloomin' little bird" start singing above the trench. And now, at length, I was certain that that bloomin' little bird, could his song have been translated, had been singing, "God rest you merry, gentlemen, let nothing you dismay."

"JOURNEY'S END"

Three principal actors in the war play now duplicating in New York its brilliant success in London. From left to right: Henry Wenman as Trotter, Colin Keith-Johnston as Stanhope, and Leon Quartermaine as Osborne.

Steichen

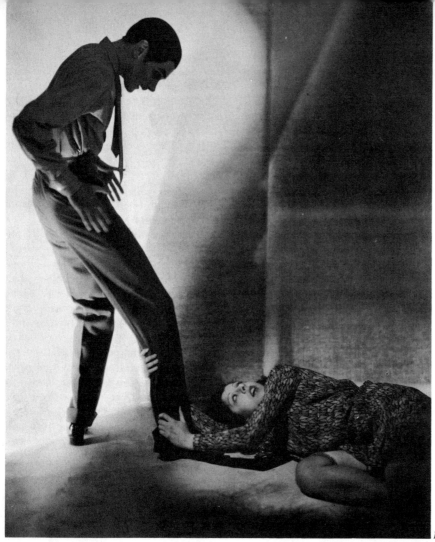

Hoyningen-Huene

CLIFTON WEBB
and
LIBBY HOLMAN

The electrifying number "Moanin' Low" — as sung by Miss Holman and danced by Mr. Webb — is the climax of the brilliant new revue The First Little Show

HELEN MORGAN

The wistful Miss Morgan, whose singing of "My Bill" in the Edna Ferber–Jerome Kern play Show Boat *has made musical-comedy history*

Steichen

A Duel Without Seconds

DJUNA BARNES

THE Baron and Baroness Otterly-Hans-clever were two at dinner, each immured in a lonely little canopy of light flung by the candles at either end of the long table. The third course had been served, and the Baron had helped himself to three cutlets in place of his usual two; for, now that his dueling days were practically over, he had no need to keep free of fat. The Baroness sat with lowered eyes, breaking her bread in silence and thinking of the days that were no longer.

Silent and preoccupied they both were, while between them the long, hard expanse of mahogany mocked them with a false gaiety of silver and glass and with shadows of candlelight that danced along its bland surface like ghosts of the company whose laughter it once had known. There was silence, too, in the room that brooded darkly over the lonely couple—silence heavy and complete save for the whisper of the butler's feet as he moved pallidly in the dimness beyond the high, brocaded chairs. But to the Baroness the very silence was loud with echoes of the past, and to her wistful eyes the fleeting shadows now seemed to take form, almost to assume the outlines of phantom guests crowding around the table in a staccato pattern of talk and color as vivid as in the days, not so long ago, when this same room had buzzed with conversation, had rung with laughter. So strong was the illusion that she half-turned her head toward the place on her right hand where the old Duke of Yarhoven, with his daughters, had been accustomed to sit—then to her left, where the bosoms, bright with medals, of famous generals and politicians had once swelled with confidence and gaiety. She sighed now as she recalled, one by one, those delightful friends of a happier day. . . . There had been the lanky Hoving twins, eager young sports-women whose laughter rang across a draw-ing-room in a kind of prolonged, double echo like the baying of hounds, making everyone think of pink coats and crisp, autumn fields so that they all felt enor-mously cheerful, even the sundry officers suffering from malaria contracted while doing the right thing by the colonies. There had been actresses, statesmen, princes, even a king—and always, like the charming, sentimental refrain running through an operetta, there had been that assortment of wistful little wives whose husbands had been sent out of their own country to do some kind of political injustice in another.

But those days were tragically over; and now the Baron and his Baroness were alone, and as lonely as dethroned royalty. The money which had once been so plentiful had diminished until now it hardly served to cover the pheasants with their appro-priate dressing. Their riches were gone, their friends were gone; before them lay nothing but a thin and dreadful solitude. But while the Baroness grew hourly frailer and more despairing, her husband seemed unaffected by their misfortunes. Indeed, looking at him now down the grim length of that deserted table, she reflected that he seemed to live entirely in the past; placid, pink, and stupid, he busied himself only with his history of dueling from the six-teenth century up to his own time—when, he assured everyone who would listen, he had been no mean hand at the fine art himself. He carried a long and nasty scar across his right cheek to attest to his verac-ity, and although the story of that scar altered brilliantly from year to year, it gave him tremendous *cachet*.

WHEN he had first met his future Baron-ess (she had been Gertie Platz, then, and sweetly gullible) he had assured her that it was but a month old, having been won in defense of her beauty and fair name; but scarcely had the glow in her heart be-gun to brighten into something akin to love for her valiant defender, when she overheard him telling the Duchess of Yar-hoven that he had come by his scar one unfortunate night in Madrid when he had righted a wrong half a mile out of town. In the succeeding years (there had been twenty) he had changed the story as often as he could find anyone to tell it to; it was, variously, on a point of personal honor that he had been wounded, for the honor of the church, for the honor of his coun-try, for the honor of a woman . . . but it was always a highly entertaining tale. In the early days, the Baroness had been thrilled. She winced and breathed faster as he drew out, in an illustrative gesture, his bloody rapier; she shuddered and paled, and murmured: "You are wonderful!" But, God of custom, that was long ago! Now her nostrils quivered slightly, and she turned her head away.

As her friends deserted her, and her life narrowed to a barren path of debt and despair, this once great lady's smile had come to be, of late, a little iced; her infre-quent laughter a trifle shrill. Lines appeared about her fine eyes, and her step was slower as she walked in her lonely garden and listened to her gardener talk of winter packing for the strawberries and the gen-tler flowers. Alas, she knew too well why her friends had left her; as vividly as though it had been carved by a bitter blade upon her mind and heart, she could trace the first indication of disaster to that dread-ful evening, five years ago, upon the occa-sion of their fifteenth anniversary ball, when the most deplorable, the most tragic event of her life had taken place.

THE Baron, that night, had just been tell-ing the pretty wife of General Koenig how he had come by his scar in Budapest, fight-ing beside the blue Danube in waltz time with an adversary who would not keep step, when one of the Hoving twins, with a long, resounding wail (the acoustics of the Baron's mansion being peculiarly per-fect for rendering anguish) screamed that she had been robbed not only of her mother's emerald pendant but of her father's father's time-piece, as big as a turnip and wound with a key in the shape of a spade, which she valued not so much because it was her grandfather's as because it was worth a thousand British pounds, its equiva-lent in dollars, its twin in marks, and its replica in lire. To this day, the Baroness shuddered as she recalled the stark silence that had followed the announcement of this loss, then the excited hum of voices as the guests began hastily to compute the loss in various currencies. Uncomfortable pauses there had been, too, lips tightened with un-spoken doubts, eyes that rested a little too long, a little too thoughtfully on other eyes. . . . All the curious, eager, yet reluctant suspicion that is so easily roused among friends dwelt like an evil fog in that bril-liant room. The thing had been hushed up, of course, although neither pendant nor watch was ever found, and there the matter might have ended; but from that day the Baroness, her eyes shadowed with anxiety, noticed that at each of her parties that followed something of value was lost. Her drawing-room lacked spontaneity after that; fewer and fewer guests came, and always there was that nervous expectation of some-one rising to proclaim the loss of a jewel, or—worse still—considerably hurrying away, murmuring something about having misplaced a cuff-link or a tie-pin, a brace-let or a ring. The servants were questioned, and several were dismissed under suspicion;

but still the thefts continued, and the Baroness grew as thin as a leaf in the wind, and seldom, now, raised her tired eyes to the faces of those friends who were left to her. Soon, even the last of these drifted away, and the Baron and Baroness Otterly-Hansclever were alone; alone, and somehow, she felt, disgraced.

It occurred to her now, as she tasted a salad-dressing that seemed almost utterly tasteless, that had she been a younger woman she would have wept, and opened her heart to her husband. But armored and inert as he was among his papers and notes on dueling, he, too, was lost to her. So she ate in silence, turning over and over in her mind the thought that had been ripening there like a dark and cruel seed, that their honor had gone unavenged. Not only had their guests been despoiled, but their own family plate had disappeared, piece by piece, and even her own little rope of pearls could not be found. Was there, she thought fiercely, no alternative, no fu-

ture for the Otterly-Hansclevers but to sit supinely, while the dark hand of disgrace closed upon them and their friends, one by one, turned surely and dreadfully away?

Why did the Baron say nothing, do nothing? Was he so engrossed in the history of dueling that he had no time nor inclination to fight when it was needed? Well . . . of what avail was the delicate art of dueling against the grim, evanescent shadow that hovered over them? Their adversary was the phantom, Doubt; so would the battle be a ghostly one. And she alone could fight it. Her fingers tightened around the worn silver of her salad-fork, and in her eyes a resolve grew until they seemed like liquid pools of fire in her tired face. Yes, she alone would avenge the honor of the Otterly-Hansclevers . . . and she would prove in the doing that faint blood was not her portion.

When the Baron had kissed her hand and excused himself for a long night

among his papers, as was his wont, she mounted slowly to her apartments. The rooms waited emptily for her, for her own maid had been dismissed not long ago, since they could afford no servants except the old butler and the gardener; but she walked across the threshold as proudly as though trumpets went before her. A duty awaited her—one last gesture to accomplish in defense of the honorable name she had assumed in marriage; and it was a gesture which must be accomplished beautifully, exquisitely. She must die.

She knew how she would die, knew that it would be by her own pistol which her mother had given her on her wedding day "in case of burglars." A handle encrusted in diamonds it had, and a long, gleaming barrel. No one had ever seen it but her husband and herself, and they had laughingly locked it away in the secret drawer of an escritoire—for, as the Baron said, "With a master of the rapier, a duelist of international fame in the house, what need could we have of pistols?" Often, in the years that had followed, she had looked at it fondly and had locked it away again.

Tonight it would serve.

Slowly she lit the tall, twisted candles in their heavy sconces; one by one the tiny flames wavered, hesitated, then grew into small spires of light, pale and steady in the high shadows of the room. The Baroness drew the curtains. . . . So, she reflected, must her courage grow and crystallize until it burned without faltering, and then—as the flame of a candle is extinguished in a breath, so would she die, quickly and alone. Her heart beat faster as she moved toward the drawer in which she knew the pistol lay. Then she paused, a hand at her breast, a dreadful indecision surging within her. Was it, after all, the best thing to do? Would her husband, her friends, know how truly, by this act, she had kept her tryst with honor, had sacrificed herself to an ideal? Or would they merely think her melodramatic? Would it, perhaps, be better to go on living, sleeping, eating, trying to forget? . . . No! To die was the only vindication—and to die magnificently, by candle-light, the diamonds in her pistol flashing a last challenge to the heartless world.

She moved to the escritoire, and put out her hand toward the fateful drawer. The words, "Death, honorable and alone" came to her in a half-whisper, but as she tried to say them, her breath caught in a little knot of pain at the base of her throat. She trembled . . . but she did not falter. She pulled out the drawer, and thrust in her hand.

For one instant she stood as if turned to stone. Then she gave a faint, inaudible cry. The pistol was gone.

Hoyningen-Huene

JOSEPHINE BAKER

A new portrait of the famous American entertainer appearing once again in the Folies Bergère, *Paris*

Beaton

THE SITWELLS—SACHEVERELL, EDITH, and OSBERT

The Sitwells, three porcelain exquisites, proceeding in unison with an almost persuasive concentration from one to another baroque posture, like the syllables in a charade that make no sense separately but may gather some meaning when assembled: Osbert is memorable for his superb *Triple Fugue and Other Stories, Before the Bombardment* and, recently, *England Reclaimed;* Edith for her bizarre and brittle poems in *Sleeping Beauty;* and Sacheverell for his brilliant studies of southern and German baroque art. Perhaps they are gravely mad; perhaps they are fabulous comedians; certainly they would resent any accusation of usefulness. But the wonderful and really heartening part of it all is that they always keep perfectly straight faces, so that no one can ever afford to laugh; nor can you and I.

This Modern Living

A Study of the Difficulties Which a Complex Civilization Presents for the Women of Today

ARNOLD BENNETT

AN EXAMPLE is worth ten general statements of what is. I give an example, known to me, of the rôle of a woman in this modern living. Her husband is a busy professional man. He is also a man not notable for tidiness, and has to be followed about in the house by a wife who transforms his disorder into her order. His profession necessitates various social contacts, so that the pair are frequently entertained and frequently entertain. In practice the entertainer is of course his wife. The husband comes in and enlivens the meal; but it is the wife who has organized the meal. For certain reasons the entertaining and the being entertained involve late nights. But the wife must be up early, for she escorts her young children to school, and, no matter what time the mother has gone to bed, the school exacts punctuality. She often drives the car, and—more troublesome—she parks and garages it.

Like most of us she is always preoccupied with the two grand problems of this modern living: satisfactory domestic service, and making both ends meet. She always designs her own frocks and sometimes makes them. When the pair go away for a holiday she first packs for herself and then packs for her husband, who cannot be trusted to pack for himself. She keeps the family accounts. She battles with tradesmen, and with pedagogues, and with the ill-health of the family, for when a malady supervenes she is the nurse as well.

"Well," you say, "there is nothing very extraordinary in all that."

Admitted. But I have incidentally to add that the wife also follows a profession.

ANOTHER example: a modern couple, at whose house I attended a dinner of over thirty covers. It was a good dinner, served with perfect tranquillity and without delay.

The point is that they had no servants—only a morning help. An intimate guest here and there inobtrusively assisted, according to previous arrangement. I was so intrigued by this amazing feat of entertaining that, being of an inquisitive and informal disposition, I said to my hostess after the dinner was finished:

"I want to see your kitchen."

The kitchen, radiant as a kitchen in some Ideal Home exhibition, was utterly empty of débris. In the scullery all the dirty crockery lay neatly assorted in piles to await the advent of the help the next morning.

MacDonald

ARNOLD BENNETT

Such is this modern living. It is very different from the ancient living which even I, who am not yet quite as old as Methuselah, can well remember. All the new developments affect women more than men. For both sexes there are more, and more various, interests demanding physical and mental activity. We have more games, more holidays, more diversions, more public spectacles, more change, more entertaining, and more arguments—particularly about the national welfare and the relations and comparative value of the sexes; indeed more everything, except perhaps sleep.

But men had always their present interests. Men are doing nothing today which they did not do aforetime. Women are now doing all sorts of things which they used not to do and which then they were not expected to do; and speaking broadly they are besides still doing all the things which they used to do. The demands on the energy of women have tremendously multiplied. The women of this age have to be, and are, political, financial, sociological, criminological, artistic, scientific, intellectual. They must and do keep abreast of every manifestation of human activity. They must and do take part with intelligence and knowledge in all discussions. They read the "woman's page" of newspapers. But they read the other pages too. Books, plays, films, murders, politics, sports, fluctuations in the stock market—these and a hundred other matters all come within the scope of their comprehension and their criticism.

WHEN men "join the ladies" their conversation is no longer narrowed down to suit the limitation of lesser minds; it continues in full, wide stream. Women still see things differently from men, and always

will; but they do see. Formerly they did not see; for they merely did not look.

Add to all this the influence of two other indisputable facts. First, that the woman's business of running a home has become much more difficult than it was. Second, that women give much more time and brains and enthusiasm to personal appearance than they did. And you will wonder how on earth women contrive to get through with the job of living on the old time-allowance of twenty-four hours a day.

And you will not wonder at the complaint which you hear on all sides about the resulting excessive strain upon their nervous energy. This complaint is justified. If women in old days did not live excitingly enough, they now live too excitingly.

WOMEN somehow cannot leave out trifles. They will not admit that trifles are trifles. They are reorganizing their existences without having properly grasped the great truth that the basis of good organizing is a sense of proportion.

The first-rate organizer is never in a hurry; he is never late; he always keeps up his sleeve a margin for the unexpected. This is so well known that everyone in need of help goes by instinct to the busy, organized man. It is only the ill-organized, busy person who has no spare time for others. Women on the contrary are too often in a hurry. In addition to expecting too much from human nature, they expect too much from clocks; they have a superstitious notion that, when it is convenient to them, the hands of clocks will cease to move.

One final suggestion. Time was always precious, but never so precious as in this modern living. The aim is continually to save time. Now in certain states of mind the best way to save time is to waste it. One of the most furious and successful workers of the twentieth century made a habit of spending a day a week in bed. I rather doubt whether any woman would be capable of a procedure so drastic; nor would I dare to demand it of any woman. But I would respectfully suggest to every woman who feels herself "rushed" that between one task and the next she should lie down, relax her muscles, shut her eyes, and empty her brain for five minutes. She would lose the five minutes, but she would most assuredly gain more than five; and she would gain, too, the invaluable sensation of serenity in the modern storm.

Nominated for the Hall of Fame: 1929

LYTTON STRACHEY

Because he is probably the ideal biographer; because in the ten years since he wrote *Eminent Victorians*, the market has been deluged with psychoanalytical biography; because he is the interpreter to the world of Victoria and Elizabeth and their times; because this portrait was painted by Roger Fry; and finally because of his latest and successful book, *Elizabeth and Essex*.

VIRGINIA WOOLF (*below*)

Because she is the first woman of English letters; because, despite the fact that her style is advanced and her subject matter recondite, she has become a popular novelist; because she has exerted a tremendous influence on her fellow writers, and finally because *Orlando* has made her a favorite with the public as well as with the intelligentsia.

Hagemeyer

ROBINSON JEFFERS

Because he is one of the first among contemporary American poets; because he has embodied the vitality of the California coast in his poems of tragic terror; and because his new poem *Cawdor* is the final part of a powerful modern trilogy.

Reinberg

SIGRID UNDSET

Because she is one of the best known of Scandinavian novelists; because as the daughter of an archaeologist she absorbed the knowledge of the ancient Norsemen which has since become the background for her novels; and finally because she has won the Nobel Prize for literature, which she has donated to charity.

JEAN GIRAUDOUX

Because he is one of a noted group of French writing diplomats; because his novel *Siegfried* and the play made from it presented a new and sophisticated viewpoint on Franco-German problems; and finally because, on leave from his diplomatic duties, he is at work on a new novel.

The Art of Dying

PAUL MORAND

"THERE is nothing that I seek information about as willingly as the way people die: what were their last words, their attitude, how did they look? If I were a writer of books, I should write an annotated record of deaths." This is a passage from Montaigne. Today, the thought has almost lost its meaning, for death, whether it occurs wholesale, as in war, or retail, in our own times is surrounded by exceeding banality. Witness the death agonies (as reported by the newspapers) of such illustrious men as Clemenceau, Foch, Lenin, Curzon. Our great men die in almost the same manner, and with words upon their lips that resemble each other even more closely—since they were borrowed by the deceased from their pious historians.

"It is an unfortunate man who does not know how to die," said Seneca. But who knows how to die? Who has meditated upon his eventual demise, or prepared the final farewell he will take from the living? Death, which we force ourselves never to think about, at last finds us stupefied, terror-stricken with fear or shocked into silence. If, by some extraordinary circumstance, we do not entirely lose our heads and remember that the moment is a solemn one which should be commemorated with a few words, we are incapable of finding anything to utter but venerable stereotypes. To us moderns should be applied the remark of the accomplished Abbé Gassendi in the eighteenth century: "I was born knowing not why. I have lived knowing not how. I die knowing neither why nor how."

The reason for this is that we have lost at the same time our scientific assurance and our faith in the beyond. We no longer embark majestically for the Great Divide as our atheist fathers did; but our departure is even less characterized by the trembling religious ecstasy of our devout grandsires. We have not, as they had, a ready answer to the enigma of death. Gripped by the mad excitement of living, we seldom worry about it. But let it graze us in passing for even an instant, as in sickness, accident, or the demise of someone dear to us, and the question crowds in upon us. Our habitual indifference is suddenly supplanted by an anxious avidity to know everything. We impugn the voiceless dead, who, even if they could speak, could not find words in our earthly language to describe their superhuman experience; to enlighten us on the mystery of the death agony, although we are familiar enough with the axiom: "When a dying man talks, he talks for the gallery." He sees himself dying, but he does not feel himself dying. He knows nothing yet of the frightful dissolution to come. He is still alive; as alive as we are. And it is very foolish to expect from him anything but a spectacle: be it edifying, honorable, or humiliating to human dignity. Nevertheless, we moderns have forgotten the rules for this very spectacle. The art of dying, like the art of living, alas, is lost. To find instances of this we need only to search in the past—in the pages of history. There we see the Emperor Augustus, when his last moment comes, has himself dressed in purple, rouged, and the crown put on his head.

"Am I a good comedian?" he asked, smiling.

To him, as to all the ancients, death was not sad. The Greeks depicted it in the shape of a handsome youth and declared wisely that the beloved of the gods died young. Life, to them, was "the hotel for a day," or else, as in Menandros, "a voyage," which ended sooner or later in a blossoming field of daffodils—the Nether Regions. To die was merely "to fall asleep at the end of a beautiful day," and the truly wise man always held himself in readiness to depart.

The ancients met death with a countenance calm, serene, and sometimes even merry. Everyone is familiar with the death of Socrates: "My friends," he said, "we owe a rooster to Æsculapius." And to his wife Xantippe, who lamented his innocent death, he said with a laugh, "Would you prefer to see me die guilty?"

I have much admiration for simple, unassuming ways of crossing the fatal threshold, without ostentation or formality. This is the only way humans may attain to the sublime naturalness of animals, who do not indulge in any cowardly complaining, or vainglorious boasting before their demise but obey only the noble impulse to hide themselves to die alone.

The Orientals have always practiced supreme reserve and modesty. The son of Confucius suffered a cruel death agony. His children wanted to move him to a softer couch, but one to which his social rank in that country of rigorous *tchin* did not entitle him. "No," the dying man objected, "my only desire is to die according to the rules." (Four thousand years later, the impoverished Oscar Wilde replied to the friends who wanted to summon a famous physician: "I do not wish to die beyond my means.")

IT MAY have been a similar concern for etiquette rather than the pompous realization of his importance which inspired the famous phrase of Marcus Aurelius: "An emperor should die standing up."

But that is doubtful. The ancients were beginning to lose their manly virtues. Great Caesar himself died with a complaint on his lips: "You too, Brutus!" And when Brutus killed himself, his pretentious utterance was: "Virtue, thou art but a name!" The world was becoming solemn and tearful; Christianity was in the air, and Septimus Severus expressed an almost Christian antithesis when he said: "I have been everything—and everything is nothing."

Jesus himself suffered a weak moment when he said on the Cross: *"Eli, Eli, lama sabachthani?"* After that he died courageously, but not silently, for he murmured: "Father, forgive them, for they know not what they do." This set the example for forgiving one's enemies which, from that time on, most dying rulers felt obliged to emulate.

There was one notable exception, however. Emperor Julian the Apostate, who fought Christianity all his life, died with a cry of hatred: "The Galilean has bested me!" But after him, nothing but sickly-sweet, whining deaths, or pompous, preaching, moralizing ones. Man became conscious of his importance; he no longer considered himself an insignificant link in the chain of beings, an obscure atom; but as an individual who treasures his life, and thinks highly of parting from it.

THE Middle Ages are full of the abject fear of death, which was increased by the fear of damnation. This was the period of the Dances of Death, of Holbein, of Dürer's etchings, of skeletons and tibiae, of sorcerers with their elixirs and strange compacts with the Devil. To escape the tortures of his inquisitioners, Galileo, terrified, disowned his great discovery. Although, to be sure, a moment later he affirmed: *"Eppur, si muove!"* But who can tell if that were not simply the absent-mindedness of the scholar who, in the pursuit of his idea, is oblivious of the world around him.

We have to skip two centuries to find

once more the elegance of the ancients. The French language contains a popular phrase, "death with few words." It reflects especially the national virtue of France, good taste (a virtue which Rousseau and his romantic successors came very near losing).

Montaigne, quoted before, said that no life should be judged until it is ended. Doubtlessly he thought, like the ancients, that *in morte veritas,* or, as in the proverb, that "the last words are the best." At the supreme moment it often occurs that man betrays all that is at the bottom of his soul, revealing himself in voluntary or involuntary avowals that give the lie to his whole past life. Everybody knows that Voltaire was a firm and militant atheist, and yet he asked for the holy rites and took the last sacrament like a good Catholic; after that he searched for an excuse in the endeavor to square himself with posterity; "When one dies at Surate," he said, "one has to hold a cow's tail in one's hand." The famous blasphemy throughout Europe.

The Spanish writer, Lope de Vega, asked his physician with great insistence if he was quite certain that he was going to die, if there was not the slightest chance of his recovery. He had a revelation to make, he said, of such a nature that, after he had made it, life would become impossible for him. Upon the physician's affirmation that he had only a few more seconds to live, he exclaimed in a loud voice: "Well—Dante makes me sick!"

How true and touching was the lament of the English poet Wolcot: "My youth!" And how refreshing the naturalness with which Mme. du Barry, at the sight of the guillotine knife, fought, yelled and screamed for help; her cries twisting the nerves of the mob so that it almost interceded in her behalf. The Terror might have been less bloody if the victims had shown less resignation; if they had, like Louis XV's favorite, pleaded for a respite: "How pressing you are, O cruel goddess!"

BUT death is not always cruel; sometimes it is even welcome. "This lovely thing, peace!" whispered young Alfred de Musset, as he died after a life of love, suffering and excesses.

Talleyrand, defrocked priest, grand lord of regicide, who was a minister under Napoleon and betrayed him for Louis XVIII, moaned on his death-bed in the presence of his sovereign: "I am suffering the torments of Hell!"—"Already?" murmured Louis XVIII.

It is claimed that drowning persons see their entire lives pass before their eyes. I wish that this was a privilege accorded to all forms of death, and that the last moment of consciousness might contain a condensed view of our whole existence, and be expressed in a few words which would sum up everything. Napoleon was a fine example of this. His last words, uttered with eyes closed, were: "My son . . . the army . . . Desais . . ." (Desais was the friend of his youth, killed at Marengo.)

And Goethe, who at the death of his son had spoken so resolutely: "Forward march! Yonder the tombstones!" sighed: "More light!" Alas for these beautiful words, so often quoted! They are not always authentic. If one can believe an eyewitness, Fräulein Seidler, Goethe is said to have addressed his sister-in-law very simply with the words: "Give me your dear little hand!"—And that recalls the story of the American general, reputed to have died with a holy name on his lips. What he really said was: "Jesus, I'm shot!"

Let us distrust historical phrases: they have been bestowed too generously, particularly on those dead least capable of uttering them. Old Patru said that during one's last moments one only talks from weakness or from vanity. Is it so painful then to keep still, when eternal silence is awaiting us? For my part, my preference is for taciturn deaths, those in which the lips do not deliver up their secret, those in which the eyes are turned away to gaze upon the Invisible. Their majesty surpasses all majesty of the human order; it is, to us, incommensurate.

Beaton

IRVING BERLIN and MRS. BERLIN

A family portrait

With audiences still responding to the melodies of "With You," and "There's Danger in Your Eyes, Chérie" from the film *Puttin' On the Ritz,* Mr. Berlin is working on the score for a new picture called *Love in a Cottage.* But the theatre has not lost him; he will begin rehearsals of the new Music Box show, to be produced in the Autumn. His wife, Ellin Mackay, contributed to the earliest pages of *The New Yorker* those clever articles on society which, in the opinion of many, helped to establish that magazine as one of our wittiest journals.

HAROLD LLOYD

Comic of the films

Ever since Mr. Lloyd joined Hal Roach in 1914 and made one-reel comedies, he has soared in popularity, offering perilous competition to Charlie Chaplin as a top box-office comic attraction. His best-known antics on celluloid have been *Grandma's Boy, Safety Last, Why Worry?, Girl Shy, For Heaven's Sake,* and *Hot Water.* His recent success, *Welcome Danger,* represents his first venture in talking films.

ED WYNN

Comic of the theatre

He has been on the stage since he was fifteen. His first successes were as Joe King in *The Follies of 1914,* as Nut Sundae in *Ziegfeld Follies of 1915,* and as star of *The Passing Show,* 1916. One success has followed another until it seems rare indeed to find a Broadway season without him. The latest vehicle for his buffoonery is *Simple Simon.*

Two-Time

A Clever Woman's Devious Designs Make at Least One Angle of a Triangle Too Acute for Comfort

MARGARET CASE HARRIMAN

NINETEEN THOUSAND—nineteen thousand, five hundred—twenty thousand. Mona Venneris, looking up from the writing-table, caught her reflection in the carved Florentine mirror that hung above it, and with the hand that held the silver pencil anxiously smoothed a line from her forehead. The doctor had told her that she *must* relax. But how was she to relax, how ever to escape from this small, impending doom of white paper that, terrible in its simplicity, lay before her?

She owed, to various shops, dressmakers and tradespeople, twenty thousand dollars. And she had six hundred and thirty-seven dollars in the bank.

It was not that her husband was ungenerous; her allowance was as large as that of any woman she knew. But she needed more, somehow, than they did. George couldn't seem to understand that her kind of beauty was difficult to dress, that her feet were too narrow for any but custom-made shoes, that her health required massage . . . there were a hundred things that made her different from other women—and more expensive.

There had been a scene, the last time, over her unpaid bills, and George had paid them reluctantly. But he had said flatly, then, that if she ever got into debt again, she would have to get herself out of it alone.

"I shall put a notice in all the papers," George had said, starkly, "that I will not, in future, be responsible for my wife's debts." She remembered the ugly bone that sprang out in his jaw when he had told her that. She knew then that he meant it. And his contempt for her had been exceeded only by her contempt for him, which was simply colossal, being the contempt of an unreasonable woman for a reasonable man.

Frightened, she had tried to economize after that. But she found it impossible to make her life over entirely, and as she had organized it, it cost a great deal. So she had sunk once more, gradually, into the warm, falsely soothing sea of extravagance, and these bills were the result—not only bills, but grim, insinuating letters from wary merchants who probably, she thought, brooded darkly upon her as they lay awake of nights in their comfortable houses built by the customers who, unlike her, promptly paid their bills.

There was only one envelope that did not contain a request for payment; an advertisement from some obscure firm of jewelers, ironical in its suggestion that she buy more

jewels. Mona pushed it aside. Obviously, she could not go to George again about her bills; his last announcement had been final. She wished now that she hadn't lied to him about so many of her accounts, pretending that they had been paid. Once in debt, she reflected, it was almost impossible to get clear of it unless one were allowed to start afresh; and now, in addition to the bills acquired since she and George had discussed it last, there were those she had withheld from him, had lied to him about so that her fault might seem less. She had, too, pawned or sold as many of her jewels as she dared—forfeiting some of them to the pawnbrokers because she hadn't enough money to pay the interest.

Her thoughts, aching in her mind, turned to Jacques. He would want to help her. He was always sending her presents—an ancient ivory, a jeweled boudoir clock, a goddess in crystal—and there was, with each gift, the suggestion that he would like to give her more. But she had never dared ask him for money; his tender (and, to her) ridiculous reverence for her would have revolted at that.

Desperately, she raised her eyes to the mirror that hung above her. But it reflected none of the panic in her heart—only the cool thoughtfulness of her face; a face that had—in the high tension of the upper lip, the thin arch of the nostrils and the carriage of the dark head, held always high and a little back—an eager, receptive quality that was, in some strange, definite way, insatiable.

Tomorrow she would be thirty-one, and she was very tired. It was curious, she often thought, that life, which begins so spontaneously and naturally, should be maintained with success—for a woman, at least—only by a complicated structure of artifice, a series of spectacular poses.

She hid the bills hurriedly in a drawer, as her husband stood in the doorway. Mona closed her eyes over the impatience in them. Tall and a little gaunt, George was fond of describing himself as "fair-minded," and always came into a room as though he were looking for something unpleasant. This was through no fault of his own; it was the way his nose was built.

"Birthday present," he said briefly; "it's tomorrow, isn't it?"

She saw that his hand was outstretched, and that from it a diamond necklace rippled like water in sunlight, swinging and spar-

kling as the warm, swift wings of color from its depths flew over the mirror, the wall, the surface of the table.

"George, darling!" . . . but after the first moment of pleasure, her interest was entirely in the contemplation of the necklace and not at all in George. She could at no time think amiably of a man who admired her so little.

But the necklace was beautiful. He clasped it around her throat, and dropped a kiss, as brief and as direct as an incision, on the top of her head.

"That's for being a good girl, and paying all your bills," he said, peacefully; then added, his eyebrow suddenly acute, "they *are* all paid?"

"Of course, George!" She lied to him so automatically that it did not even interrupt her absorption in the necklace.

He was looking at himself in the glass, leaning close, flattening the hair at his temple, feeling his jaw as though he had just invented it. "Are we dining home tonight?"

Mona turned to him swiftly, her hand still at her throat. "Oh, I'm so sorry! I promised to dine out tonight. . . . I thought you'd be playing bridge, or something. . . ."

"That's all right. Who are you going out with—Jake?"

"His name is *Jacques*, dear."

He was turning the pages of a magazine on the table. "His name is Jacob Rice, and I'll bet his wife calls him Jake. I don't see—" he was speaking slowly now, apparently interested in the magazine. "I don't really see why you have to go to dinner with him every time he asks you."

She looked at him sharply. "Well, I *don't* have to—but he's so nice, I hate to hurt his feelings. And his wife will never go anywhere—she's simply impossible." She laughed ungracefully, moving the crystal bottles on her dressing table.

George put the magazine down. "Well. Have a good time." He waved a thin, vague hand at her, and was gone.

Alone, Mona put up her hand again to feel the rich frost of diamonds at her throat. But her face was dark with discontent. If only George had given her the money instead!

She dared not sell the necklace, nor replace it with an imitation. George was cleverer than she, she reflected, when she had dressed and her maid was holding the chinchilla wrap—still unpaid for—that would accent the devious simplicity of her long black velvet gown. Even if Jacques were to give her an expensive birthday present, she would not dare sell that either, for fear of being discovered. Her hand shook with nervousness as she caught up her evening bag, a crisp circle of rhinestones. A white card, brushed from the table, fluttered to the floor, and Mona looked at it vaguely. Then she smiled, slowly. But it was not until she was in the taxi that was taking her to meet Jacob Rice that she unclasped the diamond necklace from her throat and hid it in a pocket of the rhinestone bag.

Mona's deprecations were always pretty to watch—small, perfect gestures, made of swiftly curving brows and a pensive circle of the mouth. Now she swayed like a flower toward Jacob Rice, sitting at a table for two in a restaurant just ugly enough to be the smartest in New York. "But you mustn't think of giving me a birthday present, Jacques!" she was saying. "You have given me so many beautiful things, and there's nothing I want now, except . . ."

"Except? Except?" The plump, neat contours of Jacob Rice trembled with eagerness, and his voice poured thickly from his throat like honey from a spoon. "Whatever it is, you shall have it, then. For is it not thirty-one years ago tomorrow that my blossom was born?" He sat back and clasped his hands romantically.

Mona allowed herself a moment of acute, private distaste; then she smiled. "Well, it's only that I know of a dealer in very rare jewels who has a marvelous bargain, a diamond necklace. I've seen it—and of course, if you *were* to buy it for me, Jacques, I could tell my husband it wasn't real, or something—that part could be easily arranged. But—" She paused, and permitted a gentle, selfless melancholy to dwell briefly in her eyes.

"His name?" Jacob Rice was holding a fat gold pencil briskly above a memorandum pad.

"Jacques, you mustn't!"

"Nonsense! You want this necklace. I want to buy it for you. I will go tomorrow morning."

"No," she said hastily. "I'd go in the afternoon, if I were you. I believe," she added slowly, "that he is seldom in before noon."

"Afternoon, then." He wrote the name she gave him on the pad, and put it in his pocket. "Tomorrow night you dine with me, and I will give it to you."

Mona hesitated. "I don't think I ought to dine with you two nights in succession," she objected, remembering George, "but I can lunch with you day after tomorrow. You can give it to me then."

It was with something less than her usual aversion that she watched him drink romantically out of the glass where her lips had touched it.

Mona Venneris sat alertly, next morning, in the office of Mr. Loewenstein the jeweler. On the desk between them the diamond necklace sparkled, debonair in the morning sun.

"You understand perfectly, Mr. Loewenstein?" she was saying. "You are to sell this necklace to Mr. Jacob Rice, who will call this afternoon—and to no one else. He will pay you thirty thousand dollars for it. Of this amount, I am to have twenty thousand dollars—you are to keep the rest. I have," she added, smiling prettily, "no way of proving to you my perfect right to do this, unless you take my word that the necklace is mine to sell."

The sympathetic eye of the jeweler dwelt briefly upon the slim lines of caracul that lay tranquil upon her narrow shoulders. He bowed.

"I should like you, of course, to give me a receipt for the necklace. And, of course, it will not be necessary to mention my name in the transaction." She rose, pulling the mink collar high about her chin.

Jacob Rice, alone in his room six hours later, watched the necklace tremble and shine in the glow from a lamp sleek with amethyst quartz and amber silk. The necklace was his—he had paid Loewenstein thirty thousand dollars for it. But the delight in Jacob's light blue eyes was not only the joy of possession, nor even the delicate privilege of pleasing Mona. It was the excitement of having made a good bargain. For, upon leaving Loewenstein, he had stopped shrewdly at another jeweler's to have the diamonds appraised; and had been told that they were worth sixty-five thousand dollars. So now, his heart closed warm and tight over the delicious secret of his bargain, he brooded happily over the diamonds as he dressed for dinner. Around him the room lay complacent in a rich design of tapestries, silver and mahogany the color of wine, and its air was faintly traced with pungent odors from the kitchen. It had never seemed curious to Jacob that his home, impeccable on Park Avenue, should always smell definitely of good meat and fresh vegetables cooking. He liked it, as he liked the laconic and comfortable presence of his wife.

It occurred to him, as he placed the necklace carefully in a drawer, to regret that he could not, under the circumstances, tell Jenny about it.

Mona, at luncheon with Jacob Rice the next day, was no longer deprecating. She was eager, now, and very charming.

"My birthday present, darling?" she suggested, when she had taken off her gloves and lit a cigarette. "Have you got it?"

"Of course, I have got a birthday present! Would I forget a birthday present for the most beautiful girl in all the world?"

She looked up sharply, through a thin spray of cigarette-smoke. "*A* birthday present? But surely, you bought the necklace for me?"

His hands curved in a vast gesture of distaste. "That necklace was not suitable to my little flower—too flashy, vulgar. . . ."

"But you *did* buy it! Loewenstein told me—" She stopped abruptly.

"Well, yes . . . I bought it." Jacob hesitated, then leaned confidentially across the table. "I will tell you the truth, Mona, because you are so good and so honorable yourself that I know you will understand it. I got to thinking, Mona, after I brought the necklace home last night . . . about my wife. I have neglected her." His plump hand fell heavily, contritely upon the tablecloth. "I have not given her all I could, and she has been a good wife. She has never complained. And I got to thinking, Mona, about the necklace, that it would be a good investment for her if—well, if anything happened. And then she had black bean soup for dinner, just for me because I like it, and so . . . I gave her the necklace, Mona."

Black bean soup . . . through the panic of Mona's mind, the ludicrous phrase ran shrieking like a thin hot wire. Jacob was smiling now, and searching in his pocket.

"But I have for my blossom a birthday present as delicate and fine as herself. For her tiniest finger, a pinky-ring . . . so!"

And tenderly, he slipped upon her finger a platinum ring, set with a fairly good pearl.

Child Prodigies

Variation on an old nightmare, presenting our own little wonders, virtuosos and worse

"WEE WILLIE WINKLE" BEEBE

TEDDY ("SCOOTER") DREISER

BABY BEA LILLIE AND YOUNG WILL HAYS

MRS. TULLY'S LITTLE BOY

GEORGIE ("PORGIE") BERNARD SHAW

MASTER HEYWOOD BROUN

With the stage, screen and radio becoming increasingly infested with child prodigies of violin, piano, literature and chess-playing, *Vanity Fair,* always on the alert, introduces on this page a few prodigies of its own. So here, jaded reader, is a patter of little feet that *is* a patter of little feet!

At the top of the page is Master William ("Wee Willie Winkle") Beebe, the boy winkle-magnet, to whose busy net a million winkles and one walrus have already succumbed. Next is little Teddy Dreiser, the only child in America who can write 500,000 sentences without one predicate. Beattie Lillie, baby film starlet, and her playmate, young Will Hays, are snapped on the California sands, while Master Jim Tully —a slightly burnt child who loves the fire—is shown putting his foot into a pail because nobody wants him to put his foot into a pail. The mite in the swing is Georgie ("Porgie") Bernard Shaw, who is about to abandon this pastime for his favorite sport of sliding down the cellar door into the Theatre Guild; and finally young Broun, posing in informal attire before reciting that lovely verse, dedicated to himself, "The Deep-Tangled Heywood."

"THE GREEN PASTURES"

A special study by Edward Steichen, of the March of Moses and the Israelites to the Promised Land, in Marc Connelly's new Biblical play, enacted entirely by Negroes, which is New York's greatest current success

The Mystery of Stroppingwallingshire Downs

How an Explanation Was Suddenly Provided for the Ghostly Manifestations in a Gloomy Old Castle

PHILIP WYLIE

I SHALL never forget my first glimpse of Wipping Castle, caught as I bicycled across Woppingham Tufts, that lonely marl of peat between Little Downing and Hemps. So ancient is it that I could almost catch the clang of armour over the sere and treeless mere which lay with a weird composure under the shelves of mist.

Battersea himself opened the door and the instant I saw him I knew that he was a man suffering from some deep-seated concern. His face was marked with deep furrows. His broad shoulders were bowed. He spoke in a hollow, sepulchral voice. "Welcome to Wipping Castle."

The ominous words chilled me. Even then, I thought, I could turn my cycle back and avoid a forbidding adventure. Then I heard the portal slam behind me and I realized that no Englishman, however frightened, could make so untoward a move.

A grave and it seemed to me agitated butler conveyed me to my rooms in the older wing of the castle. I changed and descended to meet the other guests.

The game of bridge in progress continued with a strained effort, as if each of the players was uneasy. I stood behind Mabs Middlebay until dinner was announced. I felt a short-lived relief at the change it brought, but even over Battersea's rather staggering cuisine hung the same morbid repression I had perceived earlier in the evening.

Dinner ended at last with something like a sigh. With coffee the conversation gained a heavy momentum but it was not until my host entered it that it took a revealing turn.

"Speaking of natural phenomena," he began with a purposeful languor, "did any of you ever hear of the Wipping Spectre?"

Mabs Middlebay dropped her cup and it broke in two halves. "Yes," she said.

"Well," he said, "it's loose again."

"Loose?" I inquired with a casualness I did not feel. "Then it must have been chained up?"

Battersea nodded. "With shackles on its bony feet and a stake through its heart."

"Goodness. And how do you know it is loose?"

Battersea spoke cryptically. "You were his friends. That is why you are all here tonight. See for yourselves that Wipping Spectre is loose." His finger touched a button. There was a distant groan and a portion of the drawing-room wall slid back revealing the most dreadful thing I ever beheld. It was the body of Lord Dreweringham and through his heart was a dagger. Lady Battersea fainted.

Save for the sound of Lady Battersea's fall, no one stirred. "Dreweringham," I gasped.

"And Wipping Spectre got him. It's the Wipping dagger."

No need to tell me that. Dreweringham was one of six—the last of the line. The Spectre was said to be the ghost of an ancestor who had sworn to obliterate his descendants. Wickwire was a cousin. Caspar Hoyt another cousin whose forefathers had colonized America. I saw the thing like a flash. And Betts—beautiful Betts—she, too, would be a victim of the machinations of the monster.

That thought had scarcely crossed my mind when the very stones of the castle were rent by a piercing scream. It rose soprano and dreadful and seemed to say something about, "In the garden—oh!"

I leaped through the French windows. The thing was probably out there. My legs propelled me onto the lawn. Blackness swallowed me. At that instant the corpse of a musty moon slid from behind a veil of clouds. The scream was repeated, and I was in the nick of time to see a human hand vanishing under the murky waters of the moat.

I am not a brave man. When I used to go down to Oxford I was, in fact, known rather as a timid man. Yet, impelled by a sort of magnetic force, I plunged into the weedy mere and grasped a form. For an instant I fought and blundered with it. Coming to the surface I caught sight of a figure and knew that Battersea would be with me in a moment. Presently I felt his arm pawing the air for mine. Together we hauled the unconscious Betts up onto the sward.

I shudder to recall what happened then. Even in my most careless instants I shall remember it. Out of the nearby bush came a peculiar call. Chilled by the pond, clammy with dread, I felt my very blood run cold. The whole scene was illuminated by an eerie, lurid light and I saw with my very eyes a human skeleton swaying on a rack of ancient timbers that resembled a gallows. Madly I rushed toward it. With loathing I grappled the thing. I tore it down and it fell in a clatter that was music to ears that had expected to hear nothing.

Perhaps two hours later we were sitting together again in the drawing room—a pale but wholly composed company. Explanations were in order and we looked toward Battersea. He smiled and spoke.

"I was afraid this little week-end was going to be a failure. When the postman did not arrive, I knew it. So I invented the ghost and bribed Betts and Dreweringham here to assist me. It rather surpassed my expectations. The skeleton was rather neat for a man who isn't handy with paint and tools, what? But I'll never try it again. I'll just rely as usual for the entertainment of my guests on my annual subscriptions to a dozen copies of *Vanity Fair*."

P. G. WYLIE

Beaton

GARY COOPER

One of the screen's strong silent men is the lank and cavalier young man called Gary Cooper. His destiny led him from a Montana cattle ranch to California in 1924 and he became—not surprisingly—a "cowboy" extra in films. What is unusual, he emerged from obscurity with hurricane velocity in the spectacular film success *Wings*. This paved the way for him to appear opposite Marlene Dietrich in her first American talking picture, *Morocco*. It seems to *Vanity Fair* that a thoroughly successful career lies ahead of him.

Tired Men and Business Women

GEOFFREY KERR

New York April 7

Henry Downe
  Book-Cadillac Hotel Detroit

HOPE YOU LIKE YOUR NEW POSITION AM MISSING YOU TERRIBLY HERE DARLING AND BY THE WAY I HAVE SLIGHTLY LESS THAN NO MONEY AT ALL

ETHEL

Detroit April 7

Mrs Henry Downe
  823 Park Avenue New York City

YOU HAVE YOUR ALLOWANCE WHICH IS ALL I CAN AFFORD

HENRY

New York April 8

Henry Downe
  Book-Cadillac Hotel Detroit

WOULD BE TERRIBLY GRATEFUL FOR ANY DONATION HOWEVER SMALL

ETHEL

Detroit April 8

Mrs Henry Downe
  823 Park Avenue New York City

SO WOULD I STOP MUST REMIND YOU ONCE MORE THERE WAS A THING CALLED THE STOCK MARKET

HENRY

New York April 9

Henry Downe
  Book-Cadillac Hotel Detroit

HAVENT A STITCH OF CLOTHING

ETHEL

Detroit April 9

Mrs Henry Downe
  823 Park Avenue New York City

STAY IN BED

HENRY

New York April 10

Edwin Baggs
  Baggs and Company Department Store
  Fifth Avenue New York City

HAVE YOU ANY JOBS IN YOUR STORE THAT I COULD DO

ETHEL DOWNE

New York April 10

Mrs Henry Downe
  823 Park Avenue New York City

VERY PROBABLY STOP COME DOWN AND SEE ME TOMORROW MORNING

EDWIN BAGGS

New York April 11

Henry Downe
  Book-Cadillac Hotel Detroit

FAILING IMMEDIATE CONTRIBUTION AM TAKING JOB IN DRESS DEPARTMENT WITH BAGGS AND CO

ETHEL

Detroit April 11

Mrs Henry Downe
  823 Park Avenue New York City

AFRAID CONTRIBUTION IMPOSSIBLE STOP TERRIBLY SORRY BUT EXCEEDINGLY HARD TO MAKE ENDS MEET ON ASSISTANT VICE PRESIDENTS SALARY STOP NEVERTHELESS PLEASE HAVE PATIENCE AND UNDERSTAND THOROUGHLY I FORBID YOUR GOING TO WORK FOR BAGGS AND COMPANY OR ANYONE ELSE

HENRY

New York April 12

Henry Downe
  Book-Cadillac Hotel Detroit

HAVE TAKEN JOB WITH BAGGS

ETHEL

Detroit April 21

Edwin Baggs
  Baggs and Co Fifth Avenue New York
  City

I UNDERSTAND MY WIFE IS WORKING FOR YOU IN SOME CAPACITY STOP SHOULD BE EXTREMELY GRATEFUL IF YOU WOULD DISCHARGE HER
    HENRY DOWNE BOOK-CADILLAC HOTEL DETROIT

New York April 21

Henry Downe
  Book-Cadillac Hotel Detroit

YOUR WIFE INVALUABLE STOP DISCHARGE OUT OF QUESTION STOP ON CONTRARY HAVE JUST PROMOTED HER

EDWIN BAGGS

•

New York April 28

Martin Shayer
  Ambassador Hotel Chicago

HOPE YOUR BUSINESS IN CHICAGO IS ATTENDED TO STOP WHEN ARE WE SAILING

AGATHA

Chicago April 28

Mrs Martin Shayer
  850 Madison Avenue New York City

AWFULLY SORRY BUT EUROPE QUITE IMPOSSIBLE THIS YEAR

MARTIN

New York April 29

Martin Shayer
  Ambassador Hotel Chicago

WHY

AGATHA

Chicago April 29

Mrs Martin Shayer
  850 Madison Avenue New York City

PATRIOTISM DUE TO LAST YEARS CRASH STOP WILL BE HOME TOMORROW

MARTIN

New York April 30

Mrs Henry Downe
  Baggs and Co Fifth Avenue New York
  City

CAN YOU GET JOB FOR ME BAGGS AND CO

AGATHA SHAYER

New York May 1

Mrs Martin Shayer
  850 Madison Avenue New York City

YES YOU CAN START MONDAY

ETHEL DOWNE

•

Detroit May 8

Martin Shayer
  850 Madison Avenue New York City

MY WIFE IS WORKING WITH BAGGS AND COMPANY STOP FEEL THIS REFLECTS ON ME STOP PLEASE ASK YOUR WIFE TO USE HER INFLUENCE WITH ETHEL TO PERSUADE HER TO RESIGN
    HENRY DOWNE BOOK-CADILLAC HOTEL DETROIT

Detroit May 9

Mrs Martin Shayer
  850 Madison Avenue New York City

ETHEL IS WORKING WITH BAGGS AND COMPANY STOP FEEL THIS IS A MISTAKE STOP PLEASE USE YOUR INFLUENCE WITH HER TO PERSUADE HER TO RESIGN
    HENRY DOWNE BOOK-CADILLAC HOTEL DETROIT

New York May 10

Henry Downe
  Book-Cadillac Hotel Detroit

WOULD GLADLY DO SO BUT AM WORKING FOR BAGGS AND COMPANY MYSELF AND ETHEL IS MY BOSS

AGATHA SHAYER

•

New York May 17

Dwight Gamble
  Clift Hotel San Francisco

BAGGS AND COMPANY ARE PESTERING ME TO PAY MY BILL CAN YOU LET ME HAVE A CHECK

HELEN

San Francisco May 18

Mrs Dwight Gamble
  370 East Seventy Second Street New York City

OUT OF THE QUESTION DEAR SO SORRY YOU MUST STALL

DWIGHT

New York May 19

Mrs Henry Downe
  Baggs and Company Fifth Avenue New York City

HAVE YOU ANY INFLUENCE WITH FINANCIAL DEPARTMENT OF YOUR FIRM THEY ARE WORRYING ME ABOUT BILL

HELEN GAMBLE

New York May 19

Mrs Dwight Gamble
  370 East Seventy Second Street New York City

COME DOWN TOMORROW MORNING MAY BE ABLE TO ARRANGE SOMETHING

ETHEL DOWNE

San Francisco May 20

Mrs Dwight Gamble
  370 East Seventy Second Street New York City

CAN PAY BAGGS AND COMPANY ONE HUNDRED DOLLARS MONTHLY ASK IF ARRANGEMENT ACCEPTABLE

DWIGHT

New York May 21

Dwight Gamble
  Clift Hotel San Francisco

EVERYTHING SATISFACTORILY ARRANGED AM WORKING FOR BAGGS AND COMPANY MY SALARY CREDITED AGAINST BILL

HELEN

●

Detroit May 25

Mrs Henry Downe
  823 Park Avenue New York City

HAVE LOST MY JOB OF ASSISTANT VICE PRESIDENT CAN YOU LEND ME SOME MONEY

HENRY

New York May 26

Henry Downe
  Book-Cadillac Hotel Detroit

CAN MAKE YOU SAME ALLOWANCE YOU MADE ME

ETHEL

New York May 28

Mrs Martin Shayer
  c/o Baggs and Company New York City

WHAT ABOUT DINING WITH ME ONE NIGHT THIS IS STILL OUR HOME WHY NOT GIVE UP YOUR WORK FOR ONE EVENING

MARTIN

New York May 28

Martin Shayer
  850 Madison Avenue New York City

CERTAINLY DARLING BUT NOT AT HOME STOP WOULD YOU LIKE TO COME TO BANQUET GIVEN BY BAGGS AND COMPANY WEDNESDAY NIGHT AT COMMODORE HOTEL

AGATHA

New York May 29

Mrs Martin Shayer
  c/o Baggs and Company New York City

IN A WORD COMMA NO

MARTIN

●

Detroit June 5

Mrs Henry Downe
  823 Park Avenue New York City

DESPERATELY HARD UP WOULD BE THANKFUL FOR ANYTHING YOU CAN SPARE

HENRY

New York June 5

Henry Downe
  Book-Cadillac Hotel Detroit

YOU HAVE YOUR ALLOWANCE WHICH IS ALL I CAN AFFORD

ETHEL

●

San Francisco June 8

Mrs Dwight Gamble
  370 East Seventy Second Street New York City

EVERYTHING ALL RIGHT NOW MADE EIGHTY THOUSAND DOLLARS LAST WEEK SO HOW ABOUT QUITTING BAGGS AND COMPANY

DWIGHT

New York June 9

Dwight Gamble
  Clift Hotel San Francisco

SHALL NEVER QUIT BIG BUSINESS MUCH TOO FASCINATING

HELEN

●

Chicago June 15

Mrs Martin Shayer
  c/o Baggs and Company New York City

CAN YOU MANAGE TO LEAVE YOUR JOB FOR JULY AND AUGUST WE CAN TAKE CHEAP HOLIDAY IN MAINE

MARTIN

New York June 15

Martin Shayer
  Ambassador Hotel Chicago

NO DARLING BUT BAGGS AND COMPANY ARE SENDING ME ON BUYING TRIP TO PARIS WILL TAKE YOU ALONG

AGATHA

●

Detroit June 20

Mrs Henry Downe
  823 Park Avenue New York City

THINGS HOPELESS HERE SHALL BE IN NEW YORK SUNDAY

HENRY

New York June 20

Henry Downe
  Book-Cadillac Hotel Detroit

HAVE ARRANGED FOR YOU TO START WORK AT BAGGS AND COMPANY MONDAY UNDER ME

ETHEL

Nominated for the Hall of Fame: 1930

LAWRENCE TIBBETT

Because he was given an ovation, at the age of twenty-six, when he appeared at the Metropolitan Opera House in *Falstaff;* because the young Californian has been heard all over the United States in concerts; because he is interested in aviation; and finally because his first talking picture, *The Rogue's Song,* has been so successful.

IVAN PETROVITCH PAVLOV

Because he is the greatest living physiologist; because his *Lectures on Conditioned Reflexes* is an epoch-making book; and finally because he recently refused an official Soviet celebration of his birthday, as he hates communism, although the Soviet voted him $50,000 and diverted traffic so as not to disturb his laboratory dogs.

Phelan

A. P. HERBERT

Because he is the A.P.H. of *Punch;* because he published *The Secret Battle* ten years before *All Quiet,* and *The House by the River,* a great murder story, five years before S. S. Van Dine; because his new novel, *The Water Gypsies,* is so old-fashioned that it is original; and finally because he is a practical believer in beer and skittles.

PAUL HINDEMITH

Because he is the leader of atonal music in Germany; because his string music focused upon him the attention of European critics; because his music has since become a cause of discussion among audiences everywhere; and finally because of the great success of his latest opera, *Cardillac.*

Sander

JOHN DEWEY

Because he is the leading contemporary American philosopher; because his writings have had great influence in China and Russia; because he is a lecturer, an educator and an authority on world politics; and finally because his greatness was suddenly recognized by the public and the press upon the recent celebration of his seventieth birthday.

HENRY LUCE *(right)*

Because he originated the news-magazine idea; because at the age of thirty-two he is the successful editor and publisher of *Time* and *Fortune* magazines; because he was once a humble newspaper reporter on the *Chicago Daily News;* and lastly because he claims that he has no other interests outside of his work, and that this work fills his waking hours.

PAUL KLEE *(below)*

Because he is an exceptionally fine violinist as well as a distinguished painter; because he has developed a new and personal concept in art; because his work is discussed in France as much as in Germany; and finally because an exhibition of his paintings has just been on view at the Museum of Modern Art in New York.

KNUTE ROCKNE *(left)*

Because he is the greatest football coach in the history of the American gridiron; because he is at present supervising a series of six football films which will familiarize the American public with the finer points and most brilliant moments of the game; and finally because his compelling personality and inspired coaching have earned him the warm admiration and friendship of sportsmen everywhere.

JOHN RUSSELL POPE

Because he is the architect who seems, by some miraculous means, to have designed most of the distinguished museums, stations, clubs, churches, and residences in New York; because he was the architect for America's recently completed war monument at Montfaucon, in France; and finally because a noble memorial to Theodore Roosevelt is about to rise in New York—the creation of his hands and brain.

Steichen

LUCREZIA BORI

Born neither Bori nor (as is sometimes supposed) Borgia but Lucrezia Borjia in Valencia, Spain, Madame Bori made her debut in *Carmen* at Rome in 1908. She joined the Metropolitan Opera Company in 1912 and has been one of its glowing luminaries ever since—gladdening the hearts of New York's music lovers in the stellar roles of such operas as *Traviata, Faust, Rigoletto, La Bohême* and *Madame Butterfly,* and now in Deems Taylor's *Peter Ibbetson.*

WALTER DAMROSCH

A new portrait by Steichen of the leading figure in the musical life of contemporary America. Mr. Damrosch was born in Breslau in 1862 and came to the U.S. with his father in 1871. He founded the Damrosch Opera Company in 1890 for the production of Wagner's music. In 1907 he organized the New York Symphony Orchestra into a permanent one and, after twenty-four years as its head, resigned to become counsel of the National Broadcasting Company, a position he has held ever since.

Steichen

The Barretts of Wimpole Street, a play by Rudolf Besier based on the courtship and elopement of Elizabeth Barrett and Robert Browning, not only affords Katharine Cornell a significant role, but marks her debut this season as an independent producer. While she was on the Coast, with *Dishonored Lady,* she cabled to England for the American rights, arranging for the British actor, Brian Aherne, to play Robert Browning and for her husband, Guthrie McClintic, to direct the production. The play is a psychological study of the power of Elizabeth Barrett's father over his daughter and of his attempts to frustrate her marriage with Browning.

KATHARINE CORNELL

As Elizabeth Barrett Browning

Who's Zoo?

In all of Italy
There's no old meany
Who can make
A monkey of Mussolini.

BENITO MUSSOLINI

GEORGE WICKERSHAM

Says walrus Wickersham,
"I am melancholy.
To tackle that prohibition gag
Was folly.
Saddest
Of all amphibians am I,
Who perish in the wet—
Yet die in the dry!"

HERBERT C. HOOVER

Mr. Hoover is not worried,
Unlike this pet,
Whose brow is furried.
The tireless watchdog
Of our nation,
He has a firm grip
On the sitchee-ation.

This pleasant, mild
and wind-blown poodle
Has less than nothing
In his noodle;
'Twixt him and Mr. Albert E.
There's thus no relativity.

ALBERT EINSTEIN

190

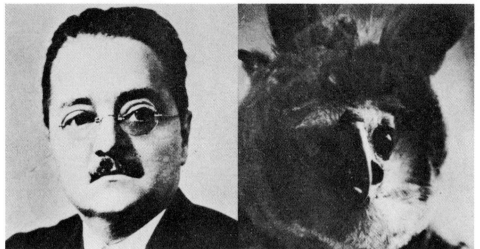

ALEXANDER WOOLLCOTT

From Paul Eiper's *Animals Looking at You*

Vanity Fair presents a new social pastime to its readers, a game called Who's Zoo? the object of which is to find (with the aid of photographs of your friends, or preferably in-laws, and those snapshots you took in the zoological gardens) human resemblances in the Animal Kingdom. The prize to be a hand-tooled volume of Darwin's *Origin of Species,* which makes very comfortable reading in the hospital.

Children, this grumpy,
Fearsome fowl
Is known as
Alex Woollcott Owl.
He swoops
From the shadows in a trice
And snaps up
Poor little writing-mice.
He might
Be married like me or you
If only he had to wit to woo.

Muray

THE YOUNG SISTERS

JOHN D. ROCKEFELLER   *Acme*

The sluggish loris,
I sadly fear,
Couldn't play nine holes
In less than a year.
Unlike John D.,
He is cross at times,
And never, never
Hands out dimes.

Loretta, Sally
And Pollyann
Are fluffy,
Sweet Young kittens.
But they'd scratch
The hide off any man
Who asked them
To work for a pittens.

·Le Départ—the Grand Prix, Longchamps

Raoul Dufy—Painter of Paris

CURIOUSLY, Raoul Dufy, the most Parisian of Parisian painters, was born in Havre, where he spent his early years. Although he seemed hopelessly launched upon a business career, his keen interest in drawing and painting finally led him to abandon commerce for art. Today he is known as one of the most sophisticated of modern French painters. A part of his fame has indubitably resulted from his choice of the ultra-fashionable world as his pictorial background.

The three scenes represented on these pages are but a small part of the number of his works which present to us the various aspects of the sport of Kings, he and Degas apparently being at one in thinking a race horse an extremely stimulating inspiration for a painter.

He has likewise devoted much attention to social scenes on the Riviera and at other fashionable French watering places, which he has also depicted from his advanced and mundane point of view.

Dufy, whether or not one has been captivated by his work, is indubitably a genius —a master of the gay, the ironic, the particolored, the inventive in art. No matter how serious the scene he depicts, there is bound to be a note in it of humor and fancy, the note of a care-free soul in bondage to no school or tradition. He is an illustrator and engraver of the first order, a lithographer, and a superlative water colorist as well, and in the field of designing fabrics no European artist is better known than he. Among the more popular fabrics which he has designed are those

illustrating race courses (jockeys, horses, paddocks), scenes on the Riviera, in the West Indies, and fanciful sketches conceived against Parisian backgrounds. A curious coincidence is that though he and his friend, Henri Matisse, have painted much the same scenes in the same part of the South of France, the resulting works have represented the opposite poles of art, showing that two geniuses can see the same thing in ways that are diametrically opposed. His painted works have met with ready acceptance in America, and there is hardly a collector of modern art in New York who has not accumulated examples of his work. His recent exhibition at the Valentine Galleries was a success, and other works shown at the Reinhardt Galleries also received much attention.

Aux Courses—a scene at Auteuil

Pesage—weighing in at the Deauville Trial

"THE CLOWN IN WHITE" BY RENOIR

This portrait, which is of his son Jean as Pierrot, belongs to Renoir's early middle period. It remained with the artist until his death at Cagnes in 1919 and then passed into the possession of his son Claude. The canvas illustrates the master's direct simple style—as he developed it, with a vital accent on reality, beyond his early impressionistic manner.

Lord of the Loin-Cloth

A Portrait of Mahatma Gandhi

GEORGE SLOCOMBE

A CYNICAL posterity may decide that Gandhi is the only truly remarkable man of our time. It may dismiss Mussolini as a Napoleon of *opéra bouffe;* Lenin as a fortuitous combination of Lincoln and Richelieu; Wilson, Foch and Clemenceau as shadows enormously exaggerated by the mists of war. But for Gandhi the book of history must be turned back many leaves, almost to its beginning, before a prototype can be found. Yet history alone contains no figure comparable with the Indian Mahatma. From Moses and Spartacus down to William the Silent and Mazzini, the leaders of nations seeking their liberation resemble him in little. His ancestry is rooted in mythology alone.

But even the heroes of mythology have presented fewer facets to the irreverent caricaturist. Even in the East, where racial and physical types are more strongly and more picturesquely differentiated than in the West, the appearance of Gandhi is singular. A tiny, brown, wasted body, narrow, bony shoulders, a large, shaven wrinkled head, very mild eyes gleaming behind enormous lenses, a wide, smiling, almost toothless mouth, a very meek, faint voice speaking an English compounded of the eloquence of John Stuart Mill and the imagery of the Hebrew Bible, a child's vivacity, a quick sense of humor, a mood alternating between simple gaiety and a brooding, a silent melancholy. He looks like a mendicant. He speaks like Socrates. He is at the same time prophet and politician, saint and sophist. He can reconcile the most mystical self-abnegation, the highest morality, the austerity of an anchorite of the desert, and an Indian peasant woman's warmth of heart with a ruthless and hair-splitting casuistry.

BUT his casuistry is the casuistry of Jesus, not that of a Jesuit. His influence is based on love, and not merely on respect. He charms and conquers as successfully as he awes. If not utterly without vanity, he is utterly without pride. He would not, he told me recently, in contradiction of a story which had gained credence, prostrate himself at the feet of the Prince of Wales, but if an untouchable struck him in the face, in memory of the wrongs done him by his high-caste Hindu fathers, he would stoop and embrace his feet. He shows an Oriental indifference to human life, but a Western sense of pity. But unlike the Occidental humanitarian, he pities the oppressor more

MAHATMA GANDHI

than the oppressed. Sometimes he appears more like a world reformer than an Indian Nationalist. It seemed last year as if he hoped to force the Christian civilizations of the West to return to Christianity, even if all India must be crucified to accomplish that conversion. If the end justifies it he is willing to suffer indefinitely, in his own person and in that of his followers. During the Delhi negotiations which preceded the suspension of the Civil Disobedience movement this year he showed an unexpected indifference to the early release of the Congress prisoners in Government jails. "They are not in a hurry to be released," he remarked stoically.

With the single exception of Rabindranath Tagore, Gandhi is the only Oriental who during his lifetime has succeeded in impressing himself upon the mind and the imagination of the West. He has accomplished this by a curious combination of physical eccentricities, mental vision, and moral personality. His physical personality is better known to Europeans than that of their kings and presidents, and to Americans than that of Hoover. When he arrived in Marseilles on his way to the London Round Table Conference, setting his sandaled feet on European soil for the first time in fifteen years, he was mobbed by admirers like a movie star. With the inspiration born of genius, or of his own rigid simplicity of character, he disdained the harsh social conventions in England, and the even harsher rigors of the climate, and entered London in a loin-cloth.

He might have succumbed to the murmured blandishments of the Viceroy, and adopted more conventional and more adequate clothing, and thus have appeared merely faintly ludicrous to the man in the street. But the gentle and smiling Gandhi in a loin-cloth, with a simple white shawl over his thin shoulders, surrendering himself like a meek sacrifice to the dangerous chills of London, and the contempt and prejudice of a white race—the challenge was too clear, the odds too unequal. His moral victory was won from the moment he stepped on English shores. He might die of the climate. He might return to India, as he feared, with empty hands. But henceforth he was a symbol in England. He had stepped from the mists of legend into the cold light of political reality.

UNTIL now, he had been a myth. His long years of campaigning for the Indian immigrants in South Africa, his inauguration over a generation ago of passive resistance as a weapon with which to combat social injustice, his many imprisonments, his many hunger-strikes, his ultimate triumph, were ignored or forgotten. His part in the recruiting of Indian soldiers to fight England's battle in the World War passed almost unnoticed. Even the explosion of the Khilafat agitation in India, and Gandhi's first Civil Disobedience movement, created but little attention in a world full of other troubles. It needed the Indian National Congress challenge at Lahore on January 1st, 1930, its demand for complete independence for India, and Gandhi's subsequent preparation of the second Civil Disobedience movement, his dramatic march to the sea in the spring of last year, his illicit salt-making on Dandi beach, and finally his arrest and incarceration in Yeravda Prison as a prisoner of state, to make him suddenly a world figure of the first importance.

Then the true purport of his challenge became clear. He had menaced the very existence of the British Empire. He represented, in his gentle but indomitable personality, its greatest enemy. The threat of an obscure Jewish agitator to the Empire of the Caesars was trivial in comparison. Gandhi was not merely a religious force. He was a political power which was rapidly uniting all India. He had defied the British Empire to maintain its power in India. He had mobilized against the greatest political and administrative machine in the world—a machine which functioned with the aid of a reasonable coercion, an admirable respect for law, an intelligent bureaucracy responsible to, but not seriously hampered by, a docile democracy—the shattering force of a single preposterous idea. He defied its visible and formidable weapons, its Army, Navy, Magistrature and Police Force, with an invisible and intangible arm—the double-edged but ambiguous arm of Truth and Non-Violence.

HE ORDERED his followers to disobey certain laws which he, in common with the authors of the American Constitution and its recent amenders, judged immoral, but not to resist the legal penalties for their disobedience. On his command the peasants refused to pay taxes, and watched with folded arms, if bitter eyes, the seizure and forced sale of their meager possessions in default. Congress volunteers attempted to raid Government salt depots and were beaten into insensibility, and in one district trampled under the hoofs of police horses. They persisted in holding prohibited meetings, and were dispersed with violence. They went to prison until all the jails were filled, and the authorities were obliged to herd their prisoners in concentration camps surrounded with electrified barbed wire.

All India saw the amazing spectacle of proud Sikhs, to whom a blow is an insult to be wiped out in blood, stoically bearing punishment on heads and shoulders from the bamboo staves of policemen, and the even more amazing spectacle of Indian women of high birth abandoning the seclusion of purdah to lie prostrate in the dust of the streets, or the mud of monsoon rains while embarrassed British police officers and awed native constables impotently endeavored to disperse them without a shameful or a dangerous use of violence.

The organized if pacific law-breakers of Gandhi brought the Government of India within measurable distance of collapse. While its spokesmen in public persisted in announcing the failure of Civil Disobedience, in private they admitted that effective government in India was at an end. The revenues of the provincial governments fell to one half. The central government was forced to balance its budget by launching large and inadequately subscribed loans at high interest on the London market. The nerves of governors, magistrates, tax-collectors and police officials were strained to breaking point. The lawless elements in the country, affected by the general political unrest, but undisciplined by the stern moral code of Congress, came more and more frequently into collision with the police. Even the young men of the Congress party, impatient at the slow maturity of the fruits of Civil Disobedience, and unre-

strained by the moral and political guidance of their imprisoned leader, showed signs of dissatisfaction at the pace of the movement, and hinted that the time for non-violence had passed.

It was at this juncture that the Indian delegates to the Round Table Conference, notably Sir Tej Bahadur Sapru and Mr. M. R. Jayakar, the Nawab of Bhopal and the Maharajah of Bikanir, succeeded in inducing the late Labour Government to announce an amnesty for the imprisoned Congress members in order that they might examine the suggestions for a Federal scheme for India approved by the Conference, and in subsequence inducing Mr. Gandhi to recommend the suspension of Civil Disobedience.

Gandhi yielded, although without conviction. As he told me when I saw him in Yeravda Prison last year, his life has been a succession of compromises. He did not believe in the pledges and assurances brought to him from London as representing the honest intentions of the British government towards India, but he was willing to test them. Besides, he feared for the sorely strained temper of his people. They were not, he feared, sufficiently disciplined in passive resistance to survive the harsh ordeal of non-violence. He could not accept a triumph gained at the price of blood shed by Indians. The bodies and the lives of his countrymen alone must pay the bitter cost of Swaraj. So he consented to a truce, and after a long and difficult discussion with other Congress leaders, and particularly with the unrelenting young Socialist, Pandit Jawaharlal Nehru, the brilliant son of Gandhi's old friend and ultimate jail companion, the late Motilal Nehru, his counsels of compromise gained the day.

But the truce is only temporary. Gandhi does not believe that Swaraj will emerge from the resumed Round Table Conference now sitting in London. He has, it is true, tacitly renounced his original demand for independence so far as the right of India to secede from the British Empire is concerned. He will be satisfied with the implicit, although not publicly recognized, rights of the self-governing Dominions. And he is now content to exact, as an immediate or early grant, the essential substance of self-government for India, the gov-

ernment of India by Indians without the control of a British Parliament. But he has no belief that either the MacDonald-Baldwin-Samuel Government or its predecessor would concede real self-government, or that a British Parliament would vote the measure. Nevertheless, as he told me on his recent arrival in Europe, he is "an irrepressible optimist," and he hopes against hope that the political horizon, now gloomy, and even desperate, may change.

His critics in England, like the Mohammedan politicians in India, frequently accuse him of representing only the high-caste Hindus, who, they suggest, are preparing to usurp power in the country at the expense of other racial or religious communities, and particularly at the expense of the sixty million outcaste Hindus, or untouchables. The truth is that Gandhi, although born a Hindu of high caste, has discarded all but the essentials of Hindu philosophy. He is as remote from the fanatical leaders of the Hindu Mahasabha as he is from the abject toadying politicians or sectarian diehards of the Moslem League. Like the Congress whose mandate he carries, he is non-partisan and non-sectarian. But if he dominates the Congress by his moral authority, his political wisdom, and his prodigious charm of character, he is intellectually and emotionally alien to the hard, brilliant and irreconcilable young realists who compose the new generation of nationalists in India.

He is a prophet where they are merely politicians. He has at once a mystical and an intensely primitive vision of India. He has, as Lenin had, a subtle and sympathetic understanding of the peasant and his problems. But in Gandhi's case it is an understanding born, not of opportunism, but of pity and of love. He incarnates, in his own person and in the deliberate austerity of his own life, the uncountable silent multitudes in India, who are sunk in poverty and despair, and for whom neither Hindu nor Moslem nor even Untouchable politicians can speak with the conviction which springs from intimate contact and intuitive comprehension.

Gandhi is not in a hurry. He does not believe that a great cause can be won cheaply. You would think that he had abandoned the dream of seeing India's liberation during his lifetime. For, although his years are counted, and at 62 he has already passed the short life-span enjoyed by his predecessors in the leadership of Indian Nationalism, he shows no anxiety over the future. Possibly the truth is that he is certain of the means, but less certain of the end. In non-violent resistance he has found the only sublime and even the only effective weapon with which to combat oppression. He will go on resisting evil to the end. But perhaps he has already sagely divined that to evil there is no end.

Acme

WINSTON CHURCHILL

Winston Churchill is the most interesting man in England. He is more than interesting; he is a phenomenon, an enigma. How can a man so versatile and so brilliant avoid being considered volatile and unsound? He will live in English history long after those who have made it are forgotten, for he is an Anglo-American freak, and England loves her freaks devotedly (once they are safely dead). Before he was twenty-six, he had seen more fighting than the oldest general. He was a Member of Parliament before he was twenty-seven, a Member of the Ministry before he was thirty-one, and a full-blown Cabinet Minister at thirty-four. Since then, he has been Minister of Commerce, Colonies, Navy, Munitions, Home Affairs, War, Air and Treasury. He devised the Antwerp and the Dardanelles campaigns, and it was not his fault that they failed. He adopted the device of tanks for trench warfare, and it was not his fault that they were used too soon. It is largely to him that the Irish settlement is to be attributed. He is the best living writer of English narrative prose. He is a landscape painter and can do anything from playing polo to brick-laying. His dominant qualities are imagination, courage and loyalty; his dominant defect, impatience. He is a man who leads forlorn hopes, and when the hopes of England become forlorn, he will once again be summoned to leadership.—*Harold Nicolson*

Von Horn

ROBERT MONTGOMERY

Robert Montgomery's stage career started when he was hired to play seven "bits" in a William Faversham play. This was followed by seventy-two weeks in stock during which he played mostly old men. Finally he achieved Broadway in the play *Possession,* and made his film debut in a picture called *So This Is College.* He has been, in turn, a rich man's son, a deck hand on a tanker and a railroad mechanic's helper; he now gets fifteen hundred fan letters every week, likes Scotties, Ravel and Irving Berlin, writes short stories, plays the piano and sings an elegant tenor. *Shipmates* was his first starring picture, and then *The Man in Possession.* He will shortly be seen in *A Family Affair.*

EDNA BEST
and
HERBERT MARSHALL

Edna Best and Herbert Marshall were married three years ago, while they were both appearing in *The High Road,* before a New York audience which had applauded them in their earlier play, *These Charming People.* Edna Best was already known for her enchanting performance as Tessa in *The Constant Nymph,* and Herbert Marshall had played in New York in *The Voice from the Minaret* with Marie Lohr as far back as 1921. He is the son of an English actor, Percy Marshall, and started life as a chartered accountant in London before the stage got him. His most recent play in New York was Philip Barry's *Tomorrow and Tomorrow.*

Steichen

NORMA SHEARER
and
IRVING THALBERG

This blissful pair are Norma Shearer, smartest of film actresses, and her husband, Irving Thalberg, head of production for the Metro-Goldwyn-Mayer Company.

Born in Montreal, Miss Shearer came to New York in 1920 to enter the films, then went to Hollywood, where she met her future husband. Legend has it that at first his youthful appearance led her into thinking he was an office boy, a *faux-pas* she finally lived down by marrying him three years later. Miss Shearer's current schedule calls for two new films, *Strange Interlude* and *Smilin' Through.*

Steichen

Beaton

INA CLAIRE

Miss Claire, whose marital life with John Gilbert was recently one of the concerns of the nation, made her stage debut in vaudeville, graduating a few years later to the Ziegfeld *Follies* of 1915 and 1916. The next year she established herself as one of our best comediennes in Belasco's *Polly with a Past,* a position she maintained in such plays as *The Gold Diggers, The Last of Mrs. Cheyney* and the revival of *Our Betters.* She is currently starred in a screen version of Donald Ogden Stewart's *Rebound.*

Steichen

MARGARET SULLAVAN

Into a waning theatrical season there has sprung an actress of a timbre of which Broadway is sadly in need. Her name is Margaret Sullavan, and when she opened in *A Modern Virgin,* her first New York play, she was instantly hailed as a player of great charm, clarity and vitality—in words of one syllable, "a find."

Born in Norfolk in 1910, she could hardly wait till she had finished college to rush off to Boston and study interpretive dancing. One thing led to another until a journey to the big city won her a place with a touring company of *Strictly Dishonorable.* The rest is history.

Steichen

NAZIMOVA

Into that rare company of Pavlova, Nijinsky and Garbo—known only by their last names—belongs Nazimova. The matchless performances of the celebrated Russian tragedienne in *The Wild Duck*, *Hedda Gabler*, *The Cherry Orchard* and *War Brides* have been rivaled only by Madame Nazimova's own consummate artistry in Eugene O'Neill's massive trilogy, *Mourning Becomes Electra*, which illumines the current New York theatre season.

201

Nominated for the Hall of Fame: 1931

NICHOLAS ROOSEVELT

Because he is the Minister to Hungary and a man of ability and versatility; because, though still in his thirties, he has achieved renown as a world traveler, foreign correspondent, soldier, author, diplomat, and editorial writer for *The New York Times;* and because he has enriched our knowledge of foreign lands.

Wide World

WALTER DISNEY

Because he is the creator of an immortal and irresistible hero of the animated cartoons—Mickey Mouse; because he inspired *Silly Symphonies;* and because, while still a young man, he has produced a new form of amusement—the synchronized and animated cartoon.

Wide World

SIR JAMES JEANS

Because he has translated abstruse scientific facts into the simple language of the man in the street; because his books on astronomy have been best-sellers; because he is research associate at Mt. Wilson Observatory; and finally because he has recently completed a successful lecture tour in this country.

GRAND DUCHESS MARIE

Because she is the granddaughter of Czar Alexander II; because she nursed in the front line throughout the war; because her book, *The Education of a Princess,* is a best-seller; and finally because, a royal refugee in an alien land, she is ambitious, hard-working, gay and philosophical.

DR. HARRY EMERSON FOSDICK

Because he is one of the most sincere, cerebral clergymen of our times; because he has reconciled science and religion in the minds of countless thousands; because, unlike many of his contemporaries, he has never sought publicity from his pulpit; and finally because his sermons show that it is possible to combine economic wisdom with idealism.

THOMAS HITCHCOCK, JR.

Because he is an outstanding figure in international polo; because, as a member of the Lafayette Escadrille, he was the hero of some of the most glamorous episodes of the World War; because he comes of a family noted for its sportsmanship; and because he graduated into polo from steeplechasing.

Culver

Acme

HOWARD DIETZ

Because he is a young American lyricist whose lyrics are both intelligent and witty; because he was the author of the revue *Three's a Crowd,* and co-author of *The Band Wagon;* and finally because, besides his artistic avocations, he is also general publicity director for the Metro-Goldwyn-Mayer film corporation.

Phyfe

LINCOLN STEFFENS *(right)*

Because he is the veteran reporter of his age; because as a journalist, magazine editor and foreign correspondent, he has, in fine, ringing prose and with sly humor, reported every aspect of the American and European scenes; because his *Autobiography* is a volume which in vitality and significance compares with *The Education of Henry Adams;* and finally because, although he has intimately known the high and the low, the rich and the poor, he is still a gentle, optimistic and Socratic seeker after truth and wisdom.

DAPHNE DU MAURIER

Because George du Maurier, author of *Trilby* and *Peter Ibbetson,* was her grandfather, and Sir Gerald, actor-manager, her father; because she follows their romantic traditions in *The Loving Spirit,* a successful first novel; because, in spite of youth and beauty, she lives in what she calls an "intelligent solitude."

GABRIELLE CHANEL

Because she was the first to apply the principles of modernism to dressmaking; because she numbers among her friends the most famous men of France; because she combines a shrewd business sense with enormous personal prodigality and a genuine if erratic enthusiasm for the arts; and finally because she came to America to make a laudable attempt to introduce chic to Hollywood.

RENÉ CLAIR

Because he directed the French film *Sous les Toits de Paris,* a talking picture which achieved instant success; because his present film, *Le Million,* excels in interest his last, and its technique could be profitably studied by Hollywood; and finally because, although only twenty-eight years old, he has been a journalist, the author of several books, a gentleman of fashion, a traveler, and the propounder of more theories on the future of the art of the cinema than have emerged from Hollywood in a decade.

Hoyningen-Huene

203

The Babe

PAUL GALLICO

THERE is, in all Christendom, no other figure quite like the great, ugly baseball player, christened George Herman Erhardt, who is now known as Babe Ruth; and there is no other nation on the face of the globe better fitted to harbor him, cultivate him, and for that matter, actually bring him into being, than these goofy United States of America.

In France they might call him something like *Le Gros Bébé*—but, then, he never could exist in France, because the Gallic temperament is not suited to baseball. The Frenchman could never stomach a close decision around second or home plate without beating someone over the head with a goldheaded cane. In Germany, he would be known as *Der Starke Ruth,* and his tremendous and overweening personality would be resented or misunderstood. In England, where nobody would ever call anybody Babe, he would probably be known unhumorously as Georgie Ruth.

The rise, the existence, the *being* of Ruth is purely an American phenomenon, like those other phenomena—crooners, Andy Volstead, the Valentino funeral, million dollar prizefight purses, skyscrapers, peanuts, chewing gum and the freedom of the press. Ruth's nickname, "Babe," is so much a part of our national consciousness that the strange message spelled out in letters six inches high across the top of any afternoon paper, "Babe Conks No. 36" or "Bam Busts Two," is not, as an English or French cryptologist might imagine, a code for "Come home, all is forgiven," but a very simple presentation of the news that Ruth has hit his 36th home run, and that he has made two homers in one game.

Americans called him Babe because he looks like anything else but and the sports writers re-nicknamed him the Bambino— also for no good reason, as there is no Italian in him—and then characteristically they shortened it to Bam.

The Sultan of Swat, the Colossus of Clout, the Behemoth of Bust, the Bambino and the Slambino, all mean one and the same person, Ruth, a ball player owned by the New York Yankees, whose extraordinary coordination of eye, brain, and muscle, coupled with an enormous frame and the most powerful wrists in the game, enable him to hit more home runs than any other man in the world. . . .

Ruth is an American Porthos, a swashbuckler built on gigantic and heroic lines, a great athlete, a Golem-like monster, a

huge, vital, vulgar fellow in whose bosom surge all the well-known elementary emotions and whose tear ducts lie close to the surface. He lives—ye gods, how he lives!— wholeheartedly, with complete gusto. He is one of the most completely alive men I have ever known. He loves to eat, to sleep, to royster and horseplay, to drink beer and play cards with companions, to play ball, to play golf, to swear and shout and laugh. Everything about him is big—his frame, his enormous head surmounted by blueblack curly hair, his great blob of a nose spattered generously over his face, his mouth and his hands—only his ankles are strangely slim like a woman's.

He talks in loud tones, he laughs uproariously, his voice is a basso-profundo and rumbles forth from the caverns of his chest like Kilauea. His greeting to all is "Hello kid," and his conversation is ripe, rich and barroomy. He talks like a sailor whose every third word is an oath and to whom oaths are so completely idioms of conversation that they are no longer oaths.

RUTH is a beloved figure and the greatest single attraction in the entire world of sport. Dempsey simply isn't in it with him, a statement that will disturb the cult of Dempsey worshipers no end, but the fact is too patent to call for proof. In one baseball season, Ruth draws more people through the turnstiles of the ball-parks than Dempsey has drawn in his lifetime. The Yankees play steadily to fifteen and twenty thousand patrons a day during the week,

and over Saturday and Sunday, against opponents high in the League standing, to crowds of sixty and seventy thousand. When Ruth is removed from the line-up for one reason or other, the crowds are cut in half.

The Babe is the only man I have ever known as spectacular in failure as he is in success. His home run is a magnificent thing, a poem of rhythm and timing. The bat meets the ball with a distinctive and peculiar sound all of its own—veterans will say "There she goes," just from the sound, and the ball, a diminishing speck, soars from the inclosures over the top tier of the farthest stands. A strike-out is just as impressive. Ruth is not constituted to do anything unimpressively. When he misses the ball, the force of his swing whirls him around until his legs are twisted like a German pretzel. Sometimes he swings himself clear off his feet. Every miss is its own guarantee of honest effort.

Nobody ever strikes the Babe out with his bat on his shoulder. He takes three healthies at the ball, *andante furioso,* each one more vicious and murderous than the last. Each miss draws a delighted roar from the crowd, or rather a grand and public shudder at the might of this man, and a sigh for what would have happened if he had connected.

THE effect of a home run upon an immediate cross section of any part of the audience is curious and inexplicable. The ball has fled the park. The Babe trots around the base paths with his arms close to his sides, taking little mincing steps on his small feet, and occasionally tipping the peak of his cap to acknowledge the roar of approbation and the patter of applauding hands. Look at your nearest neighbor. You find him acting in a manner that under any other circumstance would call for a spell at Bellevue under close observation. He is grinning from ear to ear, shaking his head from side to side, making strange noises, and thumping the nearest person to him on the back. He is acting like a man who has just been told by the nurse that it's a boy. He looks into his neighbor's face to make sure that there is equal appreciation registered thereon. He lights a fresh cigar and settles back in utter contentment.

There are some men to whom has been given the faculty of living all of their lives in newsprint. They have a natural attraction for headlines. These are very apt to become our heroes. Sometimes, like Lindbergh or Tunney, they object to the hot spotlight we turn upon them night and day, upon their private lives, their ills, their triumphs, their personal and domestic problems, an illumination which does not even spare the obstetrical chamber. Then we are liable to be impatient with a modesty which we feel is obtuse and selfish, and which denies satisfaction to our besetting sin—curiosity—not minding our own business.

THERE has never been any complaint about Ruth's modesty. The only walls he has ever known have been the parallel columns of the newspapers. Even his sins are public and certainly his expiations have been notably so. In 1925 at Asheville, North Carolina, he fell victim to the gluttony that has beset him for years—the gluttony one is liable to find in a poor boy who has never had enough good things to eat and suddenly finds himself with money to eat all he wants. Now gluttony with Ruth is not your stuffy napkin-in-collar, bring-me-a-steak-smothered-in-pork-chops kind. The beginning of the tummyache that was felt around the world was engendered by a wayside collation consisting of nine or ten greasy railroad-station frankfurters mounted on papier-mâché rolls, and washed down with some eight bottles of green, red, and yellow soda pop. Anyway, they shipped him up North on a stretcher, and the whole nation trembled with every turn of the wheels that brought him home. He was tucked into a cot in St. Vincent's Hospital, in grave danger of relinquishing his hold upon his great, mortal body, and hung between life and death for many days—on Page One. Bulletins were issued from the sickroom. Little boys brought nosegays, or congregated outside the high walls of the hospital, and looked up at the window of the room wherein lay the stricken hero. The presses lay in wait with pages of obituaries, and editorials announced the impending catastrophe as a national calamity. Even in England, the penny papers watched at his bedside. That IS fame. He recovered, he convalesced, and the nation sent a great sigh of honest relief up into the ether.

Back in 1922 Babe had a bad year. He was intractable, he drank, he fought with Judge Landis, the high priest of baseball, he abused umpires, he committed the gravest sin in baseball, that of chasing a fan up the stands. Also, he played poor baseball, although he had just signed a contract for five years at $52,000 a year, the largest salary ever paid a player up to that time.

At the annual dinner of the Baseball Writers Association, Ruth met Senator Jimmy Walker. The Senator was a baseball lover and an admirer of the Babe. He told Ruth that he owed it to the boys of the nation to behave himself. Later when Ruth was called upon to speak, he arose, gulped, and then with tears rolling down his enormous face he solemnly promised the kids of America that he would reform. He swore off drinking (in large quantities). He reformed.

The scene, the speech, the promise, the great reformation rang through the headlines. Here was a great and touching thing, usually seen only in the privacy of the parlor, where the prodigal son breaks down and promises that he will sin no more. Ruth became everybody's son. Everybody forgave him. Everybody went out to the ball yard the following year to see how his repentant prodigal was making out. He made out very nicely, hammering out 41 home runs, increasing to 46 the following year, then dropping to 25, due to his shortened playing year (the Great Tummyache), and then increasing his output again until in 1927 he had amassed the amazing total of 60.

THE man is a hero out of Horatio Alger or Burt L. Standish. He rose from Rags to Riches, Sink or Swim, Do or Die. He is the prototype of every hackneyed hero of juvenile (and adult) dollar literature come to life. The Alger books used to tell us that a poor boy could eventually triumph over temptation and adversity and acquire wealth and position, but nobody ever knew of anyone who really did.

Ruth came from the slums of Baltimore. He was an orphan. He went to a reform school. At St. Mary's Industrial School in Baltimore, he played baseball. He was a natural athlete. At the age of 20, Jack Dunn, the owner of the famous Baltimore Orioles, took him out of the school on the tip of one of the brothers. Dunn sold Ruth to the Boston Red Sox where his rise to fame was almost instantaneous, curiously enough, as a pitcher and not as a great slugger and outfielder.

Thereafter he began to amass folder after folder of news clippings, and photographs, the surest gauge of success. There are fourteen envelopes stuffed with clippings, and seven folders of pictures, seventeen inches deep in the New York *Daily News* Morgue alone. Run through these clippings and you will find no single item of his life omitted, no matter how trivial, from the appearance of a boil on his neck to the mystery that enshrouded the birth of his daughter by his first wife. (He claimed the child was born in February, whereas his wife declared it had happened in June.) Everything is there, his contract squabbles with his owner, his trials with speed cops and the demon rum, his every physical ailment from chipped ankles to flu, pneumonia and tonsil snatching. You find him in the movies, on the stage, engaged in fights on the ball field, suspended by his manager, barnstorming against Landis's orders and suffering punishment therefor. You witness his grief at the grave of his first wife, his courtship, and his marriage of his second, his yearly struggle with avoirdupois, his casual winter golf games, his lawsuits, his sentimental journeys to the bedsides of sick youngsters.

THE Babe has become a member of every family in the country that cares anything about Sport, and a great many that don't. No one goes to see him play ball impersonally. No one can look impersonally upon a public figure about which so much is known. British athletes are presented in the glossy print weeklies wearing blazers and smoking pipes, and that is that. The Frenchman makes a fuss over his athletic hero while he is on the scene, but promptly forgets him between games or matches. The Germans react coldly towards their own world's heavyweight prizefight champion, Schmeling. A professional athlete relegating political and national news to page two in Europe is simply unthinkable. But snoopiness is a national disease with us. We are a nation of gossips and Walter Winchell is our prophet. Snoopiness, our unceasing thirst for information about people in the public eye, and the activity of our press in supplying this information, has built up an orphan boy and a reform school graduate to a high estate where he receives as large a salary as the President of the United States, and far more sustained publicity. It could only occur, we are told, in a democracy, hence we are a democratic nation. It is about the only remaining proof left to us.

Ordeal by Cheque

WUTHER GRUE

Los Angeles, Calif. Aug 30th 1903 No. ___
HOLLYWOOD STATE BANK 90-984
6601 Santa Monica Boulevard
Pay to the order of Goosie Gander Baby Shoppe $148.50
One hundred & forty-eight 50/100 Dollars
Lawrence Exeter

Los Angeles, Calif. Sept 2nd 1903 No. ___
HOLLYWOOD STATE BANK 90-984
6601 Santa Monica Boulevard
Pay to the order of Hollywood Hospital $100.00
One hundred Dollars
Lawrence Exeter

Los Angeles, Calif. Oct 3rd 1903 No. ___
HOLLYWOOD STATE BANK 90-984
6601 Santa Monica Boulevard
Pay to the order of Dr. David M. McCoy $475.00
Four hundred & seventy five Dollars
Lawrence Exeter Sr.

Los Angeles, Calif. Dec 19th 1903 No. ___
HOLLYWOOD STATE BANK 90-984
6601 Santa Monica Boulevard
Pay to the order of California Toyland Co. $83.20
Eighty three 20/100 Dollars
Lawrence Exeter Sr.

Los Angeles, Calif. Oct 6th 1909 No. ___
HOLLYWOOD STATE BANK 90-984
6601 Santa Monica Boulevard
Pay to the order of Palisades School for Boys $1,250.00
Twelve hundred & fifty Dollars
Lawrence Exeter Sr.

Los Angeles, Calif. Apr 18th 1910 No. ___
HOLLYWOOD STATE BANK 90-984
6601 Santa Monica Boulevard
Pay to the order of City Bicycle Co. $52.50
Fifty two 50/100 Dollars
Lawrence Exeter Sr.

Los Angeles, Calif. Aug 26th 1915 No. ___
HOLLYWOOD STATE BANK 90-984
6601 Santa Monica Boulevard
Pay to the order of Columbia Military Acad. $2,150.00
Twenty-one hundred & fifty Dollars
Lawrence Exeter Sr.

Los Angeles, Calif. Sept 3rd 1921 No. ___
HOLLYWOOD STATE BANK 90-984
6601 Santa Monica Boulevard
Pay to the order of Hollywood-Cadillac Co. $3,885.00
Thirty-eight hundred & eighty-five Dollars
Lawrence Exeter Sr.

Los Angeles, Calif. Sept 7th 1921 No. ___
HOLLYWOOD STATE BANK 90-984
6601 Santa Monica Boulevard
Pay to the order of Wilshire Auto Repair Service $288.96
Two hundred & eighty-eight 96/100 Dollars
Lawrence Exeter Sr.

Los Angeles, Calif. Oct 15th 1921 No. ___
HOLLYWOOD STATE BANK 90-984
6601 Santa Monica Boulevard
Pay to the order of Stanford University $339.00
Three hundred & thirty-nine Dollars
Lawrence Exeter Sr.

Los Angeles, Calif. June 1st 1923 No. ___
HOLLYWOOD STATE BANK 90-984
6601 Santa Monica Boulevard
Pay to the order of Miss Daisy Windsor $25,000.00
Twenty-five thousand Dollars
Lawrence Exeter Sr.

Los Angeles, Calif. June 9th 1923 No. ___
HOLLYWOOD STATE BANK 90-984
6601 Santa Monica Boulevard
Pay to the order of French Line, Ile de France $585.00
Five hundred & eighty-five Dollars
Lawrence Exeter Sr.

Los Angeles, Calif. Aug 23rd 1923 No. ___
HOLLYWOOD STATE BANK 90-984
6601 Santa Monica Boulevard
Pay to the order of Banque de France $5000.00
Five thousand Dollars
Lawrence Exeter Sr.

Los Angeles, Calif. Feb 13th 1926 No. ___
HOLLYWOOD STATE BANK 90-984
6601 Santa Monica Boulevard
Pay to the order of University Club Florists $76.50
Seventy-six 50/100 Dollars
Lawrence Exeter Sr.

Los Angeles, Calif. June 22nd 1926 No. ___
HOLLYWOOD STATE BANK 90-984
6601 Santa Monica Boulevard
Pay to the order of University Club Florists $312.75
Three hundred & twelve 75/100 Dollars
Lawrence Exeter

Los Angeles, Calif. Aug 11th 1926 No. ___
HOLLYWOOD STATE BANK 90-984
6601 Santa Monica Boulevard
Pay to the order of Riviera Heights Land Co $56,000.00
Fifty-six thousand Dollars
Lawrence Exeter

Los Angeles, Calif. Oct 30th 1926 No. ___
HOLLYWOOD STATE BANK 90-984
6601 Santa Monica Boulevard
Pay to the order of Renaissance Interior Decorators $22,000.00
Twenty-two thousand Dollars
Lawrence Exeter

Los Angeles, Calif. Nov 18th 1926 No. ___
HOLLYWOOD STATE BANK 90-984
6601 Santa Monica Boulevard
Pay to the order of Beverly Diamond & Gift Shoppe $678.00
Six hundred & seventy-eight Dollars
Lawrence Exeter

Los Angeles, Calif. Nov 16th 1926 No. ___
HOLLYWOOD STATE BANK 90-984
6601 Santa Monica Boulevard
Pay to the order of Hawaii Steamship Co $560.00
Five hundred & sixty Dollars
Lawrence Exeter

Los Angeles, Calif. Nov 21st 1926 No. ___
HOLLYWOOD STATE BANK 90-984
6601 Santa Monica Boulevard
Pay to the order of Lawrence Exeter, Junior $200,000.00
Two hundred thousand Dollars
Lawrence Exeter

Los Angeles, Calif. Nov 22nd 1926 No. ___
HOLLYWOOD STATE BANK 90-984
6601 Santa Monica Boulevard
Pay to the order of Ambassador Hotel $2,250.00
Twenty-two hundred & fifty Dollars
Lawrence Exeter

Hansen

WARING, DURANTE, and ARNO

Presenting an informal glimpse of the popular bandleader whose "Pennsylvanians" are becoming synonymous with good dance music, the beloved comedian who recently starred on Broadway in Cole Porter's *The New Yorkers,* and the gifted cartoonist now producing a musical comedy, *Here Comes the Bride,* with book, sets and costumes by—you guessed it—Peter Arno.

CLARK GABLE

The rapid rise to fame of this gray-eyed youth is one of the weekly seven-day wonders of Hollywood. It is unique in that it is the result of the unprecedented flood of feminine "fan mail" which clamored for his screen presence, rather than of the usual planned studio campaign.

Mr. Gable was born on February 1, 1901, in Cadiz, Ohio. Of pure Pennsylvania Dutch stock, he was educated at nearby schools and at Akron University where he took a business course. This experience evidently decided him to be an actor, and for the next few years he played in stock companies from Texas to Oregon, toured with Jane Cowl in *Romeo and Juliet,* and appeared in several plays in Los Angeles. He eventually reached New York in Arthur Hopkins' *Machinal.* A few more plays followed, then the inevitable films, his first being *The Painted Desert.* His next will be *Hell's Divers.*

Twilight of the Ink-stained Gods

Two Barons of the Native Press, and How Their Contrasting Journalisms Have Eclipsed the Editors

ALVA JOHNSTON

IN 1896, William Randolph Hearst went from San Francisco to New York to buy the *Journal,* and Adolph S. Ochs went from Chattanooga to New York to buy the *Times.* In the thirty-five years since then the two men have revised American journalism. Ochs specialized in information, Hearst in entertainment; together they abolished the older type of daily journalism which specialized in opinion.

The great figures in nineteenth-century journalism were editors; today they are publishers. A newspaper is no longer a political adventure but a business. The change seems to be for the better. Under the new dispensation the press has discarded much of the evangelical hate and fury which were the major infirmities of the old organs of opinion. In his long career Ochs has given the press lessons in tolerance and fair play; Hearst has taught it how to amuse a few score millions daily. Ochs undermines the editorial writer by setting the fashion of presenting an unbiased factual record on which the reader can form his own opinion; Hearst, with his comics, miscellaneous columns and various syndicates features, dulls the appetite of the reader for solemn exhortation on the editorial page.

The nineteenth-century newspaper was basically a political pamphlet. Greeley, Raymond, Reid, Dana and Bryant were orators in print. Non-partisan treatment of news was entertained as an ideal, and fitfully practiced, but news was commonly expected to corroborate editorial dogma. The James Gordon Bennetts were great newsgatherers, but their eccentricities and personal feuds prevented them from treating the news dispassionately. Pulitzer, both a fact-digger and a crusader, was slightly more interested in shaping events than recording them. Ochs seems to have been the first great journalist to have treated news with consistent objectivity over a long period of years.

The Hearst influence has been deprecated as unedifying; the Ochs influence as tending, by its frigid impartiality, towards indifference to moral issues; but the twentieth-century press shows improvement over the nineteenth, even when the tabloids are taken into account. The master vice of the old school of journalism was a malevolent self-righteousness. The ferocity of the American newspaper, disguised as superheated public virtue, was commented on by foreign writers on American institutions from de Tocqueville to Bryce. The press was conscious of a divine commission to punish evil-doers and members of the opposing political party; the editor to some extent supplanted the cleric as the custodian of the hot vengeance and the rod of heaven. The newspaper was too often a daily vial of Old Testament wrath, and the editor an ink-stained Jehovah. The moral arrogance and persecuting ethical savagery of the American press shocked Dickens in the forties and Kipling and Stevenson in the eighties. Down to the turn of the century and later, the standard mode of flattering a journalist was to allude to his "vitriolic pen." Curious results ensue when an editor fails to make the distinction between himself and God. Dickens presented the classic picture of the rage of a journalistic Messiah when the will of heaven was frustrated by the captain of a transatlantic packet who failed to make good with the usual courtesy of a free case of champagne. The old streak of godliness still manifests itself occasionally, as when a publisher explains that he prints columns of circulation-building divorce evidence as a deterrent to sin. But, generally speaking, theocratic journalism is disappearing from the daily papers and flourishing only in weekly journals of opinion.

NEITHER Hearst nor Ochs has been an inventor or a pioneer in the publishing field, but they have developed their conceptions of journalism in such clear-cut fashion and so successfully that their methods have been widely copied. Although most American newspapers today show the influence of both Hearst and Ochs, the two men have had little effect on each other. Ochs has refused to make room in *The New York Times* for the comic strip and other variegated features of the Hearstian type. Hearst shattered the tradition of journalistic anonymity by aggressively building up the names of his writers; Ochs, until recently, maintained the policy that the newspaper writer should be nameless. The Ochs ideals of colorless news and restrained editorial comment have not, however, converted Hearst.

The influence of Ochs has been gradual, but very far-reaching. He has moderated the tone of the American press, improved its manners and taught it the difficult distinction between fact and notion. Hearst forced his journalistic developments on the country by the direct method of invading most of the large cities with his newspapers; many of his competitors reluctantly became Hearst disciples in order to meet Hearst competition. Ochs has impressed his personality on the fourth estate in a different way. His great commercial success with one newspaper (its stock went up under Ochs from $10 to $6,000 a share) caused newspaper publishers all over the country to study his methods; a large section of the press adopted Ochs impartiality in news and headlines in the hope that Ochs prosperity would follow.

Hearst, both through his own newspaper chain and through the hundreds of Hearst-influenced dailies, appears before the public as a minstrel and sage, ethical guide, social coach, financial adviser, confidant and strategist in affairs of the heart, culinary tutor, educator, house mother, prophet, purveyor of warm data on high life. As against this, Ochs is only a vendor of information; but unadulterated information, correctly branded in the headlines and, as a rule, dispassionately annotated in the editorials. Ochs opened the eyes of the American press to the great market which existed for hobby-free, grudge-free, impersonal, non-reforming, non-crusading journalism, a journalism with no friends, no fees, no *bête noire*, no sacred cow.

THE contrast between Hearst and Ochs is nowhere greater than in their use of power. Hearst always has his heavy artillery in action in behalf of his candidates, crusades and causes. Every day of his life he strives to exert his influence to the utmost. Ochs, on the other hand, is a hoarder of influence; he uses it economically, parsimoniously. He has a theory that a newspaper dissipates its influence by exerting it. The bugle call editorial, the horsewhip editorial, the Judgment Day editorial are not found in his publication; but a few mild words there sometimes have a surprising effect. Mayor Walker, usually the most indifferent of officials to newspaper attack, called all his department heads together a year ago, scolded them and warned them, all because an editorial gently critical of his administration had appeared in the *Times.* Last winter another editorial suggested that, in their furious personal abuse of President Hoover, the Democrats in Congress were displaying their historic instinct for ruining their political prospects; immediately the order, "Stop riding Hoover," went out from the Democratic great headquarters. Hearst cannot produce magical effects like these, but by huge expenditures of printer's ink, he makes his influence heavily felt. Let anyone, who thinks that Hearst has lost his influence, go forth and campaign for our entrance into the League of Nations and the World Court.

Ochs and Hearst have some traits in common. Each is possessed by a demoniacal industry. Each is an extreme individualist, little influenced by anything but a desire to please himself. Neither is a money-grubber. Hearst has more than once injured his own standing and impaired the value of his properties by fanatical zeal for unpopular causes. Ochs, in his first year in New York, when his paper was tottering on the verge of insolvency, rejected a fat advertising contract because it had an almost invisible Tammany string on it; a little later he estranged his biggest advertiser by refusing to propagandize for subway facilities near an advertiser's store.

In most respects the two men are opposites. Ochs has no fads, no whims, no causes; never ran for political office; never attempted to create a President or a Coroner; never sought to tamper with the map of the world; has no social ambitions, lives simply, is one of the few rich men who has no opinions on Old Masters. Hearst has always been deep in politics; served twice in Congress; created political parties of his own when the old ones did not suit him; ran, unsuccessfully, twice for Mayor of New York and once for Governor, being beaten for the Mayoralty once by a false count; presented his countrymen, according to some historians, with the Spanish-American War; lives regally; has Senators, Mayors, Governors, judges, princes and miscellaneous celebrities at his beck and call, is something of a connoisseur and one of the world's chief collectors of armor. Ochs has had a placid, humdrum career, finding no relish in controversy; Hearst finds life most piquant when indignant citizenry makes bonfires of his newspapers, when great auditoriums are packed by anti-Hearst rallies, when he is being anathematized in Congress and when he receives such a thirty-third-degree accolade as that of being excluded from France. Hearst has been a national figure for more than thirty years; Ochs is little known today except in his own profession, where his lightest word is accepted as revelation.

Their starts in life were very different. Hearst, the son of one of the wealthiest men in America, left Harvard after the sophomore year and began experimenting in 1887 with the San Francisco *Examiner* which his father acquired in payment for a bad debt. Pioneer manners were not yet wholly extinct in San Francisco. The horse pistol was still a literary accessory. Personal journalism was never rougher, not even in the days of Thomas Jefferson, arch-patron of publicity. Ochs, a poor boy, started as a printer's devil at Knoxville, Tennessee. He once told a group of teachers of journalism that his success had been due to heavy responsibilities which were thrust on him at a tender age: as a printer's devil he was afraid to go home alone at night because he had to pass a cemetery; he therefore always waited to go home with the foreman; the foreman, a tippler, applied himself to his bottle and made young Ochs do all the work of getting out the paper. Under this early forcing process young Ochs developed swiftly; at 21 he owned a paper in Chattanooga; at 30 he was one of the most successful publishers in the South. Hearst came to New York at the age of 33 with an enormous fortune behind him and cocksure confidence as to his future. In the same year Ochs, then 39, arrived in New York diffident, hesitating, overawed by the big city. When H. H. Kohlsaat urged him to negotiate for the *Times,* Ochs said, "I don't think I'm big enough to run it." "Don't tell that to anybody and nobody will find it out," Kohlsaat replied. His success since then has been an everfresh surprise to Ochs.

Hearst built a chain of twenty-five newspapers, developed feature syndicates and a worldwide news service, movie interests, newsreels and a string of magazines ranging from the *Connoisseur* in England to *The American Druggist*. Ochs, aside from an adventure in Philadelphia, devoted himself to his one metropolitan daily, the most valuable newspaper property in the world. Frank Munsey, after years in trying to operate a newspaper chain, said, "Mr. Ochs, you are the wisest man I know. No man is big enough to run more than one newspaper."

While Ochs has established a new canon of impartiality and of indifference to politics, he is commonly mislabeled as a "conservative" newspaperman. It would be more accurate to call him a conservative sensationalist, or a neutral between conservatism and sensationalism. Under sober headlines and restrained opening paragraphs he does full justice to the spacious scandals of the time, always endeavoring, however, to treat individuals as humanely as circumstances permit. He prints two words for one by Hearst on shockers and thrillers like the Hall-Mills, Peaches-Browning and Snyder-Gray cases. Ochs has no fear that the public will be hurt by plenty of red meat, but there is no Rabelaisian wink in his treatment of gaudy themes.

Ochs boasts that his paper has no policy. Hearst has policies and very complicated ones, but there is nevertheless considerable freedom of opinion within his organization.

The eclipse of the editor by the publisher is usually thought to have lessened the influence of the press. It is true that newspapers often make spectacular failures in attempting to force their opinions on their readers. The voter will not vote the way the papers tell him to. The paradox of modern journalism is that the news has gained influence at the expense of the newspapers. The news has escaped from control and become totally unmanageable. The publisher, whether he likes it or not, must print the news, or the reader will go elsewhere for it. When a reader forms his opinion from the news columns, the editorial columns do not reverse it. The newspaper can pick and choose to some extent, but it cannot, under current competitive conditions, suppress much important news without suppressing itself. This is the great advance of twentieth-century journalism over the nineteenth. Incidentally, this dominance of impartial reporting over journalistic politics hardly exists outside of the United States.

Neither the Hearst pattern nor the Ochs pattern is destined to be the final newspaper formula. The defect in Ochs' journalism is that its conscientious objectivity sometimes causes it to read like the *Congressional Record*. There is still room in America for digging and crusading in the Pulitzer manner. However, it is impossible to combine all merits or all faults in one newspaper, or chain of newspapers. Formulas seldom last long in journalism. A great paper reflects the qualities and defects of a great man. The Hearst-Ochs phase will last until other great personalities change the scene.

Impossible Interview

John D. Rockefeller, Senior, versus Josef Stalin

JOHN D: I never thought that even I would live to see Russia turn into a commune. Dear, dear! All that iron and steel and oil, crying out for intelligent exploitation. And nobody profiting a bit by it. STALIN: The people profit. JOHN D: The people? Oh, yes. Of course they profit —afterwards. STALIN: Afterwards? JOHN D: After decent intervals of character-building deprivation, during which industrial leaders prepare lovely periods of progress and prosperity for them. STALIN: Now that sounds like my five-year plan. JOHN D (*delighted*): It does? (*Peering at him*) Do *you* run this plan? (*Stalin nods.*) Can the people still take it? STALIN: Take it from me, they take it. JOHN D: Well, well. (*Drops a dime in Stalin's outstretched hand.*) Thank heavens, dear boy, you've restored my faith in human nature.

COVARRUBIAS

Impossible Interview

Greta Garbo versus Calvin Coolidge

GRETA (*who has been keeping cool with Cal*): You haf been here three hours, and what haf you said? Nothink, absolutely *nothink*. CAL: Words are cheap. There are over four hundred and fifty-five thousand four hundred and twenty-three words, not counting vowel sounds, in the Webster's Standard Dictionary. But it was not words that made this great country what it is today. It was actions. Actions speak louder than words. It is possible to calculate that there have been four hundred and sixty-four major actions. GRETA: Stop! (*A half-hour's silence.*) CAL: Stop what? GRETA: Stop talking. I wish to t'ink. (*Three-quarters of an hour elapse.*) CAL: And, what do you think, Miss Garbo? GRETA: I t'ink I go home. CAL: Oh, Miss Garbo! (*The next silence lasts an hour.*) Wal, I reckon that whether I choose to or not, I must run. The missus is waiting. GRETA: Vel, I'm sick of this argument, anyway.

Smiles on the Faces of Tigers

CHARLES FITZHUGH TALMAN

"SPEAKING of tigers," remarked Mr. Camille de Courcy, as he accepted a chocolate drop from Seraphina and settled down more comfortably in the wicker chair—"I don't suppose any of you ladies ever tasted tiger croquettes?"

The girls said "No" in chorus, while Mrs. Matilda muttered "Stuff and nonsense!" over her knitting, but at the same time drew her chair a little closer.

"Strange to say, neither have I," continued Camille. "During my visits to India I have often asked for them at hotels and restaurants, but never succeeded in getting them. Of course I have frequently eaten tiger steaks, tiger-tail soup and tiger à la king, and I have found them delicious. Nevertheless I have always been a little nervous about eating tiger meat served in any style, ever since a curious experience I had with it."

"Please tell us about it," begged the girls.

"Please don't," interposed Mrs. Matilda.

"I was living in Calcutta at the time," said Camille. "It was my first visit to India, and I was just beginning to get accustomed to the ways of the country. I found the people there very hospitable, but they had one fault. They loved to make fun of a newcomer by telling him all sorts of ridiculous stories. They tried this with me, but, though I was new to India, I had traveled enough in other countries to know a thing or two, and I did not swallow all the strange tales that my Indian acquaintances told to me.

"One of my best friends in Calcutta was a retired British army officer named Colonel Bottlewood. I used to lunch with him sometimes at his club, and he always entertained me during the meal with incredible stories about his Indian experiences. He was a jovial old soul, and I enjoyed his society so much that I never risked offending him by expressing doubts about the truth of his stories. At the same time I was often scandalized at his efforts to deceive me."

"You must have been," remarked Mrs. Matilda in a tone of withering sarcasm. "You are so truthful yourself that it must horrify you to hear anybody tell a fib."

"Not always," said Camille. "It depends on circumstances. For instance, when I asked Seraphina a few moments ago to hand me the chocolate drops, you asserted quite positively that they were all gone, though you must have known that the box was half full, as you had just taken one yourself. I was not at all shocked to discover that you had made a false statement, because I real-ized that it was prompted entirely by your desire to protect my health from the bad effects of eating too much candy. I did not thank you at the time, but I do now with all my heart."

Mrs. Matilda so far forgot her dignity as to stick out her tongue at Camille, but he took no notice of this demonstration.

"The Colonel," he went on, "had no good excuse for telling me untruths, and his conduct was all the more reprehensible because he claimed to be a very religious man. He went to church regularly and taught Sunday school besides. Moreover, I found, on inquiry, that the stories he told me were not much more untruthful than those he told people who had lived in India all their lives. In fact, he had a reputation throughout the country for drawing the long bow.

"One day, after I had been acquainted with him for several months, I joined him at the club, and we sat down to tiffin, as luncheon is called in India. When we were seated, the Colonel asked me whether I would have a B. and S., and I said yes, thank you, I would."

"What is a B. and S.?" inquired Seraphina.

"Biscuit and sugar," replied Camille. "In India it is quite customary to take sugared biscuits several times a day in order to ward off the feverish effects of the climate. The Colonel generally took two or three during tiffin, and these seemed to stimulate his imagination. After he had taken a second one, his stories always became so interesting that I felt only slightly grieved over their untruthfulness, especially if I had taken two sugared biscuits myself.

"HAVING consumed his first B. and S., the Colonel studied the bill-of-fare, and then ordered tiffin for us both. For the first course we had fried elephant's ears on toast."

"Dear me!" exclaimed Seraphina, and Adeline inquired whether they were good.

"Only fair," said Camille. "They were tough. When the Colonel noticed how tough they were, he declared that the elephant had undoubtedly belonged to a rajah in reduced circumstances. As he made this remark, the Colonel rubbed his fingers over the side of his nose; a gesture which, as I knew from experience, meant that he was now in the mood for story-telling. He went on to explain that when a rajah became so poor that he could no longer afford to keep a servant to swing a *punkah*, or ceiling-fan, over him at night, he generally trained an elephant to sit at his bedstead and fan him by flapping its ears.

"'Of course,' he said, 'this process soon makes the elephant's ears very tough and stringy, and also the loss of sleep is so bad for the animal's nerves, that before very long the poor beast is fit only to be converted into food. As there are always a great many rajahs in reduced circumstances in India, tough elephant's ears are found in almost every butcher-shop, and one can hardly blame the steward of the club for buying them sometime, by mistake.'"

Adeline said she thought that was a cruel way to treat a poor elephant.

"So it is," agreed Camille, "but I don't believe there was a word of truth in what the Colonel told me. Servants' wages are low in India, and it would certainly cost a rajah a great deal more to feed an elephant than to hire a man or a boy to fan him at night. No, I thought, even then, that the Colonel was merely drawing on his imagination when he explained the toughness of the elephant's ears, and I was quite sure he was when he told me, before we had finished our tiffin, about his amazing experiences in hunting pink elephants in Upper Burma. I had never been in Upper Burma myself, but when I was informed that the pink elephants in that part of the world climb trees and swing from branch to branch by their trunks, I had my doubts, even if I was too polite to express them.

"The Colonel had just finished telling me about cutting down an enormous calabash tree in order to dislodge an elephant that had taken refuge in the upper branches, when the servants brought in the next course, which consisted of tiger steak and vegetables. The tiger meat was not at all tough and I found it excellent, but the Colonel grumbled a little about it. He said that, although he could not be quite certain, he more than half suspected that the tiger had devoured a deputy-commissioner, shortly before being shot.

"'SOME people,' he said, 'do not object to a slight flavor of deputy-commissioner in broiled tiger, but I have never fancied it myself.'

"He then proceeded to explain that the flavor of a tiger's flesh depends in a marked degree upon the animal's diet, and that Indian epicures, when eating tiger, are very particular about the kind of human beings the animal has been feeding on.

"'I have a rather dull palate myself,' the Colonel went on, stroking his nose harder than ever, 'and I must confess that I cannot always tell positively from the taste of tiger meat whether the animal has been eating Europeans or natives, or living, as some tigers do, on a mixed diet. There are, however, many people in India who, at the first mouthful of a tiger steak, can give you almost a complete list of the tiger's meals for several weeks before it was bagged, and a good deal of information about each meal besides. For instance, if my friend Major Bomonjee, of the Bombay Native Forces, were here, he would be able to tell us without hesitation, not only whether this tiger had recently eaten a deputy-commissioner, but also, if such was the case, how old the unfortunate gentleman was, and whether he was married or single.'

"The Colonel then proceeded to relate how, some years before, Major Bomonjee and another Indian epicure had both fallen in love with a lady in Bombay who was celebrated for her beautiful hair and her matchless complexion. The Major had been especially attracted by her hair and the other epicure, whose name was Jeejeebhoy, by her complexion, and they had frequent disputes as to which of these two features was the more charming.

"One day they were dining together, when a particularly juicy tiger steak was set before them. The Major was the first to taste it. As he held a piece on his fork, and even before he had put it into his mouth, he detected a certain aroma about it that caused him to turn pale. When he had swallowed his first mouthful he groaned. Jeejeebhoy then took a bite of the meat, and he groaned too. They exchanged glances, and exclaimed 'Dora!' at the same time.

"Dora was the name of the lady who had the beautiful hair and the matchless complexion. She had gone for a stroll the day before in a neighboring jungle and had never returned, but her two lovers knew nothing of her disappearance until the flavor of the tiger steak revealed to them the dreadful fate that had overtaken her. They were quite overcome with grief to discover that they were partaking of the very tiger who had partaken of Dora. It was almost like eating Dora herself.

"Of course the two gentlemen had often devoured her with their eyes; they had probably told her, on occasions, that she looked good enough to eat; and they had certainly often complimented her on her excellent taste. But they were now viewing her charms from an entirely new angle, so to speak. It was this unique experience which presently led them to two startling discoveries.

"THE first one was made by the Major. He had been eating his tiger meat in sorrowful silence when suddenly he laid down his knife and fork, bestowed a triumphant look upon his companion, and exclaimed, 'Jeejeebhoy, you're a gazoot!' Jeejeebhoy pretended not to understand what the Major was driving at, but there was a sheepish expression on his face, and he had to confess that he *was* a gazoot when the Major declared, in the most positive terms, that Dora's famous complexion had been due entirely to cosmetics. The cosmetical flavor of the tiger's meat was exceedingly faint, but it was easily detected by the wonderfully acute palates of the two epicures.

"The Major did not crow over his rival long, however. Seized with an idea, Jeejeebhoy selected a bit of the tiger that was somewhat underdone and therefore had not lost much of its original flavor. Placing this in his mouth, he held it there for five minutes, while he tasted with the utmost attention; at the end of which time he swallowed the morsel, sat back in his chair, and gazed gloatingly into the eyes of the Major. 'Bomonjee,' he exclaimed, 'you are another!' By an almost superhuman feat of tasting, he had discovered that Dora's hair, of which the Major had been so much enamored, was a wig!

"After relating this story, which was, with three or four exceptions, the most incredible I have ever heard in the course of my world-wide travels, the Colonel gave his nose one final stroke, remarked that India is indeed an extraordinary country, and asked me to excuse him as he had to conduct a Bible class at the Y. M. C. A. He then hurried away—and that was the last I ever saw of him.

"A FEW days later I was much grieved to learn that the Colonel himself had been devoured by a tiger. Almost immediately afterward, the beast was shot by a hunting party, and some steaks and cutlets from it were served up at the same club where I had listened to the Colonel's remarkable narratives. As I happened to be lunching there, I had the sad but interesting experience of eating part of the tiger that had eaten the Colonel.

"I did not notice anything peculiar about the flavor of the meat, but after lunch, while talking with a number of gentlemen in the smoking room, I did something that I have ever since believed was entirely due to the influence of the food I had just eaten, as there does not seem to be any other possible way to account for it. The conversation turned on the subject of snakes. Somebody told a story about an unfortunate boa constrictor that accidentally tied itself in a hard knot and was never able to get untied, and as soon as I heard this improbable tale, a much more remarkable snake story suddenly flashed into my mind.

"Somehow it seemed as if the Colonel had come back to life and was telling it to me. Before I realized what I was doing, I began to relate the story, although there was not a word of truth in it. For the first and last time in my life, I told a deliberate out-and-out falsehood and felt no shame whatever about doing so. While I was telling the story I rubbed my nose so hard that I raised a blister on it, and that is one reason why I have always felt convinced that my untruthfulness on that occasion was the result of eating a small portion of the tiger that had devoured my untruthful friend, Colonel Bottlewood."

"Wasn't it lucky you didn't eat a *large* portion?" sneered Mrs. Matilda. "The effects might never have worn off."

"Perhaps so," returned Camille, "but in that case I should have been spared the mortification I felt when they did wear off and I realized how untruthful I had been. I was so much ashamed of the snake story I had told at the club that I afterward looked up all the gentlemen who had heard it and asked them not to believe it. They were kind enough to say they wouldn't, and so, I am glad to say, nobody was deceived by my story.

"The snake in my story mistook its own tail for that of another snake and swallowed itself *entirely*," said Camille, "but it was an exceptionally absent-minded snake. And besides, as I told you before, my story was not true."

Camille stroked his nose at this point, but it may have been only to brush away a fly.

Acme

Charles Lindbergh, the first man to fly across the Atlantic, and Mrs. Lindbergh (the former Anne Morrow) take off in their plane from New York for Maine, first stop on their flight to the Orient.

THE LINDBERGHS

RICHARD BYRD

Admiral Richard Evelyn Byrd, director of public relations for the Antarctic, is equally at home at either pole. His latest book, *Little America,* contrary to what the title might indicate, has nothing to do with the kiddies, but is an account of the life at our southern extremities.

Keystone

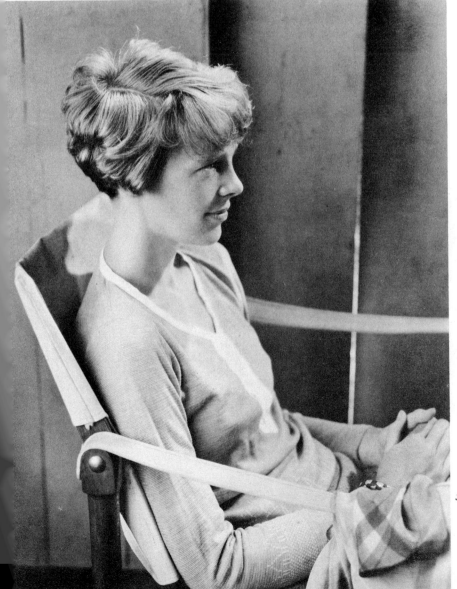

Steichen

AMELIA EARHART

A recent portrait by Steichen of the world's premiere aviatrix who was the first woman pilot to fly across the Atlantic alone.

215

THE THINKER—BY AUGUSTE RODIN

SPORTING INTELLECTION—TUNNEY

COSMIC COMEDY—CHARLES CHAPLIN

RING REVERIE—GEORGES CARPENTIER

MANAGERIAL MEDITATION—CONNIE MACK

HOLY DELIBERATION—GANDHI

FINANCIAL CEREBRATION — MORGAN

STATESMANLY COGITATION—L.GEORGE

POLITICAL VACILLATION—BORAH

MATERIAL ABSTRACTION—BISHOP CANNON

As a Man Thinketh

Thought, we are told, is valuable only in proportion as it is generative. Here are thoughtful men of action—of action varied in purpose and accomplishment, but nevertheless decisive in the scheme of things—posed in casual duplication of Rodin's immortal Thinker. Tunney, erstwhile prizefighter, ponders the technique of political battle; Chaplin plans a cosmic gag that will enrapture humorless critics; Carpentier and Connie Mack study how men may win in games; Gandhi's pensiveness, Lloyd George's whimsical imperialism, and Borah's passionate American insularity change the course of empire. Morgan scratches the surface of a great financial situation, and the brain of Bishop Cannon defends Methodism against liquor-sodden liberals.

The Pearly Beach

LORD DUNSANY

WE COULD not remember, any of us at the Club, who it was that first invented the twopenny stamp on cheques. There were eight or nine of us there, and not one of us could put a name to him. Of course a lot of us knew, but we'd all forgotten it. And that started us talking of the tricks memory plays. Some said memory didn't matter so much; some said it was looking forward that mattered most in business, or even watching closely what was going on around you now. And at that Jorkens stepped in. No, memory was the thing, he said; he could have made more by a good steady memory than by any amount of looking into the future.

"I don't see how that could be," said a stock-broker, who had just bought Jaffirs at 62, on pretty good information that they would go to 75. As a matter of fact they fell to 59¼.

But Jorkens stuck to his point. "With a good all-round memory," he said, "I could have made millions."

"But how?" asked the stock-broker.

"Well, it was this way," said Jorkens. "I had a rather nice pearl in a tie-pin. And things weren't quite going the way I liked; financially, I mean. Well, to cut a long story short, I decided to hock my pearl. I remember waiting till it was dark one winter's evening, so as to get to the pawnshop decently unobserved. And I went in and unscrewed the pearl off its pin, and saw it no more. That put the financial position on a sound basis again; but I came out a little what you call ruefully, and I suppose my face must have shown it, and I was sticking back what was left of my gold pin into my tie. Funny how anyone could have noticed all that, but I've observed that when people are a little bit drunk they sometimes do. Anyway there was a tall man leaning against a wall, a man I had never seen before in my life, and he looked at me in a lazy sort of way, not troubling to move his head, only his eyes, and even them he seemed barely troubling to turn and keep open; and he said, 'You want to go to Carrapaccas beach. That's where you want to go.' And he gave me the latitude and longitude. 'Pearls to be had for the gathering there,' he said.

"AND I asked him what he meant, why he spoke to me. I asked him all kinds of things. But all he would say was, 'You go to Carrappas beach,' not even giving it the same name the second time.

LORD AND LADY DUNSANY

"Well I jotted the latitude and longitude down on my shirt-cuff, and I thought the thing over a lot. And the first thing I saw as I thought things over was that the man was perfectly genuine; he had probably had this secret for years, and then one day he had had a drop too much, and had blurted the thing out. You may say what you like against drink, but you don't find a man to tell you a thing like that, just because he's sorry for you for losing a pearl, when he's sober. And mind you the Carrappas beaches, or whatever he called them, were there. The longitude was a long way East, and the latitude a lot South, and I started one day from London, heading for Aden. Did I tell you all this was in London? No place like it for starting on journeys. Well, I started from London and came again to Aden. I had a very curious romance there once.

"SO I came to Aden and began looking about. What I was looking for was three sailors; I fancied we could do it with that; and one of those queer small boats with green keels. Sails, of course. Well, I found two sailors; just the men I was looking for. One was named Bill, and the other the Portugee, though both looked English to me so far as I could tell. And they could get another man who was a half-wit, who they said would do very well. The beauty of that was that only two had to be in it. I told them at once it was something to do

with treasure, and they said that the third hand could be left on board when the rest of us went ashore, and would be quite happy singing a song that he sang. I never knew what his name was; Bill and the Portugee used just to shout at him, and he would always answer. His home was Aden; I never learned where the other two came from. Well, I told Bill the latitude and the longitude, and we slipped out in a tiny ship one morning from Aden, sailing towards India. And it was a long, long time before we came to Carrappas beach, or whatever it was. And day after day the sky was the same blistering blue, till sunset flamed in our faces, gazing back over the stern, and there came every evening behind us the same outburst of stars, and all the way the half-wit sang the same song; only the sea altered. And at last we got there, as Bill had promised we would, a tiny bay with a white beach shining, shut off by rocks from the rest of the coast, and from the inner land by a cliff, a low cliff steep behind it. The little bay was no more than fifty yards long. We cast anchor then, and I swam ashore with Bill and the Portugee, and the third hand sat on the deck singing his song. All that the drunken man had said was more than true. I hardly like to call him drunken, when I think what he did for me, all out of pure kindness. But you know what I mean; he had had a few drinks and they had made him quick to notice things and quick to feel for other people, and perfectly truthful; you know the old proverb. Probably, too, the drinks had brightened his memory, even to tiny details like latitude and longitude. I shall never forget the peculiar crunch as we walked. The pearls were mostly the size of good large peas, and seemed to go down to about six or eight inches onto a hard grey sand; but to that depth of six or eight inches along that fifty yards, and from the sea to the cliff, the beach was entirely composed of them. From sea to cliff was about fifteen yards, so that if you multiply that by fifty yards for the length, and by half a foot for the depth, you will see how much that was of solid pearls. I haven't done the sum myself. They didn't go out under the sea. It was nothing but dead oyster shells there. A funny little current scooped around that bay. We could see it doing it still, though the shells were all empty now; but once it must have idly gathered those pearls, and idly flung them onto the little beach, and roamed away into the Indian Ocean beyond the gaze of man. Well, of course, there was nothing to do but to fill our pockets, and we set about doing that, and it was a very curious thing—you may hardly believe me —but it was all I could do to get Bill to fill more than one pocket. Of course we had to swim back to the ship, which makes a reasonable explanation, but it wasn't Bill's reason at all. It was simply a fear he had of growing too rich. 'What's it worth?' he kept saying of his one pocketful. 'Over two hundred thousand,' I said at a guess. 'Can't see the difference between two hundred thousand and four hundred thousand,' Bill would say.

"'There's a lot of difference,' I'd tell him.

"'Yes, when I've spent the two hundred thousand,' Bill would go on.

"'Well, there you are,' I'd say.

"'And when will that be?' Bill would answer.

"I saw his point.

"AND another thing he was very keen on. Bill seemed to have read of men who had come by big fortunes: won lotteries and one thing and another; and according to Bill they went all to pieces quickly, and Bill was frightened. It was all I could do to get him to fill the other pocket. The Portugee was quietly filling his, but with an uneasy ear taking in all Bill's warnings. You know there was something a bit frightening about all that wealth. There was enough of it to have financed a war, or to have ruined a good-sized country in almost any other way. I didn't stay more than a few minutes after my pockets were full, to sit on the beach and let the pearls run through my fingers. Then we swam back to the ship. I said to Bill, 'What about one more load of pearls?' For it seemed a pity not to. And Bill said only, 'Up anchor.' And the Portugee said, 'I expect that's best.' And the half-wit stopped his song and got up the anchor, and we turned homeward towards Aden.

"In little more than a fortnight we came to that cindery harbor, safe with our pearls. And there we sold a few in a quiet way, without waking suspicion, and paid the half-wit a thousand pounds for his wages, and went on to Port Said. The three of us took cabins on a large ship bound for London, in order to sell our pearls, and late one evening we came into Port Said and were to sail on next morning. By the time we'd paid off the half-wit and paid for our cabins we hadn't much ready money left, but Bill said he knew how to get some. Bill had gone pretty slow on drinks since he got the pearls, but gambling was a thing he would never give up. 'We can afford it now,' he used to say, which is of course what you never can do. So we went ashore at Port Said, and took our pearls with us, as we'd none of us trust all that

out of our sight. And we came to a house Bill knew. Now, wasn't it a curious thing that Bill, who wouldn't trouble to put another two hundred thousand pounds in his pocket, was keen as mustard to make a hundred pounds or so in a Port Said gambling den? And it wasn't that he'd altered his mind about his pocketfuls of pearls being enough: he was never going back to that bay. Again and again I suggested it, but there was some sort of terror about that little white beach of pearls that seemed to have got hold of him.

"I wasn't keen on the gambling myself, but it seemed only friendly to keep an eye on the other two. So I slipped a revolver into my pocket and came with them. And I was probably drawn too by that feeling one used to have that, if the name of Port Said should turn up in a conversation, one has seen all that there is to see there. One liked to be able to say, if any particular den was mentioned, 'Oh yes, I dropped fifty pounds there.'

"I dropped more than that.

"Anyway we came to the house; and Bill and I and the Portugee went in; and soon we were playing and winning. The stakes aren't high downstairs, and you usually win there. In fact that downstairs room reminded me of a trail of grain over grass leading up to a trap. Upstairs the stakes were much higher, and upstairs we asked to go. A Greek ran the show downstairs, the sort of Greek you might meet at night in the shadier parts of Port Said, and very often did. The man upstairs was a Greek too, but not the kind that you would count on meeting; he seemed worse than what I'd been warned against. As we walked in he looked at us, each in turn, and it was when he looked at you that his eyes seemed to light up, and the blood seemed to pale in his face, and all the man's power and energy went to those eyes.

"'High stakes here,' he said.

"I nodded my head, and Bill and the Portugee began to babble something.

"'Got the stuff?' snapped the Greek.

"The man's style irritated me. I suppose I lost my temper. Certainly Bill and the Portugee looked pretty angry at the way he was speaking to us. I never answered a word to him. I merely slipped a hand into my pocket and brought out a handful of pearls, all gleaming in the ugly light of that room. And the Greek looked at them with his lips slowly widening, for a long while before he spoke. And then he said, 'Pearls,' in quite a funny small voice. And I was just going to say Yes. It was like a page in a book, like a page with a picture of a man in a dingy room with pearls in his hand, just going to speak; you turn the page and come on something quite different, nothing to do with pearls, no

room, and nobody speaking. Just silence and open air. And then the voice of a man coming up out of deeps of silence, saying the same thing over again, but with words that didn't as yet bring any meaning. A long time passed like that. Then the words again, and this time they seemed to mean something, if only one steadied oneself and tried to think.

"'He fainted in the street,' a man was saying.

"I was in a street right enough: I could see that as soon as I looked. And a man I had never seen before was saying that to a policeman. Fainted indeed! There was a lump on my forehead the size of two eggs, not to mention a taste in my mouth that I always get after chloroform."

"And the pearls?" blurted out the broker.

"The pearls," said Jorkens, and a sad smile shone for a moment. "Men found unconscious at night in the streets of Port Said never have pearls on them."

Jorkens remained shaking his head for a long time. "I suppose not," said someone to break the silence and bring him back to his tale.

"No," said Jorkens.

And after a while, in a voice that seemed low with mourning for his few weeks of fabulous wealth, Jorkens gave us what was left of his tale. "I never saw Bill or the Portugee again. Living or dead I never found trace of them. I took the policeman back to the house of the Greek, and was easily able to identify it. The downstairs room was the same as ever and I identified the man who ran it, as soon as we were able to wake him up and get him to come out of bed. What I couldn't do was to find the upstairs room, or even the staircase that led to it. As far as I could see we went all over the house, and I could neither say what had happened nor where it had happened, while the Greek was swearing by all kinds of things, that to him and the policeman were holy, that nothing had happened at all. How they'd made the change I was never able to see. So I just withdrew my charges, and gave the policeman baksheesh, and got back to the ship, and never saw any of my pearls again, except one that got lost in the lining, or ever saw trace again of the upstairs Greek. I got that one pearl in the lining fitted on to my tie-pin. Carrappas or Carrapaccas I could not find on any map, and no one I questioned in twenty sea-ports had ever heard of either; so that one pearl back in my tie-pin was all I got out of the kindly advice of the drunken man by the wall."

"But the latitude and the longitude," said Terbut, with the quiet air of one playing a mate.

"You see, *that*," said Jorkens, "was what I couldn't remember."

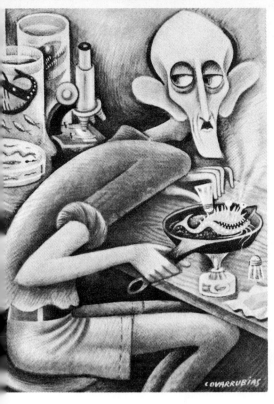

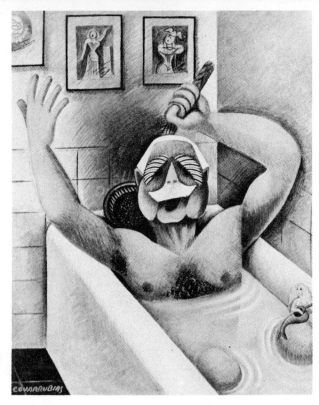

Mr. Otto Kahn, the opera impresario and banker extraordinaire, tries out that famous bathtub aria, "You're an Old Smoothie"

Professor William Beebe, gourmet and ichthyologist, secretly fries his new discovery, instead of pickling it for posterity

Private Lives of the Great

Mrs. Emily Price Post, social arbitress, in a moment of quiet abandon chez elle

THE THREE BARRYMORES

To play together in Rasputin

For the first time on any stage or screen, Lionel, Ethel, and John, the three members of our premier theatrical dynasty, will appear together in the motion picture *Rasputin,* a high melodrama centering on the court intrigues of that mad, lubricious monk. Lionel is to play Rasputin, a fine, full-bodied role, beautiful Ethel is to be the lovely, if feckless, Czarina, and John will play Prince Paul.

Bull

YEHUDI MENUHIN

The prodigy

At the age of sixteen, his music is fresh, astonishingly mature and vigorous. Born in New York, of Russian-Jewish parents, he spent his youth in San Francisco, where he first demonstrated his genius on a violin at the age of four. Like Heifetz, Zimbalist, and Elman, he was an accomplished concert violinist at the age of nine. He speaks five languages, enjoys swimming, tennis, sweets and driving a motor car. His adorations are his priceless Stradivarius, and Bach. He has given concerts to widely appreciative audiences in nearly every capital of the world. This year he is to appear in eighty-four concerts in the United States, the first of them to be in Carnegie Hall, in December.

Hoyningen-Huene

Lydia and the Ring-Doves

KAY BOYLE

THE laurel tree grew up to the window, and in the spring its white flowers opened, not quite, but edging on to fullness, and it blossomed with reserve. In the month of April they were scattered all over the tree's brow like a milky veil.

The other ornaments it wore were the ring-doves who came there to mourn. "Ah, God, ah, God!" they sobbed aloud in the branches. They peered through their bright relentless eyes for sustenance and fluttered the black lace of feathers on their throbbing throats. "Ah, God, ah, God!" they murmured of the frugalness of England, and laid their heads sideways to hark for Lydia opening her window.

Lydia gave them bread on the eaves and tried to stroke them. In all the strange country, they in their grieving had come closest to her heart. The bit of the sill with the rain or the sun lying on it, and the rosy eyes of the birds upturned to her were the simplest things she had found in England. Everything else there had a name and a form, a rooted life that set any being of the new world outside.

She tossed out the last of the crumbs and set her feet down on the floor. Here was her bedroom filled, for a wonder, with sun. And there in the glass, the reflection of the woman who had come to England to unbury the dead. She saw her own wise pale face with the deep lines of concern in the cheeks, and the heavy auburn braids wound twice around. Whatever gray there was in her hair lay carefully hidden underneath, concealed by the coils, as if the hands of a red Indian had been laid gently to her head. Almost forty, she thought grimly, and come to England to prove my identity.

She knew she belonged to the great: to the Earls and Dukes of Kingston-upon-Hull. The great, the great, she thought, and she turned again to look from the window. She had come to this place to lay her fingers on them. Dead great men to give her balance and background for her single life. She had never felt the want of money, but this other thing she had always wanted: the dignity of knowing what her own people had been.

"The Kingston titles became extinct on the duke's death without children on September 23, 1773," had been written, but town-records and family Bibles she would unearth to prove that this was not so. She wanted nothing the great might have left behind on earth, except the satisfaction. She was never at ease with the blood in her own body if she could not know where it had flowed before. If there were any great men living now, surely they never came through Kingston. She stood at the window thinking that if ever a man of proud blood set foot on the path that ran smartly up the garden, the doves would change their tune and the laurel tree would burst widely into flower. If ever a sign of the great came walking through the hedge below, the white kernels of the laurel buds would unfurl completely like corn popping in the pan. The doves would cease their moaning, and instead shout: "Caesar! Caesar!"

The first time the vegetable-man stopped his cart in the lane, all the doves rose out of the branches and went circling over the house.

The vegetable-man halted in the lane, and there called out the names of all his vegetables as if he were summoning them to rise. His face was bleached and fair under the singular gold lick of his pompadour. He wore his shirt-sleeves rolled up, and a pair of washable trousers. The horse in the shafts of his cart was slick and round and firm, and it cropped the half-apple off his palm, sneezed in a shower, tossed its bit in its mouth and lipped its master's bare light arm. The doves fled down and lighted on the side of the open cart, and Lydia held her breath at the sight of all this happening below.

In a little while, as she watched, two young goats as shy as deer came stepping down the lane as if in answer to his voice. They came to the brink of his shadow and nibbled shyly at the cabbage-leaves that the vegetable-man ripped off and threw away. Lydia saw that he had a gentleness for animals, whatever kind they were; he had a special gift for each one of them and they followed behind him when he went away.

THE vegetable-man had slapped the horse's flank with the flat of his hand, and the beast lifted up one leg and then the other, slowly, laboriously, bearing the cart away. The two little goats went stepping delicately behind him, and into the boughs of the laurel tree the doves returned and paced back and forth bemoaning. "Ah, God, ah, God!" they said in grief and dropped their Chinese white. And how strange, how strange, thought Lydia softly, that a man of the common people, a huckster, should have that wondrous gleaming poise and goodness in him. He seemed to her as clean and straight as a torch burning through frailty and through confusion to the very core of dignity that she had come to England to find.

On the third day that he came, she found she was going austerely down to buy a bunch of radishes from him. His clear blue eyes were on her as she took her pick. The little goats were shy of her, and the vegetable-man lifted one fair hand and laid it gently on the young goat's blunt-horned head.

"Good-afternoon," she said, and a curious agitation shook her.

"Good-afternoon, Miss," the vegetable-man said.

Just as she opened her purse, the doves came circling down around them. The flock of them settled in a row on the side of the cart and the feathers of their throats filled up with sound. The thin naked bird-feet clung quivering to the timber edge, and suddenly one dove dipped his head forward towards Lydia and snatched a radish-leaf from the bunch in her hand.

"Them's Barbary doves," said the vegetable-man. "I got Runts and Carriers at home as neat as anything you ever saw."

It was strange to hear him speak; strange that any man should speak of birds as though they were so dear to him. Lydia could not lift her eyes to his face as she paid the coppers out.

"Sometimes when the wind's wrong," said the vegetable-man, "there's any number of Carriers get blown out of their way and comes down for shelter."

Lydia looked up at him, touching her brow with her hand as if to re-arrange her hair but shielding her eyes from his uncanny gaze.

"I takes them home and cares for them until they're strong enough to take to the air again," he said gently; gently as a mother might have spoken of her young. Gently, thought Lydia, as her own mother had never spoken. It was wrong for a man, for a young man to be so wise in mercy. Lydia looked straight through his clear eyes into the concern for what might become of a heart that stood there open like a refuge for any creature that cared to come.

"Carrier pigeons going over?" she murmured mindlessly to conceal her confusion.

"Pigeons or doves," said the vegetable-man. "It's all one and the same. Whatever you call them, they've all got a little ring around their foot, one just like the other. With a message sealed up in it just the same. I've had Frillbacks and Tumblers," he said to her. "But the Trumpeters are the sweetest of them all."

"How do you know?" asked Lydia, and her throat was dry with wonder.

"They haven't no pedigree," said the vegetable-man. "They're riff-raff. That's what makes them the sweetest."

Lydia's heart went still for a moment, and she saw the melting eyes of the young goat under his caressing hand, and the birds close about him as if he were endowed with pure Franciscan flesh.

The next day he passed, when she heard his voice calling out between the hedge-rows, she went down the stairs with her straw purse in her hand. Two English housewives were buying carrots and onions, with care, and the two little goats were straying in his wake.

"Good-afternoon, Miss," said the vegetable-man to Lydia.

"Good-afternoon," said Lydia. When she looked into his pale eyes the color flew into her face.

When the strange women returned to their houses, the ring-doves took courage and descended, murmuring, in a sudden gust of rain. The vegetable-man threw back his head to scan the heavens.

"I don't like the looks of it," he said to Lydia, and she saw the words taking shape in his long strong lifted throat.

"Which way is the wind?" she said.

"It's coming off the channel," the vegetable-man answered. "It's a bad way for any birds as are up. It's sure and certain to blow hard tonight."

He stripped off the outer leaves of the cabbage she had chosen, and turned to see if the young goats found it to their liking. It comes of love, thought Lydia. All the endowment of perception that he has, it comes from nothing else but a wide brooding love. She saw him bent away, selecting the rosy faces of the apples for her. Everything he had on the cart she wanted a part of. She wanted to climb back to her room with a sample to taste of everything he had tended and brought to fullness. And suddenly he turned around with the apples in his hands and said to her:

"I was talking to my mother last night about the color of your hair."

Lydia's hand fled up to her heart and she saw the ring-doves whirl away.

"Ah, don't!" she said sharply. "You mustn't speak like that to me!"

His gaze was clear and guileless.

"It's such a pretty color," he said. "I meant you no offense."

She turned with her vegetables, and without a word walked sternly to the rooming-house. Just as she passed the threshold, a remnant of wind spun about her head and

unloosened a mesh of her closely braided hair; it licked across her eyes, straight out, as fierce as fire in the cheerless place.

In the day after the storm she went down into the garden and saw the havoc right and left. Here was a bough snapped off, and here the bruised flowers laid low by the rain. She walked the length to the end, and there under the hedge she saw a pigeon lying. His wings were stretched out as a cross from his drenching breast, and there was a great hoop of naked flesh around each wounded eye. Lydia fell on her knees with a cry and lifted the gray bird up in her hands. He was living, for he stirred wildly in her fingers, and she laid his failing beak against her own warm mouth. She bore him up to her room and dried his feathers with the softest linen. She heard her own voice crooning above him, soothing and wooing him as she spread him, like a fan, before the fire.

"My darling, my darling," she whispered to the heedless scrolls of his fine ears. She would have given all she possessed to know a few words of his tongue.

About his ankle was the bracelet, just as the vegetable-man had said it would be. And where it joined was sealed the little message near his claw.

"You were so brave, so brave, my darling," she said to him. She could see him flying low in the storm over the anger of the Channel waves, flying all night from the other side, following the direction that his heart's compass told him was true. "You were so brave all night," she said, "and nothing shall ever harm you."

She wanted to pluck the terror from his eye and cast it forever away. She put the pigeon in a small basket and carried him on her arm to the little cottage where the vegetable-man lived in the village.

"I've brought you a pigeon that was blown down by the wind," she said. They stood looking at each other, but now she felt no confusion. "I knew you would take care of it," she said, "until it could fly on again."

"Yes," said the vegetable-man, and he put his hand in gently to lift the pigeon from the basket. "I'll put it in with the others," he said, and his hand brushed hers in passing. "It's skin and bone. I'll put it in the coop and feed it up for a day or two."

She followed him back to the wire place where a dozen or less pigeons were gathered, pecking at corn and flying over the wet black mud.

"I found them three this morning," said the vegetable-man, pointing out three drenched and shivering birds to her. The little green blinds of their lids were drawn up over their eyes. "They pick up overnight with corn and meal," he said, and he released Lydia's pigeon.

In the week, Lydia brought him two more pigeons who fell in the lane before

the house, worn out by the wind that would not die. She set out in the morning with a bright easy sense of pleasure, and as she took the way to his cottage she could feel her heart beating soft with love. The birds were dear to her now, and the flowers that sprang up in the hedges, and nothing had ever been dear to her before. It was the best time in England, it was May, and her heart was stirring wondrously with spring. When she thought of the dead, it now seemed that they had taken on life to her. She could fancy the Duchess of Kingston stepping regally down this very lane, shining with pleasure because she was going shamelessly to tryst with a common man, a countryman, and a tide of blood ran warm in Lydia's face.

THE sun was high above the trees and the vegetable-man and his mother had already sat down to table. When Lydia came breathlessly in through the door she found them sitting at either side of the cloth with their plates steaming richly in the sun.

"Oh, I'm sorry!" said Lydia. "I just found another pigeon!"

"The fourth!" said the old woman. "Ah, you're too good to us, ma'am! If I set you a table to yourself, ma'am, would you sit down and have a bite to eat?"

"Oh, no, I couldn't trouble you!" said Lydia, but suddenly her eye fell upon the platter before them and she saw the shape of the food they were about to take: there were fresh peas from the garden set all around in the gravy, and in the center was the form of a little roasted bird. Her tongue was so parched that she could scarcely bring speech to it. She pointed with one finger at the bird on the plate.

"What happened, what happened," she said after a moment of terror, "what happened to the pigeon I brought on Monday?"

The vegetable-man shook his head and looked grieving at her.

"The poor little chap," he said with emotion. "He died during the night."

"Oh!" said Lydia. She felt her face go white and her heart was failing. "What about the two I brought on Wednesday?" she said. The walls of the room made a swoop like the flight of birds. And still the vegetable-man stood shaking his head in grief at her.

"Dead," said the vegetable-man and he opened his empty hands before her.

"Henry has a painless way of doing away with them," said the little old woman brightly. "He just holds their heads under in a glass of water."

"Oh!" said Lydia. "Oh!" she said, and she picked up her little basket. She felt her blood shuddering and shuddering throughout her body. "Yes," she said, "oh, yes, painless." And she fumbled her way out the door.

ALBERT EINSTEIN

The greatest living scientist

Born in 1879 at Württemberg, Professor Einstein began work on the theory of relativity in 1905, and this most prodigious contribution to physics in our time was completed by 1915. He has received honorary degrees from universities in six countries and was awarded the Nobel Prize in 1921. He is now once again, but sans benefit of ballyhoo, visiting America.

Bieber

H. G. WELLS

The prolific writer and prophet

The famous English author of some seventy books arrived in America a short while ago, twinkly-eyed but full of dire prophecies about the future of civilization. After exposing himself to the rigors of the American interviewers, the bland little man departed. The twinkle had deepened, but so had his prognostications of international gloom.

Steichen

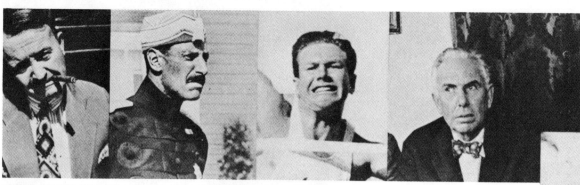

QUERY—BARNEY OLDFIELD   ANGER—KING CHRISTIAN   STRAIN—CHARLES PADDOCK   DISTRUST—THEODORE DREISER

AMUSEMENT—QUEEN MARY

SLYNESS—AL CAPONE   FEAR—"LEGS" DIAMOND

PATERNITY—SINCLAIR LEWIS

HOPE—ADOLF HITLER   CONTEMPT—JAMES J. WALKER

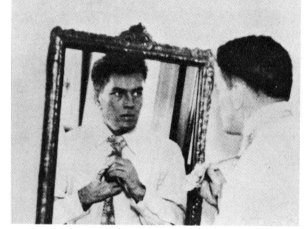

DOUBT—GENE TUNNEY

Vanity Fair's School for Actors

On these pages are a group of people important in public life, but none of whom, with the exception of the Vallees—here photographed on their honeymoon in what we hope is a non-professional moment— is in any sense a professional actor. Yet *Vanity Fair* has caught mirrored upon their faces such a variety of expression, running the gamut of tenderest love to deepest pain, that it is hard to believe that each of them was not, in reality, being directed at the time by a von Sternberg or an Eisenstein. Actors could study them with profit; and laymen who find that public characters are colorless will enjoy in future searching the rotogravures for an occasional expression which will demonstrate anew the comforting platitude that famous people are after all human.

QUIZZICAL—PRINCE OF WALES

PERPLEXITY—WINSTON CHURCHILL

GUILE AND SUSPICION—MUSSOLINI AND THE KING

ENTRATION—ELLSWORTH VINES

LOVE—MR. AND MRS RUDY VALLEE

BOREDOM—JOHN HAY WHITNEY

SE—PIERRE LAVAL   POLITESSE—ROBERT WAGNER   IRRITATION—LLOYD GEORGE

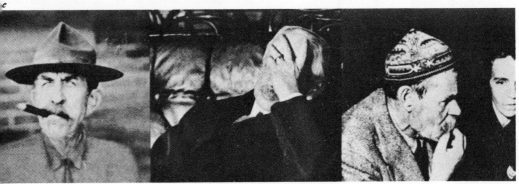

RMINATION—BILL MURRAY   MEDITATION—BISHOP JAMES CANNON   BROODING—MAXIM GORKY

WHIMSY—CALVIN COOLIDGE

Joyful James

CLARE BOOTHE

THE one conspicuously unimportant thing about James Joseph Walker, Mayor of the City of New York, seems to be his political record; the one fact of importance—the existence of his irresistible charm. During his six years as Manhattan's Chief Executive the personal popularity of this "small little man" has grown in direct ratio to the shrinkage of his political prestige. In fact, his prestige has now shrunk to such a microscopic point, and his popularity expanded to such splendid proportions, that he no longer belongs to the realm of politics, but to the realm of legend and literature. His delicate avoidance of all the tedious minutiae of civic government, his touching faith in the ability of his more or less able subordinates to enact the dreary duties of his office, his blind obedience to the dictates of the Tammany Sachem, John F. Curry, and his childish belief in the infallibility of the Tammany machine, are usually ascribed to the Mayor's neglect, incompetency or inefficiency. It is more reasonable to suppose, however, that these sins of omission spring from the instinctive wisdom of a man, who, being cast in one rôle by fate, knows that his genius lies in the development of another. With an alchemy rare to the purlieus of city halls, James J. Walker has transformed the rôle of Mayor from a political one into a dramatic

one, and has elevated that office from the low level of civic jobbery to the lofty altitude of art. He has, with a hedonism as refreshing as an attic breeze, swept from himself all the stuffy encumbrances, and heretofore solemn obligations, of office, retaining only, for his greater personal glorification, the aura of influence (which attaches to the holding rather than the practicing of public office); and has emerged from the City Hall chrysalis the perfect Casino butterfly. It is this significant transformation which baffles and eludes the Mayor's critics. It is the misapprehension of his rôle, and his character, of his spiritual, rather than his physical whereabouts, that permits men of the astuteness of Seabury, Holmes and Wise to slash away at the empty cocoon of Walker's political tenure in the vain hope of destroying the charming insect which has sprouted wings and is no longer there. They attack the shadow and not the substance. Of course, they are justifiable and admirable in their noble zeal and in their moral indignation, and the majority of Greater New York's citizens appreciates and applauds these efforts towards a better civic government. But when it appears that such Utopian desires may be fulfilled only by the ousting of James J. Walker from his office, the average voter's moral concepts become somewhat clouded by his emotional

approval of Jimmie. For the Mayor—well, the Mayor is a thoroughly charming fellow. . . .

The reader will therefore find it more amusing, if less profitable, to drop at once any consideration of Mr. Walker's political disqualifications, avoiding altogether what *The New York Times* so bitterly refers to as "corruption and contentment," and what the Messrs. Wise and Holmes so poignantly describe as "the incompetence, ineffectiveness, unfitness and grave dishonor of the Mayor," and to proceed with the infinitely more instructive and entertaining analysis of *what* makes this man so charming.

The answer is not quite as simple as it seems, as you must know if you have ever had even a short conversation about the Mayor with someone who is personally acquainted with him. You probably have: there are many such people, for the mercurial James' list of acquaintances—most of whom call him by his first name—embraces all branches of human activity, from tap dancers to kings, from bus-boys to presidents, from bartenders to financiers, from bookies to members of the Racquet Club, and from the soigné elegants of Park Avenue and Palm Beach to movie queens and crooners.

His is a wide democracy. But this is not the secret of his success. Hand-shaking,

Wise-Cracker

His Honor, the Mayor

Vacationist

Citizen

Broadway Playb[oy]

Married Man

Song-Wri[ter]

back-slapping, indiscriminate fraternizing have always been pet activities of the politician. Walker, however, differs in this, importantly: he does not appear in his contacts to be extending the right hand for a shake and the left for a vote. He conveys rather the impression that he enjoys the meeting, and that his geniality is disinterested and unselfish. He has a genius for becoming intimate with people in an incredibly short time, and the compensating knack of freeing himself of the consequences of his own sociability. He is, in fact, so winning that he puts the average person on his honor not to presume upon His Honor's affability. Moreover he tempers this excessive camaraderie by a lateness for all appointments which is proverbial. An irritated Glasgow editor said of him, "He will meet you in December if you make a date for May." But even in this fault he is democratic and consistent. He kept Calvin Coolidge waiting 35 minutes at the White House; he overslept at the Legion Parade in Paris, and the Legion Parade had been his excuse for going to Paris; he failed altogether to appear for his rendezvous with Gandhi in London—but on the other hand he was an hour late for his own wedding to Janet Allen in 1912. And it is conceivable that this was a pretty important occasion in his life.

Many attribute his great charm to his wit. The truth is that he is only occasionally witty. More often he merely wisecracks. He is, as a matter of fact, a master of this exclusively American brand of broad and cynical humor. The effectiveness of his wit does not lie so much in its penetration, in its subtlety, in its ability either to illuminate a situation or discountenance an opponent, as it resides in its nimbleness. The Mayor's mind, if not deep, is most extraordinarily alert. His tongue is quick to pluck a perception from his mind, and to translate it immediately into popular and salty idiom. His is not the well-calculated, bitter wit of a man who has thought things out to their ultimate absurdities, but neither is it *l'esprit d'escalier*. When he stands before the Legislature and tells men old enough to be his fathers that "no woman was ever ruined by a book"; * when he sasses the Board of Estimate; when he refers to the Central Park Casino as his "uptown office," and himself as New York's "nightmayor," when he twits his investigators with far more effect than they investigate him, when he welcomes moving picture actresses or princes at City Hall, then his speech is impudent, intensely American, and very much Jimmy Walker. The French would—in fact they did—call him *un gamin*.

He is by inclination and action a play-

* Defeat of the Clean Books Bill, Albany, 1923.

Tammanyite

Speaker   *Lawyer*   *World Traveler*

Society Man

Social Register Pet

boy. He likes prize fights, musical comedies, film studios, race tracks, night clubs and gay resorts. And he is genuinely fond of the people who form and frequent these milieus. He is at heart a sport. He even has the sport's weakness for flashy attire. They call him "Jimmie, the well-dressed man," but this is a misnomer. He is neat, but gaudy. From the point of view of the hinterland, he looks the part of the perfect "city-slicker." Urban sophisticates, in spite of his inventiveness in the matter of berets, find his taste theatrical. His coat lapels shine with satin or are languorous with velvet, and his pinched-in waistline would be the scandal

of Savile Row. Silk braid sweeps about the lapels, pockets, cuffs of his dinner coat. He wears pointed shoes, tight collars, brightly colored shirts, and rumor has it that his dressing gown and pajamas are peculiarly restless in character. He is, in a word, "natty." But it is a nattiness which, like his handshaking, his wit and his choice of friends is unstudied. It was adopted with no audience in view, except perhaps the natural wish to catch a feminine eye, and the even more natural desire to satisfy Jimmie Walker when Jimmie Walker looks lingeringly upon his own trim image in a cheval glass. His sartorial effect—like his tardiness—dates back to the days when he was New York's "boy Senator." Unlike Herbert Hoover's pontifical collar or Calvin Coolidge's spick and span farm overalls, it is not a symbol of democratic equality with the working man. Neither is it, like Al Smith's deplorable Brown Derby, a symbol of sentimentality applied to the process of vote getting. It is, if anything, a symbol of his own brand of political iconoclasm, which has it that the way to remain a public official is never to act or dress like one.

Walker is an ardent believer in the hedonist trinity: wine, women and song. He himself once quoted "Give me the writing of a nation's songs and I care not who makes its laws." In fact, he is more proud of the second-rate songs he has composed than of the few first-rate laws and reforms which he has—if only by sheer force of good nature, or the almost physical need of exercising his uncommon talents as a political strategist and tactician—given to the city. He is, admirably enough, no apologist for his beliefs and neither privately nor publicly tries to hide his pleasant faith behind a mask of hypocrisy. Rather, he boasts of it, and when other public servants point a scandalized finger, he challenges, "I will match my private life with any man's." He means it. Thus, having been made privy to his pleasures, five million citizens of New York turn with indignation upon the remaining million who would dare criticize a man's *public* life when his *private* life remains such an open book. He assumes the form of the eternal prodigal in the eyes of his fellow citizens, as he so loves to call them . . . and fellow citizens they are—not in the five boroughs of Manhattan, but in the five senses of man.

This is why, although the press complains that his jaunts are only convenient political getaways, the voters smile upon his frequent "vacations" to Bermuda, to Europe, to Lake Placid, to California or to Florida. . . . They travel vicariously with him, just as, vicariously, they go to prize fights and musical comedies and night clubs, sharing his amusements, his friends, and even his frequent "colds in the head." There is in Walker's attitude toward pleasure a persuasive and admirable consistency. When he was elected Mayor in 1926, although he promised that, in spite of the fact that he wore a top hat well, his intention was not to be a "picture post-card Mayor," he also said New York would find in him "no grouch"; and again "The more smiles we can get into official life, the better off the city will be." Naturally, different people smile at different things, and whereas Seabury finds certain aspects of Walker and his régime far from laughable, the majority of the people consider Jimmie's extra-mayoral antics entertaining and stimulating enough.

He was hailed six years ago as the Jazz Mayor, alias Sunny Jimmie Walker, the Tammany Troubadour, and when he answered to these names he was sailing—as he continues to sail—under no false colors.

And herein lies the charm of Jimmie Walker. He has a perfect sense of values: he knows what is important to him as an individual—that is the thing he does. In other words, he honestly loves life. Not only does he love life, and looking upon it finds it good, but he also—and here is a qualifying point not to be ignored—he loves a brand of life *only to be found on Manhattan Island*. Jimmie is a brilliant example of the city man who is happy: who indulges in metropolitan pastimes and pleasures, not to the destruction of his soul, but to the utter and sweet fulfillment of his own personality. His speech, thought, actions, desires are harmoniously adjusted to the rhythm of city life. "My city—but right or wrong my city," Walker was quoted as saying. A natural corollary to this city worship is his genuine affection for city dwellers. This often betrays him into rank sentimentalism, as when he told Mabel Willebrandt, who had spoken disparagingly of the district where Al Smith was born, "There comes out of the slums, if they be slums, as fine a womanhood and manhood as has ever been known in this country."

It is at moments such as these, when his deep-rooted loyalties are challenged, that the Mayor's sentimentality falls like a damp blanket over his bright Irish wit, and in the steam that arises from his volatile and heart-felt convictions about Tammany, Ireland, motherhood, Manhattan and his own political integrity, his listeners find their faces wet with tears. . . . "It's my emotional tonsils," James confided to a friend after one such exhibition.

At any large civic gathering—a prize fight for instance—Joyful James will receive a tremendous ovation. What the citizenry of New York applauds is not the Mayor, nor his office, but a man, set in a high place, who still has the vitality to enjoy life, the warmth to love it, and the sentiment to weep over it. His alleged incompetency, inefficiency, futility in office, his apparently blatant pleasure seeking, his unbounded effrontery and ofttimes tasteless impudence, his present shady political background of fabulous tin boxes and besmirched uniforms, of graft and corruption—all these things are forgotten in the tender mist that dims the eyes when one is confronted by a human being who, although beset by all sorts of temptations and inducements to travel the straight and narrow path, and exposed to the dank heritage of puritanism and moroseness which hangs in the American air, still has the grace to enjoy life, and the wit to disport himself merrily on the

thorny Primrose Path of metropolitan dalliance.

If the enemies of this dapper little gentleman are searching for a way most likely to destroy him, surely the character of his popularity should give them a clue. It is personal, not political. Let them reversely apply the same theories of press agentry to the case of the mellowed Jimmie as, for example, Ivy Ledbetter Lee applied to the once universally despised Rockefeller. Let them carry the war into the enemy's camp. Let them attack not the Mayor as an official whom they wish to prove corrupt, but as a legend which they can prove is false. They should destroy, in the subtle way of such things, his reputation for joy, for boundless pleasure, for merriment: or paint him as a gloomy, sinister, humorless grouch who is rapidly becoming dyspeptic. (Several years ago Walker's popularity received a severe setback when he let it be known that he was indefinitely on the water wagon. Popular opinion drove him rapidly again to drink.) Let them print stories that he was seen scowling with boredom at a prize fight, or looking with disapproval upon a current leg show, or saving his pennies, instead of betting them upon the ponies, or economizing on his neck-ties, or not laughing at George Jessel's jokes, or arriving at dinners on time, or making marked-down puns and flat-falling wisecracks, or junketing to Europe, not to flee investigation or regain his recklessly spent health, but to escape from the tedium of New York nights.

It is a waste of time, of energy and the coin of the land to try to oust him on legal or political grounds. Everyone knows that it is an unwritten law that court jesters have the right, by wit and sprightly mockery, to sit upon any throne they can snatch. There is only one effective way to banish them: to prove—if you can—that they are in reality dull fellows, sad at heart and, in unobserved moments, cantankerous. That they are, in short, no better than Kings, and not nearly as reliable.

It is over a year ago that John Haynes Holmes addressed a New York mass meeting of 3100 Indignant Citizens in Carnegie Hall, and prophesied to them that in 100 days the "small little man" would have a befitting post—that of ex-Mayor. . . . James Joseph still visits his desk in City Hall at convenient intervals, and will continue to do so until January, 1933. It is doubtful that he will stand for a third term, or even that the people will stand for him. In which case, he will take his erratic executive and legislative gifts, and his brilliant oratorical ones to Washington, D.C., where, as Congressman or Senator, he will continue to play the lovable Peter Pan of Politics—the Playboy of Tammany Hall.

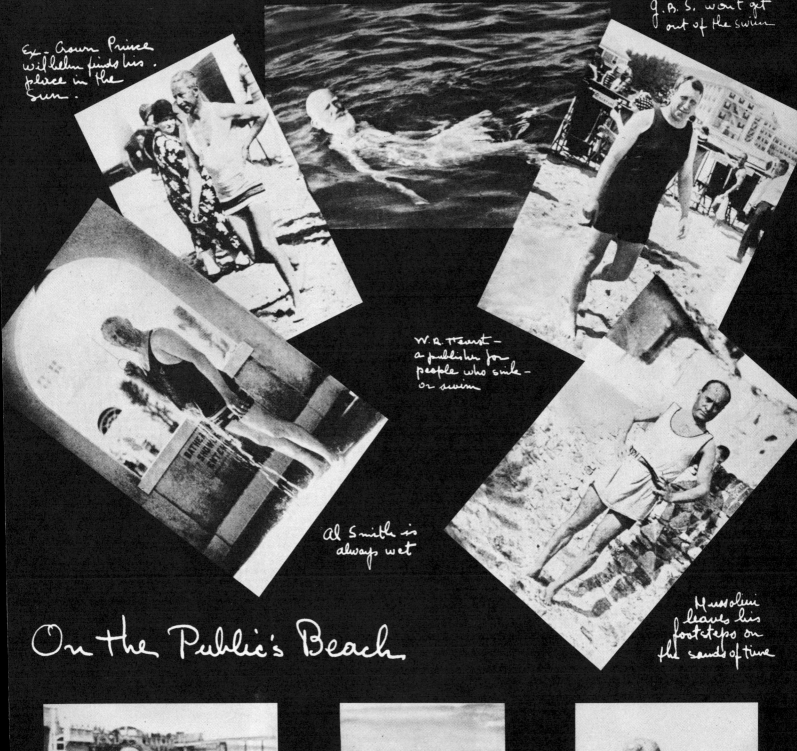

Ex-Crown Prince Wilhelm finds his place in the Sun.

G.B.S. won't get out of the swim

W. R. Hearst — a publisher for people who sink — or swim

Al Smith is always wet

Mussolini leaves his footsteps on the sands of time

On the Public's Beach

Little Sammy Untermyer tries a swimming suit

The Prince of Wales, a good catch

Otto Kahn watches the divas in the high C's.

Nominated for the Hall of Fame: 1932

JAMES TRUSLOW ADAMS

Because he is in the front rank of living American historians, placed there by his Pulitzer Prize book, *The Founding of New England,* and by *The Adams Family;* because he is a descendant of America's Spanish governor-general of 1558; and because his last book, *The Epic of America,* continues a sturdy best-seller.

Wide World

Keyst

Abbott

JAMES JOYCE *(left)*

Because he is the author of one of the supremely beautiful lyrics in English poetry; because he has devoted himself more vigorously to the novel as a literary form than anyone since Flaubert; and finally because *Ulysses* has been called the only epic of our time.

Acme

Steichen

PRINCESS ELIZABETH

Because she is the eldest child of the Duke and Duchess of York; because her bearing and appearance combine to make her resemble the storied Princess Charming; because in the natural course of events she may complete a quartet of reigning women whose first three members were the glamorous Elizabeth, the sober Anne, and the epochal Victoria.

PEARL BUCK *(left)*

Because she is one of the few Americans who have deeply penetrated Chinese life and culture; because her epic of the Chinese peasant, *The Good Earth,* now in its twenty-second edition, was recently awarded the Pulitzer Prize; because her new novel, *Sons,* a sequel to *The Good Earth,* will appear this fall.

ROLAND YOUNG

Because, besides being an actor famed for his pseudo-solemn and hilarious impersonations, he writes amusingly, draws ably, and directs with originality; because he is to appear in a film entitled *A Billion-Dollar Scandal;* because he is the country's leader in the fine art of collecting historic walking-sticks—with one of which he stands pictured here.

How Unlike We Are!

HAROLD NICOLSON

THE other day I read, for the second time, that excellent compilation by Professor André Siegfried, entitled *America Comes of Age*. Why the eminent Alsatian should imagine that the United States had only recently reached maturity passes my comprehension. But that is beside the point. The point is that towards the end of his book, M. Siegfried informs his compatriots that the United States and Great Britain understand each other better than do other foreign nations. I admit that the Professor may have found it necessary to disabuse his compatriots of their facile belief that the United States will tend, in every case, to take the side of France as against that of England, of La Fayette against Lord North. Were such an opinion held in the Quai d'Orsay (which it is not), an unfortunate misapprehension might arise. M. Siegfried is thus justified in warning France against a fallacy. For all that, I do not really believe that Great Britain and the United States understand each other better than do other foreign countries. On the contrary, I feel that we understand each other less. We in England have a clearer idea of what is going on at the back of the French mind, or even of the German mind, than we have of those recondite and rapid emotional processes which constitute the public opinion of America. You in the United States have often more understanding of the German mentality than you have of the mentality of Westminster. A month on this continent has taught me one extremely valuable lesson. It has taught me that I understand nothing about the United States whatsoever. It is for this reason that I desire, before any knowledge intervenes, to write about the British and American characters. I agree with Oscar Wilde—"ignorance is a delicate fruit: touch it, and the bloom is gone." I therefore write upon this invidious topic while the bloom is still as dust upon the damask of my ignorance.

WE ARE taught by our internationalists of today to cultivate what they call "the will to understand." The spirit may be willing, but the flesh is weak. Clearly, what one foreign nation notices most about another foreign nation is not the similarities which render each of them types of the same genus, but those dissimilarities which sunder them the one from the other. I am not struck, for instance, by the fact that the people of the United States dress much the same as those of the once United Kingdom.

I am struck by the fact that whereas American women have very tidy hair, the women of Great Britain have hair which is not tidy in the least. My attention, again, is less aroused by the curious circumstance that our two languages are, at more than one point, strikingly allied, as by the fact that when I pronounce the short "o" upon that excellent contrivance, the American telephone system, the operator, for all her comradely willingness, is unable to understand. It seems strange to me that words like "rock," "Bobby," "lock," "hot," should, in

the two languages, have diverged so strikingly in intonation. The long "o" is even more difficult than its short brother. The expression "Old Gold" is not one, for instance, which any Englishman can use without causing merriment in the drug store. I have abandoned my attempts to order rolls for breakfast: "toast" is what I say now: and with toast I have to rest content.

The gulf which sunders us is, however, more than lingual. There exists between the

Englishman and the American of 1933 a profound psychological rift which becomes apparent in many curious ways. There is, for instance, this business about laughing. I am one of those—and there are many of us—who like American stories. They are rather long, of course, but then your distances are so great and your club-cars so comfortable. Yet I have frequently gained the impression that the American narrator is left with the conviction that I, as a British auditor, have not seen his point. In almost every case, I *have* seen his point.

Steichen

HAROLD NICOLSON

I have smiled at the point, and if it has been a very good point I have even chuckled. But I haven't laughed. Englishmen, unless they possess exceptional teeth and an unreserved manner, very seldom laugh. And the American assumes therefrom that they have not seen his joke. This, I find, is a very current and damaging illusion. Nothing destroys amity so quickly as an unshared sense of humour. It is an illusion which I should wish to disperse.

A second, and more corrosive, difference is

our divergent standards of privacy. I do not say that the dumb individualism of the Englishman is a wholly attractive quality. Yet our secretive instincts are general and profound. I do not say, conversely, that the American has no sense of privacy, since one has only to probe a slight distance to be met with a strong-box of reserve. All I say is that the proportions of what goes on in public and what goes on in private are, in England and America, very different proportions. Thus you Americans are distressed by our absence of foreground, and tend to imagine that behind our cold frontages there is little more to be discovered. And we British are disconcerted by your width of foreground and tend to imagine that behind that lavish exuberance there can be little room for depths of individuality. I believe that both of us, in so imagining, are making a mistake. We are confusing manner with temperament. The Englishman hides his private feelings behind a drop-curtain; the American hides his behind a conventional performance at the front of the stage. Yet in both cases there is much that is important which takes place behind.

A FURTHER cause of mutual misunderstanding is, of course, this question of just being shy. When an American becomes shy, he is apt to raise his voice, to laugh loudly, and to allow the wings of the eagle to flap upon the air. When an Englishman, as so frequently happens, becomes shy, he puts on a boot-face, by which I mean a face like a boot. Neither of these manifestations is very agreeable—yet the sensitiveness which they are devised to hide is, in fact, a most attractive quality. It would be a good thing if all Americans, when they observe a boot-face in an Englishman, were to assume that he is just feeling shy. It would be a good thing if all Englishmen, when they hear an American beginning to raise his voice above the average, were to assume that he also is afflicted by this delightful ineptitude. For I have observed that when once Englishmen and Americans can conquer their instinctive shyness of each other they agree splendidly. On such occasions I feel that M. André Siegfried may be right. Only, as occasions, they are extremely rare.

There is also a whole area of possible misunderstanding offered by the circumstance that our habit of expression is one of under-statement, whereas the American habit is one of over-statement. This applies, not to jokes only, but to expressions of approval or distaste. An Englishman hesitates in all circumstances to employ the superlative; an American is apt to expect it.

The Englishman, moreover, has been trained to calm. The American has been trained to act as a live wire. Here in fact we touch upon something which is more than a difference of manner but is actually a difference of temperament. The Englishman inherits a long tradition of muddled optimism: the element of muddle renders him unexpectant, the element of optimism renders him silently cheerful. The American, on the other hand, has for the last three hundred years lived in an atmosphere of tense excitement: it is not surprising that, what with revolutions, frontiers, manifest destinies and bull markets, his nerves by now should be a trifle frayed. He tends therefore to be irritated by the placidity of the Englishman. Whereas the latter is dismayed by the hustle of the American. They are apt, in each case, to attribute either the stolidity or the restlessness to pose. Yet in fact the one arises from a torpid liver and the other from strained nerves. If we accept these things from the outset—if we refuse to be so foolish as to attribute to affectation all mannerisms which we do not understand—then indeed we can observe in each other the very valuable qualities which these mannerisms conceal.

YES, our dissimilarities are very apparent. There are moments even when I feel that a German visitor to this America might find himself more at home than any Englishman. He would find again that lack of individual self-confidence, that preference for corporate action, which are so marked a feature of his own gregarious countrymen. He would welcome the frequent noticeboards and public injunctions; he would share the love of speed and size; he would appreciate the graphs, the statistics and the belief in knowledge as opposed to learning. He would feel at home with the brownstone houses, the wreaths at Christmas, the half-drawn window blinds, the disregard of personal appearance among the clerical orders, the vast Sunday newspapers, that habit of putting one's address on the back of envelopes, the large helpings in restaurants, the way people are good at cooking hare and venison, the keys, the luggage-checking and the other precautions against theft.

There are moments when I feel the above. But, as moments, they are neither very intelligent nor lasting. In my saner moods I welcome the fact that now that the lion and the eagle are both in a pretty mess they may cease for a year or two to growl and peck. They may even—and why not?—come to respect each other for the curious qualities which the other lacks. We on our side may cease to feel indignant at a prosperity which America has herself temporarily—let us say—disavowed. We may forgive her even for having ousted us from the position of the greatest Power in the world. And on her side America may come to feel that the old lion, in that she suffers much from bed-sores, is not so militant a creature after all. The United States may even forgive us for having got there first. It is a good thing for Englishmen to remember that our forefathers had at least something to do with the settlement of this continent. It is a good thing for Americans to recollect that they also, if they desire thus to think, are inheritors of our tradition. It is unnecessary, and indeed unwise, to expect that such common acquirements should create either a maternal or a filial feeling. Yet after all they do constitute a bond not easily soluble.

IT IS pleasant to think of such things. Yet is it very wise? Am I not, in my present mood of gratitude towards America, allowing soft music to lull my awareness? I do not believe that amity between nations can durably be based upon pleasant feelings. It can be based only upon hard thinking. The harder I think the more different do we seem. Behind a façade of similarity stretch whole acres of vast differences. The Englishman essentially is territorial; the American of today is urban. The Englishman is fond of nature; the American, like the ancient Roman, is afraid of her. The American likes cities; we hate them. Surely these contrasts, generalized although they be, are real contrasts? And as such, almost fundamental? By identifying our differences we may, however, isolate and emphasize our similarities. I hope so. And when it comes to the last analysis—how likable we both are! And how unlike!

Steichen

PAUL ROBESON

The dark emperor

The most important movie production next month will be Eugene O'Neill's *The Emperor Jones*. First produced by the Provincetown Players in November 1920, starring the late Charles Gilpin, the play was made into a turbulent opera by Louis Gruenberg and presented, with Lawrence Tibbett, last winter at the Metropolitan Opera House. Now, under the enterprising auspices of John Krimsky and Gifford Cochran, it has reached the screen. Paul Robeson, Phi Beta Kappa scholar and indomitable athlete, actor and singer, appears in it as Brutus Jones, the Pullman porter who became a king.

Now There Is Peace

RICHARD SHERMAN

THE long, book-lined room was over-heated, and the air above the radiators shimmered in upward waves. Outside, in the gray December street whose traffic sounded faintly muffled through the magenta-draped windows, snow had begun to fall: but of the three people seated near the fire, only the boy noticed the flakes, which seemed to be coming not from the sky but from the pavement below. The woman's gaze was on the portrait over the mantel, and the man looked into the coals.

Then the man shifted, and traced a thin, dry finger over the leather of his chair.

"It was very kind of you to come," he said. "I know how precious your holiday time at home must be, and Mrs. Bentham and I appreciate your courtesy."

"Yes, sir," the boy answered, and blushed. "I mean—I mean I was glad to come."

The woman's eyes left the portrait, to rest on her folded hands.

"Perhaps, Edward, if you would explain to—" She turned: "Your first name is Martin, isn't it?" The boy nodded, and she again regarded her hands. "Perhaps if you would explain to Martin why we have asked him here . . ."

Martin spoke quickly. "I know. You wanted me to tell you about—" And then he stopped, confused.

"About Arthur," Mr. Bentham said, and at the name his wife's hands unclenched slowly.

"But I can't tell you anything." The words came even more rapidly now, as if this was all he had to say and as if after he had said it he would leave them there alone. "You see, this is my first year at the school. Your—Arthur was my Senior Counselor, but I didn't really know him. He was older than I am, and—"

"Yes, yes." Mr. Bentham nodded. "Dr. Abbott told us all that. Indeed, it was the fact that you were only slightly acquainted with him that caused us to send for you."

"Tell him what you want, Edward."

"What we want. Yes, my dear." He rose and began to pace the room, retreating into a shadowy corner and then reappearing. "We are planning," he said, "a small memoir to Arthur, a little book or pamphlet which we hope will be a tribute to his memory. A tribute to the sort of boy he was, and an inspiration to others."

"Oh," said Martin.

"I have talked with various friends of his, his chums, and each has volunteered to write a short paragraph or two about him. Dr. Abbott and several of the instructors have also signified their willingness, even their desire, to contribute too. We want to have as many different points of view as possible. Dr. Abbott gave me your name as one who might picture Arthur as he seemed to a new boy."

There was a silence in the room, a silence broken only by the dull murmur of the street outside and the sound of Mrs. Bentham's nervous breathing. Martin himself said nothing, had no opportunity to say anything, for almost at once Mr. Bentham continued.

"I believe that I am not overstating the case," he announced, "when I say that Arthur was an unusual boy. Since his death we have received many letters, some even from strangers, testifying to his all-round physical and mental brilliance. Though of slight build, he was a splendid athlete—"

For the first time, Mrs. Bentham lifted her head and met her husband's gaze.

"So splendid they killed him," she said.

"My dear, we have discussed that so often. Simply because one boy is killed in one football game—"

"Killed for sport. Like a bull. . . . It wasn't as if he enjoyed playing." Martin thought that she was going to cry, but she did not. Instead, she returned to her former attitude of lowered eyes and folded hands.

"A splendid athlete," Mr. Bentham went on, his face serene. "A distinguished student, a leader in church and social service work—yet not a prig—and extremely popular with his classmates."

"He was." The boy's voice was earnest, and it held a note of relief. "Everybody liked him. He was a big man at the school."

Mr. Bentham smiled. "He was indeed. 'Always be a leader,' I often told him. And he remained a leader to the end."

"Yes. The end," Mrs. Bentham said, and then her eyes found Martin's. "You say they liked him. Did you like him too?"

He replied without hesitation. "Of course; though I didn't see much of him. You see, he was always so busy."

At the mantel Mr. Bentham had paused, and was looking upward.

"Here," he said. "This is a painting of him, done last summer when he was just eighteen."

The boy did not move.

"Come over this way," Mr. Bentham commanded. "The light is better here."

Rising slowly from his chair, Martin went toward him.

"It's a very good likeness, isn't it?" he said. "He was—he was always smiling."

"It's more than a likeness," the man answered. "It is symbolic of Arthur, just as Arthur was symbolic of the best in boyhood, in young manhood. And that is what we want this memoir to be too. We shall call it 'Arthur Bentham: the Record of a Happy Boyhood.'"

Looking about the room now, Martin saw that everywhere there were relics of the son who had been killed. On the mahogany desk stood two large photographs of him; a catcher's mitt hung incongruously near a family shield; and on a table lay several copies of the school paper of which he had been the editor.

"It is a source of great comfort to us," Mr. Bentham resumed, not as if he were speaking to Martin but as if he were addressing a larger audience, "that Arthur's short life was a completely joyous one. Fortunately we were able to surround him with all the material advantages that any boy could wish; and also we tried—and I believe succeeded—to mold his moral and mental character to a point nearing . . ." he fumbled, "to a point nearing perfection. He lived in the sunlight always. Never did he give us cause for grief or worry."

There was a pause.

"Edward," Mrs. Bentham said. "Perhaps Martin is not interested in all that."

"Oh, but I am," Martin put in, embarrassed; "I—I. . . ."

"Of course he is." Mr. Bentham's tone to his wife was sullen, almost cold. "And so will other boys be, and their parents. In a way, you see," he continued, turning to Martin, "this book will be a guide to adolescence. Not of course that it will be a moral preachment—we want it to be gay and high-spirited, as Arthur was, and vigorous and manly too. But by re-creating his happy life, year by year, and by giving the testimonies of his friends and his teachers as to his character—by doing that we will be helping other parents and their sons."

"Martin." Mrs. Bentham stood and waited for him to come to her.

"Martin, why is it that you don't want to write for Arthur's book?"

Involuntarily he caught his breath in a sharp little gasp.

"But I haven't said—"

"Phyllis, my dear." Mr. Bentham turned from the portrait to face them. "Of course Martin wants to do it."

"No, he doesn't. Do you?"

For a moment the three of them were silent. Then the boy looked at the rug.

"No," he said.

Mr. Bentham started slightly, and a flush began to creep up his cheeks. Then he said, with quiet dignity, "I am very sorry. I had thought that anyone would welcome the privilege of—"

"Don't, Edward."

The room had grown darker now, and outside the snow was falling thicker, whiter. Martin looked not at the man but at his wife. Her face, obscure in the gloom, gave no sign of what was in her mind.

"I—I'd better go," he said, and headed toward the door. Mr. Bentham had already turned away, and was fingering a sheaf of papers. His back was stony, outraged.

"Good-by," said Martin.

Mr. Bentham did not even look up.

Hurrying down the wide, dim hall, he heard light footsteps behind him, and, turning, saw Mrs. Bentham.

"Wait," she called.

He stopped, in a sort of alcove. Immediately she was near him, very · near.

"Tell me," she said, in a low, pleading voice; a voice different from that which she had used in her husband's presence.

"It's nothing," he answered. "I'd like to do what he asks, but—"

It was as if she had not heard him at all.

"Tell me about Arthur."

She was almost touching him now—a slight, frail woman, only a little taller than he was, with great eyes. And then she placed a hand on his lapel, lightly.

"Don't think that you will hurt me. Nothing can hurt me now. But I want to know everything about him. You have no right to keep anything from me, bad or good. Don't you understand?"

"It isn't bad. I never knew of him to do or say anything that was bad."

"What is it then? Why don't you wish to write about him? Is it that you think the idea is sentimental? It *is* sentimental, but—but his father wants it."

"No. No, it isn't that."

Her hand fell away from his coat. "Then you won't tell me. You will go now and leave me knowing that there was something in Arthur's life that was a secret. Something that you, who saw him only a few times, were aware of but won't share with me."

Their eyes met in a long glance. And then Martin began to speak, uneasily.

"It isn't important. I told you it wasn't important. . . . I liked him a lot, even the first time I saw him. He was nice to me, not conceited the way most Senior Counselors are. He talked to me about my studies, and about what activities I should go out

for. 'If ever you get in trouble,' he said, 'or if you're homesick, come and see me.' He was that way with everybody."

"Yes." She knew.

"One afternoon, the day before he was —the day before the game, I went to him. I didn't have anything on my mind, except maybe that I was a little homesick, as he said I might be. I knocked at his door, and no one answered. Then I knocked again, and waited. Somehow I felt that he was there, and I thought maybe he hadn't heard me. So I opened the door. I shouldn't have done it, but I did." He stopped, but the pressure of her hand made him go on.

"He was crying. That's all. He was sitting in a chair with his head down and he was crying. You see, it's really nothing at all. But I can't forget it."

He waited for her to speak.

"Why should he cry?" he asked. "He was always laughing when people were around. Why should he cry up there alone?"

Mrs. Bentham's voice was hardly a whisper.

"I found him that way once, too," she said. "A year ago."

"And don't you know why either?" He was insistent now; demanding. "Didn't he tell you?"

She had turned away from him, and was looking at the closed door at the end of the hall.

"He didn't have to tell me," she said. "I knew."

"But I can't understand. . . ."

Now she was facing him again, and she placed her hands on his shoulders.

"I don't know who your mother and father are," she said. "But tell them to let you be what you are, not what they want you to be."

For a moment he waited for her to continue, and when he saw that she only wanted to be left alone he turned away and began to walk down the hall. At the head of the stairs she called, "Thank you, Martin."

He walked down the stairs and out of the house and into a world of white.

DR. FREUD

And his subconscious

"My, How You've Grown"

ALICE IN WONDERLAND; AND MRS. HARGREAVES, INSPIRATION FOR "ALICE"

LITTLE LORD FAUNTLEROY ("LEAN ON ME, GRANDPA!"); AND VIVIAN BURNETT

A TYPICAL GIBSON GIRL DRAWING; AND MRS. GIBSON, THE ORIGINAL MODEL

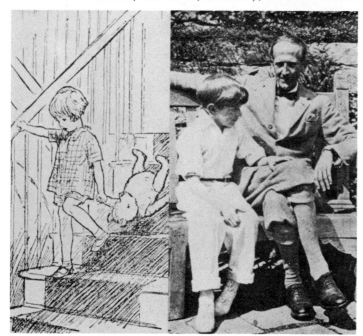

CHRISTOPHER ROBIN WITH WINNIE-THE-POOH; AND WITH A. A. MILNE

Here, shown as they look today, are a few of the people who once inspired some of the most celebrated characters in fiction: Alice Liddell, the original Alice in Wonderland, now Mrs. Reginald Hargreaves, who crossed the ocean at eighty to hear Nicholas Murray Butler make speeches about her; Vivian Burnett, Little Lord Fauntleroy, son of Frances Hodgson Burnett; Mr. Milne with his son, Christopher Robin, for whom and about whom he wrote his verses; and Mrs. Gibson, the model for her husband's famed Gibson Girls. All of which proves that people and time don't stand still even if treasured memories do.

Sister Aimée: Bernhardt of the Sawdust Trail

JOSEPH HENRY STEELE

FIVE THOUSAND souls, panting for salvation and starved for life, crowd the seats of the mighty Four Square Gospel Temple at Los Angeles. Before them is a stage completely equipped to give elaborate theatrical performances. Microphones carry the play-by-play account of mass-salvation to a sanctified broadcasting station conducted by the Temple. In the pit sits a thirty-piece orchestra. An army of ushers go up and down the aisles, selling *The Bridal Call* (monthly) and *The Foursquare Crusader* (weekly), both published by the religious promoter who has made Billy Sunday look like a piker. A choir of 200 voices occupy special sections on either side of the main stage.

Act One. The orchestra bursts into entrance music and Sister Aimée Semple McPherson Hutton marches down the middle aisle, while her husband tells the audience how she looks. She is attired, appropriately, in a flowing chiffon dress of snow-white purity. From her broad shoulders hangs a blue cape reaching to her heels. Her hair, formerly reddish-brown but now blond, is waved and meticulously arranged. She takes her post and reads from a paper. An invocation? No, a list of the prominent people who are attending her celestial circus. She blesses them to echoes of amens. Then her real show begins.

The evangelist becomes as busy as eighteen political campaign managers on an election night. She speaks into microphones, into telephones; she signals instructions, conducts the choir and leads in the singing, makes a sermon, plays a part in the sacred operas of her own composition, prompts the players, greets late arrivals, makes notes with a pencil, whispers to messengers. She shouts and chants and sings and as her husky voice resounds in far corners, her dynamic personality electrifies every person in the hall.

Act Two. The orchestra plays what sounds very much like circus music. And the ushers take up the collection. The choir sings "Everybody Happy." A morphine addict awkwardly testifies to his conversion. But when the money is gathered into the fold, the next act is ready.

Act Three. Almost anything. Today it may be a baptismal ceremony. There is a large tub on the stage in which as many as three hundred sinful bodies have been doused into spiritual purification in one night. Or it may be one of Sister's sermons

Blossom of an Evangelist

done against a stage setting and broadcast into thousands of homes. Five thousand soul-starved people gaze at her hungrily; those near enough touch the hem of her garments. And nobody seems to realize that they are witnessing the apotheosis of a histrionic girl, who, like Mary Pickford and Marie Dressler, was born in Canada, and that they are under the spell of the greatest showman of our times, the Bernhardt of the sawdust trail, the Duse of the camp-meeting. They are listening to the only living woman whose first name alone is sufficient to carry a headline on the front page of any North American newspaper; to the only woman since the pagan days who has become a high priestess in her own right.

AIMÉE is peculiarly the product of postwar go-getter philosophy. Beside her, Billy Sunday pales into a ten-twent-thirt performer and Bishop Manning is a tyro in the art of publicity. Future historians cannot neglect Aimée in their summation of this era's highlights. She belongs to the glittering galaxy that includes Phineas T. Barnum, William Jennings Bryan, Harry Houdini and Greta Garbo. Her life and her character have been prismatic and kaleidoscopic. She has had collapses, disappearances, honeymoons, operations, marriages, rejuvenations, blood transfusions and voice culture. She has sued and been sued. She has been a focus for rumor and suspicion. She is vulgar, colorful, stimulating, greedy, vibrant, willful, good-natured, tireless. She believes blindly in her own destiny. She has been called a saint and a Main Street Sybarite; a nympholept and a holy disciple. She has been hated and loved; mocked and worshiped; followed and betrayed. She has been called a contradiction,

a healer and a destroyer. And she has made a fortune at it. No one knows how much she is worth; religious institutions are not taxable and she is Los Angeles' greatest religious institution. The Temple has brought in millions and the property itself is worth a million. The head of the Temple commissary recently declared, "When Sister asked for a love offering once a month, we used to get as high as $10,000 on a single Sunday." She is, by all odds, the most successful actress of our day.

And like all successful actresses she has fought her way up from the Ontario high school to the boards of her sanctified theatre, through the old route of love, work, trial and error. She is the religious equivalent of Clara Bow. At the age of 17, Aimée was snatched from high school by the irresistible combination of love and religion. Robert Semple, a young evangelist (who was also a boilermaker), gave her the two potions simultaneously. How this happened is eloquently told in her own book, *In the Service of the King.* Semple asked her to become his wife and before she could recover her breath he suggested that they kneel in prayer and ask the Heavenly Father's will. "Robert prayed as we knelt side by side, hand in hand. I couldn't pray for the lump in my throat. But I closed my eyes very, very tight. The room seemed filled with angels who lined either side of the golden, sunlit path of life that stretched away into the vista of coming days of glorious and joyful service; a path that led to the city of the King; and therein walked Robert and I, hand in hand." Thus history repeated itself; Joan of Arc, too, had once communed with angels.

She went to China with her husband. He died there. Her daughter, Roberta Star, was born. She returned to the United States and found her mother, "Ma" Kennedy, in the Salvation Army. She met and married Harold McPherson, a grocery salesman. She bore him a son, Rolf. (McPherson divorced her in 1921 on the grounds of desertion.) McPherson subsequently told an interviewer that Aimée had "a dual personality" and was possessed of objectionable "wild cat habits at home."

In the meantime, Aimée found that the sawdust trail was a long and winding one. She washed dishes, played the piano, traveled with camp meetings and gained in experience. She found a bargain in an old tent, patched it and began an Odyssey of the Atlantic coast. During these beginnings she was publicity manager, musical director, pianist, preacher, altar worker, closer of the tent and putter-out-of-the-lights, not to mention editor and publisher of a magazine whose subscribers served as advance agents for her meetings.

The struggle from obscurity to fame and fortune had taken eight years—1917 to 1925—into which she had poured her great store of vitality and energy; but now her goal was reached. She had power, money, influence, fame. And now romance reared its head. Kenneth G. Ormiston, her radio operator, suddenly became a sympathetic and agreeable man to her, instead of a mere cog in her wholesale house of souls. The thirty-five-year-old, dynamic, red-headed woman was swept away.

Soon Mrs. Kennedy protested that the choir was gossiping about Aimée's conversations with Ormiston, she on the platform, Ormiston in the radio tower. First she used to hear the voice; it used to tell her, "You sound tired tonight, Mrs. McPherson," or "You have done splendidly tonight!" When she met the owner of the voice for the first time, she drove him home. And so it went. Presently Ormiston's wife appeared before Ma Kennedy and threatened to name Aimée as corespondent in a divorce suit. The evangelist found herself in an impossible situation, as for years she had preached against the remarriage of divorced persons. So, in January, 1926, she left for a tour of the Holy Land and Europe. It was, probably, an attempt to escape, although it was rumored that Ormiston might have accompanied her. However, he put in an appearance at the Temple while Aimée was still traveling in foreign lands, and was going through one of her rejuvenations.

Aimée returned from this flight to face the problem she had temporarily escaped. At last, unable to combat this peculiarly personal devil, she performed her greatest miracle: she walked out into the sea that sunny afternoon of May 18, 1926, and emerged in the sands of the Mexican desert near the Arizona border, at 1:30 a.m. on June 23rd.

Sister Aimée's sitting, standing, jack-knife dive, which so ravished the great American gullibility, took place at Ocean Park, California. Like some fabulous Mickey Mouse character, she dove into the sad sea waves, and wending her way through the bowels of the earth she came up a month later on the sands of the Arizona desert. She called it her "kidnaping." Whatever it was, it was worthy of the great Houdini himself. Thousands of followers were in a frenzy of sorrow. She was thought to have drowned. Mourners and weepers lined the seaside praying for her recovery. Mrs. Kennedy told the Temple crowds that she was convinced Aimée was dead. On May 23rd, Robert Browning, a 26-year-old proselyte, leapt into the sea, saying, "I am going after Sister," and was drowned. Ma issued a formal statement on May 25th that she had given up all hope of Aimée being alive. Ormiston, who had been absent, came to Los Angeles on May 27th, and again disappeared. Police searched for him and he wrote them sneering letters. By June 7th the search had died out for both Aimée and Ormiston.

Then suddenly Sister Aimée became reincarnated in the town of Agua Prieta, across the border from Douglas, Arizona. She fell, gasping and unconscious, on the doorstep of a Mexican sheepherder at Douglas, and announced herself as the one and only Aimée. It was a very strange thing, indeed. She declared that she had been kidnaped by "Rosie" and "Steve," driven to "a shack," and "held for ransom." She said she escaped through a window and had walked 20 miles across the international border line. The fact that her shoes appeared unscuffed and her gingham dress still fresh did not discount her story, she insisted. It was then that she uttered the famous line, "That's my story and I'm going to stick to it."

Aimée went up before the grand jury on charges of perjury, but the case died.

On June 28th, Ma Kennedy added another glowing chapter to the family marital record by wedding Guy Edward "What-a-Man" Hudson. Following the disconcerting discovery that Hudson had not yet divorced a previous wife, they separated, and three months later, after Hudson's entanglements had been dissolved, were remarried. Incidentally, Hudson's nickname is of Ma's own coinage. During the brief separation from him she lamented loud and long to the press about the tragedy of an "empty bed." But before Ma was ecstatically re-wed, Rolf McPherson, Aimée's 18-year-old son, married Lorna Dee Smith, a Temple school girl, younger than himself. And while all this was going on, Sister Aimée had met and become interested in David L. Hutton, concert singer, song composer and man of many other talents. They were engaged—after a short prayer to determine the wisdom of the procedure—in June of 1930, or

The Early Years: Clutching the Bible   *The Middle Years: Calling on Heaven*

Ormiston: Or, Temple Trouble

Before the Crash: Aimée and "Ma" Kennedy, with Lily-Pads

thereabouts, according to Aimée's statements months later to the press. But they managed to keep their love secret until the date of their marriage, Sept. 13. The ceremony was performed in a chartered airplane, with a reporter in attendance, on the flying field at Yuma, Arizona. It was dawn. They had traveled all night, but Aimée got back to Angelus Temple in time to conduct her Sunday morning service that same morning at 10:30!

Once again Aimée Semple McPherson Hutton became page-one news. This time she went for it big. All manner of love-nest photographs were taken and distributed to the press. Radio broadcasts were made from the nuptial chamber. Kisses and embraces were exchanged from the stage of the Four Square Gospel Temple called Angelus. Her multitudes of followers sang sweet hosannas and themselves received some share of vicarious ecstasy from the white-robed bride. That Aimée had lost only her heart was evidenced, however, by a pre-nuptial contract which effectually denied to the groom any claim on his spouse's goods and chattels.

Meanwhile Ma was having trouble with Hudson. Ma claimed she had spent her bank-roll on Hudson, that he had not earned a nickel since their marriage, that he had spent her money on his liquor, and that he was now "What-a-Flop" Hudson. Hudson left her and essayed a theatrical tour making speeches with special matinées for women only. In a public statement Hudson declared "Ma was no gilded lily." Burning with rage, Ma filed suit for $100,000 claiming defamation of character. Hudson, in turn, tried to raise enough money to finance a half-million-dollar slander suit against Ma.

Now Aimée, without her mate, is embarked on a trip to the Holy Lands—and the Riviera. She is seeking health, relaxation, rejuvenation. Her active proselytism of the Four Square Gospel is for the moment forgotten, but she is doubtless gathering new impressions, inspirations and experiences in the contemplation of the sins of her unregenerate brothers and sisters in many lands. The vocal fruits of these voyagings will inevitably again raise the roof of the Temple, and storm the gates of Heaven, when she returns.

How she will resume the pulpit of the Temple; what she will do next; how her amazing career will end; these are questions only a bold prognosticator will venture. Aimée is not a guessable quantity. The average life of an actress is somewhere between five and ten years. Very few have held their public for longer periods. But Aimée is to be classed only with the Duses and Bernhardts, and it is quite possible that she may give "farewell performances" for the rest of her life.

Aimée: Bible in Action

Aimée's Daughter: Bible at Rest

Joy: Aimée Marries off Her Son

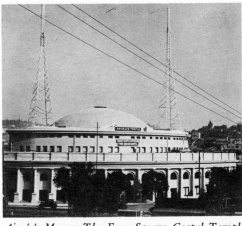

Aimée's Mecca: The Four Square Gospel Temple

Aimée Rejuvenata, Surrounded by Husband

"Ma" Kennedy, also Rejuvenata

Aimée Ill, but Not Camera-shy

White Poppies Die

NANCY HALE

WHEN William Derry came to New York to start work in an office, it was middle June and hotter than anything he had ever known or heard of. All the parties there at college had been around graduation time, the pretty girls and all his good friends wearing white flannels, and the soft jazz music and the light assurance of those early June nights lay far, far behind him and he was in a different world. He was lonely and depressed.

He knew that this summer represented the start of his career, but he hadn't known the start of his career would be just this way. The heat and the dust and the lassitude took all the punch out of it. He would have liked to show application and quickness at the office, but he couldn't, with the windows open and the sound of midsummer riveting pouring in, the other men slopping around in damp shirt-sleeves, and the stenographers dozing sweatily over their machines. It was all hot and ugly and dreamy, a drifting through routine. The vice-presidents departed for the country early each afternoon, and there wouldn't have been anybody to notice efficiency if he had been able to show any. He used to stand by those wide, blank, open windows and look over New York Harbor, thinking about cool white sailboats and tennis-courts and girls in thin pink dresses. No one of his twenty-two seashore summers had ever given him an idea of the relentless, evil heat he felt now.

There was nowhere to go in the long nostalgic evenings. He lived at his college club and at first he sat around and drank with other young men but later he became an addict of his loneliness and learned the strange sad flavor of the streets at night. He went to movies with the tired unenthusiastic crowds that go to summer movies in the city, and he sat near limp people whom he did not know in speakeasies, drinking Tom Collinses that did not cool him off, and walked along the streets slowly, watching the yellow headlights of cars and listening to the stifled booming, and hoping without hope that something beautiful and cool and delicate and romantic would happen to him. He did not even give his desire the name of Girl. All the girls he knew were out of town, and his one or two attempts at taking stenographers out to dinner had shown him that they were not pretty, or unusual, or anything the magazine stories said they were.

The strangeness of his meeting Miss Aria Dana did not really surprise him because he was still young enough to believe that wonderful and impossible adventures were part of his birthright. He only thanked Fortune for leading him to the iron fence over the brink of the East River, and for keeping him there staring across the flickering water until that misty figure drifted up to the fence near him, hardly tangible in the arc-lit darkness.

She had turned her bent head suddenly and looked toward him with a sort of intent indirection.

"Instead of its being soothing to come out and look at the river, it's more depressing still."

She said this and then looked back at the river, moodily. He realized that she did not care whether he replied or not. It was even possible that she had not seen him at all, but only a form in human shape at whom she cast her disappointed conviction.

William thought desperately that he must not reply like some stupid college boy, to shatter the moment. If he spoke at all he must speak from her mood of profound disillusion, from an impersonal haze that had forgotten conventionality, communicating in limbo with another lost spirit. If he were to say something banal he would be unworthy of the adventure Fortune had dropped him.

He waited as long as he could and said, "If you stare at the river long enough the water hypnotizes you and you forget everything."

She looked at him piercingly. Or perhaps she was not looking at him at all. Then she looked back in the direction of the river, and continued silent for a long time. William had begun to think that his impossible interlude had come to an end, that she had forgotten even whatever astral shred of him she had noticed, when she turned entirely around and threw her head back restlessly.

"Do you like Pernod?" she asked. "Let's go away from here. I have a garden and we can go and sit in it."

Assuming her unaffected abruptness as best he could William strolled down the street with her without a word. Not half a block away she stopped and unlocked a door with a latch-key. Without turning on any lights she closed the door and started to walk back through the house. William stumbled after her with his heart beating.

They emerged through a glass door into a dim garden with a brick terrace on which were chairs. They sat down and she got up again and disappeared into the house. William sat in the darkness trying to measure the event. He did not know where he was, or what was in the house, or how the woman looked, or what was going to happen. But he had entirely forgotten his sticky load of lonely dissatisfaction.

Suddenly a harsh electric light bulb flashed on above him, white and glaring. He saw the colors of things—red chairs, white board fence, and beds and beds of budding green plants. The woman walked out of the house with a glass of whitish liquid in either hand, and gave him one, calmly.

She was tall and dark, with a thin face and a rather heavy figure. She sat down in the other chair and set her glass on the ground. She did not seem aware of the violence of the light, any more than she had of the utter darkness. Her face had something fascinating about it, a kind of unconsciousness of ordinary things that fulfilled William's most romantic guesses of her. She seemed to be about thirty, although she had a curiously exhausted look. She had no possible relation to any kind of human being he had ever seen before, although he could not tell precisely why, because she was not beautiful, not brilliant, not anything except terribly different.

He drank the top off his drink; he did not like it, it tasted of licorice. He had no idea what was expected of him, but he suspected that it was nothing; he was fairly sure that she was only half aware of his being there. She did not drink her drink at all; she picked it up once and looked at it, then put it down and did not touch it again.

To relax his nerves he rose and walked along the zig-zag bricking of the garden paths that were so starkly marked out in the strong light. Once his wandering pace made him step off the path into one of the flowerbeds. The woman spoke sharply.

"Look out. Be careful of the plants."

"Yes," he said. "What kind of plants are they?"

"White ones," she said. "They are white flowers."

This was something he could understand a little better, he thought. That she should have a pose, that she should grow masses of white flowers in her city garden, was something a strange woman might do. She might have a passion for white; perhaps everything in the house was white.

He wondered if he should make love to her. He didn't want to in any familiar way that meant wanting to kiss a pretty girl; but as part of an inscrutable adventure it seemed important.

But after a silence of ten or fifteen minutes she looked up at him blindly.

"Go away now," she said. "I can't have anyone around any longer." She rose and stood facing him, with her fingers touching his shoulder, looking strangely into his face. He thought his heart would stop beating as he waited to see what she would do. But she only turned her head aside and sat down, as if she had forgotten that he was still there.

He walked through the house and let himself out of the front door. On the way through the hall he glanced into the rooms. They were nothing beautiful or romantic in themselves. Completely mediocre furniture and a neglected air, dark mirrors and pictures filled them. There was nothing white to be seen. But their abandoned look was more mysterious than the most enchanting order could have been. Closing the door William found himself in a vestibule, with cards in boxes which showed that the house was divided into apartments. On the box for the ground floor apartment he read this name, "Miss Aria Dana."

Outside he found that he was still trembling, and ran as fast as he could for four blocks, to dispel the high tension that was in him. It took him hours to go to sleep, but it was excitement and not loneliness that kept him awake.

In the next few days he found his life running at a new pitch. He thought incessantly of how he might approach the woman again, but what would be the most romantic manner, or whether she would want to see him, he could not decide. His memory distorted his view of her, and a beauty grew around her remembered face. He could not forget the strange, unsolved enticement he had imagined in her blind-eyed face when he had left her. He knew he must see her again, and not let her drift off like a shadow. After several evenings of this wondering and remembering and exaggerating he rang her bell at midnight of a night early in July. The doorhandle rattled automatically, and he opened it and walked in.

The rooms were brightly lighted and full of people. They were not very attractive people. They were most of them in a flabby and soiled middle-age, and most of them were drinking. They looked at William with casual unconcern and went on talking in loud voices.

William found Miss Aria Dana sitting on a small sofa in the room furthest from

the door with a heavy black-haired man who had his arm around her.

"Have I seen you before?" she asked, waving a hand at William. "Ask the nice young man what his name is, Tom."

"You brought me in for a drink one evening ten days or so ago," William said. He was staring at the woman's face. Instead of being tranced and dreamy, it was satisfied, carnal, and full of powdery lines. "My name is William Derry."

The heavy man in the dusty business suit and the square-toed shoes slipped his arm closer around her shoulders. These shoulders looked fleshy beneath thin black chiffon. She patted the bluish jowls with one hand, and reached the other to William.

"It's hot in here, isn't it?" she said. "Let's go out in the garden and cool off. Have you ever seen my garden?"

"Yes, I've seen it," William said.

"I'll bet you have," the heavy man said.

The flowers had bloomed since he had seen them, and the beds were now a mass of white poppies blowing in the light evening wind, lit by the light falling through overhead windows. The woman walked beside William. She slipped her arm through his.

"Were you really here once?" she asked. "Isn't it terrible the things I don't remember anything about? What did we do?"

"We didn't do anything," he said. "You were as if you were in a trance."

"Oh," she said briefly, glancing at him. She drew his arm nearer. "What am I going to do about that man in there?" she asked in a near-whisper. "He won't go away and I don't want him hanging around here. I don't like his looks. I don't know what he is."

"Why don't you tell him to go away?"

"Oh, I can't do that. I'll have to be nice to him. Oh, I couldn't do that."

"I'll tell him to get out."

"Oh no. Oh no. He mustn't get mad. Here," she said, pulling William's head down and kissing him. He was disgusted at the dry, stale touch of her. "Now I must go in and see what he's doing."

In the house she went directly to the heavy man and put her arm around him. He responded with a great loose hug. William stared at them for a few moments, bewildered and repelled. Then he left.

He fell asleep puzzling over what seemed an incredible discrepancy. He could not make one piece of his two experiences. Almost he could have believed that one of the times he had been dreaming. Next morning he made an effort and put the whole rather nasty business out of his head.

Three days later William went out to dinner with one of the men he sometimes saw around the club. There were two girls, one en route to Bar Harbor, the other the

sister of William's friend. William immediately found points in common with the sister. They knew the same people, they had only by accident missed meeting before, and they liked all the same sports. William found himself invited for the week-end to the sister's family's house on Long Island, an invitation loudly seconded by the brother, who was full of wonderment why he had not thought of it himself before. William, looking at the pretty nose and the red mouth of Eleanora, wondered too.

HE HAD a marvelous week-end, the sort of time he knew and loved, and that he had missed so disconsolately from his desk at the office. Eleanora was wonderful, one of the nicest girls he had ever met, perhaps the nicest. She came in town once or twice a week, braving the stifling heat especially to have lunch with William. Something excitingly more than a friendship was forming between them. For William, the introspective evening walks along the exhausted streets, the miserable restlessness of the long hot days, the strange unreal adventure with Miss Aria Dana were all vague nonsense of the past.

But although he had dismissed Miss Aria Dana from his mind, he had not forgotten her. Sometimes after he got into bed at night he remembered those two strange and incompatible evenings of the early summer, and tried to make sense of them. He wondered whether she had been able to get rid of the blue-jowled man who had made her look so frightened in the garden and whether today she was the strange magic spirit of the first evening or the coarse woman he had seen on his second encounter. The first evening she had been distant, as though drugged, and the second time common and uninteresting. On the whole he was glad to have abandoned such esoteric and mysterious episodes for a kind of life he knew and enjoyed— Eleanora, city luncheons, country week-ends.

But one late afternoon a latent accumulation of curiosity made him ring, on an impulse, the doorbell of Miss Aria Dana. He was let in by the automatic catch.

A colored servant showed him through to the garden. Miss Aria Dana was standing among the flowerbeds, looking cool and almost beautiful in white. She had nipped off one of the seed-pods that were beginning to form on the poppy plants, but when she saw William she dropped it. Her hand was soft and fresh in William's.

"How do you do," she said. "I was so sorry you left that dreadful party so suddenly, but I quite understand why you did. I'm afraid I'm completely incompetent at keeping tiresome people out of my house. My one protection is that people seldom come."

RONALD COLMAN

Idol of the screen

Mr. Colman, after being teamed with Vilma Banky in a series of romantic films, rose to even greater fame in *Beau Geste* and *Bulldog Drummond*. His latest vehicle, in which, with amazing conviction, he plays the title role, a Middle-Western doctor, is *Arrowsmith,* adapted from Sinclair Lewis' Pulitzer Prize novel.

Mr. Colman is admittedly something of a recluse. His unobtrusive, self-confident British charm, his casual preciousness, his reticent manner, which are entirely refuted by the intensive pride that crackles in his brown eyes—these saving qualities have done much to make him so popular on the screen.

Steichen

William could not take his eyes off her. She seemed brilliant and curiously refreshed, with bright eyes and a look of strength. He stood there on the garden path with her, watching her smile at him. Nervously he pinched off one of the seedpods close below his hand and played with it while they talked. A whitish liquid oozed out and wet his hand, and he dropped the pod and wiped his fingers with his handkerchief.

This time the woman did not seem lost or preoccupied. She talked to William entertainingly and with a great deal of balance and polish, with a quality of maturity which flattered him. She talked of trivial things and skipped gaily over the surfaces of broader subjects. She sent for a glass of iced tea, which the colored servant brought to him. William had a very good time, and let himself out of the house with a surprised satisfaction. He had loved the conversation, and he was left with a feeling of having been acting in a play. He had made a good many remarks which had sounded clever to him and which apparently sounded clever to Miss Aria Dana.

Although he was now more than ever at a loss to explain this woman, he found himself impatient to see her again. His queer little adventure had borne fruit after all. The woman was clearly brilliant, temperamental and of the world. Eleanora's expert chatter of sports sounded a little flat to him after the grown-up conversation in the garden. Three or four days later he presented himself at the door of Miss Aria Dana's apartment, again in the afternoon, late. He had to wait some time before the door-handle gave out its clatter.

He walked straight through the house before he met anyone. He came to the glass door to the garden and looked out. To his bewilderment the treasured beds were torn up, demolished; a man was bending over the scattered plants, throwing them together into a heap. He turned at a step and saw the colored servant.

"Is Miss Dana at home?"

"No *suh,*" the woman drawled nasally. "De men done came and took *her* away dis mawnin', Didn't leave no word what *Ah* was to do, an' *Ah's* got two weeks pay comin' to *me.*"

"What men? What do you mean?"

"*Ah* dunno *what* men. Dey came oveh de fence out deah, 'n' one of 'em took *her* away in the big black car, 'n' d'other ones dey jus' dug up de whole giarden like you see. One of 'em's diggin' yet."

William walked hesitantly out to where the man's back was still bent over the wilting pile of green. The man straightened up at his step on the brick walk, and he was heavy and blue-jowled and dressed in a dusty suit and square-toed shoes.

"Well, what do *you* want?" he demanded. William recognized the dark face that Miss Aria Dana had once patted with her hand.

"I wondered where Miss Dana had gone. The servant said a man took her away this morning. I wondered—if she is in any trouble—"

"She's got trouble all right. But don't you worry about her. She'll be safe right where she is, young man."

"But what happened? What are—?" He kicked the soft green heap of plants.

The man looked at him, his mouth drawn down at one corner.

"Poppy plants, young man. Pretty white poppies. *Papaver somniferum* if you want their pet name. Opium."

"But—I didn't know you could grow opium around here—why—"

"You didn't, eh? Take a look around some of these empty lots some day, and maybe you'll see, if the boys haven't dug them up already. Keeps us busy."

William turned toward the house.

"Hey," the man said. "What are *you* doing around her, anyway? Haven't I seen you before—around here, too? Hey, you, come here."

William caught his breath. He ran through the house and out of the front door. As on that other night, earlier in the summer, he ran as fast as he could for four blocks. Still running, he looked behind him. But there was no one but a few people strolling limply along in the late afternoon heat. He stopped running.

President Roosevelt's Inauguration

Depicted by Miguel Covarrubias

The artist has caricatured many of the celebrities who were present in Washington on the eventful day of March 4, 1933. The following list, keyed to the diagram at right, shows who's who.

1. President F. D. Roosevelt
2. Chief Justice Hughes
3. Mrs. Franklin D. Roosevelt
4. Vice-President Garner
5. Ex-President Hoover
6. Mrs. Herbert Hoover
7. Ex-Vice-President Curtis
8. Alfred Emanuel Smith
9. James Farley
10. Professor Raymond Moley
11. Louis Howe
12. Senator Joe Robinson
13. Bernard Mannes Baruch
14. Owen D. Young
15. Senator William Gibbs McAdoo
16. Governor Albert Cabell Ritchie
17. Senator Claude Swanson
18. Senator Pat Harrison
19. Governor Herbert Lehman
20. Senator Thomas Walsh
21. John W. Davis
22. Senator Carter Glass
23. Norman Davis
24. Newton D. Baker
25. Henry L. Stimson
26. Andrew Mellon
27. Ogden L. Mills
28. J. P. Morgan
29. Ambassador Paul Claudel
30. Sir Ronald Lindsay
31, 32. Oriental Ambassadors
33. Mark Sullivan
34. Walter Lippmann
35. Gentlemen of the Press
36. General John Pershing
37. The Forgotten Man
38. The U.S. Navy

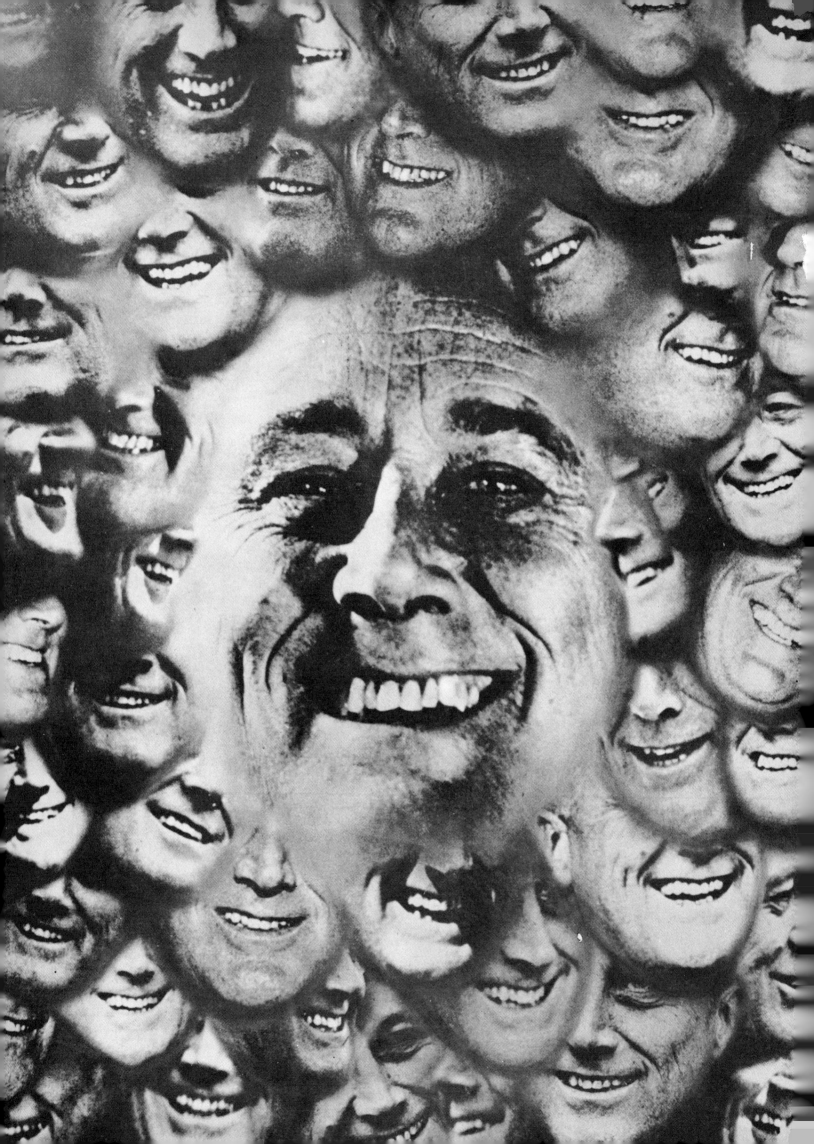

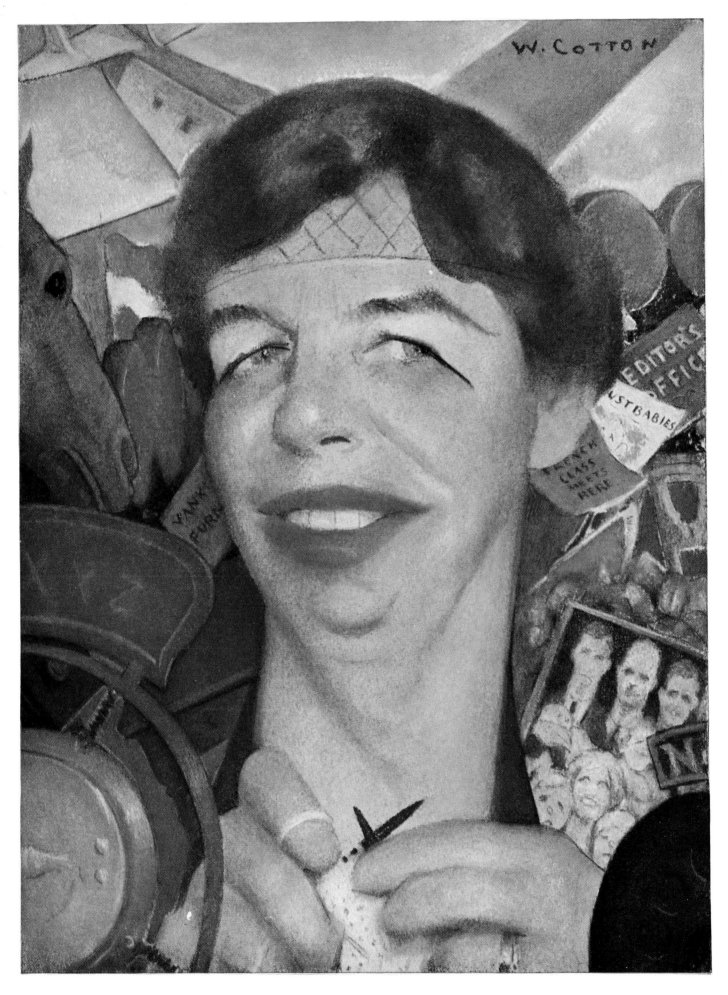

F.D.R.—and MRS. ROOSEVELT

The laughing cavalier, and the national dean of women

"PETROUCHKA"

Tamara Toumanova, Leon Woizikovsky and David Lichine
latest protagonists of Stravinsky's great ballet, presented
Count de Basil's visiting Monte Carlo Ballet Russe. Maître
ballet for the spirited young company is Léonide Massine.

Dixie Nocturne

A Parody Revelation of the Southern Heart

FRANK SULLIVAN

AT A fashionable Mayfair gathering I came across a wisp of a slip of a girl from below the Mason-Dixon Line. Gay, vivacious, charming, she was like a breath of the old South, the South I had known, the South of women who were gallant and men who were pure. I should scarcely have been a scion of the Maffles of Maffle Co't-house, Maffle County, Virginia (a hard-drinking, hard-riding, hard-loving clan, suh) had I remained unmoved by the charm of this fragile echo of my beloved Dixie.

Her eyes were two pools of violet velvet. Her hair was soft and silken, like the Spanish moss that hung from the old Spanish moss tree in front of the manse, and she wore a hat that was like a hat from the old hat tree that stood in the front hall of the manse.

HER laugh was silvery, like the sound of the hunting horn echoing through the oaks on a crisp autumn morning. We Maffles kept the finest pack of possums in the Old Dominion. The Maffle didn't exist who wasn't a born hunter. We were all at home in the saddle. My grandmother, at seventy, had a seat that was the envy of half the Midlothian Turnpike. I myself, when scarcely more than a babe, had known that never-to-be-forgotten quickening of the pulse that comes when the hunter hears from the depths of the bayou the distant bayouing that can have but one meaning. The possums have treed their hound!

Ah, well . . . I sighed and returned to earth. The young whippersnapper who had been dancing attendance on the little lady had vanished for the moment. I lost no time in grasping my opportunity. I went over and gave her the rich old bow used these three centuries by the Maffle men in saluting blondes of the first magnitude.

"Ma'am," I said to her, "may I have the honor of permitting myself to ask you to do me the favor of allowing me to pay you a compliment?"

My, but it was a relief, in this age of blunt, ungracious treatment of the fair sex, to hear a gentleman of the old school like myself address a lady in such courtly fashion.

She gazed up at me shyly.

"Why, of co'se, Cuhnel."

She knew I was a colonel! You can't fool a Southern girl.

"Then, ma'am, may I say that to me you are like a breath of the old South, the South of women who were gallant and men who were pure."

"Oh, Cuhnel," she said, and her voice seemed to me like the soft susurrus of a boll weevil and his loved one munching their way through a Georgia cotton patch. Somehow it brought back my childhood days on the old plantation. Night, and the harvest moon, a great red disk hanging low over the cabins in the slave quarters. The sound of distant banjo music and the care-free laughter of pickaninnies. And as I looked at the little missie at my side I could fairly see my old mammy.

Aunt Cindy Mammy. Dear old soul. How many times I had sought consolation in her vast and comfortable bosom for some real or fancied tragedy of childhood, a stubbed toe—or *any* kind of toe. Aunt Cindy Mammy may have been black but her heart was big enough for any kind of toe, stubbed or unstubbed. We children all used to rush to that capacious bosom for comfort in time of sorrow. Few bosoms were so rushed as hers. (Of course, those were the days, the good old days, when a bosom was a bosom, and vast herds of bosom ranged the western plains. With the advance of civilization the bosom gave way and is now practically extinct.)

A voice recalled me from my revery.

"Of co'se, Cuhnel, speaking of So'the'n men being puah, times have changed since y'all were a lad. For instance, take Mr. William Faulknah's Popeye. . . ."

Her voice had the silvery quality of corn liquor bubbling in a Tennessee mountain still. Again it took me back to the plantation and I thought of Aunt Cindy Mammy's husband, old Uncle Cindy Pappy. Lazy, good-for-nothin', wuthless old cuss. All day long he'd sit in the sun, a-sunnin' hisse'f and whittlin'. (He could whittle any tune you named, by ear. We boys used to try to stump him but we never could.) I can see him now, as if he were yesterday. His soul may have been black, but he had a mustache that was whiter than snow. It was a scraggly kind of no-count, droopy old mustache and Aunt Cindy Mammy used to make fun of it and call it his "po' white 'tache."

A voice recalled me from my revery.

"Cuhnel, where y'all from?" the little girl with the voice like the susurrus of munching weevils was saying.

"The Old Dominion, ma'am. Colonel Yancey Maffle of Maffle Co'thouse, Maffle County, Vahginia. Master of possums of the Maffle Hunt. At your service, ma'am. Where might you be from?"

"Ah come from Tay-am-puh," she said, "Tay-am-puh, Flo'da."

Tay-am-puh!

Once before, in the Long Ago, I had known one who could gargle a two-syllable word like Tampa into three syllables, and as the little missie talked on in her soft jargon I thought bitterly of that other one and of a fateful night under a sycamore in the garden. I was home on leave from Shiloh. We talked, the two of us there in the moonlight under the sycamore. "You are beautiful," I said. "Why have we never met before tonight, lovely stranger? Where do you come from?" And the whisper came, "Tay-am-puh. Ah come from Tay-am-puh." "My, but you are beautiful in that pink sprigged dimity gown," I whispered. . . . But hark! What's that? Voices. The clank of sabers. Lights. And then the stern voice of my cousin, Colonel Zeb Maffle of Jubal Early's Zouaves: "So, Captain Warehouse, it is you. Allow me to congratulate y'all on yore perfect So'the'n accent. Gentlemen, we have at last trapped the cleverest spy in the No'the'n ahmy." And with a deft upswing of his sabre, Cousin Zeb ripped the muslin frock from my vis-à-vis and revealed a young man in the blue of Sherman's cavalry.

It took years to restore my faith in women after that betrayal.

A voice recalled me from my revery.

"No, indeed," the little missie from Tampa was saying, "So'the'n men are fah from puah these days, thank goodness. And how."

And how! I thought of those how cakes, or hoe cakes, as we used to call them, of Aunt Cindy Mammy's. We youngsters used to love them—Cousin Julia Peterkin, Cousin Octy Roy Cohen, Miz' Elly Glasgow, Massa Lancey Stallings, Cousin Al Jolson, Cousin Dubose Heyward and myse'f. I can taste those hoe cakes yet.

A voice recalled me from my revery.

"What's that I see in yore eye, Cuhnel Maffle?" Miss Tampa was saying, tenderly.

"Nothin', little missie, nothin' at all."

"Oh, yes 'tis, Cuhnel, oh, yes 'tis," she said, softly.

"Jus' an old man's memories, little missie, jus' an old man's memories."

"Now, don't you fret, Cuhnel," said she.

"'I'm not frettin', Missie. Don't you trouble that little golden head of yours. . . .'"

"Ivory, Cuhnel," she corrected, "ivory."

". . . that little ivory head of yours, about me. Just you let me sit here beside you. I'll fetch me a chair."

"No, Cuhnel," she insisted, "let me fetch that chayah. I'm young and strong. Y'all are toopototottit."

"What?" I exclaimed.

"What?" she repeated.

"What did you say I was?"

"You mean when I said y'all were toopototottit?"

"Yes. That's it. What's it mean?"

"Toopototottit? Why, Cuhnel, it jus' means—ah reckon it jus' means toopototottit. Jus' what it says. Too po' to tote it."

"Toopodatatota," I repeated. "There *is* no such word. There couldn't be."

Her eyes flashed.

"Cuhnel Maffle," she said, icily, "whether or not y'all realize it, y'all are contradicting a So'the'n lady."

I bowed. "Ma'am, accept my deepest apologies. If you say so, there *is* such a word as toodapadooda. . . ."

"Toopototottit," she corrected.

"Yes, ma'am, and I will fight the man who says there isn't."

"Oh, Cuhnel." She smiled, gratefully, and her voice sounded like the scarlet jasmine that used to sing in the whippoorwill tree down by the edge of the miasma. I minded the day after General Lee summoned Cuhnel Grant to Appomattox and told him he was willing to call the Civil War a draw. Father assembled the slaves underneath the big magnolia tree in the drawing room and told them they were free. Old Black Caesar took on, something pow'ful, and wouldn't budge, but Aunt Cindy Mammy had an idea. She went no'th, took her old recipe for hoe cake batter with her; added a little gum arabic and glue, and put the result on the market as a preparation for unkinking kinked hair. She made a fortune from it.

Ah, dear old friends—Aunt Cindy Mammy, Uncle Cindy Pappy, Old Black Caesar, Slate Gray Caesar (his son), Light Tan Caesar (Slate Gray's son), White Caesar (Light Tan's son). The years fade and people fade with them.

A voice recalled me from my revery. It was the young whippersnapper this time who had returned to rejoin her.

"Come on," he was saying. "The old bozo's asleep. Shake a leg. This music is hot."

"Is it hot!" I heard Miss Tampa echo. "Ah'll say. Oh, mistah, burn mah clothes." And they shivered off together on the dance floor, leaving me to my Memories.

MR. JUSTICE HOLMES

First citizen of the land

Captain Oliver Wendell Holmes, wounded in action at Antietam and Fredericksburg, was not just the soldier son of the man who wrote *The Autocrat of the Breakfast Table;* he was a promising student of law. Soon after the Civil War, he was admitted to the Massachusetts bar. Always interested in jurisprudence more than in lawyering, the second Holmes became editor of the *American Law Review* and professor in the Harvard Law School. In the eighties he was appointed associate justice of the Massachusetts Supreme Court, and at the turn of the century became chief justice there. In 1902 he was appointed to the United States Supreme Court, a position that he has resigned after just thirty years of service. Mr. Justice Holmes' career has not been that of routine judgeship; it is the career of a thinker who has been alive to all the changes of the day, ready to interpret old statutes in terms of modern reality. During his three decades on the high bench he built up a notable record of dissent, handing down minority opinions which championed advanced ideas on free speech, labor conditions, and the use of the Fourteenth Amendment. Yet he has never subscribed to radical measures of social control; basically he is a skeptic, holding to the gospel of trial and error. In a day of mighty cleavage such as this, he stands on a rock of liberalism, convinced neither of the sanctity of the Founding Fathers, nor of the necessity of Karl Marx, nor of the all-importance of his own idea of law. Now about to reach his ninety-second birthday, dean of his profession, leader and scholar, artist of thought and word, he stands as the first citizen of the nation.

TIME
AND A HALF

Our Own Newsweeklymagazine Glances Over and Off the News in TIME'S *Supercilious Manner · By John Riddell*

NOTE: Encouraged by the popularity of TIME, the newsweeklymagazine which caroms off the news of each week at a bright supercilious tangent, the editors of *Vanity Fair* have requested Mr. Riddell in turn to skim the surface of current events and report them for our own readers in the glancing manner of Messrs. Luce & Martin's flip young weekly.

LETTERS

Correction

Sirs:

In your issue of Jan. 19, at p. 9, col. 3, you state: "Among those present was pigeon-toed, knock-kneed, cross-eyed H. Tecumseh Schmalz" etc. etc.

Nearly omniscient TIME, holding the mirror up to nature, neglected to mention that I also have one leg shorter than the other, suffer from a nervous twitch.

H. TECUMSEH SCHMALZ

The Rookery,
Metuchen, N. J.

◆

Royal Family's Whoopee

Sirs:

Is it true that King George of England cannot write his own name, Queen Mary dunks her bread in her coffee, the Prince of Wales has to be poured into bed after a whoopee party?

T. P. GOEHEGAN

South Boston, Mass.

No, it is not true that King George of England cannot write his own name, Queen Mary dunks her bread in her coffee, the Prince of Wales has to be poured into bed after a whoopee party. Always fair & broad-minded toward Great Britain, TIME would be the last to spread such rumors about her royal family. It is also untrue that last year they set fire to seven orphan asylums, robbed a church, have colored blood, are descendants of the Kallikaks & Jukes.

◆

Curt, Clear, Complete

Sirs:

I am a little girl aged 3 yrs., 5 mos., & think your magazine swell, your style dandy, your news curt, clear, complete. Please let me have a yr.'s subscription.

EFFIE E. SIMPKINS, JR.

Naples, Iowa.

SAMUEL FINLEY BREESE HOSTETTER
If the iceman . . . hadn't started

NATIONAL AFFAIRS

THE PRESIDENCY

Historic Conference

Bandy-legged, asthmatic Mrs. Tessie Messersmith rolled up her sleeves, trudged through a room of the White House last week with mop & pail of soapy water. Object: to mop the floor. Behind closed doors she heard two men arguing excitedly, recognized voices of Herbert Clark ("Smiley") Hoover & Franklin Delano ("Old Potato", TIME, Sept. 26, 1932) Roosevelt. Scrubwoman Messersmith set down pail, stooped at keyhole to listen. The door opening, she stepped back suddenly to avoid pudgy President-reject Hoover (TIME, Nov. 8, 1932), jammed her left foot into the pail of water, clumped out of the room with the pail stuck on her foot. Boiled Mrs. Messersmith later: "I couldn't make out a word that was said . . ."

THE CONGRESS

Opening Session

His round face red & perspiring, shaggy-browed John ("Nance") Garner reached behind him for a dangling suspender-strap,* hoisted it over his right shoulder, fastened it onto his right front suspender-button. Beside him ubiquitous Mrs. Garner (TIME, June 9, July 21, et seq.) brushed his velour hat, laid out matches, pipe, keys, clean handkerchief. Speaker Garner groped behind him again for the second dangling suspender-strap, hoisted it over his left shoulder, accidentally let go, the suspender snapped back & spanked him smartly. Fumed Speaker Garner: "What the goddam!" "What did you say, dear?" asked Mrs. Garner. "I was thinking about Congress," replied Speaker Garner, hoisting strap over his left shoulder again & fastening it securely this time on left front suspender-button. "Don't forget your gavel," said Mrs. Garner, wiping a spot of egg off his chin, waving goodbye to him from the window of the Washington Hotel as he hurried up the street for the opening session (TIME, Jan. 27, Feb. 3, et seq. for further developments in this interesting session, $.15 the issue, $5.00 the year, *advt.*).

CRIME

Crime-of-the-Week

From Montclair, N. J., fat-buttocked Mrs. Samuel Finley Breese Hostetter took the 10:17 a.m. train into New York, went to Saks-Fifth Avenue to exchange some Christmas presents, match a spool of silk. Leaving Saks at 3:00 p.m., Shopper Hostetter caught the 3:27 train back to Montclair. One hour later bandits & police engaged in a shooting fray in front of Saks, seven onlookers were killed, scores wounded. Said Shopper Hostetter to her husband, tired constipation-wracked

*Cautious Speaker Garner wears suspenders, a belt.

Samuel Finley Breese Hostetter, that night: "And to think I was right there only an hour before it happened, if Maudie hadn't called up in time this morning or the clock had been wrong I might have caught a later train* instead & arrived in town just in time for the whole thing because look, I'd probably of been right there in the midst of it if for instance the ice-man had been late this morning or else the car hadn't started and I'd missed that earlier train, I'd probably of just been coming out of Saks at exactly the time it was going on, and . . ."

FOREIGN NEWS

GREAT BRITAIN

Club-footed Mrs. Tessie Messersmith stooped beside a closed door in the House of Parliament last week, listened through the keyhole to voices of Norman ("Beaver") Montagu and Ramsey ("Ramsey") MacDonald arguing excitedly. The door opening, Charwoman Messersmith stepped back suddenly, jammed her left foot into a pail of water, clumped out of the room pail-on-foot. Said Mrs. Messersmith later: "Hi couldn't make out a word that was said . . ."

FRANCE

Bat-eyed, moustache-bearing Madame Thérèse Messersmith stooped beside a keyhole in the French Chamber of Deputies last week, rose again suddenly to avoid non-fur-bearing Premier Paul- ("Here Today") Boncour, jammed her left foot into a pail of water. Said Mme. Messersmith later: "I couldn't make out *un mot* that was said . . ."

JAPAN

Hare-lipped Mrs. Pitti Sing Messersmith jammed her left foot into a pail of water, clumped out of the Japanese House of Congress last week. Said Mrs. Messersmith later: "I don't speak Japanese . . ."

ART

Peeping Tom

Lowering his crossed eyes modestly, bald-headed, lecherous Albert Matthew Printwhistle—his friends call him "Jojo"—acknowledged the plaudits of art connoisseurs and critics yesterday. Occasion: the first exhibit of Artist Printwhistle's unusual collection of sculptures in dough. "It's very simple," said Artist Printwhistle. "While I am sitting in a restaurant waiting for my order, I always pick out a piece of the (Continued on page 250)

*A later train lvs. Montclair 12:43 p.m., arrv. Manhattan Transfer 2:09 p.m., does not run weekdays or Sundays.

soft part of my bread and roll it back and forth between my fingers into a little ball. Sometimes when the waiter is slower than usual I can roll ten or fifteen of these little balls or spheroids in different odd shapes or colors, depending if my fingers are very clean. At first I simply dropped them on the floor, but later I got this idea of rolling different designs and keeping them. I'm afraid some are a little stale now."

A recluse, Artist Printwhistle likes turnips, walking in the rain, Maltese cats; hates bull-fighting, Theodore Dreiser, violets, bread-pudding. Four years ago his wife ran away with the chauffeur, today he smokes hashish, has been arrested twice for forgery, once as a Peeping Tom.

MISCELLANY

"Time brings all things"

Error

In Beelzebub, Indiana, Arthur Filene, drug-clerk, lost his diamond-ring while fishing four years ago, caught a fish yesterday, found a diamond-ring inside. Ring was not his, Angler Filene threw back the fish.

Prodigy

To Mrs. Nero Pasquale McVitty, 40, wife of a Winsted, Conn., farmer, was born last week a purple calf with two heads which weighed 41 pounds, had feathers, a small beard.

M.D.

In Nehi, Nebraska, I. Killem Kwik is a doctor, I. Ketchum and U. Cheatham lawyers.

Believe-it-or-Not

In New York, N. Y., Robert Louis Ripley, a cartoonist, makes his whole living writing little items like these.

SPORT

Prizefight

Rheumatic, toothless Mrs. Tessie Messersmith rolled up her sleeves, trudged into empty, echoing Madison Square Garden at 5:00 a.m. with mop & pail of soapy water. Object: to mop the floor. Beside the deserted boxing-ring she saw a torn ticket-stub, picked it up, read "Sharkey vs. Schmeling...." Delivering a series of imaginary uppercuts, jabs, hooks, Scrub-woman Messersmith feinted, side-stepped, pedaled backward, jammed her left foot into the pail of water. Mused Mrs. Messersmith, clumping out of the Garden pail-on-foot: "I wonder who won...."

PEOPLE

"Names make subscribers." This week these people will buy a copy of Time:

Opening world's largest theater last week, John D. ("Roxy") Rockefeller entertained thousands of friends at the first performance. Visitors marveled at world's largest murals, world's largest auditorium, world's largest chandelier, handsome oil-painting in world's largest lobby showing the Rockefellers holding world's largest bag.

◆

Named the Most Forgotten Man of 1932 in undergraduate poll at Peachum University, Peachum, Vt., were: Charles ("Sitting Bull") Curtis, with 197 votes; Mrs. Ella Anti Boole, with 186 votes; Patrick James ("My Parents Were Half-Irish, Half-White") Hurley & Bishop James Ivar Kreuger Cannon, tied for third place with 177 votes each; Reverend Deets Pickett, Mrs. Charles Whoopee Peabody, Francis Scott McBride, Reed Smoot, 98 votes each; a Herbert Clark Hoover, 3 votes.

◆

Ill lay: Politician Henry Ford, Actress Ethel Barrymore, Scrubwoman Tessie Messersmith, of appendicitis, pneumonia, housemaid's-knee, in Dearborn, Hollywood, Manhattan respectively.

MILESTONES

Died, Mrs. Tessie Messersmith, 66, scrub-woman; of influenza contracted by getting her left foot wet too often; in Manhattan.

American Potentates Past and Present

In the act of blessing our national pastime

WILLIAM HOWARD TAFT

1933

HERBERT C. HOOVER

AL SMITH

WARREN G. HARDING

FRANKLIN D. ROOSEVELT

CALVIN COOLIDGE

JIMMY WALKER

WOODROW WILSON

History Repeats

"The thing that hath been, it is that which shall be; and that which is done is that which shall be done; and there is no new thing under the sun." In 1850, Jenny Lind, the Swedish Nightingale, came across the sea to sing in New York, and hysterical crowds tossed winter roses at her feet and drew her carriage through the snowy streets. In 1933, a buxom young woman known as the Songbird of the South, one Kate Smith, holds the radio audience of a continent in a state of chronic hypnosis, makes a personal appearance in a New York theatre, and is mobbed by her fans at the stage door. In 1853, Dion Boucicault culled an American fortune as a playwright and actor immensely popular with his audiences, who overlooked his lack of histrionic profundity and adored his Irish wit. Today, we have Noel Coward, whose annual American debuts are attended with fantastic excitement. Thus we echo the past with the ever-recurrent miracle of great personalities. For every Henry Ward Beecher in Brooklyn's Plymouth Church, there will later be an S. Parkes Cadman, similarly a churchly oracle on public events, holding forth from the same pulpit. Instead of bending the knee before the luster of The Divine Sarah, with her fuzzy bangs and magic eyes, we are now a nation spellbound by the flickers of pain across the face of The Glamorous Swede: and we replace Edwin Booth's Melancholy Dane with Walter Hampden's, in the same flowing black velvet—and scarcely know the difference.

NOEL COWARD, 1933   ACTOR-PLAYWRIGHT   DION BOUCICAULT, 1853

AL SMITH, 1933   DEFEATED POLITICAL ORATOR   STEPHEN A. DOUGLAS, 186

MAX SCHMELING, 1933   EX-HEAVYWEIGHT CHAMPION   JOHN L. SULLIVAN, 1872

MARY WIGMAN, 1933   DANCE SENSATION   MARY TAGLIONI, 18

WALTER HAMPDEN, 1933   SHAKESPEAREAN ACTOR   EDWIN BOOTH, 1865

GRETA GARBO, 1933   THEATRICAL IDOL   SARAH BERNHARDT, 1879

JASCHA HEIFETZ, 1933   MASTER VIOLINIST   OLE BULL, 1865

S. PARKES CADMAN, 1933   BROOKLYN CLERIC   HENRY WARD BEECHER, 1865

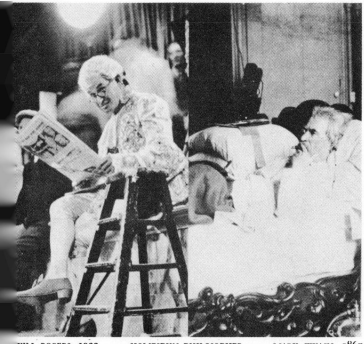

WILL ROGERS, 1933   HOMESPUN PHILOSOPHER   MARK TWAIN, 1865

KATE SMITH, 1933   POPULAR SONGBIRD   JENNY LIND, 1850

Inflation for Ida

FRANK SULLIVAN

ONE day not long ago I was in my study engaged upon some research when my seven-year-old niece, Ida, came romping in, seized a bottle of ink and poured the contents over my head. The minx knows full well her old uncle hasn't the heart to scold her for interrupting him, and she takes advantage of it.

"What is oo doin', nonkie?" she asked.

I gave her a good kick in the shin.

"Talk English, or get out of here," I ordered.

"Well, hell's bells," she protested, rubbing the injured tibia. "All I wanted to know was what you were doing."

"I'm doing some research on inflation."

"What's inflation?"

"Don't you know?"

"No. What is it?"

"Never mind. Do you know what fiat money is? Do you know at what figure France pegged the franc in 1927?"

"No."

"Do you know how to peg a franc?"

"Nope."

It was incredible. I was amazed. The world shaken by a tremendous economic upheaval, yet this girl, possible future mother of Presidents, knew nothing of inflation. I could scarcely believe my ears, and told Ida so frankly.

"I can scarcely believe my ears," I said.

"I can understand that," she said, gazing at the organs in question.

Yet Ida is an intelligent tot. Well then, I reasoned, if she does not understand inflation, neither do her 120,000,000 fellow Americans, for when it comes to the fine point we are all pretty much tots—all Idas together in this great Melting Pot of the West, trying to pour red ink on our Uncle.

Hence this explanation of inflation. I sim-ply wanted to do my bit to make inflation clear to my fellow countrymen.

Inflation isn't really hard to understand. If we bear that in mind, it will be half the battle, and half a battle is better than a battle. It's the inflationists who try to explain inflation who are really hard to understand. They do not speak the language of the average man of the street, for the street is where the average man is today. I do, and shall, speak the language of the average man, and woman, of the street.

De foist t'ing youse has got to get t'rough your beans (language of average man of street) is that currency, whether fiat, scrip or mazuma, is governed by Grantham's Law, or something that sounds like that. Grantham's Law is simply this: Centuries and centuries ago there was no such thing as money, and there is practically no such thing as money today. This proves Grantham's main contention (for which he was roundly hissed at one memorable meeting of the Royal Society) that everything runs in cycles.

Okay, honey (language of woman of street), what did they use for money when there was no money? The answer is, they bartered.

What is barter? Let me illustrate by a simple example. Let us say you have no money. Granted? But you have got a cow. Now then, your neighbor, John D. Rockefeller, Sr., has three dozen eggs, a horse, a bolt of cloth and Rockefeller Center. It so happens that you are in need of three dozen eggs, a horse and a bolt of cloth. It also happens that Mr. Rockefeller wants a cow quite badly. Let us say that Mr. Rockefeller has no money, either. Granted? Very well, what happens? You go to Mr. Rockefeller and you say to him, "I will give you my cow for your eggs, horse and that bolt of cloth." He replies, "All right, and I will also throw in Rockefeller Center," but you say, "Oh no you won't." So you give him the cow and he gives you the eggs, horse and cloth.

That is barter.

With the advance of civilization, however, it became apparent that the system of barter would not work in a highly organized community. First, there was the difficulty of keeping a cow in a modern city apartment, and second, as Oswald Spengler pointed out, it was impossible to get the average man in the street reconciled to saying "You bet your bottom cow."

Money took the place of barter, and with money came inflation. Now then, the best way to make inflation clear to the non-technical mind is in terms of wheat. If wheat brings 33⅓ cents a bushel in the open market, a dollar at par (which is to say with the French franc at $0.0392 and the Polish zloty at $0.1122) will buy two bushels of wheat; no, three. Now, the price of bar silver in London in 1931 (in terms of pence, pence and pence) was 14 19-32. I give the average, not the low or high. In the same year the total stock of money in the United States was $9,079,623,698. Let us simplify matters and say it was $9,079,-623,700. With wheat at 33⅓ that $9,079,-623,698 would buy three times that many bushels, *but*—there always seems to be a "but," doesn't there?—if we have inflation that same dollar that heretofore bought three bushels of wheat will only buy four. In other words, as the value of the dollar is inflated, the price of the wheat, together with its by-products such as imitation ivory, vegetable oils, oleomargarine, etc., is forced up or down and the result is called dumping.

NOW that is absolutely all there is to this bugaboo inflation, and why the pedants have made such an intricate matter of it, and such a pother and to-do, is altogether beyond me. I have not space or time to go into the question of fiat money, nor shrinkage, nor the fluctuation of the gold ounce, nor fixed obligations, nor the rôle that wampum has played in the development of our American monetary system. I doubt if they are important. I do not believe I mentioned the fact that our gold holdings in 1931 were $4,051,473,000, but that is not important. Neither shall I dwell on the fact that I copied all these statistics out of the World Almanac. It is not important either.

The important thing is to understand inflation, so that if we of the United States are forced into it we shall go into it with our eyes open, though blackened.

Steichen

Beaton

SOMERSET MAUGHAM

An Englishman of genius

Above is a formal portrait of the author who first tasted triumph with *Of Human Bondage*. His latest play, *For Services Rendered,* a record of post-war Britain, valiantly bears the Maugham stamp of gall and wormwood.

CARL SANDBURG

An American genius

An informal portrait of the poet, singer of prairie and industrial sagas, translator of the ugly into the beautiful, poet of the present.

DR. STEPHEN S. WISE

The rabbi

Dr. Wise is leader of American protest against the Hitler anti-Semite campaign. Born in Budapest, he came to America at the age of one, and has founded and directed hundreds of societies, including the American Zionist movement. He has a leonine head, a voice of muted thunder and the strength of an ox.

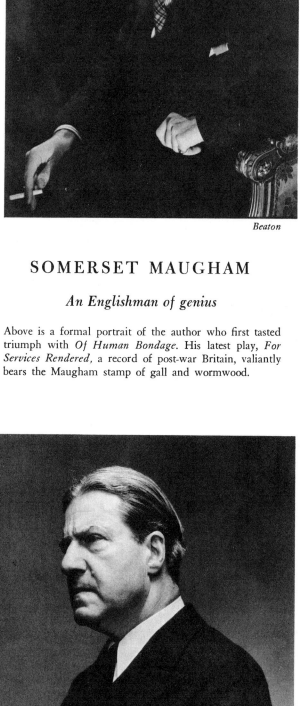

Steichen

Hutchinson

ROBERT M. HUTCHINS

The youngest national oracle

Mr. Hutchins is President of Chicago University. Precocious as leader and organizer, he became dean of Yale's Law School at twenty-nine, and head of one of the country's most influential universities two years later. Called the "Nicholas Murray Butler of the West," he seems on his way to becoming a national oracle, and possible presidential timber.

FIORELLO LA GUARDIA

"The Little Flower"

The Italian La Guardia is preparing for bloody local battle against the Irish gentlemen of Tammany. Losing his place in Congress after representing New York for sixteen years, he is entering the lists as a Republican and Fusion candidate for Mayor. Defeated in the race for Mayor of New York against Walker in 1929, he focused his insurgent and explosive tactics on Congress; but now he re-enters the lists in his native city, calling on new loyalties.

Nelson

Nominated for the Hall of Fame: 1933

ARCHIBALD MACLEISH *(left)*

Because his poetry is sinewy and masculine in spirit yet finely wrought in form; because after having graduated from the Harvard Law School he abandoned a promising legal career to devote himself to writing; because he walked and rode muleback over Cortez' route in Mexico to authenticate his Pulitzer-prize-winning *Conquistador;* and because though a *Fortune* editor he still writes poetry.

Etting

CARESSE CROSBY

Because for most of a decade she has made her Paris home an influential meeting-place of international exiles, from the James Joyces and D. H. Lawrences to the Hemingways and the youngest and brightest; because since the death of her writer husband she has increased her service to American letters by forming her own publishing firm and circulating cheap editions of good American books throughout Europe; because she is a disciple of flexibility, living as Caresse Crosby for seven years in Paris after she had lived as Polly Peabody for seven years in Boston.

Pinchot

SUMNER WELLES

Because as the forty-one-year-old Ambassador to Cuba he has demonstrated a clearheadedness and a discernment which many an older diplomat would be proud to claim; because, although he has only recently reached national prominence, he had already proved his ability by his work in Santo Domingo and Honduras; and because he can use his experience in his new post as Assistant Secretary of State in charge of Latin-American affairs.

Ewing

Van Vech

ALINE BERNSTEIN

Because as America's foremost woman scenic designer, who has worked with the Theatre Guild and Eva Le Gallienne's group, she contributed much to the success of *The Dybbuk, Reunion in Vienna,* and *Alison's House;* because she was born on the site where Macy's now stands; and because she has just completed a novel.

H. T. WEBSTER *(left)*

Because, as regular cartoonist for a succession of big syndicates, he has held a mirror up to the American people; because his various series, "The Timid Soul," "Life's Darkest Moment," etc., are becoming part of the national legendry; and because when recently, at the height of his career, "writer's cramp" lost him the use of his right hand, he learned to draw equally well with his left.

Nelson

Thoughts on Sin—and Advertising

(Speech Delivered to the American Association of Advertising Agencies)

FRANK CROWNINSHIELD

I WANT to talk to you a little about sin! I mean its origins; some of the pleasures to be derived from it and the laws, in America, that are supposed to control it.

There is a new bill before Congress which will still further limit the fields in which Americans may sin. This bill was originally fathered by Professor Rex Tugwell, but has now become the lean, adopted and unhappy child of Royal S. Copeland, the Senator from New York.

The measure is devised to prevent the manufacture of, traffic in, and what might be called the "over-romantic" advertising of certain foods, drinks, drugs, garments, cosmetics and other articles intended to make life a little happier for the ladies.

I am told that Professor Tugwell, aware perhaps that he was, because of the Puritan austerity of his life, a little unfitted to draft such a bill, turned the heavy task over to his friend, Mr. David F. Cavers, a professor of law in Duke University. And if the provisions of this bill may seem to you a little autocratic and mandatory, I would remind you that the prime begetters of it—Messrs. Cavers, Tugwell and Copeland—are named, respectively, David, Rex and Royal. And I will ask you how, from names like those, we could have expected any bill that was not biblical, imperial and autocratic in its import?

If there is anything which an American lawmaker likes to do it is to prohibit people from indulging in some form of pleasure, particularly if it is a pleasure which he himself is too old, too cynical or too anemic to enjoy. The only point, for example, which our lawmakers overlooked, when they tried to prevent drinking in America, was that Americans happened to like drinking. They liked it so much, in fact, that, according to Mr. Choate, the annual consumption of *illicit* spirits and liquors is now twice as great as our annual consumption of liquors and spirits, legal and illegal, before Washington decided to prohibit drinking entirely.

All of our intricate laws prohibiting gambling resulted, in the years immediately preceding the depression, in the greatest and most disastrous orgy of gambling which the world has ever known. And the laws with regard to modesty, on the stage and on the beaches, which were intended to promote the four-piece dancing suit and the six-piece bathing costume, were so cleverly drafted that naked women now appear nightly in our theaters while women at beaches wear practically no bathing suits at all. And so the story invariably goes.

I have lately come to think that the lawmakers who, in Washington, are trying to keep us from what they call sin, have lost sight of the fact that a little sin is today a very pleasant corrective for being forced to live what the Government so euphemistically calls a "controlled and regimented life."

The first example of Senator Copeland's particular sort of prohibition goes back about 10,000 years; to a garden party arranged by a very human and beautiful young woman. Eve, from whom all our sinful impulses sprang, was told that she could, with impunity, eat of all the fruits in the garden *save one*. And when she was so informed, it was a matter of only two minutes before she was not only eating the forbidden fruit with gusto but passing on the less desirable pieces to her husband. And it was that prohibition that completely disrupted the first recorded nudist camp in history.

And then, 10,000 years later, Professor Tugwell, modestly enacting the rôle of the Creator, and walking in his Washington garden in the cool of the day, drafted a bill of thirty or more pages, the chief purpose of which was to tell, not one woman, but 50,000,000 women, what they can or cannot eat, what they can and cannot wear, what they may or may not drink, and how and how not they may attract the attention of gentlemen—whether legal consorts, acquaintances or total strangers.

Now, the truth is that most women are not quite as afraid of sin as the professors of law would like us to believe. A witty Englishman once said that while twenty years of sin and romance made a woman look a little like a ruin, twenty years of married life gave her something of the appearance of a public building. And I am confident that the great majority of all the ladies in America would prefer to look like the Parthenon, for instance, than to take on the appearance of, let us say, Professor Tugwell's Department of Agriculture.

The origin of the American Revolution was, quite simply, that George III—a well-meaning but extremely stupid man—was constantly making lists of things which the colonists could not do. In good time they became fed-up with his prohibitions and became fed-up with his prohibitions and taboos. If they had been told that they could do pretty much as they pleased it would be a good ten to one bet that we would today be a law-abiding English colony, with a balanced national budget to solace us, a regular diet of mutton and sprouts, a pleasant cricket field in every village, and a dish of hot tea usually in our hands.

I would call to Senator Copeland's attention the case of the purest of all advertised products. (I think there can be no harm in saying *entre nous,* and away from the microphone, that I am speaking of Ivory soap.) He should remember that the manufacturers of that soap took great pains to point out that only 99 per cent of it was pure. To me, the really intriguing thing about Ivory soap has always been that *one* per cent of impurity.

Mr. Procter, the more virtuous of the two, wished to make it 100 per cent pure. But Mr. Gamble, a better salesman and much more a man of the world, held out for only 99 per cent. But if the two partners had known the American people as well as you and I know them, they would have insisted on as high as a 10 per cent impurity, and then gone on to explain that that 10 per cent was entirely made up of apricot brandy, Astrakhan caviar, paté de foies gras and absinthe. If they had done that, they would today have the American soap market at their mercy.

And it is the same with the food we eat. You have only to tell a man that a food is pure and that it is good for him, and you will sicken him of it instantly. Show any sensible man a carrot, a plate of spinach, a glass of buttermilk and some Swedish bread, and tell him that that is his dinner, and he will tell you that he would rather eat no dinner at all. But if you offer him a lobster salad, a dish of hot biscuits, a Welsh rarebit, a cup of coffee and a good cigar—all of them extremely detrimental to the health—where would his manhood be then?

We must remember that most American women lead rather monotonous and humdrum lives, particularly the housewives in whose supposed behalf this bill has primarily been drafted. Their life is a drab affair at best; washing, cooking, cleaning, tending children, and waiting for dreary husbands to return from dreary offices. Such women need romance. They crave glamour and color. They must nurse the thought that they may still be beautiful and happy and capable of generating the fire of love; that when they meet Clark Gable at Mrs. Vanderbilt's dance, they will be able, because they have put exactly the right perfume in their hair, to exact from him a complete and immediate surrender. The older of them want to be Mae West; the younger would like to be Jean Harlow.

And those happy dreams and illusions of theirs are built up for them by the advertising pages. Such pages spell romance to them. They are the magical carpets on which they ride out to love, the secret gardens into which they wander in order to escape the monotony of their work-a-day world and the banality of their well-meaning husbands.

After a single hour's reading of the advertising pages, 10,000,000 American housewives, salesgirls, telephone operators, typists, bookkeepers and factory workers daily see themselves as *femmes fatales,* as Cleopatra, as Helen of Troy, or even as Ninon de L'Enclos, who, at seventy-five, was still deriving an ecstasy from her love affairs.

For romance, to women, is very often only another name for *morale.* The American woman feels that she can be a better wife, a better worker, if she can only believe that glamour is to be her lot. She wants to nourish the illusion that, with the right kind of face cream, or mouth wash, and a little aid from the beauticians, she will become a creature whom Dante would have loved and Casanova would have died for—with a skin like a May morning, hair like a golden mist and a form that will dazzle all men and antagonize all women. All these things does a woman sigh for. And, miraculously enough, all these things can she have—and have them very inexpensively, from the shelves of the drug stores.

I have tried to show what an exciting and fascinating realm this world of the magazine advertisements has become, to the average American woman, and how greatly it contributes to her courage and morale, and I am wondering whether Washington will find it in its heart to shatter so much innocent glamour and romance.

I suppose that all we can do is to join together in praying that a majority of our Congressmen will turn out to be human beings at heart; that they will not insist upon taking what this bill calls *sin* from the mouths of the poor, and that Professor Tugwell will mercifully forget that he is Rex and Senator Copeland that he is Royal.

MARIE DRESSLER

The grand old lady

On Marie Dressler's sixty-fourth birthday, last November, more than 500,000 fans joined the Marie Dressler Birthday Club, sent her telegrams, letters, flowers, cakes, and gave testimonial dinners which numbered governors, senators and opera singers among the guests. President and Mrs. Roosevelt entertained her at dinner at the White House, and Hollywood friends gave her a 500-pound birthday cake. This climaxed, in a way, the fifty-year career of Miss Dressler, born Leila Koerber in Coburg, Canada.

Steichen

Steichen

DOLORES DEL RIO

Star out of Mexico

Lolita Dolores Asunsolo de Martinez was born on a ranch in Durango, Mexico, and educated in a convent in Mexico City. At fourteen, she was taken to Spain and presented at court; at sixteen, she married the late Jaime Del Rio, an Oxford graduate and a playwright. In 1925, Edwin Carewe, traveling in Mexico, saw her dance at a charity bazaar and brought her to Hollywood to play the French peasant in the screen version of *What Price Glory*. She has remained there ever since, now married to the director Cedric Gibbons. Her next film will be *Dance of Desire*.

Steichen

MAURICE CHEVALIER

L'homme fatal

Maurice Chevalier was born in poverty on the Lower East Side of Paris, where he knew hunger, pain and the dubious benefits of hard labor. He was discovered by Mistinguett after the war and was her partner for many years. In 1928, Paramount brought him to America and launched his cinema career. Like Chaplin, Jolson, Garbo, he is not far short of genius in what is known in the vernacular as putting the personality across. He has vast charm, unrivaled stage presence, and the sort of personal magnetism which makes whatever he does unimportant in comparison to the apparently effortless exploitation of his own essential self. His first American film was *Innocents of Paris;* his best, *The Love Parade*. His favorite diversion is roaming through Paris disguised as an apache; his greatest hatred is going to parties.

Little Caruso

WILLIAM SAROYAN

PLAYING cards at Breen's, I suddenly felt his presence in the city, like swift and sweeping excitement, all over Frisco, from the Ferry Building to the Sunset Tunnel, and a half hour later, at midnight, I saw him push through the swinging doors and walk down the length of the bar, in a terrific hurry, the way he always was, and I knew it was the same old fight, between my cousin Mano, a small dark fellow of twenty-two in a neat twelve-dollar suit, wanting to be the greatest tenor of all time, and his incredible and insane impetuosity, his everlasting unrest.

"God Almighty," I said.

"We've got no time to lose," he said. "I have been all over the public library looking for you. Is this where you spend all your time these days? What's come over you, anyway?"

"What's the matter?" I said.

"I got kicked out of the house this morning," he said, "but I'll sing from the stage of the Metropolitan Opera House in New York, if it's the last thing I do. Can I see you alone a minute?"

I got up from the table and walked with him to the door.

"Let's go up the alley," he said. "I want to sing La Donna E Mobile."

"Never mind that," I said. "Have you any money for a room tonight?"

"I haven't a nickel," he said, "but wait till you hear me sing. I caught a freight this morning, and I practiced all the way up."

"Don't make it too loud," I said. "They'll run us in for disturbing the peace."

"They wouldn't dare arrest a man with my voice," he said.

He sang the song and made something in me laugh from the beginning of time to the end of it, because he did not sing, he shouted, thrusting himself beyond the limitations of his body, outward, into the night, into the vastness of the universe, the endlessness of time, making a marvelous noise in the city. And it wasn't La Donna E Mobile: it was the cry of all of us who are seeking immortality on earth, in our own time, and the only thing I could think was, God Almighty.

"My diction is better than Gigli's," he said. "If Otto Kahn could hear me, I'd be sent to Italy in three minutes."

"I've got a dollar and thirty cents," I said. "I'll get you a room for the night, and I'll see you tomorrow."

I found a clean four-bit room for him in a small hotel on Columbus Avenue, and he said, "The world will remember you as the man who helped the greatest tenor of all time when he was broke and friendless. Leave me a half dozen cigarettes because I can't wait to get going."

I left him half a package of cigarettes, and went home. In the morning I took him a safety razor and a half dozen blades, two pairs of socks, and three clean shirts. Playing carefully, I won enough gambling to keep him going for two weeks. He went to every theatre and night club in town, begging everybody he saw to let him sing La Donna E Mobile, but they wouldn't let him do it.

"They don't know who I am," he said, "but I'll show them. I'm getting a boat to Italy because I want to walk in the streets where Caruso walked. Don't you think I look a lot like him?"

He spent a week sitting in the Seamen's Hall on Howard Street, but there were no boats to Italy, so he took the next best thing and got a job as wiper on a boat to Rio.

"Nothing is going to stop me from moving the hearts of people everywhere," he said. "I wrote some letters to Otto Khan and Deems Taylor and a couple of other people, but I can't wait. This trip to South America is just the thing for me. The answers will come General Delivery," he said. "Hold the letters till I get back."

I WENT to the General Delivery window of the Post Office for two weeks, and the only letter that came addressed to him was one from a girl back in our home town. She wrote bitterly, saying that she had really loved him once, but that it was all over now because he was not the sort of person to marry and settle down and make a name for himself. I kept the letter a month, and then tore it up.

The day he got back I was in Breen's, and I saw him tear through the swinging doors, looking furious, and the old laugh came up in me again, and I was glad he hadn't fallen off the boat and drowned.

"I can't figure you out," he said. "I've been half way around the world, busting my neck trying to establish myself, and you sit in this ungodly joint playing cards. I met a singing teacher in Rio and he said I would be a sensation in the next three years, but I can't wait. What did Otto Kahn say, anyway? Did Deems Taylor answer my letter?"

I thought I ought to lie and tell him Otto Kahn was interested in his voice, but I couldn't do it. Then I remembered that while he was gone Otto Kahn had died, and I said, "I've got bad news for you, Mano. Otto Kahn passed away while you were in Rio."

"Everything is against me," he said. "Just when I need him most, Otto Kahn dies. For the love of Mike, don't tell me

---

Opposite: "MONKEYS IN A TROPICAL FOREST" BY ROUSSEAU

Henri-Julien Rousseau (1844–1910) was a French artist who rose to fame independent of tradition and wholly uninfluenced by the art of his time. He was the first modern "primitive" and his art—the expression of a simple, ageless folk idiom—has always captured the imagination with its strange and fascinating appeal.

This picture, painted in the early 1900s, is from the collection of Mrs. Charles Payson. It exemplifies Rousseau's quaint, exotic style, his primitive quality, and the suave and decorative clarity with which he especially colored his jungle paintings.

Deems Taylor is dead, too. What did Deems say?"

"Well," I said, "I understand Deems Taylor is traveling in Europe. I think he is going to be away for another year."

"All I need is a decent contract," he said. "I know what I can do, but nobody else does."

He had a little money saved, and he stayed in Frisco until the money was gone. Then, humiliated but angry, he went back to his home town, and during the next six months I received an average of three letters a week from him.

"The power of my voice is increasing every day," he said, "and it won't be long before I can be heard from here to the Rainier Brewery, fourteen blocks away. On a clear day I can do it now, but the wind has got to be with me. . . .

"I am going to make boxes for Mouradian this summer. I've got to earn enough money to get to New York this fall because once I get there I will electrify everybody with my singing. If you get down this way, be sure and see me at Mouradian's packing house, in East Bakersfield, because I want you to hear me sing *O Sole Mio.*"

Two weeks ago I got fed up with the city and began longing for the valley where I was born, for the hot sun and the vineyards and the clarity of life there, the clarity that is driving the whole race of us all over the world, making us want to do tremendous things. I hitch-hiked from Frisco to Bakersfield and went straight out to Mouradian's packing house. Mano was in a corner, at a bench, standing on a platform because he was too small to work well from the floor, furiously nailing boxes, but not singing.

"You're just the fellow I want to see,"

he said. "I am disgusted with everything, and the way I feel now, I don't know whether I'll ever be able to sing again because this humiliation is getting to be too much for me. Everybody thinks I am nobody because I am in overalls, nailing boxes. Nobody can tell from the way I act that I am the greatest living tenor on earth, and it's burning me up."

"What you are doing," I said, "is only a means to an end. You'll be in New York this fall and everything will be swell."

"But I can't wait," he said. "I hate this atmosphere. It is destroying everything fine in me."

He didn't stop making boxes, but talked while he brought the hatchet down on the nails, bang bang bang, talking and moving his powerful arm with great rhythm.

Fifty young Filipinos stood in the packing house, packing grapes, talking along in their language while they worked, making a low and steady mumble in the heat.

"Listen to them," said Mano. "My voice will be ruined. Never before in the history of the world has a great artist suffered such humiliation as this. I need to be alone, always, so that I can let my voice grow."

He was very bitter and I didn't know what to tell him.

Then something happened that makes me laugh every time I think of it. One of the Filipino boys was having a little fun, throwing grapes at another Filipino boy who was pasting labels on boxes just beyond where Mano was working. One of the grapes went wild and hit Mano on the neck.

Mano was nailing away nicely, but when the grape hit his neck, the rhythm of his movements came to a sudden and furious stop, and he was mad. He got off the platform and walked around his bench, the

hatchet still in his hand, and lifted high.

"Who threw that grape?" he said, only it was more than speech, just as his singing was less, and more, than singing. The old insane fury.

All the boys were talking along cheerfully until they heard Mano's voice. Then the whole packing house became very quiet.

"Who threw that God-damn grape?" he said. "I'll bust the head of any bastard who throws a grape at the greatest lyric tenor in the world."

A full minute he stood before them, waiting for one of the boys to say some word, or make some false move. There were fifty of them, but they knew they were in the presence of some mighty and glorious power in man, and they were afraid, and I myself was afraid.

"If I get hit with a grape again," he said, "I'll find out who threw it and I'll bust his head. You don't know who I am, but I know."

He walked back to his bench, stepped onto the platform, and began again to nail. "You see," he said sullenly, "I am humiliated because no one knows who I am."

"Take it easy," I said. "I know who you are. You are the greatest lyric tenor alive, and everybody else will know it the minute you get to New York."

And I'm telling you, I wasn't fooling, either. My cousin Mano *is* the greatest living tenor on earth because he *thinks* he is, and nothing is going to stop him from walking out on the stage of the Metropolitan Opera House in New York and electrifying everybody with the fury of his personality, not even the untimely passing of Otto Kahn, the aloofness of Deems Taylor, or the fact that his voice isn't worth a damn.

Opposite: "THE JAPANESE FAN" BY MONET

Claude Monet (1840–1926) ranks secure as the founder of Impressionism. Crying "Let there be light!" he and Renoir wrested French painting from the devitalizing clutch of classicism. Monet's luminous palette bespoke the impressionist concept of nature as a spectrum, matter as disintegrated light. "The Japanese Fan," a portrait of the first Madame Monet, was painted in 1876 when the artist was thirty-six, and is now in the collection of Lord Duveen. The attitude of the figure and the general tone and texture of the canvas reveal the influence of Japanese art on Monet—shortly before he began painting the smoky, evanescent landscapes for which he is now so much better known.

NORMA SHEARER

JOAN CRAWFORD

MARLENE DIETRICH

The sum total of Hollywood sex appeal—Mlle. X, the golden-mean average in cinema beauty

RUTH CHATTERTON

HELEN HAYES

GRETA GARBO

Here you have the composite feminine motion-picture star, who is made of sugar and spice and everything nice, not to mention Marlene Dietrich and eight other high-priced honeys of the screen. The resultant beauty is gained by superimposing on one another the photographs of the nine women stars shown on this page. Together they form the ideal.

Male and Female

PEGGY SHANNON

DOROTHY JORDAN

JOAN BENNETT

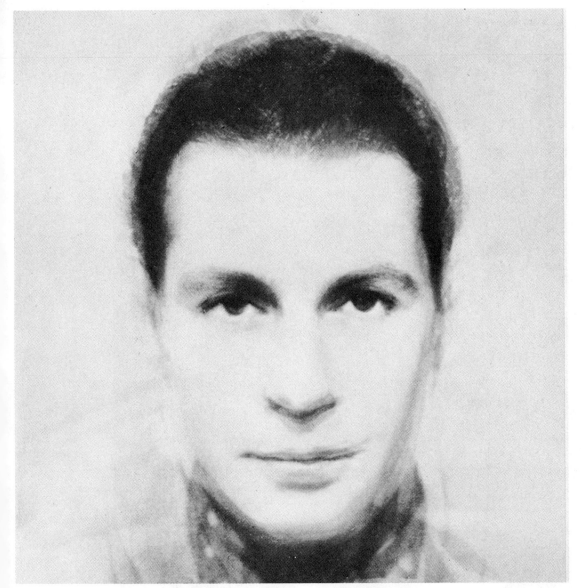

Mr. Y—not quite so effective, but still a charming young man, albeit a trifle effeminate

GARY COOPER

FREDRIC MARCH

GEORGE BRENT

And here is the ideal male star, made up of nine well-known Hollywood men, not one of whom entirely appealed to *Vanity Fair*'s editors, so they put them all together and look what they got. Each feature of his face is a composite of the same feature in nine different men, so it should spell perfection in the final composite picture of our hero.

FRANCHOT TONE

RICHARD ARLEN

ROBERT MONTGOMERY

JOHNNIE WEISMULLER

DICK POWELL

GEORGE RAFT

We Create Them

Steichen

LESLIE HOWARD

Notwithstanding the fact that Talbot Jennings' play, *This Side Idolatry,* closed in London after a run of ten days, Mr. Gilbert Miller will defiantly bring it to Broadway, with Leslie Howard in the rôle of Shakespeare. Mr. Miller figures—and perhaps rightly—that what is a failure in London is often a hit in New York, and vice versa. In addition, Leslie Howard's American popularity, for some curious reason, is about triple what it is on his native heath. Mr. Howard first came to America fourteen years ago and audiences promptly lionized him. Since then he has been a local hero, on both stage and screen. His last Broadway appearance was in *The Animal Kingdom,* his last movie *Berkeley Square.*

The Murder in Le Mans

JANET FLANNER

WHEN, in February 1933, the Papin sisters, cook and housemaid, killed Madame and Mademoiselle Lancelin in the respectable provincial town of Le Mans, a half dozen hours from Paris, it was not a murder but a revolution. It was only a minor revolution—minor enough to be fought in a front hall by four females, two on a side. The rebels won with horrible handiness. The lamentable Lancelin forces were literally scattered over a distance of ten bloody feet, or from the upper landing half way down the stairs. The physical were the most chilling details, the conquered the only dull elements in a fiery, fantastic struggle that should have remained inside Christine Papin's head and which, when it touched earth, unfortunately broke into paranoiac poetry and one of the most graceless murders in French annals.

On the day he was to be made a widower, M. Lancelin, retired lawyer, spent his afternoon at his respectable provincial club; at 6:45 he reported to his brother-in-law, M. Renard, practicing lawyer at whose table they were to dine at 7 *en famille,* that, having gone by the Lancelin home in the rue La Bruyère to pick up his wife and daughter Geneviève, he had found the doors bolted and the windows dark—except for the maids' room in the attic, where, until he started knocking, there was a feeble glow. It had appeared again only as he was leaving.

Two lawyers this time set off for the Lancelin dwelling, to observe again the mansard gleam fade, again creep back to life as the men retreated. Alarmed (for at the least a good dinner was drying up) the gentlemen procured a brace of policemen and a brigadier, who, by forcing Lancelin's window, invited Lancelin to walk into his parlor, where he discovered his electric lights did not work. Two of the police crept upstairs with one flashlight and the brother-in-law. Close to the second floor the trio humanely warned the husband not to follow.

ON THE third step from the landing, all alone, staring uniquely at the ceiling, lay an eye. On the landing itself the Lancelin ladies lay, at odd angles and with heads like blood puddings. Beneath their provincial petticoats their modest limbs had been knife-notched the way a fancy French baker notches his finer long loaves. Their fingernails had been uprooted, one of Geneviève's

Horst

JANET FLANNER

teeth was pegged in her own scalp. A second single orb—the mother's, this time, for both generations seemed to have been treated with ferocious non-partisanship—rested short-sightedly gazing at nothing in the corner of the hall. Blood had softened the carpet till it was like an elastic red moss.

The youngest and third policeman (his name was Mr. Truth) was sent creeping toward the attic. Beneath the door a crack

of light flickered. When he crashed the door, the light proved to be a candle, set on a plate so as not to drip, for the Papins were well-trained servants. The girls were in one bed in two blue kimonos. They had taken off their dresses which were stained. They had cleaned their hands and faces. They had, the police later discovered, also cleaned the carving knife, hammer and pewter pitcher which they had been using and put them neatly back where they belonged—though the pitcher was by now too battered to look tidy. Christine, the elder (Léa, the younger, was never after to speak intelligibly except once at the trial), did not confess; she merely made their mutual statement: they had done it. Truth took what was left of the candle—the short-circuiting electric iron had blown out the fuse again that afternoon and was at the bottom of everything, Christine kept saying, though the sensible Truth paid no attention—and lighted the girls downstairs, over the corpses and out to the police station. They were still in their blue kimonos and in the February air their hair was wild, though ordinarily they were the tidiest pair of domestics in Le Mans.

Through a typographical error the early French press reports printed the girls' name not as Papin which means nothing, but as Lapin which means rabbit. It was no libel.

The scene of the murder

The death-dealing Papin sisters

Waiting trial in the prison, Christine, who was 28 years of age and the cathartic of the two, had extraordinary holy visions and unholy reactions. Léa who was 22 and looked enough like her sister to be a too-long-delayed twin, had nothing, since the girls were kept separate and Léa thus had no dosage for her feeble brain.

Their trial at the local courthouse six months later was a national event, regulated by guards with bayonets, ladies with lorgnettes and envoys from the Parisian press. As commentators *Paris-Soir* sent a pair of novelists, the Tharaud brothers, Jean and Jérôme, who, when they stoop to journalism, write of themselves as "I" and even won the Goncourt Prize under this singular consolidation. Special scribes were post-hasted by *Détective,* hebdomidal pennydreadful prosperously owned by the *Nouvelle Revue Française,* or France's *Atlantic Monthly.* *L'Œuvre,* as daily house organ for the Radical Socialist Party (supposedly friendly to the working classes till they unfortunately shot a few of them in the recent Concorde Riot), sent Bérard, or their best brain.

The diametric pleas of prosecution and defense facing these historians were clear: either (a) the Papins were normal girls who had murdered without a reason, murdering without reason apparently being a proof of normalcy in Le Mans; or else (b) the Rabbit sisters were as mad as March Hares, and so didn't have to have a reason. Though they claimed to have one just like anybody else, if the jury would only listen: their reason was that unreliable electric iron, or a mediocre cause for a revolution. . . . The iron had blown out Wednesday, been repaired Thursday, blown again Friday, taking the houselights with it at 5. By 6 the Lancelin ladies, in from their walk, had been done to death in the dark, *for the dead do not scold.*

While alive, Madame had once forced Léa to her housemaid knees to retrieve a morsel of paper overlooked on the parlor rug. Or, as the Tharauds ponderously wrote in their recapitulation of the crime, "God knows the Madame Lancelins exist on earth." This one, however, had been rare in that she corroborated Léa's dusting by donning a pair of white gloves, she commentated on Christine's omelettes by formal notes delivered to the kitchen by Geneviève —both habits adding to the Papins' persecution complex, or their least interesting facet. Madame also gave the girls enough to eat and "even allowed them to have heat in their attic bedroom," though Christine did not know if Madame were kind, since in six years' service she had never spoken to them, and if people don't talk, how can you tell? As for the motive for their crime, it was again the Tharauds who, all on the girls' side, thus loyally made it clear as mud: "As good servants the girls had been

highly contraried" when the iron blew once. Twice "it was still as jewels of servants who don't like to lose their time that they became irritated. Perhaps if the sisters had been less scrupulous as domestics the horror which followed would never have taken place. And I wish to say," added Jean and Jérôme, without logic and in unison, "that many people still belong to early periods of society."

Among others, the jury did. They were 12 good men and true, or quite incompetent to appreciate the Papin sisters. Also, the trial lasted only 26 hours, or not long enough to go into the girls' mental rating though the next 40 or 50 years of their lives depended on it. The prosecution summoned three local insane-asylum experts who had seen the girls twice for a half hour, and swore on the stand that the *prisonnières* were "of unstained heredity"—i.e., their father having been a dipsomaniac who violated their elder sister, since become a nun; their mother having been an hysteric "crazy for money"; a cousin having died in a madhouse and an uncle having hanged himself "because his life was without joy." In other words, heredity OK, legal responsibility 100 per cent.

Owing to the girls' weak, if distinguished defense—high-priced French lawyers work cheaply for criminals if bloody enough, the publicity being a fortune in itself—their equally distinguished psychiatrist's refutation carried no weight. Their lawyer was Pierre Chautemps, cousin to that Camille Chautemps who, as Prime Minister, so weakly defended the French Republic in the recent Boulevard St.-Germain Riots; their expert was the brilliant Parisian professor, Logre, whose "colossal doubt on their sanity" failed to count since under cross examination he had to admit he had never seen the girls before even for 5 minutes; just knew all about them by sitting back in his Paris study, ruminating. He did, too, but the jury sniffed at the stuck-up city man.

Thus, they also missed Logre's illuminating and delicate allusion to the girls as a "psychological couple" though they'd understood the insane-asylum chief's broader reference to Sappho. Of paramount interest to twelve good men and true, the girls' incest was really one of the slighter details of their dubious domesticity. On the jury's ears Christine's prison visions also fell flat. Indeed it was not until six months after she was sentenced to be beheaded that these hallucinations were appreciated for their literary value in a scholarly essay entitled *Motifs du Crime Paranoïaque: ou Le Crime des Sœurs Papins,* by Docteur Jacques Lacan, in a recent Surréalist number of the *intelligentsia* quarterly, *Minotaure.*

In court, however, Christine's poetic visions were passed over as a willful concoction of taradiddles that took in no one—ex-

cept the defense, of course. Yet they had, in the limited data of lyrical paranoia and modern psychiatry, constituted an exceptional performance. Certain of the insane enjoy strange compensations; having lost sight of reality they see singular substitutes devoid of banal sequence, and before the rare spectacle of effect without cause are pushed to profound questions the rest of us are too sensible to bother with. "Where was I before I was in the belly of my mother?" Christine first inquired, and the fit was on. She next wished to know where the Lancelin ladies might now be for, though dead, could they not have come back in other bodies? For a cook she showed, as the Tharauds said, "a bizarre interest in metempsychosis," further illuminated by her melancholy reflection, "Sometimes I think in former lives that I was my sister's husband." Then while the prison dormitory shuddered, Christine claimed to see that unholy bride hanging hanged to an apple tree, with her limbs and the tree's limbs broken. At the sad sight crazed Christine leapt in the air to the top of a ten-foot barred window where she maintained herself with muscular ease. It was then that Léa, whom she had not seen since their incarceration six months before, was called in as a sedative. And to her Christine cried with strange exultation, "Say yes, say yes," which nobody understands to this day. By what chance did this Sarthe peasant fall like the Irish Joyce in the last line of *Ulysses* on the two richest words in any tongue—those of human affirmation, *Yes, yes. . . .*

Thus ended the lyrical phase of Christine's seizure, which then became, maybe, political. At any rate she hunger-struck for three days, like someone with a cause, went into the silence, wept and prayed like a leader betrayed, traced holy signs with her tongue on the prison walls, tried to take Léa's guilt on her shoulders and, when this failed, at least succeeded in freeing her own of her strait-jacket.

"Wasn't all of that just make-believe?" the prison officials later asked her. (All except escaping from the strait-jacket, of course, or a reality that had never occurred in French penal history before.) "If monsieur wishes," said Christine politely. Both the girls were very polite in prison and addressed their keepers in the formal third person, as if the guards were company who had just stepped in to the Lancelins' parlor for tea.

During the entire court proceeding, report on visions, vices and all, from 1:30 after lunch of one day to 3:30 before breakfast of the next, Christine sat on the accused bench with eyes closed. She looked like someone asleep or a medium in a trance, except that she rose when addressed and blindly said nearly nothing. The judge, a kind man with ferocious mustaches was, in his interrogation, finally forced to examine his own conscience, since he couldn't get Christine to talk about hers.

"When you were reprimanded in your kitchen, you never answered back but you rattled your stove-lids fiercely; I ask myself if this was not sinful pride. . . . Yet you rightly think work is no disgrace. No, you also have no class hatred," he said with relief to find that he and she were neither bolsheviks. "Nor were you influenced by literature, apparently, since only books of piety were found in your room."

(Not that printed piety had taught the girls any Christian mercy once they started to kill. The demi-blinding of the Lancelins is the only criminal case on record where eye balls were removed from the living head without practice of any instrument except the human finger. The duplicating of the tortures was also curiously cruel; Christine took Madame in charge, the dull Léa followed suit by tending to Mademoiselle; whatever the older sister did to the older woman, the younger sister repeated on fresher flesh in an orgy of obedience.)

As the trial proceeded, the spectators could have thought the court was judging one Papin cadaver seen double, so much the sisters looked alike and dead. Their sanity expert had called them Siamese souls. The Papins' was the pain of being two where some mysterious unity had been originally intended; between them was a schism which the dominant, devilish Christine had tried to resolve into one self-reflection, without ever having heard of Narcissus or thinking that the pallid Léa might thus be lost to view. For, if Christine's eyes were closed to the judges, Léa's were as empty in gaze as if she were invisible and incapable of sight. Her one comment on trial for her life was that, with the paring knife, she had "made little carvings" in poor spinster Geneviève's thighs. For there, as her Christine had said, lay the secret of life. . . .

When the jury came in with their verdict Christine was waiting for them, still somnambulant, her hands clasped not as in prayer but as if pointing down into the earth. In the chill pre-dawn both sisters' coat-collars were turned up as if they had just come in from some domestic errand run in the rain. With their first effort at concentration on Léa, whom all day the jury had tried to ignore, the foreman gave her 10 years' confinement and 20 of municipal exile. Christine was sentenced to have her head cut off in the public square of Le Mans which, since females are no longer guillotined, meant life—a courtesy she, at the moment, was ignorant of.

When Christine heard her sentence of decapitation, in true belief she fell to her knees. At last she had heard the voice of God.

Bruehl

ETHEL WATERS

In As Thousands Cheer

There comes a moment early in the Irving Berlin–Moss Hart show *As Thousands Cheer* when Ethel Waters steps out on the stage and the theatre suddenly becomes alive. With a gentle wriggle of her hips and a grin as radiant as Christmas on her face, she sings the hit song "Heat Wave."

Where Did You Come from,
Baby Dear?

*Showing that the paternal impulse is likely
to rear its head in the least expected quarters*

Acme

At ninety-five, John D. Rockefeller is still susceptible to the patter of tiny great-grandchildren's feet.

Babe Ruth, for years the idol of American youth, has one unfailing fan in his daughter.

James Joyce, the much-censored, fondly dandles his grandson, Stephen—Joyce, not Dedalus.

Primo Carnera, tamed to timidity by a publicity camera and a bouquet of neighbors' children.

Tony Canzoneri, grooming a lightweight, teaches the young idea how to shoot a fearless right

272

Actor into Philanthropist

Showing how Clifton Webb transforms himself into the likeness of John D. Rockefeller, Sr. The photographs (at right) were taken in the actor's dressing room

Clifton Webb, in the flesh unadorned

First touch—greasepaint foundation

Close-up: the incrustations of age

Putting in the wrinkles

The final touch: the wig

Mr. Rockefeller—né Clifton Webb

Noel Coward chats with a Bright Young Thing—Daniel Massey, son of the Raymond Masseys.

In one of the scenes of *As Thousands Cheer*, New York's gayest revue of the past year, the audiences are treated to the spectacle of Mr. Webb, giving a hilarious impersonation of Mr. Rockefeller. In the pictures above (taken by Nelson) Mr. Webb lets *Vanity Fair* readers in on the secret of how he achieves the magic metamorphosis from his own dapper and sardonic self into this almost eerie simulacrum of the great oil king. (Mr. Rockefeller conveniently appears at the top of the page opposite.)

273

GARBO

As Queen Christina

Two "stills" from the new Metro-Goldwyn-Mayer motion picture show the most publicized face of modern times. The film, shortly to be released, is under Rouben Mamoulian's direction. John Gilbert plays opposite Garbo.

The Movies Take Over the Stage

What Will Happen to the Legitimate Theatre When the Hollywood Directors Come to Broadway

GEORGE JEAN NATHAN

THE NEWS that the motion picture companies, operating in combination, have bought out the New York theatrical producers and taken over their theatres *in toto* for the coming season naturally came as something of a surprise to those of us who rely for our information, during the summer months, on the pony express to the Westchester Embassy and Atlantic Beach clubs. There had been rumors, of course, but we smilingly and loftily had waved them aside, like so many week-end invitations to Quogue, L. I. The idea was unthinkable, unbelievable. Yet the fact now confronts us.

On September 1, according to the announcements, the movie industry will be in complete control of the legitimate stage and its drama, with Mr. Irving Thalberg and Mr. Louis B. Mayer of the Metro-Goldwyn company, Mr. Samuel Goldwyn and Mr. Joseph Schenck of the United Artists and Twentieth Century companies, the Messrs. Cohen, Cohn, Cone, Coyne, Garfunkel, Katz, Satz, Zukor and Lustvogel of the Paramount company, and the Messrs. Selznick, Sheehan, Kraftsuppe, Laemmle, Ganzbrust, Franklin, Lasky and the eighteen Warner Brothers of the various other companies as a board of governing directors and general overlords.

With this impressive array of names, the situation looks encouraging. It may be true that Mr. Goldwyn, in his own film field, took Zola's Nana and converted her into an Edward Childs Carpenter ingénue; it may be true that Mr. Thalberg took O'Neill's Nina Leeds and converted her into a virginal Florence Nightingale; it may be true that Mr. Katz, or whatever his brother-in-law's or uncle's or cousin's name is, took *Peg o' My Heart* and introduced scenes showing Peg dancing in her birthday clothes at a National Republican Committee stag smoker; but, after all, let us not forget that Mr. Gilbert Miller called Bourdet's *Le Sexe Faible The Sex Fable* when he produced it in New York, that Mr. Guthrie McClintic took Obey's simple little *Lucrèce* and made it indistinguishable from a Cecil De Mille production, minus only an opal bathtub, and that the Theatre Guild, besides actually playing George O'Neil's *American Dream* backwards, has rejected as utterly unimportant and insignificant plays by O'Casey, Pirandello—and for many years—Eugene O'Neill, in favor of the

masterpieces of Dawn Powell, the Siftons, A. A. Milne and David Liebovitz.

As I say, the situation, despite the pitiful grunts and grousings of Mr. Brock Pemberton, who produces about one play in every three years, and of Mr. Percy Hammond, who has to come in all the way from Easthampton, Long Island, to review it—the situation, as I say, looks encouraging. Particularly when we peruse the preliminary plans of the movie executives.

According to the Hollywood announcements, the season will officially be opened with an all-star $350,000 revival of Verneuil's two-character play, *Jealousy*. There will be eighty-five people in the cast, including Clara Bow, Jean Harlow, Carole Lombard, Toby Wing, Mae West, Joan Blondell, Anna Sten, Claudette Colbert, Conchita Montenegro, Dolores del Rio, Ginger Rogers, Myrna Loy, and a swimming pool. It has not yet been decided whether men will be included in the cast or not.

Following close upon the heels of this colossal production will come Katharine Cornell's presentation of Shakespeare's *Romeo and Juliet,* with Miss Cornell appearing in the nude. Basil Rathbone who, under the present theatrical dispensation, has been playing Romeo to Miss Cornell's Juliet on the road, is to be replaced, by way of giving a little life and vitality to the stale classic, with James Cagney. The third presentation, due on September 26, is to be a new American drama, by Mr. Louis B. Mayer's brother-in-law, called *Sex!!!* It is possible, says the announcement, that the title may be changed to *Sex!!,* but several conferences will have to be held before a definite decision is arrived at.

IN OCTOBER, we are promised four great productions. Norma Shearer, under the artistic personal direction of Mr. Thalberg, is billed to do Ibsen's *The Master Builder,* rewritten by Ben Hecht and Charles MacArthur, with Busby Berkeley in charge of the choreography. Madison Square Garden has been leased for the presentation and Samuel Rothafel, the beloved "Roxy," will have charge of the stage lighting and lobby decorations. Next will come a "musical romance" with a great cast of 700, to be produced in the Little Theatre. The rôle of the little orphan princess will be filled by May Robson, while that of the amorous

Grand Duke Adolpho will be played simultaneously by the Four Mills Brothers. If the Four Mills Brothers are occupied at the time making shorts, it is announced that their place will be taken by the Three Radio Rogues. Johnny Weissmuller is to have the rôle of the old crippled inn-keeper. Oscar Straus will compose the score, which is to be rewritten by Gordon and Ravel. During the second act, the whole audience will be moved up to the balcony that it may, from that point of vantage, enjoy a bird's-eye view of the chorus maneuvers and so not miss the Hollywood effects contrived by cameras swung aloft on derricks.

AS THE treat following, we are to be given a fine novelty called *An Evening With the Stars.* Booked for the Guild Theatre, the entertainment is to consist of personal appearances by ten rare film artists, to wit, Richard Dix, Buddy Rogers, John Gilbert, Clive Brook, Boris Karloff, Joan Crawford, Helen Twelvetrees, ZaSu Pitts, Mitzi Green, and Lupe Velez. Mr. Dix will appear in an open-front white sport shirt, will frown intellectually in scholarly silence for ten minutes, and will conclude his performance by saying, "I want to thank all my loyal fans for the wonderful reception they have given me this evening. I feel mighty proud, I can tell you!" Mr. Rogers will play the saxophone for five minutes and beat on trap drums for five more, all to a lovable boyish smile, whereafter he will step to the footlights (in this instance supplanted by a row of powerful navy searchlights) and say, "I want to thank all my loyal fans for the wonderful reception they have given me this evening. I feel mighty proud, I can tell you!" Mr. Gilbert will come on, nose and all, and vouchsafe the ladies in the audience twenty minutes of hintful and passionate, if somewhat regrettably fossilized, love looks, after which he will say, "I want to thank all my loyal fans for the wonderful reception they have given me this evening. I feel mighty proud, I can tell you!" Mr. Clive Brook will smoke a pipe and emulate Mr. Dix by frowning intellectually in scholarly silence for fourteen minutes, after which, being British, he will vary his colleagues' averments by saying, "I wish to thank all of my loyal fans for the jolly reception they have accorded me this evening. I feel jolly well set up about it, I say, I say!"

Mr. Karloff will make himself up like a two-months-old corpse and will lie in state on the stage for eighteen minutes, the audience being privileged to pass in front of the bier and to touch and feel him. Being an artist who takes his art seriously and so not wishing to step out of the picture, Mr. Karloff will say nothing but will have an attendant, dressed as a grave-digger, pass out handbills informing the audience that he wants to thank all his loyal fans for the wonderful reception they have given him that evening and that he feels mighty proud, he can tell them.

Miss Crawford's part in the program will consist of a beauty lecture. She will show the ladies in the audience how, by the application of two quarts of tomato juice cocktails, a can of Sherwin-Williams carmine paint, and a large brush dipped into a pail containing half a dozen old red flannel union suits, milady's mouth may be made to look like a lovely and tempting exploded watermelon. After the lecture Miss Crawford will prettily and demurely thank her loyal fans for the wonderful reception they have given her. Miss Twelvetrees, who believes in the use of but *one* quart of tomato juice cocktails on her lips and who hence is ethereal, will pout sweetly at the gentlemen in the audience for ten minutes, thus inculcating in them an overpowering *Heinweh* for the Poillon Sisters, and Miss Pitts will open her eyes like a new baseball park and go in for wistfulness in a big way, after which both ladies will coyly finger their skirts and thank *their* loyal fans for the wonderful reception. Little Mitzi Green, who now weighs almost as much as Jim Tully, will come on in rompers and be very kiddy cutie, delighting the audience, as extra good measure, with a boop-a-doop song. Then she will lisp, "I wanna thank all my thweet fanth for thith wunnerful retheption." Finally, Miss Velez will appear and will give, in quick succession, nine imitations of an orthodox young Mexican woman imitating Hollywood's picture of an uncontrollable and devastating flood of yohimbin. Miss Velez, breathless and exhausted by the strain of her efforts, and eager to put on her old-fashioned nightgown and have a nice hot glass of Ovaltine before going quietly to bed, will pause long enough to say in over-broken English, "Me wants to tank my frens for zis warnerful recepçion what zey have given me zis evening."

It promises to be a big night, whatever Mr. Brooks Atkinson may say. Speaking for myself, I have ordered two new suits of evening clothes.

Another big November item will be a revised version of Bernard Shaw's *Back to Methuselah,* with not merely the first but *all* of the scenes in the Garden of Eden. Adam will be Buster Crabbe, with forty Eves.

The following production, it is hoped, will be one of the real box-office sensations of the season. It will be a revival of *Little Women,* which, you will recall, when done on the screen was a gold-mine because of Katharine Hepburn's presence in it. In order to ensure an even greater box-office success on the stage, the movie executives will cast the play not only with Miss Hepburn but with her family, including father, mother, brother, sister, two uncles and aunts, and former husband, Sid Grauman.

The outstanding production planned for December will be the Wampas Babies in a dramatic epic of gangster life entitled, *Shoot Her in the Pants, the Coat and Brassière Are Mine.*

Further plans for 1935 include a new play by John Monk Saunders for Sidney Blackmer, who will be supported by George M. Cohan, Walter Hampden and Walter Huston.

FANNY BRICE
and
SALLY RAND

Fan dancing, which has swept the world like wildfire, reaches its apex in its two best-known exponents: Fanny Brice of the *Ziegfeld Follies,* whose inspired insanity is the toast of the town, and Sally Rand of the Chicago World's Fair and the Paradise Club in New York.

Hoyningen-Huene

CARY GRANT

Born Archie Leach (the name under which he trouped for five years as a comic acrobat all over England and America), this rising young film actor has appeared successfully with Marlene Dietrich in *Blonde Venus* and now with Mae West in *She Done Him Wrong*. Warm, dark, and handsome, he is one of *Vanity Fair*'s candidates for future screen stardom.

Bruehl-Bourges

MAX BAER

A studio portrait of the world's heavyweight champion who draws his public from every audience except the legitimate stage

MAE WEST

Miss West has taken over the education of screen audiences the world over in her inimitable, indescribable film She Done Him Wrong

Hoyningen-Huene

And Now

And so the time comes when I can tell the story of my life

GERTRUDE STEIN

The year 1933–34 proved to be Gertrude Stein's annus mirabilis. When her life story, The Autobiography of Alice B. Toklas, was published, following serialization in The Atlantic Monthly, it was chosen by the Literary Guild, thus insuring it a wider audience than either author or publisher ever expected. Then came the production of the Stein-Thomson opera, Four Saints in Three Acts, which, during its month's run in New York, became the talk of the town, for one reason or another; was re-opened by popular demand for an additional fortnight; and is to go on tour this autumn. At that time, too, Miss Stein is to visit the United States, after thirty years of residence in Paris, to deliver a series of lectures at various universities. She has nearly finished a new volume of reminiscences.

Vanity Fair views all this with a certain smugness, for it has been publishing Miss Stein's work at various times for seventeen years. Her first contribution, in 1917, was called "Have They Attacked Mary. He Giggled," and was said to be a portrait of Henry McBride, the New York art critic. A year later Vanity Fair published her poem, "The Great American Army"; and in 1923 her portrait of Jo Davidson and a short story, "Miss Furr and Miss Skeene"; in 1924 "If I Told Him," a portrait of Picasso.

In the following article (which is written in a not too difficult style) Miss Stein tells us her reactions to her popular success.

THE other book was gay, this one will not be so gay. The other had peace and war. This one has peace and only peace and so it is not going to be so gay. It is going to be rather sad. When there has been a long peace after there had been a long war, there is a monotone and something of a moan. That is where we are today. There is a great deal to say about where we are today and what is happening every day.

What happened from the day I wrote the autobiography to today and what do I think about it all, about what happened every day.

I make my bow.

I have always quarreled with a great many young men and one of the principal things that I have quarreled with them about was that once they had made a success they became sterile, they could not go on. And I blamed them. I said it was their fault. I said success is all right but if there is anything in you it ought not to cut off

G E R T R U D E   S T E I N

the flow not if there is anything in you. Now I know better. It does cut off your flow and then if you are not too young and you are frightened enough you can begin again but if you are young or if you were young when you succeeded then when you get frightened it makes it worse not better.

That is the advantage of being older when you get frightened it starts you going, when you are young and you get frightened it just stops you more than ever. Just think of animals and children and you will understand.

What happened to me was this. When the success began and it was a success I got lost completely lost. You know the nursery rhyme, I am I because my little dog knows me. Well you see I did not know myself, I lost my personality. It has always been completely included in myself my personality as any personality naturally is, and here all of a sudden, I was not just I because so many people did know me. It was just the opposite of I am I because my little dog knows me. So many people knowing me I was I no longer and for the first time since I had begun to write I could not write and what was worse I could not worry about not writing and what was also worse I began to think about how my writing would sound to others, how could I make them understand, I who had always lived within myself and my writing. And then all of a sudden I said there it is that is what was the matter with all of them all the young men whose syrup did not pour, and here I am being just the same.

They were young and I am not but when it happens it is just the same, the syrup does not pour.

It did not frighten me, I was enjoying myself I was spending my money as they had spent their money all the other painters and writers that I had blamed and condemned and here I was doing the same thing. And then the dollar fell and somehow I got frightened, really frightened awfully frightened just as all of them had gotten frightened really frightened these last years, but luckily for me being older the fright has made me write. I say luckily for me because I like to write. It is what I like best. I like it even better than spending money although there is no pleasure so sweet as the pleasure of spending money but the pleasure of writing is longer. There is no denying that.

ALL this is to introduce what happened since the writing of the autobiography and a great many things have happened.

In the first place Picasso and I are no longer friends. All the writers about whom I wrote wrote to me that they liked what I wrote but none of the painters. The painters did not like what I wrote about them, they none of them did. They just, as Henry McBride afterward told me that Matisse did, they shuddered.

I remember when there was the first big show at the autumn salon, I imagine about 1905, of Cézanne, his really first serious public recognition, they told the story that he was so moved he said he would now have to paint more carefully than ever. And then he painted those last pictures of his that were more than ever covered over painted and painted over. Perhaps it is like that.

But to tell it all just as it had happened because of course a great deal has happened not only to me and to everybody I knew but to everything else. Once more Paris is not as it was.

When Picabia came to see us in the country he told me that there had been three young Spaniards who showed their pictures in 1904 and 1905 at a small furniture shop at Montmartre. The other two were Picasso and the unknown, the one who did the café and the one everybody has forgotten, and the third was himself Picabia. They were to have another show together the following winter but by that time Picasso and we had discovered each other and they did not have their show together. This is what Picabia told me and I was very surprised as at that time I never heard of Picabia.

When he was younger and young Picabia was very Spanish or rather very Cuban. He had the rather boring quality of the Cubans that mixture that one finds also in the South Americans of the old civilization that has not become new and the new civilization that never becomes new. Therein very different from Northern America which is all new, the old gets lost before it becomes new because the new is always becoming new.

Picabia now has lost a great deal of the Cuban. His grandfather was of course extremely French. He told us a nice story the other day. He never sees his French cousins any more although he has quantities of them but they all, he and the French cousins, do from time to time go to see the old concierges, janitors, Alsatians, who were caretakers for his grandfather and they ask the news about each other, and what, said they all to the concierge, is Picabia like now, they were all interested because he had just been given the legion of honor and a picture of his had just been accepted by the Luxembourg, and what, said Picabia to the concierge, did you answer when they asked you. Why I said exactly like his grandfather. And that is the true story of something that has been important in painting.

There was another funny photographic link. In those early days a photographer came to Paris and knew us all. He was Steichen. He had been one of Steiglitz' men and came over very excited about photography. Pretty soon he decided that ordinary painting did not interest him, one could do all that with photography, that is to say that the photographs of pictures looked just like the photographs of real landscapes or of still lives if they were good pictures, and so there must be something else and so he became very interested in modern painting and was one of those who told Steiglitz and the rest of them all about it.

ONE other funny thing happened at that time that I had forgotten all about and was reminded by a very nice letter from Lee Simonson. In those early days Simonson very young and very New York came to Paris. At Harvard he had been defending Monet and he came to Paris intending to carry on the crusade. He came to a Paris where there was no Monet to defend. Of course there was no Monet to defend. He was very upset by this but we all liked him because he told it to us.

Another thing in a little later than those days, in fact just after the war. Janet Scudder was getting tired of sculpture, she wanted to be a painter and paint. She said she always had wanted to be a painter and now the time had come. So she painted some pictures and wanted to send them to the new spring salon. There is a rule at the spring salon that a member of one cannot exhibit at another and Janet was a member of the old spring salon and so she could not exhibit at the new and she suggested to Alice B. Toklas that she Janet would exhibit under her name and Alice was amused and consented. Of course no one else was told anything about it. The picture was accepted and hung and we went over to look at it and brought home a catalogue. That evening Picasso came to the house. I showed him the catalogue. What he said, she has always painted and I never knew it. No I said she had never painted before she just painted this one picture and sent it to the salon and it was accepted. It is not possible he said angrily, it is not possible. Nobody who has never drawn or painted a picture can paint a first picture and send it to any

Gertrude Stein's studio on the rue de Fleurus in Paris

salon and have it accepted, it is not possible. But there you are, I said. It is not possible he answered stubbornly. He was terribly upset. He said that would upset everything if it were possible. The salons may not be great painting but you have to have a technique to pass the jury and if you never painted before it is not possible. He was so upset that I began to laugh. What is the story he demanded. I told him and he was so relieved. I knew he said that it was not possible. It just could not be possible otherwise nothing would have any meaning.

Even now A. B. Toklas gets catalogues of paints sent to her faithfully by art shops in hopes that she will yet paint another picture.

But now. Paris has changed and I have changed and I am no longer frightened and I will just as well change again but at present it is all very changed.

I write the way I used to write in The Making of Americans, I wander around. I come home and I write, I write in one copybook and I copy what I write into another copy-book and I write and I write. Just at present I write about American religion and Grant, Ulysses Simpson Grant, and I have come back to write the way I used to write and this is because now everything that is happening is once more happening inside, there is no use in the outside, if you see the outside you see just what you look at and that is no longer interesting, everybody says

so or at least everybody acts so and they are right because now there is no use in looking at anything. If it is going to change it is of no interest and if it is not going to change it is of no interest and so what is the use of looking, everything you see is what nobody looks at and so just as so long ago everything went on inside now everything goes on inside. Incidentally, there is a new young painter and when I know more about him I will tell about him.

And so the time comes when I can tell the history of my life.

GUSTAVE V OF SWEDEN, IN ACTION

KING FUAD OF EGYPT VISITS CLEO, HIS FAVORITE BISON

Culver Service

Even Kings Relax

Six assorted monarchs shown happily at play

"FORE!" FOR THE AGHA KHAN

KING OF SIAM, UNMOUNTED

KING CAROL OF RUMANIA (*left*) IN HIS EASTER BONNET

KING GEORGE AND QUEEN MARY HAVE FUN ON THEIR DAY OFF

Beaton

CECIL BEATON, THE PHOTOGRAPHER, AT EASE

MISS GERTRUDE LAWRENCE, ENGLISH ACTRESS, RELAXES, AMID CHIFFON

Celebrities in Bed

Four assorted personalities shown relaxing

MISS EDITH SITWELL HAS HER MORNING TEA AND CRUMPETS

The subject of our Great Ones in bed is one to intrigue the imagination of the masses. That they do go to bed is a premise we must all take for granted, since visual proof of it is difficult to snare. At considerable pains, and risk to life and limbs, *Vanity Fair*'s photographers have assembled the accompanying photographs which show our lions *couchant* on divers beds. Here you may see Gertrude Lawrence, swathed in chiffons, furs and satins; Edith Sitwell, wearing a turban in lieu of a nightcap; and, in addition, Dr. Einstein's blanket and the modest cot of Cecil Beaton.

Acme

ALBERT EINSTEIN, READY FOR A NAP

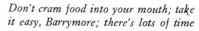

Don't whisper in public, and this goes for Mrs. James Roosevelt and Mrs. Cornelius Vanderbilt too. Fie, ladies!

Don't cram food into your mouth; take it easy, Barrymore; there's lots of time

Don't dunk, Senator Long; remember your constituents

Don't point, Governor of the Bank of England or not, don't point

Don't put your elbow on the table, G. B. Stern; no nice novelist does

Hey, You—
Mind Your Manners!

Tchk-tchk! Mrs. Emily Post has her work cut out for her among these celebrities, here depicted committing nine varieties of mayhem on the social graces. A Vanderbilt whispering in public—what, indeed, is the world coming to? In presenting (with raised eyebrows) this little object lesson in what not to do, *Vanity Fair* makes no comment, except, again, to say, *tchk-tchk.*

Don't rub the nose while eating; offender, Billy de Beck (Barney Google)

Don't syphon water out of your mouth, Mr. Montgomery—please!

Don't drink beer (or anything else) while wearing a hat, Mr. Irvin Cobb

Don't slouch in your witness chairs, mes petits Mdivanis; remember noblesse oblige

The Bucharest Du Barry

Lupescu Perpetuates the Grand Tradition of the Royal Favorite

JOHN GUNTHER

THEY say in Bucharest, those who know (and in Bucharest there are plenty who know), that old Papa Lupescu came to his daughter Magda some months ago, walking the hundred yards that separate his automobile accessories shop from the royal palace, and proceeded to lecture her smartly. There was scandal in Bucharest. The amorous court was being amorous again. King Carol had settled, as it were, down. But his younger brother Nicholas was acting up. Nicholas was about to commit marriage with a girl not exactly regal. "Daughter, daughter!" old Lupescu scolded. "What kind of a family are you getting mixed into!"

Indeed, the point might be made that Magda Lupescu, the King's Favorite, is the most respectable person in Rumania. She lives in a country monstrously corrupt and monstrously licentious, but her fidelity to King Carol, a scamp, is notorious. She sins in the flesh but shines in the spirit; she is loyal, she is discreet, and she has character. Being a King's Favorite is one of the most conspicuous jobs going, and inside Rumania she fills it unostentatiously. She is the most famous female in the kingdom, but probably not twenty people outside her immediate circle have ever seen her.

Magda Lupescu is a striking anachronism. Kings are dull folk these days. Royal mistresses, like court jesters, have practically been driven from the field by the cruel rationalizations of the twentieth century. Magda Lupescu is a last, but not forlorn, survivor. Yet, conservatively speaking, there must be about 100,000,000 women in the world today who cherish the secret, perilous wish to be mistress to a king. Lupescu alone has made the grade.

Louise de La Vallière was the daughter of an officer; Magda Lupescu of a Jewish junk-dealer. Nell Gwynn sold oranges in Drury Lane; Lupescu frequented that most inveterately Balkan of hotels, the Athena Palace of Bucharest. Lola Montez was born in Limerick, Ireland, went to Spain and India, and was mistress of Mad King Ludwig of Bavaria; Lupescu's stage has been smaller, but she picked a king who isn't, for all his peccadillos, crazy. Her mileage is good. Montez lasted a year as King's Mistress; Du Barry five years; La Vallière seven years. Lupescu has been with Carol since 1924.

She met him, so the gossips say, by a pleasant bit of trickery. She knew that he

MAGDA LUPESCU

was returning to Bucharest one fine evening after dinner in Sinaia, and she contrived to ambush him along the lonely mountain road. She planted herself there, tore off some of her clothes, let down her red hair, and staggered into the searchlights of his car. He lurched to a stop, "rescued" her, and carried her back to Bucharest and destiny.

Her flaming hair and vigorous good looks burst for the first time in the tabloids of the world a year later, when Carol "abdicated." It has been said that he gave up his crown for her, but this is not exactly true. Carol was the victim of a frameup, and the comely person of Lupescu no more than a lever in the hands of his enemies, the Bratianu brothers, who really ruled Rumania. They were out to "get" Carol, the unruly crown prince. They did. Carol was shipped out of the country to attend the funeral in London of Dowager Queen Alexandra, in 1925, and he took Lupescu with him. Reaching Milan on his return, he found messages from the Bratianus to come back to Rumania at once, without his mistress, or forfeit the crown. Carol had been victimized in other matters by the Bratianus and he lost his temper, telegraphing them to go to hell. The Bratianus persuaded King Ferdinand and Queen Marie, Carol's parents, to accept the renunciation at its face value; Carol was instantly disinherited and his royal honors removed, and the "abdication" accepted. Thus began the five years of his

exile, during which Lupescu never once left his side.

They lived first at Neuilly, near Paris, and then on the Riviera. They did not have much money. Newspaper men have seen Lupescu on the back porch of a modest villa, doing the family washing. Her hold on Carol grew. She made him forget his first wife, Zizi Lambrino, and his second, Helene of Greece; she made him remember, when Ferdinand died and his son Michael took the throne, that he was still King of Rumania. When Carol flew back to Bucharest in June, 1930, and grabbed the crown from Michael's head, she followed him in a week or two—smuggled across the frontier in a black wig.

The situation was piquant. Queen Helene had divorced Carol in exile. He made her tentative offers of reconciliation, because he wanted coronation, and he could not be crowned without a queen. Helene would accept only if Carol promised to give up Lupescu. This he resolutely refused to do. Irritated at Helene, he presently removed her from the country, and Lupescu became the queen in everything but name. Ever since, she has been the virtual ruler of Rumania.

Lupescu was installed in a comfortable villa on the outskirts of town. Officially, Carol could not be seen with her. So a sort of double court grew up: inside the regular circle Carol and Lupescu founded an inner camarilla. Carol spent less and less time in the official court. He could not bear to be separated from Lupescu. Soon the double domicile in Bucharest became a nuisance, and he came to prefer residence in Sinaia, the summer capital. In Bucharest he was hemmed in by whispers and whisperers; in Sinaia, a lovely mountain village a couple of hours from Bucharest, he created a sort of private Zenda all his own. Carol spends most of his time in Sinaia now. Sinaia became the headquarters of the Lupescu clique.

Lupescu is practically an ideal mistress. She has no desire to marry Carol. She could, if she wanted to, at the snap of a finger; but she knows full well that this might mean the end of the dynasty. She is not avaricious, and he has never given her more than normal gifts. She lets him play around—a bit— when he wants to. She has not burdened him with children (and Madame de Montespan, be it remembered, inflicted on Louis XIV no fewer than seven). She is a sensible adviser on politics. Her influence on him is enormous.

Politics may, however, be her doom, and if she falls Carol may fall with her.

People say freely in Bucharest that Michael will again be king before Carol dies—that it would not be utterly surprising if Carol should skip, if things get too hot, again in Lupescu's company. It takes a lot of dreary work to be a king, even in Rumania. Ciro's and Chantilly were ever so much more fun. Lupescu may prefer ironing shirts to ironing out the incessant contradictions of Rumanian domestic politics. Not that she would need to do the washing nowadays. If Carol hasn't saved something from his pretty civil list, all Rumania's a fool.

ist assassinated the prime minister, Jon Duca, on December 30, 1933, and the country (which is unused to such masculine deeds) all but expired in panic.

The Iron Guard movement was so particularly dangerous for Carol because it had a concrete object for its antisemitism—Lupescu. The King's Mistress is Jewish. Lupescu came to incarnate the discontent of the rich, sprawling country. Rumania was smothering under its glut of grain. Salaries were unpaid. The budget was split wide open. The peasants were starving. For these ills Lupescu, a conspicuously shining target for calumny, came to be blamed. Violent outbursts against her began—because she is Jewish, because she is the heart of the camarilla, because she keeps the King out of

Monsieur Titulescu, who is not interested in mistresses, royal or otherwise. Carol was torn between the woman he loved and the man whose services were indispensable. Titulescu demanded that he break up the Sinaia clique, and discharge not only the two men whom Maniu had tried to get rid of the year before, but even General Stangaciu, the chief of police, and young Poui Dimitrescu, Carol's own private secretary, and next to Lupescu the most powerful personage in all backstairs Rumania. Carol was confronted with the necessity of dismissing his cronies in order to get what he needed more—a government. Titulescu is a voluble and pertinacious man. He won. Carol's friends went. Titulescu consented to enter the government, and Rumania, such as it is, was saved.

Behind this struggle, the core of which was the person of Lupescu, much more than the petty warfare of Ins and Outs in Rumania was at stake. What was at stake was the position of Rumania in Europe. Traditionally a loyal member of the Little Entente and an ally of France, the Rumanians had begun to veer toward Germany. The Iron Guard was Fascist. The army was discontented with French policy. Carol himself is, after all, a Hohenzollern. Like all countries, Rumania is in the business of nationhood for what it brings her, and it seemed, at the turn of the year, that affiliation with Germany might bring her most, as Germany began to supersede France as *the* European power.

Even Titulescu did not dare ask the dismissal of Lupescu herself. He is no fool, Titulescu. He realizes that no one can ask Carol that and survive. Moreover, he represents a strong pro-French tendency, and so does Lupescu because she remembers happily her years in Paris and because she knows that a pro-Hitler, anti-Semite government in Rumania would give her short shrift indeed. The other Du Barry perished on the guillotine. Lupescu and Titulescu, emotional antagonists, became strategic allies. While the clique was blown up and most of Carol's intimates exiled, Lupescu stayed.

Then, in April, 1934, thirty army officers were suddenly arrested, charged with a fantastic plot to murder Lupescu and the King. The chief conspirator was none other than Colonel Vladimir Precup, the brilliant officer who had engineered Carol's return to Rumania in 1930, and one of his best friends. Precup, the story goes, went to the palace, and demanded that the King dismiss the lovely Magda. The King threw him out and ordered him shadowed. It was known that the army was being corrupted by Iron Guard influence. A military court had freed the Iron Guardists responsible for the Duca murder. Precup, desperate, organized a conspiracy to kill not only Lupescu but the

Champagne supper on the Riviera: Carol, Lupescu, and friend

But more likely than voluntary departure is the possibility—still remote—that Carol may be kicked out, and largely on Lupescu's account.

In February, 1933, the battle against Lupescu reached its first climax. The Jesuit Transylvanian leader, Julius Maniu, was prime minister at the time, and he demanded the dismissal from office of two men high in the Sinaia camarilla. Carol proved stronger in this first fierce clash. The king's cronies were retained in their posts, and Maniu was dismissed.

During the next year a formidable revolutionary movement grew in Rumania, partly encouraged by Maniu's party. An organization known as the Iron Guard (or Knights of the Archangel Michael), mustered 200,000 fanatics pledged to the "cleansing of Rumania," the rebirth of its national life—and the extermination of the Jews. It was one of the sub-Hitler quicksilvers streaming across Europe. It sought to put Rumania into Fascist hands. An Iron Guard-

Bucharest, because on account of her he cannot be crowned.

The Duca killing left Rumania shaken. Foreign office functionaries showed their fright with disconcerting candor. Carol's Sinaia palace was guarded by frozen-faced sentries every hundred yards. Carol missed a great opportunity to show that bullets which could kill a prime minister could not scare a king when, at the last moment, he funked appearing at Duca's funeral. It was said that the Iron Guardists had prepared a death list of twenty or thirty people doomed to assassination—with Lupescu as Number One.

Enter, then, Monsieur Nicolas Titulescu, the smartest living Rumanian, the only Rumanian with real international prestige, and a character of peculiarly fabulous quality. He refused to enter the new government as its foreign minister until Carol promised some drastic housecleaning. For a week a titanic struggle took place behind the scenes between Lupescu, the King's Mistress, and whole royal family, by bombing them at Easter service in Bucharest cathedral. Only in this way might Rumania be "cleaned," he and his fellow officers thought. But Precup was caught, and after a sensational trial he and his confederates got ten years in prison. Presumably Carol and Lupescu may now live in peace.

Carol, his friends say, will never give her up. Her own fidelity is likely to be as constant, even though, as Emerson said, every hero becomes a bore at last. She has had an amusing life and has proved that in Rumania at least vice is its own reward, and very sweet, too. She has no wedding ring; but Carol has given her a kingdom. Du Barry lost her head, but smart Magda Lupescu will never lose hers, even in the non-decapitatory sense.

Over the body of Nell Gwynn the prelate who became Archbishop of Canterbury preached the funeral sermon. All the patriarchs of Rumania would do like service for Lupescu. But she is probably not to be tempted by spiritual rewards.

KATHARINE HEPBURN

Bryn Mawr's celebrated alumna and Hartford's pride

She has enhanced the quality of the screen with her luminous portrayals in *Bill of Divorcement, Morning Glory* and as the unforgettable Jo in *Little Women.*

Beaton

The Street

ALLAN SEAGER

"YES, it's spring all right. The big elm is just turning green. Looks like a green mist over the boughs. And the hunch-backed old lady is digging and raking at that patch of lawn in front of her house."

It was spring now. For three months he had not seen a tree, lying there in the clean bare room. But Whitaker, in the bed by the window, could see the street below. He was always talking, as he was talking now, about the old lady, about the first green shoots and foliage, and about the little typist— he said she was a typist and pretty too— who passed every morning and evening. All day long he lay there, sick and still, staring at the gray wall and listening enviously to Whitaker. His vision of the street he could not see grew like a mosaic on the wall. Every day Whitaker gave him something new—a dog-fight or a householder smoking in his garden. These he would insert carefully into the whole and trim and polish until the wall almost became a window through which he too could see the street.

THERE was nothing else to do but listen. Books had grown stale and reading hurt his eyes. When his friends came to visit him they said always the same thing. Of course he was not feeling better. Didn't they understand that tuberculosis was not like the colic? One didn't get well over night. The only thing was to lie and contemplate one's navel and wonder how the trees looked in the street outside.

He wished he had the bed by the window instead of Whitaker. Then he could look out and watch not only the leaves unfurl and the flowers spring up but the people in the street as well. If he could see them coming and going, it would be quite easy for him to feel himself a part of things again. Besides, he thought, Whitaker preened himself on having such a fine place, though God knows there was no reason why he should. The doctor had assigned the beds. And Whitaker had begun to use what seemed a superior tone, as if one could not understand what a motor or a hand-organ was, or even a tree. He was certain it was a superior tone. As if one were a child. Yes, it was clear that Whitaker held one end of the thread that led back into what he was coming to call "life." And he was coming to hate Whitaker because he held it. At first he was astonished at his own baseness. He had always regarded himself as a decent fellow. He did not know that confinement and disease can taint decency. "Silly nonsense. It is all really beneath my notice. I am thirty years old. I am a man and men do not—" The naïveté of the process disgusted him but he went through it like a rosary every day for a while and sometimes he was polite to Whitaker afterward. As the days went by, all alike, he hated Whitaker simply and did not think about the baseness.

Whitaker's heart attacks evened things up. They were the price he paid for the best bed. It was quite reasonable. One could not have everything gratis. Sometimes in the night Whitaker would sit upright in the bed choking and panting. His heart would beat two hundred to the minute. It was very hard to get enough air into his rotting lungs. At the first movement he would be sharp awake and he would watch Whitaker's shoulders heave and his head jerk. Then with a feeling of condescension he would press the button to call the night nurse. Usually she could relieve Whitaker but often when it was very bad, doctors would be called. They came partly dressed and yawning. They would lean over Whitaker in the dark room and talk in low voices. The paroxysms were dangerous when they went on too long, for both his lungs were partly collapsed, and if his heart were not slowed down, he might die for lack of air. Resting on his elbow in the far bed, he would watch with secret satisfaction as if justice were being done. Even in the night when he was waked from sleeping, he was angry with Whitaker.

ALL through the hot summer when the empty days sped quickly by the window, the anger grew and festered in him like a sore he could not leave alone. His rare spasms of remorse were short and his thoughts returned to it with a kind of maddening gravity. He would recite to himself, like an old tale from a story-book, the walking tour in Brittany or his battle with the trout, but just as he was ready with the net, had got a firm footing in the swirling water, Whitaker would begin about some children in the street and he would be snatched back to be hot and sick again in his cursed narrow room. "Twisting the knife," he thought bitterly. He was sure Whitaker knew it hurt always to hear about the street and never to see.

At dusk his fever rose and as the room grew dim his head ached and the daytime clarity vanished. When he looked at the pale oblong of the window, it seemed to him a gateway and beyond it were all the joy and brightness he had been forced to forsake. If he could only stand by the gate and look out—but no, there was Whitaker, like a demon guarding the way. It was the gateway to life, and in the darkness Whitaker's gaunt face began to assume the shape and hollows of a skull. He was Death of course. Echoes and memories of the church arose in his mind, confusing him. Phrases about Death and Life, solemn and distorted, he remembered from hymns and prayer-books. If he could vanquish Death, why, he would be granted everlasting Life.

"The little typist just passed. She's got a posy."

"And you would kill her if you had the chance, just as you would kill me," he would mutter to himself. Suddenly one night he saw his course clearly: he would not press the button. When he heard Whitaker begin to twitch and pant he would not press the button. The nurse would not come and Whitaker would die. Through the steaming days of the late summer, when the street outside was full of people that he could not see; while Whitaker lay describing with brutal completeness these men and women who were well and strong, who could walk up and down the city and go on holidays, he stared at the bare gray wall smiling over his secret. The nurse would find him when she made her rounds. The doctors would come, shaking their heads and clucking. They would wheel him out on a stretcher with a sheet over him. Then he would have the bed by the window. He would look out upon the world again and this would make him well. No, the next time—or the time after—he would not press the button.

So he became slyly polite. Instead of hearing Whitaker in a barbed and sullen silence, he began to reply, even to question him with false vivacity. This was difficult for when he looked toward the other bed, he felt a horrible disgust. The endless nights of fever had imprinted the image of Death on Whitaker. Even though the sun was in the room, he saw the fleshless sockets and the bone. He always thought of Whitaker as "He" now, and in dealing with such an adversary one must be courteous so that he may not suspect. By this time he never doubted that he was right. He was even righteous.

One evening when the autumn rains had set in, and the wind pried at the window, Whitaker lay supported by his pillows, looking out.

"You should see the lamps flicker in the street. Winter will be here soon."

"See Him, see Death," he thought, "high over the city, urging on in his heart the winds and the cold. He wants the year to die also."

If he could watch over the city from that vantage point—it seemed to him a tower—he would bring back the year. Firm on that parapet, he would have the power, somehow, to make this bleak season blossom as the rose. That was it: "Blossom as the rose." He would make it warm and pleasant, not cold like the night outside and never so hot as his head felt now, but warm and green with bright flowers, and the people would be happy always. But he must have the tower so he could watch and see that nothing went wrong. Death stood in the way, and over Him he must gain the victory.

A sigh came from the other bed. Whitaker was asleep.

If it could only happen tonight! Punishment was long overdue. It must happen tonight, for had He not lounged there at His ease contriving evil things in His heart, monstrous things against the year itself? Surely these wicked desires would weigh heavily on His heart and make it beat too fast. This was but just retribution, the wages of sin. Soon.

THE wind spat hard raindrops against the window. He turned and muttered seeking a cool place on the pillow. Suddenly there was a gasp and Whitaker lurched upright in his bed panting and choking. Dim against the window like a shadow, he could see Him writhe and struggle for air. It sounded like a dog that had run too far. This was the time. Now He would die. He smiled quietly into the darkness and waited for Him to stop heaving and panting and shaking the bed and die. It was a very bad attack, and at the end Whitaker gave a series of long dry sobs. Presently the sobbing stopped and the room was still, except for the echo of the wind. He looked over

cautiously. At last. He was dead. In the morning when the street shone in the sun, he would go to the tower and keep watch over the city.

In the morning the bed next the window was empty. When the house physician made his rounds, he asked him, "Would it be possible for me to have that bed there?"

The physician wore a white coat. He stood making notes in a book. "Why yes, I think so," he said. "Pity you didn't hear poor Whitaker last night. You might have saved him."

"I save Him?"

"Yes, you could have pressed the button for the nurse."

"Yes. I might have."

The doctor went out and the nurses moved him to the bed by the window. Calmly, without haste, he arranged the pillows, making ready to look out as one who had come into a kingdom. But when he looked, it was not into a sunlit street. There were no trees. Below him was a rear courtyard of the hospital, a blank place, and all day long it was quite empty.

MISTINGUETT

The lady of the fabled legs

Mistinguett was born just outside of Paris in, probably, 1875. After many years in obscure French music halls, she made her Paris debut in 1907, at the *Folies-Dramatiques*. Her one American appearance was in 1923, in a Shubert revue. She is still the greatest revue star in Europe, and is back again this season at the *Folies-Bergère*.

A Valentine for Mr. Woollcott

DOROTHY PARKER

WHEN I was young and charming—at which time practically nobody in the land was safe from buffalos—the literary quarters of the town were loud with indignation against the dark and infrequent crime of log-rolling. Indignation, in fact, is a rather small word for the fury of feeling that spread and deepened until it became generally accepted that anyone who would praise a friend would steal a horse. You might set fire to widows, deflower orphans, or filch the flags from soldiers' graves, and still be invited to all the literary teas; but if you admired, in print, the traits and achievements of any member of your acquaintance, your jig was up. And if you couldn't stand up and put a revolver to your head, like a man, the only thing for you to do was to streak for Port Said, and become Hoppy Dick, the human derelict.

The fear of becoming a log-roller was put into me during my formative years, and there was a good long stretch during which, in my endeavors to keep clean of the ugly charge, I said only the vile of my nearest and dearest. If there were not enough outrageous things to be said in honesty, I made them up and swore by them. It was nice work, while it lasted, only pretty soon I didn't have a friend in the world and became known as the Lone Wolf. Then I found that, with a refreshing suddenness, the tumult against log-rolling had ceased, and it was as safe to write honestly of a friend as if you were in your own bed. I do not know quite what happened. Perhaps,

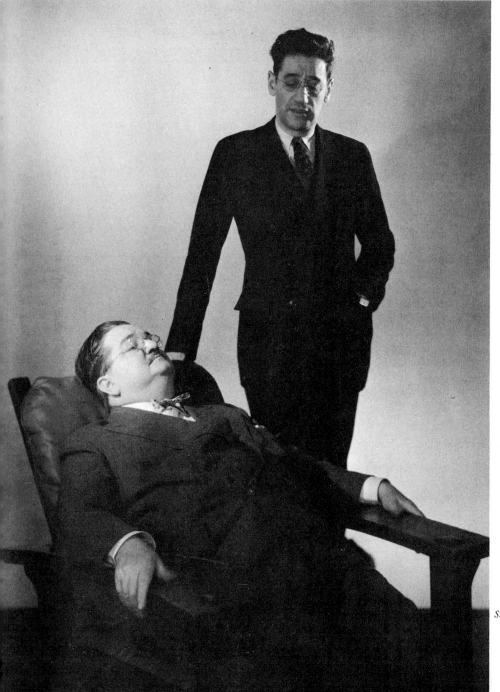

GEORGE S. KAUFMAN
and
ALEXANDER WOOLLCOTT

Steichen

as your morning paper will tell you, everything is ever so much better now, or perhaps people found they had enough troubles without bothering their curly heads over the tributes wrung from one writer to another. Anyway, there is little or no shuddering about log-rolling going on these days, and it is with a blessed sense of emancipation that I may here set down a few facts in the life of Mr. Alexander Humphries Woollcott—whom I have known for fourteen years and never a cross word—without feeling that if I don't say he is illiterate, venal, and a love-child, I must live out my days a marked woman.

ALEXANDER WOOLLCOTT was born in Phalanx, no kidding, New Jersey, in a gently strange community of which his grandfather was a founder. The idea was that everybody was to live in one vast establishment, which still stands large as life, and raise their own food and live happily ever after; and so, apparently, they did. It seems to have been an enchanted existence, perhaps due in part to the presence of a beguiling gentleman who got back to Mother Earth by painting his room in three great stripes of brown, green, and blue, and taking daily sand-baths. The father of the infant Alexander was a man of introspective nature who kept getting his feelings hurt and moving to another town, and dutifully the family went where he did, even unto Kansas City. Nor has Kansas City forgotten that the boy who was to grow up to be co-author of *The Channel Road* once dwelt there; today a splendid bulldog named Alexander Woollcott, to the very point of spelling it with all those double letters, is one of the prides of the place.

We next find our hero in Philadelphia, I forget by what process of reasoning, where he lived alone through his high school days and supported himself by his precocious pen. He reviewed books, and there was some pretty fast work done about taking them around the corner and selling them as soon as he had damned their contents. Once he entered an essay contest, won in a walk, and was awarded a gold medal, which he quickly sold, for sentiment was not yet in him. In Philadelphia he met some enthusiastic alumni of Hamilton College, so that was where he went next and back there he still goes whenever he is allowed time. It is to Hamilton, I think, that he will go when he dies, if he is good.

Then he came to New York—don't we all?—found that he was a reporter and ripped his nerves to fringe working on murder cases. So they made him dramatic critic, possibly to give him a chance to sit down. Then came That War, which occasionally creeps into his writings, and then he came back to more dramatic criticism, and then he began shooting out in all directions. But always his love, his sweet, his ladye faire is the stage, and he cannot stay long away from her. With his friend George Kaufman he wrote *The Channel Road,* of which I can only say that I didn't see it, and later he was persuaded—I imagine someone dropped a hat—to tread the boards himself in a play called *Brief Moment,* which, in an engaging manner, he stole right from under its star's pretty little nose. His part required him to lie around on couches a good deal and utter wearied epigrams and experienced advice—a rôle of which Mr. Donald Ogden Stewart remarked that no matter how thin you sliced it, it was still Polonius.

Still he is faithful to the stage, although his bi-weekly outings with her wicked stepsister, the radio, might be considered mild cheating. He loves to talk over the radio, he actually loves it; and certainly his civilized gossip along the air has gained him thousands of friends—which in his case was painted lilies to Newcastle. But the play is ever the thing with him, and his and Mr. Kaufman's *The Dark Tower* is, it seems to me, as skilled and entertaining an exhibit as you will find in the town. And I wish to God that were higher praise.

APART from his work—or perhaps because of it—he has, I think, the most enviable life I know; and it is all his own doing. He plans the pattern of his days, sees its whole fine shape and all its good colors, and then follows it. He is predisposed to like people and things, in the order named, and that is his gift from Heaven and his career, also in the order named. He has, I should think, between seven and eight hundred intimate friends, with all of whom he converses only in terms of atrocious insult. It is not, it is true, a mark of his affection if he insults you once or twice; but if he addresses you outrageously all the time, then you know you're in.

Alexander Woollcott has been told he looks like Chesterton, but he seems to me to resemble less Chesterton than one of his paradoxes. He is a vast man, not tall; mightily built, with tiny hands and feet. Caricatures of himself always delight him, no matter how they were intended. His apartment is hung with black-and-white libels of Woollcott. That apartment is just what you've always wanted, and so, I am sure, has he. It stands over the East River, so that through a great sheet of plate glass you can look across to Welfare Island or look down and see the corpses drifting lazily by, and there is one whole blessed room given over to shelf above shelf of books about murder. Murder is Mr. Woollcott's other love; it is, to date, unrequited.

It is a shade sad, for one who lives from hand to sheriff, to know that Alexander Woollcott has that apartment, all for his own, and then keeps leaving it. In the first place, he is encumbered with a passion for rather huge dogs, and as soon as he enters delightedly into their possession, he has to take country houses for them. And, besides, he travels like a forest fire. Turn your back, and the man is in Shanghai. He sails invariably with a bleeding heart for those he leaves behind, and three days out he has a complete new outfit of dear ones. It is his boast that, were he lifted from the thousand arms of his friends and dropped in some small, strange town, in two weeks the affairs of that town would be his affairs and if someone mentioned New York to him, he would have to think for several minutes before he could place it. But I think, myself, he ought to smile when he says that.

He is at the same time the busiest man I know and the most leisured. He even has time for the dear lost arts—letter-writing and conversation. It is a good thing to hear real, shaped, shining talk, in these days when halves of sentences are left hanging miserably in the air, with nothing better to sustain them than an "at least, I mean," or an "oh, *you* know." And it is a good thing to know that someone is writing letters and, as a reward, receiving them. It makes you feel that all *that* is being taken care of, and so you can just sit back and take off those heavy shoes. The Lord alone knows where he finds the hours for all he does, though I suppose that those who have always enthusiasm have, also, always time. Alexander Woollcott's enthusiasm is his trademark; you know that never has he written a piece strained through boredom. Sometimes, indeed, there are those who feel that he lets himself be carried away, though in a winning way, and gives perhaps over-generously of his sentiments in his printed words. It was Howard Dietz, God bless him, who, on reading one curiously lace-edged bit of prose, referred to its author as Louisa M. Woollcott.

Alexander Woollcott likes to work; I give you my word, he likes working. He does it rapidly and surely and, you know darn well, expertly. And he likes it. That is the worst thing I know about him; to me, the sight of someone enjoying work is the affront direct. Well. That's the way he is. He is my friend—he can do no wrong. I suppose. Maybe it would be better to slide over that side of him, if the phrase does not conjure up too difficult a picture, and go on to the best thing I know about him. That is that he does more kindness than anyone I have ever known; and I have learned that not from him but from the people who have experienced it.

(*Note to Mr. Woollcott: Dear Alex, now will you marry me? Dorothy.*)

Nominated for the Hall of Fame: 1934

ROBERT MOSES

Because in his new position as Park Commissioner of New York City he will have an opportunity to try to fulfill his ambition of eliminating nightmare bottlenecks; and because he is partly responsible for that most beautiful of civic playgrounds, Jones Beach.

Blank & Stoller

Steichen

ELISSA LANDI

Because after studying to be a ballet dancer, a pianist, and a mezzo-soprano, and becoming proficient in all three, she decided to be an actress; because being an actress has not prevented her from publishing four novels; because she has redeemed an unbroken succession of bad pictures by her good performances; and because she is the daughter of Countess Zenardi-Landi and the granddaughter of Empress Elizabeth of Austria.

SHIRLEY TEMPLE

Because she was a motion-picture actress at three and a star at five; because she sings in tune and dances tap and ballet without a tumble; because, in *Little Miss Marker,* she made a delightful entertainment out of a sorry picture; and because she has won the heart of America without losing her own head.

Fox

VINCENT SHEEAN

Because, though most widely known as the author of *The Tide,* he is a true eclectic, having been a war correspondent at twenty-one, head of a world radio expedition, a prisoner in the Riff, besides speaking four languages fluently; because he is now devoting his time to writing; and because, after such a career, he resents being considered a Richard Harding Davis character.

CLARE BOOTHE BROKAW

Because she has written a play, *Naomi's Daughter;* because her book, *Stuffed Shirts,* was an authentic and merciless satire on New York society; because she is now writing a newspaper column; because she was formerly managing editor of *Vanity Fair;* and because she combines a fragile blondness with a will of steel.

Pinchot

Blunders in Print

Some of the Great Calamities, Oddities, and Strokes of Malice
Perpetrated by Word-mauling Type-Setters or Numskull Reporters

EDMUND PEARSON

WHEN Thomas W. Lawson entered his yacht in the trial races, to choose a defender for the *America's* Cup, one especially enthusiastic reporter followed the fleet down the harbor. Returning in the dusk of the evening, his soul aglow, he composed a column or two, full of lyric rapture, for the *Boston Evening Transcript.* He struck his top note in this sentence: "Both yachts presented a gorgeous appearance as they rounded the outer mark, well heeled over, their crews perched up to windward, their bronze bottoms shining in the ruddy light of sunset."

This example of what *Punch* used to describe as "Things We Would Have Expressed Otherwise" shows that we sometimes hastily adopt the phrase "printer's error" for what is really the author's fault. The printer, has, in reality, dutifully followed copy. It is a question which has the most destructive power: the writer or the compositor? The type-setter is able to work wonders; and by juggling a single letter he may turn a sweetly solemn thought into something to provoke the snickers of the irreverent.

Thus, when the vice-president, Theodore Roosevelt, succeeded to the highest office, on the death of President McKinley, the brief ceremony took place in a private residence in Buffalo. A New York editor, impressed by the significance of the event, desired to contrast it with the splendor of a recent coronation in Europe. But—the compositor, coming to the word "oath" in the editor's manuscript, struck the wrong key for the first letter, and the sentence appeared: "For sheer democratic dignity, nothing could exceed the moment when, surrounded by the Cabinet and a few distinguished citizens, Mr. Roosevelt took his simple bath, as President of the United States."

And the fact that the devil sometimes gets into the types seemed clear when a London newspaper copied the passage in order to comment upon it. The blunder was *repeated* in the quotation, and the vision was renewed of the President, not with one hand resting on the Bible, but vigorously splashing in his tub.

These mistakes love to cluster around the eminent and the dignified. New York never had a more worthy citizen than James Lenox, whose rare books are among the chief treasures of the New York Public Library. All the greater was the horror of Laurence Hutton, preparing an article for *Harper's Weekly,* when he came within an ace of reminding New Yorkers that they ought to be grateful for "the receipt of the vest buttons of James Lenox." What he meant to say was "vast benefits."

Once I attended a meeting of librarians in the Yosemite Valley, going there for the purpose of speaking a few wise words. Leading me, on the program, was a distinguished woman, who, like myself, had once been a librarian, but, unlike me, had become a celebrated novelist and poet. The type-setter, who printed the program, was so niggardly as to omit the letter "l" from one important word, so that this blameless lady was announced to speak on: "Books From the Pubic Angle."

Two or three cynics remarked that most books, nowadays, are written from that angle. However, the novelist had no such cause for complaint as had Mr. Witter Bynner, when he read his poems in Des Moines. One of the newspapers reported the event, and (although Des Moines lacks not for songsters) desired to make clear the name of the chief bard on this occasion. Again, a stingy compositor omitted one letter ("e," this time) so that Mr. Bynner was described as "the pot of the evening." Nobody could have taken it more graciously. He remarked: "They probably thought it was a recital of chamber music."

SPEAKING of music recalls a discovery of Arthur Guiterman's when editing a weekly which was printed in the same shop as the *Musical Courier.* The rule of the shop was "No abbreviations," and the head proof-reader was laughing over a mistake in a Boston concert program. "Gounod's Fourth Mass" had been converted into a regimental history by being printed, "Gounod's Fourth Massachusetts." At this moment, Mr. Guiterman happened to glance at some of the *Courier* proofs, in which a careful compositor had expanded "Bach's Fifth *Ave Maria*" into "Bach's Fifth Avenue Maria."

Occasionally, when an error appears in the proof, it is best to leave bad enough alone. Bret Harte must have been a very young editor, and inexperienced in correcting proof, when he was conducting the *Weekly Gazette* of Red Dog—if that's the name of the mining camp. He wrote the obituary notice of a most respectable lady, Mrs. Euphemia McGilligan, and closed with the remark that "above all the ladies of this town, she was distinguished for her charity." This came back from the press-room: "distinguished for her *chastity.*" Instead of making the correction, he merely put a mark of query on the margin of the proof, with the result that, next day, Red Dog saw in its newspaper, that "Mrs. McGilligan above all the ladies of this town, was distinguished for her chastity (?)".

The blunders of foreigners, in translating English, are a needed consolation to both Briton and Yankee. They soothe us in hours of humiliation, when we have perpetrated one of those mistakes recounted in Brander Matthews' hilarious essay "On the French spoken by those who do not speak French."

Familiar though it be, there is always delight in the story of the Frenchman who translated Cibber's play, *Love's Last Shift,* as *La dernière chemise de l'amour,* and the farce, *Hit or Miss,* as *Frappé ou Mademoiselle.* Less known, perhaps, is the explanation of the Parisian scholar, who was struggling to render *Macbeth* in French, and gave the cry of the witches, "Hail! all hail!" as *"grêle, toujours grêle"* on the ground that "it always snows in Scotland." A French traveler in Utah, sixty years ago, wrote of the head of the Mormon Church as "Brigham *le jeune,*" and I have seen a very intelligent French book on American journalism, whose author had been stumped by the Cleveland *Plain Dealer.* He called it *Le simple marchand.*

Arnold Bennett said of limericks that "the best ones are entirely unprintable." And this, harrow and alas, is, in a measure, true of those printed blunders which excite raucous laughter in the smoking-room (Victorian phrase!) and cause the hair of publishers to turn prematurely white.

Newspapers have paid heavy damages for the accidental transposition of a letter or two, with results which were too close to libel. Even today, in London newspaper offices, the tale is told of the spiteful compositor on *The Times,* who inserted into the report of a stodgy speech by an eminent Cabinet Minister, a remark concerning his choice of amusements, which made single copies of that edition of *The Times* fetch £5 in the clubs.

PROOF-READERS on Washington papers still shudder at the fate of their two brethren who were given the sack for failing to notice the omission of a single syllable with results which justly ruffled the most austere of our recent Presidents. And on Boston's Washington Street, newspaper men always seem to hear the tramp of feet, as the Mayor of a Massachusetts city, flanked by attorneys, all breathing fire and slaughter, came to certain editorial offices to demand a retraction and apology for a misprint, although it passed the wit of man to devise any apology which was not worse than the original offense. And all for an error in one letter!

One historic calamity occurred in the press-room of a rural newspaper; a careful publication, a sort of family farm-journal, catering to the virtuous inhabitants of a county in the central part of the State of New York. At that remote period, forty years ago, there was occasionally to be found among type-setters a black sheep—a fellow of low and coarse tastes. Such a man, in this press-room, had a set of lascivious verses, in manuscript. Desiring a few proofs, for friends who were similarly debased, he set the thing in type, pulled the proofs, and—left the type standing! My informant, an editor, blushed as he recalled the incident, and assured me that *he* had always been told that these verses contained no single couplet which would not have horrified François Rabelais. A day later, as the paper was going to press, came the sudden need for two or three sticks of matter. Someone grabbed the dreadful verses, without examining them, and in they went!

For the next six months the mail of the unfortunate publishers contained little else than the vituperation of indignant farmers, or farmers' wives, terminating their subscriptions. To this day, the editor of the paper is regarded by many of his neighbors as the willful corrupter of youth, and an active polluter of the American home.

Certain words are a standing peril to the type-setter. The frequent confusion of "mortal" with "moral" is an example. Mr. H. B. Wheatley cites an address to the good

Dr. Watts, by a minor poet named Standen, in which the versifier was made to chant:
    With thought sublime
    And high sonorous words, thou
        sweetly sing'st
    To thy *immoral* lyre.

A collision between a train and a cow, reported in a newspaper, ended with the remark that the engineer "putting on full steam, dashed up against the cow, and literally cut it into *calves*." A young lady, for her wedding, chose a double quartet of her most charming friends to precede her as she marched up the aisle. But the newspaper gave an unfortunate impression, when it said: "The bride was accompanied to the altar by *tight* bridesmaids." The word "window" has harassed the editors of all English-speaking countries, but it was nevertheless astonishing to find *House & Garden* remarking casually: "Nothing gives a greater variety to the appearance of a house than a few undraped *widows*."

A report that, after a speech, at a political meeting, "the crowd rent the air with their *snouts*" is one of those things to make Mr. Franklin Adams remark "Stet!" When a little girl wrote, in an examination paper, "Congress is divided into civilized, semi-civilized and savage," Mark Twain commented: "Surely it is unwise to let the young know everything."

The Bible, the earliest of printed books, and the most often re-printed, has been famous for its errors. The most celebrated, which constitutes the mark of the "Wicked Bible," seems to have been held intentional, since King Charles the First's printers, Barker and Lucas, were fined £300 for leaving the word *not* out of the Seventh Commandment: "Thou shalt commit adultery." Collectors still esteem the "Wicked Bible." The Bible of 1551, with its line in the Ninety-first Psalm: "Thou shalt not nede to be afraied for eny Bugges by night" does not really contain, at this point, any misprint. The modern translation is: "Thou shalt not be afraid for the terror by night" and the meaning is the same. The curious word is used by Hamlet

("With ho! such bugs and goblins in my life") in the same sense—bugbears. A really mischievous tampering with a sacred text is said to have been done by students who broke into the offices of the Clarendon Press, and hunted up the forms for the Prayer Book, especially the marriage service. By changing one letter, k for v, they made the minister's inquiry to the bridegroom read: "Wilt thou love her, comfort her, honour, and keep her in sickness and in health; and forsaking all others, keep thee only unto her, so long as ye both shall *like?*"

Slips of the pen, or of the types, are closely allied to slips of the tongue. The head of a large system of branch libraries once addressed the forty ladies who presided, individually, over the separate libraries. There had been some cases of insubordination among the janitors, and the chief now astonished his female audience by announcing, solemnly: "Ladies, you are all to understand that each of you is to be her janitor's mistress."

When one has dealing with the printing-press, and attempts to make a bad matter better, the result, as I have said, is not always joyous. That distinguished music critic, the late Philip Hale, once prepared an article for a Boston newspaper, about a concert by the Boston Symphony Orchestra. In the article, Mr. Hale wrote: "During the performance of this number, the kettle-drummer sat, like Buddha, regarding his navel."

This was printed in the noon edition, and fell under the managing editor's eye.

"What's this? What's this?" he sputtered. "That word must come out!"

"But," he was reminded, "the stereotype is cast. It's on the press."

"Never mind," said the boss. "Get a chisel. Cut it out."

The presses were stopped, the offending word excised. And in all later editions of the paper, Bostonians were enabled to read:

"During the performance of this number, the kettle-drummer sat, like Buddha, regarding his——."

Bruehl-Bourges

"MARY OF SCOTLAND"

A dramatic moment from Maxwell Anderson's hit play which stars Helen Hayes as Mary and Helen Menken as Elizabeth

Steichen

GEORGE GERSHWIN

The high priest of modern American music

He is responsible for such diverse milestones in the history of music as *Girl Crazy,* "An American in Paris," *Of Thee I Sing* (the first musical revue to win the Pulitzer Prize) and the immortal "Rhapsody in Blue," which he was busily composing when Mr. Steichen took this picture. Mr. Gershwin has just completed the score for his first opera, *Porgy and Bess.*

Nelson

MOSS HART
and
COLE PORTER

A new pair of collaborators shown here working on Jubilee, their forthcoming and much publicized musical show

LOUIS ARMSTRONG

A characteristic photograph of the maddest monarch of hot music, who is startling Gotham this season at Connie's Inn on Broadway

Bruehl-Bourges

CONSTANCE BENNETT

Popular lady of the screen

A new portrait of the actress whose next motion picture will be *The Firebrand,* a story based on the life of Cellini. Fredric March will play opposite Miss Bennett in the role of the amorous Florentine.

Hoyningen-Huene

Hoyningen-Huene

CHARLES BOYER

Film star from France

Following his success on the Paris stage in *L'Insoumise,* and on the European screen in *La Barcarolle d'Amour,* young M. Boyer is now hoping to carve himself a niche in Hollywood. This photograph was taken on the set of the musical *Caravan,* his first American film.

HOPE WILLIAMS and NOEL COWARD

A new movie team

When Paramount releases the latest Ben Hecht–Charles MacArthur production, *Miracle on Forty-Ninth Street,* it will introduce a new pair of film stars, simultaneously making their movie debut, but not hitherto unknown in the legitimate theatre. They are those two bright people, Miss Hope Williams and Mr. Noel Coward. Advance reports predict that Mr. Coward will give Gary Cooper and the other Hollywood heartrenders a run for their money, while Miss Williams emerges an even more triumphantly tart comedienne than she was in those Broadway hits *The New Yorker* and *All Good Americans.* The cast also includes Julie Haydon, highly touted as a great "find," and Alexander Woollcott.

Nelson

The Time and the Place

As Well as the Girl. Twelve Variations on a Popular Social Theme

FRANK FENTON

She got up

Benvenuto Cellini

I SAW that she was a good, virtuous and worthy woman. Furthermore, she was delectably beautiful, but I shall abstain from undue prolixity. Some hours later I left her in extreme good spirits. She kissed me and smiled when I took my departure, laughing.

Thomas Wolfe

STORM titans mangled through his memories. From a stark precipitous and vengeful height he gazed down at her. The hills lolled like black fevered tongues of a sick earth and the night shouted wild songs to its slinking creatures! Oh, song of the night! Oh, song of the bleak intrepid and starshot darkness! Oh, two whose lonely crosses stand, and youth's innocence and love hangs crucified! Gaze at each other across the scanty feet that measure all eternity! Oh, night! Oh, bloody savage cross! Oh, youth!

Dostoyevski

HE FELT now that this was the moment all the somber days of suffering had in reality been awaiting, as animals of the earth grow restless in devious incomprehensible torments, awaiting the first blossoming of Springtime, and he closed his eyes, as though a deep shadow fled his body, and he heard himself murmuring very softly, "I love you, Tatiana Riaboushinka, I love you, I, your Fydor Fydorovitch!"

Aldous Huxley

"OH, FRANCES," he expostulated, "must we go on making false-faces at each other, like psychological children, while the world is growing up all about us?" She shrugged with a grimace of annoyance, which he was quick to perceive. He turned and walked to the door, his head bowed in thought. Then he turned. She was watching him intently.

William Saroyan

OH I laugh and I weep and I am alive when I remember! The two of us like melting stars! And me there, and the words flooding, Oh, I love you! I love you! And there we were!

Gertrude Stein

AND having the touch there, it all coming about like that and being what it seemed then not of then but of how it was and still being there and not going away or having been at all having been going away or having ever been at all having been going away and knew it then not going away.

Mae West

HE STOOD there like a lamb in the slaughter-house. "Whaddya want for breakfast?" she asked him.

Joseph Conrad

SHE came closer like a sudden mirage that whetted his strange thirst. The sea was in their limbs then. It stormed, and then afterwards came peace, as of closed eyes, shutting out other sounds save their breathing, and other sights save their eyes, filled with a curious tenderness and peril.

Jim Tully

I LEANED across the table. It reeked of beer. The labels curled wetly from the bottles. Through the fog of smoke and drunkenness her face was a painted cameo. The hard scarlet mouth deepened and softened. The laugh fell from her eyes like mascara. "Go up stairs?" I said. She got up.

Harold Bell Wright

HE TOWERED above her. She seemed so fragile beside him, so weak now and defenseless. He was a strong man and she was only a weak girl. Suddenly he ceased to struggle with himself. He would master her there and then! How pure she was! He thought of his mother in Connecticut. "Miss Dearborn," he said, with curious huskiness, "I do not wish to impose my will upon you, but I am only a man and I can no longer resist the temptation to ask for your hand! You are a good woman and my love is deep and true and, I believe, worthy!"

Dorothy Parker

AS SHE looked at him critically she knew that she was going to love him forever—all that night.

F. Scott Fitzgerald

WITH a subtle movement, almost lynx-like, she was inside his sinewy arms, and he was saying, almost inaudibly, as though from a distance, "Dear, dear baby."

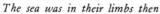

Sketches by Vertès

And he closed his eyes   *The sea was in their limbs then*   *. . . as though from a distance . . .*

Bruehl-Bourges

JOAN CRAWFORD

Perennial modern

Born Lucille Le Sueur and later known as Billie Cassin, she became Joan Crawford for the first time in the 1925 film *Sally, Irene and Mary*. After starring in the 1928 film *Our Dancing Daughters*, she spanned the bridge from silent to talking pictures and has played in *Possessed*, *Dancing Lady* and *Forsaking All Others*. Divorced Douglas Fairbanks Jr. in 1933 and married Franchot Tone this year.

Steichen

ELISABETH BERGNER

Cited by Alexander Woollcott as "probably the ablest actress in the world today," Miss Bergner has achieved a spectacular triumph—on the Continent, in London and now in New York—as the gallant gamine Gemma Jones in Margaret Kennedy's play *Escape Me Never*. She will soon play in a film version of *As You Like It,* opposite the promising young English actor Laurence Olivier.

CHARLES LAUGHTON

This distinguished British character actor hops periodically from London to Hollywood. After finishing *Ruggles of Red Gap,* an hysterical success for Paramount, he forthwith embarked for London, and was back again, nip and tuck, in time for *Les Misérables.* This time, after finishing *Mutiny on the Bounty* for MGM, he goes to England to make *Cyrano de Bergerac* with Merle Oberon as Roxane, then back again to play Louis XVI to Norma Shearer's Marie Antoinette. Such is life on the bounding main for Claridge's ex-pantry clerk, now Hollywood's most highly prized importation.

Steichen

THE LILLIE IN OUR VALLEY

"Whom are you getting at, eh?" caroled Beatrice Gladys Lillie when, at the age of fourteen, she was known to nearly every concert-hall goer in Canada as a "character costume vocalist and impersonator." Other songs in her surprisingly extensive repertoire were "My Pretty Kickoppo," "Nicoleenie" and "The Strawberry Girl." Two years later, in London, André Charlot heard her burlesquing a serious arietta and signed her up on the spot. Since then

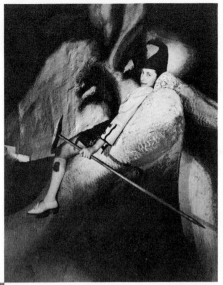

Oleo, I'm Queen of the Tyrol

A geisha's motto: It's better with your shoes off

Striking a chord on the barroom till

La Flamme de Paris

Miss Lillie has soared like a lark, into the dizziest heights of popularity, both here and abroad. Her main interests at present are (1) starring in the Winter Garden success, *At Home and Abroad,* for which these photographs were taken; (2) singing in the night club Montmartre; (3) Harrow-on-the Hill, in England, where her son, Sir Robert Peel, is at school.

Nelson

MIRIAM HOPKINS

In Becky Sharp

Based on Thackeray's *Vanity Fair, Becky Sharp* represents a milestone in movie-making as the first full-length motion picture in technicolor. The extravaganza was directed by Rouben Mamoulian, and designed in color by Robert Edmund Jones.

Bruehl

JEAN HARLOW

Beauty and the Beast

First exploited on the screen for various anatomical reasons, Jean Harlow later astounded the public by developing from the platinium blonde siren of *Hell's Angels* into an expert comedienne who, in *Red Dust* and *Dinner at Eight,* became simultaneously a box-office sensation and the critics' delight. Miss Harlow's marriages and rumored romances have made newspaper history; she is the author of an unpublished novel, and she holds, furthermore, the unofficial dice record at Agua Caliente casino with thirty-four straight passes.

Hurrell

The Blind Spot

JOHN VAN DRUTEN

"DO YOU two know each other?" his host asked, and Fred's face assumed a polite expression, preparatory to saying that he had never had the pleasure of meeting the lady, when, suddenly, he noticed her smile, which told him very clearly that he had. He adjusted his features hastily, said: "Know each other?" very heartily, and then sat down beside her, talking hard and very fast in the hope that his forgetfulness might have escaped her.

They could not, he reflected, have met more than once, nor, then, for very long, because she was attractive to a point which he must have remembered had he ever sat and talked to her before, so that perhaps his heartiness just now had been a trifle overdone. But, after all, she could very easily have taken it as the measure of his gladness in finding her again, and so regard it as a compliment that he would, in any case, have genuinely liked to pay her. She was pretty, very pretty when you looked at her, in the nicest, most unobtrusive way; what his mother would have called "good style"; with pretty, softly curling brown hair, gray eyes, a straight nose and the nicest teeth and smile. She smiled a lot while he talked to her, smiling kindly, interestedly, listening, being amused and attentive, saying very little, but always the right things. She was a delightful person, and he wished that he knew who she was.

It was a shock when, later, someone told him, and he realized that he had met her at least three times before, had sat next to her at lunch, danced with her, even, and that each time he had liked her, had made particular note of what a very sweet and charming person she was, and each time had forgotten her, having to be introduced afresh on their subsequent meeting. It was as though her face, that friendly, pretty, gentle face, were drawn in some evaporative ink of which no trace remained in his memory half an hour after he had left it.

"Ethel Wickersham," he groaned to himself. "Oh God, I hope she didn't notice! She noticed last time. I hope she didn't notice tonight."

A week later it happened again. "Have you two met before?" and this time he had already committed himself and answered "no" before she looked up and gave him that faintly pleading smile, asking for recognition, which told him that he ought to have known her. "Mrs. Wickersham," his hostess added, and his heart turned over in embarrassment. "But of course we know

each other," he said, "how silly of me. Do forgive me." And she smiled again and forgave him, and he thought again how nice she was as she listened to him talking, said the right things and asked the right questions. But this time when he went away he knew that it would happen every time they met, that he would never remember her, that there was nothing about her to which he could pin his recollection.

He asked questions about her and learned that she was Hank Wickersham's first wife; they had been divorced about three years. Julia, the present Mrs. Hank, whom he knew slightly, was a hard and noisy, though very distinctive woman, and he found himself wondering why Hank, who was the jolliest and most agreeable of men, should ever have exchanged Ethel's pretty sweetness for Julia's stridency. "Perhaps he could never remember her," he said to himself, laughingly, and suddenly, for one split second, believed it to be true, believed that there really was in Ethel some quality of indistinctness that made her impossible to remember, and believed, too, that she knew it or suspected it and that she was made unhappy by it.

And that was the moment when he knew for certain that, do what he might, he himself would never be able to remember her; his brain was always going to balk at her; it would become an obsession with him, and the more he told himself: "I must, I must, I *must* remember her next time," the more that cog would catch in his memory and deny him recognition of her. Once he had conceived that fantasy about her, some deep and psychopathic urgency in his unconscious self was going to force him always to prove it true, struggle as he might against it.

After that, he began going to parties in a state of trepidation, and found himself always standing about smiling tentatively and ingratiatingly at strange women in case they might be Ethel Wickersham. He made a good many new friends in this manner, and after a while the dread began to lessen, until the thing happened all over again, the meeting, the lack of recognition and the reintroduction, with the sickening horror of a recurring nightmare; and, as a prophylactic, he took to inquiring from his host or hostess at all subsequent parties whether Mrs. Wickersham was among the guests.

For a while he drew blank, learning that she had gone to Florida, but on one evening, nearly a year after he had first met

her, he received the answer: "Yes, she's over there in that corner."

Fred did not turn around.

"Tell me," he said, "what she's got on. Describe it exactly," and then went over to the woman in green with the coronet of leaves in her hair, and, in a voice thrilling with satisfaction, greeted her.

"Good evening, Mrs. Wickersham!" Was it his fancy, or was there really gratitude in the look she gave him, gratitude for recognition at last? He did not know, but he sat down beside her, remaining there for the entire evening, trying to burn her features into his brain, rising to leave when she did, and offering to take her home, not as a matter of duty, but because she was so nice, so charming. And because she was so nice, so really sweet and sympathetic, they did not go straight to her home, but to a night club, and then to another and another until it was five o'clock, by which time Fred liked her so much that he asked her to marry him, and she accepted.

He awoke in panic the next morning. He was engaged to Ethel Wickersham, and he would not know her if he met her. He called her up, rushed round to see her, took her out to buy the ring. It was a short engagement and, while it lasted, he took care always to call for her if they went out together, never to meet her any place, in restaurants or other people's houses, where he might fail to recognize her. There was a dreadful day when he passed her on Fifth Avenue, thinking "I know that woman" as he did so, and she came up abreast of him as he stood waiting for the light to change, laid her hand on his arm and said, "Darling, what's the matter? Didn't you see me?" He passed it off apologetically with a remark about business and preoccupation, but he was in a cold sweat for the remainder of the day, and urged the precipitation of their marriage all he could.

It was she who insisted on a church wedding, and he on her wearing a proper wedding dress so that, since he might not fetch her, he would at least be able to recognize her as the one in white satin with the veil.

It was a very happy marriage. He was right in his estimate of her as the nicest, sweetest woman he had ever met; they were free, frank and open with each other, with only one reservation. They neither of them ever mentioned the number of times it had taken him to recognize her before he proposed. Everyone in New York noticed and remarked on how devoted they were, how they never went anywhere without each other, how Fred seemed always to be devouring her with his eyes, following her with them if she left his side for a moment. He had little peculiarities about her, forbidding her ever to wear a hat in her own home during the day, when there were other women present, even at lunch if he were going to be there; he gave her a large, very striking and unusual brooch which he insisted on her wearing always, even with dresses or with other jewelry that it did not suit. He was very uxorious, and was apt at large parties, when he could not see her in the crowd, to shout loudly: "Where's my wife? I want my wife," and to go on shouting until she came to him from wherever she was and stood beside him, saying: "Darling, you *are* absurd," with a funny, pleading, frightened smile, in answer to the look of relief that passed across his face.

And then one night, about six months after they were married, came their first separation. It was for an evening only, but it was the first time that they accepted separate engagements. There was an invitation to a party at which Fred, for business reasons, felt that he ought to be present. They had arranged to dine with Ethel's family, whom Fred had never liked. Ethel did not care much for them either, but she had a sweet, strict sense of duty towards them.

"You go to the party, darling," she said. "I'll make your peace with the family, and, if I can, I'll get away early and join you at the Warburtons'. How's that?"

All the old panic flooded back.

"No, don't do that," he said, with sudden urgency. "Don't you come on. I'll leave there early. It's only a question of showing up for a little while. I'll be away by twelve, and come straight home. Don't you come on."

He kissed her lovingly as he said good-by to her while she was dressing.

"Do you mind if I don't wear your brooch tonight, darling?" she asked. "Mother's never liked it, and if you won't be there . . ."

In a way it was relief to be without her at the party, to be free of that perpetual sense of watchfulness, and yet he missed her sweetness, realized afresh how very happy they were in their marriage. He watched the clock for the earliest moment at which he could leave and rejoin her. It was a big party and he passed through the crowds, exchanging greetings as he went. His host, Bill Warburton, came up to him with a woman whose face, a pretty one, seemed vaguely familiar.

"Do you know this charming lady?" Bill asked. His tone was facetious, so that Fred replied, "I think so," with an equally ironic gravity.

The three of them stood talking for a while, and then Bill left them.

"Glad to see me?" she inquired sweetly, intimately, so Fred was taken momentarily aback. He had not thought that their previous acquaintance, whatever it was, justified quite that degree of familiarity.

"What do *you* think?" was his answer, and then other people came up to them so that they were swept into a group for the next hour, without chance of private conversation. He was surprised at the number of times that she smiled at him, and then, as the group broke up, she moved beside him.

"Want to go?" she whispered. "Let's."

Fred felt that a feather would have been an adequate weapon for flooring him. Who was this woman? Obviously, in the words of Aubrey Tanqueray, they were not strangers to each other, but it was a little brazen, he thought, the way she did not mind their being seen leaving together.

At the entrance, where the doorman hailed a taxi for them, someone delayed him for a moment, so that she ran ahead to escape the wind.

"I've told him the address," she said, as he settled down beside her, and then, when the taxi started, nestled against him.

"God, she's a pushover," Fred thought, as his arm went dutifully around her.

"I'm glad you hadn't left," she said, and turned her face to his. He kissed her, wonderingly, and she lay back restfully against him. He was acutely embarrassed.

"Look, darling," he said after a minute. "There's something, maybe, that I ought to tell you."

"What's that?"

"Well, you probably don't know. After all, it's some time since we've seen each other, but . . . Well, I'm a married man now. Maybe you hadn't heard. It did all happen rather suddenly, but, well, I'm crazy about my wife . . . so . . . Well, you understand . . . she's waiting home for me, so if I leave you at your door . . ."

He had not known quite what reaction he expected, but it was not what he received. She drew away from him, turned, looking at him.

"Don't, Fred," she said. "Don't talk like that. I don't like it."

"I'm sorry," he replied. "But it's true."

"Don't, Fred," she repeated, and now there was fear in her voice. "Please don't go on."

"Yes, but . . ."

"I tell you I don't like it. You do it too well."

"Hell," he said angrily. "You think I'm kidding."

"Well, aren't you? Aren't you?" She stared at him as they passed a street lamp, which enabled them to read each other's features. Hers were aghast. "Fred! Fred!" she cried, and then: "Oh, God, I knew it. Oh, I knew it," and burst into tears, refusing his gestures and his words of comfort. Once only she stopped, looking up to say: "I'm glad you're crazy about her, all the same," and then wept again until the taxi stopped, to his surprise, at his apartment.

"Good night," she said, "you go to your wife . . . if she's there."

"She will be," he replied. "Where shall I tell him . . . for you?"

"I'm going to an hotel," she answered. "I'll tell him. Good-by, Fred." She caught at his sleeve as he was going. "Kiss me good-by," she said.

He kissed her, and she clung for a moment. Then he left her, puzzled and dismayed. Women, he told himself, were unaccountable. Ethel was not home when he entered the apartment. "She's stayed late at her mother's," he thought, and sat down to wait for her. He waited all night.

Next day he heard from her lawyers. The grounds were "Mental cruelty."

Steichen

"ROMEO AND JULIET"

Katharine Cornell and Basil Rathbone

After the most strenuous feat of trouping the American theatre has known in the past twenty years, Miss Cornell would certainly appear to have exploded the theory: "The road is dead." Last year she took her repertory of three plays—*The Barretts of Wimpole Street, Candida,* and *Romeo and Juliet* —to seventy-five cities. She gave 225 performances, covered 17,000 miles and grossed a total of 650,000 dollars. She now brings a highly polished *Romeo and Juliet* to Broadway.

LOU GEHRIG

Batting champion

For the first time, the star of Hungry Lou Gehrig, known also, due to certain architectural amplitudes, as "Biscuit Pants," will shine, this year, as the highest-salaried player in the American League. With Babe Ruth now in alien corn as co-manager of the Boston Braves, this pleasant, burly son of a *gemütliche* German lady on Morningside Heights will be the main attraction at the Yankee Stadium.

Nelson

JOE LOUIS

Brown Bomber

On June 25, at the Yankee Stadium in New York, Mr. Louis will quarrel with Primo Carnera, the quondam champion, for fifteen rounds. Joe was born in Alabama, twenty-one years ago. He is six feet, one inch, tall, weighing two hundred pounds. The best weapons in his armory are a supply of short, swift punches, which he deals with either hand. He seldom scowls or smiles, and he reads the Bible often.

Nelson

HELEN JACOBS

Queen Helen II

Somewhere on the back courts of Wimbledon, Helen Jacobs is whetting the deceptive chop-strokes that have made her, three times, the ranking woman tennis player of America but not—yet—of England. When the Wimbledon meeting begins on June 24, the gayest ever because of the King's Jubilee, Queen Helen II will have another try at the English crown, since she has been balked, for years, on the famous Center Court by her regal predecessor, Mrs. Helen Wills Moody, and, in 1934, by the little English Sunday-school teacher, Dorothy Round. This year, after Mrs. Moody startled everyone by suddenly emerging from retirement, she will probably appear at Wimbledon to resume the Jacobean wars.

Steichen

Nelson

JESSE OWENS

Dark lightning

Below is the phenomenal 100-yard star, 200-yard world's record holder, broad-jump champion and 220-yard-hurdle champion. Mr. Owens hopes to win new laurels with the U.S. team at the Olympic games in Berlin next summer.

The Bums at Sunset

THOMAS WOLFE

SLOWLY, singly, with the ambling gait of men who have just fed, and who are faced with no pressure of time and business, the hoboes came from the jungle, descended the few feet of clay embankment that sloped to the road bed, and in an unhurried manner walked down the tracks toward the water tower. The time was the exact moment of sunset, the sun indeed had disappeared from sight, but its last shafts fell remotely, without violence or heat, upon the treetops of the already darkening woods and on the top of the water tower. That light lay there briefly with a strange unearthly detachment, like a delicate and ancient bronze, it was no part of that cool, that delicious darkening of the earth which was already steeping the woods—it was like sorrow and like ecstasy and it faded briefly like a ghost.

Of the five men who had emerged from the "jungle" above the tracks and were now advancing, in a straggling procession, toward the water tower, the oldest was perhaps fifty, but such a ruin of a man, such a shapeless agglomerate of sodden rags, matted hair, and human tissues, that his age was indeterminate. He was like something that has been melted and beaten into the earth by a heavy rain. The youngest was a fresh-skinned country lad with bright wondering eyes: he was perhaps not more than sixteen years old. Of the remaining three, one was a young man not over thirty with a ferret face and very few upper teeth. He walked along gingerly on tender feet that were obviously unaccustomed to the work he was now putting them to: he was a triumph of dirty elegance—he wore a pin-striped suit heavily spattered with grease stains and very shiny on the seat: he kept his coat collar turned up and his hands thrust deeply into his trousers pockets—he walked thus with his bony shoulders thrust forward as if, in spite of the day's heat, he was cold. He had a limp cigarette thrust out of the corner of his mouth, and he talked with a bare movement of his lips, and a curious and ugly convulsion of his mouth to the side: everything about him suggested unclean secrecy.

Of the five men, only the remaining two carried on them the authority of genuine vagabondage. One was a small man with a hard seamed face, his eyes were hard and cold as agate, and his thin mouth was twisted slantwise in his face, and was like a scar.

The other man, who might have been in his mid-fifties, had the powerful shambling figure, the seamed brutal face of the professional vagabond. It was a face and figure that had a curious brutal nobility; the battered and pitted face was hewn like a block of granite and on the man was legible the tremendous story of his wanderings—a legend of pounding wheel and thrumming rod, of bloody brawl and brutal shambles, of immense and lonely skies, the savage wildness, the wild, cruel and lonely distance of America.

This man, somehow obviously the leader of the group, walked silently, indifferently, at a powerful shambling step, not looking at the others. Once he paused, thrust a powerful hand into the baggy pocket of his coat, and drew out a cigarette, which he lit with a single motion of his hard cupped hand. Then his face luxuriously contorted as he drew upon the cigarette, he inhaled deeply, letting the smoke trickle slowly out through his nostrils after he had drawn it into the depths of his mighty lungs. It was a powerful and brutal gesture of sensual pleasure that suddenly gave to the act of smoking and to the quality of tobacco all of their primitive and fragrant relish. And it was evident that the man could impart this rare quality to the simplest physical acts of life—to everything he touched—because he had in him somehow the rare qualities of exultancy and joy.

All the time, the boy had been keeping step behind the man, his eyes fixed steadily upon the broad back of the vagabond. Now, as the man stopped, the boy came abreast of him, and also stopped, and for a moment continued to look at the man, a little uncertainly, but with the same expression of steadfast confidence.

The bum, letting the smoke coil slowly from luxurious nostrils, resumed his powerful swinging stride, and for a moment said nothing to the boy. Presently, however, he spoke, roughly, casually, but with a kind of brutal friendliness:

"Where yuh goin' kid?" he said. "To the big town?"

The boy nodded dumbly, seemed about to speak, but said nothing.

"Been there before?" the man asked.

"No," said the boy.

"First time yuh ever rode the rods, huh?"

"Yes," said the boy.

"What's the matter?" the bum said, grinning. "Too many cows to milk down on the farm, huh? Is that it?"

The boy grinned uncertainly for a moment, and then said, "Yes."

"I t'ought so," the bum said, chuckling coarsely, "Jesus! I can tell one of youse fresh country kids a mile off by the way yuh walk. . . . Well," he said with a rough blunt friendliness, in a moment, "stick wit me if you're goin' to the Big Town. I'm goin' that way, too."

"Yeah," the little man with the mouth like a scar now broke in, in a rasping voice, and with an ugly jeering laugh:

"Yeah. You stick to Bull, kid. He'll see yuh t'roo. He'll show yuh de—woild, I ain't kiddin' yuh! He'll take yuh up to Lemonade Lake an' all t'roo Breadloaf Valley—won't yuh, Bull? He'll show yuh where de ham trees are and where de toikeys grow on bushes—won't yuh, Bull?" he said with ugly yet fawning insinuation. "You stick to Bull, kid, an' you'll be wearin' poils. . . . A-a-a-ah! yuh punk kid!" he now said, with a sudden turn to snarling viciousness.

"Wat t'hell use do yuh t'ink we got for a punk kid like you?—Dat's duh trouble wit dis racket now! . . . We was all right until all dese kids began to come along! . . . Wy t'hell should we be boddered with him!" he snarled viciously. "Wat t'hell am I supposed to be—a noice maid or sump'n? . . . G'wan, yuh little punk," he snarled viciously, and lifted his fist in a sudden backhand movement, as if to strike the boy. "Scram! We got no use fer yuh! . . . G'wan, now. . . . Get t'hell away from here before I smash yuh one."

The man named Bull turned for a moment and looked silently at the smaller bum.

"Listen, Mug!" he said quietly in a moment. "You leave the kid alone. The kid stays, see?"

"A-a-a-ah!" the other man snarled sullenly. "What is dis anyway?—A—noic'ry, or sump'n?"

"Listen," the other man said, "yuh hoid me, didn't yuh?"

"A-a-ah. t'hell wit it!" the little man muttered. "I'm not goin' t' rock duh cradle f'r no punk kid."

"Yuh hoid what I said, didn't yuh?" the man named Bull said in a heavy menacing tone.

"I hoid yuh. Yeah!" the other muttered.

"Well, I don't want to hear no more outa your trap. I said the kid stays—and he stays."

The little man muttered sullenly under his breath, but said no more. Bull continued to scowl heavily at him a moment longer, then turned away and went over and sat down on a handcar which had been pushed up against a tool house on the siding.

"Come over here, kid," he said roughly, as he fumbled in his pocket for another cigarette. The boy walked over to the handcar.

"Got any smokes?" the man said, still fumbling in his pocket. The boy produced a package of cigarettes and offered them to the man. Bull took a cigarette from the package, lighted it with a single movement, between his tough seamed face and his cupped hand, and then dropped the package of cigarettes in his pocket, with the same spacious and powerful gesture.

"T'anks," he said as the acrid smoke began to coil luxuriously from his nostrils. "Sit down, kid."

The boy sat down on the handcar beside the man. For a moment, as Bull smoked, two of the bums looked quietly at each other with sly smiles, and then the young one in the soiled pin-stripe suit shook his head rapidly to himself, and, grinning toothlessly with his thin sunken mouth, mumbled derisively: "Cheezus!"

Bull said nothing, but sat there smoking, bent forward a little on his knees, as solid as a rock.

It was almost dark; there was still a faint evening light, but already great stars were beginning to flash and blaze in cloudless skies. Somewhere in the wood there was a sound of water. Far off, half-heard and half-suspected, there was a faint dynamic throbbing on the rails. The boy sat there quietly, listening, and said nothing.

ETHEL MERMAN
and
WILLIAM GAXTON

"They're the Top"

Miss Merman and Mr. Gaxton as they appear in the show-stopping "You're the Top" number from Cole Porter's lively revue *Anything Goes*.

Steichen

GRACE MOORE

Now of the movies

A behind-the-scenes photo of the Tennessee soprano whose new motion-picture triumph, *Love Me Forever,* has followed close on the heels of her sensational London Jubilee success. Miss Moore studied in Washington, D.C., and in Europe and was first seen on the New York stage in Irving Berlin's *Music Box Revue.* She joined the Metropolitan Opera Company of New York in 1928 and made her debut in *La Bohême.*

Bruehl-Bourges

Steichen

ROSA PONSELLE

The newest Carmen

Since 1918, when Caruso found in her his Leonora for *La Forza del Destino,* Rosa Ponselle has shouldered the cares of almost every dark-eyed opera heroine in the Metropolitan Opera's repertoire. This season she adds to her triumphs as an interpreter the role of Carmen, a heroine last seen at the Metropolitan when Jeritza sang the part in 1931. Rosa Ponselle made her professional debut at the age of fourteen, providing vocal and piano accompaniment at the local nickelodeon. Later she entered vaudeville with her sister. Then, once Gatti-Casazza and Caruso had heard her sing, she was engaged for the Met as a leading dramatic soprano.

Steichen

LOTTE LEHMANN

In Der Rosenkavalier

If she had obeyed her father's wishes, Miss Lehmann would have been a German school-teacher, a sad and sedentary fate for a woman who has developed one of the richest and most beautiful soprano voices in the world. Instead, she studied in Berlin, and eventually was offered a contract at the Vienna Opera. Vienna has been her home for the last eighteen years; she has sung over fifty roles and this season will sing *Der Rosenkavalier* at the Metropolitan.

KIRSTEN FLAGSTAD

Norwegian Valkyrie

Across from Norway, Kirsten Flagstad comes a second time, with the great soprano voice which was first and unforgettably heard at the Metropolitan Opera last February in *Die Walküre*. This season, she rejoins the Metropolitan. Out in California, Madame Flagstad has just finished impersonating Wagner's various Brünnhildes for the San Francisco Opera Company. Her winter program calls, additionally, for fifty concert appearances, plus radio moments for General Motors and Ford.

Steichen

Nominated for the Hall of Fame: 1935

Jevons

THOMAS WOLFE

Because he is the author of the current best-seller, *Of Time and the River;* because, after graduating from the University of South Carolina and taking an M.A. degree at Harvard, he taught English for six years at New York University; because he was awarded a Guggenheim Fellowship for study abroad in 1930–31; and because he has now sneaked off to Europe again, to elude the tea-leaves of a literary triumph in America.

CLIFFORD ODETS

Because he is the year's three-star playwright, whose *Waiting for Lefty, Till the Day I Die,* and *Awake and Sing!* clicked in unison on Broadway; because he took a part in the first-named play, and has several years of acting for the Group Theatre and the Theatre Guild to his credit; because he is a sincere and practical spokesman for the underdog; and because he resolutely declines to heed the siren beckonings of Hollywood, preferring to work on a fourth play for next season.

AGNES DE MILLE

Because she is a dance-recitalist of the first rank; because she is the daughter of William de Mille, scriptwriter of *Strongheart* and *The Warrens of Virginia;* because she designs the costumes and choreography for her own recitals; and because she has contributed original ballet creations to the stage shows of the Roxy Theatre in New York and the Leicester Square Theatre in London.

Vogue Studios

IGOR and SVIAPOSLAV STRAVINSKY

Because they are father and son who peaceably worship the same mistress, namely music; because Igor Stravinsky, whose compositions were an alarming revolution to the prewar world, has won himself a niche in musical history; because Stravinsky *fils,* twenty-four years old, is a pianist already acclaimed by European critics for his spontaneous and lucid playing; and because Stravinsky *père* is now conducting a series of piano concerts in our principal cities.

DMITRI SHOSTAKOVITCH

Because at twenty-nine he is the musical luminary of Soviet Russia; because *Lady Macbeth of Mtsensk,* the second of his two operas, was given last winter at the Metropolitan by the Cleveland Symphony; because his works embody the realism and vigor which mark the Soviet ideal; and because he has written the music for numerous sound films, five of which have invaded this country—*The Youth of Maxim* last, *Love and Hate* next.

Domanski

Pinchot

LILLIAN HELLMAN

Because she is author of *The Children's Hour,* one of the most literate, sensitive, and human dramas in the contemporary theatre; because she is only twenty-nine, writes a fine prose, and plays what is credibly reported as a wicked game of poker; and because a second play by her is scheduled for early production.

CORNELIA OTIS SKINNER

Because she is a gifted exponent of the taxing art of solo-drama; because, after impersonating all *The Wives of Henry VIII* in a six-scene monologue, she did the same thing to *The Loves of Charles II;* because she writes her own sketches, and has contributed stories to several magazines; because she studied at Bryn Mawr and the Sorbonne; and because her father is Otis Skinner, the distinguished actor.

JOHN MASON BROWN

Because he is the dramatic critic of the *New York Evening Post* and for two years has scored highest among the Broadway appraisers, on a basis of the number of hits and flops he predicted correctly; because he is an alumnus of the late George Pierce Baker's "47" Workshop at Harvard; because he has written several able books on theatrical criticism—the last called *Letters from Greenroom Ghosts.*

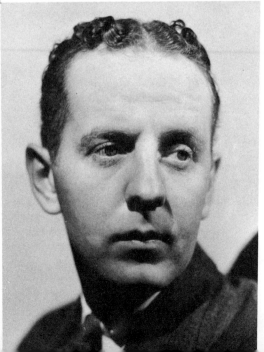

Compensation Instinct

G. B. STERN

I TOLD myself, after the orgy, that it had not been self-indulgence but the Compensation Instinct. This was the incident:

It was late afternoon on the eve of Easter Sunday. I was in London because (it is no use veiling the bare fact) nobody had asked me for Easter. I am not exaggerating (I hope) when I say that hundreds of my friends had invited me for Christmas and (literally) thousands for Whitsun, but for Easter I was Love, Locked Out. You remember the picture? It hung in my night-nursery as a child, and made a powerful impression on me. "Love, Locked Out" is a picture of the child Cupid with his chubby naked back towards us, pressing with all his might, but pressing in vain, against a closed front door. I could never quite shake off the habit of identifying myself with "Love, Locked Out" whenever I was derelict, forsaken and unwanted.

Which brings us nicely round again to the eve of Easter Sunday. I was on my way home from the National Gallery, thinking that if I improved my mind, that would learn 'em to leave me out of their Easter weekends. Once there, I thoroughly enjoyed myself.

On my way home, a craving for peppermint creams suddenly assailed me. It beat on me with such strong waves that it was like a physical encounter. Not chocolate peppermint creams, but pure white ones, round as a penny, about a quarter of an inch thick, of the velvety texture of pansy petals. I had been on a diet for some time.

I stood still in Piccadilly Circus on the Haymarket side, and slowly turned my head to the left. And there, dear children, believe it or not, was Crullers' sweet-shop, where they make the best peppermint creams of all.

I swear that I had the longing first, and saw the shop afterwards.

"Luckily," I said to myself, "you'll not have to pull yourself together and fight temptation. This door will not open suddenly and let you down flat. Luckily these are the Easter holidays; and even had it been an ordinary Saturday, it's past closing time." And to verify this comforting assurance, I tried the door. It opened immediately, and precipitated me half-way into the shop. Quickly I drew back, closed the door again, and marched on.

BUT now there were no solid barriers of brass and wood and iron between me and my desire. Only The Spirit of Austerity in single combat with The Spirit of Self-Indulgence.

You see, apart from diet, I could just remember what one felt like, after one had given way to peppermint creams.

Three times I reached the corner of Lower Regent Street; and three times, slowly, I paced back again. Unfortunately, on the third time, I suddenly remembered that I had not bought an Easter present for Sylvia: nothing to put on her plate under the table-napkin the next morning. "The girl will be disappointed," I murmured tenderly. "Glutton is her middle name."

So I went into the shop and I bought a chocolate egg. And then carelessly I added: "You might throw in half a pound of peppermint creams." No, I don't know quite what I meant by "throw in." It seemed to mitigate the crime.

I only live seven minutes' walk away from that shop, and during every second of that seven minutes I had to fight the lust to tear open my box of peppermint creams and begin eating them in the sight of all, walking down Piccadilly. I don't like to think what would have happened had somebody attempted to take them away from me. My strength was as the strength of ten because my heart was pure. Sir Galahad. (I could never square that assertion of his with Nannie's proverb that self-praise was no recommendation.)

I walked more quickly, and leapt up the stairs to my apartment on the second floor. If I could have passed through my front door without stopping to use the latchkey, I would have. I did not stop to gather up and read four delicious-looking letters and two urgent telephone messages waiting for me in the hall. I got into my room, tore open the box, snatched away the paper, stuffed in two-peppermint-creams-and-then-another-two-and-then-another-three-and-then-one. That checked the craving until I could take off my hat, coat and gloves. Then, at a much slower pace, I ate another five. Urgency was satisfied, and so was the second stage of appreciation and delight.

I PUT the box away in a drawer; yet I knew that this was not final. Twice I returned to the drawer, but only taking one cloying cream each time. After the second, I shut the drawer *firmly*.

"—And that's that," I said. And this time I believed that that was indeed that; the rest of the creams, and not many were left, would wait until tomorrow brought back zest and appetite again.

Presently I wandered to the drawer, slowly opened it, and, hating the very sight and taste of those round gleaming cool white pennies, nibbled another.

By this time I was feeling very large and very sick. My self-respect was gone for good. All this, mind you, I had anticipated when I first discovered that Crullers' was open at the Haymarket corner of Piccadilly. All of this I would remember equally accurately next time I had a craving for peppermint creams. Memory takes place in one part of you, and desire in another.

Peppermint creams. I went off and drank some brandy; and while I drank it, I thought of vinegar and sharp apples, and of other lovely refreshing things: the bite of anchovies, for instance, on the smoothly glutted throat.

Peppermint creams. I wandered into the bathroom and washed my face over and over again in cold running water, hoping vaguely that thus I would wash away self-contempt and the universal prevalence of peppermint creams. Then I had some more brandy.

And then, with lagging step and nausea on my palate, I went back to the drawer where I had put away the peppermint creams, took out the box, and hid it at the back of another drawer, a very secret drawer, and arranged silk handkerchiefs and scarves to make the hiding-place more convincing.

And after that, I had another.

"After action has been taken as the outcome of the strongest impulse or of the strongest desire, without any deliberation, there may ensue an attempt to justify the act on rational grounds."

So I prefer to think, against all appearances, that I am not a monster of self-indulgence; and that this little incident I have described, has about it an appeal of wistful universality.

You see (you do see, don't you?) it was just compensation for Love, Locked Out. Nobody had wanted me for the Easter holidays. Please don't forget that I had hundreds of invitations for Christmas, and (literally) thousands for Whitsun.

That door of Crullers' was a symbolical door. . . .

Even if those were not symbolical peppermint creams.

"ETHAN FROME"

Starring Ruth Gordon, Raymond Massey and Pauline Lord

These three are the stars of *Ethan Frome,* the heart-pinching tale of a crusty New England farmer, which Edith Wharton so brilliantly wrote and which Owen and Donald Davis have now dramatized with Lowell Barrington. In all its bitterness this story of three who live together, more dead than alive, with no peace, has been produced by Max Gordon.

Steichen

PETER LORRE

In the film Crime and Punishment

About three years ago, an extraordinary German film called *M* was shown here in America, where it duplicated the distinguished critical triumph it had already achieved over the period of a year in Europe. In this film based on the horrendous child murders in Dusseldorf, the leading role was portrayed by one Peter Lorre, a Hungarian actor, who gave a magnificent and chilling portrayal of the pathological killer. The screen's foremost exponent of unhealthy and curious terror, he is, in private life, quiet, friendly, unassuming and intelligent. He is now thirty-one, is married to a German actress, likes to sketch in charcoal, and is an ardent wrestling fan.

Nelson

Bruehl

MARLENE DIETRICH

In her new film, Desire

The amazing Miss Dietrich began her career as a violinist and made her debut as an actress on the Berlin stage in *Broadway*. After working with Max Reinhardt for four years she came to the attention of American film audiences for her fine performance as the heartless heroine of *The Blue Angel*, a German film. She was soon lured to Hollywood, and her first American film was *Morocco*, in which she played opposite Gary Cooper.

318

The Mesdames Kilbourne

ALLAN SEAGER

ROGER KILBOURNE had a bad head. The shaking of the train did not help the pounding in his skull, and still less the thought that he had made a mess of his three months' leave, and, for that matter, of his life. It would be his life, unless he damned well pulled himself together and had the thing annulled, or something legal done to it. The view from the compartment window gave him no solace, although he had long looked forward to seeing it again. It was remarkably the same as he remembered it, and duller—the same mist, the same little fields fenced with stone and hedgerows, here and there a row of pollards, and more, if anything, of the ugly red brick houses.

He turned his head and surveyed his new wife with distaste. Her face was hidden in the *Daily Express,* and he surmised that she was reading the racing news. He began to talk to her, feeling that he owed something to his caste at least, if not to her.

"Alice," he said. The newspaper came down. She was pretty enough, smiling at him, but there was too much rouge, too much lipstick. Now what was he going to say?

"You know the trains on the Continent?"

"I've never been out there."

"No matter. You see they have three warnings on the window sills of all Continental trains, in three languages. '*E pericoloso sporgersi*'—that's Italian. It means 'It is dangerous to lean out.' Then the French, '*Défense de se pencher en dehors,*'—it is forbidden to lean out. And finally, German, '*Nicht hinauslehnen.*' The Italians are the most courteous—they point out the danger, and leave the rest to you. The 'frogs' command you, and the Germans shrug it off without any explanation, just 'Don't lean out.' I suppose if *we* bothered to have a sign at all, it would say, 'The Company will not take responsibility for injuries incurred while leaning from the carriage.' Sums the countries up rather, don't you think?"

"Shall we ever go to the Continent, Roger?" she asked.

"I may have to go over to the Paris office before my leave's up."

"Oh, I say, that will be nice."

There it was again, the Cockney echo in her voice. It would definitely not do to inquire too closely, or he might learn that the wife of his bosom had been someone's second maid. He was a bloody fool to have married her, and on three days' acquaintance.

Kilbourne had gone down from Cambridge to take a banking job in the Sudan. At the time he had felt what he was certain was the exhilaration of the Empire builders, somewhat watered down, to be sure, since there were no longer any warlike niggers down there. But the excitement had worn off in three years of routine drudgery, and he had become addicted to gin and old copies of *Sketch* and *The Tatler.* He wrote to his mother every day, fearful, at the beginning of his stay, that the gin might show in the writing, but gradually the fear disappeared as he got used to it. He was very fond of his mother, and he wanted, most of all, to get back to her, more, he used to think on days when the sweat made his hand stick to the pages he was writing on, than the smell and feel of England. He had, as a little boy, played in the garden, by the hollyhock row, and she had come one day and knelt in front of him, and taken him by the shoulders and looked into his eyes a long time. Then she had begun to cry, and she had murmured in a choked voice, "Oh, my darling boy," and she had embraced him very tightly. It was this mood of trust—and compassion, really, since he felt that she had been somehow unhappy—that he tried to recapture in his letters. In them he was careful to send his love to "dear Old Dad." Dear Old Dad was a country vicar.

At the end of his three-year term in the Sudan, Kilbourne was given the usual three months' leave. He hurried to London, counting every hour *en route,* and, directly he landed, sent his mother a telegram, saying that he would come down on the late train.

He was very glad to be back, and he spent the afternoon strolling through the city. He ordered two suits from his tailor, and bought several neckties in the Burlington Arcade. It did not occur to him to ring up any of his friends because he was saving the story of his Sudanese adventures for his mother; not that they were very exciting, and she had read about them in his letters anyway, but they seemed to belong first to her. It was a foggy day, and he liked the smell of the coal smoke mingled with the fog. He examined shop windows, and gave a good many sixpences to beggars, and generally overflowed with kindness and good feeling.

After a lavish dinner enlivened by a bottle of claret and followed by a fine brandy, he thought it might be fun to poke about Piccadilly until time for his train. The statue of Eros was still firm on its pedestal, and he could remember from his childhood the hansom cabs that used to trot sedately up the great curve of Regent Street. He drank a beer at the Brasserie out of sentiment, since he had once been thrown out of the Brasserie after a Varsity match while he was still at Cambridge. Then he began to walk up toward Leicester Square, delighting in the firm English faces of the crowds in the red and blue reflections of the electric signs. He avoided the clump of harlots at the mouth of Wardour Street, gaped a moment at the movie palace, and went into a hotel for a drink. The music of a jazz band led him into the dining room, and he thought it might be pleasant to sit down and watch the dancing.

It was there that he met his future wife. She sat alone at the next table with a glass of yellow liqueur before her, a dark lovely girl in a blue satin. After a moment, he got up and asked her to dance. On the floor, he remarked that there was a fog outside; that it was damned odd that a lovely creature like herself should be sitting there alone; and he hoped that they would have several other dances together. She helped him out by admiring his dancing, and asking him if he lived in London. They got on splendidly during the music, and as they returned to her table, she said, "I'm sorry but I must ask you for ten shillings."

He was surprised, but she explained that she was a professional dancing partner. He took out a £5 note, and with an air of careless extravagance told her to tell him when he had danced it up. He was having a very good time, and he completely forgot his train.

After several drinks, he told her the story of his adventures in the Sudan, embellishing them suitably, and the longer he talked, the more charming, to his notion, she became. At midnight, he asked if he might see her home. It had been damned lonely in Africa.

She had a flat in Maida Vale, and at the door, she said, "Would you like to come in? I have some gin."

With a tingling in his spine, he went in. He knew that he would spend the night with her, and he had never spent the night with a girl before.

He thought she was wonderful, and by the time the darkness weakened in the east, he had told her all about his life. He was, only twenty-four, and he was certain he loved Alice.

During the next three days, she made up for all the long hot nights of work, and for all his loneliness. She was gentle; she was kind; and she was beautiful. Roger felt a convulsion which he was certain was love and he married her on the third day. They celebrated in several night clubs.

And now he was taking his wife, a former professional dancing partner, to meet his parents, the Reverend and Mrs. Henry Kilbourne, the Vicarage, Dry Sandford, Berks.

As the train passed landmarks which were more and more familiar, the ties he had broken in London began to knit themselves together again, and he felt increasingly unhappy that he had forsaken his mother.

When they approached the Vicarage, his mother saw them coming. She was a tall, heavy woman. Her face was a healthy red, and her plump cheeks were curtailed by fringes of gray bobbed hair. She wore a camel's-hair sweater, a shapeless green dress, and on her feet were flat-heeled shoes with a single strap across the instep. Behind the window curtains, she stood quivering with a jealous rage she had always known she would feel when her son brought home a wife.

Blushing with shame, Roger opened the door, and accepted his mother's long embrace. After her kiss, she held him and looked deep into his eyes as if she expected to find in them a sign of his defection. Then, stiffening her face, she turned to Alice.

"Mother, this is my wife, Alice."

She said to Alice, "How d'you do?" and shook hands. "Your father is in the study, Roger."

Roger hurried into the stuffy little room, and shook hands morosely with his father. The two men returned to the living room, and Mrs. Kilbourne took Alice by the arm, saying to the Vicar, "Henry, this is Roger's wife." It was all done quietly, and it was very painful for everyone, except, it seemed, the Vicar. He took his glasses out of a case,

squinted through them, and said jocosely, "Why, you're very pretty, my dear." He kissed her on the cheek, led her to a couch before the fire, and began to talk with her.

Mrs. Kilbourne, hearing the Cockney taint in Alice's voice, and remarking the rouge, and the cheap clothes, saw immediately that it was not loss she was suffering, but insult. Roger had insulted her. He had married a shop-girl, or worse. Mrs. Kilbourne looked Roger in the eye, and he rose dutifully.

"You will excuse me, if I speak to Roger?" she said to the couch.

They left the room, and presently they were heard climbing the stairs.

Alice looked at her father-in-law in the firelight. He was a meek little man, somewhat dirty, with a bald head and a gray fringe around it. His soiled clerical collar stood out a half-inch too large around his withered neck. Yet he had fine hands and he had been kind to her. She decided to tell him the truth. They all knew it anyway.

"You know, sir, that I'm a professional dancing partner?"

"What fun! We hear the London orchestras every night over the wireless, but I haven't danced, my dear, why, I haven't danced in twenty years."

"But don't you see, sir—"

"Call me Dad, Alice. I am your Dad, you know."

"Well—Dad, I'm not right for Roger really, I know it, and—"

"Why not, pray, you're a lovely girl, and strong enough for his children." Here he patted her hip. "And you love him, don't you?" He looked at her anxiously.

"Yes, I love him all right." It was very Cockney, her pronunciation, but it was sincere.

"Well then, I shouldn't worry. Of course, it is a surprise, and Roger's mother would

have him married to a duke's daughter if she could, but the stock needs refreshing, and I like you, my dear. Don't you worry."

Roger joined them silently and the maid brought in the tea. It was a rather special tea with eggs and an almond cake.

"Where's your mother, Roger?" his father asked.

"She'll be down presently she said."

The Vicar busied himself with the tea, slicing cake and pouring. Then they waited for Mrs. Kilbourne.

"Perhaps I'd better fetch her," the Vicar said.

He mounted the stairs slowly to his wife's bedroom. He found her hanging from a scarf to an old lamp hook in the ceiling. A stool lay overturned on the floor. He cut her down swiftly and laid her on the bed to listen for her heartbeat. There was none. Then he rang for the maid. She came, gave a little scream at Mrs. Kilbourne's body, and he sent her for the doctor.

The Vicar came down the stairs.

"Roger," he said, "your mother has hanged herself. Go to her."

And then to Alice, "My wife, Alice, my wife. Roger's mother. We were married thirty years, and yet"—he started to walk up and down—"and yet, you know." The old man stopped and stared, through the walls themselves, she thought, and back into the heart of thirty years. "You know, Alice, I've always hated her. God forgive me, I've hated her."

Upstairs, kneeling beside the bed, remembering his mother in the garden with the hollyhocks, Roger spoke to her corpse.

"Mother, mother darling," and with the words, all his childhood rushed back and the tears streamed down his face. "I'll always hate her. Always."

Below, in the crook of the Vicar's arm, Alice wept.

Omega

I. S. V.-PATCÉVITCH

President, The Condé Nast Publications Inc.

IT WAS a heartbreaking decision that Condé Nast (Publisher) and Frank Crowninshield (Editor) had to make in 1936, when under the pressure of the mal-economics of the depression of the Thirties it became impossible to continue the publication of *Vanity Fair* and keep its head above water, so to speak. The last issue of *Vanity Fair* as a separate magazine appeared in February 1936, and from then on some of its features—principally in the realm of art, theatre, and specialized articles — were incorporated in the editorial content of *Vogue,* its elder sister.

Ever since, for all the senior members of the Condé Nast publishing organization—including myself — the revival of *Vanity Fair* has remained an unrealized dream.

When Frederic Bradlee and Cleveland Amory came to see me, some two years ago, to discuss their idea of assembling and editing an anthology of material published in *Vanity Fair* — partly as a memorial to Frank Crowninshield — I readily and gladly offered to throw open to them the files of the magazine and to assist them in every way pos-

Rawlings

CONDÉ NAST and FRANK CROWNINSHIELD
Publisher and editor of Vanity Fair, 1914-1936

sible. Here at last, I felt, were two courageous souls willing to undertake the gigantic task of sifting, out of some 15,000 pages of printed matter and some 50,000 illustrations, the quintessence of the era during which this magazine reflected, in its inimitable way, the golden Twenties.

The volume you have just read and looked through is the result of their monumental work. The selection of what to put in and what to leave out was a difficult one, and frustrating in some respects. Many of the photographs were no longer available; and the original plates — including those of the color documents for which *Vanity Fair* was so famous — had been melted down during the copper shortage of World War II when the metal was needed for other purposes.

Nevertheless, I hope you will agree that the liveliness and timeliness of the old *Vanity Fair* have not been lost; that they have been recaptured and projected in the pages of this volume for both old and young to reminisce over and to enjoy. Perhaps the book will also inspire new talents today and tomorrow.

Acknowledgments

Grateful acknowledgment is made to the owners and publishers of the following copyright materials for permission to reprint. Unless otherwise indicated below, U.S. copyright is in the name of The Condé Nast Publications Inc. The first date given is that of the original copyright; the second, if any, indicates the date of renewal.

Djuna Barnes. "A Duel Without Seconds" (1929, 1957).

The Executor of the Estate of Max Beerbohm. "A Very Critical Gentleman" by Max Beerbohm (1928, 1956).

Clare Boothe. "Joyful James" (1932, 1960).

Charles Brackett. "Adam and Eve" (1919, 1947).

Brandt & Brandt. "The Bucharest Du Barry" by John Gunther (1934). "The Art of Dying" by Paul Morand (1930, 1958).

Mrs. Richardson Bronson. "The Golden Age of the Dandy" by John Peale Bishop (1920, 1948).

James Brown Associates, Inc. "The Incredible Jeritza" by Deems Taylor (1922, 1950).

Helen Choate. "Song" (1924, 1952).

Miss D. E. Collins. "The Soul of Skylarking" by G. K. Chesterton (1920, 1948).

Coward-McCann, Inc. "The Ballad of Yukon Jake" from *The Ballad of Yukon Jake* by Edward E. Paramore, Jr. Copyright 1921, 1949 Edward E. Paramore, Jr. Reprinted by permission of the publishers.

The Literary Trustees of Walter de la Mare and The Society of Authors. "Life," "The Old House," and "Silver" by Walter de la Mare (1925, 1953).

Doubleday & Company, Inc. "This Modern Living" by Arnold Bennett (1929, 1957). "Custer's Last Stand" from *A Parody Outline of History* by Donald Ogden Stewart; copyright 1921 George H. Doran Company. Reprinted by permission.

The Dowager Lady Dunsany. "The Pearly Beach" by Lord Dunsany (1932, 1960).

Mrs. Charles Ellis. "Wild Swans," "The Singin' Woman from the Wood's Edge," "Spring," and "Weeds" by Edna St. Vincent Millay. Copyright 1920, 1948 by Edna St. Vincent Millay.

Farrar, Straus and Cudahy, Inc. "One Evening" by Colette (1924, 1952).

Janet Flanner. "The Murder in Le Mans" (1934).

Foyer des Artistes, Librairie Plon. "The Public and the Artist" by Jean Cocteau (1922, 1950).

Mrs. Gilbert W. Gabriel. "God Rest You Merry, Gentlemen . . ." by Gilbert W. Gabriel (1929, 1957).

Donald C. Gallup. "And Now" by Gertrude Stein (1934).

Paul Géraldy. "Modern Love—by a Modern French Poet" (1919, 1947).

William Gropper. "Not on Your Tintype" (1935).

Harcourt, Brace and Company, Inc. "Memorabilia" from *Poems 1923–1954* by E. E. Cummings; copyright 1925 Horace Liveright, renewed 1953 by E. E. Cummings. "Burbank with a Baedeker: Bleistein with a Cigar," "A Cooking Egg," "The Boston Evening Transcript," and "La Figlia Che Piange" from *Collected Poems 1909–1935* by T. S. Eliot; copyright 1936 Harcourt, Brace and Company, Inc. "New Hampshire Again" from *Good Morning, America* by Carl Sandburg; copyright 1928, 1956 by Carl Sandburg. "Rhyme and Relativity" (five parodies) from *Heavens* by Louis Untermeyer; copyright 1922 Harcourt, Brace and Company, Inc., renewed 1950 by Louis Untermeyer. All the foregoing reprinted by permission of Harcourt, Brace and Company, Inc. For permission to reprint the four poems by T. S. Eliot, acknowledgment is made also to Faber and Faber, Ltd.

Harper & Brothers. "The Social Life of the Newt" from *Of All Things* by Robert Benchley; copyright 1921 Harper & Brothers, renewed 1949 by Gertrude Benchley. "Mrs. Fiske: An Artist and a Personality" from *Grotesques* by Mary Cass Canfield, copyright 1927 Harper & Brothers, renewed 1955 by Mary Cass Canfield. Reprinted by permission of the publishers.

Joseph Hennessey. "A Group of Artists Write Their Own Epitaphs," "The Theory and Lizzie Borden," and "The Captain's Memoirs" by Alexander Woollcott (1925–27–29, 1953–55–57).

Estate of Beatrice Houdini. "Confessions of a Jail-Breaker" by Harry Houdini (1919, 1947).

Houghton Mifflin Company. "The Weather-Vane Points South" (1919, 1947) from *Complete Poetical Works of Amy Lowell.* Reprinted by permission of the publishers.

Aldous Huxley. "The Importance of the Comic Genius" (1924, 1952).

Mrs. Alva Johnston. "Twilight of the Inkstained Gods" by Alva Johnston (1932, 1960).

Robert T. Jones, Jr. "Mental Hazards of Golf" (1928, 1956).

George S. Kaufman. "Big Casino Is Little Casino" (1925, 1953).

Geoffrey Kerr. "A Western Disunion" (1926, 1954) and "Tired Men and Business Women" (1930, 1958).

Alfred A. Knopf, Inc. "The Movies Take Over the Stage" from *Passing Judgments* by George Jean Nathan; copyright 1934 George Jean Nathan. "Love Song," and "A Strange Story" from *The Collected Poems of Elinor Wylie;* copyright 1932 Alfred A. Knopf, Inc. Reprinted by permission of the publishers.

Estate of the late Mrs. Frieda Lawrence. "Deserted Battlefields" by D. H. Lawrence (1928, 1956).

Walter Lippmann. "Blazing Publicity." Copyright 1927, 1955 Walter Lippmann.

Anita Loos. "The Force of Heredity, and Nella" (1915, 1943).

Monica McCall, Inc. "The Blind Spot" by John van Druten. Copyright 1935 John van Druten.

Compton Mackenzie. "The Outlived Thing" (1928, 1956).

Mme. Renée Henri Masson. "The Last Day" by Michel Corday (1927, 1955).

André Maurois. "The Birth of a Great Artist" (1927, 1955).

Scott Meredith Literary Agency, Inc., and A. P. Watt & Son. "All about the Income Tax" by P. G. Wodehouse (1919, 1947).

Lili Darvas Molnar. "A Leavetaking" (One-Act Play) by Ferenc Molnar. Copyright 1932 Review of Reviews Corp., renewed 1960 by Lili Darvas Molnar.

Harold Nicolson. "How Unlike We Are!" (1933).

Harold Ober Associates, Inc. "The Babe" by Paul Gallico (1932, 1960). "White Poppies Die" by Nancy Hale (1933). "Two-Time" by Margaret Case Harriman (1930, 1958). "Time and a Half" by John Riddell (Corey Ford) (1933). "Now There Is Peace" by Richard Sherman (1933). "The Mystery of Stroppingwallingshire Downs" by Philip Wylie (1930, 1958).

Viola Pastkowski Papini. "The Man Who Lost Himself" by Giovanni Papini (1920, 1948).

Dorothy Parker. "Men: A Hate Song" (1917, 1945), "The First Hundred Plays Are the Hardest" (1918–20, 1946–48), and "A Valentine for Mr. Woollcott" (1934).

Mrs. Mary S. Pearson. "The Murder of Captain White" (1926, 1954) and "Blunders in Print" (1935) by Edmund Pearson.

Random House, Inc. "Have They Attacked Mary. He Giggled" by Gertrude Stein (1917, 1945). Reprinted from *Selected Writings of Gertrude Stein* by permission of the publishers.

Marie Rodell and Joan Daves, Inc. "A Sort of Defense of Mothers" by Heywood Broun (1927, 1955).

William Saroyan. "Little Caruso" (1934).

Charles Scribner's Sons. "The Bums at Sunset" (1935) from *From Death to Morning* by Thomas Wolfe. "David Garrick to John Barrymore" (1923) from *Glamour* by Stark Young. Reprinted by permission of the publishers.

Gilbert Seldes. "Fred Stone and W. C. Fields." Copyright 1924, 1952 Gilbert Seldes.

Charles G. Shaw. "Three Americans" (1927, 1955).

Mrs. Robert E. Sherwood. "Charlie Chaplin and His New Film, *The Gold Rush*" by R. E. Sherwood (1925, 1953).

Simon and Schuster, Inc. "The Street" and "The Mesdames Kilbourne" by Allan Seager. Copyright 1934 and 1936 respectively by Allan Seager.

George Slocombe. "Lord of the Loincloth." Copyright 1931, 1959 George Slocombe.

Joseph Henry Steele. "Sister Aimée, Bernhardt of the Sawdust Trail." Copyright 1933 Joseph Henry Steele.

G. B. Stern. "Compensation Instinct." Copyright 1935 G. B. Stern.

Frank Sullivan. "Dixie Nocturne" and "Inflation for Ida." Copyright 1933 Frank Sullivan.

Carl Van Vechten. "The Black Blues" (1925, 1953).

The Executors of the late Sir Hugh Walpole. "William Somerset Maugham" by Hugh Walpole (1919, 1947).

A. Watkins, Inc. "Lydia and the Ring-Doves" by Kay Boyle (1932, 1960).

Willis Kingsley Wing and A. P. Watt & Son. "On the Approach of Middle Age" by Somerset Maugham (1923, 1951).

For permission to reproduce "White Plumes" by Matisse, which appears on page 134, acknowledgment is made to the present owners, The Minneapolis Institute of Arts, The William Hood Dunwoody Fund.

Index of Illustrations